The Civilization of the Italian Renaissance

A Sourcebook

The Civilization of the Italian Renaissance

A Sourcebook

Kenneth R. Bartlett
University of Toronto

D. C. HEATH AND COMPANY
Lexington, Massachusetts   Toronto

Address editorial correspondence to:
D. C. Heath and Company
125 Spring Street
Lexington, MA 02173

Photo Researcher: Rose Corbett Gordon

Cover Photograph: Melozzo da Forli, *Pope Sixtus IV and His Nephews* (1477), Pinacoteca Vaticana, Rome (Scala/Art Resource, New York). See also page 255.

Cover Design: Dustin Graphics

Published simultaneously in Canada.

Printed in the United States of America.

International Standard Book Number: 0-669-20900-7

Library of Congress Catalog Number: 91-70288

10 9 8 7 6 5 4 3 2 1

Preface

The Renaissance, perhaps more effectively than any other period, encourages both the scholar and the student to transcend the boundaries of traditional disciplines. The study of the Italian Renaissance in particular reflects a multidisciplinary imperative that has defined the way in which the years between about 1300 and 1550 have been approached, beginning with Burckhardt more than 130 years ago. No single method of study, nor any single disciplinary structure, can serve to explicate or describe the remarkable efflorescence of culture that gives the Italian Renaissance its definition in the popular imagination.

The Italian Renaissance was a time in which the broad expression of human experience was developed in a dramatic manner and recorded in various ways from the monuments of high culture to the simple documents of daily life. Each of these has a part to play in the creation of the complex image of the age, and each should be permitted to speak for itself. Consequently, rather than present a synthetic history of the Renaissance in Italy, this book offers a wide selection of materials written during the period. In addition, some of the texts of classical antiquity written by Quintilian and Cicero, which provided the models for much Italian humanistic endeavor, have been included. Since few students now read or even study Latin, such sources are not known to them, and the reference of writers such as Petrarch or Bruni to the testimony of ancient authors is not readily understood.

I have also attempted to balance the celebrated products of humanists with illustrations of the continuing power of orthodox religion and the rituals of the community. Artists appear as taxpayers and friends as well as in their customary roles as exceptional creative geniuses; panderers and poets take their place alongside popes and princes. Therefore, I hope that after studying the representative selections in this anthology students will come to appreciate the variety of Renaissance life and the interpenetration of high and popular culture and the realities of work and family for even the most gifted artist or powerful prince.

This collection of readings is the immediate result of teaching both in a university history department and in an interdisciplinary program of Renaissance Studies. It was clear to me from the beginning that there was need for a sourcebook that included material from a great many aspects of Renaissance life, that reflected the latest interests in teaching and research, and that would stimulate students to pursue the study of the Renaissance by providing them with instructive and intrinsically appealing primary-source materials. Each chapter focuses on a different facet of the Italian Renaissance, and although there is a very rough chronological order, the selections are structured as much according to theme as chronology. Similarly, I have tried to vary the types of materials presented as well as the lengths. In some instances, for example, short extracts from chronicles or official records appear; in others I have offered longer selections from literary works or treatises. I hope that this variation will also assist both the instructor and the student in their teaching and learning.

Many people helped in the creation of this book. My first debt is to my students and colleagues at Victoria College in the University of Toronto, where I have spent twenty-five years as both student and teacher. The establishment of the Renaissance Studies Programme at Victoria in 1978 did much to develop interest in the study of the Renaissance at all levels, and our students are now beginning to continue the tradition by teaching others. The staff at D. C. Heath and Company has been exemplary, especially James Miller, who devised this project with me, Karen Wise, who carried it through with unfailing professionalism and good cheer, and Margaret Roll, who did such a splendid job of securing the permissions for this anthology. Finally, as ever, there is my wife Gillian, who has assisted me in so many ways during the production of this book and who remains my greatest support.

                                                                K. R. B.

Contents

✦ CHAPTER VI *Marriage, the Family, and Women*   *139*

I

Introduction

❖

It is but in our own day that men dare boast that they see the dawn of better things. . . . Now indeed, may every thoughtful spirit thank God that he has been permitted to be born in this new age, so full of hope and promise, which already rejoices in a greater array of nobly gifted souls than the world has seen in the thousand years which preceded it. (Matteo Palmieri, *Treatise on the Civil Life*)

This is the ideal of the Renaissance in Italy, an ideal that was consciously developed and manifested by the men and women of the time. In many ways the Renaissance was the first self-conscious historical period, created as a reaction against the culture, institutions, and principles of the Middle Ages. Even the term Middle Ages *was invented by Renaissance historians to define what they called the "Gothic" (that is, barbaric) valley separating the two cultural peaks of antiquity and Italy in the late fourteenth to the sixteenth centuries.*

The purpose of this book is to introduce the Italian Renaissance through a survey of its historical development and through examples of those statesmen, writers, artists, and ordinary citizens who defined it. In so doing, there will emerge a composite picture of the period and a more complete understanding of the nature of the efflorescence of culture that is associated with the Renaissance in Italy.

INTRODUCTION: THE RENAISSANCE

To define the Renaissance it is necessary to begin in the period itself, an historical epoch defined by the writers and historiographers who created it. Beginning in the fourteenth century, Italian scholars and writers described their world as something new, something special, something

1

dramatically different from what had preceded it. Their vision of the Middle Ages was as a barbarous and savage time that lacked refinement. Some representative examples over three centuries should indicate this. First, Giovanni Boccaccio (d. 1375) wrote the following in his biography of the poet Dante:

This was that Dante granted by the special grace of God to our age. This was that Dante who was first to open the way for the return of the Muses banished from Italy. It was he who revealed the glory of the Florentine idiom. It was he who brought under the rule of due numbers every beauty of the vernacular speech. It was he who may truly be said to have brought dead poetry back to life.

Next, compare a selection from the following century, from Matteo Palmieri's Treatise on the Civil Life, *written about 1435.*

Thus the noble achievements of our far-off ancestors (i.e., the men of ancient Rome) are forgotten, and have become impossible to modern men. Where was the painter's art till Giotto tardily restored it? A caricature of the art of human delineation! Sculpture and architecture, for long years sunk to the merest travesty of art, are only to-day in process of rescue from obscurity; only now are they being brought to a new pitch of perfection by men of genius and erudition. Of Letters and liberal studies at large it were best to be silent altogether. For these, the real guides to distinction in all the arts, the solid foundation of all civilization, have been lost to mankind for 800 years and more. It is but in our own day that men dare boast that they see the dawn of better things. For example, we owe it to our Lionardo Bruni that Latin, so long a bye-word for its uncouthness, has begun to shine forth in its ancient purity, its beauty, its majestic rhythm. Now, indeed, may every thoughtful spirit thank God that it has been permitted to him to be born in this new age, so full of hope and promise, which already rejoices in a greater array of nobly-gifted souls that the world has seen in the thousand years that have preceded it. If but our distressed land enjoy assured peace, most certainly shall we garner the fruits of the seed now being sown. Then shall we see these errors, deep-seated and long reputed, which have perverted every branch of knowledge, surely rooted out. For the books which an age of darkness puts forth into the world are themselves—how otherwise?—dark and obscure, and in their turn darken all learning by their subtleties and confusion. . . . But I see the day coming when all philosophy and wisdom and all arts shall be drunk from the pure fountain head—the great intelligences of old. . . . By way of illustration, it is not so long ago that a man would spend a large portion of his working life in the intricacies of Latin grammar. Inferior masters, teaching from perverse manuals, mingled grammar with philosophy, with logic, and heterogeneous learning, reducing it to an absurdity.

But now we rejoice in seeing our youth entering on the study of Latin by such order and method that in a year or two they come to speak and write that language with a fluency and correctness which it was impossible that our fathers could ever attain to at all.

Finally, here are the words of Giorgio Vasari, from his Lives of the Painters, *1550:*

The admirable sculptures and paintings buried in the ruins of Italy remained hidden or unknown to the men of this time who were engrossed in the rude productions of their own age, in which they used no sculptures or paintings except such as were produced by the old artists of Greece [i.e., Byzantium], who still survived, making images of clay or stone, or painting grotesque figures and only coloring the general outline. These artists were invited to Italy for they were the best and indeed the only representatives of their profession. With them they brought the mosaic, sculpture, and painting as they understood them, and thus they taught their own rough and clumsy style to the Italians, who practiced the art in this fashion up to a certain time, as I shall relate.

As the men of the age were not accustomed to see any excellence or greater perfection than the things thus produced, they greatly admired them, and considered them to be the type of perfection, barbarous as they were. Yet some rising spirits, aided by some quality in the air of certain places, so far purged themselves of this crude style that in 1250 Heaven took compassion on the fine minds that the Tuscan soil was producing every day, and directed them to the original forms. For although the preceding generations had before them the remains of arches, colossi, statues, pillars or carved stone columns which were left after the plunder, ruin and fire which Rome had passed through, yet they could never make use of them or derive any profit from them until the period named.

Up to the present, I have discoursed upon the origin of sculpture and painting, perhaps more at length than was necessary at this stage. I have done so, not so much because I have been carried away by my love for the arts, as because I wish to be of service to the artists of our own day, by showing them how a small beginning leads to the highest elevation, and how from so noble a situation it is possible to fall to utterest ruin, and consequently, how these arts resemble nature as shown in our human bodies, and have their birth, growth, age and death, and I hope by this means they will be enabled more easily to recognize the progress of the renaissance of the arts, and the perfection to which they have attained in our own time. And again, it ever it happens, which God forbid, that the arts should once more fall to a like ruin and disorder, through the negligence of man, the malignity of the age, or the decree of Heaven, which does not appear to wish that the things of this world should remain stationary, these labors of mine, such as they are (if they are worthy of a happier fate), by means of the things discussed before, and by those which remain to be said, may maintain the arts in life, or, at any rate, encourage the better spirits to provide them with every assistance, so that, by my good will and the labors of such men, they may have an abundance of those aids and embellishments which, if I may speak the truth freely, they have lacked until now.

Obviously, then, writers and thinkers in the Renaissance itself saw themselves as special, different, and having more in common with the style and principles of the classical world of ancient Rome than in the intervening Middle Age. Also, from the examples just given, certain elements emerge that will be shown to characterize the Renaissance in Italy. These are the return to a classical style of Latin prose, the growing significance of the vernacular languages, and a return to naturalism in art. Thus the Italian Renaissance did define itself and identify its own contributions to history by distinguishing itself from its immediate past. In this way one can see the development of the modern discipline of history, a Renaissance art. Unless an historian can see the past as something distant and remote, he or she lacks the perspective to study it with objectivity. The Middle Ages saw the past as a continuum beginning with the creation, because the purpose of its study was to trace and understand insofar as possible the unfolding of God's plan for humanity. The great moments were theological: the creation, the events of the Bible, the incarnation, the establishment of the Christian Roman Empire, and the spread of faith. Their world was theocentric—God-centered—not anthropocentric—human-centered. Humanity was not in control of its own world in this medieval vision because human causality always had to bow to divine causality.

Because of their attitude toward the more distant past, especially the past of ancient Rome, however, the scholars of the Renaissance sought to transcend the period of the Middle Ages and return as much as possible to classical antiquity. Consequently, they invented other tools to help them do so: archeology to discover physical traces of the antique world; numismatics to use the huge numbers of surviving ancient coins and medals to learn about the economies, iconography, history, and even physical characteristics of the ancients; and philology to assist in the search for a true classical style in Latin and later Greek, such as textual editing to get back to what the ancients actually wrote, clearing away the accretions of centuries of copying errors, commentaries, and interpolations. Renaissance scholars wished to recover the intellectual heritage of the ancient world, so they developed these means to do so in order to define themselves better in terms of the culture they wished to emulate.

Why did the sensitive and learned scholars and statesmen of the fourteenth and fifteenth centuries in Italy believe the Middle Ages to be barbarous and unsympathetic? Why was there the need to return to classical antiquity? This issue is central to any understanding of the Italian Renaissance in all its manifestations, including such psychological and abstract qualities as self-confidence, ideals of beauty, styles of architecture, modes of learning and education, and even individual self-awareness.

In effect, beginning in the late fourteenth and early fifteenth centuries, Italians believed that they had much more in common with the civilization of the ancient world than with the age immediately preceding their own. Florence, the city that exemplified so many Renaissance values and structures, provides a useful example. Florence was a republican city-state ruled by a merchant patriciate dependent on manufacturing, long-distance trade, and banking for its wealth and power. Consequently, Rome in the century before Christ, the age of Cicero, was more congenial to Florentines than the feudal, agrarian, monarchical period of the Middle Ages. Thus, when the rulers of Florence needed a model, an ideology on which to build their lives and their state, the ancient world provided one almost ready made, a model that was accessible, comprehensible, sympathetic, relevant, and self-supporting. Moreover, this model was especially powerful because fourteenth-century Italians also identified themselves as the heirs of the greatness of Rome, which they sought to recover, at least culturally.

Nevertheless, when the age of the Renaissance is addressed, certain images and ideas come to mind, ideas determined by a century of scholarship, a tradition largely begun by one man, Jacob Burckhardt. In 1860, Burkhardt wrote a book entitled The Civilization of the Renaissance in Italy. *It was not really a history book but one of the earliest and greatest of a whole new way of looking at the past, an original method that synthesized many aspects of the intellectual, social, and cultural elements of a society into a singular, unified vision to create a study of a mentality, a point of view that can be identified immediately as "Renaissance." Burckhardt's German word for this was* Kulturgeschichte; *the English is* cultural history *or* interdisciplinary history.

What is significant is that Burckhardt was an art historian and aesthete who saw the world very much from the perspective of art and culture rather than political history. Second, his book was arranged topically so that he was looking at the Renaissance not as a developing period of time but as a series of different facets of the same experience. This is the method through which Renaissance studies are often still approached today. Ideas such as the recovery of antiquity, the dignity of human beings, unbridled egoism, and naturalism all inform his book, not because he imposed this vision on the past, but because, as has been shown, these were the elements that observers in the Renaissance itself saw as their defining characteristics.

Burckhardt had a long succession of disciples, the most important of whom identified the central role of humanism in the creation of the Renaissance mentality. Humanism can be described as a method of teaching and studying classical texts so as to understand their essential meaning and the application of the lessons learned to a world ruled by leisured, wealthy laypeople whose access to power was as much through their talents and accomplishments as through their births.

This connection between humanism and the definition of the Renaissance is critical. In part this is because the Middle Ages were not as dark as fourteenth- and fifteenth-century Italians believed and in part because any historical period like the Renaissance that is not bound by precise temporal or geographic limits must be reducible to some coherent principles.

Humanism, then, developed into a belief—whether true or false—held by Italians of the fourteenth and fifteenth centuries that they were indeed different and separated from the values and styles of the Middle Ages. Although it can be shown easily that the styles and themes employed in Renaissance art and literature were borrowed from antiquity, they also were used during the Middle Ages, often skillfully. It was simply that the Renaissance used these principles differently. What is significant is that more than the form was reproduced (for example, exact anatomy or certain ancient literary genres): the vital, dynamic spirit behind the form was recaptured. Thus this humanist perspective was a self-perpetuating, self-defining belief that brought Italians of the Renaissance closer to their ancient models and provided a guide to life and letters, education and politics, morals and ethics, and art and culture simply because these Renaissance Italians accepted as true that these classical elements could be brought back to life rather than merely copied. These ancient principles, then, could be shaped into a functional code of behavior, a statement of belief or an ideology to animate a ruling elite, that is, the well-educated, independent, urban mercantile bourgeois inhabitants of the city-state republics or petty despotisms of the peninsula.

This identification of humanism as an animating spirit or ideology is fundamental because it answers so many questions and allows an interpretation of the Renaissance as something other than a block of time. The Renaissance becomes, then, a vital idea, a concept, a self-definition that can be traced through republics like Florence, where it had special importance and application, to smaller warrior principalities like Urbino, to papal Rome, and ultimately, to the great dynastic kingdoms of northern Europe, whose traditions were completely different, but whose ruling elites fell prey to a modified version of this animating spirit, this ideology, because it equally met so many of their social, cultural, educational, and psychological needs.

Therefore, in response to the question, "What is the Renaissance?" one can reply that it was an historical force characterized by certain principles to which the educated elite conformed and which consequently transformed their entire mentality into a world view heavily dependent on classical models and values filtered through Italian experience of the *fourteenth, fifteenth, and sixteenth centuries and ultimately grafted to a wide variety of constitutional structures that took on immediately recognizable and identifiable aspects. Despite the differences of time and space, therefore, Petrarch would have much to say to Leon Battista Alberti or even Leonardo da Vinci or Castiglione because each of these men shared important aspects of a similar humanist ideology of the Renaissance.*

THE CLASSICAL HERITAGE

*T*he significance of the classical world to the Renaissance has been shown to have been fundamental. As a result, the search for remnants of the classical past became an obsession among Italian humanists. Recovering lost, partial, or garbled ancient books drove scholars to rummage through the monastery and cathedral libraries of Europe looking for manuscripts. It is largely because of these efforts that the corpus of Latin literature known today exists. Works by such important authors as Quintilian, Lucretius, Vitruvius, Cicero, and Apuleius were found and transmitted in clear, well-edited copies to posterity. In so doing, the classical past that was to provide so much of the humanist perspective of the Renaissance became available.

In particular, Renaissance scholars were interested in works of rhetoric and moral philosophy, or ethics. These ancient texts provided an important element of guidance in the search for an appropriate cultural model. Eloquence and virtue were closely identified by the ancients: Good people were equated with good letters and—so necessary in a republic such as Florence—good government. Thus the discovery of lost or partly lost works such as On the Early Education of the Citizen-Orator by Quintilian (Marcus Fabius Quintilianus, c. A.D. 35–100) was reported with great excitement in humanist circles. The humanist Leonardo Bruni wrote to Poggio Bracciolini concerning the recovery of a complete text of the Roman author: "Oh wondrous treasure! Oh unexpected joy! Shall I see you, Marcus Fabius, whole and undamaged, and how much will you mean to me now? . . . Please Poggio, satisfy this deep desire of mine as quickly as possible, so that if kindness means anything I may see him before I die."

✦ *Quintilian*

*M*arcus Fabius Quintilianus (c. A.D. 35–100) was born in Spain but received his rhetorical education in Rome. He returned to Spain as a young man, however, to practice law, but he accompanied Galba, the *governor of Spain, who had become emperor in* A.D. *68, back to Rome, where he soon acquired a reputation as a formidable rhetorician and teacher. Quintilian stressed ethics and morality as necessary elements in a rhetorical education. In* A.D. *88 he was appointed master of what may have been the first publicly funded school in Rome and was acknowledged the greatest teacher in the imperial capital. The Emperor Domitian bestowed consular rank on Quintilian after he had retired from teaching and had made a considerable fortune from teaching and the law.*

On the Early Education of the Citizen-Orator *dates from about* A.D. *95 and reflects the mature rhetorician's principles of education. Morality, ethics, clarity, and elegance all join to form good speech, or oratory, which Quintilian defined as a good man speaking well.*

The complete text of On the Early Education of the Citizen-Orator *was discovered by Poggio Bracciolini in the monastery of St. Gall in 1416. This discovery added greatly to Quintilian's importance as a theorist of education and one heavily used by such humanist writers and teachers as Pietro Paolo Vergerio and Vittorino da Feltre. The model Quintilian proposes, in which virtue, learning, and eloquence all combine to form the ideal citizen, became central to the Renaissance.*

ON THE EARLY EDUCATION OF THE CITIZEN-ORATOR

We are to form, then, the perfect orator, who cannot exist unless he is above all a good man. We require in him, therefore, not only consumate ability in speaking, but also every excellence of mind. For I cannot admit that the principles of moral and honorable conduct are, as some have thought, to be left to the philosophers. This is true because the man who can duly sustain his character as a citizen, who is qualified for the management of public and private affairs, and who can govern communities by his counsels, settle them by means of laws, and improve them by judicial enactments, can certainly be nothing else but an orator. Although I acknowledge, therefore, that I shall adopt some precepts which are contained in the writings of the philosophers, yet I shall maintain with justice and truth that they belong to my subject and have a peculiar relation to the art of oratory. If we constantly have occasion to speak of justice, fortitude, temperance, and other similar topics, so that a cause can scarcely be found in which some such discussion does not occur, and if all such subjects are to be illustrated by invention and elocution, can it be doubted that, wherever power of intellect and copiousness of language are required, the art of the orator is to be there pre-eminently exerted?

SOURCE: Marcus Fabius Quintilianus, *On the Early Education of the Citizen-Orator,* ed. by J. J. Murphy, trans. by J. S. Watson (Indianapolis, Ind.: Bobbs-Merrill, 1965), pp. 6–8. Reprinted by permission of James J. Murphy.

These two accomplishments, as Cicero very plainly proves, were, as they are joined by nature, so also united in practice, so that the same persons were thought at once wise and eloquent. Subsequently, the study divided itself, and, through want of art, it came to pass that the arts were considered to be diverse; for, as soon as the tongue became an instrument of gain, and it was made a practice to abuse the gifts of eloquence, those who were esteemed as eloquent abandoned the care of morals, which, when thus neglected, became, as it were, the prize of the less robust intellects. Some, disliking the toil of cultivating eloquence, afterward returned to the discipline of the mind and the establishment of rules of life, retaining themselves the better part, if it could be divided into two —but assuming, at the same time, the most presumptuous of titles, so as to be called the only cultivators of wisdom, a distinction which neither the most eminent commanders nor men who were engaged with the utmost distinction in the direction of the greatest affairs and in the management of whole commonwealths ever ventured to claim for themselves; for they preferred rather to practice excellence of conduct than to profess it. That many of the ancient professors of wisdom, indeed, both delivered virtuous precepts, and even lived as they directed others to live, I will readily admit; but, in our own times, the greatest vices have been hidden under this name in many of the professors. They did not strive by virtue and study to be esteemed philosophers, but adopted a peculiarity of look, austerity or demeanor, and a dress different from that of other men, as cloaks for the vilest immoralities.

But those topics, which are claimed as peculiar to philosophy, we all discuss everywhere. For what person (if he be not an utterly corrupt character) does not sometimes speak of justice, equity, and goodness? Who even among rustics, does not make some inquiries about the causes of the operations of nature? As to the proper use and distinction of words, it ought to be common to all who make their language an object of care. But it will be the orator who will understand and express those matters best, and if he should ever arrive at perfection, the precepts of virtue would not have to be sought from the schools of the philosophers. At present it is necessary to have recourse, at times, to those authors who have, as I said, adopted the deserted, but pre-eminently better, part of philosophy, and to reclaim, as it were, what is our own, not that we may appropriate their discoveries, but that we may show them that they have usurped what belonged to others.

Let the orator, therefore, be such a man as may be called truly wise, not blameless in morals only (for that, in my opinion, though some disagree with me, is not enough), but accomplished also in science, and in every qualification for speaking—a character such as, perhaps, no man ever was. But we are not the less, for that reason, to aim at perfection, for which most of the ancients strove; though they thought that no wise man had yet been found, they nevertheless laid down directions for gaining wisdom. For the perfection of eloquence is assuredly something, nor does the nature of the human mind forbid us to reach it; but if to reach it be not granted us, yet those who shall strive to gain the summit will make higher advances than those who, prematurely conceiving a despair of attaining the point at which they aim, shall at once sink down at the foot of the ascent.

✦ *Cicero*

*M*arcus Tullius Cicero (106–43 B.C.) was perhaps the most famous orator who ever lived. He was born at Arpinum in 106 B.C. and studied rhetoric, philosophy, and law in Rome and Greece. Returning to Rome in 76 B.C., he distinguished himself as a lawyer and was elected consul in 64 B.C. Exiled in 58 B.C. by his enemies for political reasons, he returned the next year to resume his political and legal career, which lasted until Caesar's victory in 47 B.C. This event eclipsed Cicero's ambitions because of his opposition to Caesar's dictatorship. It was during this period of enforced leisure that Cicero produced so many of his literary works.*

Caesar's assassination in 44 B.C. brought Cicero again into a leading position in the senate. He used his eminence and powerful oratory to attack Mark Antony in his Philipics, *in an attempt to ensure the reestablishment of the republic. The hatred he had aroused in Antony resulted in Cicero being murdered by Antony's soldiers in 43 B.C.*

Before the fourteenth century, Cicero was not well understood by medieval authors, who saw him more as a contemplative, misogynistic thinker. Petrarch's discovery of Cicero's letters to his friend Atticus in 1345 made the political Cicero visible once more, largely to Petrarch's unease. However, by the end of the century, this attitude had changed sufficiently under the influence of civic humanism to permit Coluccio Salutati (who had discovered the familiar letters in 1394) to praise Cicero's political activity, and Salutati's student, Pietro Paolo Vergerio, answered Petrarch's letter to the shade of Cicero by asserting the essential value of the active life.

THE ORATOR

Nor, while he is acquainted with the divine order of nature, would I have him ignorant of human affairs. He should understand the civil law, which

SOURCE: Marcus Tullius Cicero, *The Orator*, trans. by H. Hubbell (Cambridge, Mass.: Harvard University Press, 1971), pp. 395, 397, and 421. Reprinted by permission of the publishers and the Loeb Classical Library.

is needed daily in practice in the courts of law. What is more disgraceful than to attempt to plead in legal and civil disputes when ignorant of the statutes and the civil law? He should also be acquainted with the history of the events of past ages, particularly, of course, of our state, but also of imperial nations and famous kings; here our task has been lightened by the labor of our friend Atticus, who has comprised in one book the record of seven hundred years, keeping the chronology definite and omitting no important event. To be ignorant of what occurred before you were born is to remain always a child. For what is the worth of human life, unless it is woven into the life of our ancestors by the records of history? Moreover, the mention of antiquity and the citation of examples give the speech authority and credibility as well as affording the highest pleasure to the audience.

Thus equipped, then, he will come to the pleading of causes: and first he must be acquainted with the different kinds of causes. For he will clearly recognize that there can be no dispute in which the controversy does not arise either about fact or about words: in the case of fact the dispute is about the truth of the charge, its justification or its definition; in the case of words whether they are ambiguous, or contradictory. For if there is ever a case in which one thing is meant and another expressed, this is a kind of ambiguity which usually arises from the omission of a word; in this case we see that there are two meanings, and that is the characteristic of ambiguity. As there are so few kinds of causes, the rules for arguments are likewise few. There are, according to the usual theory, two sources from which they may be drawn; one, inherent in the case itself, the others external to it.

It is the treatment of the subject matter, then, that makes the speech admirable; the facts themselves are easy enough to acquire. For what remains that is subject to the rules of art, except to begin the speech in such a manner as to win the favor of the audience or to arouse them or to put them in a receptive mood; to set forth the facts briefly, clearly and reasonably, so that the subject under dispute may be understood; to prove one's own case and demolish the adversary's, and to do this not confusedly, but with arguments so conclusive as to prove what is the natural consequence of the principles laid down to prove each point; finally to pronounce a peroration either to inflame or to quench the passion of the audience?

❖ ❖ ❖

Even if these rules are necessary, as I think, still there is more glory in using them than in teaching them. That is true in general, and particularly true of this case. For it is true of all important arts as of trees, that their lofty height pleases us, but their roots and stems do not to the same degree; yet the latter are essential to the former. As for me, however, whether it is that well-known verse forbidding to

> Blush to own the art you practice

that will not allow me to conceal my delight, or it is your desire which has extorted this volume from me, nevertheless I have felt obliged to make reply to those who I suspected would find something to criticize. But even if the facts were not as I have stated them, who would be hard or unfeeling enough to refuse me the favor of devoting myself to letters, now that my forensic practice and my public career have fallen in ruins, rather than to idleness, which is impossible for me, or to grief, against which I put up a bold front? Literature was once my companion in the court and senate house; now it is my joy at home; nor am I busied merely with such matters as form the subject of this book, but with even greater and weightier themes. If these are brought to completion, I am sure my forensic efforts will find a proper counterpart even in the literary labors of my seclusion. But we must now return to the discussion which we have begun.

BRUTUS

I, on the other hand, did not cease from efforts to increase such gifts as I had by every type of exercise, and particularly by writing. To pass over much in this period and in the years which followed my aedileship, I was made praetor, and because of great popular favor towards me I stood first among the candidates chosen. For not only my constant activity and industry as a pleader, but also my style of speaking, more thoroughly considered than the conventional manner of the forum, had by its novelty drawn the attention of men to me. I say nothing of myself; I shall speak rather of others. Of them there was not one who gave the impression of having read more deeply than the average man, and reading is the well-spring of perfect eloquence; no one whose studies had embraced philosophy, the mother of excellence in deeds and in words; no one who had mastered thoroughly the civil law, a subject absolutely essential to equip the orator with the knowledge and practical judgment requisite for the conduct of private suits; no one who knew thoroughly Roman history, from which as occasion demanded he could summon as from the dead most unimpeachable witnesses; no one who with brief and pointed jest at his opponent's expense was able to relax the attention of the court and pass for a moment from the seriousness of the business in hand to provoke a smile or open laughter; no one who understood how to amplify his case,

SOURCE: Marcus Tullius Cicero, *Brutus*, trans. by G. Hendrickson (Cambridge, Mass.: Harvard University Press, 1971), pp. 279 and 281. Reprinted by permission of the publishers and the Loeb Classical Library.

and, from a question restricted to a particular person and time, transfer it to universals; no one who knew how to enliven it with brief digression; no one who could inspire in the judge a feeling of angry indignation, or move him to tears, or in short (and this is the one supreme characteristic of the orator) sway his feelings in whatever direction the situation demanded.

ON DUTIES

The principle that applies most broadly to the three remaining virtues is the one that holds together the society of humans among themselves or what might be called the "community of life." It has two parts: justice, in which virtue's splendor is unsurpassed and from which good men derive their reputation; and, related to justice, generosity, which may also be called kindliness or beneficence.

The first function of justice is to see that no man shall harm another unless he has been wounded by wrongdoing. The second is to see that each man uses public property for public benefit and his private property for himself. In nature nothing is private property. Property becomes private by longstanding occupation, that is, people once settled on vacant land; or by conquest, that is, someone gained control in a war; or by a law, by a contract, a stipulation or by casting of lots. It is on this principle that the Arpinates own the land of Arpinum and Tusculum belongs to the Tusculans. The definition of individual private possessions is analogous. It follows that each man should remain in possession of what he obtains for himself, since what had once naturally been shared becomes each man's own. It follows from this that whoever craves another's possessions violates a basic condition of human society.

Plato wrote brilliantly on this point: "We have not been born for ourselves alone; our native land claims a portion of our origin, our friends claim a portion." The Stoics like to repeat that everything that comes into being in the world is created for the benefit of man, that even men themselves are born for mankind's sake, that people can be helpful among themselves, one to another. The Stoics say that we should follow nature's lead in this and that we should contribute to the public benefit by the mutual interchange of obligations, by both giving and receiving. By our skills, by our efforts, by our capacities we should thus link men together into a human society.

Trust is basic to justice. By trust I mean stability and truth in promises and in agreements. I may risk repeating a discovery of the Stoics: they conduct industrious research into the derivations of words and they would

SOURCE: Marcus Tullius Cicero, *De Officiis (On Duties)*, trans. by H. Edinger (Indianapolis, Ind.: Bobbs-Merrill, 1974), pp. 12–16. Reprinted by permission of Macmillan Publishing Company.

have us believe that men devised the word "trust" (*fides*) because what an individual promises "is done" (*fiat*). Of course, the derivation will probably seem rather forced to some people.

There are two classifications of injustice. One part includes those who act unjustly. The other part includes men who, even if they have the power to do so, fail to protect from abuse those people against whom other men commit violence. The man who unjustly does harm to someone else, either in anger or because some other passion arouses him, acts as if he were striking a companion. But the man who does not avert an act of violence, or offer resistance if he has the power, is just as much at fault as if he betrayed his parents, or friends, or his fatherland. Those crimes that men commit deliberately to cause harm often arise from fear. I mean that a man who makes up his mind to harm someone else fears that he might suffer some injury himself unless he commits the crime. On the whole, however, men resort to criminal activity to get possession of what they crave. Greed is the clearest motive of crime.

Now men pursue wealth both for the basic needs of life and for the easy enjoyment of pleasures as well. More ambitious men, however, desire wealth because it leads to power and the ability to obligate other people. Not long ago, for example, Marcus Crassus said that no one who wants to be the chief power in the state has sufficient property unless he can maintain an army on his income. Men also take pleasure in impressive furnishings and luxurious living along with elegance and abundance. Yet these are the objects that stimulate an unending desire for wealth. Of course, no one should criticize an increase in a family's estate that harms no one else, but it should never involve breaking the law. Blindness to the claims of justice seizes men (and most people do not resist it) when they have received an ambition for military commands, or public offices, or glory. The quotation from Ennius:

> No society is sacred,
> No trust is safe in questions of kingdom

has a rather wide application. Whatever is by definition a sphere in which not more than one person can be first, usually stirs up such competition that it is extremely hard to maintain a [sacred] society. The recklessness of Julius Caesar recently made this clear. He twisted every divine and human law to get the ruling position that he imagined in some distorted fancy should belong to him. It is unfortunate in this matter that the craving for office, for command, for power and glory usually occurs in people of the finest energy and most brilliant ability. This fact provides an additional warning against any weakness in this area.

In all cases of injustice it makes a vast difference whether the crime arises from some mental aberration, which is usually brief and temporary, or whether it is deliberate and premeditated. Crimes that occur because of some momentary disturbance are less blameworthy than those that men commit after meditation and preparation. This is sufficient discussion of the actual commission of injustices.

As for protection of the weak, several causes may be mentioned why men overlook and abandon this duty. Perhaps they wish to avoid unpopularity, or hard work, or expense. Or indifference, laziness, or weariness, or some private concerns and preoccupations hamper them so much that they allow people whom they ought to shelter to remain unprotected. For this reason you have to examine whether what Plato says about philosophers is adequate. He says that because they are busy searching for truth and because they condemn and despise what most men pursue eagerly and usually fight over among themselves, for these reasons philosophers are men of justice. They pursue one [type of justice] by inflicting a wrong so they do not harm anyone, . . . they fall into another. Their concern for learning hobbles them, and so they abandon people whom they should protect. He therefore thinks that they would not be inclined to participate in government unless they were compelled to do so. Yet their participation would be more reasonable if it were voluntary, because a right action is only just on the condition that it is voluntary. There are also men who, because they concentrate on protecting their private interests or because they have some dislike for mankind in general, say that they are minding their own business and to all appearances do not do anyone else any criminal harm. They escape one category of injustice but fall into another, because they abandon the society of life by devoting neither attention, nor any effort, nor any of their abilities to it.

Since I have set forth two categories of injustice and added the reasons for each group, and since I have previously established the features that define justice, we shall easily be able to decide what a man's obligation is for each occasion, unless we are excessively self-centered. Concern for other people's interests is hard to arouse. I grant that Chremes in Terence "thinks nothing human alien to himself." Nevertheless our decisions about others differ from those about ourselves, because we have more feeling for and experience of the things that will turn out successfully or adversely for ourselves than for the things that affect others. We see other men's affairs across a long intervening gulf, as it were. So philosophers who strictly forbid you to act when you have any reason to doubt whether your action is just or unjust, are good teachers. Justice stands out brightly by itself, while the mere fact of doubt indicates a suspicion of wrongdoing.

II

Petrarch

INTRODUCTION

*F*rancesco Petrarca (Petrarch) was born in 1304 in the Tuscan town of
Arezzo not far from Florence, the son of an exiled Florentine notary
who had been driven from his native city by the same series of proscrip-
tions that had exiled the poet Dante in 1302. Petrarch's father took his
family out of Italy to Avignon, where the papacy had been established,
in order to escape from the dangers and insecurities of Rome. In Avignon,
he was granted a position in the Curia, the pope's court.

For his education, Petrarch was sent to the University of Montpellier
to study law, but all that young Francesco learned there was an abiding
love for the Latin classics, especially Cicero, as well as a deep understanding of and appreciation for Provençal love lyrics. Subsequently, Petrarch
was sent to Bologna to pursue his legal studies. Back in Italy, the young
man made a number of important and lasting friendships among the
wealthy and sophisticated students at the university. Of these, his association with the great Roman noble family of the Colonna would prove
to be the most important.

When back in Avignon, in the church of St. Clare, on Holy Friday
1327, Petrarch saw the woman whose image was to inspire him for the
rest of his life: Laura. In this woman Petrarch believed he had encountered perfect, ideal love, and he proceeded, like his compatriot Dante
with his Beatrice, to celebrate her and his love in every way, most especially in his lyric poetry.

Eventually, however, in order to receive a benefice from the pope,
Petrarch formally entered the Church as a cleric, assisted by the patronage of the Colonna family. Soon after, he traveled to Rome to see the
Holy City. While he was there, however, Petrarch was seduced by the
ruins of the ancient world, the physical remains of the Roman Empire,

17

already well known to him through his reading of Latin literature, and Petrarch's intuitive and temperamental love of classical antiquity was greatly strengthened by this personal contact with its remains.

Petrarch returned to Avignon and built a small villa in the Vaucluse, where he produced the greatest part of his work. These writings, especially his Italian love sonnets to Laura—a genre he perfected—made him very famous. Indeed, he became so celebrated as a poet that the citizens of Rome invited him to the city to be crowned with laurel on the Capitoline like the great Latin poets of the ancient world, the first in 1300 years.

After a number of years of wandering, living at the courts of Italian princes or serving as their envoy, Petrarch took ill outside the city of Padua and was taken to a villa he owned in the Euganean Hills at Arquà (now appropriately called Arquà Petrarca). There he died in 1374.

The great importance of Petrarch is as a transitional figure between the older values of the Middle Ages and the new ideals of Renaissance Italy. Because of the very contradictions and confusions that are evident in Petrarch, he can be seen to illustrate the formative period of Renaissance humanism. What humanism was in essence was the ideology of the Renaissance, a new method of education and thought that was designed to replace the scholastic model of the Middle Ages, which Petrarch so hated. Whereas Dante had not only accepted scholasticism but even made it his organizing world view, Petrarch detested it.

Petrarch disliked medieval scholasticism for a number of reasons. First, he thought that the style of Latin in which scholastic works were written was barbarous and loathesome and very unlike the style of Latin authors of the Golden Age, such as Cicero, who had become Petrarch's model in his youth. In short, scholastic Latin was ugly and unaesthetic, and Petrarch wished a return to the pure Latin of the classical period. Second, Petrarch disliked what the scholastics wrote. He saw no value in the esoteric arguments about minute—and, he believed, irrelevant— points of faith. Educated Christians had, after all, the guidance of the early Fathers of the Church, such as St. Augustine, who required no commentaries or glosses and who wrote, moreover, in a clear, classical style.

Third, Petrarch was most concerned with man's humanity—who he was and the purpose for which he was born—as he himself remarks in On His Own Ignorance: *"What is the use, I beseech you, to know the nature of quadrapeds, fowls, fishes and serpents and not know or even neglect man's nature, the purpose for which we are born and whence and whereto we travel?" This central concern with self and with human, earthly experience dominates all of Petrarch's works. He wished to encourage not only the potential power of the individual but also a new relationship with nature and literature and the past; he believed that his experience on earth had validity, value, and significance and that his self was worthy of knowing.*

LETTER TO POSTERITY

It is possible that some word of me may have come to you, though even this is doubtful, since an insignificant and obscure name will scarcely penetrate far in either time or space. If, however, you should have heard of me, you may desire to know what manner of man I was, or what was the outcome of my labors, especially those of which some description or, at any rate, the bare titles may have reached you.

To begin with myself, then, the utterances of men concerning me will differ widely, since in passing judgment almost every one is influenced not so much by truth as by preference, and good and evil report alike know no bounds. I was, in truth, a poor mortal like yourself, neither very exalted in my origin, nor, on the other hand, of the most humble birth, but belonging, as Augustus Caesar says of himself, to an ancient family. As to my disposition, I was not naturally perverse or wanting in modesty, however the contagion of evil associations may have corrupted me. My youth was gone before I realized it; I was carried away by the strength of manhood; but a riper age brought me to my senses and taught me by experience the truth I had long before read in books, that youth and pleasure are vanity—nay, that the Author of all ages and times permits us miserable mortals, puffed up with emptiness, thus to wander about, until finally, coming to a tardy consciousness of our sins, we shall learn to know ourselves. In my prime I was blessed with a quick and active body, although not exceptionally strong; and while I do not lay claim to remarkable personal beauty, I was comely enough in my best days. I was possessed of a clear complexion, between light and dark, lively eyes, and for long years a keen vision, which however deserted me, contrary to my hopes, after I reached my sixtieth birthday, and forced me, to my great annoyance, to resort to glasses. Although I had previously enjoyed perfect health, old age brought with it the usual array of discomforts.

I have always possessed an extreme contempt for wealth; not that riches are not desirable in themselves, but because I hate the anxiety and care which are invariably associated with them. I certainly do not long to be able to give gorgeous banquets. I have, on the contrary, led a happier existence with plain living and ordinary fare than all the followers of Apicius,[1] with their elaborate dainties. So-called *convivia*, which are but vulgar bouts, sinning against sobriety and good manners, have always been repugnant to me. I have ever felt that it was irksome and profitless to invite others to such affairs, and not less so to be bidden to them

---

1. Proverbial gourmet from the age of Tiberius.

SOURCE: Excerpts from D. Thompson (ed. and trans.), *Petrarch: A Humanist Among Princes.* (New York: Harper and Row, 1971), pp. 1–13. Reprinted by permission of HarperCollins Publishers.

myself. On the other hand, the pleasure of dining with one's friends is so great that nothing has ever given me more delight than their unexpected arrival, nor have I ever willingly sat down to table without a companion. Nothing displeases me more than display, for not only is it bad in itself, and opposed to humility, but it is troublesome and distracting.

I struggled in my younger days with a keen but constant and pure attachment, and would have struggled with it longer had not the sinking flame been extinguished by death—premature and bitter, but salutary.[2] I should be glad to be able to say that I had always been entirely free from irregular desires, but I should lie if I did so. I can, however, conscientiously claim that, although I may have been carried away by the fire of youth or by my ardent temperament, I have always abhorred such sins from the depths of my soul. As I approached the age of forty, while my powers were unimpaired and my passions were still strong, I not only abruptly threw off my bad habits, but even the very recollection of them, as if I had never looked upon a woman. This I mention as among the greatest of my blessings, and I render thanks to God, who freed me, while still sound and vigorous, from a disgusting slavery which had always been hateful to me.[3] But let us turn to other matters.

I have perceived pride in others, never in myself, and however insignificant I may have been, I have always been still less important in my own judgment. My anger has very often injured myself, but never others. I make this boast without fear, since I am confident that I speak truly: While I am very prone to take offense, I am equally quick to forget injuries, and have a memory tenacious of benefits. I have always been most desirous of honorable friendships, and have faithfully cherished them. But it is the cruel fate of those who are growing old that they can commonly only weep for friends who have passed away. In my familiar associations with kings and princes, and in my friendship with noble personages, my good fortune has been such as to excite envy. I fled, however, from many of those to whom I was greatly attached; and such was my innate longing for liberty, that I studiously avoided those whose very name seemed incompatible with the freedom that I loved. The greatest kings of this age have loved and courted me. They may know why; I certainly do not. With some of them I was on such terms that they seemed in a certain sense my guests rather than I theirs; their lofty position in no way embarrassing me, but, on the contrary, bringing with it many advantages.

---

2. While it is tempting to see here a reference to Laura, there are chronological difficulties. The period of life described (*adolescentia*) extended from age 15 to 28, but Petrarch's attachment to Laura lasted until her death many years later. Perhaps we must simply accept this as one of those not infrequent instances where Petrarch has altered the account of his life.
3. Though a cleric, Petrarch was the father of two illegitimate children: Giovanni, born in 1337; and Francesca, born six years later.

I possessed a well-balanced rather than a keen intellect, one prone to all kinds of good and wholesome study, but especially inclined to moral philosophy and the art of poetry. The latter, indeed, I neglected as time went on, and took delight in sacred literature. Finding in that a hidden sweetness which I had once esteemed but lightly, I came to regard the works of the poets as only amenities. Among the many subjects which interested me, I dwelt especially upon antiquity, for our own age has always repelled me, so that, had it not been for the love of those dear to me, I should have preferred to have been born in any other period than our own. In order to forget my own time, I have constantly striven to place myself in spirit in other ages, and consequently I delighted in history; not that the conflicting statements did not offend me, but when in doubt I accepted what appeared to me most probable, or yielded to the authority of the writer.

My style, as many claimed, was clear and forcible; but to me it seemed weak and obscure. In ordinary conversation with friends, or with those about me, I never gave any thought to my language, and I have always wondered that Augustus Caesar should have taken such pains in this respect.[4] When, however, the subject itself, or the place or listener, seemed to demand it, I gave some attention to style, with what success I cannot pretend to say; let them judge in whose presence I spoke. If only I have lived well, it matters little to me how I talked. Mere elegance of language can produce at best but an empty renown.

My parents were honorable folk, Florentine in their origin, of medium fortune, or, I may as well admit it, in a condition verging on poverty. They had been expelled from their native city,[5] and consequently I was born in exile, at Arezzo, in the year 1304 of this latter age which begins with Christ's birth, July the twentieth, on a Monday, at dawn. My life up to the present has, either through fate or my own choice, fallen into the following divisions. A part only of my first year was spent at Arezzo, where I first saw the light. The six following years were, owing to the recall of my mother from exile, spent upon my father's estate at Incisa, about fourteen miles above Florence. I passed my eighth year at Pisa, the ninth and following years in Farther Gaul, at Avignon, on the left bank of the Rhone, where the Roman Pontiff holds and has long held the Church of Christ in shameful exile.[6] It seemed a few years ago as if Urban V was on the point of restoring the Church to its ancient seat, but it is clear that nothing is coming of this effort, and, what is to me the worst of all, the

---

4. Suetonius, *Life of Augustus*, p. 87.
5. Petrarch's father, a "White" Guelph, was banished by the victorious "Black" Guelphs on October 20, 1302 (nine months after the expulsion of Dante, whom he had known).
6. The French pope, Clement V (1305–14), had moved the papal court to Avignon in 1309.

Pope seems to have repented him of his good work, for failure came while he was still living.[7] Had he lived but a little longer, he would certainly have learned how I regarded his retreat. My pen was in my hand when he abruptly surrendered at once his exalted office and his life. Unhappy man, who might have died before the altar of Saint Peter and in his own habitation! Had his successors remained in their capital he would have been looked upon as the cause of this benign change, while, had they left Rome, his virtue would have been all the more conspicuous in contrast with their fault.[8]

But such laments are somewhat remote from my subject. On the windy banks of the river Rhone I spent my boyhood, guided by my parents, and then, guided by my own fancies, the whole of my youth. Yet there were long intervals spent elsewhere, for I first passed four years at the little town of Carpentras, somewhat to the east of Avignon: in these two places I learned as much of grammar, logic, and rhetoric as my age permitted, or rather, as much as it is customary to teach in school: you know how little that is, dear reader. I then set out for Montpellier to study law, and spent four years there, then three at Bologna. I heard the whole body of the civil law, and would, as many thought, have distinguished myself later, had I but continued my studies. I gave up the subject altogether, however, so soon as it was no longer necessary to consult the wishes of my parents.[9] My reason was that, although the dignity of the law, which is doubtless very great, and especially the numerous references it contains to Roman antiquity, did not fail to delight me, I felt it to be habitually degraded by those who practice it. It went against me painfully to acquire an art which I would not practice dishonestly, and could hardly hope to exercise otherwise. Had I made the latter attempt, my scrupulousness would doubtless have been ascribed to simplicity.

So at the age of two and twenty I returned home. I call my place of exile home, Avignon, where I had been since childhood; for habit has almost the potency of nature itself. I had already begun to be known there, and my friendship was sought by prominent men; wherefore I cannot say. I confess this is now a source of surprise to me, although it seemed natural enough at an age when we are used to regard ourselves as worthy of the highest respect. I was courted first and foremost by that very distinguished and noble family, the Colonnesi, who, at that period, adorned the Roman Curia with their presence. However it might be now, I was at that time certainly quite unworthy of the esteem in which I was held by them. I

---

7. Urban V (1362–70) left Avignon in April, 1367; returned there from Rome in September, 1370; and died on December 19 of the same year.

8. Petrarch had sent metrical epistles to Urban's predecessors, Benedict XII (1334–42) and Clement VI (1342–52), urging them to restore the papacy to Rome.

9. Petrarch left Bologna in April, 1326, probably on receiving news of his father's death. His mother had died some years earlier.

was especially honored by the incomparable Giacomo Colonna, then Bishop of Lombez,[10] whose peer I know not whether I have ever seen or ever shall see, and was taken by him to Gascony; there I spent such a divine summer among the foot-hills of the Pyrenees, in happy intercourse with my master and the members of our company, that I can never recall the experience without a sigh of regret.[11]

Returning thence, I passed many years in the house of Giacomo's brother, Cardinal Giovanni Colonna, not as if he were my lord and master, but rather my father, or better, a most affectionate brother—nay, it was as if I were in my own home.[12] About this time, a youthful desire impelled me to visit France and Germany. While I invented certain reasons to satisfy my elders of the propriety of the journey, the real explanation was a great inclination and longing to see new sights. I first visited Paris, as I was anxious to discover what was true and what fabulous in the accounts I had heard of that city. On my return from this journey I went to Rome, which I had since my infancy ardently desired to visit. There I soon came to venerate Stephano, the noble head of the family of the Colonnesi, like some ancient hero, and was in turn treated by him in every respect like a son. The love and good-will of this excellent man toward me remained constant to the end of his life, and lives in me still, nor will it cease until I myself pass away.

On my return, since I experienced a deep-seated and innate repugnance to town life, especially in that disgusting city of Avignon which I heartily abhorred, I sought some means of escape. I fortunately discovered, about fifteen miles from Avignon, a delightful valley, narrow and secluded, called Vaucluse, where the Sorgue, the prince of streams, takes its rise. Captivated by the charms of the place, I transferred thither myself and my books. Were I to describe what I did there during many years, it would prove a long story. Indeed, almost every bit of writing which I have put forth was either accomplished or begun, or at least conceived, there, and my undertakings have been so numerous that they still continue to vex and weary me. My mind, like my body, is characterized by a certain versatility and readiness, rather than by strength, so that many tasks that

---

10. Some thirty miles southwest of Toulouse. Giacomo had been elected bishop in 1328. He died in 1341.
11. It was during this summer of 1330 that Petrarch formed his lifelong friendship with "Socrates" (the Flemish Ludwig van Kempen, chanter in the chapel of Cardinal Giovanni Colonna), who resided at Avignon; and with "Laelius" (a Roman, Lello di Pietro Stefano dei Tosetti), who also resided at Avignon until the cardinal's death in 1348. Many of Petrarch's letters are addressed to these two friends.
12. As a household chaplain Petrarch was an active member of the cardinal's staff from 1330 to 1337, and an occasionally active member for another ten years. This was his first ecclesiastical appointment. On his ecclesiastical career, see E. H. Wilkins, *Studies in the Life and Works of Petrarch* (Cambridge, Mass., 1955), pp. 3–32.

were easy of conception have been given up by reason of the difficulty of their execution. The character of my surroundings suggested the composition of a sylvan or bucolic song.[13] I also dedicated a work in two books upon *The Life of Solitude*, to Philip, now exalted to the Cardinal-bishopric of Sabina. Although always a great man, he was, at the time of which I speak, only the humble Bishop of Cavaillon.[14] He is the only one of my old friends who is still left to me, and he has always loved and treated me not as a bishop (as Ambrose did Augustine), but as a brother.

While I was wandering in those mountains upon Friday in Holy Week, the strong desire seized me to write an epic in an heroic strain, taking as my theme Scipio Africanus the Great, who had, strange to say, been dear to me from my childhood. But although I began the execution of this project with enthusiasm, I straightway abandoned it, owing to a variety of distractions. The poem was, however, christened *Africa*, from the name of its hero, and, whether from his fortunes or mine, it did not fail to arouse the interest of many before they had seen it.[15]

While leading a leisurely existence in this region, I received, remarkable as it may seem, upon one and the same day,[16] letters both from the Senate at Rome and the Chancellor of the University of Paris, pressing me to appear in Rome and Paris, respectively, to receive the poet's crown of laurel.[17] In my youthful elation I convinced myself that I was quite

---

13. Petrarch conflates his first stay in Vaucluse (1337–41) with his third (1345–47); for the *Bucolicum Carman* and the *De Vita Solitaria* were both begun during the latter period. Petrarch began one or more major works during each of his four periods of residence at Vaucluse.

14. Philippe de Cabassoles, whose diocese included Vaucluse, was about Petrarch's age, and they shared similar tastes for books and country life. Philippe became cardinal in 1368, cardinal-bishop in 1370, and died in 1372.

15. Begun in 1338 or 1339, the *Africa* was never finished; and aside from a fragment that circulated during Petrarch's lifetime, it was not published until after his death. It proved something of a disappointment to Coluccio Salutati and others after they had seen it.

16. September 1, 1340.

17. Albertino Mussato had been crowned with laurel in Padua in 1315; and Dante had been offered a crown by Bologna but had declined (see *Paradiso* XXV, 1–9 on his desire to receive the crown in Florence). For the whole complicated question see E. H. Wilkins, "The Coronation of Petrarch" (*The Making of the "Cansoniere" and Other Petrarchan Studies* [Rome, 1951], pp. 9–69), who concludes: "the sum of the matter would seem to be that Petrarch succeeded, after persistent and varied efforts, in getting two invitations to receive the laurel crown; that the specific basis for the invitations was a rather limited amount of published Latin verse, together with the knowledge that he was engaged in the writing of a grandiose epic; that he had convinced the Colonna family and Roberto de' Bardi [Chancellor at the University of Paris, and a Florentine] that he was in truth a great poet; that their sense of his poetic worth was presumably enhanced by their knowledge that he was engaged in the writing of historical works and by the obvious range of his classical scholarship; and—just

worthy of this honor; the recognition came from eminent judges, and I accepted their verdict rather than that of my own better judgment. I hesitated for a time which I should give ear to, and sent a letter to Cardinal Giovanni Colonna, of whom I have already spoken, asking his opinion. He was so near that, although I wrote late in the day, I received his reply before the third hour on the morrow. I followed his advice, and recognized the claims of Rome as superior to all others. My acceptance of his counsel is shown by my twofold letter to him on that occasion, which I still keep. I set off accordingly; but although, after the fashion of youth, I was a most indulgent judge of my own work, I still blushed to accept in my own case the verdict even of such men as those who summoned me, despite the fact that they would certainly not have honored me in this way, had they not believed me worthy.

THE ASCENT OF MOUNT VENTOUX[1]

Today I made the ascent of the highest mountain in this region, which is not improperly called Ventosum. My only motive was the wish to see what so great an elevation had to offer. I have had the expedition in mind for many years; for, as you know, I have lived in this region from infancy, having been cast here by that fate which determines the affairs of men. Consequently the mountain, which is visible from a great distance, was ever before my eyes, and I conceived the plan of some time doing what I have at last accomplished today. The idea took hold upon me with especial force when, in re-reading Livy's *History of Rome*, yesterday, I happened upon the place where Philip of Macedon, the same who waged war against the Romans, ascended Mount Haemus in Thessaly, from whose summit he was able, it is said, to see two seas, the Adriatic and the Euxine.[2] Whether this be true or false I have not been able to determine, for the mountain is too far away, and writers disagree. Pomponius Mela, the cosmographer—not to mention others who have spoken of this occurrence—admits its truth without hesitation; Titus Livius, on the other hand, considers it false. I, assuredly, should not have left the question

---

possibly—that the beauty of some of his belittled Italian lyrics was in their minds" (p. 35).

1. *Epistolae Familiares* IV, 1, to Dionigi da Borgo San Sepolcro, whom Petrarch probably met in 1333 in Paris, where Dionigi, an Augustinian friar, was professor of theology and philosophy at the University. In 1339 King Robert called Dionigi to Naples, where he died in 1342. This letter was ostensibly written from Malaucène on April 26, 1336; but Billanovich (*Petrarca letterato*, pp. 193–98) considers it fictitious and assigns it to 1352–53. For an excellent assessment of the problem, see Hans Baron, *From Petrarch to Leonardo Bruni, Studies in Humanistic and Political Literature* (Chicago and London, 1968), pp. 17–20.
2. Livy XL, 21, 2–22. Mount Haemus (now Mount Balkan, in Bulgaria) is in Thrace, not Thessaly.

long in doubt, had that mountain been as easy to explore as this one. Let us leave this matter to one side, however, and return to my mountain here—it seems to me that a young man in private life may well be excused for attempting what an aged king could undertake without arousing criticism.

When I came to look around for a companion I found, strangely enough, that hardly one among my friends seemed suitable, so rarely do we meet with just the right combination of personal tastes and characteristics, even among those who are dearest to us. This one was too apathetic, that one over-anxious; this one too slow, that one too hasty; one was too sad, another over-cheerful; one more simple, another more sagacious, than I desired. I feared this one's taciturnity and that one's loquacity. The heavy deliberation of some repelled me as much as the lean incapacity of others. I rejected those who were likely to irritate me by a cold want of interest, as well as those who might weary me by their excessive enthusiasm. Such defects, however grave, could be borne with at home, for charity suffereth all things, and friendship accepts any burden; but it is quite otherwise on a journey, where every weakness becomes much more serious. So, as I was bent upon pleasure and anxious that my enjoyment should be unalloyed, I looked about me with unusual care, balanced against one another the various characteristics of my friends, and without committing any breach of friendship I silently condemned every trait which might prove disagreeable on the way. And—would you believe it—I finally turned homeward for aid, and proposed the ascent to my only brother, who is younger than I, and with whom you are well acquainted.[3] He was delighted and gratified beyond measure by the thought of holding the place of a friend as well as of a brother.

At the time fixed we left the house, and by evening reached Malaucène, which lies at the foot of the mountain, to the north. Having rested there a day, we finally made the ascent this morning, with no companions except two servants; and a most difficult task it was. The mountain is a very steep and almost inaccessible mass of stony soil. But, as the poet has said, "Remorseless toil conquers all." It was a long day, the air fine. We enjoyed the advantages of vigor of mind and strength and agility of body, and everything else essential to those engaged in such an undertaking, and so had no other difficulties to face than those of region itself. We found an old shepherd in one of the mountain dales, who tried, at great length, to dissuade us from the ascent, saying that some fifty years before he had, in the same ardor of youth, reached the summit, but had gotten for his pains nothing except fatigue and regret, and clothes and body torn by the rocks and briars. No one, so far as he or his companions knew, had

---

3. Petrarch's brother Gherardo was probably born in 1307; studied with him at Bologna; shared the fashionable life at Avignon; and became a monk in 1342.

ever tried the ascent before or after him. But his counsels increased rather than diminished our desire to proceed, since youth is suspicious of warnings. So the old man, finding that his efforts were in vain, went a little way with us, and pointed out a rough path among the rocks, uttering many admonitions, which he continued to send after us even after we had left him behind. Surrendering to him all such garments or other possessions as might prove burdensome to us, we made ready for the ascent, and started off at a good pace. But, as usually happens, fatigue quickly followed upon our excessive exertion, and we soon came to a halt at the top of a certain cliff. Upon starting on again we went more slowly, and I especially advanced along the rocky way with a more deliberate step. While my brother chose a direct path straight up the ridge,[4] I weakly took an easier one which really descended. When I was called back, and the right road was shown me, I replied that I hoped to find a better way round on the other side, and that I did not mind going farther if the path were only less steep. This was just an excuse for my laziness; and when the others had already reached a considerable height I was still wandering in the valleys. I had failed to find an easier path, and had only increased the distance and difficulty of the ascent. At last I became disgusted with the intricate way I had chosen, and resolved to ascend without more ado. When I reached my brother, who, while waiting for me, had had ample opportunity for rest, I was tired and irritated. We walked along together for a time, but hardly had we passed the first spur when I forgot about the circuitous route which I had just tried, and took a lower one again. Once more I followed an easy, roundabout path through winding valleys, only to find myself soon in my old difficulty. I was simply trying to avoid the exertion of the ascent; but no human ingenuity can alter the nature of things, or cause anything to reach a height by going down. Suffice it to say that, much to my vexation and my brother's amusement, I made this same mistake three times or more during a few hours.

After being frequently misled in this way, I finally sat down in a valley and transferred my winged thoughts from things corporeal to the immaterial, addressing myself as follows: "What thou hast repeatedly experienced today in the ascent of this mountain, happens to thee, as to many, in the journey toward the blessed life. But this is not so readily perceived by men, since the motions of the body are obvious and external while those of the soul are invisible and hidden. Yes, the life which we call blessed is to be sought for on a high eminence, and strait is the way that leads to it. Many, also, are the hills that lie between, and we must ascend, by a glorious stairway, from strength to strength. At the top is at once the end of our struggles and the goal for which we are bound. All wish to

---

4. Perhaps an allusion to Gherardo's choice of the monastic life in contrast to Petrarch's secular career.

reach this goal, but, as Ovid says, "To wish is little; we must long with the utmost eagerness to gain our end." Thou certainly dost ardently desire, as well as simply wish, unless thou deceivest thyself in this matter, as in so many others. What, then, doth hold thee back? Nothing, assuredly, except that thou wouldst take a path which seems, at first thought, more easy, leading through low and worldly pleasures. But nevertheless in the end, after long wanderings, thou must perforce either climb the steeper path, under the burden of tasks foolishly deferred, to its blessed culmination, or lie down in the valley of thy sins, and (I shudder to think of it!), if the shadow of death overtake thee, spend an eternal night amid constant torments." These thoughts stimulated both body and mind in a wonderful degree for facing the difficulties which yet remained. Oh, that I might traverse in spirit that other road for which I long day and night, even as today I overcame material obstacles by my bodily exertions! And I know not why it should not be far easier, since the swift immortal soul can reach its goal in the twinkling of an eye, without passing through space, while my progress today was necessarily slow, dependent as I was upon a failing body weighed down by heavy members.

One peak of the mountain, the highest of all, the country people call "Sonny," why, I do not know, unless by antiphrasis, as I have sometimes suspected in other instances; for the peak in question would seem to be the father of all the surrounding ones. On its top is a little level place, and here we could at last rest our tired bodies.

Now, my father, since you have followed the thoughts that spurred me on in my ascent, listen to the rest of the story, and devote one hour, I pray you, to reviewing the experiences of my entire day. At first, owing to the unaccustomed quality of the air and the effect of the great sweep of view spread out before me, I stood like one dazed. I beheld the clouds under our feet, and what I had read of Athos and Olympus seemed less incredible as I myself witnessed the same things from a mountain of less fame. I turned my eyes toward Italy, whither my heart most inclined. The Alps, rugged and snow-capped, seemed to rise close by, although they were really at a great distance; the very same Alps through which that fierce enemy of the Roman name once made his way, bursting the rocks, if we may believe the report, by the application of vinegar. I sighed, I must confess, for the skies of Italy, which I beheld rather with my mind than with my eyes. An inexpressible longing came over me to see once more my friend[5] and my country. At the same time I reproached myself for this double weakness, springing, as it did, from a soul not yet steeled to manly resistance. And yet there were excuses for both of these cravings, and a number of distinguished writers might be summoned to support me.

---

5. Giacomo Colonna had been in Rome since 1333.

Then a new idea took possession of me, and I shifted my thoughts to a consideration of time rather than place. "Today it is ten years since, having completed thy youthful studies, thou didst leave Bologna. Eternal God! In the name of immutable wisdom, think what alterations in thy character this intervening period has beheld! I pass over a thousand instances. I am not yet in a safe harbor where I can calmly recall past storms. The time may come when I can review in due order all the experiences of the past, saying with St. Augustine, 'I desire to recall my foul actions and the carnal corruption of my soul, not because I love them, but that I may the more love thee, O my God.' Much that is doubtful and evil still clings to me, but what I once loved, that I love no longer. And yet what am I saying? I still love it, but with shame, but with heaviness of heart. Now, at last, I have confessed the truth. So it is. I love, but love what I would not love, what I would that I might hate. Though loath to do so, though constrained, though sad and sorrowing, still I do love, and I feel in my miserable self the truth of the well known words, 'I will hate if I can; if not, I will love against my will.' Three years have not yet passed since that perverse and wicked passion which had a firm grasp upon me and held undisputed sway in my heart began to discover a rebellious opponent, who was unwilling longer to yield obedience. These two adversaries have joined in close combat for the supremacy, and for a long time now a harassing and doubtful war has been waged in the field of my thoughts."

Thus I turned over the last ten years in my mind, and then, fixing my anxious gaze on the future, I asked myself, "If, perchance, thou shouldst prolong this uncertain life of thine for yet two lusters, and shouldst make an advance toward virtue proportionate to the distance to which thou hast departed from thine original infatuation during the past two years, since the new longing first encountered the old, couldst thou, on reaching thy fortieth year, face death, if not with complete assurance, at least with hopefulness, calmly dismissing from thy thoughts the residuum of life as it faded into old age?"

These and similar reflections occurred to me, my father. I rejoiced in my progress, mourned my weaknesses, and commiserated the universal instability of human conduct. I had well-nigh forgotten where I was and our object in coming; but at last I dismissed my anxieties, which were better suited to other surroundings, and resolved to look about me and see what we had come to see. The sinking sun and the lengthening shadows of the mountain were already warning us that the time was near at hand when we must go. As if suddenly wakened from sleep, I turned about and gazed toward the west. I was unable to discern the summits of the Pyrenees, which form the barrier between France and Spain; not because of any intervening obstacle that I know of but owing simply to the insufficiency of our mortal vision. But I could see with the utmost clearness, off to the right, the mountains of the region about Lyons, and to the left the bay of Marseilles and the waters that lash the shores of Aigues Mortes, although all these places were so distant that it would require a journey of several days to reach them. Under our very eyes flowed the Rhone.

While I was thus dividing my thoughts, now turning my attention to some terrestrial object that lay before me, now raising my soul, as I had done my body, to higher places, it occurred to me to look into my copy of St. Augustine's *Confessions*, a gift that I owe to your love, and that I always have about me.[6] In memory of both the author and the giver, I opened the compact little volume, small indeed in size, but of infinite charm, with the intention of reading whatever came to hand, for I could happen upon nothing that would be otherwise than edifying and devout. Now it chanced that the tenth book presented itself. My brother, waiting to hear something of St. Augustine's from my lips, stood attentively by. I call him, and God too, to witness that where I first fixed my eyes it was written: "And men go about to wonder at the heights of the mountains, and the mighty waves of the sea, and the wide sweep of rivers, and the circuit of the ocean, and the revolution of the stars, but themselves they consider not."[7] I was abashed, and, asking my brother (who was anxious to hear more) not to annoy me, I closed the book, angry with myself that I should still be admiring earthly things who might long ago have learned from even the pagan philosophers that nothing is wonderful but the soul, which, when great itself, finds nothing great outside itself. Then, in truth, I was satisfied that I had seen enough of the mountain; I turned my inward eye upon myself, and from that time not a syllable fell from my lips until we reached the bottom again. Those words had given me occupation enough for I could not believe that it was by a mere accident that I happened upon them. What I had there read I believed to be addressed to me and to no other, remembering that St. Augustine had once suspected the same thing in his own case, when, on opening the book of the Apostle, as he himself tells us, the first words that he saw there were, "Not in rioting and drunkenness, not in chambering and wantonness, not in strife and envying. But put ye on the Lord Jesus Christ, and make not provision for the flesh, to fulfil the lusts thereof."[8]

---

6. In the last year of his life Petrarch gave his copy of the *Confessions* to Luigi Marsili, an Augustinian friar who had settled in Florence and was to be an important influence on Salutati and Niccolo Niccoli. For the great importance of Augustine in this period, see P. O. Kristeller, "Augustine and the Early Renaissance," *Review of Religion* VIII (1944), 339–58.

7. *Confessions* X, 8, 15. On the alleged date of the ascent, Petrarch was in his thirty-second year, as was Augustine at the end of his conversion.

8. Romans 13, 13–14, quoted in *Confessions* VIII, 12, 29.

LETTER TO THE SHADE OF CICERO[1]

Your letters I sought for long and diligently; and finally, where I least expected it, I found them. At once I read them, over and over, with the utmost eagerness. And as I read I seemed to hear your bodily voice, O Marcus Tullius, saying many things, uttering many lamentations, ranging through many phases of thought and feeling. I long had known how excellent a guide you have proved for others; at last I was to learn what sort of guidance you gave yourself.

Now it is your turn to be the listener. Hearken, wherever you are, to the words of advice, or rather of sorrow and regret, that fall, not unaccompanied by tears, from the lips of one of your successors, who loves you faithfully and cherishes your name. O spirit ever restless and perturbed! in old age—I am but using your own words[2]—self-involved in calamities and ruin! what good could you think would come from your incessant wrangling, from all this wasteful strife and enmity? Where were the peace and quiet that befitted your years, your profession, your station in life? What Will-o'-the-wisp tempted you away, with a delusive hope of glory; involved you, in your declining years, in the wars of younger men; and, after exposing you to every form of misfortune, hurled you to a death that it was unseemly for a philosopher to die?[3] Alas! the wise counsel that you gave your brother, and the salutary advice of your great masters, you forgot. You were like a traveler in the night, whose torch lights up for others the path where he himself has miserably fallen.

Of Dionysius[4] I forbear to speak; of your brother and nephew, too; of Dolabella[5] even, if you like. At one moment you praise them all to the skies; at the next fall upon them with sudden maledictions. This, however, could perhaps be pardoned. I will pass by Julius Caesar, too, whose well-approved clemency was a harbor of refuge for the very men who were

---

1. *Epistolae Familiares* XXIV, 3. This collection closes with a book of letters addressed to Cicero, Seneca, Varro, Quintilian, Livy, Asinius Pollio, Horace, Virgil, and Homer (see Mario E. Cosenza, *Petrarch's Letters to Classical Authors*, Chicago, 1910). Like Azzo da Correggio, Petrarch took refuge in Verona, where he discovered in the cathedral library a volume containing the sixteen books of Cicero's *Letters to Atticus* (along with Cicero's correspondence with his brother Quintus and with Brutus), which he copied and which gave him the inspiration to form collections of his own letters. On Cicero's significance for Petrarch, see Hans Baron, "Cicero and the Roman Civic Spirit in the Middle Ages and Early Renaissance," *Bulletin of the John Rylands Library* XXII (1938), 72–97, esp. pp. 85–88.

    While in Verona Petrarch must have become acquainted with Dante's son, Pietro, to whom he addressed a metrical epistle (see Wilkins, *Studies*, pp. 33–47).
2. From the *Epistle to Octavian* 6 (wrongly attributed to Cicero).
3. Cicero was murdered by Antony's henchmen.
4. A freed slave, teacher to his son Marcus.
5. Husband of Cicero's daughter, Tullia.

warring against him. Great Pompey, likewise, I refrain from mentioning. His affection for you was such that you could do with him what you would. But what insanity led you to hurl yourself upon Antony?[6] Love of the republic, you would probably say. But the republic had fallen before this into irretrievable ruin, as you had yourself admitted. Still, it is possible that a lofty sense of duty, and love of liberty, constrained you to do as you did, hopeless though the effort was. That we can easily believe of so great a man. But why, then, were you so friendly with Augustus? What answer can you give to Brutus? If you accept Octavius, said he, we must conclude that you are not so anxious to be rid of all tyrants as to find a tyrant who will be well-disposed toward yourself. Now, unhappy man, you were to take the last false step, the last and most deplorable. You began to speak ill of the very friend whom you had so lauded, although he was not doing any ill to you, but merely refusing to prevent others who were. I grieve, dear friend, at such fickleness. These shortcomings fill me with pity and shame. Like Brutus, I feel no confidence in the arts in which you are so proficient. What, pray, does it profit a man to teach others, and to be prating always about virtue, in high-sounding words, if he fails to give heed to his own instructions? Ah! how much better it would have been, how much more fitting for a philosopher, to have grown old peacefully in the country, meditating, as you yourself have somewhere said, upon the life that endures for ever, and not upon this poor fragment of life; to have found no fasces, yearned for no triumphs, found no Catilines to fill the soul with ambitious longings!—all this, however, is vain. Farewell, forever, my Cicero.

Written in the land of the living; on the right bank of the Adige, in Verona, a city of Transpadane Italy; on the 16th of June, and in the year of that God whom you never knew the 1345th.

---

6. Cicero's *Philippics* are a series of fierce attacks on Antony.

III

Florence in the Renaissance

INTRODUCTION

F *lorence became the leading state of Tuscany through its importance as a banking and manufacturing center. Because of Florence's Guelf (papal) allegiance, Florentine bankers were given special concessions in collecting and disbursing papal taxes and revenues. Also, the excellent woolen cloth produced by the city's clothmakers, the city's largest industry, added even more to its wealth and power.*

By the end of the thirteenth century, the wealthy merchant class of Florence wanted political power and social prestige that would be commensurate with their new economic power, but the traditional authority of the old noble, feudal families blocked them. Eventually, however, the commune (city government) of Florence achieved increasing independence from the landed feudal aristocrats of the rural contado *(countryside) and their urban magnate associates. This was accomplished by using the authority of the guilds to create a participatory regime in which those rich urban laypeople who were members of a merchant or craft organization (or guild) increasingly determined the political and economic affairs of the city. After 1283, only those citizens who had matriculated in a guild could hold office in Florence, and after the celebrated 1293 Ordinances of Justice, the rural and urban nobility were humbled by being excluded from all important civic positions by having the fortified towers on their city palaces pulled down and by having to post large bonds to ensure their obedience to the new merchant regime.*

This success of the newly rich guild members did not result in a harmonious government. Factional squabbles, personal rivalries, and the continuing interference of the old nobility meant that the commune was unstable politically. Various measures were attempted to bring stability, such as entrusting the rule of the city to a foreign overlord, first the son of the King of Naples and later to an adventurer, Walter of Brienne. However, these failed experiments simply indicated the danger inherent in an unstable republican regime, especially the danger of surrendering the liberty of the city to a signore (prince).

The Black Death of 1348 also had a devastating effect on the city, killing perhaps half its population of about 90,000. Soon after, war and economic unrest caused by the severe dislocation of the plague resulted in extreme instability and discontent among the poorer citizens. In 1378, this explosive situation erupted into the Ciompi revolt, in which the poorest members of society, the disenfranchised woolworkers, or ciompi, led by renegade aristocrats, established a very broadly based government in which the ciompi were represented through their own guild. The wealthy, established merchants and "middle class" property owners of the city reacted with fear and outrage, overthrowing in 1382 the ciompi and the regime of lesser guildsmen that succeeded it and erecting in its place a much more closed, oligarchic form of government in which the tradesmen of the fourteen lesser craft guilds willingly allowed the rich merchants of the seven greater guilds (really mercantile cartels) to rule the city in their own interests.

This oligarchic government faced a number of critical challenges, especially the attempt of Giangaleazzo Visconti, the ruler of Milan, to conquer all of north and central Italy and incorporate the territory into a greater Milanese state. Among the major states north of the papal dominions, only Florence withstood Visconti so that when Giangaleazzo died unexpectedly in 1402 and with him his ambitious aggression, Florence felt that the city had withstood its greatest threat because of the love of liberty felt by its people and enshrined in its republican constitution. Although only a very small percentage of Florentines (perhaps 3 percent) could hold public office at any one time, there began a myth of Florentine republican liberty, closely associated with the Roman republic, which animated the civic humanism of its political and educated classes. In this way, the humanism of Coluccio Salutati and Leonardo Bruni merged with the constitutional structure of the commune.

This humanistic, oligarchic republic continued until 1434, at which time it was captured by the faction led by Cosimo de' Medici, the immensely rich head of the Medici bank. Cosimo did not overtly change the constitution; he merely managed it in the interests of his faction. He successfully included many disgruntled citizens and followed a policy that was attractive to the great majority of the political classes. He also helped bring peace to the entire Italian peninsula through shrewd diplomatic arrangements, and he used his great wealth to assist in the operation of the city's finances. When he died in 1464, he was revered as "Pater Patriae," the father of his country.

His son, Piero, was an ill man who was not as successful in meeting the needs of the various factions and interest groups within Florence. As a result, his regime was seriously challenged, but he managed nevertheless to pass the Medici authority on to his own son, Lorenzo, in 1469. Lorenzo, called, "The Magnificent," was the apogee of Medicean Florence in terms of culture. He continued his grandfather's policies as far as possible, but he behaved more as a prince than as a republican magistrate or even factional leader. He engaged in personal diplomacy and used the resources of the republic to enhance his position and that of his family. A war with the pope resulted in an attempt by a rival banking family, the Pazzi, to kill him and his brother and restore the old oligarchic republic without Medicean manipulation. The plot failed, although Lorenzo was wounded and his brother Giuliano was killed. What was proved by the plot more than anything else was the continued power the Medici had over the allegiance of Florentines of all classes. There was no popular rally to the Pazzi, and the commune decided to continue its war against the pope, despite the knowledge that it would end if Lorenzo were deposed and handed over to Sixtus IV.

After Lorenzo's death in 1492, the rule of the city passed to his son, Piero. Piero was incapable of sustaining the Medici control of the city and was driven out in 1494 as a consequence of the French invasions. A very broadly based republic, heavily influenced by the millenarian prophecies of the Dominican Girolamo Savonarola, was erected. This republic, which had to face the collapse of the Italian state system following the intervention of the French and the Spanish in the peninsula, lasted until 1512, when the pope used a Spanish army to restore the Medici.

Lorenzo's son, Giovanni, had been elected pope as Leo X, and Florence became an adjunct not only of the Medici but also of papal interests. The destruction of papal and Medici authority (Lorenzo's nephew, Giulio, had been elected Pope Clement VII) following the sack of Rome in 1527 resulted in the Medicis again being thrown out of Florence and another republic being declared. This last Florentine republic lasted until 1530, when it, too, was extinguished by a Spanish papal army. In its place was established a Medici principality ruled first by the wicked Alessandro de'Medici and after his assassination in 1537 by Cosimo de' Medici, who began the hereditary Medici monarchy as the first Duke of Florence and eventually Grand Duke of Tuscany.

✦ Giovanni Villani

Giovanni Villani (c. 1276–1348) was the great late medieval–early Renaissance chronicler of Florence. He was a banker by profession, but he was stimulated by a visit to Rome during the Jubilee of 1300 to write a history of his own city. Although he enjoyed many forward-looking characteristics, such as an interest in statistical information and astute political and psychological insight, his reliance on such elements as divine providence links Villani closely with the medieval vernacular chronical tradition. His chronicle ends abruptly during his description of the Black Death of 1348 because the chronicler himself fell victim to the plague. His work was continued by his brother, Matteo, who carried the chronicle until 1363, the year he, too, succumbed to another plague; one final year was added by Matteo's son, Filippo, bringing the Villani family chronicle to an end in 1364.

SELECTIONS FROM *THE CHRONICLE OF GIOVANNI VILLANI*

Villani Writes His *Chronicle*

And being on that blessed pilgrimage in the sacred city of Rome and seeing its great and ancient monuments and reading the great deeds of the Romans as described by Virgil, Sallust, Lucan, Livy, Valerius, Orosius, and other masters of history . . . I took my prompting from them although I am a disciple unworthy of such an undertaking. But in view of the fact that our city of Florence, daughter and offspring of Rome, was mounting and pursuing great purposes, while Rome was in its decline, I thought it proper to trace in this chronicle the origins of the city of Florence, so far as I have been able to recover them, and to relate the city's further development at greater length, and at the same time to give a brief account of events throughout the world as long as it please God, in the hope of whose favor I undertook the said enterprise rather than in reliance on my own poor wits. And thus in the year 1300, on my return from Rome, I began to compile this book in the name of God and the blessed John the Baptist and in honor of our city of Florence.

The Rebuilding of Florence after 1293

The Cathedral

In the year 1296, when the city of Florence was in very tranquil state after the revolution associated with the name of Giano della Bella, the citizens agreed to renew their leading church, which was a rude affair and small for such a municipality. They resolved to lengthen it by extending it eastward [*di trerla addietro*] and to make it of marble and sculptured figures. And the foundation was laid with great solemnity on the day of St. Mary of September by the cardinal legate of the pope and many bishops. And there were present also the podestà and the captain and the priors and all the officials of Florence. And the church was consecrated to the

Source: Excerpts from F. Schevill, trans., *Medieval and Renaissance Florence*, Vol. 1. New York: Harper and Row, 1963. Reprinted by permission of James E. Schevill.

honor of God and St. Mary and given the name of Santa Maria del Fiore, although the people continued to call it by its former name of Santa Reparata. And in aid of the construction of the said church the commune ordered a subsidy of four denari on each libra paid out of the city treasury and a head-tax of two soldi on every male. And the legate and bishops endowed the church with liberal indulgences and pardons to whosoever should aid with alms.

The Palace of the Priors

In the said year 1299 the commune and people of Florence laid the foundation of the palace of the priors. They were moved to take this step because of the party divisions and the brawls resulting therefrom between the people and the magnates on the occasion of the renewal of the priors, which occurred every two months. And it did not seem that the priors, who ruled the people and the republic, were secure in the house they inhabited which belonged to the White Cerchi and lay behind the church of San Brocolo. And there, where they laid the foundation of the said palace, had formerly stood the houses of the Uberti, rebels of Florence and Ghibellines. And the ground whereon the houses had stood was converted into a piazza to make sure that the houses would never be rebuilt. And the commune bought the houses of other citizens, as, for instance, those of the Foraboschi, and raised the said palace on the purchased ground. And for the tower of the palace of the priors they utilized the tower of the Foraboschi, which was almost one hundred feet high and was called La Vacca [the Cow]. And in order that the said palace be not built on the former land of the Uberti the committee in charge placed it askew [*il puosomo musso*], which was a great imperfection inasmuch as the palace should have been given a square or rectangular shape and should not have been carried so close to the church of San Piero Scheraggio.

The Bell Tower of Giotto

In the said year [1334], on July 18, was begun the new bell tower of Santa Reparata [we observe that Villani too, much like the common people, was slow in applying to the cathedral its newer, more pretentious name of Santa Maria del Fiore] close to the front of the church on the piazza of San Giovanni. And there were present for the blessing of the first stone the bishop of Florence with all his clergy as well as the priors and the other magistrates with many people and a great procession. And the foundation was made as solid as possible. And as superintendent and overseer of the opera of Santa Reparata the commune appointed our fellow-citizen, Giotto, the most sovereign master of painting in his time, who drew all his figures and their postures according to nature. And he was given a salary by the commune in virtue of his talent and excellence.

The Black Death

The said plague was greater than among us in Pistoia and Prato . . . in Bologna and in the Romagna. It was greater also at Avignon, where the pope keeps court, and throughout the kingdom of France. But where it reaped the greatest harvest was in Turkey and among the countries beyond the sea and among the Tartars. . . . Having grown to vigor in Turkey and Greece and having spread thence over the whole Levant and Mesopotamia and Syria and Chaldea and Cyprus and Crete and Rhodes and all the islands of the Greek archipelago, the said pestilence leaped to Sicily and Sardinia and Corsica and Elba, and from there soon reached all the shores of the mainland. And of eight Genoese galleys which had gone to the Black Sea only four returned, full of infected sailors, who were smitten one after the other on the return journey. And all who arrived at Genoa died, and they corrupted the air to such an extent that whoever came near the bodies died shortly after. And it was a disease in which there appeared certain swellings in the groin and under the armpit, and the victims spat blood, and in three days they were dead. And the priest who confessed the sick and those who nursed them so generally caught the infection that the victims were abandoned and deprived of confession, sacrament, medicine, and nursing. . . . And many lands and cities were made desolate. And this plague lasted till . . . [This sentence was left incomplete as Giovanni himself fell victim to the Black Death of 1348.]

Fire

In the said year [1331], on June 23, during the night of the vigil of Saint John, a fire broke out on the Ponte Vecchio, toward the left bank, and all the shops on the bridge to the number of twenty were burned with heavy loss to many craftsmen. And two apprentices perished in the fire. . . . Further, on September 12, at dusk, a fire broke out at the house of the Soldanieri by the church of Santa Trinità in certain lowly structures housing some carpenters and a blacksmith. And six persons perished, who because of the furious blaze occasioned by the lumber and the horse-stalls were unable to escape. And again, on February 28 [1332], at oncoming night fire attacked the palace of the podestà and burned the roof of the old structure and two-thirds of the new palace from the first story up. On which account the government ordered both structures to be rebuilt in stone all the way to the roof. And a half year later, on July 16, the palace of the wool gild by Or San Michele took fire and everything was consumed from the first story up. . . . The wool gild thereupon ordered their palace to be reconstructed on a larger scale with stone vaults to the roof.

Famine

The famine was felt not only in Florence but throughout Tuscany and a large part of Italy. And so terrible was it that the Perugians, the Sienese, the Lucchese, the Pistolese, and many other townsmen drove forth from their territory all their beggars because they could not support them. Guided by wise counsel and divine pity, the commune of Florence did not do this; in fact it received and provided for a large fraction of the poor mendicants of all Tuscany. . . . It sent for grain to Sicily, ordering it to be brought to the port of Talamone in the Maremma and transporting it thence to Florence at great risk and expense. The government sent also to the Romagna and to the contado of Arezzo; and as long as the scarcity lasted, disregarding the heavy charge upon the public purse, it kept the price of the staio at half a gold florin [which would be two and a half times the normal figure] although to effect this reduction it permitted the wheat to be mixed to one-fourth its volume with coarser grain. In spite of all the government did, the agitation of the people at the market of Or San Michele was so great that it was necessary to protect the officials by means of guards fitted out with ax and block to punish rioters on the spot with the loss of hands or feet.

And in mitigation of this famine the commune of Florence spent in those two years more than sixty thousand gold florins. Finally, it was decided not to go on selling grain in the piazza but to requisition all the bakers' ovens for the baking of bread in order to sell it on the following morning in three or four shops in every sesto at four pennies for the loaf of six ounces. This arrangement successfully tamed the rage of the people since wage-earners with eight to twelve pennies a day could now buy bread on which to live, whereas formerly they had been unable to find the sum necessary to buy a whole staio of wheat.

Flood

By Thursday noon, November 4, the Arno had swollen so vastly at Florence that it covered the whole plain of San Salvi to a depth of from ten to sixteen feet. [San Salvi lay to the east of the town and the water was dammed up on the plain by the stout city wall.] And at the first sleep of night the water washed away the city wall above the Corso de' Tintori . . . for a space of over two hundred feet. Thereupon the whole volume of the flood rushed into the city with such fury that it filled all Florence. It covered and drowned the streets, some more, some less, but it was worst in the sesti of San Piero Scheraggio and Porta San Piero and Porta del Duomo. . . . In the baptistery of St. John the water rose above the altar and reached to over half the height of the columns of porphyry before the entrance. [These were the columns presented by the Pisans over two hundred years before. They are to this day in the indicated place with a line scratched on them showing the level reached by the water in 1333.] And in the palace of the commune, where dwells the podestà, it rose in the courtyard, where he pronounces justice, to the height of ten feet. . . . And in Or San Michele and in the nearby Mercato Nuovo it rose to almost four feet. . . . And the Carraia bridge fell with the exception of two arches toward the right bank. And immediately after fell the Trinità bridge, save for one pier and one arch toward the church of Santa Trinità. It was now the turn of the Ponte Vecchio. When it was choked by the logs brought down by the Arno, the waters leaped over the arches and, rushing on the shops upon the bridge, swept everything away except the two central piers. And at the Rubaconte bridge the water washed over the top at one side and destroyed the parapet at several places. . . . And the statue of Mars, which stood on a pedestal on this side of the Ponte Vecchio, fell into the Arno. . . . And when Mars had fallen and all the houses between the Ponte Vecchio and the Carraia bridge had come down and all the streets on both banks were covered with ruins—to look at this scene was to stare at chaos.

Plague

For at once began a great pestilence, from which, if one fell ill, he but rarely escaped. And more than a sixth of the citizenry perished, among them the best and most beloved of our men and women. There was no family which did not lose one and even two and three of its members. And the pestilence lasted till the approach of winter. And in the city alone more than 15,000 corpses of men and women were buried. Wherefore the city was full of grief and lamentation and people hardly attended to anything other than burying the dead. . . . In the country the mortality was not so great but there too there died a plenty; and with this pestilence there came a new scarcity on top of that of the preceding year and, in spite of the decrease of the population, the staio of grain was sold at thirty soldi. And the price would have risen higher if the commune had not made provision by importing grain by sea. . . . And on account of this pestilence the bishop and the clergy advised the holding of a great procession. It took place on June 18 and almost the whole body of citizens, men and women, followed the relics of the body of Christ, which are preserved at Sant' Ambrogio, and marched through the city till nones [3 P.M.] carrying more than one hundred and fifty lighted candles as large as torches.

Flagellants

In the said year [1310] a great marvel made its appearance. It began in Piedmont, advanced through Lombardy and the Genoese littoral, and spread thence to Tuscany and almost covered all Italy. Many people of the commoner sort, men and women and children without number, left their occupations and their cares behind them and, with the cross to point the way, went from place to place beating their bodies and crying *misericordia* and turning people to penance by persuading them to make peace with one another. The Florentines and the inhabitants of a few other cities refused to let them enter their territory and drove them away saying that they were an augury of evil to the land.

The City

Since we have spoken about the income and expenditure of the Commune of Florence in this period, I think it is fitting to mention this and other great features of our city, so that our descendants in days to come may be aware of any rise, stability, and decline in condition and power that our city may undergo, and also so that, through the wise and able citizens who at the time shall be in charge of its government, [our descendants] may endeavor to advance it in condition and power, seeing our record and example in this chronicle. We find after careful investigation that in this period there were in Florence about 25,000 men from the ages of fifteen to seventy fit to bear arms, all citizens. And among them were 1,500 noble and powerful citizens who as magnates gave security to the Commune. There were in Florence also some seventy-five full-dress knights. To be sure, we find that before the second popular government now in power was formed there were more than 250 knights; but from the time that the people began to rule, the magnates no longer had the status and authority enjoyed earlier, and hence few persons were knighted. From the amount of bread constantly needed for the city, it was estimated that in Florence there were some 90,000 mouths divided among men, women, and children, as can readily be grasped [from what we shall say] later; and it was reckoned that in the city there were always about 1,500 foreigners, transients, and soldiers, not including in the total the citizens who were clerics and cloistered monks and nuns, of whom we shall speak later. It was reckoned that in this period there were some 80,000 men in the territory and district of Florence. From the rector who baptized the infants—since he deposited a black bean for every male baptized in San Giovanni and a white bean for every female in order to ascertain their number—we find that at this period there were from 5,500 to 6,000 baptisms every year, the males usually outnumbering the females by 300 to 500. We find that the boys and girls learning to read [numbered] from 8,000 to 10,000, the children learning the abacus and algorism from 1,000 to 1,200, and those learning grammar and logic in four large schools from 550 to 600.

We find that the churches then in Florence and in the suburbs, including the abbeys and the churches of friars, were 110, among which were 57 parishes with congregations, 5 abbeys with two priors and some 80 monks each, 24 nunneries with some 500 women, 10 orders of friars, 30 hospitals with more than 1,000 beds to receive the poor and the sick, and from 250 to 300 chaplain priests.

The workshops of the *Arte della Lana*[1] were 200 or more, and they

---

1. The guild of wool merchants and entrepreneurs in the woolen industry.

Source: From R. S. Lopez and I. W. Raymond, *Medieval Trade in the Mediterranean World* (New York: Columbia University Press, 1966), pp. 71–74. Reprinted by permission.

made from 70,000 to 80,000 pieces of cloth, which were worth more than 1,200,000 gold florins. And a good third [of this sum] remained in the land as [the reward] of labor, without counting the profit of the entrepreneurs. And more than 30,000 persons lived by it. [To be sure,] we find that some thirty years earlier there were 300 workshops or thereabouts, and they made more than 100,000 pieces of cloth yearly; but these cloths were coarser and one half less valuable, because at that time English wool was not imported and they did not know, as they did later, how to work it.

The *fondachi* of the *Arte di Calimala*,[2] dealing in French and Trans-alpine cloth, were some twenty, and they imported yearly more than 10,000 pieces of cloth, worth 300,000 gold florins. And all these were sold in Florence, without counting those which were reexported from Florence.

The banks of money-changers were about eighty. The gold coins which were struck amounted to some 350,000 gold florins and at times 400,000 [yearly]. And as for deniers of four petty each, about 20,000 pounds of them were struck yearly.

The association of judges was composed of some eighty members; the notaries were some six hundred; physicians and surgical doctors, some sixty; shops of dealers in spices, some hundred.

Merchants and mercers were a large number; the shops of shoemakers, slipper makers, and wooden-shoe makers were so numerous they could not be counted. There were some three hundred persons and more who went to do business out of Florence, and [so did] many other masters in many crafts, and stone and carpentry masters.

There were then in Florence 146 bakeries. And from the [amount of the] tax on grinding and through [information furnished by] the bakers we find that the city within the walls needed 140 *moggia*[3] of grain every day. By this one can estimate how much was needed yearly, not to mention the fact that the larger part of the rich, noble, and well-to-do citizens with their families spent four months a year in the country, and some of them a still longer period.

We also find that in the year 1280, when the city was in a good and happy condition, it needed some 800 *moggia* of grain a week.

Through [the amount of] the tax at the gates we find that some 55,000 *cogna* of wine entered Florence yearly, and in times of plenty about 10,000 *cogna* more.

Every year the city consumed about 4,000 oxen and calves, 60,000 mutton and sheep, 20,000 she-goats and he-goats, 30,000 pigs.

During the month of July 4,000 *some* of melons came through Porta San Friano and they were all distributed in the city. . . .

---

2. The guild of importers, refinishers, and sellers of Transalpine cloth. Their name is derived from Calle Mala, the "bad street," where their shops were located.
3. The *moggio* was a dry measure equal to 16.59+ bushels.

[Florence] within the walls was well built, with many beautiful houses, and at that period people kept building with improved techniques to obtain comfort and richness by importing designs of every kind of improvement. [They built] parish churches and churches of friars of every order, and splendid monasteries. And besides this, there was no citizen, whether commoner or magnate, who had not built or was not building in the country a large and rich estate with a very costly mansion and with fine buildings, much better than those in the city—and in this they all were committing sin, and they were called crazy on account of their wild expenses. And yet, this was such a wonderful sight that when foreigners, not accustomed to [cities like] Florence, came from abroad, they usually believed that all of the costly buildings and beautiful palaces which surrounded the city for three miles were part of the city in the manner of Rome—not to mention the costly palaces with towers, courts, and walled gardens farther distant, which would have been called castles in any other country. To sum up, it was estimated that within a six-mile radius around the city there were more than twice as many rich and noble mansions as in Florence.

✦ *Giovanni Boccaccio*

*G*iovanni Boccaccio was born in Paris in 1313, the illegitimate son of a Florentine father and a French mother. His father wished him to enter business, and he was sent to Naples to learn the profession. However, Boccaccio disliked mercantile affairs, so his father arranged for him to study canon law, but that discipline was equally uncongenial. Boccaccio's true vocation was letters, which he pursued at the highly polished court of King Robert of Naples. There Boccaccio also began a love affair with the king's natural daughter, Fiammetta, who stimulated Boccaccio's poetic imagination.

The economic dislocation caused by the collapse of two large Florentine banks and the mortality of the Black Death of 1348 required Boccaccio to return to and remain in Florence to assist his father. There he began his literary production in earnest, producing many of his Italian works. After about 1350, Boccaccio wrote the Decameron, a collection of tales told by aristocratic young Florentines as they sought refuge from the plague, an event described by the author with chilling effect. This great book is a complex vision of Italian society at all levels in the middle of the fourteenth century. Sensitive, humorous, elegant, and very popular, it became the model for an entire genre of such collections, and its language was suggested by Pietro Bembo as the ideal example of Italian vernacular style.

However, in the 1350s, Boccaccio fell increasingly under the influence of Petrarch and entered into a close friendship with the older poet. Boccaccio began to write more in Latin and more of a religious, devotional, and philosophical nature. He wrote against women and love, and he entered into the detailed study of Dante, whose biography he wrote and for whose Divine Comedy he produced a commentary. Also, he became interested in the study of Greek and was instrumental in having a chair in that language established at the University of Florence, although he never succeeded in mastering the language himself.

Despite these personal and literary links to Florence, Boccaccio left the city to reside briefly again in Naples on two occasions and in Venice. However, he found no greater respect outside his ancestral city, so he returned to Florence, where in 1373 he was granted a public readership for the study of Dante. Only a year after this recognition, though, Boccaccio took ill and had to resign his professorship. Boccaccio died in the following year.

A DESCRIPTION OF THE PLAGUE FROM
THE DECAMERON
First Day

Here begins the First Day of the Decameron, *wherein first of all the author explains the circumstances in which certain persons, who presently make their appearance, were induced to meet for the purpose of conversing together, after which, under the rule of* Pampinea, *each of them speaks on the subject they find most congenial.*

Whenever, fairest ladies, I pause to consider how compassionate you all are by nature, I invariably become aware that the present work will seem to you to possess an irksome and ponderous opening. For it carries at its head the painful memory of the deadly havoc wrought by the recent plague, which brought so much heartache and misery to those who witnessed, or had experience of it. But I do not want you to be deterred, for this reason, from reading any further, on the assumption that you are to be subjected, as you read, to an endless torrent of tears and sobbing. You will be affected no differently by this grim beginning than walkers confronted by a steep and rugged hill, beyond which there lies a beautiful and delectable plain. The degree of pleasure they derive from the latter will correspond directly to the difficulty of the climb and the descent. And just as the end of mirth is heaviness,[1] so sorrows are dispersed by the advent of joy.

---

1. Proverbs 14, 23.

Source: Giovanni Boccaccio, *The Decameron,* trans. and with an Introduction by G. H. McWilliam (Harmondsworth: Penguin Books), pp. 49–60. Reproduced by permission of Penguin Books Ltd.

This brief unpleasantness (I call it brief, inasmuch as it is contained within few words) is quickly followed by the sweetness and the pleasure which I have already promised you, and which, unless you were told in advance, you would not perhaps be expecting to find after such a beginning as this. Believe me, if I could decently have taken you whither I desire by some other route, rather than along a path so difficult as this, I would gladly have done so. But since it is impossible without this memoir to show the origin of the events you will read about later, I really have no alternative but to address myself to its composition.

I say, then, that the sum of thirteen hundred and forty-eight years had elapsed since the fruitful Incarnation of the Son of God, when the noble city of Florence, which for its great beauty excels all others in Italy, was visited by the deadly pestilence. Some say that it descended upon the human race through the influence of the heavenly bodies, others that it was a punishment signifying God's righteous anger at our iniquitous way of life. But whatever its cause, it had originated some years earlier in the East, where it had claimed countless lives before it unhappily spread westward, growing in strength as it swept relentlessly on from one place to the next.

In the face of its onrush, all the wisdom and ingenuity of man were unavailing. Large quantities of refuse were cleared out of the city by officials specially appointed for the purpose, all sick persons were forbidden entry, and numerous instructions were issued for safeguarding the people's health, but all to no avail. Nor were the countless petitions humbly directed to God by the pious, whether by means of formal processions or in any other guise, any less ineffectual. For in the early spring of the year we have mentioned, the plague began, in a terrifying and extraordinary manner, to make its disastrous effects apparent. It did not take the form it had assumed in the East, where if anyone bled from the nose it was an obvious portent of certain death. On the contrary, its earliest symptom, in men and women alike, was the appearance of certain swellings in the groin or the armpit, some of which were egg-shaped whilst others were roughly the size of the common apple. Sometimes the swellings were large, sometimes not so large, and they were referred to by the populace as *gavòccioli*. From the two areas already mentioned, this deadly *gavòcciolo* would begin to spread, and within a short time it would appear at random all over the body. Later on, the symptoms of the disease changed, and many people began to find dark blotches and bruises on their arms, thighs, and other parts of the body, sometimes large and few in number, at other times tiny and closely spaced. These, to anyone unfortunate enough to contract them, were just as infallible a sign that he would die as the *gavòcciolo* had been earlier, and as indeed it still was.

Against these maladies, it seemed that all the advice of physicians and all the power of medicine were profitless and unavailing. Perhaps the nature of the illness was such that it allowed no remedy: or perhaps those people who were treating the illness (whose numbers had increased enormously because the ranks of the qualified were invaded by people, both men and women, who had never received any training in medicine), being ignorant of its causes, were not prescribing the appropriate cure. At all events, few of those who caught it ever recovered, and in most cases death occurred within three days from the appearance of the symptoms we have described, some people dying more rapidly than others, the majority without any fever or other complications.

But what made this pestilence even more severe was that whenever those suffering from it mixed with people who were still unaffected, it would rush upon these with the speed of a fire racing through dry or oily substances that happened to be placed within its reach. Nor was this the full extent of its evil, for not only did it infect healthy persons who conversed or had any dealings with the sick, making them ill or visiting an equally horrible death upon them, but it also seemed to transfer the sickness to anyone touching the clothes or other objects which had been handled or used by its victims.

It is a remarkable story that I have to relate. And were it not for the fact that I am one of many people who saw it with their own eyes, I would scarcely dare to believe it, let alone commit it to paper, even though I had heard it from a person whose word I could trust. The plague I have been describing was of so contagious a nature that very often it visibly did more than simply pass from one person to another. In other words, whenever an animal other than a human being touched anything belonging to a person who had been stricken or exterminated by the disease, it not only caught the sickness, but died from it almost at once. To all of this, as I have just said, my own eyes bore witness on more than one occasion. One day, for instance, the rags of a pauper who had died from the disease were thrown into the street, where they attracted the attention of two pigs. In their wonted fashion, the pigs first of all gave the rags a thorough mauling with their snouts after which they took them between their teeth and shook them against their cheeks. And within a short time they began to writhe as though they had been poisoned, then they both dropped dead to the ground, spreadeagled upon the rags that had brought about their undoing.

These things, and many others of a similar or even worse nature, caused various fears and fantasies to take root in the minds of those who were still alive and well. And almost without exception, they took a single and very inhuman precaution, namely to avoid or run away from the sick and their belongings, by which means they all thought that their own health would be preserved.

Some people were of the opinion that a sober and abstemious mode of living considerably reduced the risk of infection. They therefore formed themselves into groups and lived in isolation from everyone else. Having withdrawn to a comfortable abode where there were no sick persons, they locked themselves in and settled down to a peaceable existence, consuming modest quantities of delicate foods and precious wines and avoiding all excesses. They refrained from speaking to outsiders, refused to receive news of the dead or the sick, and entertained themselves with music and whatever other amusements they were able to devise.

Others took the opposite view, and maintained that an infallible way of warding off this appalling evil was to drink heavily, enjoy life to the full, go round singing and merrymaking, gratify all of one's cravings whenever the opportunity offered, and shrug the whole thing off as one enormous joke. Moreover, they practiced what they preached to the best of their ability, for they would visit one tavern after another, drinking all day and night to immoderate excess; or alternatively (and this was their more frequent custom), they would do their drinking in various private houses, but only in the ones where the conversation was restricted to subjects that were pleasant or entertaining. Such places were easy to find, for people behaved as though their days were numbered, and treated their belongings and their own persons with equal abandon. Hence most houses had become common property, and any passing stranger could make himself at home as naturally as though he were the rightful owner. But for all their riotous manner of living, these people always took good care to avoid any contact with the sick.

In the face of so much affliction and misery, all respect for the laws of God and man had virtually broken down and been extinguished in our city. For like everybody else, those ministers and executors of the laws who were not either dead or ill were left with so few subordinates that they were unable to discharge any of their duties. Hence everyone was free to behave as he pleased.

There were many other people who steered a middle course between the two already mentioned, neither restricting their diet to the same degree as the first group, nor indulging so freely as the second in drinking and other forms of wantonness, but simply doing no more than satisfy their appetite. Instead of incarcerating themselves, these people moved about freely, holding in their hands a posy of flowers, or fragrant herbs, or one of a wide range of spices, which they applied at frequent intervals to their nostrils, thinking it an excellent idea to fortify the brain with smells of that particular sort; for the stench of dead bodies, sickness, and medicines seemed to fill and pollute the whole of the atmosphere.

Some people, pursuing what was possibly the safer alternative, callously maintained that there was no better or more efficacious remedy against a plague than to run away from it. Swayed by this argument, and sparing no thought for anyone but themselves, large numbers of men and women abandoned their city, their homes, their relatives, their estates and their belongings, and headed for the countryside, either in Florentine territory or, better still, abroad. It was as though they imagined that the wrath of God would not unleash this plague against men for their iniquities irrespective of where they happened to be, but would only be aroused against those who found themselves within the city walls; or possibly they assumed that the whole of the population would be exterminated and that the city's last hour had come.

Of the people who held these various opinions, not all of them died. Nor, however, did they all survive. On the contrary, many of each different persuasion fell ill here, there, and everywhere, and having themselves, when they were fit and well, set an example to those who were as yet unaffected, they languished away with virtually no one to nurse them. It was not merely a question of one citizen avoiding another, and of people almost invariably neglecting their neighbors and rarely or never visiting their relatives, addressing them only from a distance; this scourge had implanted so great a terror in the hearts of men and women that brothers abandoned brothers, uncles their nephews, sisters their brothers, and in many cases wives deserted their husbands. But even worse, and almost incredible, was the fact that fathers and mothers refused to nurse and assist their own children, as though they did not belong to them.

Hence the countless numbers of people who fell ill, both male and female, were entirely dependent upon either the charity of friends (who were few and far between) or the greed of servants, who remained in short supply despite the attraction of high wages out of all proportion to the services they performed. Furthermore, these latter were men and women of coarse intellect and the majority were unused to such duties, and they did little more than hand things to the invalid when asked to do so and watch over him when he was dying. And in performing this kind of service, they frequently lost their lives as well as their earnings.

As a result of this wholesale desertion of the sick by neighbors, relatives and friends, and in view of the scarcity of servants, there grew up a practice almost never previously heard of, whereby when a woman fell ill, no matter how gracious or beautiful or gently bred she might be, she raised no objections to being attended by a male servant, whether he was young or not. Nor did she have any scruples about showing him every part of her body as freely as she would have displayed it to a woman, provided that the nature of her infirmity required her to do so; and this explains why those women who recovered were possibly less chaste in the period that followed.

Moreover a great many people died who would perhaps have survived had they received some assistance. And hence, what with the lack of appropriate means for tending the sick, and the virulence of the plague, the number of deaths reported in the city whether by day or night was so enormous that it astonished all who heard tell of it, to say nothing of the people who actually witnessed the carnage. And it was perhaps inevitable that among the citizens who survived there arose certain customs that were quite contrary to established tradition.

It had once been customary, as it is again nowadays, for the women relatives and neighbors of a dead man to assemble in his house in order to mourn in the company of the women who had been closest to him; moreover his kinsfolk would forgather in front of his house along with his neighbors and various other citizens, and there would be a contingent of priests, whose numbers varied according to the quality of the deceased; his body would be taken thence to the church in which he had wanted to be buried, being borne on the shoulders of his peers amidst the funeral pomp of candles and dirges. But as the ferocity of the plague began to mount, this practice all but disappeared entirely and was replaced by different customs. For not only did people die without having many women about them, but a great number departed this life without anyone at all to witness their going. Few indeed were those to whom the lamentations and bitter tears of their relatives were accorded; on the contrary, more often than not bereavement was the signal for laughter and witticisms and general jollification—the art of which the women, having for the most part suppressed their feminine concern for the salvation of the souls of the dead, had learned to perfection. Moreover it was rare for the bodies of the dead to be accompanied by more than ten or twelve neighbors to the church, nor were they borne on the shoulders of worthy and honest citizens, but by a kind of gravedigging fraternity, newly come into being and drawn from the lower orders of society. These people assumed the title of sexton, and demanded a fat fee for their services, which consisted in taking up the coffin and hauling it swiftly away, not to the church specified by the dead man in his will, but usually to the nearest at hand. They would be preceded by a group of four or six clerics, who between them carried one or two candles at most, and sometimes none at all. Nor did the priests go to the trouble of pronouncing solemn and lengthy funeral rites, but, with the aid of these so-called sextons, they hastily lowered the body into the nearest empty grave they could find.

As for the common people and a large proportion of the bourgeoisie, they presented a much more pathetic spectacle, for the majority of them were constrained, either by their poverty or the hope of survival, to remain in their houses. Being confined to their own parts of the city, they fell ill daily in their thousands, and since they had no one to assist them or attend to their needs, they inevitably perished almost without exception. Many dropped dead in the open streets, both by day and by night, whilst a great many others, though dying in their own houses, drew their neighbors' attention to the fact more by the smell of their rotting corpses than by any other means. And what with these, and the others who were dying all over the city, bodies were here, there and everywhere.

Whenever people died, their neighbors nearly always followed a single, set routine, prompted as much by their fear of being contaminated by the decaying corpse as by any charitable feelings they may have entertained towards the deceased. Either on their own, or with the assistance of bearers whenever these were to be had, they extracted the bodies of the dead from their houses and left them lying outside their front doors, where anyone going about the streets, especially in the early morning, could have observed countless numbers of them. Funeral biers would then be sent for, upon which the dead were taken away, though there were some who, for lack of biers, were carried off on plain boards. It was by no means rare for more than one of these biers to be seen with two or three bodies upon it at a time; on the contrary, many were seen to contain a husband and wife, two or three brothers and sisters, a father and son, or some other pair of close relatives. And times without number it happened that two priests would be on their way to bury someone, holding a cross before them, only to find that bearers carrying three or four additional biers would fall in behind them; so that whereas the priests had thought they had only one burial to attend to, they in fact had six or seven, and sometimes more. Even in these circumstances, however, there were no tears or candles or mourners to honor the dead; in fact, no more respect was accorded to dead people than would nowadays be shown towards dead goats. For it was quite apparent that the one thing which, in normal times, no wise man had ever learned to accept with patient resignation (even though it struck so seldom and unobtrusively), had now been brought home to the feeble-minded as well, but the scale of the calamity caused them to regard it with indifference.

Such was the multitude of corpses (of which further consignments were arriving every day and almost by the hour at each of the churches), that there was not sufficient consecrated ground for them to be buried in, especially if each was to have its own plot in accordance with long-established custom. So when all the graves were full, huge trenches were excavated in the churchyards, into which new arrivals were placed in their hundreds, stowed tier upon tier like ships' cargo, each layer of corpses being covered over with a thin layer of soil till the trench was filled to the top.

But rather than describe in elaborate detail the calamities we experi-enced in the city at that time, I must mention that, whilst an ill wind was blowing through Florence itself, the surrounding region was no less badly affected. In the fortified towns, conditions were similar to those in the city itself on a minor scale; but in the scattered hamlets and the countryside proper, the poor unfortunate peasants and their families had no physicians or servants whatever to assist them, and collapsed by the wayside, in their fields, and in their cottages at all hours of the day and night, dying more like animals than human beings. Like the townspeople, they too grew apathetic in their ways, disregarded their affairs, and neglected their possessions. Moreover they all behaved as though each day was to be their last, and far from making provision for the future by tilling their lands, tending their flocks, and adding to their previous labors, they tried in every way they could think of to squander the assets already in their possession. Thus it came about that oxen, asses, sheep, goats, pigs, chickens, and even dogs (for all their deep fidelity to man) were driven away and allowed to roam freely through the fields, where the crops lay abandoned and had not even been reaped, let alone gathered in. And after a whole day's feasting, many of these animals, as though possessing the power of reason, would return glutted in the evening to their own quarters, without any shepherd to guide them.

But let us leave the countryside and return to the city. What more remains to be said, except that the cruelty of heaven (and possibly, in some measure, also that of man) was so immense and so devastating that between March and July of the year in question, what with the fury of the pestilence and the fact that so many of the sick were inadequately cared for or abandoned in their hour of need because the healthy were too terrified to approach them, it is reliably thought that over a hundred thousand human lives were extinguished within the walls of the city of Florence? Yet before this lethal catastrophe fell upon the city, it is doubtful whether anyone would have guessed it contained so many inhabitants.

Ah, how great a number of splendid palaces, fine houses, and noble dwellings, once filled with retainers, with lords and with ladies, were bereft of all who had lived there, down to the tiniest child! How numerous were the famous families, the vast estates, the notable fortunes, that were seen to be left without a rightful successor! How many gallant gentlemen, fair ladies, and sprightly youths, who would have been judged hale and hearty by Galen, Hippocrates and Aesculapius (to say nothing of others), having breakfasted in the morning with their kinsfolk, acquaintances and friends, supped that same evening with their ancestors in the next world!

The more I reflect upon all this misery, the deeper my sense of personal sorrow; hence I shall refrain from describing those aspects which can suitably be omitted, and proceed to inform you that these were the conditions prevailing in our city, which was by now almost emptied of its inhabitants, when one Tuesday morning (or so I was told by a person whose word can be trusted) seven young ladies were to be found in the venerable church of Santa Maria Novella, which was otherwise almost deserted. They had been attending divine service, and were dressed in mournful attire appropriate to the times. Each was a friend, a neighbor, or a relative of the other six, none was older than twenty-seven or younger than eighteen, and all were intelligent, gently bred, fair to look upon, graceful in bearing, and charmingly unaffected. I could tell you their actual names, but refrain from doing so for a good reason, namely that I would not want any of them to feel embarrassed, at any time in the future, on account of the ensuing stories, all of which they either listened to or narrated themselves. For nowadays, laws relating to pleasure are somewhat restrictive, whereas at that time, for the reasons indicated above, they were exceptionally lax, not only for ladies of their own age but also for much older women. Besides, I have no wish to supply envious tongues, ever ready to censure a laudable way of life, with a chance to besmirch the good name of these worthy ladies with their lewd and filthy gossip.

And therefore, so that we may perceive distinctly what each of them had to say, I propose to refer to them by names which are either wholly or partially appropriate to the qualities of each. The first of them, who was also the eldest, we shall call Pampinea, the second Fiammetta, Filomena the third, and the fourth Emilia; then we shall name the fifth Lauretta, and the sixth Neifile, whilst to the last, not without reason, we shall give the name of Elissa.

Without prior agreement but simply by chance, these seven ladies found themselves sitting, more or less in a circle, in one part of the church, reciting their paternosters. Eventually, they left off and heaved a great many sighs, after which they began to talk among themselves on various different aspects of the times through which they were passing. But after a little while, they all fell silent except for Pampinea, who said:

'Dear ladies, you will often have heard it affirmed, as I have, that no man does injury to another in exercising his lawful rights. Every person born into this world has a natural right to sustain, preserve, and defend his own life to the best of his ability—a right so freely acknowledged that men have sometimes killed others in self-defense, and no blame whatever has attached to their actions. Now, if this is permitted by the laws, upon whose prompt application all mortal creatures depend for their well-being, how can it possibly be wrong, seeing that it harms no one, for us or anyone else to do all in our power to preserve our lives? If I pause to consider what we have been doing this morning, and what we have done on several mornings in the past, if I reflect on the nature and subject of our conversation, I realize, just as you also must realize, that each of us is apprehensive on her own account. This does not surprise me in the least, but what does greatly surprise me (seeing that each of us has the natural feelings of a woman) is that we do nothing to requite ourselves against the thing of which we are all so justly afraid.

'Here we linger for no other purpose, or so it seems to me, than to count the number of corpses being taken to burial, or to hear whether the friars of the church, very few of whom are left, chant their offices at the appropriate hours, or to exhibit the quality and quantity of our sorrows, by means of the clothes we are wearing, to all those whom we meet in this place. And if we go outside, we shall see the dead and the sick being carried hither and thither, or we shall see people, once condemned to exile by the courts for their misdeeds, careering wildly about the streets in open defiance of the law, well knowing that those appointed to enforce it are either dead or dying; or else we shall find ourselves at the mercy of the sum of our city who, having scented our blood, call themselves sextons and go prancing and bustling all over the place, singing bawdy songs that add insult to our injuries. Moreover, all we ever hear is "So-and-so's dead" and "So-and-so's dying"; and if there were anyone left to mourn, the whole place would be filled with sounds of wailing and weeping.

'And if we return to our homes, what happens? I know not whether your own experience is similar to mine, but my house was once full of servants, and now that there is no one left apart from my maid and myself, I am filled with foreboding and feel as if every hair of my head is standing on end. Wherever I go in the house, wherever I pause to rest, I seem to be haunted by the shades of the departed, whose faces no longer appear as I remember them but with strange and horribly twisted expressions that frighten me out of my senses.

'Accordingly, whether I am here in church or out in the streets or sitting at home, I always feel ill at ease, the more so because it seems to me that no one possessing private means and a place to retreat to is left here apart from ourselves. But even if such people are still to be found, they draw no distinction, as I have frequently heard and seen for myself, between what is honest and what is dishonest; and provided only that they are prompted by their appetites, they will do whatever affords them the greatest pleasure, whether by day or by night, alone or in company. It is not only of lay people that I speak, but also of those enclosed in monasteries, who, having convinced themselves that such behavior is suitable for them and is only unbecoming in others, have broken the rules of obedience and given themselves over to carnal pleasures, thereby thinking to escape, and have turned lascivious and dissolute.

SELECTIONS FROM *THE LIFE OF DANTE*

Proem

Solon, whose bosom was reputed a human temple of divine wisdom, and whose sacred laws are manifest proof to modern men of ancient justice, used frequently to say, as some relate, that all republics, like men, walk and stand on two feet. With sound judgment he declared the right foot to be the punishment of every crime, and the left the remuneration of every virtuous deed. He added that if either of these two things through carelessness or corruption be neglected, the republic that so acts must unquestionably walk lame; and that if she should be so unfortunate as to sin against both these canons, almost certainly she could not stand at all. Moved, then, by this commendable and obviously true precept, many ancient and illustrious peoples did honor to their men of worth, sometimes by deification, again by a marble statue, often by splendid obsequies, now by an arch of triumph, and now by a laurel crown, according to the merits of their lives. The punishments, on the other hand, that were meted to the culpable, I do not care to rehearse.

By virtue of these honors and corrections, Assyria, Macedonia, Greece, and finally the Roman Republic expanded, reaching with their deeds the

Source: G. Boccaccio and L. Bruni Aretino, *The Earliest Lives of Dante*, edited by F. Bassetti-Sani (New York: Ungar, 1963), pp. 9–12 and 18–41. Reprinted by permission of Ungar Publishing Co.

ends of the earth and with their fame touching the stars. But their modern successors, and especially my Florentines, have not only followed feebly in the footsteps of these noble exemplars, but have so far departed therefrom that ambition usurps all the rewards of virtue. Wherefore it is with the greatest affliction of mind that I, and whoever else views it with the eye of reason, see evil and perverse men raised to high places, to the chief offices and rewards, and good men banished, depreciated, and debased. What end the judgment of God reserves for such action, let them consider who hold the helm of this vessel, for we of the humbler throng are borne on the wave of fortune, and are not partakers in their guilt.

Although what has been said above could be verified by countless cases of ingratitude, and by instances of shameless indulgence plain to all, it will suffice for me to instance one case alone, in order that I may the less expose our faults, and that I may come to my principal purpose. Nor is the case in point an ordinary or slight one, for I am going to record the banishment of that most illustrious man, Dante Alighieri, an ancient citizen and born of no mean parents, who merited as much through his virtue, learning, and good services as is adequately shown and will be shown by the deeds he wrought. If such deeds had been done in a just republic, we believe they would have earned for him the highest rewards.

O iniquitous design! O shameless deed! O wretched example, clear proof of ruin to come! Instead of these rewards there was meted to him an unjust and bitter condemnation, perpetual banishment with alienation of his paternal goods, and, could it have been effected, the profanation of his glorious renown by false charges. The recent traces of his flight, his bones buried in an alien land, and his children scattered in the houses of others, still in part bear witness to these things. If all the other iniquities of Florence could be hidden from the all-seeing eyes of God, should not this one suffice to provoke his wrath upon her? Yea, in truth. Of him who, on the other hand, may be exalted, I deem it fitting to be silent.

Indeed, the close observer sees that the modern world has not only departed from the pathway of the former world, whereon I touched above, but that it has turned its feet in quite the opposite direction. Wherefore it seems manifest that if we and others who live contrary to the above-cited maxim of Solon remain on our feet without falling, the reason must be that the nature of things has changed, as we often notice, through long operation, or that God unexpectedly and miraculously sustains us through the merits of some action of our past; or else, perchance, his patience awaits our repentance. If this in due time does not follow, let none doubt that his wrath, which with slow pace moves to vengeance, reserves for us treatment so much the more grievous as fully to compensate for his delay.

But inasmuch as we should not only flee evil deeds, albeit they seem to go unpunished, but also by right action should strive to amend them, I, although not fitted for so great a task, will try to do according to my little talent what the city should have done with magnificence, but has not. For I recognize that I am a part, though a small one, of that same city whereof Dante Alighieri, if his merits, his nobleness, and his virtue be considered, was a very great part and that for this reason I, like every other citizen, am personally responsible for the honors due him. Not with a statue shall I honor him, nor with splendid obsequies—which customs no longer hold among us, nor would my powers suffice therefor—but with words I shall honor him, feeble though they be for so great an undertaking. Of these I have, and of these will I give, that other nations may not say that his native land, both as a whole and in part, has been equally ungrateful to so great a poet.

And I shall write in a style full light and humble, for higher my art does not permit me; and in the Florentine idiom, that it may not differ from that which Dante used in the greater part of his writings. I shall first record those things about which he himself preserved a modest silence, namely the nobleness of his birth, his life, his studies, and his habits. Afterwards I shall gather under one head the works he composed, whereby he has rendered himself so evident to posterity that perchance my words will throw as much darkness upon him as light, albeit this is neither my intention nor wish. For I am content always to be set right, here and elsewhere, by those wiser than I, in all that I have spoken mistakenly. And that I may not err, I humbly pray that He who, as we know, drew Dante to his vision by a stair so lofty, will now aid and guide my spirit and my feeble hand.

Family Cares, Honors, and Exile of Dante

It is the general nature of things temporal that one thing entails another. Domestic cares drew Dante to public ones, where the vain honors that are attached to state positions so bewildered him that, without noting whence he had come and whither he was bound, with free rein he almost completely surrendered himself to the management of these matters. And therein fortune was so favorable to him that no legation was heard or answered, no law established or repealed, no peace made nor public war undertaken, nor, in short, was any deliberation of weight entered upon, until Dante had first given his opinion relative thereto. On him all public faith, all hope, and, in a word, all things human and divine seemed to rest. But although Fortune, the subverter of our counsels and the foe of all human stability, kept him at the summit of her wheel for several years of glorious rule, she brought him to an end far different from his beginning, since he trusted her immoderately.

In Dante's time the citizens of Florence were perversely divided into two factions, and by the operations of astute and prudent leaders each party was very powerful, so that sometimes one ruled and sometimes the other, to the displeasure of its defeated rival. In his wish to unite the divided body of his republic, Dante brought all genius, all art, all study to bear, showing the wiser citizens how great things soon perish through discord, and how little things through harmony have infinite growth. Finding, however, that his auditors' minds were unyielding and that his labor was in vain, and believing it the judgment of God, he at first purposed to drop entirely all public affairs and live a private life. But afterwards he was drawn on by the sweetness of glory, by the empty favor of the populace, and by the persuasions of the chief citizens, coupled with his own belief that, should the occasion offer, he could accomplish much more good for his city if he were great in public affairs than he could in his private capacity completely removed therefrom.

O fond desire of human splendors, how much stronger is thy power than he who has not known thee can believe! This man, mature as he was, bred, nurtured, and trained in the sacred bosom of philosophy, before whose eyes was the downfall of kings ancient and modern, the desolation of kingdoms, provinces, and cities, and the furious onslaughts of fortune, though he sought naught else than the highest, lacked either the knowledge or the power to defend himself from thy charms.

Dante decided, then, to pursue the fleeting honor and false glory of public office. Perceiving that he could not support by himself a third party, which, in itself just, should overthrow the injustice of the two others and reduce them to unity, he allied himself with that faction which seemed to him to possess most of justice and reason—working always for that which he recognized as salutary to his country and her citizens. But human counsels are commonly defeated by the powers of heaven. Hatred and enmities arose, though without just cause, and waxed greater day by day; so that many times the citizens rushed to arms, to their utmost confusion. They purposed to end the struggle by fire and sword, and were so blinded by wrath that they did not see that they themselves would perish miserably thereby.

After each of the factions had given many proofs of their strength to their mutual loss, the time came when the secret counsels of threatening Fortune were to be disclosed. Rumor, who reports both the true and the false, announced that the foes of Dante's faction were strengthened by wise and wonderful designs and by an immense multitude of armed men, and by this means so terrified the leaders of his party that she banished from their minds all consideration, all forethought, all reason, save how to flee in safety. Together with them Dante, instantly precipitated from the chief rule of his city, beheld himself not only brought low to the earth, but banished from his country. Not many days after his expulsion, when the populace had already rushed to the houses of the exiles, and had furiously pillaged and gutted them, the victors reorganized the city after their pleasure, condemning all the leaders of their adversaries to perpetual exile as capital enemies of the republic, and with them Dante, not as one of the lesser leaders, but as it were the chief one. Their real property was meanwhile confiscated or alienated to the victors.

This reward Dante gained for the tender love which he had borne his country! This reward Dante gained for his efforts to allay the civic discord! This reward Dante gained for having given all his care to the welfare, the peace, the tranquility of his fellow-citizens! It is manifest from this how void of truth are the favors of the people, and how little trust may be placed therein. He in whom, but a short time before, every public hope, all the affections of the citizens, every refuge of the people, seemed to be placed, suddenly, for no just cause, for no offense or crime, is furiously driven into irrevocable exile, and all by means of that very Fame who aforetime had frequently been heard to lift his praises to the stars. This was the marble statue raised to the eternal memory of his virtue! With these letters was his name inscribed on tables of gold among the fathers of his country! By such commendatory reports were thanks rendered him for his good deeds! Who, then, in view of these things, will say that our republic does not halt upon this foot?

O vain confidence of mortals, by how many lofty examples art thou continually reproved, admonished, and chastised! Alas! if Camillus, Rutilius, Coriolanus, the two Scipios, and the other ancient worthies have passed from thy memory through lapse of time, let this recent instance make thee pursue thy pleasure with more temperate rein. Nothing in this world has less stability than popular favor. There is no hope more insane, no counsel more foolish than that which encourages one to trust therein. Let our minds, then, be lifted up to Heaven, in whose everlasting law, in whose eternal splendors, in whose true beauty, is clearly manifest the stability of Him who moves all things according to reason; and thus, leaving transitory things, we may, to avoid deception, fasten our every hope on Him, as on a fixed goal.

Rebuke of the Florentines

O ungrateful fatherland! What madness, what recklessness possessed thee, when with unwonted cruelty thou didst put to flight thy most precious citizen, thy chief benefactor, thy supreme poet? Or what has since possessed thee? If perchance thou excuse thyself, laying the blame of thy evil purpose on the general fury of the time, why, when thy wrath had ceased and thy peace of mind was restored, and when thou hadst repented of the deed, didst thou not recall him? Ah! be not loth to reason a little with me, thy son, and receive what righteous indignation makes me say, as from a man who desires that thou amend, and not that thou be punished.

Does it seem to thee that thou art glorious in so many and so great titles that thou shouldst have wished to banish from thee that one, the like of whom no neighboring city can boast? Ah! tell me with what victories, what triumphs, with what virtues and worthy citizens art thou resplendent? Thy riches, a thing transient and uncertain; thy beauties, a thing fragile and failing; thy luxuries, a thing effeminate and reprehensible—these make thee famous in the false judgment of the people, who ever look more to appearances than to the truth. Alas! wilt thou glory in thy merchants and the artists in whom thou dost abound? Fool-ishly wilt thou do so. The former with constant avarice ply a servile trade, and art, which once was ennobled by men of genius, in that they made it their second nature, is now corrupted by this very avarice, and become of no account. Wilt thou glory then in the sloth and cowardice of those who, calling to mind their ancestors, would gain within thy walls high station in that nobility which they work against by robbery, treachery, and deceit? Worthless glory will be thine, and the scorn of those whose opinion has a fitting basis and firm stability.

Alas! wretched mother, open thine eyes and see with some remorse what thou has done. Be ashamed, thou that art reputed wise, for the false choice thou hast made in thine errors. Ah! if thou didst not have such counsel in thyself, why didst thou not imitate the actions of those cities which are still famous for their praiseworthy deeds? Athens, one of the eyes of Greece, equally splendid in learning, eloquence, and military power, when on her rested the rule of the world; Argos, still glorious in the titles of her kings; Smyrna, for ever to be revered for the sake of Nicholas, her bishop; Pylos, renowned for her aged Nestor; Cyme, Chios, and Colophon, splendid cities of the past—none of these was ashamed nor did they hesitate in their most glorious days eagerly to discuss the birthplace of the poet Homer, each city affirming that he has drawn from her. So strong did each one make her claim that it is not certain whence he did come; and the dispute still continues, for all make equal boast of this great citizen. And Mantua, our neighbor, from what does she derive greater fame than from the fact that Virgil, whose name they still hold in great reverence, was a Mantuan? So acceptable to all is he that his image is seen not only in public but also in many private places, showing that, notwithstanding the fact that his father was a potter, he was the ennobler of them all. Sulmona glories in Ovid, Venosa in Horace, Aquino in Juvenal, and so with many others, each arguing her claim to her son.

It had been no shame for thee to have followed the example of these cities, for it is not likely that without cause they have been so fond and tender toward such citizens. They realized what thou likewise couldst have known and canst now, namely, that the ever-enduring influence of these men, even after the ruin of the cities themselves, would keep their names eternal; even as now, published throughout the world, they make the cities known to those who have never seen them. Thou alone, blinded by I know not what infatuation, hast chosen a different course, and, as if full glorious in thyself, has not cared for this splendor. Thou alone, as if the Camilli, the Publicoli, the Torquati, the Fabricii, the Fabii, the Catos, and the Scipios had been thine, and by their splendid deeds had made thee famous, not only hast suffered thine ancient citizen Claudian to fall from thy hands, but hast neglected thy present poet and hast driven him from thee, banished him, and wouldst have deprived him, had it been possible, of thy name. I cannot escape being ashamed in thy behalf.

But lo! not fortune, but the natural course of things, has been so favorable to thy vicious appetite that it has performed by its eternal law what thou in brutal eagerness wouldst willingly have done, if he had fallen into they hands—slain him. Dead is thy Dante Alighieri in that exile to which thou, jealous of his worth, didst unjustly condemn him. O crime immemorable, that the mother should envy the virtue of any of her sons! Now at last art thou free from anxiety. Now by reason of his death thou livest secure in thy faults, and canst end thy long and unjust persecutions. He cannot, dead, do that to thee which, living, he never would have done. He lies beneath another sky than thine, nor mayst thou think ever to see him more, save on that day when thou shalt see all thy citizens examined and punished by a just judge.

If then hatred, anger, and enmities cease at the death of any one, as is believed, begin to return to thyself and thy right mind. Begin to be ashamed of having acted contrary to thine ancient humanity. Begin to wish to appear a mother, and no longer a foe. Pay the debt of weeping to thy son. Proffer him thy maternal pity, and him whom thou didst cast out when he was alive, yea, didst banish as a suspect, desire at least to recover now that he is dead. Restore thy citizenship, thy bosom, thy favor to his memory. Verily, for all that thou wert ungrateful and arrogant toward him, yet ever like a son he held thee in reverence. Never did he wish to deprive thee of the honor that would come to thee through his works, as thou didst deprive him of thy citizenship. Notwithstanding his exile was a long one, he always called himself, and wished to be called, a Florentine. Ever he preferred thee above all others, ever he loved thee.

What, then, wilt thou do? Wilt thou always persist in thine iniquity? Shall there be in thee less of humanity than in barbarians, whom we find not only to have demanded the bodies of their dead, but to have been ready to die manfully in order to recover them? Thou desirest that the world consider thee the granddaughter of famous Troy, and the daughter of Rome. Surely children should resemble their fathers and grandfathers. Priam in his grief not only begged for the body of the dead Hector, but bought it back by the payment of much gold. And the Romans, as some believe, brought the bones of the first Scipio from Liternum, albeit for good reasons he had forbidden it at his death. Though Hector by his prowess was long the defense of the Trojans, and Scipio was the liberator not only of Rome, but of all Italy, and though none can properly credit two like services to Dante, yet is he not to be held in less esteem. There was never yet a time when arms did not give way to learning.

If thou didst not at first, when it would have been most fitting, imitate the deeds and example of these wise cities, amend now and follow them. There was none of the seven that did not build a true or a false tomb for Homer. And who doubts that the Mantuans, who continue to honor the fields and the poor cottage at Piettola that belonged to Virgil, would have erected a splendid tomb for him, if Octavian Augustus, who transported his bones from Brindisi to Naples, had not ordered that the spot where he laid them should be their perpetual resting-place? Sulmona wept long merely because a spot in the island of Pontus held her Ovid. Parma, on the other hand, rejoiced in the possession of Cassius. Strive to be, therefore, the guardian of thy Dante. Beg for him. Perform this act of humanity even if thou have no desire to recover him. By this pretense partially rid thyself of the reproach previously incurred. Beg for him. I am certain that he will not be returned to thee, but thou, at the same moment, wilt have shown thyself to be full of pity, and in thine innate cruelty wilt rejoice in not recovering him.

But to what do I encourage thee? I can scarce believe that, if the dead have aught of feeling, the body of Dante would leave its resting-place in order to return to thee. He lies with company far more to be praised than that which thou couldst afford him. He sleeps in Ravenna, a city much more to be revered than thou; and, although her age somewhat disfigures her, she was far more flourishing in her youth than thou art now. She is, as it were, a general sepulchre of most sacred persons, and there is no spot in her where one can keep from treading on venerable ashes. Who, then, would desire to return to thee and lie among thine ashes, which may be thought to preserve the wrath and iniquity that was theirs in life, and, at ill accord, to stand apart like the flames of the two Thebans?

Albeit Ravenna in ancient days was almost completely bathed in the precious blood of many martyrs, and to-day keeps their bodies out of reverence, as well as the remains of many magnificent emperors and others illustrious for their ancient families and for virtuous deeds, she rejoices not a little in having been granted by God, in addition to her other gifts, the perpetual guardianship of such a treasure as the body of him whose works hold the whole world in admiration, and of whom thou hast not known how to make thyself worthy. But certainly the joy of possessing him is not so great as the envy she bears thee in that thou holdest the title of his birthplace. And she half scorns the fact that, while she will be remembered for his last days, thou wilt be named for her for his first. Wherefore do thou remain in thine iniquity, and let Ravenna, happy in thine honors, take glory among future generations.

✦ *Short Documents Illustrating Guild,*
Political, and Commercial Activity

GUELFS AND GHIBELLINES, 1347

The lord priors have heard and comprehended the expositions and supplications made to them . . . by zealous Guelfs who are loyal to the Holy

Roman Church, to the effect that the Guelfs of the city, *contado*, and district of Florence . . . have always striven for the glory and honor of Mother Church and they intend to continue to do so with all of their power. [They assert that] there are some who are not only rebels of Mother Church, but also of the *popolo* and Commune of Florence, who have insinuated themselves into the administration and government of the city of Florence and with iniquitous and deceitful words and operations, endeavor to separate devoted and faithful children from their venerated mother. . . . So the abovementioned lord priors desire to have the Holy Roman Church as the mother of her Guelf children, and to prevent those seeking to sow discord from achieving their goals and from interfering in the administration of the Florentine republic, which is to be ruled and governed by true Guelfs. . . . In honor, praise, and reverence of the omnipotent God and the glorious Virgin, and in exaltation and augmentation of Mother Church and the magnificent Parte Guelfa . . . they provide, ordain, and decree the following:

First, no Ghibelline who has been condemned and outlawed for rebellion since November 1, 1300 . . . or who has rebelled (or will rebel in future) . . . against the *popolo* and Commune of Florence . . . or his son or descendant . . . in the male line . . . may hold any office of the *popolo* and Commune of Florence or any office in the Parte Guelfa or . . . in any guild. . . .

If any doubt should arise concerning any person or persons who are drawn for, or elected to any of the abovementioned offices, that he might be or is said to be one of those prohibited, then there should be held . . . a deliberation of the lord priors . . . [with their colleges] . . . whether or not that person should be removed from office. And if it is decided by a majority of them by secret vote . . . then he is to be removed from that office. . . .

Anyone may accuse [or] denounce [a person] and notify [the authorities] about the abovementioned cases . . . and the podestà, captain, and executor . . . must take cognizance of this and proceed by means of an inquisition, and punish and condemn [the guilty]. . . . And for proof, the testimony of six reputable witnesses suffices. . . .

THE AFTERMATH OF THE *CIOMPI* REVOLT: A COMMUNITY IN DISORDER, 1382

On Monday night, January 13, [1382], Messer Giorgio Scali, with armed men from the two new guilds [of artisans which had been created in 1378]

Source: Excerpts from G. Brucker, ed. and trans., *The Society of Renaissance Florence: A Documentary Study* (New York: Harper Torchbooks, 1971). Reprinted by permission of HarperCollins Publishers.

. . . and with their Ghibelline followers went to the palace of the captain [of the *popolo*], all together about four hundred men. From his custody, they took Scatizza, a cloth shearer, who on the following morning was to be executed by the captain. . . . He had confessed that he was planning to kill all the Guelfs and deliver the city to Messer Bernabò Visconti, lord of Milan. The next morning, the captain went to the palace of the Signoria and, narrating to the priors what had happened the night before, he resigned his office. . . . This greatly displeased the priors, their colleges, and the good citizens, and there was much talk throughout the city. . . . On Thursday morning, January 16, 1382, the captain received authority to punish whoever erred, and his office was returned to him. . . . After dinner, the captain had Giorgio Scali captured, and there was a lot of talk among the Ghibellines. . . . The militia captains armed their companies for the security of the city, and so that no disorders would break out. . . .

On Friday morning, January 17, Messer Giorgio Scali was executed for treason on the wall of the captain's courtyard. He confessed that he was going to surrender the city to Messer Bernabò Visconti of Milan, and that on the 21st, he was going to ravage the city and rob and kill all of the Guelfs. . . . On Saturday, the 18th, the cry went up: "Long live the Parte Guelfa," but no banners were displayed. And the Guelfs, all armed with swords in hand, ran through the city streets. . . . The city was peaceful and that night the Guelfs fortified themselves.

. . . On Monday morning, the 20th, Messer Donato di Ricco and Feo, the armorer, were executed on the wall of the courtyard, and immediately a disturbance broke out and [the people] shouted, "Long live the Parte Guelfa and death to the Ghibellines!" And they ran through the city streets with three flags of the Parte Guelfa. . . . The city was in arms and all of the Guelfs were in the piazza. . . . At vespers, the standard of the Parte Guelfa was given to Giovanni Cambi, and with that [banner] displayed, the entire populace marched in procession—the worthy citizens, the soldiers, the people—in an atmosphere of joy and celebration. . . . That night the city was peaceful. On Tuesday morning, the 21st, members of the guild of cloth manufacturers armed themselves, and together with the prominent citizens, they assembled in the Mercato Nuovo, and they demanded that the two new guilds be disbanded, and this was done. The houses where they met were ransacked, with all of their furnishings, arms, and papers. . . .

Then on Wednesday morning, the 22nd, the fourteen lower guilds [of artisans and shopkeepers] assembled and marched to the Piazza della Signoria. [The priors] marveled at this and asked them what they wanted. They replied that they had heard that the magnates desired to ransack the city, and they said this to disguise the fact that they wished to restore the two disbanded guilds, for they feared that they too would be barred from office. The members of the cloth manufacturers' guild armed themselves and marched to the piazza where they attacked the butchers. There was a great struggle, in which two died and several were wounded. The flags [of the Commune] and of the Parte Guelfa were brought out of the palace [of the Signoria] and carried several times around the piazza, and as a result, the people became calm. And all of the flags of the guilds were collected and brought into the palace of the Signoria.

On Thursday, the 23rd, the Signoria issued a decree that every citizen should stand with his arms and on the alert, for they feared that the fourteen lower guilds would attempt to restore the two disbanded guilds. And the seven greater guilds assembled, together with the rich and prominent citizens, in the Mercato Nuovo with a large force. . . . On Friday, the 24th, the shops, factories, and moneychangers' tables were all open and trouble erupted, whereupon the seven greater guilds assembled with the rich and worthy citizens in the Mercato Nuovo. . . . On Saturday evening, the 25th, the Guelfs marched through the city with torches and lanterns, but no one did or said anything against them. . . . And many pacts were concluded among the Guelfs, who agreed to stay united in peace and amity to maintain their status.

THE DECLINE OF THE
GUELF PARTY, 1413

In November of that year, the captains of the Parte Guelfa took counsel with a large number of Guelfs who had been assembled and also with the two regular councils. . . . With their colleges and with ninety-six Guelf co-adjutors they assumed the authority for reforming offices of the Parte with a new scrutiny, after burning and annulling all of the previous scrutinies. They were motivated to do this, because the Parte had lost much of its accustomed honor and reputation. So low indeed had it fallen that the captains had difficulty in recruiting citizens to accompany them on their processions to make the customary offerings. This resulted from the disdain felt by good and true Guelfs at seeing many Ghibellines and parvenus of low condition occupying the offices of the Parte Guelfa.

[November 16, 1413] Piero Baroncelli said that nothing is more desirable than to live in peace, to value and to conserve the status [of everyone], and to unite the citizenry. The captains [of the Parte Guelfa] say that they desire to achieve this, and that they seek to reform the Parte because it is not in a good condition. Everyone should rejoice, and if toward this end they hold a new scrutiny [for offices], that is proper. . . . But it is displeasing to hear that . . . the scrutinies should be burned, and it is even worse to hear that all scrutinies of the Commune should be burned. Everyone must deplore this. All of the troubles which have occurred in the city since 1378 had their origin in this [tampering with elections], and it has almost brought the city to destruction. On no account should it be done. Let the Signoria agree with the captains [of the Parte Guelfa] and others to have a new scrutiny . . . but no burnings. The palace [of the Parte Guelfa] is on a par with this palace [of the Signoria] in the government of the city. . . .

Rinaldo di Filippo Rondinelli said that as a result of our actions, God must regard us with loathing. We take no account of our condition, nor of the imminent dangers which threaten us. Daily we seek changes. . . . There are errors in the scrutinies of the Parte, but this results from unwise nominations. The present [reform] is not useful; rather, the Parte should be strengthened. . . . The captains should proceed with holding a new scrutiny, but nothing should be burned . . . and the Signoria should so instruct the captains. . . .

Messer Lorenzo Ridolfi said that everyone ought to honor and exalt the Parte. He who is not willing to do so is not a citizen but a rebel. . . .

Messer Rinaldo Gianfigliazzi said that as a result of the Parte's poor condition, the captains are not obeyed by the citizens when they call them to assembly, or when they ask for oblations. Since the society does not function properly, many refuse to go. . . . He and his three sons are in the bags [i.e., they were nominated for Parte office], and he has seen three or four men chosen as captains whose relatives, being Ghibellines, could not bear arms in the *contado* . . . which is a scandal to the Parte Guelfa. . . .

GUILD CORPORATIONS: WINE MERCHANTS

[Chapter 18] It is also decreed and ordained that the consuls [of the guild] are required, by their oath, to force all of the winesellers . . . who sell at retail in the city and *contado* of Florence to swear allegiance to this guild and for this guild. And for this purpose they must make a monthly search through the city and the suburbs of Florence, and if they find anyone who is not matriculated in the guild, they must require him to swear allegiance. . . . And whoever, as has been said, is engaged in this trade, even though he is not . . . matriculated in the guild . . . is considered to be a member of the guild. . . . And each newly matriculated wineseller . . . must pay . . . 5 lire to the guild treasurer . . . as his matriculation fee. . . . If, however, he is a father or son of a guild member, then he is not required to pay anything. . . .

[Chapter 20] The consuls, treasurer, and notary of the guild are required to assemble together wherever they wish . . . to render justice to whoever demands it of the men of this guild, against any and all those . . . who sell wine at retail . . . in the city, *contado*, and district of Florence. . . . [They must] hear, take cognizance of, make decisions, and act on everything which pertains to their office, and accept every appeal which is brought before them by whosoever has any claim upon any member of the guild. . . . They must record [these acts] in their protocols and render justice with good faith and without fraud on one day of each week. . . . With respect to these disputes, the consuls are required to proceed in the following manner. If any dispute or quarrel is brought against any member of the guild . . . and it involves a sum of 3 Florentine lire di piccolo or less, this dispute is to be decided summarily by the consuls, after the parties have sworn an oath, in favor of whoever appears to be more honest and of better reputation. . . . If the dispute involves 60 soldi or more, the consuls, after receiving the complaint, are required to demand that . . . the defendant appear to reply to the complaint. . . . [Witnesses are to be called and interrogated in such major disputes, and the consuls must announce their judgment within one month.]

[Chapter 21] It is decreed and ordained that each wine-seller shall come to the assembly of the guild as often as he is summoned by the consuls. . . . The consuls are required to levy a fine of 10 soldi . . . against whoever violates this [rule], and the same penalty is to be incurred by anyone who fails to respond to the consuls' order to come to the guild's offering in a church. . . . And if necessity requires that . . . the members of the guild assemble under their banner to stand guard, or to go on a march, by day or night, in the city and *contado* of Florence or elsewhere, every member of the guild is required to appear in person, with or without arms as ordered, with their standard-bearer and under their banner, or pay a fine of 10 lire. . . .

[Chapter 35] For the honor of the guild and of the members of the guild, it is decreed and ordained that whenever any member of the guild dies, all guild members in the city and suburbs who are summoned by the messenger of the guild . . . are required to go to the service for the dead man, and to stay there until he is buried. . . . And the consuls are required to send the guild messenger, requesting and inviting the members of the guild to participate in the obsequies for the dead. . . .

GUILD PHILANTHROPY

[October 20, 1421] . . . This petition is presented with all due reverence to you, lord priors, on behalf of your devoted sons of the guild of Por Santa Maria [the silk guild] and the merchants and guildsmen of that association. It is well known to all of the people of Florence that this guild has sought, through pious acts, to conserve . . . and also to promote your republic and this guild. It has begun to construct a most beautiful edifice in the city of Florence and in the parish of S. Michele Visdomini, next to the piazza called the "Frati de' Servi." [This building is] a hospital called S. Maria degli Innocenti, in which shall be received those who, against natural law, have been deserted by their fathers or their mothers, that is, infants, who in the vernacular are called *gittatelli* [literally, castaways, foundlings]. Without the help and favor of your benign lordships, it will not be possible to transform this laudable objective into reality . . . nor after it has been achieved to preserve and conserve it.

And since [we] realized that your lordships and all of the people are, in the highest degree, committed to works of charity, [we have] decided to have recourse to your clemency, and to request, most devotedly, all of the things which are described below. So on behalf of the abovementioned guild, you are humbly petitioned . . . to enact a law . . . that this guild of Por Santa Maria and its members and guildsmen—as founders, originators, and principals of this hospital—are understood in perpetuity to be . . . the sole patrons, defenders, protectors, and supporters of this hospital as representatives of, and in the name of, the *popolo* and Commune of Florence. . . .

Item, the consuls of the guild . . . have authority . . . to choose supervisors and governors of the hospital and of the children and servants. . . .

THE *CATASTO* OF 1427: THE DECLARATION OF LORENZO GHIBERTI, SCULPTOR

. . . A house located in the parish of S. Ambrogio in Florence in the Via Borgo Allegri . . . with household furnishings for the use of myself and my family . . .   0

    A piece of land in the parish of S. Donato in Franzano . . .   100-0-0

    In my shop are two pieces of bronze sculpture which I have made for a baptismal font in Siena. . . . I estimate that they are worth 400 florins or thereabouts, of which sum I have received 290 florins; so the balance is 110 florins.   110-0-0

    Also in my shop is a bronze casket which I made for Cosimo de' Medici; I value it at approximately 200 florins, of which I have received 135 florins. The balance owed to me is 65 florins.   65-0-0

    I have investments in the *Monte* of 714 florins.   714-0-0

    I am still owed 10 florins by the Friars of S. Maria Novella for the tomb of the General [of the Dominican Order, Lionardo Dati].

Obligations

Personal exemptions:

Lorenzo di Bartolo, aged 46	200-0-0
Marsilia, my wife, aged 26	200-0-0
Tommaso, my son, aged 10 or thereabouts	200-0-0
Vettorio, my son, aged 7 or thereabouts	200-0-0

I owe money to the following persons:

Antonio di Piero del Vaglente and company, goldsmiths	33-0-0
Nicola di Vieri de' Medici	10-0-0
Domenico di Tano, cutler	9-0-0
Niccolò Carducci and company, retail cloth merchants	7-0-0

Papi d'Andrea, cabinet-maker	16-0-0
Mariano da Gambassi, mason	7-0-0
Papero di Meo of Settignano (my apprentices	
Simone di Nanni of Fiesole in	48-0-0
Cipriano di Bartolo of Pistoia the shop)	
Antonio, called El Maestro, tailor	15-0-0
Domenico di Lippi, cutler	2-0-0
Alessandro Allesandri and company	4-0-0
Duccio Adimari and company, retail cloth merchants	8-0-0
Antonio di Giovanni, stationer	3-0-0
Isau d'Agnolo and company, bankers	50-0-0
Commissioners in charge of maintenance and rebuilding of the church of S. Croce	6-0-0
Lorenzo di Bruciane, kiln operator	3-0-0
Meo of S. Apollinare	45-0-0
Pippo, stocking maker	8-0-0
[Total of Lorenzo's taxable assets]	999-0-0
[Total obligations and exemptions]	1074-0-0

◆ *Leonardo Bruni*

THE EVENTS OF 1292–1293

Speech of Giano della Bella

One who tried to stop the disorder and decline of the [Florentine] Republic was Giano della Bella, a man who showed great courage and wisdom during that stormy time. He was descended from well-known men, but was himself of middling station and very popular. This leader spoke separately with many people about the power of the nobility and the excessive passivity that was destroying the people, for they kept letting individuals suffer injustice without recognizing that they were all as a group being subjected to shameful servitude. *He said it was stupid to think one would not be personally hit, when after the first people were oppressed, the force would strike others too, spreading like fire. Resistance was necessary now, and the evil must not be allowed to grow. For though the disease had been allowed to develop, it was not yet so established that it could not be healed. But if they paid little attention and everyone looked to*

Source: R. N. Watkins, trans. and ed., *Humanism and Liberty: Writings on Freedom, from 15th Century Florence* (Columbia, S.C.: University of South Carolina Press, 1978), pp. 69–73.

others to start, matters would reach the point where they would seek a cure in vain. By saying these things over and over he fired up men's minds and stiffened their resolution to take the Republic in hand. The popular classes arose and supported the effort, going forth to take the matter to the government. When the people were thus gathered at last, and different opinions were being voiced by different persons, Giano della Bella arose and spoke most fully, addressing the crowd in the following manner:

"I have always been of the same mind, good citizens of wise judgment, and the more I think about the Republic, the more I am convinced that we must either check the pride of the powerful families or lose our liberty altogether. Things have reached the point, I think, where *your tolerance and your liberty are no longer compatible.* I think too that no one of sound judgment can be in doubt which of the two is to be preferred. Though I well know how dangerous it is to talk of this, I am not afraid. *A good citizen, I think, ignores his own comfort when his country needs his advice, and he does not cut down his public statements to suit his private convenience.* Therefore I shall speak my mind freely. It seems to me that the liberty of the people consists in two things: the laws and the judges. When the power of these two things prevails in the city over the power of any individual citizen, then liberty is preserved. But when some people scorn the laws and the judges with impunity, then it is fair to say that liberty is gone. For in what sense are you free in relation to people who, with no fear of judgment, can do to you and yours whatever violence they please? Therefore think what your condition is, and consider the crimes of the nobility: tell me, any one of you, whether you think the city is free or whether it has been for some time in subjection. The answer will be easier for those who have a neighbor in the city or in the nearby country who is one of this circle of powerful men. For what do we possess, that they don't want to take? And what have they wanted to take that they have not promptly tried to take, and what don't they feel perfectly justified in taking, whether by legal or illegal ways? Our very bodies, if we will only admit it, are no longer free: remember the citizens who have been beaten, chased out of their homes, the numerous examples of arson, rape, wounding, and killing in these last years. The doers of these evil deeds are so well-known and publicly recognized that obviously they either don't care to conceal their crimes or they are unable to; they stay visible; we see men who deserve prison and torture strutting around the city with a crowd of armed retainers, terrifying us and the officials. Would anyone tell me that this is liberty? *What is the difference from tyrants who kill, expropriate, take whatever they want, and fear no judges?* And if one man destroys liberty in other states, what shall we think of ours where a great number do it all at once? We have certainly been for some time subjected, believe me, and under the empty name of liberty, we suffer shameful servitude. You may object, however, and say: no one doubts that what you say is true, but what is the cure—don't give us nothing but complaints. To this I say that we can shake this servitude from our backs with no great difficulty. For if the destruction of laws and judges is the cause of our loss of liberty, let us expel those criminals and our liberty will be restored. If you wish to be free, therefore (*which you should wish as much as you wish to live*), reinstate those two things to primary authority, and protect them with all your strength and zeal. You have many laws against violence, killing, theft, assault, and other crimes. These laws must be renewed against the powerful, I say, and *new measures must be taken for, as everyone knows, the perversity of men has increased from day to day.* First of all, I think, the punishments for crime must be increased when the powerful commit them. *Surely if you want to tie up both a powerful man and a puny one, you don't use the same kind of bonds. You tie the lion with chains, but the weak with ropes and thongs.* Punishments are the bonds of law, and likewise must be greater for great and powerful men. The ones we have don't hold them now. It seems we must stipulate also that family and household are to be included in punishments. *We should consider clan and kinsmen as complicit in the crime, for their support enables the criminal to proceed.* Two things usually prevent our judges from doing their job: difficulty in proving the case and lack of power to bring the criminals to justice. For they frighten witnesses from testifying against the powerful men, and this fear destroys the whole judgment in one stroke; and even if proofs are given, the executive is afraid to act. If you do not change these things, you will have no republic. *What are the best of laws if the judgments are made void?* So you must first of all, I think, take care of the problem of witnesses; in the case of powerful men general public knowledge must be sufficient evidence of guilt. Thus when a crime has been committed, and neighbors for some distance say that a certain powerful man committed it, the judge need not find other proofs, which will fade away because of men's fear of the powerful one; but public knowledge, as we have said, will suffice to convict. As to the second problem, putting the judges' decision into action, please pay attention—I think it is a greater matter than people realize, depending less on the officials than on the will and vigor of the public. For if the people really wants as it should to keep its power in the Republic, the decisions of the judges against the powerful persons will readily be carried out. But if the people is full of respect for others and considers them superior to itself, this will chill both the judges and the officials. All this was foreseen long ago when the Gonfaloniere di Giustizia was created, but I marvel at the diminution of his reputation and power. *It is stupid to be surprised, however, when the people itself is negligent and cold, that the people's vicars are overcome and are not brave.* And still at that time so much was omitted that the constitution was only begun rather than perfected. So the authority of the Gonfaloniere di Giustizia needs to be very much strengthened. He should, above all, I think, have at his command, not a thousand armed men as heretofore, but four thousand, to be recruited in turn from the whole people. I also think, the Gonfaloniere should reside in the same building as the priors, so that he will personally hear the complaints of the citizens and provide for the needs of the Republic. The Gonfaloniere will not remain at home whether because he is slow to hear or because, as we know has happened, he is privately persuaded to slow down his work. A third provision which was not made at that time seems to me necessary—that none of the powerful, even if they become members of a guild, can be raised to become priors, and thus put into a position to help criminals and to impede justice. *Their existing power is sufficiently burdensome to us, without adding the armor of public authority.* In this way if you resuscitate the laws, restore punishments, empower the judges to deal with powerful men, you will force them to cease from tyranny. And if they go on unrestrained, you will have to exterminate them with iron and fire as you would incurably sick limbs, putting aside that excessive and extreme patience of yours which is leading you with eyes and ears open into slavery. I have said what I think are the measures needed by the Republic and are necessary for our liberty. If they were difficult and expensive and involved a lot of labor, I would tell you that they had to be carried out anyway because of their great usefulness. As they are easy, however, and lie in your hands, who is so fallen that he would rather serve in pain and humiliation than be equal to others in right and honor? Our ancestors were not willing to serve even the Roman emperors, though the title of the nation and the dignity of the people made servitude less dishonorable. Are you willing to go on serving the vilest of men? Our ancestors bore death and wounds and loss of goods and carried on almost infinite struggles for the sake of dignity and power. You, out of fear and laziness, have submitted to tyrants who ought to be your subjects. It seems that a people, that is a vast multitude of strong men, who have conquered by their military art all their neighbors and have smashed a thousand enemy battalions, would be ashamed to fear this or that family at home and patiently to let their pride make us slaves. I shall stop now, so that my momentum does not carry me too far. For I feel too much reverence to chide the people, yet when I remember your degenerate passivity I cannot be silent and calm. I only ask you to think of your own liberty and your welfare."

IV

Humanism

> ⟞⟐⟐◆⟐⟐⟝

INTRODUCTION

*H*umanism was the central cultural and educational expression of the
Renaissance. The word itself arose from late medieval student slang.
A professor of the studia humanitatis, *that is, of humane letters or liberal
arts, was referred to as an* umanista. *And, indeed, the course of studies
followed by these* umanisti *illustrates quite well the original principles
that animated humanistic studies in the Renaissance.*

The curriculum of the studia humanitatis *consisted of rhetoric, moral
philosophy, history, and poetry. The disciplines stressed were clearly,
then, those which reflected human values and experience. In addition,
especially after the influence of Petrarch was felt widely in academic
circles, these subjects began to grow in significance at the expense of the
older scholastic disciplines so despised by Petrarch and his disciples. All
humanists admitted to certain interests; interests that have been shown
to be central to Petrarch's writings. These were the recovery, study, interpretation, and transmission of the heritage of classical antiquity; a powerful desire to transform the style and content of contemporary Latin
(and later vernacular) literature; an emphasis on moral philosophy (that
is, really, ethics) at the expense of theology and scholastic method; a
renewed and growing interest in the study and teaching of ancient Greek;
and finally, and more narrowly, a wish to return to naturalism in art,
that is, to reproduce what the eye sees.*

*The important points to stress about the early development of human-
ism are, first, that the movement was secular and, second, that it was
practical, that is, functionally defined. Humanism was a largely secular
discipline. Clerics were educated according to the old scholastic method,
in which theology was explicated by Aristotelian logic. The language and
style, even the cast of thought, of such men did not prepare them to*

71

pursue careers as secretaries, whose talents must be rhetorical and who were expected to correspond with other rhetorically trained secretaries in the new conventions of their common profession. Therefore, the great practitioners of humanism were laymen who, naturally, would impart a secular character to their writings and teachings.

Second; humanism was practical. It was designed for concrete functions, at least initially. It trained scholars to instruct their readers and to move them with their advice, and consequently, it had to be rhetorical. Also, the subjects treated in the practice of humanism tended to be highly specific and useful in the world of politics and trade. The material of this early phase of humanism, the letters, orations, and treatises of the late fourteenth and early fifteenth centuries, were thus usually concerned with the problems and pleasures of this world: diplomatic correspondence of peace and war, the documents of trade and finances, and the moral example of the ancients and how to apply it. In short, implicit in humanism was the belief that words properly expressed could influence men and events, that the style and content of language had enormous power as well as providing great delight. Moreover, as humanism spread throughout Italy, it became apparent that humanism could serve as well in princely despotism or papal Rome as in a mercantile republic such as Florence, and once the career advantages it provided for poorer young men or the cultivated polish it accorded to well-born courtiers became generally recognized, humanism was accepted increasingly in Italy as a means of educating the political, social, and economic elite. In others words, for anyone desiring a leading position in the state, humanism proved to be an excellent training.

This relationship between humanism and government should, in fact, be clear. Truth came from eloquence, and eloquence was one of the fundamental products of a humanist curriculum. The control of language and words was a natural consequence of the study of ancient literature, and all humanists believed that good words reflected good thoughts produced by good men. Hence moral philosophy, that application of ethics to daily life, created students able to distinguish good from evil and with the skill to make that difference visible to their audiences—indeed, it was their responsibility to do so.

✦ **Coluccio Salutati**

C oluccio Salutati was born in 1331 in the Florentine contado. Trained as a notary, he held various offices in Tuscany and Rome, rising briefly to be Chancellor of Lucca. He was a friend and correspondent of Petrarch and shared the older poet's views of classical literature and the importance of good Latin style.

In 1375 Salutati became Chancellor of Florence, an office he held
until his death in 1406. He used this position to encourage humanism
among the educated patricians of the city and to promote humanist
values in general. His effect as a spokesman for the republic was well
illustrated by Florence's great enemy Giangaleazzo Visconti. Visconti
remarked that a letter of Salutati was worth a contingent of cavalry.

Salutati wrote much himself, always in Latin and in a heavy, didactic
style. He was personally very devout and wavered between complete
acceptance of the role of the active layman in the state and a more
traditional respect for the contemplative ideal of the Middle Ages. Similarly, in his political thought, he represented the Florentine republic with
the full force of his intellect and erudition against the tyrant of Milan,
but he also wrote a treatise in favor of monarchy.

Salutati was, then, a transitional figure, but one who cemented
humanistic learning to the service of the Florentine republic. He was the
patron of many subsequent humanists, and he brought the principles of
humanism into the highest reaches of Florentine society and government.

LETTER TO PEREGRINO ZAMBECCARI

You write,[1] my Peregrino, that you have left the confusions and ravings
of vain love behind and have strengthened your resolve through Him who
hung on the cross for the salvation of the human race. And you add, if I
might cite your words:

> I hope, if bitter fortune not vex and disquiet me, to choose within two years,
> when I am in control of myself, a form of life that will make me master of
> my own time, and I will flee cares and the pursuit of wealth, which have up
> to the present deprived me of true freedom. Time will not make me as much
> a slave as it does you. And that you might believe that I have become another
> Peregrino: I have had an oratory constructed outside the gate of Saint Mam-
> moli,[2] in which I shall leave the relics of that mad Cupid. I will cherish and
> love the Mother of our Redeemer instead of false Giovanna, and I will leave
> you behind in this confused world attempting to flatter everyone. Farewell

---

1. This letter is not published among the known correspondence of Zambeccari, *Epistolario di Pellegrino Zambeccari*, ed. Luigi Frati, Fonti per la storia d'Italia, 40 (Rome,
   1929). Salutati's earliest correspondence with his friend on this matter is found in
   Novati, *Epistolerio di Coluccio Salutati*, 3, pp. 3–6.
2. The oratory dedicated to St. Peregrino was founded by an act drawn up in July 1398.
   Apparently Zambeccari did not heed Salutati's advice, at least in this regard: *ibid.*, 3,
   p. 295, n. 2.

Source: B. Kohl and R. Witt, eds., *The Earthly Republic: Italian Humanists on
Government and Society* (Philadelphia: University of Pennsylvania Press, 1978),
pp. 93–114. Reprinted with permission of University of Pennsylvania Press.

and spend a part of your old age on my behalf so that, if I survive you, I might be educated with your sacred words of eloquence.

I have quoted your words in context so that you might know that you wrote not in dust, which the wind scatters, nor in ice, which melts in sun and fire. Responding to you with this letter, I quoted them to this extent so that they might remain for reference. If I might enter into a friendly argument with you about some of your remarks, have you not said: "Now I have left the confusions and ravings of vain love"? Have you strengthened your resolve in our Savior, you who hope to choose (if fortune permits) a new life within two years, when you will be ready to free time for yourself? Are you to deposit the relics of mad Cupid in this your oratory? Are you going to love the Virgin Mary instead of the false Giovanna?[3] Have you strengthened yourself in Christ, my Peregrino, who loves not yet but who will love His mother, the Virgin? My Peregrino, anyone who intended to do what you say you will do would be mad! You have not yet left the remnants of a foolish love and still maintain that you are firmly tied to Christ. Do you not feel that these things are like opposites that contradict each other? Do you wish for miracles for yourself? For my part, I do not simply hope but ardently long for them.

Nevertheless, I rejoice that you who were once the blind lover of your Giovanna, and would not heed my warnings, have finally with open eyes confessed that this love was false. I am vexed and displeased, however, that, although you recognize your earthly love to be false, you have not yet given it up and not made that fruitful conversion. You still love Giovanna and not the Virgin Mary, whom you say you will cherish and love but do not love now. Why put it off, my Peregrino? Why not start today? Why draw things out by procrastinating? This commitment does not require an oratory, only your heart and mind; there is no need to postpone what can be accomplished in a moment. If you discard the foolish, false, and mad love of Giovanna, you will have to love something else. Our soul cannot not love. It is perpetual, it always grows, always thinks, always loves. If you do not come to love the Virgin Mary, it is necessary that you embrace another thing with love, or doubtless remain in love with Giovanna. Tell me, you still love Giovanna, don't you? I clearly believe you do, or you would show you loved something else. You will love Mary the Virgin instead of Giovanna. Oh happy Mary, whom you think alone worthy of this honor and on whom you direct the focus of your love, hitherto directed on Giovanna. Tell me, will you love Mary's starry eyes and the other things that once, wild with desire, you marveled

---

3. We do not know the identity of Giovanna. From earlier letters it appears that years before, as a single man, Zambeccari had tried to marry her, but she chose another. Taking a wife himself in 1384, he was never able to put Giovanna out of his mind.

at in Giovanna? If you do not love these things in Mary, she will not be loved in place of Giovanna.

But you will say: "You take my words too literally. Why do you twist everything? Why do you not understand them fairly? You plainly know what I meant." I twist nothing at all, nor do I think that one ought to neglect the significance of the words, except when it is manifest that the speaker meant something else, as Marcellus advised in the third collection of the material on legates. Nor am I able to understand more than the words mean. How do I know what you want when you do not know how to tell me? I am perhaps able to know what you ought to want; however, who but the spirit within you can know what you want?

The crux of my dispute with you is that you have confessed to me that you love Giovanna. For what else am I to believe since you have not yet established the life that you will elect, nay, hope to elect within two years if fortune does not hinder or disturb you. What else, when you write that you will deposit the relics of insane Cupid in your oratory and that you will cherish and love the Mother of our Redeemer for the false Giovanna? O if your star but returned from Ferrara, your Giovanna! O if you would see her again armed with the usual weapons! O if you looked on her again, beautiful, charming, all full of honesty and virtue, qualities that you thought you saw in her and wanted to see, even if they were not there! Then would you not say:

> This woman is the only one who has stirred my senses and sapped my will. I feel once more the scars of the old flame?

Clearly your mind would say this; your heart, your intellect, would say this; and your mouth, which speaks from a full heart, would not keep silent. O then you would be happy! O deserted oratory! O invisible and deserted Mary! But why do I go on? I am very certain that if mild Giovanna nodded with the array of her beauty, if she showed herself swept away by your love, if she cried out as in the Song of Solomon: "I swear to you, O daughters of Bologna, if you find my beloved, my Peregrino, that you tell him that I languish for love!" O, if you would hear this song, how you would act and what height of madness you would reach! What binding vow, what stipulations in your profession of faith, what principles of conduct, what religious bonds you would not break, would not abandon, would not belittle in importance, and would not dissolve!

Remember that love conquers all! Remember that, whether it is innate or caused by the stars or customs, it is common for you and other Bolognese to love too much. Remember that this is a licentious habit and practice among you, common not only to men but also to young women! Remember that when the suitor arrives he is immediately given leave to see the beloved, nay, rather, they are even allowed to join hands! Remember that young women are also allowed to rebuke a suitor (for this they call their lovers) if he neglects them. I am not maintaining that the

Bolognese are immoral because of these things, but, rather, I mean that you as a people pursue love hotly and with passion.

I shall tell you a true account, not a fable, of one of your compatriots, a Bolognese citizen, so that I might demonstrate how wildly your people fall in love. There was a man, whose name I shall omit, comparable to you in regard to family and age, not dissimilar to you in profession or in dignity, and, that I might speak truly, quite like you, a kind of other Peregrino. His fate was that he loved his Giovanna. Like yours, she was married, beautiful, upright, and honorable. The same thing happened to her husband, who was exiled because he killed another man. This lover of his Giovanna obtained a favor for her husband, as you did for the husband of yours. Finally, after considering many places for a residence in exile, the husband chose Ferrara, where he would have his permanent home with his wife. And, since he wished to have Giovanna with him, he asked the lover's help or had his wishes reported to him.

The latter, just like all lovers, or rather madmen, tending to their own ruin, procures a safe conduct for the husband so that he might please Giovanna and make himself a friend to the husband as he is a lover to the wife. The husband comes, he is thankful to everyone, and he thanks especially the lover of his wife. He packs his bags. Not only does he make preparations to depart but he leaves, taking with him his wife, who will never return.

This stupid citizen of yours, your alter ego, who helped make all this possible because of his desire for Giovanna, finally, but in vain, recognizes what he has done. Still he bears it all happily. But when he sees his soul, his heart leaving, becoming wild, he puts on his elegant and expensive imported clothing, which you call "ciambellotti," and, like a madman, follows her to the docks on the left bank of the channel from which those going to Ferrara by water, moving through a muddy valley or series of valleys, sail to the Reno or a branch of that river.[4]

There, having a breakfast prepared that certain people call a "refreshment," he shows his generosity. He takes charge of all things, arranging that Giovanna might recline on a skiff that they call a "barclum," or little boat, in order that she reach the ship safely and might board without fear or risk. After all things have been looked after, the sailor loosens the rope and seizes and fixes the tiller so that he might control the boat. Not content with fixing the tiller, he calls a friend and compels him to pole the boat, and he himself with a similar implement drives the ship away from the dock. Not only does he double the velocity of the water moving downstream, but he drives it even faster.

---

4. The Reno is a river near Bologna. In the twelfth century a canal was built, starting from the river at Casalecchi, passing through Bologna, and thereafter meandering through a plain until it rejoined the Reno near Segni.

Alas, what then was the feeling of the lover? How burdensome, how intolerable was the departure? Your fellow citizen started to rave and was smitten, running along the bank, urging Giovanna not to be afraid and the boatman to be diligent. It is said, moreover—such was his depravity —that at one point he got into the boat, and I easily believe it. I would like to have seen him—crying out phrases, rolling his eyes, nodding his head, and warning with hands—so that I could describe him.

I would, however, speak of one happening that ought to be amusing. Perhaps the persistent rain had made the banks sodden, but he, following the little ship, ran along the very edge of the bank to be as close as possible to the ship. While speaking to those directing the ship, while jumping over the rough spots with a leap, stirring up muddy pools where he landed and covering himself with the mud of the bank—for the river banks are not only dirty but deep with mud—he tripped all filthy on the bank and, leaping up, besmeared with mud, fell into the Reno. Soiled with slime and drenched with water, he was laughed at not only by spectators but by the sailors, and even by the river banks and the river itself, the weeping willows and the other trees and by the fish, all witnesses of his stupidity. Finally, as we read about Menoetes in Vergil:

> All laughed at the sight of him going overboard, swimming, And now they
> laugh to see him wringing the muddy water from his clothes.

I wish you would have seen this ludicrous spectacle, nay, I would have liked for you to have been this fellow I am describing: I wish you had seen him all slimey and dripping, entering the city and being pointed out as a foolish man, an example of mad love, and jeered at by all whom he encountered. I think you would have been equally moved and, taking this experience to heart, would have put yourself in his place like Aeneas, who, having witnessed the slaughter of Priam, thought about his own father's fate.

> Then first the full horror of it all was borne in upon me. I stood
> In a daze: the picture of my dear father came to mind,
> As I watched King Priam, a man of the same age, cruelly killed . . .
> Gasping his life away; I pictured Creusa
> Deserted, my home pillaged, and the fate of my little Julius.

Perhaps if you had seen him with his dirty face, befouled with mud and drenched with water, you would have seen your turpitude as his and your stupidity as well, so that what you would not heed by reason you would see by example and with your own eyes.

I see, my Peregrino, that among the errors conceived regarding Giovanna the light of truth shines in you and that you are drawn from one extreme to the other. But before you consider the extremes, I want you to bring yourself back to the mean. To love Mary the Virgin and to have loved Giovanna are two extremes that confront each other as if from opposite towers. You will not be able to love Mary as much as you ought. You have been given the capacity and are able to love Giovanna to a lesser extent so as not to exceed the proper limit in loving. You have loved the latter with physical love and to the point of madness, but Mary is necessarily loved for spiritual consolation and as an example of chastity. You marveled at your earthly love among transitory things; however, you shall learn that Mary is to be cherished among eternal objects that lead to eternal glory. When you love the Virgin above you, then you will be near the goal.

Hence, I urge you, my Peregrino, and I admonish you, if ever you want to learn anything from me, abandon Giovanna completely! Second, consider that you are obligated to the state and to your family, your sons and relations. After you have fulfilled these obligations, free from others, you will be able to prepare yourself for that final love and charity for Mary that does not puff up but edifies. Therefore, paying your debt, you will learn how much you owe to the highest good and in what way you, who do not yet understand, may satisfy those claims.

God has appointed you father of many and, because of many blessings, the refuge and friend to many; He has made it so that in your commonwealth you are able to do more than generally anyone else. If you desert these obligations, will God not demand these things from you? You have received a talent; do not bury it but use it. Labor! Make yourself a useful servant! Pay back in kind what was given you! Perhaps it is not actually God's will that you convert to another life. It is good and honest to love Mary, but it is better to imitate her. Know, however, that for this purpose we have no need of a man-made oratory or of solitude. Our mind, our heart, and our soul make a perpetual temple of God built not by man's hand. There our conscience lives; there our affection is examined by Him who scrutinizes the reins and the heart; by Him who wills these things from eternity, whatever they be, and not only with a good will but with the best, and who fashions them from eternity in the most equitable manner.

Indeed, He acts most justly in abandoning us so that we do evil deeds or in aiding us beforehand with his beneficent grace, that we do the good things that are done. This is the temple of the Lord that was destroyed and rebuilt in three days. It was destroyed by the descent into sin; it is restored in the triple light of penitence, that is, in the bitterness of remorse, in recognizing sins and in the shame of confession, in divulging secrets, and in making satisfaction out of contrition and lamenting the evil done. This is called the house of prayer, with the buyers and sellers excluded, that is, the commercial transactions of the temporal life in which only the acquisition of temporal possessions counts. In the doorways of this our temple stands pride, seeking superiority; avarice lies in wait, picking up what falls by chance; envy burns, desiring evil; anger rages, wanting to profit from injury; sadness mourns, seeking repose; the throat sticks, wanting to stroke the food tasted; and lust sordidly seeks the satisfaction of desire. The Lord expelled those buying and selling from the temple so that we might expel them from our temple doors. He prohibited such dealings so that we not admit them to the temple that we keep for secret matters.

Purge your temple, my Peregrino. Wish for nothing transitory; but the more beautiful things are to the eye, the sweeter to the taste and the softer to the touch; lust for them the less not only in words but also in your feelings and in deed. Do not think about peace for yourself when you can have no peace in the flesh. There will be worry in the hermitage; it does not abandon you in the oratory nor when you are alone in bed. You do not know how full of stimulation solitude is, how beset by thoughts, and how it is a prey to dangers. We praise all those things that we have not learned to fear; the active man and the contemplative man alike have their troubles. Each shade endures his own sufferings; each one is tied to something that impedes, troubles, and disquiets. Do not believe, my Peregrino, that to flee the crowd, to avoid the sight of attractive objects, to shut oneself in a cloister or to go off to a hermitage is the way of perfection. Something in you sets the seal of perfection on your work, something that receives within those things that do not touch you, nay, that are unable to touch you if your mind and spirit will restrain themselves and not seek outside. If it will not admit those external things, the square, the forum, the court, and the busy places of the city will be to you a kind of hermitage, a very remote and perfect solitude. But if remembering things absent or confronted with enticements, our mind reaches outside itself, I do not know how it is an advantage to live as a solitary. For whether it is comprehended by the senses, represented by the memory, constructed by the sharpness of intellect, or created by the desire of the feelings, it is a property of the mind always to think something.

Now, my Peregrino, tell me: Who do you think was more pleasing to God, the contemplative hermit Paul or the active man Abraham? Do you not think that Jacob, with twelve sons, so many flocks of sheep, and two wives, and so much wealth and property, was more acceptable to God than the two Macharii, Theophylac or Hilarion?[5] Believe me, Peregrino, for just as there are incomparably more who are busy in secular affairs than who are concerned with spiritual matters alone, so far more of this kind of men are accepted by God than of that group who are interested in spiritual things alone. But if you perhaps do not believe me, please believe Aurelius, who says about the title of the fifty-first Psalm:

---

5. Three of these can be identified as monks: St. Macarius of Alexandria (4th century), St. Macarius of Egypt (4th century), and St. Hilarion (4th century). Salutati probably meant the fourth, Theophylact, to be Theophylact of Alexandria, patriarch of the city in the fourth century and regarded as the friend of the monks of the desert.

Observe two kinds of men: The one composed of workers, the other of those among whom they labor; the one of the earth, the other thinking of heaven; the one weighing their hearts down into the depths, the others joining their hearts to the angels; the one trusting in terrestrial possessions wherein this world is rich, the other seeking celestial goods that a truthful God has promised. But these two kinds of men are mixed. Now I find a citizen of Jerusalem, a citizen of the kingdom of heaven having an office on earth. That is, he wears the purple; he is a magistrate, an aedile, a proconsul, an emperor; he rules the earthly republic. But he has his heart uplifted, if he is a Christian, if a believer, if pious, if he distains the things of this present world and trusts in those things belonging to the future life. That holy woman Esther was of this nature; who, although the wife of the king, faced the danger of entreating for her own people and when she prayed to her lord in the presence of God, where lying was forbidden, she said in her prayer that her regal vestments were to her like a menstruating woman's cloth.

or, as our translation runs: "You know my necessity, that I abhor the sign of pride and my glory, which is upon my head in the days of my splendor, and I detest this like the cloth of a menstruating woman." To these words father Augustine immediately added: "Therefore let us not despair of the citizens of the kingdom of heaven, when we see them do some of the business of Babylon, some terrestrial affair in the terrestrial republic; nor again should we keep congratulating all men who we see doing heavenly business." And after a few words he added: "Those amid earthly matters raise their hearts to heaven, these amid heavenly words draw their hearts to the earth."

I have quoted all these passages of father Augustine, so that you not keep flattering yourself about your man-constructed oratory or about your being closer to heavenly things, and that you not damn me for remaining in the world and justify yourself fleeing the world. Clearly your fleeing the world can draw your heart from heavenly things to earth, and I, remaining in earthly affairs, will be able to raise my heart to heaven. And you, if you provide for and serve and strive for your family and your sons, your relatives and your friends, and your state (which embraces all), you cannot fail to raise your heart to heavenly things and please God. Indeed, devoted to these things, you are perhaps more acceptable since you not only claim for yourself the coexistence of the first cause, but striving as hard as you can for things necessary to your family, pleasing to your friends, and salubrious for the state, you work together with that same cause that provides for all.[6]

I know, and at this point I do not wish to argue, that the life of those contemplating the divine object, which we ought to love above and before

---

6. When Peregrino serves his fellow men, God is not merely present, as he is when men do any act, but a special relationship arises. In helping others Peregrino is imitating God's Providence.

all things, is more sublime and more perfect than that of those devoted to activities. The former contemplate and love God. The latter, if they are perfectly motivated on account of God and love God, still minister and serve His creatures. I admit, of course, that those given to activity, because of error and crime, can be devoted to the creature on account of the creature. The contemplative is more perfect since it is of such continuous duration that, as the Truth says, Mary has chosen the best part that shall not be taken from her, from the present time and into the future she will be linked with an uninterrupted love. Just as she contemplates eternal things here, so there will she cling to and enjoy eternal things.

I grant that the contemplative life is more sublime for its high level of thought; more delectable with the sweetness of tranquility and meditation; more self-sufficient since it requires fewer things; more divine since it considers divine rather than human things; more noble since it exercises the intellect, the higher part of the soul, which among living things is the unique possession of man. I grant, finally, that it is more lovable because of itself and, as Aurelius says, that it is to be sought for love of the truth; nonetheless, the active life that you flee is to be followed both as an exercise in virtue and because of the necessity of brotherly love. Indeed, as the Philosopher has said, it is better to philosophize than to grow rich, but philosophy is not to be chosen by one needing the necessities of life. The contemplative life is better, I confess; nevertheless, it is not always to be chosen by everybody.

The active life is inferior, but many times it is to be preferred. Although the contemplative life is a matter of choice and the active life concerns necessary things, the latter is not so attached and tied to existence that it does not care about or consider acting well. Therefore do you not believe that this way of life opens a path to heaven? Moreover, eternal beatitude is an act, not a possession, and is devoted to loving, viewing, and enjoying; all discursive operations of speculation and contemplation cease in it. When we die we will see the truth as it is. Would it not, therefore, be appropriate to say that the active life follows the contemplative after death, just as the active precedes it in act while we are alive, since on earth the former produces and begets the latter.

For it was not permitted Jacob to have Rachel unless he had bought and possessed Leah as a wife for seven years. By Leah one understands the active life and by Rachel the contemplative. Now, however, just as Leah comes first in order in this life, so she comes after Rachel in the eternal life. She is always dim-sighted, however, since here below she thinks of temporal things even though with a view to God; and when she receives eternal happiness by grace she will not behold the beatific object. There is a mystery in this since Rachel died first; after a time, however, Leah was buried with Isaac and Rebecca. However, Leah was buried after Rachel, that is, the active life after the contemplative. Where was she buried? Certainly with Isaac and Rebecca. What is Isaac if not, as interpreters say, laughter and joy; what is Rebecca but great wisdom, much patience, and long suffering? From this reading and analysis of Genesis it is clear that Leah is buried with laughter and joy, with much wisdom, which is perfected in action, and much patience, which is made known through a continuation of works and labors, and with much suffering. These are the things in Isaac and Rebecca that represent the happy life.

Indeed, although we distinguish these two ways of life with words and argument, they are really mixed; no one can be so connected with material things that he does for God's sake that he entirely lacks a contemplative element; nor can a contemplative, if he lives as a man, be completely dead to secular matters. Since God is the end of all his actions, how else could he do this unless he has contemplated God and this is done from act to act? Since he must live and help his neighbor on God's behalf, the first because of his nature and the second by the order of divine law, can he always remain in a state of contemplation, unmindful of the necessities of life and doing nothing for the salvation of his fellow man?

Will he be a contemplative so completely devoted to God that disasters befalling a dear one or the death of relatives will not affect him and the destruction of his homeland not move him? If there were such a person, and he related to other people like this, he would show himself not a man but a tree trunk, a useless piece of wood, a hard rock and obdurate stone; nor would he imitate the mediator of God and man who represents the highest perfection. For Christ wept over Lazarus and cried abundantly over Jerusalem, in these things, as in others, leaving us an example to follow.

To conclude shortly, let us grant that the contemplative life is better, more divine and sublime; yet it must be mixed with action and cannot always remain at the height of speculation. Just consider father Augustine meditating and acting; now he is intent on contemplating, now on instructing; now in a certain way enjoying serving his neighbor; now thinking of God, now writing what he thinks; now resting in God, now fighting with heretics. Believe me, he will seem greater to you as an active than as a contemplative man, not only because of the infinite services derived from his deeds, which have benefited all men living in his time and in our own, but also because of the merits of the active life given him in gracious recompense.

Tell me, I pray, what will we be called to answer for in that last judgment if not works of mercy, whether neglected or unfulfilled? For the one who clothed the naked, fed the hungry, gave drink to the thirsting, buried the dead, freed the imprisoned, visited the sick, received the wanderer, will hear these happy words: "Come, blessed of my father, possess the kingdom prepared for you from the foundation of the world." If you establish yourself in Christ, do not think of solitude, for Jerome merited incomparably more in the monastic congregation than in solitude. In solitude he wept; there, I confess, he laid down the burden of sinners;

there, after his departure from the world, he became of such a nature that he could fight isolation. But in the brotherhood and the frequent human contact of the monastery, my Peregrino, he fought with heretics; criticizing the clerics, he purified and instructed them; he resisted his adversaries; he created many things and translated the sacred treasury of letters for Christianity.[7] He not only had men for followers but even used a lion for a guardian and for a beast of burden, which he did not merit in retreat.

I want you, however, if you change your form of life, to learn in society to please God not yourself, so that, departing from this confusion, you seek not your own quiet, nor any pleasure in such things even if they be honorable, but the tears of sins and the deepest affliction because of the beloved Giovanna, bewailing your errors and grinding in penitence. I hope that if you leave the world in this way you will not abandon me, as you threaten, "in this confused world attempting to flatter everyone." The latter words you spoke with great anger. In this case, since I have confidence in you, induce me to follow you or, if I would remain behind, force me by violence to stay with you. Nor will you, who began by admonishing your friend about certain matters, look forward to learning from me. Farewell, if those matters of which you write are true, and meditate on those things I have included in my answer to you. Florence, April 23 [1398].

✦ *Vespasiano da Bisticci*

*V*espasiano da Bisticci was born in 1421 and owned and operated a bookshop in Florence that provided manuscripts both to the powerful princely collectors of Italy and Europe, such as Duke Federico of Urbino and Duke Humphrey of Gloucester, and to the intellectual leaders of the humanist movement, such as Niccolo Niccoli and Poggio Bracciolini. His texts were of the most exacting standards of copying, combining excellent exemplars (texts used as models for copying) with beautiful handwriting designed for clarity and elegance.

Vespasiano also became friends with many of his customers of all ranks. Consequently, when he abandoned his manuscript copying business in 1482 as a result of competition from the introduction of printing, he used his leisure to write short biographical sketches of scholars, book collectors, and patrons who had frequented his shop. Vespasiano da Bisticci died in 1498.

---

7. St. Jerome translated portions of the Bible into Latin.

◆ *Poggio Bracciolini*

*P*oggio Bracciolini was born in 1380 and entered the humanist circle of Coluccio Salutati while the great scholar was Chancellor of Florence. Poggio developed into a fine Latinist who was employed in Rome at the papal court as a secretary, and as a result, he had the opportunity to travel to the Council of Constance (1414–1418), where he sought for lost classical manuscripts in the rich but underused monastic libraries of northern Europe. There he found previously lost works by Cicero and the complete text of Quintilian, as well as The Golden Ass of Apuleius. These discoveries not only added greatly to the literary and intellectual heritage of the ancient world, but also made Poggio famous.

Poggio wrote many works himself in Latin and developed a significant reputation as a writer. This growing fame led to his being chosen Chancellor of Florence some years before his death in 1459, an office he used to write his own history of the city.

FROM VESPASIANO'S *LIVES*

Poggio Fiorentino (1380–1459)

Messer Poggio was born at Terranuova, a Florentine village. His father sent him to the University, where he remained as a teacher, being very learned in the Latin tongue and well conversant with Greek. He was an excellent scribe in ancient characters, and in his youth he was wont to write for a living, providing himself thus with money for the purchase of books and for his other needs. It is well known that the court of Rome is a place where distinguished men may find a position and reward for their activity, and thither he accordingly went, and when his quickness of wit had become known, he was appointed apostolic secretary. Afterward he opened a scrivener's [notary's] office, and in these two vocations was known as a man of integrity and good repute. He had no mind to enter the priesthood, or to accept ecclesiastical preferment, but he took as wife a lady of the noblest blood of Florence, one of the Buondelmonti, and by her had four sons and one daughter. He was sent by Pope Martin with letters into England, and he found much to censure in the way of life of that country, how the people were fain to spend all their time in eating and drinking; indeed, by way of joke, he would tell how, when he had been invited by some bishop or nobleman to dine or sup, he had been forced, after sitting four hours at table, to rise and bathe his eyes with

Source: Vespasiano da Bisticci, *The Vespasiano Memoirs* (London: Routledge and Kegan Paul, 1926), pp. 351–357. Reprinted in W. L. Gundersheimer, ed., *The Italian Renaissance* (Englewood Cliffs, N.J.: Prentice-Hall, 1965), pp. 40–45.

cold water to prevent him[self] from falling asleep. He had many marvelous tales to tell about the wealth of the land. . . .

It was said that his [patron's] gold and silver plate was of enormous value, and that all the kitchen utensils were of silver, as were also the andirons and all the smaller articles. Another fellow citizen of ours, Antonio dei Pazzi, went thither also, and one morning, on a solemn feast, the cardinal assembled a great company for which two rooms were prepared, hung with the richest cloth and arranged all round to hold silver ornaments, one of them being full of cups of silver, and the other with cups gilded or golden. Afterward Pazzi was taken into a very sumptuous chamber, and seven strong boxes full of English articles of price were exhibited to him. . . .

When the Council of Constance was assembled, Poggio went thither, and was besought by Nicolò [Nicoli] and other learned men not to spare himself trouble in searching through the religious houses in these parts for some of the many Latin books which had been lost. He found six Orations of Cicero, and, as I understood him to say, found them in a heap of waste paper among the rubbish. He found the complete works of Quintilian, which had hitherto been only known in fragments, and as he could not obtain the volume he spent thirty-two days in copying it with his own hand: this I saw in the fairest manuscript. Every day he filled a copybook with the text. He found Tully's [Cicero's] *De Oratore,* which had been long lost and was known only in parts, Silius Italicus, *De secundo bello punico* [*The Second Punic War*], in heroic verse, Marcus Manilius on Astronomy, written in verse, and the poem of Lucretius, *De rerum Natura* [*Concerning the Nature of Things*], all works of the highest importance. . . .

Next at Constance he found Tully's letters to Atticus, but of these I have no information, and Messer Leonardo [Bruni] and Messer Poggio together discovered the last twelve comedies of Plautus, which, Gregorio Corero, Poggio, and certain others amended and set in the order which they still follow. The Verrine orations of Cicero also came from Constance and were brought to Italy by Leonardo and Poggio. Thus it may be seen how many noble works we possess through the efforts of these scholars, and how much we are indebted to them; and how greatly the students of our own time have been enlightened by their discoveries. There was no copy of Pliny in Italy; but, news having been brought to Nicolò that there was a fine and perfect one at Lübeck in Germany, he worked so effectively through Cosimo de' Medici that he, by the agency of a kinsman of his living there, bargained with friars who owned it, giving them a hundred Rhenish ducats in exchange for the book. But great trouble followed, both to the friar and to the purchasers.

After his return from Constance Poggio commenced [to be an] author, and to show his quality as a speaker. He had a great gift of words, as the study of his writings and translations will show. His letters are most delightful from their easy style, written without effort. He was given to strong invective, and all stood in dread of him. He was a very cultured and pleasant man, sincere and liberal, and the foe of all deceit and pretense. He had many witty stories to tell of adventures he had encountered in England and Germany when he went thither. As he was very free of speech he incurred the ill will of some of their learned men, and was prompt to take up his pen in vituperation of certain men of letters. He wrote a very abusive letter to Pope Felix, the Duke of Savoy, and took up the cudgels in defense of Nicolò Nicoli, on the score of his many virtues, against a learned man who is now dead. Nicolò was devoted to Carlo d'Arezzo [a humanist and academician] on account of his learning and of his excellent character, and procured advancement for him in many ways. By his influence Carlo was appointed to teach in the University in competition with the learned man before named, against whom Poggio, from his love of Nicolò Nicoli, had written his invective. The gathering at Messer Carlo's lectures was marvelous; thither came all the court of Rome, which was then at Florence, and all the learned Florentines, and from this cause arose the differences between Nicolò Nicoli and Filelfo [poet and humanist], through the great reputation which Messer Carlo had thereby gained. Poggio defended Nicolò Nicoli against an attack made by Filelfo, and on this account ill-feeling arose between Nicolò and Filelfo. As much abuse passed from one to the other, and as Cosimo de' Medici was well disposed to Nicolò and Messer Carlo, Filelfo began to trouble the state, and for his misdemeanor was banished as a rebel; so high did feeling run. To return to Messer Poggio. His fame increased all over the world wherever his works were known, and he spent in original writing or in translating all the time he had to spare after attending to his secretarial and his scrivener's office. . . .

While he tarried at Rome, enjoying the highest favor of the Pope, Messer Carlo d' Arezzo, the Chancellor of the Signoria, died at Florence and Poggio was elected to the office forthwith on account of his fame, and his appointment met with general approval. When this news was brought to him, although from his high position at the court of Rome, and the profit he made, he could not hope to better his condition, he felt a desire to return to his country, so he accepted the office and made Florence his fatherland, as it was just to do. Coming from the court of Rome, and being of a disposition open and frank, and without any leaning toward falsity or dissimulation, Poggio by his character was unacceptable to many of those who ruled their conduct by opposite maxims, saying one thing and meaning another.

It happened that an election was held and that he was put forward as a candidate, wherefore he sent word through one of his friends to the electors, who gave him favorable promises as to what they would do. Messer Poggio, who knew little of the Florentine character, took all this for truth, having yet much to learn; and after he had come to an understanding with his friend, and after the ballot boxes had been emptied, he found that he had received nothing but white beans [blackballs]. Deceit was foreign to Poggio, and up to this time he had believed that what so many citizens had said must have been near the truth; but when he saw that he had been tricked, he lost patience at the duplicity of the Florentines, and broke the peace with them, saying that he could never have believed that men would have transgressed into such evil ways, and lamenting that he had come to live in Florence. He believed that this false trick had been played on himself, and not on his friend.

After he had lived some time in Florence he was chosen into the Signoria in order to honor him with [a position of] civic dignity. When he ceased to attend the Signoria—still retaining the chancellorship and discharging his duties—he went to the Roman court, having won approval from the papal authorities by his letters from all parts of the world. Then it was that certain Florentines, of the sort which is always ready to find fault with everything, began to censure him, scheming how, by the agency of Cosimo de' Medici, who was well disposed toward him, they might drive him out of the chancellorship and put another in his place. Let everyone mark what great danger a man incurs who, with many competitors, submits to the popular vote. Messer Poggio, who was growing old, perceived he could not satisfy this demand because it was mixed up with various parties and policies, [and] decided to retire, in order to have more rest and leisure for study, and let them put another in his office.

Life in the city was uncongenial to his habits and pursuits. Cosimo was much attached to him, and would never have wished to see anyone else in the chancellorship, but when he saw that Messer Poggio cared naught in the matter, he let things take their course, otherwise he would not have allowed the change. Messer Poggio was at this time very rich through long residence at the court of Rome. He had much ready money, property, many houses in Florence, fine household goods, and a noble library: wherefore there was no reason why he should save. Having done with the Palazzo, and with time on his hands, he began upon the history of Florence, taking up the work where Messer Leonardo [Bruni] had left it, and bringing it down to his own day. In Florence it was considered a work of great merit. It had been agreed that he should pay to the state a certain annual sum so that neither he nor his children in the future should be subject to the public burdens of Florence. It came to pass that this privilege was abrogated by an additional tax which laid upon him the insupportable levy of two hundred florins. Hearing the same, Messer Poggio lost patience that the exemption granted to him should be broken in his own lifetime, and if it had not been that Cosimo, who had great influence with him, was able to moderate his anger, he might have taken some imprudent action, for he could not see that a return like this was the meet reward for all his labor. The city itself, and all those who had the Latin tongue, were under great obligations to him, to Messer Leonardo, and Fra Ambrogio [Traversari (1380–1431), humanist and theologian], the first exponents of Latin, which had lain obscure and neglected for so many centuries. Thus Florence found itself, in this golden age, full of learned men.

Among the other exceptional debts which the city of Florence owed to Messer Leonardo and to Messer Poggio may be reckoned the following: From the times of the Roman republic onward there was not to be found any republic or popular state in Italy so famous as was the city of Florence, which had its history written by two authors so illustrious as were Messer Leonardo and Messer Poggio; indeed, before they wrote all knowledge of the same lay in the deepest obscurity. If the chronicles of the Venetian republic, with its numerous men of learning, which has wrought such great deeds both by land and sea, had been written down and not left unrecorded, the renown of Venice would stand higher than it stands today. . . . Every republic ought to set high value upon its writers who may record what is done therein; as we may see from what has been done in Florence, in a narrative from the very beginning of the state, to the times of Messer Leonardo and Messer Poggio; every deed done by the Florentines being set down in Latin in a narrative appropriate to the same. Poggio let his history follow that of Leonardo, writing also in Latin, and Giovanni Villani wrote a general history in the vulgar tongue, telling of what happened in every place, mixing with it the history of Florence, and following him Filippo Villani did the same. These two [the Villanis, early Florentine chroniclers] are the only historians who exhibit these times to us in their writings.

Anyone who may have to write the Life of Messer Poggio will find many things to tell, but having had to make something by way of a commentary, this, which is written here of him, is enough for the present. . . . Before he died, having left to his children a good income as it has been already noticed, he made plans for a marble tomb in S. Croce and stated his wishes as to the erection of the same, writing the epitaph with his own hand, but afterward, while the affair was in progress, the money was put to bad use and the tomb was never built. . . .

✦ *Nicolò Nicoli*

*N*icolò Nicoli was born in Florence into a wealthy merchant family in 1364. He was not at all interested in business but was consumed with the love of classical letters. Consequently, he used his money to build a great private library of the very best copies of Latin and Greek authors then available. He encouraged the search for more lost books from the ancient world and made his own copies in his fine handwriting. In addition, he acquired a great number of ancient objects such as marble statues, coins, and medals.

He was an important member of the intellectual coterie around Leo-nardo Bruni and was a friend of most of the leading scholars of the city. He himself wrote nothing of consequence and avoided public office, lead-ing an almost contemplative scholarly life.

After his death in 1435, his fine library passed eventually to Cosimo de' Medici who further endowed it; and it forms the foundation of the Laurentian Library in Florence to this day.

FROM VESPASIANO'S *LIVES*

Nicolò Nicoli (*d.* 1437)

Nicolò was well born, one of the four sons of a rich merchant, all of whom became merchants. In his youth Nicolò, by his father's wish, entered trade, wherefore he could not give his time to letters as he desired. After his father's death he left his brothers so as to carry out his aims. He was the master of a good fortune and took up Latin letters, in which he soon became proficient. He studied under [Manuel] Chrysoloras, a learned Greek who had recently come to Florence, and although he worked hard in Greek and Latin he was not content with his progress, so he went to study with Luigi Marsigli [*d.* 1394; Florentine humanist and political writer], a learned philosopher and theologian, and in the course of some years' reading gained a good knowledge of the subjects he studied. He here acted like a good and faithful Christian, for, putting all else aside, he studied theology alone. Nicolò may justly be called the father and the benefactor of all students of letters, for he gave them protection and encouragement to work, and pointed out to them the rewards which would follow. If he knew of any Greek or Latin book which was not in Florence he spared neither trouble nor cost until he should procure it; indeed, there are numberless Latin books which the city possesses through his care. He gained such high reputation amongst men of letters that Messer Leonardo sent him his *Life of Cicero* and pronounced him to be the censor [i.e., foremost critic] of the Latin tongue.

He was a man of upright life who favored virtue and censured vice. He collected a fine library, not regarding the cost, and was always search-ing for rare books. He bought all these with the wealth which his father had left, putting aside only what was necessary for his maintenance. He sold several of his farms and spent the proceeds on his library. He was a devoted Christian, who specially favored monks and friars, and was the foe of evildoers. He held his books rather for the use of others than of himself, and all lettered students of Greek or Latin would come to him

Source: Vespasiano da Bisticci, *The Vespasiano Memoirs* (London: Routledge and Kegan Paul, 1926), pp. 395–403. Reprinted in W. L. Gundersheimer, ed., *The Italian Renaissance* (Englewood Cliffs, N.J.: Prentice-Hall, 1965), pp. 46–53.

to borrow books, which he would always lend. He was guileless and sincere and liberal to everyone. It was through his good offices that Fra Ambrogio and Carlo d'Arezzo achieved success, on account of his gifts, the loan of his books, and the fees he paid to their teachers. If he heard of students going to Greece or to France or elsewhere he would give them the names of books which they lacked in Florence, and procure for them the help of Cosimo de' Medici who would do anything for him. When it happened that he could only get the copy of a book he would copy it himself, either in current or shaped characters, all in the finest script, as may be seen in San Marco, where there are many books from his hand in one lettering or the other. He procured at his own expense the works of Tertullian and other [ancient] writers which were not in Italy. He also found an imperfect copy of Ammianus Marcellinus and wrote it out with his own hand. The *De Oratore* and the *Brutus* [by Cicero] were sent to Nicolò from Lombardy, having been brought by the envoys of Duke Filippo when they went to ask for peace in the time of Pope Martin. The book was found in a chest in a very old church; this chest had not been opened for a long time, and they found the book, a very ancient example, while searching for evidence concerning certain ancient rights. *De Oratore* was found broken up, and it is through the care of Nicolò that we find it perfect today. He also rediscovered many sacred works and several of Tully's orations.

Through Nicolò Florence acquired many fine works of sculpture, of which he had great knowledge as well as of painting. A complete copy of Pliny did not exist in Florence, but when Nicolò heard that there was one in Lübeck, in Germany, he secured it by Cosimo's aid, and thus Pliny came to Florence. All the young men he knew in Florence used to come to him for instruction in letters, and he cared for the needs of all those who wanted books or teachers. He did not seek any office in Florence [although] he was made an official in the University; many times he was selected for some governorship, but he refused them all, saying that they were food for the vultures, and he would let these feed on them. He called vultures those who went into the alehouses and devoured the poor. Master Paolo and Ser Filippo were his intimate friends, and there were few days when they would not be found at the monastery of the Agnoli, together with Fra Ambrogio and sometimes Cosimo and Lorenzo de' Medici, who, on account of Nicolò's great merits, treated him most liberally, because he had spent in books almost all that he had. His means only allowed him to live very sparingly considering his position. The Medici, as they knew this, gave orders at the bank that whenever Nicolò might ask for money, it should be given to him, and charged to their account. They afterward told Nicolò not to let himself want for anything, but to send to the bank for whatever he needed. So Nicolò, being in sore straits, heartened himself to do what he would not otherwise have done. They supported him in this way till the end of his life, and they showed the greatest courtesy in aiding him in necessity. In 1420 Cosimo fled from the plague to Verona, taking with him Nicolò and Carlo d' Arezzo and paying all their charges. Afterward, when Cosimo was banished to Venice, Nicolò was deeply grieved on account of the love he had for him, and one day he wrote a letter to Cosimo at Venice, and when he gave it to the horseman who would deliver it, he said in my presence: "Give this letter to Cosimo, and tell him, Nicolò says that so many ill-deeds are committed by the state every day, that a ream of paper would not suffice him to write them down." And he spoke these words in so loud a voice that all those present could hear them. . . .

His was a frank and liberal nature. One day when he was in company with a friar who was learned rather than pious, he addressed him, saying: "There will be few of your kind in Paradise." Another friar, Francesco da Pietropane by name, lived with a few others in the mountains near Lucca, in pious community, and was a man well versed in Greek and Latin. Nicolò showed them much favor and let them have all the books they wanted. At his death he had lent here and there more than two hundred volumes, among which were some of the Greek books which had been lent to Fra Francesco. This friar, amongst many other gifts, had that of predicting the future, and before Cosimo was banished he informed Nicolò that the year 1433 would bring great danger to Cosimo; he would either lose his life or be exiled, whereupon Nicolò sent word to Cosimo to be on his guard, for in this same year he would be in peril either of death or exile. Cosimo was loath to believe this, but these words proved true. Nicolò had a pure mind, and his conversation was that of a good and faithful Christian, for he would say that there were many unbelievers and rebels against the Christian religion who argued against the immortality of the soul, as if this were a matter of doubt. That it was a great misfortune to many that they were only able to care for their bodies, thinking of their souls, which are no way concerned with their unbridled lusts, as something which could sit in a chair, as something substantial enough to be seen with the eye. All those who were not good Christians and doubted concerning that religion to which he was so firmly attached, incurred his strongest hatred; indeed, it seemed to him stark madness to have any doubt of anything so noble which had won the support of so many wonderful men in every age.

Beyond his other remarkable qualities he had a wide judgment, not only in letters, but also in painting and in sculpture, and he had in his house a number of medals, in bronze, silver, and gold; also many antique figures in copper, and heads in marble. One day, when Nicolò was leaving his house, he saw a boy who had around his neck a chalcedony engraved with a figure by the hand of Polycleitus, a beautiful work. He enquired of the boy his father's name, and having learned this, sent to ask him if he would sell the stone; the father readily consented, like one who neither knew what it was nor valued it. Nicolò sent him five florins in exchange, and the good man to whom it had belonged deemed that he had paid him more than double its value. Nicolò afterward exhibited it as a remarkable object, as indeed it was. There was in Florence in the time of Pope Eugenius a certain Maestro Luigi, the Patriarch, who took great interest in such things as these, and he sent word to Nicolò, asking if he might see the chalcedony. Nicolò sent it to him, and it pleased him so greatly that he kept it, and sent to Nicolò two hundred golden ducats and he urged him so much that Nicolò, not being a rich man, let him have it. After the death of this Patriarch it passed to Pope Paul, and then to Lorenzo de' Medici.

Nicolò had a great knowledge of all parts of the world, so that if anyone who had been in any particular region, and asked him about it, Nicolò would know it better than the man who had been there, and he gave many instances of this. Nicolò always had his house full of distinguished men, and the leading youths of the city. As to the strangers who visited Florence at that time, they all deemed that if they had not visited Nicolò they had not been to Florence at all. Many prelates and learned youths and courtiers frequented his house, and among those who often went to see him was Messer Gregorio Correro, nephew of the Cardinal of Bologna, who himself was the nephew of Pope Gregory. This Messer Gregorio was a mirror of conduct, well read in prose and in verse, and much devoted to Nicolò. As soon as Gregorio, or any other of these youths, should come to him, he put a book into his hand, and bade him read it. There would often be, at the same time, ten or twelve noble young gentlemen with books in their hands reading; after a time he would bid them put down the books and tell him what they had been studying. Then there would be a discussion on some matter of interest so that no time might be lost. Indeed, with Nicolò the custom was absolutely different from that of other houses, where men would sit down to play or gamble at once. It chanced one day that a scholar brought some of his writings to show to him, but neither the subject nor the style of them was to Nicolò's liking. After he had read separate portions of the work, the writer begged for his opinion, but Nicolò demurred, being unwilling to vex him, and answered, "I have already to deal with several hundred volumes of authors of repute before I shall be able to consider yours" (for every writer of that time would ask him to read his work and give an opinion), and handed the manuscript back to the writer, who was much astonished, and failed to understand what his verdict was. He was very apt at composition, but his taste was so delicate that he could rarely satisfy himself. I have spoken formerly with some who have seen his Latin epistles and other elegant writings, but these were not shown to me for reasons which I fully understood.

Nicolò always encouraged promising students to follow a literary life, and he nobly aided all those who showed merit in providing them with teachers and books, for in his time teachers and books were not so numerous as they are today. It may be said that he was the reviver of Greek and

Latin letters in Florence; they had for a long time lain buried, and although Petrarch, Dante, and Boccaccio had done something to rehabilitate them, they had not reached that height which they attained through Nicolò's cultivation of them for diverse reasons. First, because he urged many in his time to take to letters, and, through his persuasion, many scholars came to Florence for study and teaching; for instance, he and Palla Strozzi induced Manuel Chrysoloras to come by providing money for his journey. He did the same for Aurispa [another celebrated Greek scholar] and other learned men, and when the question arose of spending money he would say to certain of those he knew, "I wish you would help bring over Manuel, or someone else," and then he would say what each one might give.

Nicolò patronized painters, sculptors, and architects as well as men of letters, and he had a thorough knowledge of their crafts. . . . He was a true connoisseur of all fine things. Friar Ambrogio, Messer Poggio, and Carlo d'Arezzo were his friends, and it was through him that these men of genius became public teachers in Florence in the time of Pope Eugenius. He was on terms of friendship with all the learned men of Italy, and he corresponded with them both at home and abroad.

After having done so many good deeds, and gathered together a vast number of books on all the liberal arts in Greek and Latin, he desired that these should be made accessible to everyone. He directed that, after his death, they should continue to be at the service of all, so in his will he designated forty citizens to see that the books in question should be made a public library in order that all might use them. There were eight hundred volumes of Greek and Latin. He gave directions to these forty citizens that these books should be given to Cosimo de' Medici for the library of San Marco, in fulfillment of the wishes of the testator, that they should remain in a public place for the use of those who might want to consult them. Also that it should be written in the cover of every book how it had once belonged to Nicolò Nicoli, and thus they remain to the present day. The value of them was six thousand florins. At the end of his book, *De longaevis*, Messer Giannozzo [Manetti (1396–1459)] mentions Nicolò and his way of life and the high praise he earned. Among other things he praises most highly the gift of this library, and says that he did more than Plato, Aristotle, or Theophrastus had done, for in the last testaments of Plato and Aristotle are named certain goods which they left to their children, and to others, but they made no mention of their books. Theophrastus left all his possessions privately to a friend; Nicolò alone dedicated his to the public use, therefore much gratitude is due to him. Nor was this all, for Giovanni Boccaccio at his death had left all his books to Santo Spirito, where they were kept in chests, but Nicolò decided that they ought rather to be in a library available for all, so at his own expense he built one for their reception and preservation, and for the honor of Messer Giovanni. As they were for public use he made shelves for them, and they may be seen there to the present time.

To describe Nicolò, he was of handsome presence, lively, with a smile usually on his face, and pleasant manner in conversation. His clothes were always of fine red cloth down to the ground; he never took a wife so as not to be hindered in his studies. He had a housekeeper to provide for his wants, and was one of the most particular of men in his diet as in all else, and was accustomed to have his meals served to him in beautiful old dishes; his table would be covered with vases of porcelain, and he drank from a cup of crystal or of some other fine stone. It was a pleasure to see him at table, old as he was. All the linen that he used was of the whitest. Some may be astonished to hear that he possessed a vast number of vessels, and to these may be answered that, in his day, things of this sort were not so highly prized as now; but Nicolò, being known all over the world, those who wished to please him would send him either marble statues, or antique vases, or sculpture, or marble inscriptions, or pictures by distinguished masters, or tables in mosaic. He had a fine map of the world on which all places were given, and also illustrations of Italy and Spain. There was no house in Florence better decorated than his or better furnished with beautiful things. Nicolò was now over sixty-five years of age; his life had been occupied with good deeds, and when sickness came he was fain to show how his death might be worthy of his life. He was aware that he was near his end, so he sent for Friar Ambrogio and several other holy men and begged them to stay by him till the end. He was a great friend of Maestro Paolo, who, besides being a physician, was a man of holy life, and he begged him to remain also. As he could not rise from his bed he bade them prepare an altar in his room, and all things necessary for the mass; he also made full confession, and then begged Friar Ambrogio to say mass there every morning. After the mass an epistle of Saint Paul, for whom he had the greatest reverence, would be read, and during the reading, when the friar came to any fine passage, he would beg him to stop and would reflect over what had been read, and according to Friar Ambrogio he rarely heard one of these fine passages without tears. He also told me that his fervor and his devotion were wonderful, the result of a well-spent life. He knew that his conscience was clear; that he had never deprived anyone of wealth or fame; and that he had never desired any office in which he might have to pass sentence on others. His room was always filled with those who were the servants of God; unbelievers kept away, knowing that he did not care for them.

At the end he did his religious duties with great devotion. First mass was said, then he had himself placed on the ground on a carpet, with a large number of persons kneeling around him. When the Host was presented he showed the greatest devotion, and he turned to his Redeemer and accused himself as a sinner, and as one unworthy of this holy sacrament. Those around him could scarcely restrain their tears. This wonderful grace came from his habit of always reading holy books. Having taken the sacred body of Christ from the hands of Friar Ambrogio he seemed greatly consoled, and would only speak of his own salvation or read some book of devotion or discourse with the holy men about him. These were the exercises of his last illness, and when his end came he died in the arms of Friar Ambrogio, like a holy man who from his childhood had lived a godly life.

✦ *Leonardo Bruni*

*L*eonardo Bruni was born in 1370 in Arezzo, a town in the Florentine contado. He studied Latin and Greek and was part of the circle of Coluccio Salutati. His celebrated skill at Latin earned him a position in Rome at the papal court, but he returned to Florence in 1415 to assume a position in the communal bureaucracy, rising to the high office of Chancellor of the Republic in 1427, an office he held until his death in 1444.

Bruni used his influence in the chancery to disseminate humanism, which he closely associated with the active life of the layman seeking the good of the community through service to the state. He was instrumental in creating the belief that Florentine republican liberty was the elemental factor in Florence's defeat of Milan occasioned by the death of Giangaleazzo Visconti in 1402. And, as an historian, he linked the foundation of the city not to the age of the Caesars, but to the years of the Roman Republic.

Bruni's historical writings are extremely important in the development of history as a discipline. He modeled his style heavily on that of the Roman historian Livy and exchanged belief in divine intervention for the demonstrable proof of historical causality. Events were the result of human activity, not God's plan for humanity.

Greek studies also were greatly stimulated by Bruni, whose command of the language was complete. He translated Aristotle's Ethics and Politics, as well as a number of Plato's works that had never been rendered into Latin.

Bruni argued in favor of a secular life of active involvement in the affairs of state and for the efficacy of wealth as a means of achieving the good life. He translated the pseudo-Aristotelian Economics and provided for subsequent generations of humanists an argument and an example of the virtuous citizen in the service of his fellows.

HISTORY OF FLORENCE: THE STRUGGLE AGAINST THE VISCONTI

From Book Twelve

Ambassadors from Milan described in Venice their quarrel with Florence and made their accusations. The Venetians, however, when they had heard these arguments, called certain Florentine ambassadors who were in Venice on another mission, so that they might hear all that the Milanese said and, if they wished, respond. To let the reader judge the case, I shall put down here what were the accusations of our adversaries and what were our replies. The Milanese ambassadors to Venice, therefore, when they were given audience, gave the following kind of speech against the Florentines:

"We speak to you, oh Venetians, who have been designers and mediators of truces and treaties, in complaint against those who, violating both faith and law; have destroyed our peace and truce. *For if you designed and mediated our current peace, it seems you are to some extent responsible for it.* If nothing more, you ought at least in this quarrel to hear both sides. We say that these men are chiefly to blame for their failure to keep their promises and disregard for their legal commitments and contracts. To break promises and violate faith is always disgraceful, but it is still more abominable when it brings on war and upheaval despite formal peace treaties. *For if faithfulness to oaths and the sacredness of law break down, what remains to tie men together? How can one still put trust in another? Anyone who violates faith and disregards promises in time of peace dissolves the social bonds of mankind.* You, oh Venetians, know what agreements to truce and peace were recently made, and with what solemn oaths these arrangements were sealed, but how Florence kept those oaths you have seen for yourselves just now.

"In time of peace, while no one expected them to do anything, their ambassadors went to Germany and incited Robert, who claims to be the Roman emperor, to come into Italy and fight Galeazzo of Milan, with whom they had solemnly sworn to remain at peace. They agreed to pay a great sum of money, and expressly contracted to hand this payment over only when he had invaded the land of one with whom they had just made peace, invaded his land and brought about his destruction. No one can deny that this is what their ambassadors tried to arrange, and everyone ought to wonder at such cunning and deceit. These are the same Florentines who have been sending messages and publishing documents, not only all over Italy but also in France, claiming that they, desiring only peace and tranquillity, have been attacked. Their actions now show clearly that they desire not peace but war, not tranquillity but disturbance and the downfall of others. Such is the result of spiritual restlessness and too much wealth. This city, against all the precedents set by our ancestors, has thus tried to get French and German troops to invade Italy—foreign and barbarous peoples, a clear threat to the honor of our Italian name. They have invited those whom nature herself excludes from Italy, to come and lay their yoke on us. Such is their blindness that they do not see the

Source: R. N. Watkins, ed. and trans., *Humanism and Liberty: Writings on Freedom from 15th Century Florence* (Columbia, S.C.: University of South Carolina Press, 1978), pp. 84–91. Reprinted by permission of Renée E. Watkins.

French and German invasion as the common downfall of all Italians, sure
to lay a yoke on Florence as well as on others. The Romans gained praise
and glory because, when the Cimbrians and Teutons were preparing to
invade Italy, they undertook a great military campaign and annihilated
them. By many costly battles they broke the French and liberated the
Italians. These new Romans, however, as they like to call themselves, try
even with bribes to invite the same barbarous and cruel invaders, such is
their people's restlessness, and perverse ambition, and despicable lack of
concern for their country and their race. *We all know what to call the
man who opens the gates of his country to the enemy.* They have earned
the hatred of all Italians, surely, by bribing foreigners to trample on Italian
soil.

"Galeazzo, they say, helps their Tuscan enemies. We reply that Pisa
and Siena would not need anyone's help if they were not cruelly vexed by
Florence. Because of the threat to themselves that does exist, they flock
to Galeazzo for protection. It is no disgrace to him if he defends these old
friends of his father against the depredations of Florence. It is surely
abundantly clear that Galeazzo did not seek Tuscan entanglements for
himself, but that he was called in, begged to come in by those who had
been robbed of most of their possessions, found themselves exhausted,
and yet were unwilling to submit to further damage and humiliation. Not
Galeazzo's willingness to help, but their arrogance toward their neighbors,
is to be deplored. But to conclude briefly, there are three reasons, oh
Venetians, why we were sent to you here: first to complain of a violation
of the sworn peace, second, to demand punishment of the violators in
accordance with the terms of the contract, and third, to tell you not to be
amazed if we resist by war those who broke the peace. The first of these
points is a matter of honor, the second of justice, and the third of necessity." With this, the Milanese ambassadors ended their speech.

The Florentine ambassadors heard it all and discussed it for a little
while, then made up their minds how to reply to the specific points of
the accusation. Then they spoke in the following manner for the honor
of the city:

"We consider it our gain, oh Venetians, that our enemies desired to
give a speech like this. Had they been silent, perhaps the truth would
have remained hidden, but now the provocation of their words will bring
it to light. With your encouragement and help, we made peace with
Galeazzo of Milan, and signed a treaty, thinking he would cease from
desiring to hurt and entrap us. Convinced of this, we not only put down
our arms, but put all thought of war out of our minds. He, however, like
one incapable of striving towards anything but wars and upheaval, acted
with hostility even in peace. We won't mention his condottieri and their
men who, just after peace was signed, devastated the land of our allies,
the Luccans, sacked Volterra, extorted booty and captives from San Gimig-
niano and Collegiani, and afterward brought prisoners and booty from all

this to Siena, which was in his power. He did all these things against the oath and contract of Milan, violating the integrity and good faith of his promises. We won't discuss these actions, as I say, but just pass over them. But it does seem important that during the same peace, he sent into Tuscany a greater army than before and occupied our next door neighbor, Pisa, garrisoning all the towns and castles of that city and subjecting them to his own power. He also added Siena to his dominions, an ancient town very near us. And did he not make Perugia and Assisi effectively his subjects? Did he in doing these things preserve the peace and respect the sacredness of oaths? *It is not only by knocking down walls and mounting a direct assault that one starts a war, this should be recognized, but also by building and setting up siege machinery, even if it is not drawn right up to the wall.* It was not right for Galeazzo to plan war when peace had been made, nor, after he had put down his arms, to retain an armed spirit. He surrounded us with a multitude of towns and cities to fear, he prepared something very like a siege around us, something as well constructed as siege machinery—was this not a breach of the peace? Did he not invade Tuscany against his word and violate the peace treaty? This is undeniable. The things our adversaries have said, therefore, about breakers of truces and of treaties, and about defectors from faith and promises, we say even more strongly, showing that it was he who violated the peace, he who broke promises, he who defected from faith, and he who despised the oaths he had given. We stand against this breach of faith of his part, and we say we were driven by necessity. Can anyone be so under the spell of these people and so unable to think for himself as not to see that, when the duke had put troops in Tuscany and taken Pisa, had subjected the Sienese government to his own, had made Perugia and Assisi subject cities, had by strenuous efforts gained Lucca, and was trying to do the same to Cortona, he had done all this in order again, despite the recent peace treaty, to make war on Florence? These things, therefore, he did against his faith and legal oath, violating his promises and the peace. If we made public in Italy and elsewhere that we wanted peace and tranquillity and that he was aggressing against us with his attacks, we spoke no more than the truth. *Even after making peace and swearing to it, he could not limit himself but prepared all things for our destruction; what can we suppose he would have done without oaths and peace treaties?* When he says that we are incapable of peaceful behavior, we say let him be silent and let others judge who themselves are capable of peace. He who has not let his immediate family live in security, nor his kin, nor his neighbors, nor his allies, nor nearby peoples, who subjected Verona and Padua by fraud, who now plans wholly to subjugate Tuscany, and whose greed is never satiated, is wholly unfit to say these things of us. We want peace if only we are allowed to have it. What his ambassadors say concerning the French and Germans entering Italy at our invitation makes us ask who is responsible for this; isn't it he and his restlessness and violence that are bringing them in? He is not satisfied with northern Italy but, with incredible ambition he seeks Tuscany and Rome also for himself. His greed and ambition have gone so far that he makes himself the ultimate promise of a kingdom of Italy. His words are all deceit, his deeds are all meant to trap others, he has no honor left, for his is stained and rotten. If our word does not convince you, ask the lords of Verona and Padua, whom he expelled by fraud. Ask the Pisans and Sienese, whom he wanted to rule by tyranny and succeeded in subjecting by fraud. For what he did to his own relatives is too shameful to mention. If we try to defend ourselves against so much greed and perfidy, and if some upheavals arise in Italy as a result and some foreign peoples enter, whose fault is it? Is it his who moves and attacks, or ours, who are driven by necessity to seek help from anyone we can find? The Roman emperor coming into Italy, however, ought not to seem a foreigner. The others who came in were not six hundred thousand strong, like the Cimbri and Teutons, nor were they such a force and such a multitude that Italy needed to fear them. In closing, we demand the vindication which they demand, for the violation of peace and of truce. We declare that the duke of Milan owes us some recompense for his violations and his disregard of sworn pacts. We plead with you and all powers for recognition of our rights. For as they say, *no one should be amazed if he attacks us, since everybody has grown used to seeing him make war with and without excuse.* Having faith in God and justice, we resist his violence." Thus spoke the ambassadors in reply.

The Venetians showed their approval of what the Florentine ambassadors had said, so that these would feel they had sufficiently defended the honor of the city; at the same time, as a neutral power, the Venetians tried to placate the tempers of both sides with grave and prudent words.

The following year, which was 1402, great battles were fought around Bologna. Even before the emperor's complete withdrawal, Galeazzo, elated by the way things were going for him, sent part of his forces into Bolognese territory, to overthrow if possible the new lord of that city. When the emperor had left, he sent more troops into Bolognese territory. The generals in charge of these forces were the lord of Mantua, recently come into the grace and friendship of Milan, and Pandolfo Malatesta and Ottobuono of Parma, as well as other captains. The arrival of these forces immediately put the city in great peril, for there were enough powerful exiles to make the castles and towns of the area rise up, and the citizens inside the city were not all happy about the government of the lord of Bologna either. The Florentines responded to the danger by sending the captain Bernardone with a large number of troops. They added more troops in time, as they learned of reinforcements sent to the enemy. Large forces were sent to the aid of Bologna by the lord of Padua and other allies, and the lord of Padua sent two of his sons along. All the forces of the Florentine people and of their allies, and all the forces of the enemy, were finally gathered around Bologna. Both sides made encampments around the city, but the enemy's were farther from the city and ours were closer, lying halfway between the enemy's lines and the city. The general-in-chief of the Florentine armies was Bernardone, and the armies of the enemy were commanded by Duke Alberigo.

With the armies thus arrayed for some time, the enemy, who was more numerous and stronger, finally initiated an attack on the encampment of the Florentines and their allies. Our camp was near Casaleccio, four miles outside Bologna. The defense of this spot seemed vital, because water from the Reno flows to Bologna through there; if the enemy could divert this stream the city would be in serious trouble. The enemy left camp, therefore, and mounted a sudden attack on ours. Our men met them with bitter fighting and resisted vigorously, and Bernardone was there to encourage and guide them. But the attack of the enemy was so forceful that our men retreated from the bridge over the river, and they occupied it. Then suddenly, not only over the bridge but also by other ways, they crossed the river and attacked our people; it was not a matter of feats of arms anymore but of slaughter or flight everywhere. Bernardone was captured and the other leaders were almost all taken too, except those who fled into the city of Bologna. The two sons of the lord of Padua boldly laid waste around them, but finally surrendered to the lord of Mantua. The camps were all taken by the enemy with enormous booty.

This calamity soon led to greater ruin. The Bolognese citizens of the opposition rose in insurrection, and men of various factions now dared to raise their heads against their master. There were battles throughout the city during the night. Bentivoglio fought with amazing skill and won universal praise for it. Friends and enemies alike admitted that he was the first and best of fighters. With the whole city in arms, however, and victorious enemies holding all the territory outside, the party of the opposition was able to seize one of the gates and let in the exiles and part of the enemy force. With such a multitude of enemies swarming around, Bentivoglio was captured and soon killed. Two Florentine ambassadors were in the city, Nicolò da Uzzano and Bardo Rittafè. Bardo was wounded and died soon after. Nicolò was taken prisoner and carried to Pavia, where he suffered wretchedly in prison.

Bologna after the return of the exiles received a civil government. A formal republic and formal liberty were restored. This indeed was what Galeazzo had promised the exiles. The pleasure only lasted two or three days, however. Then certain persons sent by the duke with a military force ran through the city shouting the name of Galeazzo, usurped the authority of the city's officials, and proclaimed the entire lordship of Milan. The people and the exiles were disappointed, but they had to bend their necks to the yoke of servitude.

When the Florentines heard that the army had been defeated and Bernardone taken prisoner, they were terribly frightened and anxious. When they learned that Bologna too had fallen, they were even more terrified, expecting the enemy from hour to hour. Without the general and the army, they seemed to despair completely. Had the enemy approached promptly to follow up his victory, the city could not have withstood him. The enemy, however, whether because of weariness or internal discord, let the time for action pass in useless settling down. When many days had passed and the enemy with his army had not appeared, the city gathered its spirits a little and began to rise up and repair its strength. They sent some troops against the partisans of the Ubaldini, who had rebelled after the enemy's success, and against Ricciardo of Pistoia and his followers who, upon hearing of the defeat, had captured many places. The troops the Florentines sent put a stop to such outbreaks.

Those who discussed possible means of defense against the great danger that threatened thought of two hopes; one, that Pope Boniface would go to war, the other that Venice would. There was some basis for these hopes, for the pope definitely was not pleased to see the cities of Perugia and Bologna both captured. The Venetians long before had begun to show displeasure at the growth of Milanese power. Florence tried with the utmost zeal to make an alliance with both cities. Yet both stood still and seemed horrified at the idea of actually going to war. The Venetians definitely wanted a somewhat unfair treaty of alliance, by which war would be made more at the expense of Florence than of Venice, and yet Venice would have the right of complete discretion in the matter of making peace, which they could do at any time without the consent of Florence. These conditions seemed too hard and beneath the dignity of the Florentine people.

Amidst all this came the hope of peace. The enemy seemed to want to make peace after taking Bologna, and sent representatives to Venice to propose rather reasonable conditions. The Florentines suspected deception and fraud, and finally decided to agree to the peace and to the Venetian alliance at the same time, thinking that if the peace began at the same time as the alliance, the peace would be more durable and the conditions demanded by the Venetians less important. They instructed their representatives to sign, with the addition of a few corrections, peace with the enemy and an alliance with Venice.

While the city was just doing this, word came through that Galeazzo was dead. The death was first announced by Paolo Guinisi, lord of Lucca, but it was not considered a certainty. Later it was repeated as a certainty, but a deep secret. At once letters were sent to the representatives in Venice not to agree to the peace nor to the alliance. The Venetians learned of the duke's death only from the Florentine embassy, having heard nothing before. There had been signs, however, such as some forces sent towards Tuscany through Piacenza and Lunigiana being suddenly recalled. The leaders of the army, who were still before Bologna, had received orders not to move from the spot. It now proved that Galeazzo had become ill soon after Bologna was taken. He had died somewhat later of the same illness, at the Milanese castle of Marignano. These facts had been kept secret at first. Eventually they had to be made public, and there was a magnificent funeral. It also came out that Galeazzo, while he lay ill, had passionately desired peace with Florence. Hence the attempt to send a mission to Venice and to make a new peace. He realized that his sons were still young and were being left in the midst of great danger. So he was in a hurry to make peace before he would leave the world. This would have been accomplished, too, if he had lived just a little longer. His sudden death brought such a reversal of things that those who before had hardly any hope left for their own safety were now filled with high confidence, while those who had just considered themselves victorious lost all hope of being able to resist.

THE LIFE OF DANTE

Dante's ancestors belonged to one of the oldest Florentine families. Indeed the poet in certain passages seems to imply that they were among those Romans who founded Florence. But this is most doubtful—mere supposition, as it seems to me. His great-great-grandfather, as I am informed, was Messer Cacciaguida, a Florentine knight who served under the Emperor Conrad. This Messer Cacciaguida had two brothers, Moronto and Eliseo. We do not read of any succession from Moronto, but from Eliseo sprang the family of the Elisei, who, however, possibly bore this name previously. From Messer Cacciaguida came the Aldighieri, so called from one of his sons, who received the name from the family of his mother.

Messer Cacciaguida, his brothers, and their ancestors, lived almost at the corner of the Porta San Piero, where it is first entered from the Mercato Vecchio, in houses still called of the Elisei, since their ancient title has remained to them. The Aldighieri, who were descended from Messer Cacciaguida, dwelt in the piazza at the rear of San Martino del Vescovo, opposite the street that leads to the houses of the Sacchetti. On the other side their dwellings extend toward those of the Donati and of the Giuochi.

Dante was born in the year of our Lord 1265, shortly after the return to Florence of the Guelfs, who had been in exile because of the defeat at Montaperti. In his boyhood he received a liberal education under teachers of letters, and at once gave evidence of a great natural capacity equal to excellent things. At this time he lost his father, but, encouraged by his relatives and by Brunetto Latini, a most worthy man for those times, he devoted himself not only to literature but to other liberal studies, omitting nothing that pertains to the making of an excellent man.

He did not, however, renounce the world and shut himself up to ease, but associated and conversed with youths of his own age. Courteous,

Source: G. Boccaccio and L. Bruni Aretino, The Earliest Lives of Dante, edited by F. Bassetti-Sani (New York: Frederick Ungar, 1963), pp. 82–94. Reprinted by permission of Ungar Publishing Co.

spirited, and full of courage, he took part in every youthful exercise; and in the great and memorable battle of Campaldino, Dante, young but well esteemed, fought vigorously, mounted and in the front rank. Here he incurred the utmost peril, for the first engagement was between the cavalry, in which the horse of the Aretines defeated and overthrew with such violence the horse of the Florentines that the latter, repulsed and routed, were obliged to fall back upon their infantry.

This rout, however, lost the battle for the Aretines. For their victorious horsemen, pursuing those who fled, left their infantry far behind, so that thenceforth they nowhere fought in unison, but the cavalry fought alone without the infantry, and the infantry alone without the cavalry. But on the Florentine side the contrary took place, for, since their cavalry had retreated to their infantry, they were able to advance in a body, and easily overthrew first the horse and then the foot-soldiers of the enemy.

Dante gives a description of the battle in one of his letters. He states that he was in the fight, and draws a plan of the field. And for our better information we must understand that the Uberti, Lamberti, Abati, and all the other Florentine exiles sided with the Aretines in this battle, and that all the exiles of Arezzo, nobles and commoners of the Guelfs, all of whom were in banishment at this time, fought with the Florentines. For this reason the words in the Palace read: *The Ghibellines defeated at Certomondo*, and not, *The Aretines defeated;* to the end that those Aretines who shared the victory with the Commune might have no reason to complain.

Returning then to our subject, I repeat that Dante fought valiantly for his country on this occasion. And I could wish that our Boccaccio had made mention of this virtue rather than of love at nine, and the like trivialities which he tells of this great man. But what use is there in speaking? "The tongue points where the tooth pains," and "Whose taste runs to drinking, his talk runs to wines."

When Dante returned home from this battle, he devoted himself more fervently than ever to his studies, yet omitted naught of polite and social intercourse. It was remarkable that, although he studied incessantly, none would have supposed from his happy manner and youthful way of speaking that he studied at all. In view of this, I wish to denounce the false opinion of many ignorant persons who think that no one is a student save he who buries himself in solitude and ease. I have never seen one of these muffled recluses who knew three letters. The great and lofty genius has no need of such tortures. Indeed, it is a most true and absolute conclusion that they who do not learn quickly, never learn. Therefore to estrange and absent one's self from society is peculiar to those whose poor minds unfit them for knowledge of any kind.

It was not only in social intercourse with men that Dante moved, since in his youth he took to himself a wife. She was a lady of the Donati family, called Madonna Gemma. By her he had several children, as we shall see in another part of this work. At this point Boccaccio loses all patience, and says that wives are hindrances to study, forgetting that Socrates, the noblest philosopher that ever lived, had a wife and children, and held public offices in his city. And Aristotle, beyond whose wisdom and learning it is impossible to go, was twice married, and had children and great riches. Moreover, Cicero, Varro, and Seneca, all consummate Latin philosophers, had wives, and held offices of government in the republic. So Boccaccio may pardon me, for his judgments on this matter are both false and feeble. Man, according to all the philosophers, is a social animal. The first union, by the multiplication whereof the city arises, is that of husband and wife. Nothing can be perfect where this does not obtain, for only this kind of love is natural, lawful, and allowable.

Dante, then, took a wife, and living the honest, studious life of a citizen, was considerably employed in the republic, and at length, when he had attained to the required age, was made one of the Priors, not chosen by lot as at present, but elected by vote, as was then the rule. With him in this office were Messer Palmieri degli Altoviti, Neri di Messer Jacopo degli Alberti, and others.

This priorate, of the year 1300, was the cause of Dante's banishment and of all the misfortunes of his life, as he himself states in one of his letters in the following words: "All my troubles and hardships had their cause and rise in the disastrous meetings held during my priorate. Albeit in wisdom I was not worthy of that office, nevertheless I was not unworthy of it in fidelity and in age, since ten years had elapsed since the battle of Campaldino, wherein the Ghibelline party was almost utterly defeated and effaced, and on that occasion I was present, no child at arms, and felt at first great fear, but in the end the greatest joy by reason of the various fortunes of that battle." These are Dante's own words. I wish now to give in detail the cause of his banishment, since it is a matter worthy our attention, and Boccaccio passes over it so briefly that perchance it was not so well known to him as it is to me by reason of the history I have written.

The city of Florence, which formerly had been divided by the many dissensions of Guelfs and Ghibellines, finally passed into the hands of the Guelfs, and remained for a long period in that condition. But now among the Guelfs themselves, who ruled the republic, another curse of parties arose, namely, the factions of the Bianchi and Neri. This infection first appeared among the Pistojans, particularly in the family of the Cancellieri. And when all Pistoja was divided, the Florentines, by way of remedy, ordered the leaders of these factions to come to Florence, in order that they might not cause further disturbance at home.

This remedy worked less good to the Pistojans by the removal of their chiefs than harm to the Florentines, who contracted this pestilence. For, since the leaders had many relatives and friends in Florence, from whom they received divers favors, they at once kindled a greater fire of discord than they had left behind them in Pistoja. And inasmuch as the affair was treated of *publice et privatim*, the evil seed spread to a marvelous degree, so that the whole city took sides. There was scarcely a house, noble or plebeian, that was not divided against itself, nor was there a man of any prominence or family that did not subscribe to one of these two parties. The division extended even to brothers of the same blood, one holding to this side, the other to that.

The troubles, which already had lasted several months, were multiplied not only by words, but by mean and spiteful deeds. These were begun by the youths, but were taken up by men of maturity, until the whole city was in confusion and suspense. At this point, while Dante was still of the Priors, the Neri faction held a meeting in the Church of Santa Trinita. The proceedings were profoundly secret, but the main plan was to treat with Boniface VIII, who was pope at that time, to the end that he should send Charles of Valois, of the royal house of France, to pacify and reform the city.

When the other faction, the Bianchi, heard about the conference, they immediately conceived the greatest distrust thereof. They took up arms, gathered together their allies, and, marching to the Priors, complained of the conference in that it had deliberated in private on public affairs. This was done, they declared, in order to banish them, the Bianchi, from Florence, and they therefore demanded that the Priors should punish this presumptuous outrage.

They who had held the meeting, fearing, in turn, the Bianchi, took up arms, complained to the Priors that their adversaries had armed and fortified themselves without the public consent, and affirmed that the Bianchi under various pretexts wished to banish them. They asked the Priors to punish them, therefore, as disturbers of the public peace.

Both parties were provided with armed men and with their allies. Suspicion and terror were at their height, and the actual peril was very great. The city being in arms and in a turmoil, the Priors, at Dante's suggestion, took the precaution of fortifying themselves behind the multitude of the people. And when they were thus secured, they confined within bounds the leaders of the two factions. Of the Neri faction, Messer Corso Donati, Messer Geri Spini, Messer Giacchinotto de' Pazzi, Messer Rosso della Tosa, and others, were sent to the Castello della Pieve in the province of Perugia. Of the Bianchi faction were Messer Gentile and Messer Torrigiano de' Cerchi, Guido Cavalcanti, Baschiera della Tosa, Baldinaccio Adimari, Naldo di Messer Lottino Gherardini, and others. These men were confined within bounds at Serezzana.

This action caused much trouble to Dante. Although he defended himself as a man without a party, yet it was thought that he inclined to the Bianchi, and that he disapproved of the scheme proposed in Santa Trinita of calling Charles of Valois to Florence, believing that it was likely to bring discord and calamity on the city. To add to this ill-feeling, those citizens who were confined at Serezzana suddenly returned to Florence, while those who had been sent to the Castello della Pieve remained outside. With regard to this matter Dante explained that he was not a prior at the time when the men of Serezzana were recalled, and that therefore he was not to be held accountable. He declared, furthermore, that their return was due to the sickness and death of Guido Cavalcanti, who had fallen ill at Serezzana owing to the bad climate, and died shortly afterward.

This unequal state of things led the pope to send Charles to Florence. Being honorably received into the city out of respect to the papacy and the house of France, he straightway recalled those citizens who were still confined within bounds, and later banished all the Bianchi faction. The reason of this was a plot that was disclosed by his baron, Messer Piero Ferranti. This man said that three gentlemen of the Bianchi party, namely, Naldo di Messer Lottino Gherardini, Baschiera della Tosa, and Baldinaccio Adimari, had requested him to try and prevail upon Charles of Valois to keep their party at the head of the state, and that they promised to make him governor of Prato in return. The baron produced the written petition and promise with their seals affixed. This original document I have seen, since it lies to-day in the palace with other public writings, but in my opinion it is not above suspicion, and indeed I feel quite certain that it was forged. Be that as it may, the banishment of all the Bianchi party followed, Charles professing great indignation at their request and promise.

Dante was not in Florence at this time, but at Rome, whither he had been sent shortly before as ambassador to the pope, to offer him the peace and concord of the citizens. Nevertheless, through the anger of those Neri who had been banished during his priorate, his house was attacked, everything was pillaged, and his estate was laid waste. Banishment was decreed for him and for Messer Palmieri Altoviti, not by reason of any wrong committed, but for contumacy in failing to appear.

The manner of decreeing the banishment was this. They enacted a perverse and iniquitous law with retrospective action, which declared it the power and duty of the Podestà of Florence to recognize past offenses committed by a prior when in office, although acquittal had followed at the time. Under this law Messer Cante de' Gabbrielli, Podestà of Florence, summoned Dante to trial. And since he was absent from the city, and did not appear, he was condemned and banished, and his goods were confiscated, although they already had been plundered and laid waste.

We have given the cause and the circumstances of Dante's banishment; we shall now speak of his life in exile. When Dante heard of his ruin, he at once left Rome, where he was ambassador, and, journeying with all haste, he came to Siena. Here he learned more definitely of his misfortune, and seeing no recourse, he decided to throw in his lot with the other exiles. He first joined them in a meeting held at Gorgonza, where among the many things discussed they fixed on Arezzo as their headquarters. There they made a large camp, and created the Count Alessandro da Romena their captain, together with twelve councilors, among whom was Dante. They remained here from hope to hope till the year 1304, and then, making a great gathering of all their allies, they planned to re-enter Florence with an exceeding great multitude, assembled not only from Arezzo, but from Bologna and Pistoja. Arriving unexpectedly, they immediately captured one of the gates and occupied part of the city. But in the end they were forced to retire with no advantage.

Since this great hope had failed, Dante, deeming it wrong to waste more time, left Arezzo for Verona. Here he was most courteously received by the Lords della Scala, and tarried with them for some time. And now in all humility he endeavored by good deeds and upright conduct to obtain the favor of returning to Florence through the voluntary action of the government. Devoting himself resolutely to this end, he wrote frequently to individual citizens in power and also to the people, among others one long letter which began: *Popule mee, quid feci tibi?*

But while he was still hoping to return by the way of pardon, the election of Henry of Luxemburg as Emperor occurred. This election, and the coming of Henry, filled all Italy with the hope of a great change, and Dante himself could no longer keep to his plan of waiting for pardon. With his pride of spirit aroused, he began to speak evil of the rulers of the state, calling them caitiffs and criminals, and threatening them at the hands of the emperor with deserved punishment. From this, he said, there was clearly no possible escape for them.

Yet so great was the reverence he felt for his country, that when the emperor had marched against Florence and was encamped near the gate, Dante would not be present, as he writes, although he had urged the emperor's coming. And when Henry died the following summer at Buon-convento, Dante lost all hope, for he himself had destroyed all chance of pardon by speaking and writing against the citizens in power, and no force remained whereon he could place further assurance. Void of hope, therefore, and in great poverty, he passed the remainder of his life tarrying in divers parts of Lombardy, Tuscany, and Romagna, under the protection of various lords, until finally he settled down at Ravenna, where he died.

Since we have told of his public troubles, and under this head have shown the course of his life, we will now speak of his domestic affairs, and of his habits and studies. Previous to his banishment from Florence, although he was not a man of great wealth, yet he was not poor, for he possessed a moderate patrimony, large enough to admit of comfortable living. He had one brother, Francisco Alighieri, a wife, as already mentioned, and several children, whose descendants remain to this day, as we shall show later. He owned good houses in Florence, adjoining those of Gieri di Messer Bello, his kinsman; possessions also in Camerata, in the Piacentina, and in the plain of Ripoli; and, as he writes, many pieces of valuable furniture.

He was a man of great refinement; of medium height, and of a pleasant but deeply serious face. He spoke only seldom, and then slowly, but was very subtle in his replies. His portrait may be seen in Santa Croce, near the center of the church, on the left hand as you approach the high altar, a most faithful painting by an excellent artist of that time. He delighted in music and singing, and drew exceedingly well. He wrote a finished hand, making thin, long, and perfectly formed letters, as I have seen in some of his correspondence. In his youth he associated with young lovers, and he, too, was filled with a like passion, not through evil desire, but out of a gentleness of his heart. And in his tender years he began to write love verses, as may be seen in his short work in the vernacular called the *Vita Nuova*.

◆ *Isotta Nogarola*

*B*orn in 1418 in Verona, Isotta Nogarola became perhaps the most *learned woman of the fifteenth century in Italy. She studied Latin and Greek with a pupil of Guarino, and at the age of 18 she began her own humanist correspondence, writing to Guarino himself. However, the scorn shown her by many hostile men drove her to stop writing in 1438, just two years later.*

Nogarola moved temporarily to Venice in that year but returned to Verona in 1441 and decided neither to marry nor to become a nun but to dedicate herself to sacred studies. This she did, and she managed to achieve some considerable distinction. In the early 1450s she became close to Venetian diplomat and humanist Lodovico Foscarini. The dialogue that follows represents a literary discussion between them on the relative sinfulness of Adam and Eve.

Isotta Nogarola died in 1466.

OF THE EQUAL OR UNEQUAL SIN OF ADAM AND EVE

An honorable disputation between the illustrious lord Ludovico Foscarini, Venetian doctor of arts and both laws, and the noble and learned and divine lady Isotta Nogarola of Verona, regarding this judgment of Aurelius Augustine: They sinned unequally according to sex, but equally according to pride.

Ludovico begins: If it is in any way possible to measure the gravity of human sinfulness, then we should see Eve's sin as more to be condemned

Source: M. King and A. Rabil, eds. & trans., *Her Immaculate Hand: Selected, Works By and About The Women Humanists of 1400 Italy* (Binghamton, N.Y.: MARTS, 1983), pp. 59–69. Reprinted by permission of the publisher.

than Adam's [for three reasons]. [First], she was assigned by a just judge to a harsher punishment than was Adam. [Second], she believed that she was made more like God, and that is in the category of unforgiveable sins against the Holy Spirit. [Third], she suggested and was the cause of Adam's sin—not he of hers; and although it is a poor excuse to sin because of a friend, nevertheless none was more tolerable than the one by which Adam was enticed.

Isotta: But I see things—since you move me to reply—from quite another and contrary viewpoint. For where there is less intellect and less constancy, there there is less sin; and Eve [lacked sense and constancy] and therefore sinned less. Knowing [her weakness] that crafty serpent began by tempting the woman, thinking the man perhaps invulnerable because of his constancy. [For it says in] *Sentences* 2: Standing in the woman's presence, the ancient foe did not boldly persuade, but approached her with a question: "Why did God bid you not to eat of the tree of paradise?" She responded: "Lest perhaps we die." But seeing that she doubted the words of the Lord, the devil said: "You shall not die," but "you will be like God, knowing good and evil."

[Adam must also be judged more guilty than Eve, secondly] because of his greater contempt for the command. For in Genesis 2 it appears that the Lord commanded Adam, not Eve, where it says: "The Lord God took the man and placed him in the paradise of Eden to till it and to keep it," (and it does not say, "that they might care for and protect it") ". . . and the Lord God commanded the man" (and not "them"): "From every tree of the garden you may eat" (and not "you" [in the plural sense]), and, [referring to the forbidden tree], "for the day you eat of it, you must die," [again, using the singular form of "you"] [God directed his command to Adam alone] because he esteemed the man more highly than the woman.

Moreover, the woman did not [eat from the forbidden tree] because she believed that she was made more like God, but rather because she was weak and [inclined to indulge in] pleasure. Thus: "Now the woman saw that the tree was good for food, pleasing to the eyes, and desirable for the knowledge it would give. She took of its fruit and ate it, and also gave some to her husband and he ate," and it does not say [that she did so] in order to be like God. And if Adam had not eaten, her sin would have had no consequences. For it does not say: "If Eve had not sinned Christ would not have been made incarnate," but "If Adam had not sinned." Hence the woman, but only because she had been first deceived by the serpent's evil persuasion, did indulge in the delights of paradise; but she would have harmed only herself and in no way endangered human posterity if the consent of the first-born man had not been offered. Therefore Eve was no danger to posterity but [only] to herself; but the man Adam spread the infection of sin to himself and to all future generations. Thus Adam, being the author of all humans yet to be born, was also the first cause of their perdition. For this reason the healing of humankind was celebrated first in the man and then in the woman, just as [according to Jewish tradition], after an unclean spirit has been expelled from a man, as it springs forth from the synagogue, the woman is purged [as well].

Moreover, that Eve was condemned by a just judge to a harsher punishment is evidently false, for God said to the woman: "I will make great your distress in childbearing; in pain shall you bring forth children; for your husband shall be your longing, though he have dominion over you." But to Adam he said: "Because you have listened to your wife and have eaten of the tree of which I have commanded you not to eat" (notice that God appears to have admonished Adam alone [using the singular form of "you"] and not Eve) "Cursed be the ground because of you; in toil shall you eat of it all the days of your life; thorns and thistles shall it bring forth to you, and you shall eat the plants of the field. In the sweat of your brow you shall eat bread, till you return to the ground, since out of it you were taken; for dust you are and unto dust you shall return." Notice that Adam's punishment appears harsher than Eve's; for God said to Adam: "to dust you shall return," and not to Eve, and death is the most terrible punishment that could be assigned. Therefore it is established that Adam's punishment was greater than Eve's.

I have written this because you wished me to. Yet I have done so fearfully, since this is not a woman's task. But you are kind, and if you find any part of my writing clumsy you will correct it.

Ludovico: You defend the cause of Eve most subtly, and indeed defend it so [well] that, if I had not been born a man, you would have made me your champion. But sticking fast to the truth, which is attached by very strong roots, I have set out [here] to assault your fortress with your own weapons. I shall begin by attacking its foundations, which can be destroyed by the testimony of Sacred Scripture, so that there will be no lack of material for my refutation.

Eve sinned from ignorance and inconstancy, from which you conclude that she sinned less seriously. [But] ignorance—especially of those things which we are obligated to know—does not excuse us. For it is written: "If anyone ignores this, he shall be ignored." The eyes which guilt makes blind punishment opens. He who has been foolish in guilt will be wise in punishment, especially when the sinner's mistake occurs through negligence. For the woman's ignorance, born of arrogance, does not excuse her, in the same way that Aristotle and the [lawyers], who teach a true philosophy, find the drunk and ignorant deserving of a double punishment. Nor do I understand how in the world you, so many ages distant from Eve, fault her intellect, when her knowledge, divinely created by the highest craftsman of all things, daunted that clever serpent lurking in paradise. For, as you write, he was not bold enough to attempt to persuade her but approached her with a question.

But the acts due to inconstancy are even more blameworthy [than those due to ignorance]. For to the same degree that the acts issuing from a solid and constant mental attitude are more worthy and distinct from the preceding ones, so should those issuing from inconstancy be punished more severely, since inconstancy is an evil in itself and when paired with an evil sin makes the sin worse.

Nor is Adam's companion excused because Adam was appointed to protect her, [contrary to your contention that] thieves who have been trustingly employed by a householder are not punished with the most severe punishment like strangers or those in whom no confidence has been placed. Also, the woman's frailty was not the cause of sin, as you write, but her pride, since the demon promised her knowledge, which leads to arrogance and inflates [with pride], according to the apostle. For it says in Ecclesiasticus: "Pride was the beginning of every sin." And though the other women followed, yet she was the first since, when man existed in a state of innocence, the flesh was obedient to him and [did not struggle] against reason. The first impulse [of sin], therefore, was an inordinate appetite for seeking that which was not suited to its own nature, as Augustine wrote to Orosius: "Swollen by pride, man obeyed the serpent's persuasion and disdained God's commands." For the adversary said to Eve: "Your eyes will be opened and you will be like God, knowing good and evil." Nor would the woman have believed the demon's persuasive words, as Augustine says [in his commentary] on Genesis, unless a love of her own power had overcome her, which [love is] a stream sprung from the well of pride. [I shall continue to follow Augustine in his view that at the moment] when Eve desired to capture divinity, she lost happiness. And those words: "If Adam had not sinned, etc." confirm me in my view. For Eve sinned perhaps in such a way that, just as the demons did not merit redemption, neither perhaps did she. I speak only in jest, but Adam's sin was fortunate, since it warranted such a redeemer.

And lest I finally stray too far from what you have written, [I shall turn to your argument that Adam's punishment was more severe than Eve's and his sin, accordingly, greater. But] the woman suffers all the penalties [inflicted on] the man, and since her sorrows are greater than his, not only is she doomed to death, condemned to eat at the cost of sweat, denied by the cherubim and flaming swords entry to paradise, but in addition to all these things which are common [to both], she alone must give birth in pain and be subjected to her husband. [Her punishment is thus harsher than Adam's, as her sin is greater].

But because in such a matter it is not sufficient to have refuted your arguments without also putting forward my own, [I shall do so now]. Eve believed that she was made similar to God and, out of envy, desired that which wounds the Holy Spirit. Moreover, she must bear responsibility for every fault of Adam because, as Aristotle testifies, the cause of a cause is the cause of that which is caused. Indeed, every prior cause influences an outcome more than a secondary cause, and the principle of any genus, according to the same Aristotle, is seen as its greatest [component]. In fact, [it] is considered to be more than half the whole. And in the *Posterior*

Analytics he writes: "That on account of which any thing exists is that thing and more greatly so." Now [since] Adam sinned on account of Eve, it follows that Eve sinned much more than Adam. Similarly, just as it is better to treat others well than to be well-treated, so it is worse to persuade another to evil than to be persuaded to evil. For he sins less who sins by another's example, inasmuch as what is done by example can be said to be done according to a kind of law, [and thus justly]. For this reason it is commonly said that "the sins that many commit are [without fault]." [Thus Eve, who persuaded her husband to commit an evil act, sinned more greatly than Adam, who merely consented to her example.] And if Adam and Eve both had thought that they were worthy of the same glory, Eve, who was inferior [by nature], more greatly departed from the mean, and consequently sinned more greatly. Moreover, as a beloved companion she could deceive her husband [vulnerable to her persuasion because of his love for her] more easily than the shameful serpent could deceive the woman. And she persevered longer [in sin] than Adam, because she began first, and offenses are that much more serious (according to Gregory's decree) in relation to the length of time they hold the unhappy soul in bondage. Finally, to bring my discourse to a close, Eve was the cause and the example of sin, and Gregory greatly increases the guilt in the case of the example. And Christ, who could not err, condemned more severely the pretext of the ignorant Jews, because it came first, than he did the sentence of the learned Pilate, when he said: "They who have betrayed me to you have greater sin, etc." All who wish to be called Christians have always agreed with this judgment, and you, above all most Christian, will approve and defend it. Farewell, and do not fear, but dare to do much, because you have excellently understood so much and write so learnedly.

Isotta: I had decided that I would not enter further into a contest with you because, as you say, you assault my fortress with my own weapons. [The propositions] you have presented me were so perfectly and diligently defended that it would be difficult not merely for me, but for the most learned men, to oppose them. But since I recognize that this context is useful for me, I have decided to obey your honest wish. Even though I know I struggle in vain, yet I will earn the highest praise if I am defeated by so mighty a man as you.

Eve sinned out of ignorance and inconstancy, and hence you contend that she sinned more gravely, because the ignorance of those things which we are obligated to know does not excuse us, since it is written: "He who does not know will not be known." I would concede your point if that ignorance were crude or affected. But Eve's ignorance was implanted by nature, of which nature God himself is the author and founder. In many people it is seen that he who knows less sins less, like a boy who sins less than an old man or a peasant less than a noble. Such a person does not need to know explicitly what is required for salvation, but implicitly, because [for him] faith alone suffices. The question of inconstancy proceeds similarly. For when it is said that the acts which proceed from inconstancy are more blameworthy, [that kind of] inconstancy is understood which is not innate but the product of character and sins.

The same is true of imperfection. For when gifts increase, greater responsibility is imposed. When God created man, from the beginning he created him perfect, and the powers of his soul perfect, and gave him a greater understanding and knowledge of truth as well as a greater depth of wisdom. Thus it was that the Lord led to Adam all the animals of the earth and the birds of heaven, so that Adam could call them by their names. For God said: "Let us make mankind in our image and likeness, and let them have dominion over the fish of the sea, and the birds of the air, the cattle, over all the wild animals and every creature that crawls on the earth," making clear his own perfection. But of the woman he said: "It is not good that the man is alone; I will make him a helper like himself." And since consolation and joy are required for happiness, and since no one can have solace and joy when alone, it appears that God created woman for man's consolation. For the good spreads itself, and the greater it is the more it shares itself. Therefore, it appears that Adam's sin was greater than Eve's. [As] Ambrose [says]: "In him to whom a more indulgent liberality has been shown is insolence more inexcusable."

"But Adam's companion," [you argue], "is not excused because Adam was appointed to protect her, because thieves who have been trustingly employed by a householder are not punished with the most severe punishment like strangers or those in whom the householder placed no confidence." This is true, however, in temporal law, but not in divine law, for divine justice proceeds differently from temporal justice in punishing [sin].

[You argue further that] "the fragility of the woman was not the cause of sin, but rather her inordinate appetite for seeking that which was not suited to her nature," which [appetite] is the product, as you write, of pride. Yet it is clearly less a sin to desire the knowledge of good and evil than to transgress against a divine commandment, since the desire for knowledge is a natural thing, and all men by nature desire to know. And even if the first impulse [of sin] were this inordinate appetite, which cannot be without sin, yet it is more tolerable than the sin of transgression, for the observance of the commandments is the road which leads to the country of salvation. [It is written]: "But if thou wilt enter into life, keep the commandments;" and likewise: "What shall I do to gain eternal life? Keep the commandments." And transgression is particularly born of pride, because pride is nothing other than rebellion against divine rule, exalting oneself above what is permitted according to divine rule, by disdaining the will of God and displacing it with one's own. Thus Augustine [writes] in *On Nature and Grace:* "Sin is the will to pursue or retain what justice forbids, that is, to deny what God wishes." Ambrose agrees with him in his *On Paradise:* "Sin is the transgression against divine law and disobedience to the heavenly commandments." Behold! See that the transgression against and disobedience to the heavenly commandments is the greatest sin, whereas you have thus defined sin: "Sin is the inordinate desire to know." Thus clearly the sin of transgression against a command is greater than [the sin of] desiring the knowledge of good and evil. So even if inordinate desire be a sin, as with Eve, yet she did not desire to be like God in power but only in the knowledge of good and evil, which by nature she was actually inclined to desire.

[Next, as to your statement] that those words, "if Adam had not sinned," confirm you in your view [of Eve's damnability], since Eve may have so sinned that, like the demons, she did not merit redemption, I reply that she also was redeemed with Adam, because [she was] "bone of my bone and flesh of my flesh." And if it seems that God did not redeem her, this was undoubtedly because God held her sin as negligible. For if man deserved redemption, the woman deserved it much more because of the slightness of the crime. For the angel cannot be excused by ignorance as can the woman. For the angel understands without investigation or discussion and has an intellect more in the likeness of God's—to which it seems Eve desired to be similar—than does man. Hence the angel is called intellectual and the man rational. Thus where the woman sinned from her desire for knowledge, the angel sinned from a desire for power. While knowledge of an appearance in some small way can be partaken of by the creature, in no way can it partake in the power of God and of the soul of Christ. Moreover, the woman in sinning thought she would receive mercy, believing certainly that she was committing a sin, but not one so great as to warrant God's inflicting such a sentence and punishment. But the angel did not think [of mercy]. Hence Gregory [says in the] fourth book of the *Moralia:* "The first parents were needed for this, that the sin which they committed by transgressing they might purge by confessing." But that persuasive serpent was never punished for his sin, for he was never to be recalled to grace. Thus, in sum, Eve clearly merited redemption more than the angels.

[As to your argument] that the woman also suffers all the penalties inflicted on the man, and beyond those which are common [to both] she alone gives birth in sorrow and has been subjected to man, this also reinforces my earlier point. As I said, the good spreads itself, and the greater it is the more it shares itself. So also evil, the greater it is the more it shares itself, and the more it shares itself the more harmful it is, and the more harmful it is the greater it is. Furthermore, the severity of the punishment is proportional to the gravity of the sin. Hence Christ chose to die on the cross, though this was the most shameful and horrible kind of death, and on the cross he endured in general every kind of suffering by type. Hence Isidore writes concerning the Trinity: "The only-born Son of God in executing the sacrament of his death, in himself bears witness that he consummated every kind of suffering when, with lowered head, he gave up his spirit." The reason was that the punishment had to correspond to the guilt. Adam took the fruit of the forbidden tree; Christ suffered on the tree and so made satisfaction [for Adam's sin]. [As] Augustine [writes]: "Adam disdained God's command" (and he does not say Eve) "accepting the fruit from the tree, but whatever Adam lost Christ restored." [For Christ paid the penalty for sin he had not committed, as it says in] Psalm 64: "For what I have not taken, then I atoned." Therefore, Adam's sin was the greatest [possible], because the punishment corresponding to his fault was the greatest [possible] and was general in all men. [As the] apostle [says]: "All sinned in Adam."

"Eve," [you say], "must bear responsibility for every fault of Adam because, as Aristotle shows, whatever is the cause of the cause is the cause of the thing caused." This is true in the case of things which are, as you know better [than I], in themselves the causes of other things, which is the case for the first cause, the first principle, and "that on account of which anything is what it is." But clearly this was not the case with Eve, because Adam either had free will or he did not. If he did not have it, he did not sin; if he had it, then Eve forced the sin [upon him], which is impossible. For as Bernard says: "Free will, because of its inborn nobility, is forced by no necessity," not even by God, because if that were the case it would be to concede that two contradictories are true at the same time. God cannot do, therefore, what would cause an act proceeding from free will and remaining free to be not free but coerced. [As] Augustine [writes in his commentary] on Genesis: "God cannot act against that nature which he created with a good will." God could himself, however, remove that condition of liberty from any person and bestow some other condition on him. In the same way fire cannot, while it remains fire, not burn, unless its nature is changed and suspended for a time by divine force. No other creature, such as a good angel or devil can do this, since they are less than God; much less a woman, since she is less perfect and weaker than they. Augustine clarifies this principle [of God's supremacy] saying: "Above our mind is nothing besides God, nor is there anything intermediary between God and our mind." Yet only something which is superior to something else can coerce it; but Eve was inferior to Adam, therefore she was not herself the cause of sin. [In] Ecclesiasticus 15 [it says]: "God from the beginning created man and placed him in the palm of his counsel and made clear his commandments and precepts. If you wish to preserve the commandments, they will preserve you and create in you pleasing faith." Thus Adam appeared to accuse God rather than excuse himself when he said: "The woman you placed at my side gave me fruit from the tree and I ate it."

[Next you argue] that the beloved companion could have more easily deceived the man than the shameful serpent the woman. To this I reply that Eve, weak and ignorant by nature, sinned much less by assenting to that astute serpent, who was called "wise," than Adam—created by God with perfect knowledge and understanding—in listening to the persuasive words and voice of the imperfect woman.

[Further, you say] that Eve persevered in her sin a longer time and therefore sinned more, because crimes are that much more serious according to the length of time they hold the unhappy soul in bondage. This is no doubt true, when two sins are equal, and in the same person or in two similar persons. But Adam and Eve were not equals, because Adam was a perfect animal and Eve imperfect and ignorant. [Therefore, their sins were not comparable, and Eve, who persevered longer in sin, was not on that account more guilty than Adam].

Finally, if I may quote you: "The woman was the example and the cause of sin, and Gregory emphatically extends the burden of guilt to [the person who provided] an example, and Christ condemned the cause of the ignorant Jews, because it was first, more than the learned Pilate's sentence when he said: 'Therefore he who betrayed me to you has greater sin.' " I reply that Christ did not condemn the cause of the ignorant Jews because it was first, but because it was vicious and devilish due to their native malice and obstinacy. For they did not sin from ignorance. The gentile Pilate was more ignorant about these things than the Jews, who had the law and the prophets and read them and daily saw signs concerning [Christ]. For John 15 says: "If I had not come and spoken to them, they would have no sin. But now they have no excuse for their sin." Thus they themselves said: "What are we doing? for this man is working signs." And: "Art thou the Christ, the Son of the Blessed One?" For the [Jewish] people was special to God, and Christ himself [said]: "I was not sent except to the lost sheep of the house of Israel. It is not fair to take the children's bread and cast it to the dogs." Therefore the Jews sinned more, because Jesus loved them more.

Let these words be enough from me, an unarmed and poor little woman.

V

Florentine Neoplatonism and Mysticism

INTRODUCTION

*W*ith the revival of Greek studies and the widespread rejection of medieval scholasticism based on Aristotle, there was an increasing interest in the work of Plato and his followers in the Italian Renaissance. Only a few of Plato's own writings were generally known during the Middle Ages, but the renewed intellectual connections between the Greek Byzantine Empire and the Latin West in the fifteenth century resulted in many more of Plato's works being made available in Italy.

Much of the credit for popularizing Plato must go to Marsilio Ficino, who was patronized by the Medici in Florence and who translated the entire known corpus of Plato's work into Latin, an edition that was printed in 1484. Ficino was established in the Medici villa at Careggi and began there an informal "academy" that was to include many of the most important intellectual and artistic figures of the age of Lorenzo the Magnificent: Giovanni Pico della Mirandola, Angelo Poliziano, and Michelangelo, among others. Ficino also went beyond the texts of Plato himself and integrated the work of his followers, such as Plotinus, into a more coherent philosophy than Plato himself had ever established. In addition, the mystical tradition of the Hermetics (based on the works of the so-called Hermes Trismegistus), the Cabala and other occult sources were added, which produced a body of thought of a highly abstract and diffuse nature.

In part, the use of various mystical and occult sources to broaden the Platonic corpus was an attempt by Ficino, Pico, and others to reveal absolute truth and discover the route to perfect knowledge. Moreover, these Florentine Neoplatonists believed that there was no necessary exclusion of Christian truth from this method. Indeed, Christian religion was seen as perfectly compatible with the thought of the Platonists and formed a part of the belief in the unity of all truth.

Neoplatonism flourished in the Italian Renaissance largely in learned academies and aristocratic coteries. It was not a fundamental element in the universities, although certain dialogues of Plato were used for instruction in Greek. The philosophical system was well suited to a polished, highly exclusive, and aristocratic environment because of its emphasis on the perfectability of human beings through knowledge, the belief in an ideal universe, and the explicit adherence to hierarchies. Also, it was easily and effectively applied in literature, something scholasticism was not. Writers popularized Neoplatonism in poetry, dialogues, and other literary forms so that it entered the creative imagination of Renaissance Europeans. Baldassare Castiglione, for example, used Renaissance Neoplatonism heavily to inform his very popular Book of the Courtier, and the poetry of Poliziano and Michelangelo is similarly suffused with its ideals, ideals that were transported across the Alps to influence in turn the literature of northern Europe.

✦ Marsilio Ficino

*M*arsilio Ficino (born in 1433) was the most influential of the Renaissance Neoplatonists. Educated in Latin, Greek, and medicine, he was noticed by Cosimo de' Medici, who employed him to translate all the known works of Plato into Latin, a task he accomplished between 1463 and 1469. Ficino became so completely immersed in Platonic thought that he even moved briefly away from Christianity, thinking Platonism superior.

However, Ficino recovered his faith and became a priest in 1473, although his reverence for Plato did not end. His own great philosophical work, Theologia Platonica (Platonic Theology), completed in 1474, proposed many elements of Platonic thought that were compatible with Christianity, such as the immortality of the soul and the participation of human reason in the divine order. For Ficino, human reason and will could aid the ascent of the soul toward God, and such doctrines consequently meant that Ficino's Neoplatonism was not condemned by the Church during his lifetime, although he was viewed with some suspicion.

Ficino was given a Medici villa at Careggi near Florence, and this rural retreat became the center of the famous informal Platonic Academy, with Ficino as its intellectual animator. The leading citizens, artists, and thinkers of the Florence of Lorenzo the Magnificent spent time there discussing Plato. Also, during the last years of Lorenzo's life, Ficino was engaged in the translation of Plotinus, making the most important of the ancient Neoplatonists widely available to the West for the first time.

In addition, Ficino introduced the study of occult thought into his Neoplatonism. He translated the corpus of Greek writings known as the Hermetic books into Latin in 1471. These works were believed to have been written by the Greek god Hermes, who was conflated with Egyptian deities as well. Ficino argued that although they were not Christian themselves, they partook of absolute truth through divine revelation and thus were useful in humanity's understanding of the universe. Such doctrines led Ficino to seek truth in similar mystical and magical lore, including astrology. He believed that all religions and philosophies contributed to an understanding of absolute truth and the nature of God and the universe, therefore investing them with intrinsic significance.

The expulsion of the Medici in 1494 and the rise of Savonarola were not greeted with enthusiasm by Ficino, as they were by Pico, or with disgust, as they were by Poliziano. Rather, Ficino kept to his translating, completing a Latin version of Proclus, and not becoming involved in the affairs of state. Savonarola, however, thought Ficino's work useless. Ficino died in 1499.

COMMENTARY ON PLATO'S SYMPOSIUM ON LOVE

On the Two Origins of Love and the Double Venus

Next the two kinds of loves should be discussed briefly. According to Plato, Pausanias says that Cupid is the companion of Venus. And he thinks that there must necessarily be as many Cupids as there are Venuses. He mentions two Venuses, whom twin Cupids likewise accompany. One Venus he certainly calls Heavenly, but the other Vulgar. That Heavenly Venus was born of Uranus, without any mother. The Vulgar Venus was born of Jupiter and Dione.

The Platonists call the supreme God Uranus because just as heaven, that sublime body, rules over and contains all bodies, so that supreme God is exalted over all spirits. But the Mind they call by several names. For they sometimes call it Saturn, sometimes Jupiter, sometimes Venus. For that Mind exists, lives, and understands. Its being they were accustomed to call Saturn; its life, Jupiter; its intelligence, Venus. The World Soul also we call, in the same way, Saturn, Jupiter, and Venus: insofar as it understands the celestial things, Saturn; insofar as it moves the heavenly things, Jupiter; insofar as it procreates lower things, Venus.

The first Venus, which is in the Mind, is said to have been born of Uranus without a mother, because *mother*, to the physicists, is *matter*. But that Mind is a stranger to any association with corporeal matter. The second Venus, which is located in the World Soul, was born of Jupiter and Dione. "Born of Jupiter"—that is, of that faculty of the Soul itself which moves the heavenly things, since that faculty created the power which generates these lower things. They also attribute a mother to that second Venus, for this reason, that since she is infused into the Matter of the world, she is thought to have commerce with matter.

Finally, to speak briefly, Venus is twofold. One is certainly that intelligence which we have located in the Angelic Mind. The other is the power of procreation attributed to the World Soul. Each Venus has as her companion a love like herself. For the former Venus is entranced by an innate love for understanding the Beauty of god. The latter likewise is entranced by her love for procreating that same beauty in bodies. The former Venus first embraces the splendor of divinity in herself; then she transfers it to the second Venus. The latter Venus transfers sparks of that splendor into the Matter of the world. Because of the presence of these sparks, all of the bodies of the world seem beautiful according to the receptivity of their nature. The beauty of these bodies the human soul perceives through the eyes. The soul again possesses twin powers. It certainly has the power of understanding, and it has the power of procreation. These twin powers are two Venuses in us, accompanied by twin loves. When the beauty of a human body first meets our eyes, our intellect, which is the first Venus in us, worships and esteems it as an image of the divine beauty, and through this is often aroused to that. But the power of procreation, the second Venus, desires to procreate a form like this. On both sides, therefore, there is a love: there a desire to contemplate beauty, here a desire to propagate it. Each love is virtuous and praiseworthy, for each follows a divine image.

What, therefore, does Pausanias censure in love? Indeed I shall tell you. If anyone, through being more desirous of procreation, neglects contemplation or attends to procreation beyond measure with women, or against the order of nature with men, or prefers the form of the body to the beauty of the soul, he certainly abuses the dignity of love. This abuse of love Pausanias censures. He who properly uses love certainly praises the form of the body, but through that contemplates the higher beauty of the Soul, the Mind, and God, and admires and loves that more strongly. And he uses the office of procreation and intercourse only as much as the natural order and the civil laws laid down by the prudent prescribe. About these things Pausanias speaks at greater length.

On the Painting of Love

The poet Agathon, in the manner of ancient poets, clothes this god in human form, and paints him as attractive, like men: *Young, tender, flex-*

ible or agile, well-proportioned, and glowing. Why these? Certainly these are preparations for a beautiful nature rather than beauty itself. For, of these five parts, the first three signify the temperate complexion of the body, which is the first foundation; the other two represent Arrangement, Proportion, and Aspect.

Natural philosophers have shown that the sign of a temperate constitution is soft and firm smoothness of the tender flesh. Where heat exceeds too much, the body is dry and hairy; where cold exceeds, the skin is stiff; where dryness, hard and rough; where moisture, loose, flabby, uneven, drawn. Therefore a smooth and firm tenderness of the body shows that the body's constitution in the four humors is well-balanced. This is why Agathon called Love *soft, delicate, and tender.*

Why *young?* Because this temperateness is possessed through the kindness not only of nature, but also of age. For with the passage of time, as the finer parts of the humors are dissipated, only the coarser parts remain: when the fire and air have been exhaled, an excess of water and earth prevails.

But why *agile and flexible?* So that you may understand that love is fit and ready for all motions, lest you perhaps suppose that when he said *soft,* he meant the effeminate, weak, and unfit softness of water. For that is contrary to a balanced complexion.

After these Agathon added *well-proportioned,* that is, properly formed in the Arrangement and Proportion of parts. He also added *glowing,* that is, shining in the attractive Aspect of colors. Having explained these preparations, Agathon did not say what the rest was. For it is up to us to understand that after these preparations occurs the advent of grace.

These five parts seem to be meant in the way we have said, with respect to the figure of Man, but in a different way with respect to the potency of love, for they refer to its force and quality. Love is said to be *young* for the reason that the young are usually caught by love, and those who are caught in his traps desire the youthful age. *Soft* because gentle natures are more easily caught. And those who are caught, even though formerly wild, are rendered tame. *Agile and flexible* because it flows in secretly, and flows out in the same way. *Well-proportioned and well-shaped* because it desires shapely and well-ordered things and avoids the opposite. *Glowing* because it influences the character of Man at the blooming and glowing age, and it desires blooming things. Since Agathon explains these things at length, let it suffice to have touched on them briefly.

✦ ✦ ✦

How the Soul Is Raised from the Beauty of the Body to the Beauty of God

Consider this, dear guests; imagine Diotima addressing Socrates thus.

"No body is completely beautiful, O Socrates. For it is either attractive in this part and ugly in that, or attractive today, and at other times not, or is thought beautiful by one person and ugly by another. Therefore the beauty of the body, contaminated by the contagion of ugliness, cannot be the pure, true, and first beauty. In addition no one ever supposes beauty itself to be ugly, just as one does not suppose wisdom to be foolish, but we do consider the arrangement of bodies sometimes beautiful and sometimes ugly. And at any one time different people have different opinions about it. Therefore the first and true beauty is not in bodies. Add the fact that many different bodies have the same family name, 'the beautiful.' Therefore there must be one common quality of beauty in many bodies, by virtue of which they are alike called 'beautiful.' But remember that just as this single quality is in another, namely matter, so it derives from another. For what cannot sustain itself can hardly derive from itself. Do you think it will derive from matter? Certainly not. For nothing ugly and imperfect can make itself beautiful and perfect. That which is one must derive from one. Therefore the single beauty of many bodies derives from some single incorporeal maker. The one maker of all things is God, who through the Angels and the Souls every day renders all the Matter of the world beautiful. Therefore it must be concluded that that true Reason of beauty is to be found in God and in His ministers rather than in the Body of the world. To it you will easily ascend again, I think, O Socrates, by these steps.

"If nature had given you the eyes of a lynx, my Socrates, so that you could penetrate with your vision whatever confronted you, that outwardly handsome body of your Alcibiades would seem very ugly to you. How valuable is that which you love, my friend? It is only a surface, or rather a color, that captivates you, or rather it is only a certain reflection of lights, and an insubstantial shadow. Or a vain fantasy is deceiving you so that you love something that you are dreaming rather than something that you are seeing. But lest I seem to oppose you completely, let this Alcibiades of yours be admittedly handsome. But in what part is he handsome? Truly in all his parts except in his flat nose and his higher than normal eyebrows. These parts, however, in Phaedrus are attractive. But in him the thickness of the legs is displeasing. These things are attractive in Charmides, unless his thin neck offends you. Thus if you will observe all men individually you will praise none of them in every part. Whatever is right everywhere you will gather together; you will construct in yourself a whole figure from the observation of all, so that the absolute beauty of the human race, which is found distributed among many bodies, is collected in your soul by thinking of a single image. The beauty of any individual man, O Socrates, you will scorn if you compare it to that abstract concept of yours. You possess that concept not so much thanks to bodies as to your own soul. Therefore love that concept which your soul has created, and the soul itself, its creator, rather than that external beauty, which is defective and scattered.

"But what is it that I urge you to love in the soul? The beauty of the soul. The beauty of bodies is a light; the beauty of the soul is also a light. The light of the soul is truth, which is the only thing which your friend Plato seems to ask of God in his prayers:

Grant to me, O God, he says, *that my soul may become beautiful, and that those things which pertain to the body may not impair the beauty of the soul, and that I may think only the wise man rich.*

In this prayer Plato says that the beauty of the soul consists in truth and wisdom, and that it is given to men by God. Truth, which is given to us by God single and uniform, through its various effects acquires the names of various virtues. Insofar as it deals with divine things, it is called Wisdom (which Plato asked of God above all else); insofar as it deals with natural things, it is called Knowledge; with human things, Prudence. Insofar as it makes men equal, it is called Justice; insofar as it makes them invincible, Courage; and tranquil, Temperance.

"Among these, two kinds of virtues are included; I mean the moral virtues and the intellectual, which are superior to them. The intellectual virtues are Wisdom, Knowledge, and Prudence; the moral virtues are Justice, Courage, and Temperance. The moral virtues are better known, because of their operations and their public applications. The intellectual virtues are more mysterious, because of their hidden truth. However, anyone who is brought up on the moral virtues, since he is purer than other people, can easily ascend to the intellectual virtues. For this reason I urge you to consider first the beauty of the soul which is found in the moral virtues, so that you will understand that there is one principle in all of them, by virtue of which they are all alike called 'moral.' That is, that there is a single truth of the pure life, which, through actions of Justice, Courage, and Temperance, leads us to true happiness. Therefore seek first this single truth of the moral virtues, the most beautiful light of the soul.

"But realize also that you can immediately rise above the moral virtues to the clearer truth of Wisdom, Knowledge, and Prudence, if you will consider that these virtues are granted to the soul brought up on the best moral virtues, and that in them is contained the highest form of moral life. Although you may think that the concepts of Wisdom, Knowledge, and Prudence all differ, remember that there is nevertheless a single light of truth in all of them, by virtue of which they are all alike called 'beautiful.' I advise you to love this light above all, as the highest beauty of the soul.

"But this single truth, embodied in many different virtues, cannot be the first truth of all, for, since it is distributed among many virtues, it is in something else. And whatever lies *in* another certainly derives *from* another. However, a single truth is not derived from a multitude of concepts. For what is one must derive from one. Therefore above the soul of man there must be some single wisdom which is not divided among various concepts, but is a single wisdom, from whose single truth the manifold truth of men derives.

"O Socrates, remember that that single light of the single wisdom is the beauty of the Angel, which you must honor above the beauty of the Soul. As we have shown in the above, it excels the beauty of bodies, because it is not bound by place or divided according to the parts of matter, and it is not corrupted. It also excels the beauty of the Soul, because it is completely eternal and does not move in temporal progession. But since the light of the Angel shines among the ranks of the innumerable Ideas, and since above every multiplicity there must be a unity which is the origin of all number, it must emanate from a single beginning of all things, which we call the One itself.

"Thus the perfectly simple light of the One itself is infinite beauty, because it is not soiled by the stains of Matter, as the beauty of the Body is, or changed by temporal progression, as the beauty of the Soul is, or dissipated in multiplicity, as the beauty of the Angel is. But any quality which is free from extraneous addition is called infinite by the natural philosophers. If heat exists by itself, unimpeded by cold or moisture, and not burdened by the weight of matter, it is called infinite heat, because its force is free and is not confined by any limitations of addition. Similarly, light which is free from any body is infinite, for it shines of its own nature, without measure or limit, when it is not limited by anything else. Thus the light and beauty of God, which is utterly pure and free of all other things, may be called without the slightest question, infinite beauty. But infinite beauty also requires immense love. Therefore I beg you, O Socrates, to love other things with a certain moderation and limit, but to love God with an infinite love, and let there be no moderation in divine love."

This is what Diotima said to Socrates.

✦ ✦ ✦

How God Is to Be Loved

But we, my distinguished friends, shall love God not only without moderation, as Diotima is imagined as commanding, but God alone. For the Angelic Mind is to God as the vision of our eyes is to the sun. The eye desires not only light above all else, but light alone. If we do love bodies, souls, or angels, we shall not really be loving these things, but God in them. In loving bodies we shall really be loving the shadow of God; in souls, the likeness of God; in angels, the image of God. Thus in this life we shall love God in all things so that in the next we may love all things in God. For living in this way we shall proceed to the point where we shall see both God and all things in God, and love both Him, and all things which are in Him. And anyone who surrenders himself to God with love in this life will recover himself in God in the next life. Such a man will certainly return to his own Idea, the Idea by which he was created. There any defect in him will be corrected again; he will be united with his Idea forever. For the true man and the Idea of a man are the same. For this reason as long as we are in this life, separated from God, none of us is a true man, for we are separated from our own Idea or Form. To it, divine love and piety will lead us. Even though we may be dismembered and mutilated here, then, joined by love to our own Idea, we shall become whole men, so that we shall seem to have first worshipped God in things, in order later to worship things in God, and to worship things in God for this reason, in order to recover ourselves in Him above all, and in loving God we shall seem to have loved ourselves.

SELECTIONS FROM THE LETTERS OF MARSILIO FICINO

On Law and Justice

Marsilio Ficino to the magnanimous Lorenzo de' Medici: greetings.

I promised Lorenzo, on his return to Florence from Pisa on the seventh of March, if I remember rightly, that I would write to him when he next went to Pisa. Usually I write to friends because I wish to; on the present occasion I shall write because I must. It is just to keep a promise, for law ordains it so. So accept a just and lawful letter. No! To speak more truly, whenever I wish to write, then write I must, by the law of love; when I must write, then I also wish to, for the love of law. So today you will receive a letter written of my own accord and in accordance with the law. To separate the voluntary from the just or the just from the voluntary is not lawful for anyone and is unpleasant for friends. So, Marsilio, you now both must, and wish to write to Medici.

Of what can you principally write, and which god will be your guide? Oh salvation of mankind! Oh Justice, Queen of the world! For a long time you have given me cause to write; now, I beseech you, provide material so that I may fulfil my promise as successfully with your aid, as I gave it gladly when you commanded.

That divine law by which the universe abides and is governed, kindles in our minds at their creation the inextinguishable light of natural law, by which good and evil are tested. From this natural law, which is a spark of the divine, the written law arises like a ray from that spark. Moreover,

Source: The Letters of Marsilio Ficino, Vol. 1, trans. by the Language Department of the School of Economic Science, London, Preface by P. O. Kristeller (London: Shepheard-Walwyn, 1975), pp. 145–147, 123–124, and 66–67. Reprinted by permission of the publisher.

these three laws, divine, natural and written, teach each man what justice is, so that there is scarcely any room left for sinners to plead complete ignorance as an excuse for their faults.

These three lights show the eye of the mind that justice is really a quality of will, which is directed and strengthened by reason, so that, despising threats and enticements, it decides to act only as divinity, nature and citizenship dictate. What does divinity instruct but to give back to God, from whom we receive everything, every insight of the mind, every desire of the will, the energy of every action, and the reward of work? What else does nature teach, if not that we should make wealth subject to the body, the body to the soul, the soul to reason, and reason to God?

Finally, citizenship seems to teach that each citizen should remember that he is a member of the state. Therefore it is right for men to love their country as if it were one body, and fellow-citizens as members of that body. And so a man will be considered indisputably just who reverences God as his Father and Lord with utmost piety. He will carefully restrain his feelings and emotions; he will love all men as his brothers; he will love himself in God and all men in himself; he will cleave to God with all his strength and, so far as he is able, he will unite others with himself in the divine nature. Therefore it is the duty of a just man to render each his due; to those above, honor and respect; to equals, family companionship; and to those below, support and advice.

Furthermore, when he is appointed an officer of the Government, he will have the law always in view as if it were God. He will not, indeed, consider himself a master of the law, but its faithful interpreter and devoted servant. In administering it he should punish offences impartially and with even temper. Without envy he should reward virtuous actions according to their worth. He should not give thought to his own interests but rather to those of the community. Neither should he trust in his own ability, but he should seek advice in all matters from elder men, those who are prudent and god-fearing. That, too, should remain deeply impressed on his mind.

Lay aside your proud and pompous looks, you to whom the ruler of the sea and land has given the great jurisdiction of life and death. Whatever a lesser man dreads at your hands, with that a greater Lord threatens you. Every authority is subject to a greater authority. Let that be enough about what justice is; what a just man is; and what is his duty.

Moreover, how important the fruit of just action is, is very clear, because neither home, state, army, nor business of any kind, whether of good or bad men, can endure without a just distribution, made according to merit. In fact, if it is so vital to the structure of the world that its removal would mean the world's immediate destruction, its importance for the life of men cannot be expressed. Indeed, if justice were not present amongst men either they would herd together in one place and quickly perish at each other's hands or they would live scattered to be separately torn to pieces by wild beasts. Oh eternal bond of the human race! Most wholesome cure for our sickness! Common soul of society! Justice that is blissful life! Justice that is heavenly life! Mother and Queen of the golden age, sublime Astrea seated among the starry thrones! Goddess, we beg you, do not abandon your earthly abode, lest we miserably sink into the iron age. Heavenly goddess, we beseech you, ever live in human minds, that is, in citizens who belong to the heavenly country, so that for the present we may imitate the divine life as well as we can, and that in the time to come we may live it to the full.

Farewell.

On the Duty of a Citizen

Marsilio Ficino to Piero del Nero: greetings.

Tell me, Piero, why did the fever suddenly strike me after it had attacked your uncle Bernardo? Is it that, as we are so close to each other, when the dog-star belches its flames on one of us it also sets fire to the other? May your uncle quickly recover so that Marsilio may too, or rather so that Florence may enjoy better health. If she always had such medical men as she has in this Medici, she would never be seriously ill. Such men properly perform the function of a citizen, without which the good health of the country is not preserved.

It is the duty of a citizen to consider the state as a single being formed of its citizens who are the parts; and that the parts should serve the whole, not the whole the parts. For when the profit of the part alone is sought, there is no profit at all for either part or whole. When, however, the good of the whole is sought, the good of both is assured. Therefore because of this connection the citizen ought to remember that nothing good or bad can touch one limb of the state, without affecting the others and indeed the state as a whole. And again, nothing can happen to the whole body of the state without soon affecting each limb.

Let no one, then, in this household of city say, "This is mine," and "That is yours," for everything in this vast organism belongs in a way to everyone in common. Rather let him say, "Both this and that are mine," not because they are his personal property, but because he loves and cares for them. Let each man love and reverence his country as he would the founder of his family. Let the ordinary citizen obey the ancient, well-tried laws, just as he would obey God, for such laws are not established without God. Let the magistrate remember that he is subject to the laws in just the same way as the ordinary citizen is subject to the magistrate. Let him understand that when he passes judgment he is himself being judged by God. Let him always have before him the injunction of Plato, to have regard not for himself, but the state; and not just some part of the state but the whole. In short, he should know that Heaven's highest place is reserved for the man who has done his best to model his earthly country on the heavenly one. For nothing pleases the universal ruler of the world more than the universal good.

I think that you know these and similar precepts relating to the true citizen, and I hope that you will abide by them since you lack neither instruction nor prudence. Besides, you have at home a competent teacher in this subject, about whose merits I will write another time.

Farewell. Our Giovanni Cavalcanti commends himself to you.

The Astonishing Glories of Lorenzo de' Medici

Marsilio Ficino to Niccolo Michelozzi, a true man: greetings.

O how difficult it now is, my Niccolo, how very difficult not to be consumed with envy! I for my part, Niccolo, would perhaps be unable to avoid being envious of so many magnificent qualities in a young man, which are usually associated with age, were it not that Lorenzo's qualities are mine also. Tell me, friend, who speaks more eloquently? Who appraises more shrewdly? Who soothes more gently? Who stirs men more passionately? Poets, you have long since awarded him the laurel; orators, you have recently done likewise; now let us philosophers do the same. By Jupiter, how is it that easy-going veterans are overcome so quickly, so easily, and so completely, by this hustling youngster?

But let others direct their envy elsewhere and be consumed by its gnawing. I for my part greatly rejoice and delight in what is my own; for Lorenzo belongs to me, through his unbelievable humanity. I also am Lorenzo's, because of the incomparable gift of his soul; he has bought me at a great price, that is, himself.

May God love me, Niccolo! I speak the truth when I say that no one was closer or dearer to me than the great Cosimo. I recognized in that old man not human virtue, but the virtue of a Hero. I now acknowledge within this young man all the qualities of the old man. I see the Phoenix in the Phoenix, the light in the sunbeam. That splendor of Cosimo now shines daily from our Lorenzo in many forms, bringing light to the Latin people and glory to the Florentine Republic. But enough of this for the present.

Now Lorenzo was asking in his letter whose thanks I had conveyed to him, mine or another's. Reply to him on my behalf that I wished him God's grace. For I pray that those three Graces described by Orpheus, namely splendor, joy and vigor, will support our Medici; that is, splendor of intellect, joy in the exercise of will, vigor and prosperity of body. These Graces now inspire Lorenzo from on high, and they will do so as long as he only acknowledges that he has freely received these favors from God alone.

Farewell.

21st January, 1473
Florence

✦ *Giovanni Pico della Mirandola*

*B*orn into a noble family, Giovanni Pico della Mirandola chose early in life the study of philosophy, pursuing it in Padua, Ferrara, and Paris. His intellect was prodigious; he was fluent in many languages and read many more; he had studied a great many disciplines; and he enjoyed such an attractive personality that all who knew him admired him for his character as much as for his learning.

Like other Renaissance Neoplatonists, he believed in the unity of all knowledge and sought learning wherever he could, although he pursued this belief with far more energy than most of his contemporaries. This quest for complete wisdom led him to study Hebrew philosophy, the Cabala, and other occult lore, as well as Arabic, mathematics, music, physics, and theology, in the belief that all knowledge could be reconciled. In defense of this ideal, he traveled to Rome at the age of 24 and posted 900 theses that he wished to debate with anyone who would challenge him. As a preface to these points of disputation, he wrote his Oration on the Dignity of Man.

The pope, however, condemned three of Pico's theses to be heretical, and the young man was forced to flee to Paris. However, the new pope, Alexander VI (Roderigo Borgia), with the support of Lorenzo de' Medici, forgave Pico and he returned to Florence.

In Florence, Pico was one of the bright lights of the Platonic Academy. He wrote many treatises, such as his Heptaplus, dedicated to Lorenzo, and another dedicated to Poliziano. However, of all his works, his Oration remained the most famous.

After the death of Lorenzo, Pico became increasingly attracted to the prophecies and message of Savonarola. He gave away his fortune to the poor, and he repudiated and destroyed his love poetry. Just before he was to take orders as a Dominican monk, Pico died in Florence in 1494 at the age of 31.

ORATION ON THE DIGNITY OF MAN

I have read in the records of the Arabians, reverend Fathers, that Abdala the Saracen, when questioned as to what on this stage of the world, as it were, could be seen most worthy of wonder, replied: "There is nothing to be seen more wonderful than man." In agreement with this opinion is the saying of Hermes Trismegistus: "A great miracle, Asclepius, is man." But when I weighed the reason for these maxims, the many grounds for the

Source: Giovanni Pico della Mirandola, "Oration on the Dignity of Man," in E. Cassirer et al., *Renaissance Philosophy of Man* (Chicago: University of Chicago Press, 1948), pp. 223–254. Reprinted by permission of the University of Chicago Press.

excellence of human nature reported by many men failed to satisfy me—
that man is the intermediary between creatures, the intimate of the gods,
the king of the lower beings, by the acuteness of his senses, by the
discernment of his reason, and by the light of his intelligence the interpreter of nature, the interval between fixed eternity and fleeting time, and
(as the Persians say) the bond, nay, rather, the marriage song of the world,
on David's testimony but little lower than the angels. Admittedly great
though these reasons be, they are not the principal grounds, that is, those
which may rightfully claim for themselves the privilege of the highest
admiration. For why should we not admire more the angels themselves
and the blessed choirs of heaven? At last it seems to me I have come to
understand why man is the most fortunate of creatures and consequently
worthy of all admiration and what precisely is that rank which is his lot
in the universal chain of Being—a rank to be envied not only by brutes
but even by the stars and by minds beyond this world. It is a matter past
faith and a wondrous one. Why should it not be? For it is on this very
account that man is rightly called and judged a great miracle and a wonderful creature indeed.

But hear, Fathers, exactly what this rank is and, as friendly auditors,
conformably to your kindness, do me this favor. God the Father, the
supreme Architect, had already built this cosmic home we behold, the
most sacred temple of His godhead, by the laws of His mysterious wisdom.
The region above the heavens He had adorned with Intelligences, the
heavenly spheres He had quickened with eternal souls, and the excremen-
tary and filthy parts of the lower world He had filled with a multitude of
animals of every kind. But, when the work was finished, the Craftsman
kept wishing that there were someone to ponder the plan of so great a
work, to love its beauty, and to wonder at its vastness. Therefore, when
everything was done (as Moses and Timaeus bear witness), He finally took
thought concerning the creation of man. But there was not among His
archetypes that from which He could fashion a new offspring, nor was
there in His treasure-houses anything which He might bestow on His new
son as an inheritance, nor was there in the seats of all the world a place
where the latter might sit to contemplate the universe. All was now
complete; all things had been assigned to the highest, the middle, and the
lowest orders. But in its final creation it was not the part of the Father's
power to fail as though exhausted. It was not the part of His wisdom to
waver in a needful matter through poverty of counsel. It was not the part
of His kindly love that he who was to praise God's divine generosity in
regard to others should be compelled to condemn it in regard to himself.

At last the best of artisans ordained that that creature to whom He
had been able to give nothing proper to himself should have joint possession of whatever had been peculiar to each of the different kinds of being.
He therefore took man as a creature of indeterminate nature and, assigning
him a place in the middle of the world, addressed him thus: "Neither a

fixed abode nor a form that is thine alone nor any function peculiar to thyself have we given thee, Adam, to the end that according to thy longing and according to thy judgment thou mayest have and possess what abode, what form, and what functions thou thyself shalt desire. The nature of all other beings is limited and constrained within the bounds of laws prescribed by Us. Thou, constrained by no limits, in accordance with thine own free will, in whose hand We have placed thee, shalt ordain for thyself the limits of thy nature. We have set thee at the world's center that thou mayest from thence more easily observe whatever is in the world. We have made thee neither of heaven nor of earth, neither mortal nor immortal, so that with freedom of choice and with honor, as though the maker and molder of thyself, thou mayest fashion thyself in whatever shape thou shalt prefer. Thou shalt have the power to degenerate into the lower forms of life, which are brutish. Thou shalt have the power, out of thy soul's judgment, to be reborn into the higher forms, which are divine."

O supreme generosity of God the Father, O highest and most marvelous felicity of man! To him it is granted to have whatever he chooses, to be whatever he wills. Beasts as soon as they are born (so says Lucilius) bring with them from their mother's womb all they will ever possess. Spiritual beings, either from the beginning or soon thereafter, become what they are to be for ever and ever. On man when he came into life the Father conferred the seeds of all kinds and the germs of every way of life. Whatever seeds each man cultivates will grow to maturity and bear in him their own fruit. If they be vegetative, he will be like a plant. If sensitive, he will become brutish. If rational, he will grow into a heavenly being. If intellectual, he will be an angel and the son of God. And if, happy in the lot of no created thing, he withdraws into the center of his own unity, his spirit, made one with God, in the solitary darkness of God, who is set above all things, shall surpass them all. Who would not admire this our chameleon? Or who could more greatly admire aught else whatever? It is man who Asclepius of Athens, arguing from his mutability of character and from his self-transforming nature, on just grounds says was symbolized by Proteus in the mysteries. Hence those metamorphoses renowned among the Hebrews and the Pythagoreans.

For the occult theology of the Hebrews sometimes transforms the holy Enoch into an angel of divinity whom they call "Mal'akh Adonay Shebaoth," and sometimes transforms others into other divinities. The Pythagoreans degrade impious men into brutes and, if one is to believe Empedocles, even into plants. Mohammed, in imitation, often had this saying on his tongue: "They who have deviated from divine law become beasts," and surely he spoke justly. For it is not the bark that makes the plant but its senseless and insentient nature; neither is it the hide that makes the beast of burden but its irrational, sensitive soul; neither is it the orbed form that makes the heavens but their undeviating order; nor is it the sundering from body but his spiritual intelligence that makes the angel. For if you see one abandoned to his appetites crawling on the ground, it is a plant and not a man you see; if you see one blinded by the vain illusions of imagery, as it were of Calypso, and, softened by their gnawing allurement, delivered over to his senses, it is a beast and not a man you see. If you see a philosopher determining all things by means of right reason, him you shall reverence: he is a heavenly being and not of this earth. If you see a pure contemplator, one unaware of the body and confined to the inner reaches of the mind, he is neither an earthly nor a heavenly being; he is a more reverend divinity vested with human flesh.

Are there any who would not admire man, who is, in the sacred writings of Moses and the Christians, not without reason described sometimes by the name of "all flesh," sometimes by that of "every creature," inasmuch as he himself molds, fashions, and changes himself into the form of all flesh and into the character of every creature? For this reason the Persian Euanthes, in describing the Chaldaean theology, writes that man has no semblance that is inborn and his very own but many that are external and foreign to him; whence this saying of the Chaldaeans: "Hanorish tharah sharinas," that is, "Man is a being of varied, manifold, and inconstant nature." But why do we emphasize this? To the end that after we have been born to this condition—that we can become what we will —we should understand that we ought to have especial care to this, that it should never be said against us that, although born to a privileged position, we failed to recognize it and became like unto wild animals and senseless beasts of burden, but that rather the saying of Asaph the prophet should apply: "Ye are all angels and sons of the Most High," and that we may not, by abusing the most indulgent generosity of the Father, make for ourselves that freedom of choice He has given into something harmful instead of salutary. Let a certain holy ambition invade our souls, so that, not content with the mediocre, we shall pant after the highest and (since we may if we wish) toil with all our strength to obtain it.

Let us disdain earthly things, despise heavenly things, and, finally, esteeming less whatever is of the world, hasten to that court which is beyond the world and nearest to the Godhead. There, as the sacred mysteries relate, Seraphim, Cherubim, and Thrones hold the first places; let us, incapable of yielding to them, and intolerant of a lower place, emulate their dignity and their glory. If we have willed it, we shall be second to them in nothing.

But how shall we go about it, and what in the end shall we do? Let us consider what they do, what sort of life they lead. If we also come to lead that life (for we have the power), we shall then equal their good fortune. The Seraph burns with the fire of love. The Cherub glows with the splendor of intelligence. The Throne stands by the steadfastness of judgment. Therefore if, in giving ourselves over to the active life, we have after due consideration undertaken the care of the lower beings, we shall be strengthened with the firm stability of Thrones. If, unoccupied by deeds, we pass our time in the leisure of contemplation, considering the Creator in the creature and the creature in the Creator, we shall be all ablaze with Cherubic light. If we long with love for the Creator himself alone, we shall speedily flame up with His consuming fire into a Seraphic likeness. Above the Throne, that is, above the just judge, God sits as Judge of the ages. Above the Cherub, that is, above him who contemplates, God flies, and cherishes him, as it were, in watching over him. For the spirit of the Lord moves upon the waters, the waters, I say, which are above the firmament and which in Job praise the Lord with hymns before dawn. Whoso is a Seraph, that is, a lover, is in God and God in him, nay, rather, God and himself are one. Great is the power of Thrones, which we attain in using judgment, and most high the exaltation of Seraphs, which we attain in loving.

But by what means is one able either to judge or to love things unknown? Moses loved a God whom he saw and, as judge, administered among the people what he had first beheld in contemplation upon the mountain. Therefore, the Cherub as intermediary by his own light makes us ready for the Seraphic fire and equally lights the way to the judgment of the Thrones. This is the bond of the first minds, the Palladian order, the chief of contemplative philosophy. This is the one for us first to emulate, to court, and to understand; the one from whence we may be rapt to the heights of love and descend, well taught and well prepared, to the functions of active life. But truly it is worth while, if our life is to be modeled on the example of the Cherubic life, to have before our eyes and clearly understood both its nature and its quality and those things which are the deeds and the labor of Cherubs. But since it is not permitted us to attain this through our own efforts, we who are but flesh and know of the things of earth, let us go to the ancient fathers who, inasmuch as they were familiar and conversant with these matters, can give sure and altogether trustworthy testimony. Let us consult the Apostle Paul, the chosen vessel, as to what he saw the hosts of Cherubim doing when he was himself exalted to the third heaven. He will answer, according to the interpretation of Dionysius,[1] that he saw them being purified, then being illuminated, and at last being made perfect. Let us also, therefore, by emulating the Cherubic way of life on earth, by taming the impulses of our passions with moral science, by dispelling the darkness of reason with dialectic, and by, so to speak, washing away the filth of ignorance and vice, cleanse our soul, so that her passions may not rave at random nor her reason through heedlessness ever be deranged.

Then let us fill our well-prepared and purified soul with the light of

---

1. Dionysius the Areopagite. The writings current under that name, composed by an unknown author probably about A.D. 500, were long attributed to Dionysius, the disciple of Paul, and hence enjoyed an enormous authority.

natural philosophy, so that we may at last perfect her in the knowledge of things divine. And lest we be satisfied with those of our faith, let us consult the patriarch Jacob, whose form gleams carved on the throne of glory. Sleeping in the lower world but keeping watch in the upper, the wisest of fathers will advise us. But he will advise us through a figure (in this way everything was wont to come to those men) that there is a ladder extending from the lowest earth to the highest heaven, divided in a series of many steps, with the Lord seated at the top, and angels in contemplation ascending and descending over them alternately by turns.

If this is what we must practice in our aspiration to the angelic way of life, I ask: "Who will touch the ladder of the Lord either with fouled foot or with unclean hands?" As the sacred mysteries have it, it is impious for the impure to touch the pure. But what are these feet? What these hands? Surely the foot of the soul is that most contemptible part by which the soul rests on matter as on the soil of the earth, I mean the nourishing and feeding power, the tinder of lust, and the teacher of pleasurable weakness. Why should we not call the hands of the soul its irascible power, which struggles on its behalf as the champion of desire and as plunderer seizes in the dust and sun what desire will devour slumbering in the shade? These hands, these feet, that is, all the sentient part whereon resides the attraction of the body which, as they say, by wrenching the neck holds the soul in check, lest we be hurled down from the ladder as impious and unclean, let us bathe in moral philosophy as if in a living river. Yet this will not be enough if we wish to be companions of the angels going up and down on Jacob's ladder, unless we have first been well fitted and instructed to be promoted duly from step to step, to stray nowhere from the stairway, and to engage in the alternate comings and goings. Once we have achieved this by the art of discourse or reasoning, then, inspired by the Cherubic spirit, using philosophy through the steps of the ladder, that is, of nature, and penetrating all things from center to center, we shall sometimes descend, with titanic force rending the unity like Osiris into many parts, and we shall sometimes ascend, with the force of Phoebus collecting the parts like the limbs of Osiris into a unity, until, resting at last in the bosom of the Father who is above the ladder, we shall be made perfect with the felicity of theology.

✦ Angelo Poliziano

*A*ngelo Poliziano (or Politian) was born Angelo Ambrogini in 1454 in Montepulciano, from which he took his popular name. In 1464 he moved to Florence to study Greek, Latin, philosophy, and Platonism, the last with Ficino himself. His great gifts as a Latin stylist attracted the attention of Lorenzo de' Medici, who employed him as tutor to his son, Piero. Poliziano also used this opportunity to write, editing the **Pandects** *of Justinian, among other classical works, and beginning in 1474 his* Stanzas on the Occasion of the Jousts of Giuliano de' Medici. *These poems inspired the painter Botticelli, a member of the Platonic Academy with Poliziano, to paint scenes that have since come to illustrate the art of Laurentian Florence:* Primavera *and* The Birth of Venus. *Poliziano ceased his poetry after Giuliano's murder during the Pazzi conspiracy of 1478, however, and turned instead to writing the history of that event in the manner of Roman historians.*

Furthermore, Lorenzo's wife disapproved of Poliziano as a tutor for her son, so he left Florence in 1479 for Mantua to enter the court of Francesco Gonzaga. There he wrote his Orfeo, *an attempt to recreate classical musical drama that became one of the precursors of Italian opera.*

Poliziano returned to Florence in 1480 to continue his work as an editor and Latin stylist and to assume his new position as professor of Greek and Latin at the University. His poetry in Greek and Latin indicates that he understood fully the nature of those languages and their metrical qualities. Although not a profound Neoplatonist like Ficino or Pico, Poliziano acquired considerable fame and recognition for the elegance and fluency of his verse.

After the death of Lorenzo, Poliziano grew despondent and died two years after his patron in 1494.

SELECTIONS FROM *STANZAS ON THE OCCASION OF THE JOUSTS OF GIULIANO DE' MEDICI*

XXV

Zephyr, adorned already with fair blossoms,
had banished from the mountains all the frost;
the weary pilgrim swallow, little swallow,
had flown already back into her nest;
with tenderness the murmur of the woods
ever around the morning hour was heard,
and the laborious bee, at the first sheen,
preying on this and on that bloom was seen.

XXVI

Undaunted Julus at the daylight's prime
when owls resume their clayey solitude,

Source: Angelo Poliziano, "Stanzas on the Occasion of the Jousts of Giuliano de' Medici," trans. by J. Tusiani, in *Italian Poets of the Renaissance*, (Long Island City, N.Y.: Baroque Press, 1971), pp. 92–94.

on his new-bridled, proudly running steed
started with chosen friends out toward the woods
(and under good command came right behind
the close-knit pack of many a faithful hound),
all bearing that which with the hunting goes—
arrows and horns and spits and traps and bows.

XXXVII

He was already, as he had desired,
from his companions far and far away,
and saw his steed already out of breath
just as he was one step behind his prey;
but still pursuing all his hope in vain,
into a verdant blooming mead he came.
There a gay nymph whose veil was waving white
appeared to him and soon was out of sight.

XXXVIII

Out of his sight the forest phantom fled,
and for the nymph the youth seemed not to care;
rather, he checked the bridles of his steed
and stopped him right upon that greenness fair.
But, full of wonder, he was seeing still
the fleeting figure of the nymphet there,
and a new sweetness then seemed to depart
from her fair eyes and fall into his heart.

XLIII

Full white is she, and white her dress is too,
though painted all with roses, grass, and flowers:
the golden ringlets of her golden hair
stream down upon her brow that's humbly proud.
The forest all around him is one smile
and does its best to quiet his despair.
Majestic in her bearing and yet meek,
she with one glance can tame all tempests quick.

XLIV

A limpid sweetness in her eyes is flashing,
where Cupid keeps all of his torches hid;
the air about her shines with joyous glow
whene'er she turn her glances' loving light.
With heavenly happiness her face is lit,

with privets and with roses painted bright:
all breezes listen to her heavenly words,
and sing a Latin of their own, all birds.

XLVII

Upon that greenness she was gladly sitting,
and she had woven a small gentle wreath;
her dress was painted with as many blossoms
as all about her were by Nature made.
But as her glances rested on the youth,
somewhat bewildered, lifted she her dress
and, holding up its hem with her white hand,
with blossoms on her lap was seen to stand.

LV

Then with more smiling and more joyous eyes,
whereby she made the sky above grow bright,
slowly she moved upon the youthful grass,
each step an act adorned with loving grace.
Soon a sweet keening from the forest came,
and the small birds began to weep and weep;
but under her lithe tread the grass became
white, blue, and yellow, and vermilion flame.

VI

Marriage, the Family, and Women

<figure>ornamental divider</figure>

INTRODUCTION

*T*he family was the most important association a Renaissance Italian enjoyed, more powerful than his or her allegiance to the commune, business partners, friends, or neighbors. The family, moreover, was a complex organism with a double connotation: First, there was the immediate family of parents, husband or wife, children, close relations, and household servants, most of whom would share a single dwelling; second, there was the extended family, sometimes known as kin, or **casa** or consorteria, especially in noble families.

The father was the head of the Renaissance household. He had much authority over his wife and children and could, in fact, determine many of the fundamental decisions of his children's lives, such as the occupation his sons would enter and whom his daughters would marry. The marriage of a child was indeed decided by the father without necessarily consulting the children. Other relations would be asked about the suitabilty of the proposed match, but the considerations were ones of rank, wealth, good character, usefulness of political or business connections, and health. Love rarely entered the issue at all: Marriage was primarily a means of allying families, transferring property, and ensuring the survival of the line through procreation.

Men tended to be older than their wives at the time of their marriage, 28 being an average age for men and 18 for women. The woman's family was expected to provide a dowry for her husband, and this could be very large, depending on the social position and wealth of the wife. A father with many daughters often would have to place some of them in a convent as nuns in order not to bankrupt the family completely. (A convent required a dowry, too, but a smaller one than a potential groom.) The option of daughters either not marrying or entering a convent was not really offered; unmarried secular women were considered to have a destablizing effect on the community. However, it was not uncommon for some men to remain bachelors so that the family inheritance could be kept together rather than divided among all the sons who had married and had the expense of a family.

The wider kin structure, or casa or consorteria, consisted of all those relations who bore the same name or who were equally closely connected through descent from a common ancestor. They did not necessarily include relations by marriage, since women entered the families of their husbands on marriage, although ties of loyalty and affection continued to exist. Often these extended kin groups had deep roots in the locality, living in the same neighborhood, occupying adjoining palaces or houses on the same street or around the same square, and worshipping at the same church. In this way, the influence of the extended family was great indeed, given its broad neighborhood power base and its ability to provide patronage and concentrated political pressure in the quarter of the city it dominated.

Maintaining the wealth, social position, and political ambition of a family was the responsibility of all its members. Relatives were expected to help one another in time of need, and business arrangements within families were common to keep the profits at home. Even distant relations often expected to be consulted in important matters such as marriages and major financial dealings, since the outcome would affect them directly, either improving or diminishing their social standing.

This loyalty to a wider kin, the broad definition of the family, declined as the Renaissance developed in Italy. Initially, family feuds and kin-based mercantile associations were very common, but over time, the propensity for families to take retribution into their own hands abated, and more and more outsiders were accepted into family companies as full partners. Nevertheless, the strong affinity for members of the family extending to the most distant relation remained strong and influenced every aspect of domestic life. Consequently, political and factional connections were often based on kin; business decisions were greatly influenced by the involvement of family members; and social position was very directly linked to the success of your relations in business and government.

✦ *Francesco Barbaro*

*F*rancesco Barbaro was born in Venice in 1390 into one of the great patrician families that governed the republic. He studied the classics and was a student at the celebrated University of Padua, the school within the Venetian dominions to which the noble families sent their sons for advanced education. In 1412, Barbaro received his doctorate at the university, and it was there that he came into contact with Greek studies and broader humanist ideals.

Returning to Venice in 1414, Barbaro began to study Greek seriously with the great schoolmaster Guarino of Verona, who, in fact, entered his household. Barbaro also began his own literary activities, translating important Greek texts into Latin. In 1415, Barbaro visited Florence, staying in the house of Cosimo de' Medici, where he met the humanist leaders of Florence, such as Leonardo Bruni and Nicolò Nicoli. Also, he became close friends with Cosimo's brother, Lorenzo de' Medici, the great uncle of the Magnificent Lorenzo, and wrote for him his De re uxoria (On Wifely Duties) as a wedding gift to be dedicated to the newly wed Lorenzo and his wife.

In 1419, Barbaro himself married and began the career of a Venetian statesman, a role determined for him by his birth and education. He was elected to the Senate in 1419; he subsequently held office as governor in several Venetian cities, including Verona and Vicenza; and he served as Venetian ambassador to the pope. Near the end of his career he attained the highest offices of the republic: President of the Venetian Senate in 1449 and Procurator of St. Mark in 1452. Barbaro died in 1454.

Barbaro's treatise on marriage was very popular in Italy and abroad, especially in humanist circles, where it was admired as much for its learning and style as for its content. De re uxoria is a standard humanist treatise inasmuch as it is heavily dependent on ancient Latin and Greek sources. Nevertheless, there is much of the Renaissance Venetian aristocratic perspective in the message. Marriage is a Christian state, and a dignified one worthy of a good man. Still, it is also the vehicle for the maintenance of noble lineages and through them the vitality of the republic. Marriage, then, is not just the union of two people but of two families to produce heirs who will serve the state, and in this important function, both father and mother had central roles to play.

SELECTIONS FROM *ON WIFELY DUTIES*

On the Faculty of Obedience

This is now the remaining part to be done here, in which if wives follow me, either of their own free will or by the commands of their husbands, no one will be so unfair as to think that I have not so established the duties of the wife that youth can enjoy peace and quiet the whole life

SOURCE: B. Kohl and R. Witt, eds., *The Earthly Republic* (Philadelphia: University of Pennsylvania Press, 1918), pp. 192–228. Reprinted with permission of University of Pennsylvania Press.

long. Therefore, there are three things that, if they are diligently observed by a wife, will make a marriage praiseworthy and admirable: love for her husband, modesty of life, and diligent and complete care in domestic matters. We shall discuss the first of these, but before this I want to say something about the faculty of obedience, which is her master and companion, because nothing more important, nothing greater can be demanded of a wife than this. The importance of this faculty did not escape the ancient wise men who instituted the custom that when a sacrifice was made to Juno, who was called by the name Gamelia because of her governance of marriage, the gall was removed from the victim. They were wisely warning by this custom that it was proper to banish all gall and rancor from married life. For this reason the Spartan woman's response has usually been approved by many learned men. When she was provoked by the slanderous reproaches of some mad old woman against her husband, she said: "Get out of here with such slanderous talk! When I was still a girl, I learned to obey the dictates of my parents, and now I realize that it is best to follow the wishes of my husband if I want to be what I ought to be." Therefore, let the husband give the orders, and let the wife carry them out with an even temper. For this reason that woman called Gorgo is surely not to be censured when she gave this reply to the question of whether she made advances to the husband: "No, I have not, but he comes to me." Cyrus, that great man and emperor, used to tell his troops that if the enemy advanced making a great noise, they should withstand the assault in silence, but if the enemy approached silently, then his men should go into battle with great noise and clamor. I would give the same advice to wives. If a husband, excited to anger, should scold you more than your ears are accustomed to hear, tolerate his wrath silently. But if he has been struck silent by a fit of depression, you should address him with sweet and suitable words, encourage, console, amuse, and humor him. Those who work with elephants do not wear white clothes, and those who work with wild bulls are right not to wear red; for those beasts are made ever more ferocious by those colors. Many authors report that tigers are angered by drums and made violent by them. Wives ought to observe the same thing; if, indeed, a particular dress is offensive to a husband, then we advise them not to wear it, so that they do not give affront to their husbands, with whom they ought to live peacefully and pleasantly. I think that ear guards (for so they are called because they protect the ear) are far more necessary for wives than for wrestlers, for the ears of the latter are only subject to blows, but indeed the former are subject to bills of repudiation accompanied by deep humiliation. Hence, wives must take great care that they do not entertain suspicions, jealousy, or anger on account of what they hear with their ears. Indeed, wives can often prevent such errors if they will only follow the prudent example of King Alexander, who, when someone was accused and brought before him for trial, would always stop up one of his ears so that he might later open it to the accused who might want to defend himself. Indeed, it seems that

Hermione was speaking the truth when she testified that she was brought to ruin by wicked women with whom she had been on familiar terms. Therefore, if wives should at some time become suspicious, let them stay away from slanderous women, stop up their ears, and suppress their mutterings, so that (as the proverb has it) fire is not added to fire. Let wives learn to follow that saying of Philip, that most outstanding king. This man was urged once by his courtiers to be harsher toward the Greeks who, though they had received many benefits from him, still criticized and slandered him. But he said: "What would they do if they were ever to receive bad treatment from us?" In the same way, when troublesome women say, "Your husband esteems you, who are so obedient and affectionate, only very little," then wives should answer, "What if I willingly and actively lost my modesty with my shame and my great desire for him along with my love?" A certain master found his runaway slave in a workhouse, and because the slave had been punished enough the master said: "Would that I had found you somewhere else than in this place." The wife who is angry with her husband because of jealousy and is considering a separation should ask herself this question: If I put myself in a workhouse because I hate a whore, what could make her far happier and more fortunate than this? She would see me almost shipwrecked, while at the same time she was sailing with favorable winds and securely casting her anchor into my marriage bed? Euripides, in his usual manner, greatly criticized those who were accustomed to listening to the harp while they were at dinner, for such music was better fitted to soothing anger or sadness than to relaxing those already immersed in pleasure. In similar fashion I would criticize wives who when they are happy and contented sleep with their husbands but when they are angry sleep apart and reject their husbands' affections, which through pleasantness and pleasure easily bring about reconciliation. The word Juno in Homer means "overseer of the nuptial ties," and if I remember correctly, when she spoke of Tethys and Oceanus, she declared that she would compose their differences and bring them together in lovemaking and nocturnal embraces. At Rome when there arose any differences between husband and wife, they entered the temple of the appeasing goddess where, after the spectators had been ushered out, they discussed everything frankly, and, finally, they returned home reconciled.

It was considered very good for domestic peace and harmony if a wife kept her husband's love with total diligence. At the olympic games that were dedicated to the great god Jupiter and attended by all of Greece, Gorgias used his eloquence to urge a union of all the Greeks. Melanthus said: Our patron attempts to persuade us that we should all join together in a league, but he cannot bring himself and his wife and her maid—who are only three people—to a mutual agreement (for the wife was very jealous because Gorgias was wildly enamoured of her maid). Likewise, Philip was for a long time displeased with the queen Olympias and Alexander. And when Demaratus of Corinth returned from Greece, Philip eagerly and closely questioned him about the union of the Greeks. Demaratus said to him: "Philip, I consider it a very bad thing that you are spending all your energy in bringing peace and concord to all of Greece when you are not yet reconciled with your own wife and son. Therefore, if any woman wants to govern her children and servants, she should make sure that she is, first of all, at peace with her husband. Otherwise, it will seem that she wants to imitate the very things that she is trying to correct in them. In order that a wife does her duty and brings peace and harmony to her household, she must agree to the first principle that she does not disagree with her husband on any point. But of this enough has been said.

On Love

Now we shall speak of conjugal love, whose great power and high dignity almost always created—as we know from many great thinkers—a pattern of perfect friendship. I must omit a great many topics so that I may speak primarily about what is to be observed most. I should like a wife to love her husband with such great delight, faithfulness, and affection that he can desire nothing more in diligence, love, and goodwill. Let her be so close to him that nothing seems good or pleasant to her without her husband. Indeed, I think that true love will be of the greatest help in this matter. In all matters there is no better, no shorter path than being exactly what we seem to be.

How much work, how much energy must an incompetent farmer expend if he would appear to be competent? How much learning, how much effort do unskillful physicians, or horsemen, or harp players need if they desire to seem to surpass others in fields where they are themselves completely without talent? It happens that many things generally intervene, so that the counterfeit practice of agriculture, medicine, horsemanship, and music comes to naught. If these persons take my advice, they will attain a solid and well-deserved reputation more easily, more quickly, and more surely if they suppress the spokesmen of false and overzealous praise. Since in every instance truth always overcomes imitation, the fact is that the farmer should take pains to till his fields with skill and hard work; the physician to heal men's diseases; the horseman to control unruly horses at his will; and the musician to give such delight with his song that nothing could be more pleasant or sweeter to the ears. Wherefore, if wives want to seem to love their husbands deeply, let them love them from their hearts.

In the first place, let wives strive so that their husbands will clearly perceive that they are pensive or joyful according to the differing states of their husbands' fortunes. Surely congratulations are proper in times of good fortune, just as consolations are appropriate in times of adversity. Let them openly discuss whatever is bothering them, provided it is worthy of prudent people, and let them feign nothing, dissemble nothing, and conceal nothing. Very often sorrow and trouble of mind are relieved by means of discussion and counsel that ought to be carried out in a friendly fashion with the husband. If a husband shares all the pressures of her anxieties, he will lighten them by participating in them and make their burden lighter; but if her troubles are very great or deeply rooted, they will be relieved as long as she is able to sigh in the embrace of her husband. I would like wives to live with their husbands in such a way that they can always be in agreement, and if this can be done, then, as Pythagoras defines friendship, the two are united in one. Now that this could be accomplished more easily, the people of Crete, who have for several centuries now lived under our dominion, used to permit their daughters to marry only those men with whom as virgins they had expressed mutual signs of love. The Cretans believe that those men would be more beloved by their wives if they were loved by them even before marriage. They recall that nature has so arranged and usage proven that all actions require time with few exceptions. It certainly happens that we may touch something hot and we are not immediately burned, or sometimes wood that is thrown into a fire does not always burst into flame right away. Hence, they think it is necessary for the girl to choose a husband suited to her own personality, just as one does in forming a friendship. The Cretans believe that a couple cannot properly know each other or fall passionately in love immediately. Whether the custom is a good one, I leave it to everyone to decide, but I cannot deny that it is well suited to the joy and constancy of love. I cannot pass over in silence those who seek to arouse their husbands to love by means of potions and amorous incantations. I would compare such wives to fishermen who catch fish with poison bait (as they still do in certain parts of Tuscany), and in so doing make the fish tasteless and almost inedible. Really, such women seem to be scarcely different from travelers who prefer to lead the blind than follow these who can see.

Therefore, mutual love should freely and diligently be acquired, nurtured, and preserved. This principle is illustrated by the lives and actions of the most distinguished women, and if wives imitate these they themselves will successfully meet the trials of virtue, love, and constancy. For example, Panthea wonderfully loved and delighted her husband, Abradatus, prince of Susa, and even as a captive she preserved her fidelity to him and made Cyrus a friend. In providing honorably for her husband, moreover, she did not squander his wealth but stored it. Abradatus fought valiantly against the Egyptians, who were the allies of Croesus, in order both to win the affection of Cyrus and to be a worthy husband to his wife Panthea. Then, performing his duty as a brave commander and stalwart soldier, he gave up his life in battle. Panthea, so that she might make him the most honorable sacrifice, desperately sought out his dead body and committed suicide upon it. Likewise, Cassandane so loved Cyrus that when she was about to die she found it was more bitter for her to leave

Cyrus than to depart this life. For this reason Cyrus, who did not want to act as an ungrateful husband, lamented her long after her death and ordered all those whom he governed to go into mourning in her honor. The wife of Themistocles loved him so much that it was generally acknowledged that she thought of nothing except her affection and love for her husband. For this reason it happened that the most famous leader of Greece yielded to her in all matters. Hence she was able to bring about more changes than any other Greek of her time. For whatever she wanted Themistocles also wanted, whatever Themistocles wanted the Athenians wished as well, and whatever the Athenians desired the whole of Greece desired. Thesta, the sister of the elder Dionysius, was married to Polyxenus, who, after he had been treated as an enemy by his brother-in-law, fled from Sicily. Then Dionysius called upon his sister and accused her of failing to report the flight of her husband even though she knew about it. Thesta, relying upon her reputation for constancy and outstanding virtue, responded: O Dionysius, do I seem to you to be such a vile and terrible woman that if I had known of my husband's flight I would have refused to go with him as a companion and partner in his misfortune? Indeed, it would be more acceptable to me to be called the wife of Polyxenus, the exile, than the sister of Dionysius, the tyrant. The Syracusans so admired the loftiness of her character that, after the tyrant had been expelled, they conferred royal honors on her as long as she lived. When she died men of all sorts and conditions—indeed, the entire population of Syracuse— attended her funeral. Armenia, the wife of Tigranes, is another noble example to women. For when Cyrus waged a campaign against the Assyrians, she was not able to bear the absence of her husband, so she followed Tigranes very willingly everywhere as his untiring companion through thick and thin. In Homer, Andromache showed her great affection for Hector, on whom she bestowed all her love, as in this passage:

> You are my sole father, and indeed my venerable mother, you are my sweet brother, you are my spouse, admirable in all respects.

Eventually driven insane by her husband's death, she ran through the city and wandered on the walls of Troy.

At this point I should speak of the virtue of the excellent wife Camma. Although her story is a long one, still its dignity, nobility, and distinction will be pleasing both to you and to others who will read this treatise. Therefore, we shall set about telling her story in detail. Sinatus and Sinorix, who were united to each other by blood, no doubt excelled the other tetrarchs of Galatia in power, renown, and glory. Of the two, Sinatus took as his wife Camma, who was outstanding not only in her bodily beauty but in her singular virtue as well. Thus endowed with chastity, goodness, prudence, and magnanimity, she bound the hearts of everyone to her with marvelous affection. That she was a priestess of Diana, who was especially worshipped by the Galatians, made Camma even more famous, and, on account of her own great status and that of her ancestors, she became the chief priestess. At their sacrifices, where she was always magnificently attired, she attracted everyone's eyes. For this reason Sinorix began to be smitten with her, and soon he began to plan the death of his kinsman since he feared that while her husband was still alive he would not be able to carry out his plan of seduction. Thus this evil man, blinded by his great passion, secretly succeeded in killing the unsuspecting Sinatus. Soon thereafter he urged marriage on Camma, who, courageously bearing her husband's death, waited the chance and opportunity for revenge of the impious deed of Sinorix. He continued to urge that the fatal marriage be made and he even admitted honest motives for the murder, if we may consider honest that which has been contaminated by the worst sort of crime. At first Camma rejected his entreaties, but soon her relations, who wanted to join their line forever with that of a powerful prince, urged her even more strongly to be content with marrying him. Then, as if persuaded, she agreed to marry him, and thereafter she received the young man at home and went with him to the temple of Diana, where they were to institute their marriage with a covenant and vows in the presence of the goddess. Taking a cup in her hand, as if about to make a toast, she put her lips to the rim and then gave the rest to Sinorix to drink. The cup had been filled with mead mixed with poison, and when she saw that Sinorix had drained the cup, her pleasure shone on her face and from her eyes and countenance. Turning to the statue of Diana, she spoke the following words: "O divine mother, I witness to you that I have not wanted to survive my beloved Sinatus because of love for life (because indeed the life I have led has only afflicted me with troubles, which now ended will release me from all pain) but because I was determined to survive to carry out the events of this day. Nor would I have taken any pleasure in continuing to live after the funeral of my husband, which was sorrowful to me and a calamity to his country? Only a certain hope for revenge has comforted me from time to time. And now that this vengeance had been exacted, I go to my dear and fine husband, Sinatus. And as for you, vilest of beasts, Sinorix, instead of a wedding bed, a tomb is being prepared." In a short time after the poison had spread through all the members of their bodies, first Sinorix and then Camma died.

Stratonica loved her husband Deiotarus so much that she thought she should do nothing but follow her husband's commands and interests. Therefore, she was in great grief and mourning when she saw that Deiotarus was unhappy because she had given him no heir, and that there would be no successor for his kingdom. Hence, of her own free will she provided her husband with a woman named Electra, who was handsome of face and decent in her habits, and Stratonica urged, exhorted, and persuaded her husband, who much admired the affection and constancy of his wife, to meet privately with Electra. Afterwards she cared for, educated, and instructed honorably the children born of Electra as if they had been her own.

It would be tedious if I were to recount here the earnest affection that

Tertia, daughter of Aemilius Paulus, held for P. Cornelius Scipio, or if I were to call to mind the very great love of Julia, Porcia, Artemisia, Hypsicratea, and other fine examples, which are familiar to anyone who has any familiarity at all with ancient history. There are also many things to be learned concerning the love of wives that I shall pass over intentionally. For we are confident in the great ingenuity with which wives will diligently and carefully seek out, of their own free will, ways to love and esteem their husbands. Still, we hope that those qualities which wives will develop naturally by practice will not differ too much from the precepts which have been described here.

On Moderation

The next part is concerning moderation, from which very often an enduring love between man and wife is begun, always nurtured and preserved. This quality is not only pleasing to the husband but also seems very noble to all those who hear about it. Moderation in a wife is believed to consist especially in controlling her demeanor, behavior, speech, dress, eating, and lovemaking. We shall discuss briefly these things that we have perceived either by our natural powers, learning, or experience; and since the first two qualities mentioned above amount to the same thing, we shall discuss them together.

Now demeanor, which is above all the most certain expression of the personality and is found in no living creature except man, demonstrates signs of an honest, respectful, and abstemious character. In demeanor the habits that nature might otherwise have hidden completely are detected. One's demeanor declares and manifests many things without the use of words. From the face and its movement the disposition of an individual may be known. Even in dumb animals we discern anger, pleasure, and other such emotions from the movement of the body and from the eyes, which testify and make clear what kind of emotions there are inside. Wherefore many who trust in facial characteristics maintain that one can learn many things about an individual's nature in this way. But I digress too much.

I therefore would like wives to evidence modesty at all times and in all places. They can do this if they will preserve an evenness and restraint in the movements of the eyes, in their walking, and in the movement of their bodies; for the wandering of the eyes, a hasty gait, and excessive movement of the hands and other parts of the body cannot be done without loss of dignity, and such actions are always joined to vanity and are signs of frivolity. Therefore, wives should take care that their faces, countenances, and gestures (by which we can penetrate by careful observation into the most guarded thoughts) be applied to the observance of decency. If they are observant in these matters, they will merit dignity and honor; but if they are negligent, they will not be able to avoid censure and criticism. Still, I am not asking that a wife's face be unpleasant, with a sour expression, but, rather, it should be pleasant. And her demeanor should not be clumsy but gracefully dignified. Moreover, I earnestly beg that wives observe the precept of avoiding immoderate laughter. This is a habit that is indecent in all persons, but it is especially hateful in a woman. On the other hand, women should not be censured if they laugh a little at a good joke and thus lapse somewhat from their serious demeanor. Demosthenes used to rehearse his legal speeches at home in front of a mirror so that with his own eyes he could judge what he should do and what he should avoid in delivering his speeches at court. We may well apply this practice to wifely behavior.

I wish that wives would daily think and consider what the dignity, the status of being a wife requires, so that they will not be lacking in dignified comportment. We know that Spartan wives used to go about with their faces covered, while Spartan virgins went about with their faces uncovered. When the Spartan Charillus was asked about this practice he answered: Our ancestors permitted this liberty to young virgins so that they might find husbands; but they prohibited it in married women so that they might understand that it was not their place to seek husbands but to care for and keep those they already had. Indeed, our Cretan subjects permit a similar custom. They allow their young girls to stand in their doorways and sing and joke and play games with their suitors. But when their women are married they have to stay at home, just as do those women who are dedicated to the rite of Vesta; and they can scarcely even go out, as if it would be unlawful for them even to see strange men. Who would not agree that they took this custom from Xenophon? One can easily learn from the following anecdote how much Xenophon would control the gaze of women. For when Tigranes returned home from service under King Cyrus with his kinsmen and his beloved wife Armenia, many men praised the king's manners, the size of his body, and his gracefulness. Tigranes asked Armenia what she thought of Cyrus's beauty, but Armenia, swearing before the immortal gods, answered: "I never turned my eyes away from you. Therefore, I am quite ignorant of what Cyrus's size or shape may be." That story is consistent with the principles of Gorgias, who wanted women to be shut up at home so that nothing could be known about them except their reputation. But Thucydides did not think that they merited such treatment, for he declared he had the best wife, about whom there was not the least word praising or censuring her.

We who follow a middle way should establish some rather liberal rules for our wives. They should not be shut up in their bedrooms as in a prison but should be permitted to go out, and this privilege should be taken as evidence of their virtue and propriety. Still, wives should not act with their husbands as the moon does with the sun; for when the moon is near the sun it is never visible, but when it is distant it stands resplendent by itself. Therefore, I would have wives be seen in public with their husbands, but when their husbands are away wives should stay at home. By maintaining an honest gaze in their eyes, they can communicate most significantly as in painting, which is called silent poetry. They also should maintain dignity in the motion of their heads and the other movements of their bodies. Now that I have spoken about demeanor and behavior, I shall now speak of speech.

On Speech and Silence

Isocrates warns men to speak on those matters that they know well and about which they cannot, on account of their dignity, remain silent. We commend women to concede the former as the property of men, but they should consider the latter to be appropriate to themselves as well as to men. Loquacity cannot be sufficiently reproached in women, as many very learned and wise men have stated, nor can silence be sufficiently applauded. For this reason women were prohibited by the laws of the Romans from pleading either criminal or civil law cases. And when Maesia, Afrania, and Hortensia deviated from these laws, their actions were reproved, criticized, and censured in the histories of the Romans. When Marcus Cato the Elder observed that Roman women, contrary to nature's law and the condition of the female sex, sometimes frequented the forum, sought a favorable decision, and spoke with strangers, he inveighed against, criticized, and restrained them as was required by that great citizen's honor and the dignity of his state. We know that the Pythagoreans were ordered to be silent for at least two years after beginning their studies. In this way they were not able to lie, to be deceived, or to be in error— all of which are very shameful acts—and, moreover, they could not stubbornly defend those opinions that they had not yet sufficiently investigated. But we require that wives be perpetually silent whenever there is an opportunity for frivolity, dishonesty, and impudence. When addressed, wives should reply very modestly to familiar friends and return their greetings, and they should very briefly treat those matters that the time and place offer them. In this way they will always seem to be provoked into conversation rather than to provoke it. They should also take pains to be praised for the dignified brevity of their speech rather than for its glittering prolixity. When a certain young man saw the noble woman Theano stretch her arm out of her mantle that had been drawn back, he said to his companions: "How handsome is her arm." To this she replied: "It is not a public one." It is proper, however, that not only arms but indeed also the speech of women never be made public; for the speech of a noble woman can be no less dangerous than the nakedness of her limbs. For this reason women ought to avoid conversations with strangers since manners and feelings often draw notice easily in these situations.

Silence is also often praised in the finest men. Pindar heaped praise on that outstanding Greek ruler Epaminondas because, though he knew much, he said little. In this matter, as in many others, Epaminondas followed the excellent teachings of nature, the mistress of life, who has clearly made known her thoughts on silence. She has with good reason furnished us with two ears but only one tongue, and this she has guarded with the double defense of lips and teeth. Now Theophrastus and many other men say that nature has made us with this opening so that the virute planted in us may enjoy the most pleasant and best results. As for the other senses that nature has bestowed upon us as scouts and messengers, they sometimes are sources of reliable knowledge but are very often only the conveyers of ignorance. Yet a certain Venetian citizen, whom I don't think it is necessary to name at present, praises silence only in those who cannot gain approval by their genius, authority by their wisdom, or renown by their well-wrought speeches. To this man I usually answer that the principal consideration in every matter refers to the person and to the place as well as to the time. Even if I were to concede, following his opinion, that it is usually appropriate for men to speak, still I consider such speechmaking to be, in the main, repugnant to the modesty, constancy, and dignity of a wife. For this reason the author Sophocles, who is certainly no worse than the Venetian I am discussing—and most men consider him better—has termed silence the most outstanding ornament of women. Therefore, women should believe they have achieved glory of eloquence if they will honor themselves with the outstanding ornament of silence. Neither the applause of a declamatory play nor the glory and adoration of an assembly is required of them, but all that is desired of them is eloquent, well-considered, and dignified silence. But what am I doing? I must be very careful, especially since I am treating silence, that I do not perhaps seem to you too talkative.

On Dress and Other Adornments

This is the point at which to discuss dress and other adornments of the body, which when they are not properly observed, lead not only to the ruin of a marriage but often to the squandering of a patrimony as well. All authorities who have studied these matters bear witness to this fact. If indeed one is pleased by the always praiseworthy rule of moderation, women will be recognized for modesty, and care will be taken for personal wealth and, at the same time, for the city as a whole. Here this fine precept should be followed: wives ought to care more to avoid censure than to win applause in their splendid style of dress. If they are of noble birth, they should not wear mean and despicable clothes if their wealth permits otherwise. Attention must be given, we believe, to the condition of the matter, the place, the person, and the time; for who cannot, without laughing, look upon a priest who is dressed in a soldier's mantel or someone else girdled with a statesman's purple at a literary gathering or wearing a toga at a horse race. Hence, we approve neither someone who is too finely dressed nor someone who is too negligent in her attire, but, rather, we approve someone who has preserved decency in her dress. Excessive indulgence in clothes is a good sign of great vanity. Moreover, experience and authorities have shown that such wives are apt to turn from their own husbands to other lovers. King Cyrus ought to be an example to our women that they should not strive too much to have expensive clothes, for Cyrus seems to be equal to his great name, which in the Persian tongue means "sun," both in his admirable wisdom and in his splendid moderation. When ambassadors came from the king of India to make peace with the Assyrians in the city of his uncle Cyaxares, the uncle wanted the choicest part of his army to appear before them. He sent orders to his general Cyrus to appear as soon as possible with all his troops in the courtyard of the royal palace and the large market square. Cyrus carried out these orders and came with order, dignity, and unbelievable speed, wearing only a thin garment, even though Cyaxares had sent him a purple robe, a precious necklace, and other Persian ornaments to wear so that his nephew, the general of his army, might seem all the more splendid and well-dressed. But Cyrus despised all these things greatly, and it seemed to others and to himself the highest decoration to be seen arriving ready to fight with the well-trained army almost before the royal messenger had returned to Cyaxares. A similar disdain for fine apparel would bring great honor to our wives.

Dionysius, the tyrant of Sicily, gave two very precious garments to Lysander so that his daughters might be more finely dressed. But Lysander refused the gifts and ordered the garments returned to Dionysius, saying that his daughters would be even more finely attired without the garments. Julia, the daughter of Caesar Augustus, imagined that her fine attire was sometimes offensive to her father, so one day she put on a plain dress and went to pay him a visit. When Caesar greatly approved of her new attire, she acknowledged that she was now wearing clothes that would please her father while before she had been dressing to please her husband Agrippa.

One may believe whatever he wishes. But still I think that wives wear and esteem all those fine garments so that men other than their own husbands will be impressed and pleased. For wives always neglect such adornments at home, but in the market square "this consumer of wealth" cannot be sufficiently decked out or adorned. Indeed, a great variety of clothes is rarely useful and often harmful to husbands, while this same variety is always pleasing to paramours for whom such things were invented. I am wont to compare these men who are properly called "uxorious" to those who are so pleased with splendid exteriors on their houses while they are forced to do without necessary things inside. Hence, they present a golden facade to give pleasure to neighbors and the passers-by. Such husbands are also similar to unskilled but rich barbers whom middle-aged men frequent only if they wish to have their hair arranged. Their ivory tools and elaborate mirrors are no source of wealth to them, but rather of grief, when they see the most noble young men going, to their great sorrow, to the neighboring barbershops. Moreover, sumptuous attire, magnificent clothes, and luxurious apparel give pleasure to those who frequent porticos, open courts, and sidewalks or very often promenade through the whole city. Hence, it was wisely forbidden to the women of Egypt to wear ornate shoes so that they might be prevented from wandering about too freely. Indeed, if we were to deprive most women of their sumptuous clothes, they would gladly and willingly stay at home.

Yet I think we ought to follow the custom—for good mores have so decayed—that our wives adorn themselves with gold, jewels, and pearls, if we can afford it. For such adornments are the sign of a wealthy, not a lascivious, woman and are taken as evidence of the wealth of the husband more than as a desire to impress wanton eyes. I will not dwell on the fact that this sort of wealth is more durable, and less likely to entail poverty than money put into rich clothing. Moreover, jewels and gold may often easily be of great use in business and public affairs. Who does not know how useful this sort of wealth was at a certain time to the ancient Romans, who in the time of peril during the Punic War raised money—which the ancients called the "sinews of war"—for their city, following the Oppian Law. Still I think that wives ought to display their jewels even less than the present sumptuary laws permit. Therefore, I would like them to abstain from wearing very licentious apparel and other bodily adornments, not out of necessity but because they desire to win praise by showing that "they can do without those things that they are legally allowed." But you have heard enough about attire.

On the Regulation of Lovemaking

Indeed, the fact is that as food and drink are to be regulated, so in its own fashion moderation in lovemaking ought to be observed. For lovemaking itself follows the rule of life, just as a young chick follows its mother. This fact is borne out by many examples, but we cannot at this point in our treatise begin more wisely or more aptly than from the example of nature itself. So we shall discuss briefly what we have in mind.

Indeed, the union of man and wife was first invented (as we said above), and ought to be esteemed especially, for the purpose of procreation. The couple must mainly use intercourse in the hope of procreating offspring. We can perceive and understand well enough that in most beasts there is a natural urge that leads them to follow certain rules of copulation, so that through the seed of mortal animals these same beasts are made immortal by a perpetual succession. Thus, in this way animals provide an example for us who possess a freer and nobler appetite, that we should indulge in sexual intercourse not for pleasure but only for the purpose of procreating offspring. Using the words of Julia, the daughter of Augustus,

I admonish you that when the ship is full it should admit no more passengers. Therefore, we should certainly not consider beasts to be beasts for the very reason that they never have sexual appetites when they are pregnant but only for the sake of procreation. But if a woman should transgress these limits, I wish that she will curb herself so that she will be, or at least seem to be, chaste in that sort of temperance from which chastity is derived. It would be conducive to achieving this result if, from the very beginning, husbands would accustom themselves to serving as the helpers of necessity rather than of passion. And wives should bear themselves with decorum and modesty in their married life so that both affection and moderation will accompany their lovemaking. Lust and unseemly desire are harmful to their dignity and to their husbands, even when they later say nothing about it. Herodotus writes that women lay aside their modesty together with their undergarments; if they make love with adulterers, let us acknowledge that this is true, but if wives will listen to us they will maintain their dignity with their husbands. When a certain woman was being forcibly taken by King Philip to satisfy his lust and desires, she declared: "Give me any woman and take away the light and you won't know one from the other." Now this can be justly said of adulterers. But wives, even though the light has been far removed, do not behave at all like these vile women. Does not Hesiod absolutely forbid that we should be uncovered at night? Because, as he says, the nights also belong to the immortal gods. For at all times a wife ought to do her duty, and although her body cannot be seen, still she ought always to observe decency so that she will justly seem decent to her husband even in the dark. Hence, when the wife of the famous Commodus attempted to entice her husband to use unusual and improper pleasures on her, he answered: "How far one can go in doing such things depends on the woman, but the term wife is surely a name of honor, not of pleasure." Similarly Cato the Censor expelled Manilius from the Senate because he passionately kissed his wife in the presence of his daughters. Now if it is true that it is a very base thing to kiss or passionately embrace one's wife in the presence of one's children, how much more important is it that nothing immoderate, nothing wanton should take place before the eyes that wives ought especially to please? Hiero fined Epicharmus, the comic poet, very heavily because he publicly made an indecent remark in the presence of his wife; for the dignity of marriage is so venerable that it is proper that no access should be given to the eyes and ears of strangers. The decency of the Athenians demonstrates this principle beautifully when they returned with the seals unbroken the letters they had intercepted that King Philip had sent to his wife Olympias; indeed, they held that it was completely wrong for a stranger, or even an enemy, to share the secrets exchanged between a husband and his wife.

It is therefore proper that wives always be careful and thoughtful in such matters so that they may win praise, honors, and crowns of gold. Hence, nothing should seem so pleasant and delightful that it would ever keep them from their obligation to do everything in a modest manner. In this matter wives should follow the example of many illustrious women. I do not know if Brasilla was the first among these, but surely her great deeds should not be passed over in silence in our own age. She was born of noble parents at Durazzo, as we know from the testimony of certain authors, and when she had been taken captive during a pirate raid she was in danger of being raped. But this beautiful woman, even in that great peril, preserved her sacred and uncorrupted chastity by the use of her wit, virtue, and lofty spirit; and with many words she stayed the aggression and repelled the fury of her captor, Cerič. And she struck a bargain with him that if she could preserve her chastity, she would provide him with a magic ointment that would render him immune to harm from military arms. Convinced by the argument of this fine and chaste woman and the virgin's reputation for magic, he put Brasilla under guard while she went out to gather herbs, and he eagerly awaited the concoction of the ointment. Then, with great courage, she approached Cerič and promised that she would render him safe from harm not with mere words but with herbs. After she had anointed her own neck with the ointment, she offered her throat to him. Indeed, Cerič, who rashly believed that she was quite immune, cut off her head with his sword and was amazed at such a display of chastity. What more need be said? If wives would want to be as they ought to be, there would be no need of further examples and exhortations. So that we do not further delay the discussion of those matters that we ought to treat next, we shall end our treatment of modesty here.

On the Education of Children

It remains to speak about the education of children, which is surely a rewarding and certainly the most serious of a wife's duties. Diligence in accumulation of money for the family is really worth nothing (as ancient Crates used to say) unless a great deal of care and really extraordinary amount of energy is expended on the upbringing and instruction of the children to whom the wealth is to be left. For this care children, who owe everything to their parents, are especially obligated. But if parents do not perform the task of caring for and instructing children, the children must really and truly seem deserted and abandoned. If, indeed, we acknowledge that all things are due to the authors of our life, which all mortals naturally cherish and hold on to with good reason, and what should we do if to a noble upbringing we add training in living well? On this account, if you reflect upon all the aspects of the matter, you will find that unless mothers totally repudiate the rules of nature, the duty of educating their children is so incumbent upon them that they cannot refuse this duty without great harm. For nature assigns to them an overwhelming love for their children, which they simply cannot overlook. So that this fact may be amply demonstrated, I will speak of the procreation of children before they see the light of day; but time does not allow me to digress for long, and Nature has so hidden and secluded those parts of the body that what cannot be viewed without embarrassment can hardly be discussed by us without loss of dignity. However, we shall treat those matters that we absolutely cannot omit.

In pregnancy the same blood of which women otherwise are cleansed in their monthly effusions is held back. This time, following the laws of nature, the fetus is nourished by this blood until the time of birth arrives. Then, as in all animals who give birth, the nourishment of milk is supplied. For this, Nature has made breasts, which, like bountiful fountains, nourish the young child and help it to grow gradually in all its parts. Moreover, women have been given two breasts so that if they have twins they may easily suckle and nourish them together. All these things have been thus provided with great wisdom, but they still might seem to have been done in vain except that Nature has also instilled in women an incredible love and affection for their offspring. Here the special care and diligence of Nature can be observed, for while she has placed the nipples of other animals under their stomachs, in women she has affixed them on their breasts so that they may feed their children milk and fondle them with embraces at the same time, kiss them easily and comfortably, and, as they say, receive them to their bosoms.

Thus Nature has assigned to women the duty of bearing and rearing children not only by necessity but also with her singular goodwill and love. Moreover, we can see a good argument in favor of a mother exercising great care for her newborn babies if women will but follow the habits of the terrible she-bear and other beasts. After bears have given birth to their unformed cub, they form and clean the cub with their tongues, as if the tongue were a kind of tool, so they can be justly called not just the mother of the cub but even its artificer. But why should we dwell on these small matters? Surely Nature has bestowed such good feeling toward newborn infants that we can see some animals who are timid become very brave on account of their offspring, others who are lazy become diligent, and others still who are slave to the stomach and gluttony become very abstemious. Did not even the Homeric bird endure hunger in order to provide for her young ones, and did she not cheat her own stomach to keep them fed? Therefore, mothers merit the severest censure if they neglect the care of their children and live carelessly. I would have them avoid no hardship in order to ensure that they make their children the best companions, comforters, and helpers in their old age. Therefore, if mothers would be free from reproach they should not neglect their offspring, but they should provide for both the bodies and souls of their children, and they should nourish and suckle them at their breasts. And the ones they nourished with their blood while still unknown mothers now will raise, since they are now born and have become human beings and are known and dear, since they require greatly not simply the care of a nurse but that of a mother as well. The wife of Marcus Cato the Censor fed her infant with her own milk, and this custom continues among Roman women down to the present age. In fact, because the fellowship of food and nourishment always increases friendship and love, in order to make the infants of her servants more loving to her own infants, a wife should sometimes feed them at her own breasts. We beg and exhort the most noble women to follow this example of feeding her infant her own milk, for it is very important that an infant should be nourished by the same mother in whose womb and by whose blood he was conceived. No nourishment seems more proper, none more wholesome than that same nourishment of body that glowed with greatest life and heat in the womb and should thus be given as known and familiar food to newborn infants. The power of the mother's food most effectively lends itself to shaping the properties of body and mind to the character of the seed. That may be discerned quite clearly in many instances; for example, when young goats are suckled with sheep's milk their hair becomes much softer, and when lambs are fed on goats' milk, it is evident that their fleeces become much coarser. In trees it is certain that they are much more dependent on the qualities of both sap and soil than on the quality of the seed; thus, if they are transplanted to other ground when flourishing and well leafed, you will find them changed enormously by the sap from the less fertile ground. Therefore, noble women should always try to feed their own offspring so that they will not degenerate from being fed on poorer, foreign milk. But if, as often happens, mothers cannot for compelling reasons suckle their own children, they ought to place them with good nurses, not with slaves, strangers, or drunken and unchaste women. They ought to give their infants to the care of those who are freeborn, well mannered, and especially those endowed with dignified speech. In this way the young infant will not imbibe corrupt habits and words and will not receive, with his milk, baseness, faults, and impure infirmities and thus be infected with a dangerous degenerative disease in mind and body. For just as the limbs of an infant can be properly and precisely formed and strengthened, so can his manners be exactly and properly shaped from birth. Therefore, mothers ought to be especially careful in their choice of nurses for infants; at this tender age a child's unformed character is very susceptible to being molded, and, as we impress a seal in soft wax, so the disposition and faults of a nurse can be sealed upon an infant. That very wise poet Vergil showed how important a nurse's inclinations and nature are when he described how Dido called Aeneas harsh and unyielding. Thus he has her say: "The Hircanian tigers fed you at their breasts." Likewise, that most pleasant poet Theocritus said that he detested cruel Cupid, not because he was born of his mother Venus "but because he suckled the breast of a lioness."

Therefore, women ought to consider it best, very honorable, and commendable to suckle their own children, whom they should nourish with great love, fidelity, and diligence; or they may commit this part of their duty to well-trained nurses who will esteem and care for the infants, not with a pretended enthusiasm nor out of mercenary consideration. After their offspring have passed their infancy, mothers should use all their skill, care, and effort to ensure that their children are endowed with excellent qualities of mind and body. First they should instruct them in their duty toward Immortal God, their country, and their parents, so that they will be instilled from their earliest years with those qualities that are the foundation of all other virtues. Only those children who fear God, obey the laws, honor their parents, respect their superiors, are pleasant with their equals and courteous to their inferiors, will exhibit much hope for themselves. Children should meet all people with a civil demeanor, pleasant countenance, and friendly words. But they should be on the most familiar terms with only the best people. Thus they will learn moderation in food and drink so that they may lay, as it were, the foundation of temperance for their future lives. They should be taught to avoid these pleasures that are dishonorable, and they should apply their efforts and thoughts to those matters that are the most becoming and will be useful and pleasant when they become older. If mothers are able to instruct their children in these matters, their offspring will much more easily and better receive the benefit of education. Very often we see that the commands and gifts of rulers are welcomed by their subjects, yet when these same things are bestowed by private persons they hardly even seem acceptable. Who can be unaware of what great authority the mildest and shortest reproach of a parent has on his children? Whence that wise man, Cato the Elder, instructed his offspring diligently in many subjects, including literature, so he would not be lacking in his duties as a father. Even the barbarous Eurydice ought to be judged worthy of great praise, for when she was advanced in years she applied herself to the study of literature, that monument of virtue and learning, so that, having done this, she would not only be considered the source of life to her children but could also instill in them through the bountiful condiments of the humanities the art of living well and happily. Mothers should often warn their children to abstain from excessive laughter and to avoid words that denote a rash character. That is the mark of stupidity, the evidence of passion. Moreover, children should be warned not ever to speak on those matters that are base in the act. Therefore, mothers should restrain them from vulgar or cutting words. If their children should say anything that is obscene or licentious, mothers should not greet it with a laugh or a kiss, but with a whip.

Moreover, they should teach their children not to criticize anyone because of his poverty or the low birth of his lineage or other misfortunes, for they are sure to make bitter enemies from such actions or develop an attitude of arrogance. Mothers should teach their children sports in which they so willingly learn to exert themselves that, if the occasion arises, they can easily bear even more difficult hardships. I would have mothers sharply criticized for displays of anger, greed, or sexual desire in the presence of their offspring, for these vices weaken virtue. If mothers act appropriately, their children will learn from infancy to condemn, avoid, and hate these most filthy mistresses and they will take care to revere the names of God and will be afraid to take them in vain. For whoever has been taught at an early age to despise the Divinity, will they not as adults surely curse Him? Therefore, it is of great importance to train children from infancy so that they never swear. Indeed, those who swear readily because of some misfortune are not deserving of trust, and those who readily swear very often unwittingly betray themselves. Mothers ought to teach their children to speak the truth. This was well established among the Persians, and for that reason they decreed that there would be no market squares in their cities since they believed that such places were only fit for lying, or telling falsehoods, or for swearing falsely. Mothers should teach their children to say little at all times, and especially at banquets, unless they are ordered to speak, so that children do not become impudent or talkative—qualities that ought to be especially avoided in the young. It will be an impediment to proper education if children try to explain impudently what they themselves have not yet sufficiently understood. Therefore, you should recall that saying of Cato who, when he was as a youth blamed for his silence, said: "Then I shall not harm myself at all, until I shall say those things that are not worthy of being left unsaid." If children will learn such precepts from their mothers as soon as their tender years permit, they will more happily and easily obtain the dignity and learning of their parents.

There are many other matters that I shall omit at present because they are peculiar to fathers, and I do so readily because I see that some people consider this subject of wifely duties to be so vast and infinite that the subject of fatherly duties can scarcely be sufficiently treated here. I can say nothing truer than that I never intended to discuss what might be done, but, rather, I have tried to describe what ought to be done. Therefore, who is such an unjust critic that if he will approve of a marriage done for the best reasons (just as you have done) and will, in his choice of a wife, take a woman outstanding in her morals, suitable in her age, family, beauty, and wealth, loving to her husband, and modest and very skillful in domestic matters—who, I say, would be so pessimistic in these matters that he cannot wish for all these great qualities or imagine that wives so endowed ought not to perform all these important precepts? Therefore, my Lorenzo, your compatriots ought to be stirred by your example and follow you with great enthusiasm, for in Ginevra you have taken a wife who is a virgin well endowed with virtue, charm, a noble lineage, and great wealth. What more outstanding, more worthy model could I propose than yours? What more shining, more worthy example than yours, since in this outstanding city of Florence you are most eminently connected through your father, grandfather, and ancestors? You have taken a wife whose great wealth the entire world indeed admires but whose chastity, constancy, and prudence all men of goodwill esteem highly. They consider that you are blessed and happy to have her as a wife, as she is to have you as a husband. Since you have contracted such an outstanding and fine marriage, these same men ask God Immortal that you will have the best children who will become very honored citizens in your state. These matters might perhaps seem negligible since I am treating them, but indeed they are, in their own fashion, borne out in your marriage. Thus, surely young men who follow your example will profit more than only by following my precepts; just as laws are much more likely to be observed in a city when they are obeyed by its ruler, so, since your own choice of a wife is consistent with my teachings, we may hope that these precepts will be followed by the youth.

But, Lorenzo, as my treatise begins with you, so shall it end. You now have, instead of a present, my opinion on wifely duties, and I hope that whatever has been said by me, not to admonish you (as I made clear from the beginning) but to declare our mutual goodwill, will in large measure be kindly accepted by many others. I am certain that it will be well received by you, in whose name I undertook this endeavor. If when you are reading our little commentary you find anything that perhaps seems to be well or wisely stated, attribute it to that excellent man Zaccaria Trevisan, who is worthy of every sort of praise and whose memory I gladly cherish, and to my study of Greek literature. From the latter I have culled some things that pertain to our subject and inserted them here. Although I have been occupied with this treatise for only a few months, I still am happy to think that it will bear abundant and pleasant fruit. For I have profited so much from the learning and talent of that fine and very erudite man, Guarino da Verona, who was my tutor and my closest friend from among all my acquaintances. He was a guide to me and to several other first-rate people, in understanding and advancing our study of the humanities. And he was such a fine guide that, with his help, these divine studies, to which I have devoted myself from boyhood, have become very enjoyable and profitable to me. Therefore, please accept gladly from me this wife's necklace (as I wish to call it), given on the occasion of your marriage. I know that you will esteem it greatly both because it is the sort of necklace that cannot be broken or destroyed by use (as others can) and because it is the product of my sincere friendship and of a mind that is entirely devoted to you.

♦ Leon Battista Alberti

*L*eon Battista Alberti (d. 1472) was born in Genoa in 1404, the illegitimate son of an exiled Florentine patrician. He was educated at the universities of Padua and Bologna, studying law as well as classical languages and literatures. His training resulted in a position in the papal service, which allowed him to write and practice the many arts and skills he had acquired.

The Alberti family was permitted to return to Florence through a lifting of their banishment. Leon Battista took the opportunity to visit his ancestral city, where he was much impressed with the new styles of painting and architecture developing there. Stimulated by this environment, Alberti began a treatise, **On Painting**, in 1436 that was to argue the importance of mathematical perspective for the creation of the appearance of a three-dimensional vision on a two-dimensional plane, and he stressed the importance of telling a story in composing a painting.

Alberti, who continued to serve as a papal secretary based in Rome, spent much time in other Italian cities as well, taking commissions as an architect. For the Lord of Rimini he redesigned the Church of San Francesco as a virtual pagan temple dedicated to the power of the ruling Malatesta family. In Mantua he created another church, San Andrea, which reflected the influence of classical architecture, which he saw as the ideal form of building. Even in Florence he was called on to design public and private buildings, for example, the facade of the Dominican Church of Santa Maria Novella and the beautiful palace of the Rucellai family, the facade of which incorporates the three orders of columns found in the text of the recently rediscovered Roman architect Vitruvius.

These classical principles and his great debt to Vitruvius inspired Alberti to write a treatise on architecture as well, **On Building**. This book argues for beauty through harmony and proportion, including the application to architecture of the perfect proportions found in music and the human body.

Alberti was so talented in so many areas that he has been suggested as the ideal Renaissance man. He was a painter, architect, and artistic theorist; he wrote Latin with such facility that he successfully circulated one of his own plays in jest as a lost classical comedy; he was a fine athlete and musician; he was an orator and mathematician, reducing the laws of perspective to a formula that any artist might employ; and he was an excellent writer in Italian, choosing the vernacular language for certain of his works (such as **On the Family**) to ensure their widespread popularity among all classes of readers. It is appropriate, then, that Alberti's dictum that man is the measure of all things should become a commonplace of the Italian Renaissance ideal.

On the Family was written in the 1430s while Alberti was traveling to Florence often. It is a dialogue in which various members of the Alberti family discuss the nature of the family from several perspectives, providing a wide commentary on the role of the husband, wife, children, and even servants.

THE FAMILY IN RENAISSANCE FLORENCE

Giannozzo: Let the father of the family follow my example. Since I find it no easy matter to deal with the needs of the household when I must often be engaged outside with other men in arranging matters of wider consequence, I have found it wise to set aside a certain amount for outside use, for investments and purchases. The rest, which takes care of all the smaller household affairs, I leave to my wife's care. I have done it this way, for, to tell the truth, it would hardly win us respect if our wife busied herself among the men in the marketplace, out in the public eye. It also seems somewhat demeaning to me to remain shut up in the house among women when I have manly things to do among men, fellow citizens and worthy and distinguished foreigners.

I don't know whether you will approve of my solution. I know some people are always checking on their own household and rummaging around in every nook and cranny lest something remain hidden from them. Nothing is so obscure that they do not look into it and poke their fingers in. They say that it is no shame or harm to a man to attend carefully to his own affairs and to lay down the law and custom in his own house. They point out that Niccolo Alberti, who was a very diligent person, said diligence and universal vigilance was the mother of wealth. I too admire and like this saying, for diligence always helps; but I cannot convince myself that men who are engaged in other concerns really ought to be or to seem so very interested in every little household trifle. I don't know, perhaps I am wrong about this. What do you say, Lionardo, what do you think?

Lionardo: I agree, for you are, indeed, precisely of the opinion of the ancients. They used to say that men are by nature of a more elevated mind than women. They are more suited to struggle with arms and with cunning against the misfortunes which afflict country, religion, and one's own children. The character of men is stronger than that of women and can bear the attacks of enemies better, can stand strain longer, is more constant under stress. Therefore men have the freedom to travel with honor in foreign lands, acquiring and gathering the goods of fortune. Women, on the other hand, are almost all timid by nature, soft, slow, and therefore more useful when they sit still and watch over our things. It is as though nature thus provided for our well-being, arranging for men to bring things home and for women to guard them. The woman, as she remains locked up at home, should watch over things by staying at her post, by diligent care and watchfulness. The man should guard the woman, the house, and his family and country, but not by sitting still. He should exercise his spirit and his hands in brave enterprise, even at the cost of sweat and blood. No doubt of it, therefore, Giannozzo, those idle creatures who stay all day among the little females or who keep their minds occupied with little feminine trifles certainly lack a masculine and glorious spirit. They are contemptible in their apparent inclination to play the part

SOURCE: Leon Battista Alberti, *The Family in Renaissance Florence*, trans. by R. N. Watkins (Columbia, S.C.: University of South Carolina Press, 1969), pp. 207–229. Reprinted by permission of Renee E. Watkins.

of women rather than that of men. A man demonstrates his love of high achievements by the pride he takes in his own. But if he does not shun trifling occupations, clearly he does not mind being regarded as effeminate. It seems to me, then, that you are entirely right to leave the care of minor matters to your wife and to take upon yourself, as I have always seen you do, all manly and honorable concerns.

Giannozzo: Yes, you see that's my long-standing conviction. I believe that a man who is the father of a family not only should do all that is proper to a man, but that he must abstain from such activities as properly pertain to women. The details of housekeeping he should commit entirely into their hands. I always do.

Lionardo: You, however, can congratulate yourself on having a wife who probably surpasses other women. I don't know how many women one could find as vigorous and as wise in their rule of the household as your wife.

Giannozzo: My wife certainly did turn into a perfect mother for my household. Partly this was the result of her particular nature and temperament, but mainly it was due to my instruction.

Lionardo: Then you taught her?

Giannozzo: Many things.

Lionardo: And how did you do it?

Giannozzo: Well, I'll tell you. After my wife had been settled in my house a few days, and after her first pangs of longing for her mother and family had begun to fade, I took her by the hand and showed her around the whole house. I explained that the loft was the place for grain and that the stores of wine and wood were kept in the cellar. I showed her where things needed for the table were kept, and so on, through the whole house. At the end there were no household goods of which my wife had not learned both the place and the purpose. Then we returned to my room, and, having locked the door, I showed her my treasures, silver, tapestry, garments, jewels, and where each thing had its place.

Lionardo: All those valuables, then, were assigned some place in your room, I suppose because they were safer there, better secluded and more securely locked up.

Giannozzo: Yes, but primarily so that I could look them over whenever I liked without witnesses. You may be sure, children, that it is imprudent to live so openly that the whole household knows everything. It is less difficult to guard a thing from a few persons than from all. If something is known only to a few, it is easier to keep safe. If it does get lost, it is easier to get it back from a few than from many. For this and for many other reasons, I have always thought it a good precaution to keep every precious thing I had well hidden if possible, and locked up out of the reach of most hands and eyes. These treasures, I always felt, should be kept where they are safe from fire and other disaster, and where I can frequently, whether for my pleasure or to check them over, shut myself up alone or with whomever I choose while giving no cause for undue curiosity to those outside. No place seemed more suited for this purpose than the room where I slept. There, as I was saying, I wanted none of my precious things to be hidden from my wife. I opened to her all my household treasures, unfolded them, and showed them to her.

Only my books and records and those of my ancestors did I determine to keep well sealed both then and thereafter. These my wife not only could not read, she could not even lay hands on them. I kept my records at all times not in the sleeves of my dress, but locked up and arranged in order in my study, almost like sacred and religious objects. I never gave my wife permission to enter that place, with me or alone. I also ordered her, if she ever came across any writing of mine, to give it over to my keeping at once. To take away any taste she might have for looking at my notes or prying into my private affairs, I often used to express my disapproval of bold and forward females who try too hard to know about things outside the house and about the concerns of their husband and of men in general. I used to remind her of a truth which Messer Cipriano Alberti once voiced to me. A most honest and wise man, Messer Cipriano once saw that the wife of a good friend of his was overeager to ask and inquire into the place where her husband had stayed the night and the company he had kept. He was anxious to warn her as best he could and to show her the respect he perhaps felt he owed to his friend. Finally he said to her, "I counsel you, friend, for your own good—be far more eager to learn what goes on in your own house than to find out about what lies outside it. Let me remind you as I would a sister that wise men say a woman who spies too much on men may be suspected of having men too much on her mind, being perhaps secretly anxious whether others are learning about her own character when she appears too interested in them. Think for yourself whether either of these passions is becoming to a lady of unblemished honor." Thus Messer Cipriano, and thus I too, spoke to my wife.

I always tried to make sure, first that she could not, and second that she did not wish, to know more of my secrets than I cared to impart. One should never, in fact, tell a secret, even a trivial one, to one's wife or any woman. I am greatly displeased with those husbands who take counsel with their wives and don't know how to confine any kind of secret to their own breast. They are madmen if they think true prudence or good counsel lies in the female brain, and still more clearly mad if they suppose that a wife will be more constant in silence concerning her husband's business than he himself has proved. Stupid husbands to blab to their wives and forget that women themselves can do anything sooner than keep quiet! For this very reason I have always tried carefully not to let any secret of mine be known to a woman. I did not doubt that my wife was most loving, and more discreet and modest in her ways than any, but I still considered it safer to have her unable, and not merely unwilling, to harm me.

Lionardo: An excellent lesson. You have been no less wise than fortunate if your wife has never dragged any secret out of you.

Giannozzo: Never, my dear Lionardo, and I'll tell you why. First, she was very modest and never cared to know more than was her business. Furthermore, I made it a rule never to speak with her of anything but household matters or questions of conduct, or of the children. Of these matters I spoke a good deal to her. From what I said, and by answering me and discussing with me, she learned the principles she required and how to apply them. I did this, also, my dear Lionardo, in order to make it impossible for her to enter into discussions with me concerning my more important and private affairs. This was my practice: I always kept my secrets and my notes carefully hidden; everything else of a domestic nature, I thought then and later, could properly be delegated to her. I did not, however, leave things so much in her hands as to be uninterested or not examine the details and be sure all was well managed.

When my wife had seen and understood the place of everything in the house, I said to her, "My dear wife, those things are to be as useful and precious to you as to me. The loss of them would injure and grieve you, therefore should you guard them no less zealously than I do. You have seen our treasures now, and thanks be to God they are such that we ought to be contented with them. If we know how to preserve them, these things will serve you and me and our children. It is up to you, therefore, my dear wife, to keep no less careful watch over them than I."

Lionardo: And what did your wife say to that?

Giannozzo: She replied by saying that her father and mother had taught her to obey them and had ordered her always to obey me, and so she was prepared to do anything I told her to. "My dear wife," said I, "a girl who knows how to obey her father and mother soon learns to please her husband. But do you know how we shall try to be? We shall imitate those who stand guard on the walls of the city; if one of them, by chance, falls asleep, he does not take it amiss for his companion to wake him up that he may do his duty for his country. Likewise, my dear wife, if you ever see any fault in me, I shall be very grateful to you for letting me know. In that way I shall know that our honor and our welfare and the good of our children are dear to your heart. Likewise be not displeased if I awaken you where there is need. Where I am lacking, you shall make it good, and so together we shall try to surpass each other in love and in zeal.

This property, this family, and the children to be born to us will belong to us both, to you as much as to me, to me as much as to you. It behooves us, therefore, not to think how much each of us has brought into our marriage, but how we can best maintain all that belongs to both of us. I shall try to obtain outside what you need inside the house; you must see that none of it is wasted.

Lionardo: How did she seem to take all this? Was she pleased?

Giannozzo: Very much so. She said she would be happy to do conscientiously whatever she knew how to do and had the skill to do, hoping it might please me. To this I said, "Dear wife, listen to me. I shall be most pleased if you do just three things: first, my wife, see that you never want another man to share this bed but me. You understand." She blushed and cast down her eyes. Still I repeated that she should never receive anyone into that room but myself. That was the first point. The second, I said, was that she should take care of the household, preside over it with modesty, serenity, tranquillity, and peace. That was the second point. The third thing, I said, was that she should see that nothing went wrong in the house.

Lionardo: Did you show her how to do what you commanded, or did she already have an expert knowledge of these things?

Giannozzo: Do not imagine, my dear Lionardo, that a young girl can ever be very well versed in these matters. Nor is such cleverness and cunning required from a young girl as it is from the mother of a family. Her modesty and virtue, on the other hand, must be much greater. And these very qualities my wife had in abundance. In these virtues she surpassed all other women. I could not describe to you how reverently she replied to me. She said her mother had taught her only how to spin and sew, and how to be virtuous and obedient. Now she would gladly learn from me how to rule the family and whatever I might wish to teach her.

Lionardo: And you, Giannozzo, how did you manage to teach her these things?

Giannozzo: What things? How to sleep with no other man but myself, perhaps?

Lionardo: You are wonderful, Giannozzo. Even in giving us these holy and austere lessons, you know how to joke and make us laugh.

Giannozzo: It certainly would be funny if I had tried to teach her how to sleep alone. I don't know if those ancient authors you like to read were able to teach that.

Lionardo: Everything but that. They do say, however, how they instructed their wives never, in bearing and behavior, to let themselves appear less virtuous than they really were. It is also described how they tried to persuade women, for this very reason, never to paint their faces with white powder, brazilnut dye, or other make-up.

Giannozzo: I myself, I assure you, did not omit this.

Lionardo: I would like to hear how you handled it. When I have a wife of my own I should like to know how to do something which, it seems, few husbands can manage. For everyone hates to see make-up on his wife, yet no one seems able to prevent it.

Giannozzo: In dealing with this problem, I exercised great discretion. You'll not be sorry to hear my fine method for making her detest the stuff. So, since it will be most useful to you to have heard me, listen carefully now. When I had given the house over to my wife's keeping, I brought her back to our own locked room, as I was saying. Then she and I knelt down and prayed to God to give us the power to make good use of those possessions which he, in his mercy and kindness, had allowed us to enjoy. We also prayed with most devoted mind that he might grant us the grace to live together in peace and harmony for many happy years, and with many male children, and that he might grant to me riches, friendship, and honor, and to her, integrity, purity, and the character of a perfect mistress of the household. Then, when we had stood up, I said to her:

"My dear wife, to have prayed God for these things is not enough. Let us also be very diligent and conscientious and do our best to obtain what we have prayed for. I, my dear wife, shall seek with all my powers to gain what we have asked of God. You, too, must set your whole will, all your mind, and all your modesty to work to make yourself a person whom God has heard and to whom he has granted what you prayed for. You should realize that in this regard nothing is so important for yourself, so acceptable to God, so pleasing to me, and precious in the sight of your children as your chastity. The woman's character is the jewel of her family; the mother's purity has always been a part of the dowry she passes on to her daughters; her purity has always far outweighed her beauty. A beautiful face is praised, but unchaste eyes make it ugly through men's scorn, and too often flushed with shame or pale with sorrow and melancholy. A handsome person is pleasing to see, but a shameless gesture or an act of incontinence in an instant renders her appearance vile. Unchastity angers God, and you know that God punishes nothing so severely in women as he does this lack. All their lives he makes them notorious and miserable. The shameless woman is hated by her whose love is true and good. She soon discovers that, in fact, her dishonored condition pleases only her enemies. Only one who wishes us to suffer and be troubled can rejoice when he sees you fall from honor.

"Shun every sort of dishonor, my dear wife. Use every means to appear to all people as a highly respectable woman. To seem less would be to offend God, me, our children, and yourself. To seem so, indeed, brings praise and love and favor from all. Then you can hope that God will give some aid to your prayers and vows.

"To be praised for your chastity, you must shun every deed that lacks true nobility, eschew any sort of improper speech, avoid giving any sign that your spirit lacks perfect balance and chastity. You will disdain, first of all, those vanities which some females imagine will please men. All made up and plastered and painted and dressed in lascivious and improper clothing, they suppose they are more attractive to men than when adorned with pure simplicity and true virtue. Vain and foolish women are these who imagine that when they appear in make-up and look far from virtuous they will be praised by those who see them. They do not realize that they are provoking disapproval and harming themselves. Nor do they realize, in their petty vanity, that their immodest appearance excites numerous lustful men. Such men all besiege and attack such a girl, some with suddenness, some with persistence, some with trickery, until at last the unfortunate wretch falls into real disgrace. From such a fall she cannot rise again without the stain of great and lasting infamy upon her."

Thus I spoke to my wife. To convince her still more fully of the danger, as well as of the shame, in a woman's covering her face with the powders and poisons which the silly creatures call make-up, see, dear Lionardo, what a nice lesson I gave her. There was a saint in the room, a very lovely statue of silver, whose head and hands alone were of purest ivory. It was set, polished and shining, in the center of the altar, as usual. "My dear wife," I said to her, "suppose you besmirched the face of this image in the morning with chalk and calcium and other ointments. It might well gain in color and whiteness. In the course of the day the wind would carry dust to it and make it dirty, but in the evening you would wash it, and then, the next day, cover it again with ointments, and then wash it again. Tell me, after many days of this, if you wanted to sell it, all polished and painted, how much money do you think you would get for it? More than if you had never begun painting it?

"Much less," she replied.

"That's right," said I, "for the buyer of the image does not buy it for a coating of paint which can be put on or off but because he appreciates the excellence of the statue and the skill of the artist. You would have lost your labor, then, as well as the cost of those ointments. Tell me, though, if you went on for months or years washing and redaubing it, would you make it more beautiful?"

"I think not," she said.

"On the contrary, you would spoil it and wear it out. You would scrape off the finish of the ivory. It would become rough and end up colorless, yellowed, softened by those powders. Certainly. But if those poultices could have that effect on ivory, which is hard stuff by nature and able to last forever if left alone, you can be sure, my dear wife, that they can do your own brow and cheeks still greater harm. For your skin is tender and delicate if you don't smear anything on it, and if you do it will soon grow rough and flabby. Don't deny that those things are poison. You know that all those make-up materials do contain poison. They do you much more harm than they would to ivory. You know, even the least bit of dust or a drop of sweat makes a smear on your face. No, you will not be more beautiful with that stuff, only dirty, and in the long run you will ruin your skin."

Lionardo: Did she seem to agree and to realize you were telling the truth?

Giannozzo: What sort of silly girl would fail to realize this was the truth? Besides, to make sure she did believe me, I asked her about a neighbor of mine, a woman who had few teeth left in her mouth, and those appeared tarnished with rust. Her eyes were sunken and always inflamed, the rest of her face withered and ashen. All her flesh looked decomposed and disgusting. Her silvery hair was the only thing about her that one might regard without displeasure. So I asked my wife whether she wished she were blond and looked like her?

"Heavens, no," said she.

"And why not? Does she seem so old to you? How old do you think she is?"

To that she replied most modestly that she was no judge of these matters, but to her the woman seemed about the age of her mother's wetnurse. Then I assured her of the truth, namely that that neighbor of mine was born less than two years before me and had certainly not yet attained her thirty-second year. Thanks to make-up, however, she had been left in this diseased condition and seemed old before her time.

When I saw she was really amazed at this, I reminded her of all the Alberti girls, of my cousins and others in the family. "You see, my dear wife," I said, "how fresh and lively our girls all are, for the simple reason that they never anoint themselves with anything but river water. And so shall you do, my wife," said I. "You'll not poison yourself or whiten your face to make yourself seem more beautiful for me. You are white and bright enough complexioned for me as you are. Rather, like the Alberti girls, you will just wash and keep clean with water alone. My dear wife, there is no one but me for you to think of pleasing in this matter. Me, however, you cannot please by deception. Remember that. You cannot deceive me, anyway, because I see you at all hours and know very well how you look without make-up. As for outsiders, if you love me, think how could any of them matter more to you than your own husband. Remember, my dear wife, that a girl who tries harder to please outsiders than the one she should be pleasing shows that she loves her husband less than she does strangers."

Lionardo: Wise words. But did she obey you?

Giannozzo: It is true that at weddings, sometimes, whether because she was embarrassed at being among so many people or heated with dancing, she sometimes appeared to have more than her normal color. In the house, however, there was only one time, when friends and their wives were invited to dinner at Easter. My wife, on this occasion, had covered her face with pumice, in God's name, and she talked all too animatedly with each guest on his arrival or departure. She was showing off and being merry with everyone, as I observed.

Lionardo: Did you get angry with her?

Giannozzo: Ah, Lionardo, I never got angry with my wife.

Lionardo: Never?

Giannozzo: Why should we let quarrels arise between ourselves? Neither of us ever desired from the other anything that was not wholly right.

Lionardo: Yet I imagine you must have been troubled if in this matter your wife failed to obey you as she should have.

Giannozzo: Yes, yes, true enough. But I did not, for all that, show her that I was troubled.

Lionardo: Didn't you scold her?

Giannozzo: Ha, ha, yes, in the right way. To me it has always seemed obvious, dear children, that the way to correct someone is to begin gently, put out the evil quickly, and kindle good will. This you can learn from me—it is much better to reprimand a woman temperately and gently than with any sort of harsh severity. A slave can bear threats and blows and perhaps not grow indignant if you shout at him. A wife, however, will obey you better from love than from fear. Any free spirit will sooner set out to please you than to submit to you. It is best, therefore, to do as I did and correct your wife's failing kindly but in time.

Lionardo: How did you reprimand her?

Giannozzo: I waited till we were alone. Then I smiled at her and said, "Oh dear, how did your face get dirty? Did you by any chance bump into a pan? Go wash yourself, quick, before these people begin to make fun of you. The lady and mother of a household must always be neat and clean if she wants the rest of the family to learn good conduct and modest demeanor."

She understood me and at once began to cry. I let her go wash off both tears and make-up. After that I never had to tell her again.

Lionardo: What a perfect wife. I can well believe that such a woman, so obedient to your word and so modest by her own nature, could elicit respect and good behavior in the rest of the household.

Giannozzo: All wives are thus obedient, if their husbands know how to be husbands. But some I see quite unwisely suppose that they can win obedience and respect from a wife to whom they openly and abjectly subject themselves. If they show by word and gesture that their spirit is all too deeply lascivious and feminine, they certainly make their wives no less unfaithful than rebellious. Never, at any moment, did I choose to show in word or action even the least bit of self-surrender in front of my wife. I did not imagine for a moment that I could hope to win obedience from one to whom I had confessed myself a slave. Always, therefore, I showed myself virile and a real man. Always I encouraged her to love virtue. Always I reminded her to be most disciplined. I kept her always conscious of all that I, myself, knew was right for a perfect mother of a family and wanted her to know also.

"My dear wife," I often told her, "if we want to live in peace and harmony, all our household must be well behaved and modest in their ways. You must gladly take on yourself the task of making them obedient and respectful toward yourself. Unless you yourself are very modest and self-restrained, however, you may be sure that what you cannot do for yourself you can still less produce in others. To be regarded as a very modest and restrained woman, you must be such that all vileness offends you. This will help to discipline the household, for all its members will take care not to displease you. Unless they have the highest example of chastity and decorum in you, however, do not expect them to show obedience, let alone reverence, toward yourself. Respect is something one must earn. Only character gives a man dignity, and one who wears dignity can gain respect; one who can gain respect can win obedience. One who does not live up to his own standards soon loses all dignity and all respect. Therefore, dear wife, make it your concern to be and to appear in every gesture, word, and deed most modest and most virtuous.

"A great part of modesty, remember, consists in tempering all one's gestures with gravity and a mature manner. One must temper one's mind and every word of one's speech, even within the household and among one's own family, all the more outside among strangers. I shall be truly glad if I see that you disdain the frivolous mannerisms, the habit of tossing the hands about, the chattering that some little girls do all day, in the house, at the door, and wherever they go. They talk now with this friend, now with that one; they ask a lot of questions and say a lot of things that they don't know as well as a lot that they do. All that is the way to get yourself the reputation of an irresponsible featherbrain. Silence is as it always has been, the peak of dignity and the source of respect for a woman. Talking too much has been ever the habit and sign of a silly fool. So be glad to listen quietly and to talk less than you listen. If you do talk, never on any account tell our secrets to others or be too eager to know their affairs. A woman who spends all day chattering and agitating about things that do not concern the welfare of her household, while neglecting the things that do, indulges an ugly habit and brings contempt on herself. But if you govern the family with proper diligence, you will preserve and put to good use all the resources of the household."

Lionardo: And I imagine you taught her the management of the household as you taught her other things?

Giannozzo: Don't you doubt it. Of course I did my best to make her in every way an excellent mother of the household. "Dear wife," I told her, "you should view it as your job to give the house such an orderly routine that no one is ever idle. Give everyone some suitable job to do. And where you see reliable loyalty and hard work, give all the responsibility that may properly be given. At the same time, keep your eye on what everyone is doing. Make sure that those who are busy with things that are useful and beneficial for the family are aware that you will witness their merit. If someone works more diligently and lovingly at his task than the others, be sure, dear wife, that you do not forget to praise him in their presence. Thus in the future he will long to be still more helpful every day, knowing he can count on your appreciation. The others will want to please you, too, as much as those you have praised most. Together, let us reward everyone according to his merit. In that way we shall make all our servants loyal and devoted to us and our affairs.

Lionardo: But, Giannozzo, we all know that servants and even other members of the household are apt to be persons of small intelligence. Generally if they had more capacity for work and finer feelings, they would not stay with us but would learn some other trade. Did you teach your wife how to handle rough and uncouth persons, therefore, and how to make them obey her?

*Giannozzo:*The fact is that servants are as obedient as masters are skilled in commanding. Some people, as I have observed myself, want their servants to obey them in matters where they themselves can give no direction. Others never know how to be the real master or to convince others that that's what they are. Remember, my children, no servant will listen and obey unless you know how to command. Nor will any resist and rebel if you know how to rule in a spirit of moderation and wisdom.

It is good to know not only how to make your servants obey but how to make them love and revere you. I find that the best way to make the impression of a real master is to do what I told my wife to do, talk as little as possible with her maid and even less with other servants. Too much familiarity kills respect. I also told her to give her orders in detail and at frequent intervals. She should not act like some people, who call everyone together and announce, "one of you do this," and then, when no one does it, all are equally at fault and no one is personally responsible.

I also said that she should order maids and all her servants never to leave the house without permission. They should all be on call and ready to help. She was never to give permission to all to go out at once, for there should be someone in the house on guard at any time. If anything happened, someone should always be there. I have always preferred to organize my house so that at any hour of the day or night, one person in the house was in charge in case something came up. There should also always be geese and dogs in a house, animals that are watchful and, as you know, both suspicious and affectionate. One wakes the other and calls out the whole crowd, and so the household is always safe—that is my way. To return to our subject, however, I told my wife not only never to give them all leave to go out at the same time, but also, if they came in late, to insist firmly, gently, and with deliberation on knowing the reason for it.

Besides this I said: "Since it does often happen that among servants, however obedient and reverent, occasional disagreements and conflicts arise, I charge you, dear wife, never to interfere in any such quarrel. Don't ever give any member of your household cause to feel that, in act or word, he can overstep what ought to be his bounds. Don't listen, dear wife, or show favor when one of them reports evil of another or brings an argument to you. The household full of quarrels can never abide in constancy of plan and purpose and, therefore, can never serve you well. If someone thinks that he has been injured through another's report to you and through your listening to it, he will carry a fire in his bosom and always be watching for a chance to revenge himself. In many ways he will try to make you condemn that person. He will be delighted to find that the other has committed some grave offense against the service of our house, for which he may be sent away. Should this wish of his be fulfilled, he will also feel free to contrive a similar disgrace for anyone else he dislikes. But if anyone can at his whim cause someone else to be discharged from our household, don't you see, dear wife, that he is no longer our servant, but our master? Even if he cannot quite gain his ends, he can keep our household in a state of agitation. He will be constantly thinking how, since he may have lost your good will, he can manage best for himself. He does not care at all if his profit be our loss. Even after he has left your service, such a man will keep trying to lay the blame on us and thus excuse his own past conduct. As you see, there is danger in a servant who speaks ill of the other servants and quarrels with them, whether you keep him or send him away. In either case he brings public disgrace. If you keep him, besides, you must always be changing your household staff, for people who don't want to serve our servant will always seek new masters. For this they will excuse themselves and cast the blame on you. Their words will get you a reputation for being either proud and aloof or avaricious and petty."

The truth is, my children, that when there are quarrels in the household, the masters inevitably suffer part of the harm done. But if the masters are not unwise, the house will not be quarrelsome. It is the poor judgment of the master that makes some families shameless and undisciplined and, as a result, always turbulent, poorly served, loaded with practical difficulties and public ignominy. The father of a family must detest talebearers, who are the source and cause of every quarrel, conflict, and intrigue. He should discharge them instantly. To see his household free of argument, peaceful, and harmonious should make him happy. This excellent state is one he can make sure of if he so desires. He must only do as I instructed my wife—never lend his ear or his mind to any sort of complaints or quarrels.

I further said to my wife that if a member of the household failed to obey her or to be as amenable and devoted as the peace and quiet of the family required, she should never be provoked into fighting with him or screaming at him. "It is an ugly thing," I said, "if women like you, dear wife, who are honorable and worthy of all respect, are seen with wild-eyed contorted expressions, screaming, threatening, and throwing their arms about. All the neighbors would reprove and mock you, and you would give everyone something to talk about. A woman of authority, such as I hope you, dear wife, will gradually come to be, maintains a constant modesty and dignity of manner. She would be grievously mistaken, not only if she raised her voice in reprimanding members of the household but if in commanding and discussing things she used a very loud voice. Some women talk in the house as if the whole family were deaf, or as if they wanted the whole neighborhood to hear every word. This is a sign of arrogance, a peasant habit. It suits the mountain girls who are used to calling to each other from slope to slope. You, dear wife, should admonish people with gentleness of gesture and of words, not with an air of indulgence and laxness but with calm and temperance. You must give orders in so reasonable and moderate a way that you will not only be obeyed but, because you show kindness and all the modesty compatible with your dignity, obeyed with love and devotion."

Lionardo: Where can you find such good advice for the edification of a perfect wife and mother as in these instructions of Giannozzo's? First he shows her the necessity of seeming and being most honorable and chaste; then he teaches her how to make herself duly obeyed, feared, loved, and respected. We ourselves shall be fortunate husbands if when we are married we have the wisdom to make use of your remarks, Giannozzo, and to teach our own wives to be like yours—shining examples of so many virtues!

♦ Marriage and the Family in Renaissance Florence

THE MARRIAGES OF GREGORIO DATI

In the name of God and the Virgin Mary, of Blessed Michael the Archangel, of SS. John the Baptist and John the Evangelist, of SS. Peter and Paul, of the holy scholars, SS. Gregory and Jerome, and of St. Mary Magdalene and St. Elisabeth and all the blessed saints in heaven—may they ever intercede for us—I shall record here how I married my second wife, Isabetta, known as Betta, the daughter of Mari di Lorenzo Vilanuzzi and of Monna Veronica, daughter of Pagolo d'Arrigo Guglielmi, and I shall also record the promises which were made to me. May God and his Saints grant by their grace that they be kept.

On March 31, 1393, I was betrothed to her and on Easter Monday, April 7, I gave her a ring. On June 22, a Sunday, I became her husband in the name of God and good fortune. Her first cousins, Giovanni and Lionardo di Domenico Arrighi, promised that she should have a dowry of 900 gold florins and that, apart from the dowry, she should have the income from a farm in S. Fiore a Elsa which had been left her as a legacy by her

SOURCE: Excerpts from G. Brucker, ed., *Two Memoirs of Renaissance Florence* (New York: Harper & Row, 1967), pp. 113–115, 123, 132–134; reprinted in G. Brucker, ed., *The Society of Renaissance Florence* (New York: Harper & Row, 1971), pp. 29–41, 69–70. Reprinted by permission of HarperCollins Publishers.

mother, Monna Veronica. It was not stated at the time how much this amounted to but it was understood that she would receive the accounts. We arranged our match very simply indeed and with scarcely any discussion. God grant that nothing but good may come of it. On the 26th of that same June, I received a payment of 800 gold florins from the bank of Giacomino and Company. This was the dowry. I invested in the shop of Buonaccorso Berardi and his partners. At the same time I received the trousseau which my wife's cousins valued at 106 florins, in the light of which they deducted 6 florins from another account, leaving me the equivalent of 100 florins. But from what I heard from her, and what I saw myself, they had overestimated it by 30 florins or more. However, from politeness, I said nothing about this. . . . Our Lord God was pleased to call to Himself the blessed soul of . . . Betta, on Monday, October 2 [1402] . . . and the next day, Tuesday, at three in the afternoon she was buried in our grave in S. Spirito. May God receive her soul in his glory. Amen. . . .

I record that on May 8, 1403, I was betrothed to Ginevra, daughter of Antonio di Piero Piuvichese Brancacci, in the church of S. Maria sopra Porta. The dowry was 1,000 florins: 700 in cash and 300 in a farm at Campi. On . . . May 20, we were married, but we held no festivities or wedding celebrations as we were in mourning for Manetto Dati [Gregorio's son], who had died the week before. God grant us a good life together. Ginevra had been married before for four years to Tommaso Brancacci, by whom she had an eight-month-old son. She is now in her twenty-first year.

After that [1411] it was God's will to recall to Himself the blessed soul of my wife Ginevra. She died in childbirth after lengthy suffering, which she bore with remarkable strength and patience. She was perfectly lucid at the time of her death, when she received all the sacraments: confession, communion, extreme unction, and a papal indulgence granting absolution for all her sins. . . . It comforted her greatly, and she returned her soul to her Creator on September 7. . . . On Friday the 8th she was honorably buried and on the 9th, masses were said for her soul.

Memo that on Tuesday, January 28, 1421, I made an agreement with Niccolò d'Andrea del Benino to take his niece Caterina for my lawful wife. She is the daughter of the late Dardano di Niccolò Guicciardini and of Monna Tita, Andrea del Benino's daughter. We were betrothed on the morning of Monday, February 3, the Eve of Carnival. I met Piero and Giovanni di Messer Luigi [Guicciardini] in the church of S. Maria sopra Porta, and Niccolò d'Andrea del Benino was our mediator. The dowry promised me was 600 florins, and the notary was Ser Niccolò di Ser Verdiano. I went to dine with her that evening in Piero's house and the Saturday after Easter . . . I gave her the ring and then on Sunday evening, March 30, she came to live in our house simply and without ceremony. . . .

TWO MARRIAGES IN THE VALORI
FAMILY, 1452 AND 1476

I record this event, that on July 15, 1452, Niccolò di Piero Capponi sent for me and, after many circumlocutions, he asked me if I were still in a mood to marry. I told him that I would not diverge from his judgment in this matter or in any other, for I had great faith in him and was certain that his advice would be prudent and honest. Then he told me that Piero di Messer Andrea de'Pazzi had two nubile daughters and that he was willing to give me the girl which I preferred. He was making this offer to me on Piero's behalf. I accepted the bait willingly and asked for two days' grace to confer with several of my relatives, which I did extensively, and was advised by them to proceed. After two days, I returned to Niccolò and told him to ask Piero's consent to marry the eldest whom I knew well, for up to the age of twelve we were practically raised together. [For a dowry, Bartolomeo received 14,000 florins of communal bonds, valued at 2,000 florins. His wife Caterina died on November 20, 1474, leaving two boys and six girls.] . . .

On this day, July 5, 1476, Lorenzo de' Medici [the Magnificent] told me that he wanted to speak to me, and I visited him immediately. He said that Averardo d'Alamanno Salviati had come to see him and told him that he had a daughter of marriageable age that he would willingly give her to my son Filippo, requesting that Lorenzo be the broker. I replied that this pleased me but that I wished first to speak to Filippo to learn his views, which I did that same evening. Finding my son disposed to follow my judgment and my will, on the next day I asked Lorenzo to conclude the business. He sent for Averardo and they agreed on the conditions. On July 7, Lorenzo came to my house and told me that the alliance was sealed, that Alessandra, the daughter of Averardo Salviati, would be the wife of my son Filippo with a dowry of 2,000 florins. And we formally sealed the agreement in the palace of the Signoria, with Lorenzo himself pronouncing the details of the settlement.

MARRIAGE NEGOTIATIONS: THE DEL
BENE, 1381

[February 20] In the name of God, yesterday I concluded the agreement with Giovanni di Luca [a marriage broker] for the marriage of Caterina [Del Bene, Giovanni's daughter] with Andrea di Castello da Quarata, with a dowry of 900 florins. I could not reduce that sum, although I tried hard to persuade Giovanni to adhere to the terms of our previous discussions. But things are very much up in the air, and Giovanni insisted upon it, alleging many reasons. So, to avoid the rupture of negotiations, I surrendered on this point.

Then I requested Giovanni to maintain secrecy about this affair, as we have agreed, and he said that he would give me a reply. Last night he said that it was impossible, because they wanted to discuss the matter with their relatives, who were so numerous that they couldn't keep the affair secret. However, they are very pleased with this match, and they didn't want to displease me on this point. So, after much effort, I persuaded them to keep it secret through Sunday, and then everyone is free to publicize it as he wishes. So, on the same day, our relatives and Amerigo's friends will be informed. . . .

The women of your household to whom I have spoken say that the girl wishes to have a satin gown, which seems too lavish to me. Write me your opinion. On Sunday, I will meet with Giovanni [di Luca] and we will settle this affair in one day, and also the church where the betrothal ceremony will take place. And I will do the same with Lemmo [Balducci] and will explain the reason to Giovanni. And that evening I will relate everything to our women, because Lapa says that Monna Giovanni di Messer Meo has said that Amerigo [Del Bene, Giovanni's son] has a bride and that she informed her son Niccolò.

The marriage chest will be furnished in the customary manner; it will cost between 70 and 75 florins. They will provide the ring, so that everything will be ready at the proper time. In your letter, remind me of anything that, in your opinion, should be done with respect to these marriages.

There is no further news concerning Antonia [Francesco's daughter] except that her mother was very unhappy about that negotiation at Borgo S. Lorenzo. It is my feeling that we shouldn't push this issue and annoy her further, and that we will find some other good prospect for her. You should advise us how we should proceed with the girls; that is, when we should go to see Amerigo's bride, and when the bridegroom should come to see Caterina. I think that Andrea [da Quarata] should come to our house first, and then Caterina, accompanied by our women, should go to see Amerigo's bride. Write me whether you think that Andrea should give the ring that day [of the betrothal ceremony] or not, so that we can arrange the matter beforehand. . . .

[February 21] I wrote you last night and sent the letter off this morning, and so I have little to tell you save that I met Giovanni [di Luca] Mozzi today. We agreed that the betrothal would take place on the first Sunday in Lent, and we may choose the church where it will take place. I don't think that Amerigo's betrothal should be kept secret any longer, so that they won't have any excuse for complaining. I think that on Saturday, Amerigo should go to them [the Balducci] and tell them that we are arranging to marry Caterina, as well as give him a bride. He should tell them everything, and then we can settle that business, and they will learn about it a few days before it becomes public knowledge. Amerigo will write about the deliberations of the women concerning Caterina's trousseau.

I have heard that Dora [Francesco's wife] is somewhat unhappy about this marriage, seeing that Antonia [her daughter] is still unwed. . . . I also think that Antonia may be upset when she sees Caterina's beautiful gown. I urge you to write a comforting letter to Dora, and tell her that we will find a husband for Antonia, if God wills it. Nor should Antonia be unhappy about the new gown, for I think that it will not be long before she too will have one. I shall not be pleased, if I see any discontent in a household where there should be joy.

[February 24] . . . Concerning Caterina, we have concluded the marriage agreement for 900 florins. . . . They wanted to hold the betrothal ceremony on the first Sunday of Lent, and Giovanni [Mozzi] and I agreed on that point, and also that it will take place in [the church of] S. Apollinare. We haven't yet discussed the guest list, but I think that they will want a large assembly. It is my feeling that we should hold the betrothal ceremony before the dinner, so there will be time afterwards to accept and to deliver the contract. I don't know whom they wish to give the ring, but tomorrow I will settle these matters of the guest list and the ring. The women have decided that Caterina's dress will be made of blue silk and that the gown will form part of the dowry; this was a wise decision. Tomorrow everything will be settled.

It is true that Dora, whom I have always considered a sensible woman, has been behaving in a way that redounds neither to her nor to our dignity. She has not wished to join in any part of this affair. Her attitude is so bizarre and so melancholy that she cries all day and says that your daughter [Antonia] will never be married and that you don't care. She says the most shocking things that I have ever heard, and has made your whole family miserable. I am very annoyed by her conduct, and it would please me if you wrote to comfort and correct her, so that she will be content with this affair, and not vexed.

I was with Ser Naddo [di Ser Nepo] on Saturday and told him about Caterina's marriage, and my opinions on the betrothal of the girl [Amerigo's bride] and of Caterina, and also the question of the church and the guest lists. I also informed him of the penalty [for breaking the betrothal contract] of 2,000 florins, and every other detail concerning this affair. Today Ser Naddo told me that Lemmo is content with everything, except that if Caterina's husband gives her the ring, then he wants Amerigo to give it to his daughter; otherwise not. He also says that the penalty should be no more than 1,000 florins, since the rumors of the dowry which he has provided have ruined him. Concerning the ring, he says that he wants it to be arranged in this way, to do like the others. Concerning the penalty, I told him that you had instructed me in this matter as it was agreed, and that I could not alter it without writing you. . . .

[Letter from Naddo di Ser Nepo to Francesco di Jacopo Del Bene, February 24, 1381] After you left here, Giovanni d'Amerigo sent for me to inform me of the marriage alliance which, by the grace of God, has been arranged between you and Lemmo. We discussed certain problems, among which was the fact that in the agreement was a clause providing for a penalty of 2,000 florins. After our discussion, I spoke with Lemmo and he agreed to everything except the penalty of 2,000 florins. He argued as follows: "The rumors of this large dowry which I have given are ruining me, with respect to the taxes which I pay to the Commune. And with this matter of a 2,000 florin penalty, everyone will believe that I have given a dowry of that amount, which will destroy me, and surely they [the Del Bene] should not want this to happen. However, this business has been given by Francesco and myself to Messer Bartolomeo [Panciatichi?] for arbitration, and I will abide fully by his decision." On the 24th of this month, I met Giovanni and told him what Lemmo wanted, and that he wanted a penalty of only 1,000 florins, and the reasons for this. Giovanni told me that you had so arranged matters that he could not reply without consulting you.

Speaking with all due reverence and faith, it appears to me that this issue should not disturb or impede this marriage, considering the great friendship which has always existed between you and Lemmo, and which now should be greater than ever. Moreover, you and Amerigo should desire to further his interests, and approve a penalty of 1,000 florins and no more. They entered into this marriage with a positive attitude, and so did you, and therefore I pray you as fervently as I can to be content. I am always ready to carry out your commands.

MARRIAGE NEGOTIATIONS: THE STROZZI, 1464–1465

[April 20, 1464] . . . Concerning the matter of a wife [for Filippo], it appears to me that if Francesco di Messer Guglielmino Tanagli wishes to give his daughter, that it would be a fine marriage. . . . Now I will speak with Marco [Parenti, Alessandra's son-in-law], to see if there are other prospects that would be better, and if there are none, then we will learn if he wishes to give her [in marriage]. . . . Francesco Tanagli has a good reputation, and he has held office, not the highest, but still he has been in office. You may ask: "Why should he give her to someone in exile?" There are three reasons. First, there aren't many young men of good family who have both virtue and property. Secondly, she has only a small dowry, 1,000 florins, which is the dowry of an artisan. . . . Third, I believe that he will give her away, because he has a large family and he will need help to settle them. . . .

[July 26, 1465] . . . Marco Parenti came to me and told me that for some time, he has been considering how to find a wife for you. . . . There is the daughter of Francesco di Messer Guglielmino Tanagli, and until now there hasn't been anyone who is better suited for you than this girl. It is true that we haven't discussed this at length, for a reason which you understand. However, we have made secret inquiries, and the only people who are willing to make a marriage agreement with exiles have some flaw, either a lack of money or something else. Now money is the least serious drawback, if the other factors are positive. . . . Francesco is a good friend of Marco and he trusts him. On S. Jacopo's day, he spoke to him discreetly and persuasively, saying that for several months he had heard that we were interested in the girl and . . . that when we had made up our minds, she will come to us willingly. [He said that] you were a worthy man, and that his family had always made good marriages, but that he had only a small dowry to give her, and so he would prefer to send her outside of Florence to someone of worth, rather than to give her to someone here, from among those who were available, with little money. . . . He invited Marco to his house and he called the girl down. . . . Marco said that she was attractive and that she appeared to be suitable. We have information that she is affable and competent. She is responsible for a large family (there are twelve children, six boys and six girls), and the mother is always pregnant and isn't very competent. . . .

[August 17, 1465] . . . Sunday morning I went to the first mass at S. Reparata . . . to see the Adimari girl, who customarily goes to that mass, and I found the Tanagli girl there. Not knowing who she was, I stood beside her. . . . She is very attractive, well proportioned, as large or larger than Caterina [Alessandra's daughter]. . . . She has a long face, and her features are not very delicate, but they aren't like a peasant's. From her demeanor, she does not appear to me to be indolent. . . . I walked behind her as we left the church, and thus I realized that she was one of the Tanagli. So I am somewhat enlightened about. . . .

[August 31, 1465] . . . I have recently received some very favorable information [about the Tanagli girl] from two individuals. . . . They are in agreement that whoever gets her will be content. . . . Concerning her beauty, they told me what I had already seen, that she is attractive and well-proportioned. Her face is long, but I couldn't look directly into her face, since she appeared to be aware that I was examining her . . . and so she turned away from me like the wind. . . . She reads quite well . . . and she can dance and sing. . . . Her father is one of the most respected young men of Florence, very civilized in his manners. He is fond of this girl, and it appears that he has brought her up well.

So yesterday I sent for Marco and told him what I had learned. And we talked about the matter for a while, and decided that he should say something to the father and give him a little hope, but not so much that we couldn't withdraw, and find out from him the amount of the dowry. . . . Marco and Francesco [Tanagli] had a discussion about this yesterday (I haven't seen him since), and Marco should inform you about it one of these days, and you will then understand more clearly what should follow.

May God help us to choose what will contribute to our tranquillity and to the consolation of us all. . . .

[September 13, 1465] . . . Marco came to me and said that he had met with Francesco Tanagli, who had spoken very coldly, so that I understand that he had changed his mind. They say that he wants to discuss the matter with his brother-in-law, Messer Antonio Ridolfi. . . . And he [Francesco] says that it would be a serious matter to send his daughter so far away [to Naples], and to a house that might be described as a hotel. And he spoke in such a way that it is clear that he has changed his mind. I believe that this is the result of the long delay in our replying to him, both yours and Marco's. Two weeks ago, he could have given him a little hope. Now this delay has angered him, and he has at hand some prospect that is more attractive. . . . I am very annoyed by this business; I can't recall when I have been so troubled. For I felt that this marriage would have satisfied our needs better than any other we could have found. . . .

[Filippo Strozzi eventually married Fiametta di Donato Adimari, in 1466.]

ILLEGITIMACY AND MARRIAGE, 1355

Agnola, the illegitimate daughter of Piccio [Velluti's brother], was born in Trapani in Sicily, of the proprietress of a baker's shop, or rather a lasagna shop. While Piccio was alive, he did not want to bring her here [to Florence], although my wife and I urged him to do so. After his death, Leonardo Ferrucci [Velluti's brother-in-law] went to Sicily and . . . found Agnola alive and her mother dead. He then asked me to bring her [to Florence]. But I had some doubt that she was really Piccio's child, seeing that he did not wish to bring her back, and also considering that in his will he left her 50 florins for her dowry, if she were truly his daughter. . . . But seeing that there was no other descendant in our immediate family except Fra Lottieri and myself and my son Lamberto, and my niece Tessa di Gherardo, and so that she would not fall upon evil ways, and for the love of God, I allowed her to come. She was then ten years old, and I welcomed her and I—and my family—treated her as though she were my own daughter. And truly she was the daughter of Piccio, considering her features and the fact that she resembled him in every way.

When she reached the age of matrimony, I desired to arrange a match for her, and she caused me a great deal of trouble. I was willing to spend up to 300 florins [for her dowry] but could not find anyone interested in her. Finally, after much time had passed, and with her situation not improving, she began to complain about me to relatives and others, saying that I didn't know how to get her out of the house [i.e., to marry her]. In the cloth factory which my son Lamberto was operating with Ciore Pitti, there was a factor named Piero Talenti, who was earning a [yearly] salary of 64 florins, and later he received 72 florins. And since I couldn't find any better prospect, I married her to him in May, 1355. . . .

Later there occurred the plague of 1363 . . . and first Piero's four children died, and then Piero himself, and I had to bury him. He left about 35 florins worth of household furnishings, and I had to provide mourning clothes for Agnola, and I could not get back her dowry of 160 florins. . . . Since her husband's death, Agnola has lived with me. I wanted to arrange another marriage for her, but since she is both a widow and illegitimate, I have not been able to find her a husband. So, to protect my honor and to assist her in her need, Fra Lottieri arranged for her to become a tertiary in his order in December, 1366. . . .

A BROKEN MARRIAGE, 1377

To you, lord priors . . . of the city and Commune of Florence, with reverence and tears, this petition is presented by Monna Nicolosa, widow of Giovanni di Ventura, a mercer, of the parish of S. Reparata of Florence. It is true that Duccio di Agostino di Duccio de'Benegli of S. Martino la Palma took as his wife Monna Madelena, daughter of Giovanni [di Ventura]. And having taken her, Duccio beat her and maltreated her unmercifully, and wished to kill her without any cause. With the license of the priors then in office and with their messenger, Giovanni brought his daughter back to his house. It was then formally decreed by the priors and other good men that Duccio and Agostino had to give her a certain amount of food each year. Agostino had recently left S. Martino la Palma to stay in Florence, and last July, this hypocritical and perverse man and his son Duccio . . . conspired to kill Giovanni di Ventura, an artisan and a weak man, the father-in-law of Duccio, who only a short time ago was one of the priors, and has been an official [of his guild] on several occasions. Agostino ordered Duccio to assassinate Giovanni, and also told his son Felice to help him. . . .

Moreover, Agostino loaned his horse, saddled and ready, to Duccio at his house in Florence, on which Duccio fled to Pisa immediately after the homicide, to the house of his relatives there. Desiring to put into execution this evil plan, Duccio with his companions . . . assaulted Giovanni di Ventura on a plot of land in the parish of S. Maria de Falgano di Valdisieve. . . . They struck and wounded Giovanni with knives, as a result of which he fell to the earth dead. And if it had not been for the outcry which arose, they would have gone to the farmhouse to burn it down and kill Giovanni's wife and children. . . .

Agostino and Duccio all belong to a powerful clan, the house of Benegli in S. Martino la Palma, and they are among the wealthiest and most powerful members of that family, of those who live in the *contado*. And there are more than sixty men with arms, rich and powerful, and they continue to threaten to kill Giovanni's sons. Moreover, Duccio and Agostino have forbidden anyone to cultivate the farm which belonged to Giovanni, so that the land lies idle, and they [the members of Giovanni's family] have nothing for their sustenance. So, having killed the father, [and] retained the dowry of the daughter, they now wish to starve the family, and they will continue to persecute them into the next world. . . .

THE CHILDREN OF GREGORIO DATI, 1404

Glory, honor and praise be to Almighty God. Continuing from folio 5, I shall list the children which He shall in His grace bestow on me and my wife, Ginevra.

On Sunday morning at terce, 27 April of the same year, Ginevra gave birth to our first-born son. He was baptized at the hour of vespers on Monday the 28th in the church of S. Giovanni. We named him Manetto Domenico. His sponsors in God's love were Bartolo di Giovanni di Niccola, Giovanni di Michelozzo, a belt-maker, and Domenico di Deo, a goldsmith. God make him good.

At the third hour of Thursday, 19 March 1405, Ginevra gave birth to a female child of less than seven months. She had not realized she was pregnant, since for four months she had been ailing as though she were not, and in the end was unable to hold it. We baptized it at once in the church of S. Giovanni. The sponsors were Bartolo, Monna Buona, another lady, and the blind woman. Having thought at first that it was a boy, we named it Agnolo Giovanni. It died at dawn on Sunday morning, 22 March, and was buried before the sermon.

At terce on Tuesday morning, 8 June 1406, Ginevra had her third child, a fine full-term baby girl whom we had baptized on Friday morning, 9 June. We christened her Elisabetta Caterina and she will be called Lisabetta in memory of my dead wife, Betta. The sponsors were Fra Lorenzo, Bartolo, and the blind woman.

On 4 June 1407, a Saturday, Ginevra gave birth after a nine-month pregnancy to a little girl whom we had baptized on the evening of Tuesday the 7th. We named her Antonia Margherita and we shall call her Antonia. Her godfather was Nello di Ser Piero Nelli, a neighbor. God grant her good fortune.

At terce, Sunday, 31 July 1411, Ginevra gave birth to a very attractive baby boy whom we had baptized on 4 August. The sponsors were my colleagues among the Standard-bearers of the Militia Companies with the

SOURCE: G. Brucker, ed., *Two Memories of Renaissance Florence* (New York: Harper & Row, 1967), pp. 126–128, 134–136. Reprinted by permission of HarperCollins Publishers.

exception of two: Giorgio and Bartolomeo Fioravanti. We called the child Niccolò. God bless him. God was pleased to call the child very shortly to Himself. He died of dysentery on 22 October at terce. May he intercede with God for us.

At terce on Sunday, 1 October 1412, Ginevra had a son whom, from devotion to St. Jerome—since it was yesterday that her pains began—I called Girolamo Domenico. The sponsors were Master Bartolomeo del Carmine, Cristofano di Francesco di Ser Giovanni, and Lappuccio di Villa, and his son Bettino. God grant him and us health and make him a good man.

God willed that the blessed soul of our daughter Betta should return to Him after a long illness. She passed away during the night between Tuesday and the first Wednesday of Lent at four in the morning, 21 February 1414. She was seven years and seven months, and I was sorely grieved at her death. God grant she pray for us.

On 1 May 1415, at the hour of terce on a Wednesday, God granted us a fine little boy, and I had him baptized at four on Saturday morning. Jacopo di Francesco di Tura and Aringhieri di Jacopo, the wool merchant, were his godfathers. May God grant that he be healthy, wise, and good. We named him after the two holy apostles, Jacopo and Filippo, on whose feast day he was born and we shall call him Filippo.

At eleven o'clock on Friday, 24 April 1416, Ginevra gave birth to a baby girl after a painful and almost fatal labor. The child was baptized immediately on S. Marco's Day, the 25th. We called her Ghita in memory of our mother. Monna Mea di Franchino was her godmother.

Manetto died in Pisa in January 1418. He had been very sick and was buried in S. Martino. Pippo died on 2 August 1419 in Val di Pesa in a place called Polonia. This is recorded in notebook B.

At two o'clock on the night following Monday 17 July, Lisa was born. She was baptized by Master Pagolo from Montepulciano, a preaching friar, on Wednesday at seven o'clock. God console us, amen. She died later.

Altogether Ginevra and I had eleven children: four boys and seven girls.

Offspring, 1422

The following is a list of the children begotten by me.

I was single when my first son, Maso,[1] was born on 21 December 1391—this appears on the back of page 4. Before his birth I had got Bandecca with child but she had a miscarriage in her sixth month in July 1390. After that, as I have indicated on page 5, I had eight children by my

---

1. Maso was the child born of the slave girl, Margherita, in Valencia.

second wife, Betta: five boys and three girls. Then, as I show on page 10, I had eleven children by my third wife, Ginevra: four boys and seven girls. Altogether, not counting the one that did not live to be baptized, I have had twenty children: ten boys and ten girls. Of these, Maso, Bernardo, Girolamo, Ghita and Betta are still alive. Praise be to God for all things, amen.

Caterina, my fourth wife, miscarried after four months and the child did not live long enough to receive baptism. That was in August 1421.

On 4 October 1422, at one o'clock on a Sunday night, Caterina gave birth to a daughter. We had Fra Aducci and Fra Giovanni Masi baptize her on Monday the 5th and christen her Ginevra Francesca. May God bless her.

At three o'clock on Friday, 7 January 1424, Caterina gave birth to a fine healthy boy whom we had baptized on the morning of Saturday the 8th.

The godparents were the Abbot Simone of S. Felice and Michele di Manetto. We christened the child Antonio Felice. God grant he turn out a good man.

Between eight and nine o'clock on the morning of Tuesday, 20 March 1425, Caterina had another healthy and attractive child who was baptized the following day—the 21st—which was the feast of St. Benedict. Fra Cristofano, Father Provincial of the monks of S. Maria Novella, the prior, Master Alessio, Master Girolamo, and Fra Benedetto were his sponsors. We christened him Lionardo Benedetto. God make him a good man.

At three in the morning of 26 July 1426, Caterina had a fine little girl whom we christened Anna Bandecca. The baptism was on the 27th and her sponsors were Antonino and Monna Lucia. God grant her His grace and that she be a comfort to us.

At two o'clock in the night of Monday, 28 August 1427, Caterina gave birth to a fine little girl. She was baptized on Wednesday morning the 22nd and christened Filippa Felice. The Abbot of S. Felice, Giovanni di Messer Forese Sanviati, and Giuliano di Tommaso di Guccio, who had served in the same office with me, were her sponsors. God grant she be a source of consolation to us and fill her with His grace. Our Lord called her to Himself on 19 October 1430. This appears on page 30, notebook E. May God bless her.

At about eleven o'clock on Saturday, 2 June 1431, Caterina gave birth to a girl who was baptized on Monday the 4th in S. Giovanni's and christened Bartolomea Domenica. See notebook E, page 46.

Our Lord was pleased to call to Himself and to eternal life our two blessed children, Lionardo and Ginevra, on Saturday, 6 October 1431. This appears in notebook one, page 14. Lionardo had been in perfect health twenty-four hours before his death. God bless them and grant us the grace to bear this loss with fortitude.

♦ *Niccolo Machiavelli*

SELECTIONS FROM *MANDRAGOLA*

Scene IX (Timoteo alone)

. . . Messer Nicia and Callimaco are both rich and each for diverse reasons can be well plucked. The thing must be kept dark, that's as important to them as it is to me. Be it as they wish, I'll not repent me of it. Forsooth I doubt not we shall find it hard, for Donna Lucrezia is sensible and good. But I'll work on her kindness, all women have little brains, and if one of them knows enough to say two words, there must be a sermon about it: for in the realm of the blind the one-eyed is king. And here she is with her mother, who is a very beast and will be of great use in bringing her around to my wishes.

Scene X (Sostrata and Lucrezia)

Sostrata: I'm sure you believe, daughter, that I set as much store by your honor as anybody in the world, and that I should never advise you to do anything that was not good. I have told you and I tell you again that if Brother Timoteo says that there's nothing in it to trouble your conscience, you may do it without another thought.

Lucrezia: I have never had a doubt that the longing Messer Nicia has for children would sooner or later make us do something foolish; and just on this account, whenever he has come to me with some notion, have I been jealous and suspicious of it. But of all the things that we have tried, this last seems to me the strangest; to have to submit my body to this outrage, and to cause a man to die for outraging me; I'd never have believed, no not if I were the last woman left in the world and the human race had to start all over again from me, that such a thing could have fallen to my lot.

Sostrata: I can't explain such matters, daughter; you'll talk to the friar and you'll see what he tells you, and then do as you are advised by him, by us and by those who wish you well.

Lucrezia: I'm sweating with rage.

Scene XI (Timoteo, Lucrezia, and Sostrata)

Timoteo: You are welcome both. I know what you wish to know from me. Messer Nicia has told me. Truly I have been in my books more than

SOURCE: B. Tierney and J. Scott, *Western Societies: A Documentation History*, Vol. 1 (New York: Knopf, 1984), pp. 371–373.

two hours studying this case, and after much question, I find many things both in general and in particular that are in our favor.

Lucrezia: Are you serious or jesting?

Timoteo: Ah! Donna Lucrezia, are these matters for jesting? Is that what you think of me?

Lucrezia: Father, no; but this seems to me the strangest business I ever heard of.

Timoteo: Madam, I believe you: but I would not have you say any more in this vein. There are many things which seen at a distance appear terrible, unbearable, strange; but when you come nearer to them they prove to be human, bearable, familiar; wherefore it is said that the fear is worse than the evil. And this is one of them.

Lucrezia: It's the will of God.

Timoteo: I'll go back to what I was saying at first. For the sake of your conscience you must go on this general principle: where there is a certain good and an uncertain evil, we must not forsake that good for fear of that evil. Here is a certain good, you will be with child. You will donate a soul to the Lord God. The uncertain evil is that he who lies with you after you've taken the potion, dies: but he will also find himself among those who will never die. But since the thing is dubious, it's right that Messer Nicia should run no risk. And if the act is sinful, it's only in a manner of speaking so after all, for the will is what sins, not the body: it's a sin on the grounds that it displeases your husband, and you please him: it's a sin on the grounds of taking pleasure in it, and you take no pleasure in it. Moreover the end is what you must consider in every case. Your end is to fill a seat in Paradise, to make your husband happy. The Bible says that the daughters of Lot, believing that they alone were left in the world, consorted with their father; and since their intention was good they did not sin.

Lucrezia: What would you persuade me to?

Sostrata: Let yourself be persuaded, daughter. Don't you see that a woman who has no children has no home? When her husband is dead she remains, like a beast, deserted by everyone.

Timoteo: I swear to you, Madam, by the holy sacrament, that your duty in this case is to obey your husband, though it were to eat meat on Wednesdays; which is a sin that no holy water can wash away.

Lucrezia: Where are you pushing me; father?

Timoteo: I'm urging you to things that you'll ask God to bless me for, and that next year you'll value more than now.

Sostrata: She'll do what you wish. I'll put her to bed myself to-night. What are you afraid of, idiot? There are fifty women in this land who would lift their hands to heaven for this that you'll be getting.

Lucrezia: I consent; but I don't expect to be alive tomorrow morning.

Timoteo: Have no fear, my daughter: I will pray God for you; I will say a prayer to the angel Rafael to be at your side. Go quickly and prepare for this mystery that the night will bring.

Sostrata: Rest in peace, father.

Lucrezia: God and Our Lady keep me from harm.

Everything ends happily for everyone. Callimaco arranges that he is the young man who is kidnapped and put to bed with Lucrezia. He suffers no ill effect from the mandrake, and he pleases Lucrezia so much that she decides to take him as a permanent lover. Nicia remains contentedly ignorant of the affair. One is left with a reasonable hope that Lucrezia's infertility will be overcome.

✦ Baldassare Castiglione

B *aldassare Castiglione was born near Mantua in 1478, the son of a noble courtier of the ruling Gonzaga family. After a period of polishing at the court of Milan and acquiring a deep love and knowledge of classical learning, Castiglione entered the service of the Gonzaga at Mantua in 1500, serving as a diplomat and military officer. From 1504 until 1516 he resided at the court of Urbino and became a leading figure in the service of the Montefeltro Duke Guidobaldo and his successor. Returning to Mantua, he reentered the employ of the marquis, functioning mostly as a diplomat. In 1524 Castiglione was appointed papal nuncio in Spain and soon after Bishop of Avila. He died in Toledo in 1529.*

Castiglione is mostly remembered for his Book of the Courtier, *one of the most evocative texts of the Renaissance. The book describes a series of discussions held at the court of Urbino in 1506 to define the perfect court gentlemen and lady (Book Three). The wide-ranging material in these dialogues crystallized many of the dominant ideals of the courtly aspect of the Italian Renaissance. In addition to* The Courtier, *Castiglione wrote both Latin and Italian poetry of fine quality.*

THE BOOK OF THE COURTIER

. . . I hold that many virtues of the mind are as necessary to a woman as to a man; also, gentle birth; to avoid affectation, to be naturally graceful in all her actions, to be mannerly, clever, prudent, not arrogant, not

SOURCE: Excerpts from Baldassare Castiglione, *The Book of the Courtier,* ed. by E. Mayhew, trans. by C. Singleton (Garden City, N.Y.: Anchor, 1959), pp. 206–213. Translation copyright © 1959 by Charles S. Singleton and Edgar de N. Mayhew. Used by permission of Doubleday, a division of Bantam Doubleday Dell Publishing Group, Inc.

envious, not slanderous, not vain, not contentious, not inept, to know how to gain and hold the favor of her mistress and of all others, to perform well and gracefully the exercises that are suitable for women. And I do think that beauty is more necessary to her than to the Courtier, for truly that woman lacks much who lacks beauty. Also she must be more circumspect, and more careful not to give occasion for evil being said of her, and conduct herself so that she may not only escape being sullied by guilt but even by the suspicion of it, for a woman has not so many ways of defending herself against false calumnies as a man has. But since Count Ludovico has set forth in great detail the chief profession of the Courtier, and has insisted that this be arms, I think it is also fitting to state what I judge that of the Court Lady to be, and when I have done this I shall think to have discharged the greater part of my assignment.

◆ ◆ ◆

[6] "And since words that have no subject matter of importance are vain and puerile, the Court Lady must have not only the good judgment to recognize the kind of person with whom she is speaking, but must have knowledge of many things, in order to entertain that person graciously; and let her know how in her talk to choose those things that are suited to the kind of person with whom she is speaking, and be careful lest, unintentionally, she might sometimes utter words that could offend him. Let her take care not to disgust him by indiscreet praise of herself or by being too prolix. Let her not proceed to mingle serious matters with playful or humorous discourse, or mix jests and jokes with serious talk. Let her not show ineptitude in pretending to know what she does not know, but let her seek modestly to do herself credit in what she does know—in all things avoiding affectation, as has been said. In this way she will be adorned with good manners; she will perform with surpassing grace the bodily exercises that are proper to women; her discourse will be fluent and most prudent, virtuous, and pleasant; thus, she will be not only loved but revered by everyone, and perhaps worthy of being considered the equal of this great Courtier, both in qualities of mind and of body."

◆ ◆ ◆

"Since I may fashion this Lady as I please, not only would I not have her engage in such robust and strenuous manly exercises, but even those that are becoming to a woman I would have her practice in a measured way and with that gentle delicacy that we have said befits her; and so when she dances, I should not wish to see her make movements that are too energetic and violent; nor, when she sings or plays, use those loud and oftrepeated diminutions that show more art than sweetness; likewise the musical instruments that she plays ought in my opinion to be appropriate to this intent. Consider what an ungainly thing it would be to see a woman playing drums, fifes, trumpets, or other like instruments; and this because their harshness hides and removes that suave gentleness which so adorns a woman in her every act. Hence, when she starts to dance or to make music of any kind, she ought to begin by letting herself be begged a little, and with a certain shyness bespeaking a noble shame that is the opposite of brazenness.

"Moreover, she must make her dress conform to this intent, and must clothe herself in such a way as not to appear vain and frivolous. But since women are not only permitted but bound to care more about beauty than men—and there are several sorts of beauty—this Lady must have the good judgment to see which are the garments that enhance her grace and are most appropriate to the exercises in which she intends to engage at a given time, and choose these. And when she knows that hers is a bright and cheerful beauty, she must enhance it with movements, words, and dress that tend toward the cheerful; just as another who senses that her own style is the gentle and grave ought to accompany it with like manners, in order to increase what is a gift of nature. Thus, if she is a little stouter or thinner than normal, or fair or dark, let her help herself in her dress, but in as hidden a way as possible; and all the while she keeps herself dainty and clean, let her appear to have no care or concern for this.

[9] "And since signor Gasparo asks further what these many things are that she should know about, and in what manner she ought to converse, and whether her virtues are to contribute to her conversation—I declare that I would have her know that which these gentlemen wished the Courtier to know. And, as for the exercises that we have said are unbecoming to her, I would have her at least possess such understanding of them as we may have of those things we do not practice; and this in order that she may know how to value and praise cavaliers more or less according to their merits.

"And, to repeat briefly a part of what has already been said, I wish this Lady to have knowledge of letters, of music, of painting, and know how to dance and how to be festive, adding a discreet modesty and the giving of a good impression of herself to those other things that have been required of the Courtier. And so, in her talk, her laughter, her play, her jesting, in short in everything, she will be most graceful and will converse appropriately with every person in whose company she may happen to be, using witticisms and pleasantries that are becoming to her. And although continence, magnanimity, temperance, fortitude of spirit, prudence, and the other virtues might appear to matter little in her association with others (though they can contribute something there too), I would have her adorned with all of these, not so much for the sake of that association as that she may be virtuous, and to the end that these virtues may make her worthy of being honored and that her every act may be informed by them."

[10] Then signor Gasparo said, laughing: "Since you have granted letters and continence and magnanimity and temperance to women, I am quite surprised that you do not wish them to govern cities, make laws, lead armies, and let the men stay at home to cook or spin."

The Magnifico replied, also laughing: "Perhaps that would not be so bad either." Then he added: "Don't you know that Plato, who certainly was no great friend to women, put them in charge of the city and gave all martial duties to the men? Don't you believe that many women could be found who would know how to govern cities and armies as well as men do? But I have not given them these duties, because I am fashioning a Court Lady, not a Queen. I know full well that you would like tacitly to renew the false aspersion which signor Ottaviano cast on women yesterday, representing them as very imperfect creatures, incapable of any virtuous action, and of very little worth and of no dignity compared to men: but, in truth, both you and he would be making a very great mistake in thinking so."

[11] Then signor Gasparo said: "I do not wish to repeat things that have been said already; but you would very much wish to make me say something which would hurt these ladies' feelings and make them my enemies, just as you wish to win their favor by flattering them falsely. But they are so far superior to other women in their discretion that they love the truth (even if the truth is not so much to their credit) more than they love false praise; nor do they resent it if anyone says that men have greater dignity, and they will declare that you have said surprising things in attributing to the Court Lady certain absurd impossibilities and so many virtues that Socrates and Cato and all the philosophers in the world are as nothing by comparison; for, to tell the truth, I wonder that you are not ashamed to have gone so far beyond bounds. For it should have been enough for you to make this Court Lady beautiful, discreet, chaste, affable, and able to entertain (without getting a bad name) in dancing, music, games, laughter, witticisms, and the other things that we see going on at court every day; but to wish to give her knowledge of everything in the world, and allow her those virtues that have so rarely been seen in men during the past centuries, is something one cannot endure or listen to at all.

"Now, that women are imperfect creatures, and consequently have less dignity than men, and that they are not capable of the virtues that men are capable of, is something I am not disposed to maintain, because the worthiness of the ladies here present would be enough to prove me wrong: but I do say that very learned men have written that, since nature always intends and plans to make things most perfect, she would constantly bring forth men if she could; and that when a women is born, it is a defect or mistake of nature, and contrary to what she would wish to do: as is seen too in the case of one who is born blind, or lame, or with some other defect; and, in trees, the many fruits that never ripen. Thus, a woman can be said to be a creature produced by chance and accident. That such is the case, consider a man's actions and a woman's, and conclude from these regarding the perfection of the one and the other. Nevertheless, since these defects in women are the fault of nature that made them so, we ought not on that account to despise them, or fail to show them the respect.

✦ *Laura Cereta*

*L*aura Cereta was born into an aristocratic family of Brescia. She received her early education in a convent, but at the age of nine she returned home to be educated by her father, a learned official. She was taught Latin and Greek, as well as mathematics, in which she became particularly skilled. At 15 she was married to Pietro Serino of Brescia, but he died from the plague just 18 months later. Cereta was to remain a widow for the rest of her life.

About the time of her marriage, Laura Cereta began a Latin correspondence with other humanists. Indeed, her humanist interests continued after her marriage, and her scholarly pursuits helped her recover from the loss of her husband. In 1488 she published a volume of her letters.

Many of the male humanists aware of Cereta treated her with condescension or contempt. Many did not believe that a young woman could write such elegant Latin. There were, however, a few scholars who supported her.

Laura Cereta wrote a wide range of Latin works, including invectives (perhaps the first woman humanist to do so), letters, and an important defense of humanist education for women. She died in 1499.

LETTER TO AUGUSTINUS AEMILIUS, CURSE AGAINST THE ORNAMENTATION OF WOMEN

Alone, I fled to the country, and in tranquil leisure delighted in [humane] studies. But you, meanwhile, were disturbed by my retreat, as if you seemed to consider me, a nonentity, important.

I came at the end when my husband was feverish. Dying myself, I saw him half dead. I cheered him when he seemed to revive, I wept over him when he died, I fell lifeless on his dead body, and the fatal house which awaited me for marriage admitted me to lamentation. Thus one, and that an abominable year, saw me a girl, bride, widow, and pauper. These events were ordered by fate, not by you; you were mortal and died.

I thank you for esteeming me so highly, and more so than I deserve, for I cannot be compared to women like Sarah, Esther, Sephora and Susanna, any more than a glowworm shining at night can be compared to the brilliant stars in heaven. I fear that your lofty opinion of me may spring from some other source than a carefully balanced judgment. Conjure up in your mind an ordinary woman, drab of face and drably dressed —for I care more for letters than for flashy clothes. Moreover, I have committed myself absolutely to that cultivation of virtue which can profit me not only when alive but also after death. There are those who are captivated by beauty. I myself should give the greater prize to grey-haired chastity, since in the lovely company of comely youth blaze up enticements to passion. For virtue excels the brilliance of beauty, elaborate polished artifice, and precious flowers of every tenderness. Let Mark Antony be attracted by bejewelled Cleopatra; I shall imitate the innocence of Rebecca. Let Paris seek the wandering Helen; I choose to imitate the modesty of Rachel. Wives are bewitched by rich display; more witless still are those who, to satisfy the appetite of their wives, destroy their patrimonies. Today men's love for women has made our commonwealth the imitator or rather the plunderer of the East. Luxury has thrived in this age, more than all others prodigiously vain. Let those who do not believe me attend the services of the church. Let them observe weddings packed with seated matrons. Let them gaze at these women who, with majestic pride, promenade amidst crowds through the piazzas. Among them, here and there, is one who ties a towering knot—made of someone else's hair—at the very peak of her head; another's forehead is submerged in waves of crimped curls; and another, in order to bare her neck, binds with a golden ribbon her golden hair. One suspends a necklace from her shoulder, another from her arm, another from neck to breast. Others choke themselves with pearl necklaces; born free, they boast to be held captive. And many display fingers glistening with jewels. One, lusting to walk more mincingly, loosens her girdle, while another tightens hers to make her breasts bulge. Some drag from their shoulders silken tunics. Others, sweet-scented with perfumes, cover themselves with an Arabian hood. Some boost themselves with high-heeled shoes. And all think it particularly modish to swathe their legs with fine soft cotton. Many press soft-

SOURCE: M. King and A. Rabil, *Her Immaculate Hand* (Binghamton, N.Y.: MARTS, 1983), pp. 78–80.

ened bread on their faces, many artificially smooth their skin, stretched with wrinkles; there are few whose ruddy faces are not painted with the lustre of white lead. In one way or another they strive by means of exquisite artistry to seem more beautiful than the Author of their beauty decreed. The impudence of some women is shameful. They paint their white cheeks with purple and, with furtive winks and smiling mouths, pierce the poisoned hearts of those who gaze on them. O the bold wantonness of lost modesty! O the weakness of our sex, stooping to voluptuousness! We have only to hang from our ears little ornaments trembling with precious stones and emeralds, and we shall not differ from pagans. Was it for this, by chance, that we were begotten, that we might worship in shameless devotion the idols of our mirrored faces? Did we renounce display in baptism so that, as Christian women, we might imitate Jews and barbarians?

Even the feeblest desire [for honor] should make us blush over this longing for magnificence. These insane and lustful carvings, born of arrogance, should frighten us. Mindful of the ashes from which we come, we should renounce sins born from desires. How will our lamentations prevail if heavenly anger and indignation should rage against us miserable women? If those who rebel against the king commit their necks to the axe, why should we women marvel, rebels, indeed, warriors against God, if, to avenge our sin, an army rise up against us? Rome mourns to this day the Gauls' assault. Italy, vanquished, bewails the Gothic sword. Greece suffers Mahomet's tyranny. These vicious devastations are not caused by human might but ordained by heaven [as a punishment for sins]. Let each woman dress and heal the wound from which we languish. We should seek the adornment of honor, not vulgar display, and we should pursue this life mindful of our mortality. For God the Father has decreed that the good die well.

Therefore, Augustine, you have had ample opportunity to see that I consider this splendid magnificence foolish, and I wish you would pay no attention to my age or at least my sex. For [woman's] nature is not immune to sin; nature produced our mother [Eve], not from earth or rock, but from Adam's humanity. To be human is, however, to incline sometimes to good, but sometimes to pleasure. We are quite an imperfect animal, and our puny strength is not sufficient for mighty battles. [But] you great men, wielding such authority, commanding such success, who justly discern among your number so many present-day Brutuses, so many Curiuses, Fabriciuses, Catos, and Aemiliuses, be careful: do not therefore be taken by the snare of this carefully arranged elegance. For where there is greater wisdom, there lies greater guilt. February 12 [1487].

✦ *Documents Illustrating the Lives of Poor and Marginal Women in Renaissance Florence*

THE ESTABLISHMENT OF COMMUNAL BROTHELS, 1415[1]

Desiring to eliminate a worse evil by means of a lesser one, the lord priors . . . [and their colleges] have decreed that . . . the priors . . . [and their colleges] may authorize the establishment of two public brothels in the city of Florence, in addition to the one which already exists: one in the quarter of S. Spirito and the other in the quarter of S. Croce. [They are to be located] in suitable places or in places where the exercise of such scandalous activity can best be concealed, for the honor of the city and of those who live in the neighborhood in which these prostitutes must stay to hire their bodies for lucre, as other prostitutes stay in the other brothel. For establishing these places . . . in a proper manner and for their construction, furnishing, and improvement, they may spend up to 1,000 florins. . . .

PROFITS OF PROSTITUTION[2]

[1427] . . . Rosso di Giovanni di Niccolò de' Medici . . . owns a house located at the entrance to the Chiasso Malacucina. . . . [It is rented by Biagio d'Antonio, a pork-butcher, for 12 florins per year.] . . . There are six little shops beneath that house which are rented to prostitutes, who usually pay from 10 to 13 lire per month [for a room], and this rent is never higher. The innkeeper, Giuliano, keeps the keys and he puts whoever he wishes [into the rooms].

[1433] . . . Piero di Simone Brunelleschi and his mother Antonia . . . own two houses adjacent to each other in the Chiasso Malacucina, with furnishings required by prostitutes. . . . And there are several shops underneath those houses which are also inhabited by prostitutes. . . . They also report that they keep Giovanni di Marco of Venice in these houses . . . so that he, with some boys who stay with him, can collect the rents. They

---

1. *ASF, Provvisioni*, 105, fols. 248r–248v.
2. *ASF, Catasto*, 79, fol. 347r; 498, fol. 531v.

SOURCE: G. Brucker, ed., *The Society of Renaissance Florence* (New York: Harper & Row, 1971), pp. 190–201, 281–221, 224–228, 270–273. Reprinted by permission of HarperCollins Publishers.

also state that they do not receive more than 4 florins per month from these houses and shops, on account of the depression. . . .

PROSTITUTES AND THE COURTS, 1398–1400

[Angela, wife of Nofri di Francesco, was convicted of plying the prostitute's trade without wearing the required garb, "gloves on her hands and a bell on her head." The following witnesses testified against her.]

Bartolo Gadini . . . stated that he was well informed about the contents of this process, namely that Angela had publicly sold her body for money in the parish of S. Maria a Verzaia, and that it is generally believed in the city of Florence . . . that she was and is a public prostitute. . . . Asked how he knew this, the witness said that he is Angela's neighbor, and that he saw many men openly coming to her house to copulate with her for money. . . . The witness further testified that during the previous November and December, on behalf of all of his neighbors and conforming to their will, he asked Angela to abandon her prostitute's career and live honestly. If she did so, he promised her, on behalf of the neighbors, to furnish her with a basket of bread each week for her sustenance. But Angela replied that she did not wish to give up prostitution unless her neighbors first gave her 2 florins. Otherwise she intended to pursue the whore's life since she earned much more money than the amount which her neighbors wished to give her. . . .

Antonio di Zanobi . . . testified that he had information concerning this case. . . . [He stated that] he had copulated with Angela and that for that act, she demanded 19 quattrini. Following the witness, a cloth worker from the parish of S. Frediano, Spina di Alimento, copulated with her and on that occasion he paid her a certain sum of money. . . .

Lorenzo di Riccomano . . . was and is a neighbor of Angela . . . and on several days and nights, he saw and heard men going to have carnal relations with her for money. On several occasions during this time, he reproached Angela for her dishonest and libidinous life. And he saw and heard her . . . say: "I am and I wish to remain a public whore, and I will sell my body to you for money."

This is the inquisition carried out by the excellent and honorable doctor of law, Messer Giovanni of Montepulciano, the appellate judge . . . of the city of Florence . . . against Salvaza, wife of Seze, parish of S. Lucia Ogni Santi. . . . It has come to the attention of the abovementioned judge and his court . . . that this Salvaza, wife of Seze . . . has publicly committed adultery with several persons and has sold her body for money. . . . With respect to all of these charges, the judge intends to discover the truth; and if she is found guilty of walking without gloves and bells on her head or with high-heeled slippers, to punish her according to the Communal statutes; and if innocent, to absolve her from this accusation.

This inquisition was begun by the judge against Salvaza on November 16, 1400. Sitting in tribunal in the accustomed seat of his office, the judge ordered . . . Bartolo di Bartolo, a public messenger of the Commune of Florence, to go to the home of Salvaza and order her to appear before the judge to clear herself of this accusation and to defend herself. . . .

November 16. The messenger has informed the judge and myself, the notary, that he went to the house of Salvaza and finding her there, informed her of everything herein inscribed and personally left a copy of this inquisition. . . .

November 19, 1400. Salvaza appeared personally at the residence of the judge, and since according to the statutes, no woman is allowed to enter there, the judge . . . ordered me, Jacopo de Silis, his notary, to descend to her near the entrance door . . . to hear and receive her reply, defense, and excuse. Before me, the notary, Salvaza replied to this accusation by stating that it was not true. . . . [She was then informed that she had eight days in which to furnish evidence of her innocence.]

November 24, 1400. Bartolo di Bartolo informed me, Jacopo de Silis, that he had personally informed the witnesses, identified below, from the parish of S. Lucia Ogni Santi, to appear on that same day before him at his accustomed residence to swear to tell the truth . . . concerning the statements in this accusation. . . .

The following witnesses against Salvaza were sworn in and examined by the judge and myself, the notary, on November 24, 1400.

Antonio di Ugo, parish of S. Lucia Ogni Santi . . . stated that everything in the accusation was true. When asked how he knew this, the witness replied that on numerous occasions, he had seen Salvaza enter the houses of many men—both natives and foreigners—by day and night. They played and danced with her, and did many illicit and indecent things with her, touching her and fondling her with their hands, as is done by public prostitutes. Asked whom he had seen touching and fondling her, and in whose houses, he replied that Salvaza went to the house of a certain Mancino, a Florentine citizen, and stayed with him for several days; also a certain pimp named Nanni, Niccolò, a tiler, and many others whose names he did not know. Asked about Salvaza's reputation, he replied that she is commonly regarded as a whore. When asked who voices this opinion, and where he heard it, he replied that it was the general opinion of nearly everyone in the parish. Asked about Salvaza's physical appearance and age, he replied that she is a big woman, about forty-five, quite attractive, with a dark complexion.

Vanni Migliore, parish of S. Lucia, . . . stated that he knew Salvaza, wife of Seze, very well; she lives in the street called the Prato Ogni Santi. He said that the contents of this accusation are true. When asked how he knew, he replied that he had seen many men, both citizens and foreigners, enter her house both day and night, and that she committed adultery with them. He had seen her engaged in indecent acts with them. Asked whom he had seen entering this house and participating in these indecencies, he identified a certain Martino of the parish of S. Paolo, Niccolò, a tiler, and many others whom he did not know. He stated that one night his door was closed and he was told that Niccolò had closed it. Thereupon, the witness encountered Niccolò and quarreled with him and told him that he was doing wrong. And Niccolò replied: "And I will fornicate wherever I please," and he held a key in his hands, and Salvaza was mouthing obscenities at him. Asked about Salvaza's reputation, he replied that among all of the residents of the parish, she had a bad reputation as a prostitute. Asked about her physical appearance and age, he replied that she was a large, dark woman of about forty years of age. . . .

Monna Leonarda, widow of Damello, parish of S. Lucia, . . . said that the contents of this accusation were true. Asked how she knew, she replied that she had seen many men entering Salvaza's house . . . both day and night when her husband was absent, and that men were said to have committed adultery with Salvaza. Asked whom she had seen entering the house, she replied that she had seen a certain Mancino and many others. Asked about Salvaza's reputation, she replied that she had a bad reputation and was considered a whore by nearly everyone in the parish.

Paula, wife of Lorenzo of the parish of S. Lucia, asserted that the contents of the inquisition were true. Asked how she knew this, the witness replied that she was Salvaza's neighbor and that she had often seen men enter her house, and had often heard her playing and joking with them. She also stated that on one occasion, a foreigner wished to go to Salvaza and the witness was standing on her doorstep. Feeling ashamed, the foreigner said to her: "You should go inside to your house," and then the witness went inside and the foreigner entered Salvaza's house. . . .

Margherita, widow of Ugo . . . stated that the contents of the accusation were true. When asked how she knew this, she replied that she is a near neighbor of Salvaza, and that she had often seen men enter her house. . . . The witness said that she had frequently looked through a window of Salvaza's house and had seen her nude in bed with men, engaging in those indecent acts which are practiced by prostitutes. [Salvaza was declared to be a public prostitute, and was required to wear gloves, bells, and high-heeled slippers.]

THE RECRUITMENT OF PROSTITUTES, 1379

. . . We condemn . . . Niccolò di Giunta, called Bocco, formerly of Prato and now living in the parish of S. Lorenzo, a man of low condition, life, and reputation, a kidnapper of women, violator of virgins and widows, and a panderer who persuades honest women to lead a life of sin and corruption. This Niccolò went to a house owned by Landino di Martino, in the *pieve* of S. Severi de Legravallis Marine, where there lived Meo di Venture and his wife Riguardata, an honest couple of good reputation. He had several secret conversations with Riguardata, and with cunning and deceptive words, he tried to persuade her to commit adultery. These were his words: "Monna Riguardata, I have great sympathy for your youth, since you are a very beautiful girl and you have not married well, in terms of the person and the property of your husband. You know that Meo is crippled in one arm and one leg so that he is not really a man. Of the things of this world, he has none. You know this very well, for you are poorly dressed and badly shod, and you possess nothing in this world. You have little bread and wine, and there is neither meat nor oil in your house. I have never seen such a pretty girl living in this poverty and misery. I have the greatest compassion for you, particularly since your husband is the ugliest and most wretched man in the world, and you are so beautiful. So I have decided to take you away from this misery and arrange matters so that you will lack for nothing, and you will be well clothed, as your youth and beauty require. . . ." But Riguardata did not consent to these appeals but said: "I want to stay with my husband." However, Niccolò was not satisfied with this reply but said to Riguardata: "Please don't make this your final response, but think about it. If you will do as I ask, I will make you the happiest girl in the world."

And with these and similar words, Niccolò persuaded Riguardata to commit sin. . . . In the present month of November, he went to the home of Meo and Riguardata . . . and took that woman of good condition, behavior, and reputation with him and brought her to a place called Trespiano. There, in the inn of Ceccarello of Trespiano, he kept her one day and two nights and committed adultery with her on several occasions. Then he decided to take her to the city of Bologna and place her in the public brothel of that city so that she might earn money. . . . And he would have done so if he and Riguardata had not been captured in Ceccarello's inn by one of our officials and the husband of Riguardata.

Item, this Niccolò with bland and false words persuaded Bona, the daughter of Clari and wife of Janni of Florence, who now is called Caterina, to commit sin. These were his words: "Bona, if you wish to stay with me, I will clothe you and provide you with your living expenses, if you will sell wine in my tavern. And I will pay you for your work [as a prostitute] and you may keep two-thirds and I will take one-third, and we will sell more of our wine." With these words and others, he induced her to sin and she had relations with several men. From this adultery, Bona earned money for Niccolò, against the wishes of her husband and her father Clari, and to their shame and disgrace.

Item, in the current year and the month of January, Giovanna of Borgo Citramontina was staying in Niccolò's hostel. He saw this pretty girl, poor and badly dressed. He said to her: "How do you manage alone in your wanderings? You are young, and restless feet do not gain much. I beg you to stay with men and work in my hostel and I promise never to leave you and I will clothe you very handsomely. And with these false and deceptive words, he induced Giovanna to sin . . . and kept her in the hostel. She dined with the guests and other men, so that they would pay to commit adultery with her. The money which she received from this adultery was turned over to Niccolò for his use. Then, persuaded by Niccolò, Giovanna entered the public brothel of the city of Florence. . . .

Item, when Monna Margherita of Reggio, who today lives in the house of Niccolò di Cristoforo, came to Florence with Antonio di Masso of Reggio, she stayed in the house of the above-mentioned Niccolò [di Cristoforo]. And Niccolò [di Giunta] persuaded her to commit sin. . . . And so that he might gain his evil objective more easily, he arranged with an official of the city of Florence to seize, torture, and expel Antonio [di Masso] from the city of Florence. Then he spoke to Margherita: "You have been left here alone. How are you doing? I want you to stay with me, and I promise not to bother you. And I will arrange for you to earn a lot of money, and I will provide you with fine clothes and shoes." And with these words, he persuaded her to commit sin . . . and on several occasions he committed adultery with her.

Item . . . this Niccolò, a notorious pimp, with bland and deceptive phrases had induced several married women and widows of Florence to lead a life of sin and to commit adultery with various men, with officials and nobles of Florence, and also with foreigners, in his house. [Niccolò di Giunta confessed to these crimes; he was executed.]

A PANDERER'S CAREER

. . . We condemn . . . Bartolomeo di Lorenzo, of the parish of S. Piero Gattolino of Florence, a pimp and vendor of his own flesh, a man of evil condition, life, and reputation; Stella, called Pellegrina, the daughter of Master Pace, a painter of Faenza, and wife of Bartolomeo, an adulterous woman and a violator of holy matrimony; and Jacopo di Lorenzo, called El Padovano, of Padua, an exploiter of women. . . .

Forgetting his own honor and the spiritual nature of the matrimony which he had contracted with . . . Stella on the feast day of S. Bartolomeo in August 1416, Bartolomeo had a conversation with a certain Checco of Florence, who lives in Lucca and is the operator of a brothel there. Bartolomeo said, "You know that I have a wife, Stella, and you will recall that a few days ago, we agreed that you would employ her in your brothel in Lucca. Now if you will give me 30 florins, I will consent to your keeping her in your bordello. . . ." Checco then replied to Bartolomeo, "I will give you 12 florins, or 16 at the most, and no more. For she is poorly clothed and I will have to furnish her with a new wardrobe." After this conversation, Checco departed from Pisa . . . and Bartolomeo was not able to put his iniquitous plan into effect. . . .

Item, in the present year and the month of August, Bartolomeo . . . on various days and at various times . . . sold his wife to Ser Jacopo de Interanne, to Piero of Villa Tartagli in the Florentine contado, and to Ser Jacopo di Simone of Prato. He brought them at night to his house . . . and permitted them to have carnal relations with his wife Stella, to the shame and opprobrium of Bartolomeo himself and of his wife. . . .

Item, in September of this year, he sold his wife Stella to a Florentine notary whose name he does not remember. . . . He received a wine flask full of oil as the price for this prostitution. . . .

Item, persevering in this iniquitous course, Bartolomeo took Stella with him . . . to the house of Corrado di Jacopo, a hosier, in the district of S. Martino of Chinocha of Pisa, with whom Bartolomeo and Stella dined. After dinner, all three went into the same bed, and the next morning, Corrado had carnal relations with Stella with Bartolomeo's knowledge and consent. After this intercourse, Corrado gave Stella a Florentine silver quattrino and a silk jacket with a belt as the price for her labor. Stella gave the coin to her husband Bartolomeo. . . .

Item, in his house Bartolomeo sold Stella to Antonio Biffoli of Florence, for which he received some money and a doublet. . . .

Item, he sold his wife to Nanni di Duccio, a Pisan druggist . . . who gave Stella ten Bologna pennies and a quattrino.

Item, Bartolomeo forced his wife Stella to have carnal relations on various occasions with different men for certain sums of money. . . .

Item, in the current month and year, Jacopo di Lorenzo, called El Padovano, went to Bartolomeo's house in Pisa in the Campo S. Cristoforo and abducted Stella, Bartolomeo's wife knowing and believing that she was a woman of good condition and honest life, and with force took her outside the city of Pisa, against her will and Bartolomeo's. [All three of the accused confessed to their crimes. Bartolomeo was sentenced to be whipped through the streets of Pisa and fined 1,000 lire. After paying the fine, he was to remain in prison for two years. Stella was to be whipped through the streets and remain in prison for the month of November. Jacopo was to be whipped, and required to leave Pisa by November 15.]

THE STORY OF THE SERVANT GIRL NENCIA

On this day, November 17, 1475, I record that on Wednesday, the 25th of the preceding month, . . . my wife told me that from certain signs which she had observed, our servant girl Lorenza, also called Nencia di Lazerino, had missed her period and that she appeared to be pregnant. Having learned about these indications from her, I told her to confront the girl alone and to use threats and persuasions to find out the truth from her. I had to go away, and upon my return in the evening, she told me that she had the girl alone in a room and that, after cajoling and threatening her, she had learned that the girl was pregnant by Niccolò di Alessandro Machiavelli.

When asked how this had happened, she said that after we had returned from the country last year, on November 8, she had often gone at night through the window over the roof, and then through the little window next to the kitchen hearth to Niccolò's house to stay with him. This she did most frequently when my wife was pregnant and when she was in labor. During May and June of this past year, when Niccolò's wife was ill, he often entered [the house] through that little window and slept with her on the kitchen hearth.

When I learned all this, I left the house and went to find my wife's brother, Giovanni Nelli. Since his brother Carlo had come to Florence from Pisa, I also met him and told them the story and asked them to come the next morning to have breakfast with me, and to decide on the best course of action. I did this because Giovanni had found the girl for me and had persuaded her father, who was his friend, to give her to me. So the next morning, they both came to breakfast with me, and after we had eaten, we called Nencia into my room . . . and asked her about this matter described above. She repeated the same story to us, though Giovanni, Carlo, and I warned her to be careful of what she said, because it did not seem plausible that Niccolò, who had a young and beautiful wife, would have paid any attention to her; [but] she insisted on her story. She also said that when Niccolò was at the villa (most of the time he stayed at Colombaia), he called her through the barred window of her room from his balcony, and that two or three times a week, they would stay together. It was true that she was pregnant by Niccolò and that he had promised to give her a cape and a gown.

Then, having sent Nencia from the room, Giovanni and Carlo told me that they would find Niccolò and tell him about this affair and the girl's story, and they would then report to me what he said. . . . I told them that I was content, but that I did not want the girl in my house any longer and that I thought that the girl's mother—who was staying with Giovanni—and her father should be informed, so that they would take her away. They replied that I should speak first with Niccolò and then what had to be done would be done. So, on Saturday the 28th, the eve of [the feast of] S. Simone, the twenty-third hour having already struck, I left the house and while walking toward the Ponte Vecchio, I met Niccolò . . . and told him that I wanted to talk to him. . . . I told him what Nencia had said. He replied that for six months and longer, he had wanted to tell me about this, and that he didn't know himself why he hadn't done so. The story was this. Francesco Renzi, called "L'Agata," who was the nephew of Master Raffaello of Terranuova, the physician, had told him some six months before that when he had left him in his [Niccolò's] house . . . Nencia had left the house via the roof and had gone into Niccolò's house to stay with him. This had happened on several occasions after I had returned from the villa. The truth was that he, Niccolò, had never had anything to do with her. Francesco had done this, and his only fault had been his failure to tell me.

In reply, I complained bitterly of his injury to me, which would have
been grave in any event, but which was even worse, since he was my
neighbor . . . and a close blood relation. [I said] that I had never done
anything similar to him or his father, and that I did not understand how
he could have held me in such low esteem. For both here [in Florence]
and at the villa, he was often in my company and had never said anything
to me so that I might prevent my house from becoming a bordello. He
should also consider the nature of this affair, for this girl was not a slut
but came from a good but impoverished family of Pistoia, and her father
and brothers were men of some worth. I did not want the girl in my house
any longer, and I had no choice but to inform Giovanni Nelli, who had
given her to me, or to arrange for her father and mother to come for her.
Niccolò replied that he was aware that he had injured me, but that it was
Francesco who had harmed the girl, and that his error had been in not
telling me. . . .

On Monday, the 30th, I met Giovanni Nelli and told him that I had
spoken with Niccolò. . . . Giovanni told me to be patient, since he wished
to speak to him too. On the morning of the 31st, I was walking toward
the Ponte Vecchio and I met Niccolò . . . and he told me: "Now I want
to tell you why I didn't say anything to you about Nencia and Agata. You
know that Francesco Agata is staying with Master Raffaello, and I beg you
not to mention this to him. He has a beautiful girl in his house whom I
wanted, and Francesco was my liaison, and since he had done me this
favor, I consented to his affair with Nencia. . . . I told him that this was
a fine story, but that the girl . . . said that it had been himself. . . . [I told
him] that I had spoken about this matter to Giovanni Nelli and asked him
to send for the father and take the girl away, since I didn't want her any
longer, and that Giovanni had said that he wanted to speak to him [Nic-
colò] before informing the father, to see if something could be done to
avoid scandal. . . .

On Friday the 3rd, Giovanni came to dine and spend the night with
me, and he told me that he had been with Niccolò Machiavelli in the
Mercato Nuovo that evening and he had spoken about this matter. . . . It
appeared to him, so he had told Niccolò, that in order to avoid scandal,
which would arise if the father were informed of this, they should find a
woman to care for the girl until she had been delivered, and then arrange
to give her [a dowry of] 25 florins so that she could be married and thus
save Giovanni's honor, since he had been responsible for giving her to me.
Niccolò replied that this pleased him, and while insisting strongly that it
had not been himself but rather Francesco Agata, nevertheless he said that
he wished to see if it would be possible to arrange the matter as Giovanni
had suggested. . . .

On the 12th day of the present month, Giovanni Nelli, Niccolò, and
I were together in Giovanni's shop and we agreed that Niccolò should
promise in writing to give Giovanni 100 lire for Nencia's dowry. . . . Last
night, Saturday, November 18, 1475, Giovanni Nelli came to stay with

me and told me that on that same evening, he and Niccolò Machiavelli had been with Monna Lisa, who takes care of children . . . and they had agreed to take . . . Nencia to her this morning. She promised to care for her until her delivery, and Niccolò promised to give her 5 lire each month. . . . This morning, just before the fourteenth hour, Giovanni took Nencia away to the house of Monna Lisa and my wife gave her all of her shirts and handkerchiefs and other clothes. . . .

THE TRIBULATIONS OF A SLAVE GIRL

This petition is presented to you, lord priors . . . on behalf of Maria, the daughter of Dece de Cigoli of Slavonia, formerly in bondage and now free, who in Florence is called Maria di Pippo. On July 17, 1449, she was condemned (together with a certain Crispino also named in the sentence) . . . to pay a fine of 150 lire . . . and to restore the items stolen by Maria, the slave of Bernardo di Berto di Luce, which items were taken from Bernardo's house at the behest of Maria di Pippo. She was also sent to the Stinche, to be detained there until the items stolen from Bernardo's house, or their monetary equivalent, were restored to him, and until she paid the fine of 150 lire. . . .

Early in March of the year 1449, when Maria di Pippo was in the piazza of S. Maria Bertelde, Crispino said to her: "Maria, go find Maria, the slave girl of Bernardo di Berto, the silk merchant, and tell her for me that she must come immediately to my house because I want to speak to her. After Crispino's departure, Maria di Pippo went to Maria the slave in Bernardo's house and told her what Crispino had instructed her to say. Several days later, the two Marias were in Bernardo's house and Maria the slave said to Maria di Pippo: "I went to see Crispino in his house and he told me that he has made a vow to marry a slave girl and make her free, and if I wish (since he loves me very much), that he will marry me in preference to another girl whom he knows and take me to his house in his native district. However, since the route [to his home] is long, he said that he doesn't have enough money for the expenses of the journey. He wants me to take some of my mistress's jewels, a ring and a necklace and the good pieces in the chest where she keeps her jewels, and give them to him." Then Maria di Pippo said to Maria the slave: "Maria, be careful what you do, because if you are caught, he will be hanged and you will be in trouble too." Then after several days, Maria the slave spoke to Maria di Pippo: "I told Crispino what you said and he told me not to be afraid, and that he will never leave me." Then Maria di Pippo said to Maria the slave: "If he wishes to marry you, as he says, and do for you what he promises, then you can take those things, one at a time, from the house and give them to him." Maria the slave replied: ". . . I don't want to do that; instead, I want to take the jewels and leave the house and go away all at once. If my mistress discovers that her jewels are missing, she will beat me, as she has done in the past. . . ."

Item, in the month of April 1449 after Easter, when Maria di Pippo was in the church of S. Reparata, Crispino came to her and said: "Go tell Maria the slave that if she wants to come with me, she should get ready, since I want to leave Florence." And Maria di Pippo went to see Maria the slave in Bernardo's house and told her what Crispino had said in the church of S. Reparata. . . . And Maria the slave replied to Maria di Pippo: "I don't know what to do for I am terribly afraid to leave." Maria di Pippo said: "Don't be frightened about this; now is the time to go, and what you have to do, you should do quickly." And Maria the slave replied, "I don't trust him, because I fear that he will deceive me." Then Maria di Pippo said: "Don't be afraid; you know that he is a worthy person and that he won't trick you. But you could go away with someone who would sell you."

Maria the slave then said: "I don't know how to open the chest." Maria di Pippo replied, "You should talk to Crispino." So Maria the slave went to Crispino and told him that she had found the key to the chest and showed it to him. And Crispino said to her: "Leave it with me and I will have a copy made by a locksmith. But Maria replied that she didn't want to leave it with him for fear of her mistress. . . . So Crispino gave her some wax to make an imprint of the key . . . which she made and gave to Maria di Pippo to take to Crispino. . . . He went to a locksmith to have a copy made, and took that key to Maria the slave who then tried to open the chest, but she could not open it since the key would not turn.

Then Maria the slave . . . went to the house of Maria di Pippo and told her: "Crispino gave me this key to open the chest; go and tell him that he will have to repair it." Receiving the key, Crispino repaired it and brought it to Maria di Pippo and said: "Take this key to Maria so that she can try to open the chest, and if she cannot, then take a lighted candle and blacken the key so that one can see its flaw. . . ." So both Marias went together to try the key and when they saw that it would not open [the chest], they blackened the key and tried it again. Seeing that they could not open it, Maria the slave took a bunch of keys . . . and they both began to try them, to see if there was a key which would open the chest. Then Domenico, the son of Bernardo, arrived on horseback and knocked at the door of the house. Maria the slave said to Maria di Pippo: "Go and see who is knocking at the door; I hope it isn't one of my masters." Maria then saw that it was Domenico, and Maria the slave took the bunch of keys and hid them . . . and said to Maria di Pippo: "Go into my room, for if Domenico finds you here, he will beat me to death." So Maria di Pippo hid in the room until Domenico left the house. . . .

Afterwards, in the month of May, Maria di Pippo . . . went to Bernardo's house and said to Maria the slave: "Maria, Crispino says that since you cannot find a way to open the chest, that he will come here into the house . . . and you can carry away the things that are inside and then flee." Maria the slave replied: "I don't want to do this, and you tell him not to come here to ransack the house. If I can find the key to open the chest, I will do it, but I won't do anything else. . . ." Several days later, when a locksmith (whose name they did not know) was passing through the neighborhood and was in front of Bernardo's house, Maria the slave called him and had him make a key, with which she opened the chest. Then she found Maria di Pippo and told her: "I had a key made that opens the chest." Then Maria di Pippo said: "Now that you have the key, what are you going to do? Take those things which you need and then run away." But Maria the slave replied: "I don't trust that man," to which Maria di Pippo replied: "You can really trust him." Several days later, Maria di Pippo went to Bernardo's house and said to Maria the slave: "Crispino tells me that you should give me these things, and if you don't wish to give them to me, then you should tell me what is in the chest so that he will know what he can carry away." Maria the slave said: "I don't want to tell you because I wish to take those things and carry them away myself when I want to leave. I don't want to give everything to him, because I want to keep some things for myself." Maria di Pippo replied: "You are acting wisely by not giving him everything; keep something for yourself in the event of sickness or some other misfortune. . . .

On the same day, Maria di Pippo went to Bernardo's house . . . and said to Maria the slave: "Crispino says that he thinks it is time to go away with those things." And Maria the slave replied: "It is better to go on a work day after dinner, because on feast days my mistress and my masters often come home, but on work days, they go to their shops and they don't return home so quickly." On Monday, May 19, after dinner, Maria the slave opened the chest with the key and took from it the following jewels and other objects: a pair of pearls set in gold, weighing 8 ounces; a pearl necklace, weighing 8 ounces; a diamond ornament; a large pearl . . . [and other items of jewelry and clothing] . . . valued at 200 florins or thereabouts. These objects she took to the Porta al Prato near the wall by the Arno river, where Crispino had instructed her to meet him, and she gave them to Crispino. He hid the objects in the saddlebags of his horse, and after mounting, he said to Maria the slave: "You go out [of the city] through the Porta a Faenza and I will leave by this gate. Wait for me there and I will bring another horse for you and we will go away together." When Crispino went out through the gate with these objects, he fled and abandoned Maria the slave. [Maria petitioned for the cancellation of her fine and her release from prison; the petition was approved.]

A WITCH'S CAREER

. . . We condemn . . . Giovanna called Caterina, daughter of Francesco called El Toso, a resident of the parish of S. Ambrogio of Florence . . . who is a magician, witch, and sorceress, and a practitioner of the black arts. . . . It happened that Giovanni Ceresani of the parish of S. Jacopo tra le Fosse was passing by her door and stared at her fixedly. She thought that she would draw the chaste spirit of Giovanni to her for carnal purposes by means of the black arts. . . . She went to the shop of Monna Gilia, the druggist, and purchased from her a small amount of lead . . . and then she took a bowl and placed the lead in it and put it on the fire so that the lead would melt. With this melted lead she made a small chain and spoke certain words which have significance for this magical and diabolical art (and which, lest the people learn about them, shall not be recorded). . . . All this which was done and spoken against Giovanni's safety by Giovanna was so powerful that his chaste spirit was deflected to lust after her, so that willynilly he went several times to her house and there he fulfilled her perfidious desire. . . .

With the desire of doing further harm to Giovanni's health through the black arts, and so persisting in what she had begun, she acquired a little gold, frankincense, and myrrh, and then took a little bowl with some glowing charcoal inside, and having prepared these ingredients and having lit the candle which she held in her left hand, she genuflected before the image and placed the bowl at the foot of the figure. Calling out the name of Giovanni, she threw the gold, frankincense, and myrrh upon the charcoal. And when the smoke from the charcoal covered the whole image, Giovanna spoke certain words, the tenor of which is vile and detestable, and which should be buried in silence lest the people be given information for committing sin. . . .

When she realized that what she had done against Giovanni's health was not sufficient to satisfy completely her insatiable lust, she learned from a certain priest that . . . if water from the skulls of dead men was distilled and given with a little wine to any man, that it was a most valid test. . . . Night and day, that woman thought of nothing but how she could give that water to Giovanni to drink. . . . She visited the priest and bought from him a small amount of that water . . . and that accursed woman gave Giovanni that water mixed with wine to drink. After he drank it, Giovanni could think of nothing but satisfying his lust with Giovanna. And his health has been somewhat damaged, in the opinion of good and worthy [men]. . . .

In the time when Giovanna was menstruating, she took a little of her menses, that quantity which is required by the diabolical ceremonies, and placed it in a small beaker . . . and then poured it into another flask filled with wine . . . and gave it to Giovanni to drink. And on account of this and the other things described above, Giovanni no longer has time for his affairs as he did in the past, and he has left his home and his wife and son . . . and does only what pleases Giovanna. . . .

On several occasions, Giovanna had intercourse with a certain Jacopo di Andrea, a doublet-maker, of the parish of S. Niccolò. Desiring to possess his chaste spirit totally for her lust and against his health, Giovanna . . . thought to give Jacopo some of her menses, since she knew that it was very efficacious. . . . Having observed several diabolical rites, she took the beaker with the menses . . . and gave it to Jacopo to drink. After he had drunk, she uttered these words among others: "I will catch you in my net if you don't flee. . . ." When they were engaged in the act of intercourse, she placed her hand on her private parts . . . and after uttering certain diabolical words, she put a finger on Jacopo's lips. . . . Thereafter, in the opinion of everyone, Jacopo's health deteriorated and he was forced by necessity to obey her in everything. . . .

Several years ago, Giovanna was the concubine of Niccolò di Ser Casciotto of the parish of S. Giorgio, and she had three children by him. Having a great affection for Niccolò, who was then in Hungary, she wanted him to return to her in Florence. . . . So she planned a diabolical experiment by invoking a demon, to the detriment of Niccolò's health. . . . She went to someone who shall not be identified . . . and asked him to go to another diabolical woman, a sorceress (whose name shall not be publicized, for the public good), and asked her to make for Giovanna a wax image in the form of a woman, and also some pins and other items required by this diabolical experiment. . . . Giovanna took that image and placed it in a chest in her house. When, a few days later, she had to leave that house and move to another, she left the image in the chest. Later it was discovered by the residents of that house, who burned it. . . .

She collected nine beans, a piece of cloth, some charcoal, several olive leaves which had been blessed and which stood before the image of the virgin Mary, a coin with a cross, and a grain of salt. With these in her hand she genuflected . . . [before the image] and recited three times the Pater Noster and the Ave Maria, spurning the divine prayers composed for the worship of God and his mother the Virgin Mary. Having done this, she placed these items on a piece of linen cloth and slept over them for three nights. And afterwards, she took them in her hand and thrice repeated the Pater Noster and the Ave Maria. . . . And thus Giovanna knew that her future husband would not love her. And so it happened, for after the celebration and the consummation of the marriage, her husband Giovanni stayed with her for a few days, and then left her and has not yet returned. [Giovanna confessed to these crimes and was beheaded.]

VII

Art and Architecture

INTRODUCTION

*T*he *Renaissance is traditionally identified as one of the great moments
in the history of art. Indeed, when asked to exemplify the Renaissance, most observers select an example from the world of art. The reason
for this rests with the growing accessibility of Renaissance painting and
sculpture, introducing a style in which nature is reproduced with greater
accuracy, and flat canvases or walls are turned in apparently three-dimensional visions of a universe that relates clearly to the human experience
of the observer.*

    *Human circumstances and experience are at the root of Renaissance
art. Alberti, in his treatise on painting, discusses the importance of the
storia, or narrative, of the picture. Individual human beings or small
groups of men and women linked pictorially by family, religion, class,
political allegiance, or other elements of daily experience dominate the
subject. There is a movement away from the divine, supernatural, hieratic
quality of medieval art toward one of earthly life and knowledge, even
in religious subjects. Thus the value of human experience, so visible in
every aspect of Renaissance life, is again central. Art reproduces what
the eye sees and makes individual human experience valid and worth
recording.*

    *To accomplish this, Renaissance artists developed the mechanisms
for reproducing what the eye sees. Linear perspective (turning a two-
dimensional into a three-dimensional plane) was developed at the beginning of the fifteenth century by Brunelleschi and Alberti to
define rules by which depth might be accurately portrayed. Similarly,
Renaissance artists engaged in the study of anatomy, botany, and other
sciences to assist in reproducing nature as they perceived it. Naturalism,*

then, became one of the central elements in Renaissance art. Portraits came to be increasingly exact representations of the persons depicted, both in physiognomy and in character, and by the fifteenth century, fully rounded portrait busts and bronze equestrian statues were again created for the first time since classical antiquity. Landscapes were more and more real reproductions of specific places with identifiable plants and topography.

As with other Renaissance phenomena, classical antiquity provided much of the inspiration. This is especially true of architecture and sculpture, because very little ancient painting had yet been discovered. Architects, such as Brunelleschi and Alberti, actually traveled to Rome to measure and draw ancient ruins to learn how they were constructed. The rediscovery of the Roman architect Vitruvius' Ten Books on Architecture gave a theoretical foundation to this research and provided Alberti with the model for his own text. Buildings in the Renaissance consequently absorbed the vocabulary of ancient structures. Their proportions were those of the human body, as Vitruvius taught, or were accessible and pleasing as mathematical qualities to the trained, rational mind of humanistically educated patrons and observers.

Added to this was the highly developed artisan workshop tradition of the Italian city-state. Talented aspiring artists, sculptors, and architects entered the workshop of a master and learned his skill by practicing their art under the direction of the master. This workshop tradition was particularly important in Florence because the wealth of the city attracted many of the best practitioners looking for employment and because the relatively large size of the urban patriciate made competition for the best artists very acute. This, together with the civic tradition of public patronage (exemplified by the Baptistry Doors), made Florence a center for Renaissance artistic activity and innovation. Moreover, because of the gathering of so many of the finest craftsmen, the city itself became a repository of examples of the new style. With every new painting, fresco, sculpture, palace, or church created by the most skilled artists and architects, the reputation of Florence spread as the most significant place to study and practice the rapidly developing styles of the Renaissance.

These elements of competition and patronage cannot be stressed strongly enough. Competition brought out the best of the talented men creating art in the Renaissance and gave them a livelihood in an appreciative environment where their work could serve as examples to others. Equally, discriminating patrons, such as Isabella d'Este, could work closely with a talented artist to create objects of great beauty and profundity for personal or public use. This conjunction of learned patron and talented artist—despite the occasional tension—helped drive the art and architecture of the Renaissance to its heights of excellence.

✦ *Filippo Brunelleschi*

*F*ilippo Brunelleschi (1377–1446) was a Florentine architect originally trained as a goldsmith, but he turned almost completely to the practice of architecture and engineering after losing the competition to design the Baptistry doors to Ghiberti. He was greatly influenced by the building practices of ancient Rome and even traveled to that city with the sculptor Donatello to study and measure ancient ruins to better understand their construction. It was Brunelleschi who designed the Foundling Hospital (Innocenti, 1419) and the dome on the cathedral of Florence (beginning in 1420), the Old Sacristy at San Lorenzo (after 1421), the burial place of the Medici. He also designed or participated in the building of some of Florence's most beautiful churches and chapels: the Pazzi Chapel at Santa Croce, Santo Spirito (after 1436), San Lorenzo, and the unfinished Santa Maria degli Angeli (after 1434).

The influence of classical models and of linear perspective is evident in all Brunelleschi's work. His architectural vocabulary was that of ancient Rome, mixed with local Tuscan as well as Romanesque and Byzantine elements.

✦ *Mariano Taccola*

*M*ariano di Jacopo Taccola (1382– c. 1454) was a Sienese engineer who designed machines for building large-scale bridges, port facilities, and similar major civic construction. Also, he entered the service of the Emperor Sigismund, for whom he designed military machines, and he may have assisted Sigismund in his wars against the Turks. His Ten Books on Machines (1449) was very important and well known in the fifteenth century.

A SPEECH BY BRUNELLESCHI

Pippo Brunelleschi of the great and mighty city of Florence, a singularly honored man, famous in several arts, gifted by God especially in architecture, a most learned inventor of devices in mechanics, was kind enough to speak to me in Siena, using these words: Do not share your inventions with many, share them only with few who understand and love the sciences. To disclose too much of one's inventions and achievements is one

SOURCE: I. Hyman, ed., *Brunelleschi in Perspective* (Englewood Cliffs, N.J.: Prentice-Hall, 1974), pp. 30–32.

and the same thing as to give up the fruit of one's ingenuity. Many are ready, when listening to the inventor, to belittle and deny his achievements, so that he will no longer be heard in honorable places, but after some months or a year they use the inventor's words, in speech or writing or design. They boldly call themselves the inventors of the things that they first condemned, and attribute the glory of another to themselves. There is also the great big ingenious fellow, who, having heard of some innovation or invention never known before, will find the inventor and his idea most surprising and ridiculous. He tells him: Go away, do me the favor and say no such things any more—you will be esteemed a *beast*. Therefore the gifts given to us by God must not be relinquished to those who speak ill of them and who are moved by envy or ignorance. We must do that which wise men esteem to be the wisdom of the strong and ingenious:

We must not show to all and sundry the secrets of the waters flowing in ocean and river, or the devices that work on these waters. Let there be convened a council of experts and masters in mechanical art to deliberate what is needed to compose and construct these works. Every person wishes to know of the proposals, the learned and the ignorant; the learned understands the work proposed—he understands at least something, partly or fully—but the ignorant and inexperienced understand nothing, not even when things are explained to them. Their ignorance moves them promptly to anger; they remain in their ignorance because they want to show themselves learned, which they are not, and they move the other ignorant crowd to insistence on its own poor ways and to scorn for those who know. Therefore the *blockheads* and ignorants are a great danger for the aqueducts, the means for forcing the waters, their ascending and descending both subterranean and terrestrial, and the building in water and over the water, be it salt or fresh. Those who know these things are much to be loved, but those who do not are even more to be avoided, and the *headstrong* ignorant should be sent to war. Only the wise should form a council, since they are the honor and glory of the republic. Amen.

◆ *The Competition for the Baptistry Doors*

LORENZO GHIBERTI

*L*orenzo Ghiberti (1378–1455) was a Florentine sculptor much inspired by the bronzes of classical antiquity. In 1401 he won a competition to create the bronze doors of the Baptistry in Florence, defeating seven other sculptors, including his famous contemporary, Filippo Brunelleschi.

This competition took up most of Ghiberti's life. He only completed the second pair of doors—those termed by Michelangelo to be worthy of the Gates of Paradise—in 1452.

In my youth in the year of Christ 1400, I left Florence because the air was corrupt and the city in a bad state. I left in the company of a distinguished painter who had been summoned by the Lord Malatesta of Pesaro. He had had a room made which we painted for him with the greatest diligence. . . . At this time however my friends in Florence wrote to me that the governors of the temple of S. Giovanni Battista were sending for skilled masters of whose work they wished to see proof. From all over Italy many skilled masters came to enter this trial and contest. I requested leave from the lord [Malatesta] and from my companion. When the lord [Malatesta] heard the situation he immediately granted me leave; together with other sculptors I went before the committee [of S. Giovanni Battista]. To each one were given four bronze tablets. As the trial piece the committee and the governors of that temple wanted each of us to make one narrative panel for the door. The story they selected was the Sacrifice of Isaac, and each of the contestants had to make the same story. The trial pieces were to be executed in one year and he who won would be given the prize. The contestants were these: Filippo di ser Brunellesco, Simone da Colle, Nicolò d'Arezzo, Jacopo della Quercia of Siena, Francesco di Valdambrina, Nicolò Lamberti. There were six[1] taking part in this contest, which was a demonstration of the various aspects of the art of sculpture. To me was conceded the palm of victory by all the experts and by all those who competed with me. Universally I was conceded the glory without exception. At that time it seemed to all, after great consultation and examination by the learned men, that I had surpassed all the others without any exception. The committee of the governors wanted the opinion of the experts written by their own hand. They were highly skilled men among painters, goldsmiths, silversmiths, and marble sculptors. There were thirty-four judges from the city and other places nearby. From all came the declaration of the victory in my favor by the consuls and the committee and the entire body of the Merchants' Guild which is in charge of the temple of S. Giovanni. It was conceded to me and determined that I should make the bronze door for this temple. This I carried out with great diligence. . . .

---

1. Ghiberti neglected to include himself in the count; there were seven contestants.

SOURCE: A. di Tuccio, *The Life of Brunelleschi,* ed. by H. Saal, trans. by C. Engass (University Park and London: The Pennsylvania State University Press, 1970), pp. 46, 48, 50. Reproduced by permission of the publisher.

ANTONIO MANETTI

*A*ntonio di Tuccio Manetti (1423–1497) was a Florentine architect and
humanist who is most remembered for his biography of Brunelleschi
(c. 1480), the first full-length life of an artist written in the Renaissance.

In the year of Our Lord 1401 when [Brunelleschi—Ed.] was a young man
of twenty-four, working at the goldsmith's art, the *operai* of the building
of the temple of San Giovanni had to commission the making of the
second bronze doors (which are today on the north facade) for the embellishment of the aforesaid church. While considering the reputation of the
masters of figure casting—including the Florentine masters—in order to
assign them to the one who was best, they decided, after many discussions
amongst themselves and after counsels with the citizens and artisans, that
the two finest they could find were both Florentines and that neither in
Florence or elsewhere did they know of anyone better. Those two were
the aforementioned Filippo and Lorenzo di Bartolo. The latter's name is
inscribed on the doors as Lorenzo di Cione Ghiberti as he was the son of
Cione. At the outset of this affair of the doors Lorenzo was a young man
also. He was in Rimini in the service of Signor Malatesta when he was
called to Florence for this event. The following method was employed to
choose the best one: they selected the shape of one of the compartments
from the bronze doors that had been made by non-Florentine masters in
the last century (although the design of the wax modeled figures was by
the painter Giotto) containing the story of St. John. Each of them was
given a scene to sculpt in bronze within such a form with the principal
intention of commissioning the doors to the one who came out the best
in the aforesaid test.

They made those scenes and they have been preserved to this day.
The one in the Audience Hall of the Guild of the Merchants is by Lorenzo
and the one in the dossal of the sacristy altar of San Lorenzo in Florence
is by Filippo. The subject of both is Abraham sacrificing his son. Filippo
sculpted his scene in the way that still may be seen today. He made it
quickly, as he had a powerful command of the art. Having cast, cleaned,
and polished it completely he was not eager to talk about it with anyone,
since, as I have said, he was not boastful. He waited for the time of
confrontation. It was said that Lorenzo was rather apprehensive about
Filippo's merit as [the latter] was very apparent. Since it did not seem to
him that he possessed such mastery of the art, he worked slowly. Having
been told something of the beauty of Filippo's work he had the idea, as
he was a shrewd person, of proceeding by means of hard work and by
humbling himself through seeking the counsel—so that his work would
not fail at the confrontation—of all the people he esteemed who, being
goldsmiths, painters, sculptors, etc. and knowledgeable men, had to do
the judging. While making [his scene] in wax he conferred and—humbling

himself a great deal—asked for advice constantly of people of that sort and, insofar as he could, he tried to find out how Filippo's work was coming along. He unmade and remade the whole and sections of it without sparing effort, just as often as the majority of the experts in discussing it judged that he should. The *operai* and officials of the church were advised by the very people Lorenzo had singled out. They were in fact the best informed and had been around Lorenzo's work many times: perhaps there was no one else [to consult].

Since none of them had seen Filippo's model they all believed that Polycletus—not to mention Filippo—could not have done better [than Lorenzo]. Filippo's fame was not yet widespread as he was a young man and his mind was fixed on deeds rather than on appearances. However, when they saw his work they were all astonished and marveled at the problems that he had set himself: the attitude, the position of the finger under the chin, and the energy of Abraham; the clothing, bearing, and delicacy of the son's entire figure; the angel's robes, bearing, and gestures and the manner in which he grasps the hand; the attitude, bearing, and delicacy of the figure removing a thorn from his foot and the figure bending over to drink—how complex these figures are and how well they fulfill their functions (there is not a limb that is not alive); the types and the fineness of the animals as well as all the other elements and the composition of the scene as a whole.

Those deputized to do the judging changed their opinion when they saw it. However, it seemed unfeasible to recant what they had said so persistently to anyone who would listen to them, though it now seemed laughable, even though they recognized the truth. Gathering together again they came to a decision and made the following report to the *operai*: both models were very beautiful and for their part, taking everything into consideration, they were unable to put one ahead of the other, and since it was a big undertaking requiring much time and expense they should commission it to both equally and they should be partners. When Filippo and Lorenzo were summoned and informed of the decision, Lorenzo remained silent while Filippo was unwilling to consent unless he was given entire charge of the work. On that point he was unyielding. The officials made the decision thinking that certainly they would in the end agree. Filippo, like one who unknowingly has been destined for some greater tasks by God, refused to budge. The officials threatened to assign it to Lorenzo if he did not change his mind: he answered that he wanted no part of it if he did not have complete control, and if they were unwilling to grant it they could give it to Lorenzo as far as he was concerned. With that they made their decision. Public opinion in the city was completely divided as a result. Those who took Filippo's side were very displeased that the commission for the whole work had not been given to him. However, that is what happened, and in view of what was awaiting Filippo experience proved that it was for the best.

GIORGIO VASARI

*F*or Giorgio Vasari (1511–1574), Florentine artist, architect, and art theorist and historian, see below, p. 406.

In the year 1401, it was proposed to make the two bronze doors of the church and baptistery of S. Giovanni, sculpture having advanced so greatly, because from the time of the death of Andrea Pisano there had not been any masters capable of carrying them out. Accordingly this purpose was made known to the sculptors then in Tuscany, who were invited to come, provided with maintenance and set to prepare a panel. Among those thus invited were Filippo and Donato, Lorenzo Ghiberti, Jacopo della Fonte, Simone da Colle, Francesco di Valdambrina and Niccolo d' Arezzo. The panels were completed that same year, and when they came to be exhibited in competition they were all most beautiful, each different from the other. That of Donato was well designed and badly executed; that of Jacopo della Quercia was well designed and executed, but with faulty perspective of the figures; that of Francesco di Valdambrina had poor invention and tiny figures; the worst of all were those of Niccolo d' Arezzo and Simone da Colle; and the best that of Lorenzo di Ghiberti, combining design, diligence, invention and art, the figures being beautifully made. Not much inferior to his, however, was the panel of Filippo, on which he had represented Abraham sacrificing Isaac, with a servant extracting a thorn from his foot while waiting for Abraham, and an ass grazing, which merits considerable praise. When the scenes came to be exhibited, Filippo and Donato were only satisfied with that of Lorenzo, judging it to be better adapted to its peculiar purpose than those of the others. So they persuaded the consuls with good arguments that the work should be given to Lorenzo, showing that both public and private ends would be best served thereby. This was a true act of friendship, a virtue without envy, and a clear judgment of their own limitations, so that they deserve more praise than if they had completed that work themselves. Happy spirits who, while assisting each other, rejoice in praising the work of others! How unhappy are the men of our own times, who try to injure others, and burst with envy if they cannot vent their malice. Filippo was requested by the consuls to undertake the work together with Lorenzo, but he refused, as he preferred to be the first in another art, rather than be equal or second in that.

♦ *Il Pinturicchio (Bernardino di Betto)*

*I*l Pinturicchio (1454–1513) was born in Perugio but left for Rome, where he worked with Perugino on the Sistine Chapel and painted the Borgia Apartments for Pope Alexander VI. Subsequently, Pinturicchio accepted *a commission from Cardinal Todeschini-Piccolomini, nephew of Pope Pius II (Aeneas Silvius Piccolomini), in 1502 to fresco the Piccolomini Library in the Cathedral of Siena. His patron was elevated to the papacy himself in 1503 but died a few days after.*

CONTRACT OF PINTURICCHIO WITH CARDINAL FRANCESCO DE' TODESCHINI-PICCOLOMINI FOR DECORATING THE LIBRARY IN SIENA CATHEDRAL, 29 JUNE 1502

In the name of God, Amen

Be it noted by whoever reads or sees the present writing how on this day 29 June 1502 the Very Reverend Lord Cardinal of Siena has contracted and commissioned Master Bernardino, called *el Penturicchio*, Perugian painter, to paint a Library in the cathedral of Siena, according to the conditions and agreements set out below:

That during the time he is painting it, he may not undertake any other work of painting, whether a picture or a mural, in Siena or elsewhere, which may cause the decoration of the said Library to be postponed or retarded.

Item, he is obliged to render the ceiling of the Library with fantasies and colors and small panels as lovely, beautiful and sumptuous as he judges best; all in good, fine, fast colors in the manner of design known today as *grottesche*, with different backgrounds as will be reckoned most lovely and beautiful.

Item, if the arms of the Most Reverend Monsignor are not painted on the middle of the ceiling, he shall be obliged to make a rich and beautiful coat of arms of the size necessary to be in proportion to the roof. And if it is already painted, he shall renovate it, or if it is done in marble, he shall likewise be obliged to paint, gild or embellish it as above.

Item, he is obliged, as well as doing the ceiling, to do ten stories in fresco, in which (as will be laid out in a memorandum) he is to paint the life of Pope Pius of holy memory, with fitting persons, events and apparel necessary and appropriate to illustrate it properly; with gold, ultramarine azure, green glazes and azures and other colors as are in accordance with the fee, the subject-matter, the place and his own convenience.

Item, he is obliged to render in fresco as above, touch up in *secco* and finish in fine colors the said figures, nudes, garments, draperies, trees, landscapes, cities, air and sky, funeral scenes and friezes.

SOURCE: D. S. Chambers, ed., *Patrons and Artists in the Italian Renaissance* (Columbia, S.C.: University of South Carolina Press, 1971), pp. 25–29. Reprinted by permission of Macmillan, London and Basingstoke.

Item, it is left to him to decide whether the half-lunette above each picture should be decorated with figures or filled with landscapes etc.

Item, he is obliged to render the pilasters which divide and enclose the panels in which the painted scenes will go, and the capitals, cornices, gilded bases and friezes contained within them all in good and fine colors, as are best and most beautiful.

Item, he is obliged to do all the designs of the stories in his own hand on cartoon and on the wall; to do the heads all in fresco by his own hand, and to touch up in *secco* and finish them to perfection.

Item, he is obliged to do a panel linking the pilasters under each scene, in which shall be an inscription or proper explanation of the scene painted above, and this can be written either in verse or prose; and at the base of these columns and pilasters the arms of the Most Reverend Monsignore shall be painted.

And it has been agreed by the aforesaid Master Bernardino to do the ceiling according to the requisite standard of perfection, and the ten pictures as richly and finely as appropriate; and for his salary and reward the said Most Reverend Cardinal promises to give him 1000 gold ducats of Papal Chamber (*de Camera*) as follows: first, the said Cardinal will have 200 gold ducats *de Camera* paid to him in Venice to buy gold and necessary colors, and 100 more ducats will be paid to him at Perugia for his needs and for the transport of his equipment and assistants to Siena. For this initial payment of 300 ducats the said Master Bernardino shall be obliged to give suitable good security for his execution of the work. And should God so will it otherwise, he will do what is proper and restore all the money to the said Cardinal, saving a discount for whatever part of the work he has already done. The rest his sponsors shall be held to restore in entirety to the said Cardinal, without any exception whatsoever.

Item, on completion of each panel, the said Cardinal will have 50 gold ducats *de camera* paid to him, and he will continue thus for each in turn. When all are entirely finished, he will pay him the 200 ducats outstanding.

Item, the most Reverend Cardinal promises the said Master Bernardino that he will lend him a house near the cathedral church to live in free while he is in Siena.

Item, he will allow him wood to make the scaffolding, and also arrange for him to receive sufficient lime and sand.

And because the said Master Bernardino needs corn, wine and oil while he is working on the Library, he shall be obliged to obtain these from the said Cardinal's factor, at current prices, to be discounted from the payment for his work.

And in security of the above, the contracting parties undertake the following: the most Reverend Monsignor personally pledges himself, his goods both moveable and nonmoveable, and his heirs, both present and future, to observe in entirety all the above-named clauses and agreements with Master Bernardino; and to pay him the said quantity of 1000 gold ducats *de camera* in the manner and times set forth above.

And the said Bernardino for his part promises and wholly pledges himself to observe what is detailed above with the most reverend Cardinal, and to give sufficient security for the 300 gold ducats that are to be advanced to him; also pledging his goods moveable and nonmoveable, and his heirs, present and future, that in all and every part he will observe in entirety all the things agreed and promised above, understanding that all is in good faith and without any intent to defraud.

And I, the above-mentioned Francesco Cardinal of Siena am content, and promise as above; and with faith in the truth have written these lines in my own hand, on the said day of the said month and year.

And I, the above-mentioned Master Bernardino etc.

Drawn up before me personally, public notary, with the below-named witnesses, the most Reverend Father in Christ and Lord Francesco dei Piccolomini, Lord Cardinal of Siena, and the discreet master Bernardino, alias Pinturicchio, of Perugia, painter . . . Enacted at Siena in the house of the said Most Reverend Lord Cardinal situated near the church and in the parish of San Vigilio, Siena, in the presence of the venerable and worthy Lord Francesco Nanni, canon of Sateano and chaplain in Siena cathedral, and Luca Bartolomeo Cerini of Siena, familiars of the said Cardinal; and Fortino Lorenzo, Master Marco and Luca dei Vieri, citizens of Siena, witnesses.

And I Francesco, son of Giacomo of Montalcino, public and imperial notary and judge ordinary of Siena, at present scriptor in the Archbishop's Court in Siena, have written, drawn up and registered these agreements.

✦ Isabella d'Este

B orn the daughter of Ercole I, Duke of Ferrara, Isabella d'Este (1474– 1539) enjoyed a wonderful humanist education at her father's court. At 16 she was married to Francesco Gonzaga of Mantua, for whom she often ruled because of his long absences on military campaigns. She was a brilliant patron, having excellent taste, great wealth, and civilized advisers. She patronized Leonardo da Vinci, Titian, and Perugino, for whom in 1503 she designed an allegorical subject for him to paint. Equally, she surrounded herself with men of letters, such as Castiglione and Pietro Bembo. Despite her active humanist interests, Isabella remained a devout Catholic, founding religious houses and sustaining the Church in her dominions, although she maintained a political wariness of the ambitions of the papacy.

♦ *Pietro Vanucci Perugino*

*P*ietro Vanucci Perugino (1446–1523) was born near Perugia, but he went to Florence to study painting, working in the workshop of Verrocchio, where Leonardo da Vinci also was apprenticed. In 1481 Perugino was summoned to Rome by Pope Sixtus IV to help in the decoration of the Sistine Chapel. After 1492, however, he established his own workshop in Florence, producing many paintings to meet the demand his fame engendered. As a result, Perugino became rich and respected throughout Italy. Before the end of the century, he returned to accept a major civic commission in his home town of Perugia, completing the cycle of paintings in the College of the Bankers by 1501, assisted by the young Raphael, who had entered his workshop. Around 1503 he returned to Florence, but left for Rome in 1507 to work for Pope Julius II at the Vatican.

INSTRUCTIONS OF ISABELLA D'ESTE TO PERUGINO, 19 JANUARY 1503

Drawn up at Florence in the parish of Santa Maria in Campo in the below-mentioned house, in the presence of Bernardo Antonio di Castiglione, Florentine citizen, and Fra Ambrogio, Prior of the Order of Jesuati, near Florence, witnesses.

Lord Francesco de' Malatesta of Mantua, procurator of the Marchioness of Mantua, in the best manner he was able, commissioned from Master Perugino, painter, there present, the undertaking on his own behalf and that of his heirs to make a painting on canvas, 2 1/2 *braccia* high and 3 *braccia* wide, and the said Pietro, the contractor, is obliged to paint on it a certain work of Lasciviousness and Modesty (in conflict) with these and many other embellishments, transmitted in this instruction to the said Pietro by the said Marchioness of Mantua, the copy of which is as follows:

Our poetic invention, which we greatly want to see painted by you, is a battle of Chastity against Lasciviousness, that is to say, Pallas and Diana fighting vigorously against Venus and Cupid. And Pallas should seem almost to have vanquished Cupid, having broken his golden arrow and cast his silver bow underfoot; with one hand she is holding him by the bandage which the blind boy has before his eyes, and with the other she is lifting her lance and about to kill him. By comparison Diana must seem to be having a closer fight with Venus for victory. Venus has been

SOURCE: D. S. Chambers, ed., *Patrons and Artists in the Italian Renaissance* (Columbia, S.C.: University of South Carolina Press, 1971), pp. 135–139. Reprinted by permission of Macmillan, London and Basingstoke.

struck by Diana's arrow only on the surface of the body, on her crown and garland, or on a veil she may have around her; and part of Diana's raiment will have been singed by the torch of Venus, but nowhere else will either of them have been wounded. Beyond these four deities, the most chaste nymphs in the trains of Pallas and Diana, in whatever attitudes and ways you please, have to fight fiercely with a lascivious crowd of fauns, satyrs and several thousand cupids; and these cupids must be much smaller than the first [the god Cupid], and not bearing gold bows and silver arrows, but bows and arrows of some baser material such as wood or iron or what you please. And to give more expression and decoration to the picture, beside Pallas I want to have the olive tree sacred to her, with a shield leaning against it bearing the head of Medusa, and with the owl, the bird peculiar to Pallas, perched among the branches. And beside Venus I want her favorite tree, the myrtle, to be placed. But to enhance the beauty a fount of water must be included, such as a river or the sea, where fauns, satyrs and more cupids will be seen, hastening to the help of Cupid, some swimming through the river, some flying, and some riding upon white swans, coming to join such an amorous battle. On the bank of the said river or sea stands Jupiter with other gods, as the enemy of Chastity, changed into the bull which carried off the fair Europa; and Mercury as an eagle circling above its prey, flies around one of Pallas' nymphs, called Glaucera, who carries a casket engraved with the sacred emblems of the goddess. Polyphemus, the one-eyed Cyclops, chases Galatea, and Phoebus chases Daphne, who has already turned into a laurel tree; Pluto, having seized Proserpina, is bearing her off to his kingdom of darkness, and Neptune has seized a nymph who has been turned almost entirely into a raven.

I am sending you all these details in a small drawing, so that with both the written description and the drawing you will be able to consider my wishes in this matter. But if you think that perhaps there are too many figures in this for one picture, it is left to you to reduce them as you please, provided that you do not remove the principal basis, which consists of the four figures of Pallas, Diana, Venus and Cupid. If no inconvenience occurs I shall consider myself well satisfied; you are free to reduce them, but not to add anything else. Please be content with this arrangement.

And to this manner and form the parties are referred.

Master Pietro promised Lord Francesco to devote himself with his skill to achieving the said picture over a period from now until the end of next June, without any exception of law or deed; Lord Francesco promised, in the said names, to pay for the making of the said work a hundred gold florins, in large gold florins, to the said Lord [sic] Pietro, with the agreement that of the said sum twenty gold florins, in large gold florins, should be given at present to the said Lord Pietro, painter; which the said Lord Pietro in the presence of me, the notary, and of the witnesses written above, acknowledged he had received of the said Lord Francesco, and the remainder the said Lord Francesco promised to pay to the said Lord Pietro when the said Lord Pietro completes the said work to perfection and shall give it to Lord Francesco Malatesta of Mantua. And the said Lord Pietro is obliged to complete the said work himself, bearing all the expenses for the same; with an agreement that in the event of the death of the said Master Pietro, should it happen that the said work is not completed, the heirs of the said Master Pietro shall be obliged to restore the said sum of 20 large gold florins to the said Lord Francesco Malatesta, or however much more he has had; or else, in the event of the said work not being completed on account of the death of the said Lord Pietro, that the said Lord Francesco shall be obliged to receive the said work in the form and style so far devised for it, and the said work must be valued by two experienced painters and he must take it for the price they estimate.

LETTER OF PERUGINO TO ISABELLA D'ESTE, 10 DECEMBER 1503

Most Excellent Madam

Having learnt the story which Your Ladyship commissioned from me a short while ago, it seems to me that the drawing sent to me does not correspond very well with the size of the figures, which seem to me to be very small and the height of the picture seems too great in proportion to them. I want to know what is the size of the figures in the other stories which are to go beside it, because if the whole scheme is to turn out well all the measurements must agree, or there must be very little difference. Therefore please arrange for me to be sent this information, so that I can give satisfaction to Your Excellency as is my desire. Nothing else; I recommend myself humbly, praying God keeps you well.

Florence, 10 December 1503
Your Excellency's faithful servant, Pietro Perugino

LETTER OF ISABELLA D'ESTE TO PERUGINO, 12 JANUARY 1504

Excellent friend

The enclosed paper, and the thread wound round it together give the length of the largest figure on Master Andrea Mantegna's picture, beside which yours will hang. The other figures smaller than this can be as you please. You know how to arrange it. We beg you above all to hasten with the work; the sooner we have it, the more we shall be pleased.

LETTER OF PERUGINO TO ISABELLA D'ESTE, 24 JANUARY 1504

My most illustrious Lady, Marchioness of Mantua, greeting and infinite recommendations

I sent a letter to you a month and a half ago and I have never had a reply to the said letter. I will repeat what it is about in this: I have drawn some of your figures, which come out very small; I would like Your Ladyship to send me the size of the other stories which are to accompany my story, so that they should conform; and so that the principal figures are all of one size, otherwise they will contradict each other a great deal, one being big and another small. So send me the measurements of the other figures in the other stories that you have had done, and I will at once show my diligence. Nothing further; I recommend myself to Your Ladyship.

24 January 1504
Your Pietro Perugino, painter in Florence

✦ *Leon Battista Alberti*

*F*or details of the life and work of Leon Battista Alberti (1404–1472), see above, p. 162.

ON PAINTING AND ON SCULPTURE

19. Up to now we have explained everything related to the power of sight and the understanding of the intersection. But as it is relevant to know, not simply what the intersection is and what it consists in, but also how it can be constructed, we must now explain the art of expressing the intersection in painting. Let me tell you what I do when I am painting. First of all, on the surface on which I am going to paint, I draw a rectangle of whatever size I want, which I regard as an open window through which the subject to be painted is seen; and I decide how large I wish the human figures in the painting to be. I divide the height of this man into three parts, which will be proportional to the measure commonly called a *braccio*; for, as may be seen from the relationship of his limbs, three *braccia* is just about the average height of a man's body. With this measure I divide the bottom line of my rectangle into as many parts as it will hold;

SOURCE: Leon Battista Alberti, *On Painting and On Sculpture*, trans. and ed. by C. Grayson (London: Phaidon, 1972), pp. 53–67, 95–99. Reprinted by permission of C. Grayson.

and this bottom line of the rectangle is for me proportional to the next transverse equidistant quantity seen on the pavement. Then I establish a point in the rectangle wherever I wish; and as it occupies the place where the centric ray strikes, I shall call this the centric point. The suitable position for this centric point is no higher from the base line than the height of the man to be represented in the painting, for in this way both the viewers and the objects in the painting will seem to be on the same plane. Having placed the centric point, I draw straight lines from it to each of the divisions on the base line. These lines show me how successive transverse quantities visually change to an almost infinite distance. At this stage some would draw a line across the rectangle equidistant from the divided line, and then divide the space between these two lines into three parts. Then, to that second equidistant line they would add another above, following the rule that the space which is divided into three parts between the first divided (base) line and the second equidistant one, shall exceed by one of its parts the space between the second and third lines; and they would go on to add other lines in such a way that each succeeding space between them would always be to the one preceding it in the relationship, in mathematical terminology, of *superbipartiens*. That would be their way of proceeding, and although people say they are following an excellent method of painting, I believe they are not a little mistaken, because, having placed the first equidistant line at random, even though the other equidistant lines follow with some system and reason, nonetheless they do not know where the fixed position of the vertex of the pyramid is for correct viewing. For this reason quite serious mistakes occur in painting. What is more, the method of such people would be completely faulty, where the centric point were higher or lower than the height of a man in the picture. Besides, no learned person will deny that no objects in a painting can appear like real objects, unless they stand to each other in a determined relationship. We will explain the theory behind this if ever we write about the demonstrations of painting, which our friends marveled at when we did them, and called them "miracles of painting"; for the things I have said are extremely relevant to this aspect of the subject. Let us return, therefore, to what we were saying.

20. With regard to the question outlined above, I discovered the following excellent method. I follow in all other respects the same procedure I mentioned above about placing the centric point, dividing the base line and drawing lines from that point to each of the divisions of the base line. But as regards the successive transverse quantities I observe the following method. I have a drawing surface on which I describe a single straight line, and this I divide into parts like those into which the base line of the rectangle is divided. Then I place a point above this line, directly over one end of it, at the same height as the centric point is from the base line of the rectangle, and from this point I draw lines to each of the divisions of the line. Then I determine the distance I want between the eye of the

spectator and the painting, and having established the position of the intersection at this distance, I effect the intersection with what mathematicians call a perpendicular. A perpendicular is a line which at the intersection with another straight line makes right angles on all sides. This perpendicular will give me, at the places it cuts the other lines, the measure of what the distance should be in each case between the transverse equidistant lines of the pavement. In this way I have all the parallels of the pavement drawn. A parallel is the space between two equidistant lines, of which we spoke at some length above. A proof of whether they are correctly drawn will be if a single straight line forms a diameter of connected quadrangles in the pavement. The diameter of a quadrangle for mathematicians is the straight line drawn from one angle to the angle opposite it, which divides the quadrangle into two parts so as to create two triangles from it. When I have carefully done these things, I draw a line across, equidistant from the other lines below, which cuts the two upright sides of the large rectangle and passes through the centric point. This line is for me a limit or boundary, which no quantity exceeds that is not higher than the eye of the spectator. As it passes through the centric point, this line may be called the centric line. This is why men depicted standing in the parallel furthest away are a great deal smaller than those in the nearer ones—a phenomenon which is clearly demonstrated by nature herself, for in churches we see the heads of men walking about, moving at more or less the same height, while the feet of those further away may correspond to the knee-level of those in front.

21. This method of dividing up the pavement pertains especially to that part of painting which, when we come to it, we shall call composition; and it is such that I fear it may be little understood by readers on account of the novelty of the subject and the brevity of our description. As we can easily judge from the works of former ages, this matter probably remained completely unknown to our ancestors because of its obscurity and difficulty. You will hardly find any "historia" of theirs properly composed either in painting or modelling or sculpture.

22. I have set out the foregoing briefly and, I believe, in a not altogether obscure fashion, but I realize the content is such that, while I can claim no praise for eloquence in exposition, the reader who does not understand at first acquaintance, will probably never grasp it however hard he tries. To intelligent minds that are well disposed to painting, those things are simple and splendid, however presented, which are disagreeable to gross intellects little disposed to these noble arts, even if expounded by the most eloquent writers. As they have been explained by me briefly and without eloquence, they will probably not be read without some distaste. Yet I crave indulgence if, in my desire above all to be understood, I saw to it that my exposition should be clear rather than elegant and ornate. What follows will, I hope, be less disagreeable to the reader.

23. I have set out whatever seemed necessary to say about triangles,

the pyramid and the intersection. I used to demonstrate these things at greater length to my friends with some geometrical explanation. I considered it best to omit this from these books for reasons of brevity. I have outlined here, as a painter speaking to painters, only the first rudiments of the art of painting. And I have called them rudiments, because they lay the first foundations of the art for unlearned painters. They are such that whoever has grasped them properly will see they are of considerable benefit, not only to his own talent and to understanding the definition of painting, but also to the appreciation of what we are going to say later on. Let no one doubt that the man who does not perfectly understand what he is attempting to do when painting, will never be a good painter. It is useless to draw the bow, unless you have a target to aim the arrow at. I want us to be convinced that he alone will be an excellent painter who has learned thoroughly to understand the outlines and all the properties of surfaces. On the other hand, I believe that he who has not diligently mastered all we have said, will never be a good artist.

24. These remarks on surfaces and intersection were, therefore, essential for our purposes. We will now go on to instruct the painter how he can represent with his hand what he has understood with his mind.

25. As the effort of learning may perhaps seem to the young too laborious, I think I should explain here how painting is worthy of all our attention and study. Painting possesses a truly divine power in that not only does it make the absent present (as they say of friendship), but it also represents the dead to the living many centuries later, so that they are recognized by spectators with pleasure and deep admiration for the artist. Plutarch tells us that Cassandrus, one of Alexander's commanders, trembled all over at the sight of a portrait of the deceased Alexander, in which he recognized the majesty of his king. He also tells us how Agesilaus the Lacedaemonian, realizing that he was very ugly, refused to allow his likeness to be known to posterity, and so would not be painted or modeled by anyone. Through painting, the faces of the dead go on living for a very long time. We should also consider it a very great gift to men that painting has represented the gods they worship, for painting has contributed considerably to the piety which binds us to the gods, and to filling our minds with sound religious beliefs. It is said that Phidias made a statue of Jove in Elis, whose beauty added not a little to the received religion. How much painting contributes to the honest pleasures of the mind, and to the beauty of things, may be seen in various ways but especially in the fact that you will find nothing so precious which association with painting does not render far more valuable and highly prized. Ivory, gems, and all other similar precious things are made more valuable by the hand of the painter. Gold too, when embellished by the art of painting, is equal in value to a far larger quantity of gold. Even lead, the basest of metals, if it were formed into some image by the hand of Phidias or Praxiteles, would probably be regarded as more precious than rough unworked silver. The

painter Zeuxis began to give his works away, because, as he said, they could not be bought for money. He did not believe any price could be found to recompense the man who, in modeling or painting living things, behaved like a god among mortals.

26. The virtues of painting, therefore, are that its masters see their works admired and feel themselves to be almost like the Creator. Is it not true that painting is the mistress of all the arts or their principal ornament? If I am not mistaken, the architect took from the painter architraves, capitals, bases, columns and pediments, and all the other fine features of buildings. The stonemason, the sculptor and all the workshops and crafts of artificers are guided by the rule and art of the painter. Indeed, hardly any art, except the very meanest, can be found that does not somehow pertain to painting. So I would venture to assert that whatever beauty there is in things has been derived from painting. Painting was honoured by our ancestors with this special distinction that, whereas all other artists were called craftsmen, the painter alone was not counted among their number. Consequently I used to tell my friends that the inventor of painting, according to the poets, was Narcissus, who was turned into a flower; for, as painting is the flower of all the arts, so the tale of Narcissus fits our purpose perfectly. What is painting but the act of embracing by means of art the surface of the pool? Quintilian believed that the earliest painters used to draw around shadows made by the sun, and the art eventually grew by a process of additions. Some say that an Egyptian Philocles and a certain Cleanthes were among the first inventors of this art. The Egyptians say painting was practiced in their country six thousand years before it was brought over into Greece. Our writers say it came from Greece to Italy after the victories of Marcellus in Sicily. But it is of little concern to us to discover the first painters or the inventors of the art, since we are not writing a history of painting like Pliny, but treating of the art in an entirely new way. On this subject there exist today none of the writings of the ancients, as far as I have seen, although they say that Euphranor the Isthmian wrote something about symmetry and colors, that Antigonus and Xenocrates set down some works about paintings, and that Apelles wrote on painting to Perseus. Diogenes Laertius tells us that the philosopher Demetrius also wrote about painting. Since all the other liberal arts were committed to writing by our ancestors, I believe that painting too was not neglected by our authors of Italy, for the ancient Etruscans were the most expert of all in Italy in the art of painting.

27. The ancient writer Trismegistus believes that sculpture and painting originated together with religion. He addresses Asclepius with these words: "Man, mindful of his nature and origin, represented the gods in his own likeness." Yet who will deny that painting has assumed the most honored part in all things both public and private, profane and religious, to such an extent that no art, I find, has been so highly valued universally among men? Almost incredible prices are quoted for painted panels. The

Theban Aristides sold one painting alone for a hundred talents. They say that Rhodes was not burned down by King Demetrius lest a painting by Protogenes be destroyed. So we can say that Rhodes was redeemed from the enemy by a single picture. Many other similar tales were collected by writers, from which you can clearly see that good painters always and everywhere were held in the highest esteem and honor, so that even the most noble and distinguished citizens and philosophers and kings took great pleasure not only in seeing and possessing paintings, but also in painting themselves. L. Manilius, a Roman citizen, and the nobleman Fabius were painters. Turpilius, a Roman knight, painted at Verona. Sitedius, praetor and proconsul, acquired fame in painting. Pacuvius, the tragedian, nephew of the poet Ennius, painted Hercules in the forum. The philosophers Socrates, Plato, Metrodorus and Pyrrho achieved distinction in painting. The emperors Nero, Valentinianus and Alexander Severus were very devoted to painting. It would be a long story to tell how many princes or kings have devoted themselves to this most noble art. Besides, it is not appropriate to review all the multitude of ancient painters. Its size may be understood from the fact that for Demetrius of Phalerum, son of Phanostratus, three hundred and sixty statues were completed within four hundred days, some on horseback and some in chariots. In a city in which there was so large a number of sculptors, shall we not believe there were also many painters? Painting and sculpture are cognate arts, nurtured by the same genius. But I shall always prefer the genius of the painter, as it attempts by far the most difficult task. Let us return to what we were saying.

28. The number of painters and sculptors was enormous in those days, when princes and people, and learned and unlearned alike delighted in painting, and statues and pictures were displayed in the theatres among the chief spoils brought from the provinces. Eventually Paulus Aemilius and many other Roman citizens taught their sons painting among the liberal arts in the pursuit of the good and happy life. The excellent custom was especially observed among the Greeks that free-born and liberally educated young people were also taught the art of painting together with letters, geometry and music. Indeed the skill of painting was a mark of honor also in women. Martia, Varro's daughter, is celebrated by writers for her painting. The art was held in such high esteem and honor that it was forbidden by law among the Greeks for slaves to learn to paint; and quite rightly so, for the art of painting is indeed worthy of free minds and noble intellects. I have always regarded it as a mark of an excellent and superior mind in any person whom I saw take great delight in painting. Although, this art alone is equally pleasing to both learned and unlearned; and it rarely happens in any other art that what pleases the knowledgeable also attracts the ignorant. You will not easily find anyone who does not earnestly desire to be accomplished in painting. Indeed it is evident that Nature herself delights in painting, for we observe she often fashions in

marble hippocentaurs and bearded faces of kings. It is also said that in a gem owned by Pyrrhus the nine Muses were clearly depicted by Nature, complete with their insignia. Furthermore, there is no other art in whose study and practice all ages of learned and unlearned alike may engage with such pleasure. Let me speak of my own experience. Whenever I devote myself to painting for pleasure, which I very often do when I have leisure from other affairs, I persevere with such pleasure in finishing my work that I can hardly believe later on that three or even four hours have gone by.

29. This art, then, brings pleasure while you practice it, and praise, riches and endless fame when you have cultivated it well. Therefore, as painting is the finest and most ancient ornament of things, worthy of free men and pleasing to learned and unlearned alike, I earnestly beseech young students to devote themselves to painting as much as they can. Next, I would advise those who are devoted to painting to go on to master with every effort and care this perfect art of painting. You who strive to excel in painting, should cultivate above all the fame and reputation which you see the ancients attained, and in so doing it will be a good thing to remember that avarice was always the enemy of renown and virtue. A mind intent on gain will rarely obtain the reward of fame with posterity. I have seen many in the very flower, as it were, of learning, descend to gain and thereafter obtain neither riches nor distinction, who if they had improved their talent with application, would easily have risen to fame and there received both wealth and the satisfaction of renown. But we have said enough on these matters.

✦ ✦ ✦

51. Several things, which I do not think should be omitted from these books, still remain to complete the instruction of the painter, so that he may attain all the praiseworthy objects of which we have spoken. Let me now explain them very briefly.

52. The function of the painter is to draw with lines and paint in colors on a surface any given bodies in such a way that, at a fixed distance and with a certain determined position of the centric ray, what you see represented appears to be in relief and just like those bodies. The aim of the painter is to obtain praise, favor and good-will for his work much more than riches. The painter will achieve this if his painting holds and charms the eyes and minds of spectators. We explained how this may be done when talking above about composition and the reception of light. But in order that he may attain all these things, I would have the painter first of all be a good man, well versed in the liberal arts. Everyone knows how much more effective uprightness of character is in securing people's favor than any amount of admiration for someone's industry and art. And no one doubts that the favor of many people is very useful to the artist

for acquiring reputation and wealth. It so happens that, as rich men are often moved by kindness more than by expert knowledge of art, they will give money to one man who is especially modest and good, and spurn another who is more skilled but perhaps intemperate. For this reason it behoves the artist to be particularly attentive to his morals, especially to good manners and amiability, whereby he may obtain both the good-will of others, which is a firm protection against poverty, and money, which is an excellent aid to the perfection of his art.

53. I want the painter, as far as he is able, to be learned in all the liberal arts, but I wish him above all to have a good knowledge of geometry. I agree with the ancient and famous painter Pamphilus, from whom young nobles first learned painting; for he used to say that no one could be a good painter who did not know geometry. Our rudiments, from which the complete and perfect art of painting may be drawn, can easily be understood by a geometer, whereas I think that neither the rudiments nor any principles of painting can be understood by those who are ignorant of geometry. Therefore, I believe that painters should study the art of geometry. Next, it will be of advantage if they take pleasure in poets and orators, for these have many ornaments in common with the painter. Literary men, who are full of information about many subjects, will be of great assistance in preparing the composition of a "historia," and the great virtue of this consists primarily in its invention. Indeed, invention is such that even by itself and without pictorial representation it can give pleasure. The description that Lucian gives of Calumny painted by Apelles, excites our admiration when we read it. I do not think it is inappropriate to tell it here, so that painters may be advised of the need to take particular care in creating inventions of this kind. In the painting there was a man with enormous ears sticking out, attended on each side by two women, Ignorance and Suspicion; from one side Calumny was approaching in the form of an attractive woman, but whose face seemed too well versed in cunning, and she was holding in her left hand a lighted torch, while with her right she was dragging by the hair a youth with his arms outstretched towards heaven. Leading her was another man, pale, ugly and fierce to look upon, whom you would rightly compare to those exhausted by long service in the field. They identified him correctly as Envy. There are two other women attendant on Calumny and busy arranging their mistress's dress; they are Treachery and Deceit. Behind them comes Repentance clad in mourning and rending her hair, and in her train chaste and modest Truth. If this "historia" seizes the imagination when described in words, how much beauty and pleasure do you think it presented in the actual painting of that excellent artist?

54. What shall we say too about those three young sisters, whom Hesiod called Egle, Euphronesis and Thalia? The ancients represented them dressed in loose transparent robes, with smiling faces and hands intertwined; they thereby wished to signify liberality, for one of the sisters

gives, another receives and the third returns the favor, all of which degrees should be present in every act of perfect liberality. You can appreciate how inventions of this kind bring great repute to the artist. I therefore advise the studious painter to make himself familiar with poets and orators and other men of letters, for he will not only obtain excellent ornaments from such learned minds, but he will also be assisted in those very inventions which in painting may gain him the greatest praise. The eminent painter Phidias used to say that he had learned from Homer how best to represent the majesty of Jupiter. I believe that we too may be richer and better painters from reading our poets, provided we are more attentive to learning than to financial gain.

55. Very often, however, ignorance of the way to learn, more than the effort of learning itself, breaks the spirit of men who are both studious and anxious to do so. So let us explain how we should become learned in this art. The fundamental principle will be that all the steps of learning should be sought from Nature: the means of perfecting our art will be found in diligence, study and application. I would have those who begin to learn the art of painting do what I see practised by teachers of writing. They first teach all the signs of the alphabet separately, and then how to put syllables together, and then whole words. Our students should follow this method with painting. First they should learn the outlines of surfaces, then the way in which surfaces are joined together, and after that the forms of all the members individually; and they should commit to memory all the differences that can exist in those members, for they are neither few nor insignificant. Some people will have a crook-backed nose; others will have flat, turned-back, open nostrils; some are full around the mouth, while others are graced with slender lips, and so on: every part has something particular which considerably alters the whole member when it is present in greater or lesser degree. Indeed we see that those same members which in our boyhood were rounded, and, one might say, well turned and smoothed, are become rough and angular with the advance of age. All these things, therefore, the student of painting will take from Nature, and assiduously meditate upon the appearance of each part; and he will persist continually in such enquiry with both eye and mind. In a seated figure he will observe the lap, and how the legs hang gently down. In a standing person he will note the whole appearance and posture, and there will be no part whose function and symmetry, as the Greeks call it, he will not know. But, considering all these parts, he should be attentive not only to the likeness of things but also and especially to beauty, for in painting beauty is as pleasing as it is necessary. The early painter Demetrius failed to obtain the highest praise because he was more devoted to representing the likeness of things than to beauty. Therefore, excellent parts should all be selected from the most beautiful bodies, and every effort should be made to perceive, understand and express beauty. Although this is the most difficult thing of all, because the merits of beauty are not all to be

found in one place, but are dispersed here and there in many, every endeavor should nonetheless be made to investigate and understand it thoroughly. The man who has learned to grasp and handle more serious matters, will in my view easily manage the less troublesome, and there is nothing so difficult that cannot be overcome by application and persistent effort.

56. Yet, in order that our effort shall not be vain and futile, we must avoid the habit of those who strive for distinction in painting by the light of their own intelligence without having before their eyes or in their mind any form of beauty taken from Nature to follow. They do not learn to paint properly, but simply make habits of their mistakes. The idea of beauty, which the most expert have difficulty in discerning, eludes the ignorant. Zeuxis, the most eminent, learned and skilled painter of all, when about to paint a panel to be publicly dedicated in the temple of Lucina at Croton, did not set about his work trusting rashly in his own talent like all painters do now; but, because he believed that all the things he desired to achieve beauty not only could not be found by his own intuition, but were not to be discovered even in Nature in one body alone, he chose from all the youth of the city five outstandingly beautiful girls, so that he might represent in his painting whatever feature of feminine beauty was most praiseworthy in each of them. He acted wisely, for to painters with no model before them to follow, who strive by the light of their own talent alone to capture the qualities of beauty, it easily happens that they do not by their efforts achieve the beauty they seek or ought to create; they simply fall into bad habits of painting, which they have great difficulty in relinquishing even if they wish. But the painter who has accustomed himself to taking everything from Nature, will so train his hand that anything he attempts will echo Nature. We can see how desirable this is in painting when the figure of some well-known person is present in a "historia," for although others executed with greater skill may be conspicuous in the picture, the face that is known draws the eyes of all spectators, so great is the power and attraction of something taken from Nature. So, let us always take from Nature whatever we are about to paint, and let us always choose those things that are most beautiful and worthy.

ON ARCHITECTURE

A Prudent Architect will proceed in the Method which we have been just laying down. He will never set about his Work without proper Caution and Advice. He will study the Nature and Strength of the Soil where he

SOURCE: Leon Battista Alberti, *Ten Books on Architecture*, trans. by J. Leoni (London: Alec Tiranti, 1965), pp. 192–208. Reprinted by permission of Academy Editions, London.

is to build, and observe, as well from a Survey of Structures in the Neighborhood, as from the Practice and Use of the Inhabitants, what Materials, what Sort of Stone, Sand, Lime or Timber, whether found on the Place, or brought from other Parts, will best stand against the Injuries of the Weather. He will set out the exact Breadth and Depth of the Foundations, and of the Basement of the whole Wall, and take an Account of every Thing that is necessary for the Building, whether for the outward Coat or the filling up, for the Ligatures, the Ribs, or the Apertures, the Roof, the Incrustation, for Pavements abroad, or Floors within; he will direct which Way, and by what Method every thing superfluous, noxious or offensive shall be carried off by Drains for conveying away the rain Water, and keeping the Foundations dry, and by proper Defenses against any moist Vapors, or even against any unexpected Floods or Violence from Winds or Storms. In a Word, he will give Directions for every single Part, and not suffer any thing to escape his Notice and Decree. And tho' all these Particulars seem chiefly to relate to Convenience and Stability, yet they carry this along with them, that if neglected they destroy all the Beauty and Ornament of the Edifice. Now the Rules which give the Ornaments themselves their main Excellence, are as follows. First all your Ornaments must be exactly regular, and perfectly distinct, and without Confusion: Your Embellishments must not be too much crowded together or scattered as it were under Foot, or thrown on in Heaps, but so aptly and neatly distributed, that whoever should go about to alter their Situation, should be sensible that he destroyed the whole Beauty and Delicacy of the Work. There is no Part whatsoever but what the Artist ought to adorn; but there is no Occasion that all should be adorned equally, or that every thing should be enriched with equal Expense; for indeed I would not have the Merit of the Work consist so much in Plenty as in Variety. Let the Builder fix his richest Ornaments in the principal Places; those of a middling Sort, in Places of less Note, and the meanest in the meanest. And here he should be particularly careful, not to mix what is rich with any thing trifling, nothing little with what is great, nor to set any thing too large or high in narrow or close Places; tho' things which are not equal to each other in Dignity, nor alike even in Species, may very well be placed together, so it be done artfully and ingeniously, and in such a Manner, that as the one appears solemn and majestick, the other may shew chearful and pleasant, and that they may not only unite their different Beauties for the Embellishment of the Structure, but also seem as if the one without the other had been imperfect; nor may it be amiss in some certain Places to intermix somewhat even of a coarse Sort, that what is noble may receive a yet further Addition from the Comparison: Always be sure never to make a Confusion of the Orders, which will happen if you mix the *Doric* Members with the *Corinthian*, as I observed before, or the *Corinthian* with the *Ionic*, or the like. Let every Order have its own regular Members, and those all in their proper Places, that nothing may appear perplexed or broken. Let such Ornaments as are proper to the Middle be placed in the Middle, and let those which are equal Distances on each Side, be proportioned exactly alike. In short, let every thing be measured, and put together with the greatest Exactness of Lines and Angles, that the Beholder's Eye may have a clear and distinct View along the Cornices, between the Columns on the Inside and without, receiving every Moment fresh Delight from the Variety he meets with, insomuch, that after the most careful and even repeated Views, he shall not be able to depart without once more turning back to take another Look, nor, upon the most critical Examination, be able in any Part of the whole Structure to find one Thing unequal, incongruous, out of Proportion, or not conducive to the general Beauty of the Whole. All these Particulars you must provide for by means of your Model; and from thence too you should before-hand consider not only what the Building is that you are to erect, but also get together all the Materials you shall want for the Execution, that when you have begun your Work you may not be at a Loss, or change or supersede your Design: but having before-hand made Provision of every Thing that you shall want, you may be able to keep your Workmen constantly supplied with all their Materials. These are the Things which the Architect is to take care of with the greatest Diligence and Judgment. The Errors which may happen in the manual Execution of the Work, need not be repeated here; but only the Workmen should be well looked after, to see that they work exactly by their Square, Level and Plumb-line; that they do their Business at the proper Seasons, take proper Seasons to let their Work rest, and at proper Seasons go to it again; that they use good Stuff, found, unmixed, solid, strong, and suitable to the Work, and that they use it in proper Places, and finish every Thing according to their Model.

But to the Intent that the Architect may come off worthily and honorably in preparing, ordering and accomplishing all these Things, there are some necessary Admonitions, which he should by no means neglect. And first he ought to consider well what Weight he is going to take upon his Shoulders, what it is that he professes, what Manner of Man he would be thought, how great a Business he undertakes, how much Applause, Profit, Favor and Fame among Posterity he will gain when he executes his Work as he ought, and on the contrary, if he goes about any thing ignorantly, unadvisedly, or inconsiderately, to how much Disgrace, to how much Indignation he exposes himself, what a clear, manifest and everlasting Testimony he gives Mankind of his Folly and Indiscretion. Doubtless Architecture is a very noble Science, not fit for every Head. He ought to be a Man of a fine Genius, of a great Application, of the best Education, of thorough Experience, and especially of strong Sense and sound Judgment, that presumes to declare himself an Architect. It is the Business of Architecture, and indeed its highest Praise, to judge rightly what is fit and decent: For though Building is a Matter of Necessity, yet convenient

Building is both of Necessity and Utility too: But to build in such a Manner, that the Generous shall commend you, and the Frugal not blame you, is the Work only of a prudent, wise and learned Architect. To run up any thing that is immediately necessary for any particular Purpose, and about which there is no doubt of what Sort it should be, or of the Ability of the Owner to afford it, is not so much the Business of an Architect, as of a common Workman: But to raise an Edifice which is to be compleat in every Part, and to consider and provide before-hand every Thing necessary for such a Work, is the Business only of that extensive Genius which I have described above: For indeed his Invention must be owing to his Wit, his Knowledge, to Experience, his Choice to Judgment, his Composition to Study, and the Completion of his Work to his Perfection in his Art; of all which Qualifications I take the Foundation to be Prudence and mature Deliberation. As to the other Virtues, Humanity, Benevolence, Modesty, Probity; I do not require them more in the Architect, than I do in every other Man, let him profess what Art he will: For indeed without them I do not think any one worthy to be deemed a Man: But above all Things he should avoid Levity, Obstinacy, Ostentation, Intemperance, and all those other Vices which may lose him the good Will of his Fellow-Citizens, and make him odious to the World. Lastly, in the Study of his Art I would have him follow the Example of those that apply themselves to Letters: For no Man thinks himself sufficiently learned in any Science, unless he has read and examined all the Authors, as well bad as good that have wrote in that Science which he is pursuing. In the same Manner I would have the Architect diligently consider all the Buildings that have any tolerable Reputation; and not only so, but take them down in Lines and Numbers, nay, make Designs and Models of them, and by means of those, consider and examine the Order, Situation, Sort and Number of every Part which others have employed, especially such as have done any thing very great and excellent, whom we may reasonably suppose to have been Men of very great Note, when they were intrusted with the Direction of so great an Expense. Not that I would have him admire a Structure merely for being huge, and imagine that to be a sufficient Beauty; but let him principally enquire in every Building what there is particularly artful and excellent for Contrivance or Invention, and gain a Habit of being pleased with nothing but what is really elegant and praise-worthy for the Design: And where-ever he finds any thing noble, let him make use of it, or imitate it in his own Performances; and when he sees any thing well done, that is capable of being still further improved and made delicate, let him study to bring it to Perfection in his own Works; and when he meets with any Design that is only not absolutely bad, let him try in his own Things to work it if possible into something excellent. Thus by a continued and nice Examination of the best Productions, still considering what Improvements might be made in every thing that he sees, he may so exercise and sharpen his own Invention, as to collect into his own Works not only all the Beauties which are dispersed up and down in those of other Men, but even those which lie in a Manner concealed in the most hidden Recesses of Nature, to his own immortal Reputation. Not satisfied with this, he should also have an Ambition to produce something admirable, which may be entirely of his own Invention; like him, for Instance, who built a Temple without using one iron Tool in it; or him that brought the *Colossus* to *Rome*, suspended all the Way upright, in which Work we may just mention that he employed no less than four-and-twenty Elephants; or like an Artist that in only seemingly working a common Quarry of Stone, should cut it out into a Labyrinth, a Temple, or some other useful Structure, to the Surprise of all Mankind. We are told that *Nero* used to employ miraculous Architects, who never thought of any Invention, but what it was almost impossible for the Skill of Man to reduce to practice. Such Geniuses I can by no means approve of; for, indeed, I would have the Architect always appear to have consulted Necessity and Convenience in the first Place, even tho' at the very same Time his principal Care has been Ornament. If he can make a handsome Mixture of the noble Orders of the Ancients, with any of the new Inventions of the Moderns, he may deserve Commendation. In this Manner he should be continually improving his Genius by Use and Exercise in such Things as may conduce to make him Excellent in this Science; and indeed, he should think it becomes him to have not only that Knowledge, without which he would not really be what he professed himself; but he should also adorn his Mind with such a Tincture of all the liberal Arts, as may be of Service to make him more ready and ingenious at his own, and that he may never be at a Loss for any Helps in it which Learning can furnish him with. In short, he ought still to be persevering in his Study and Application, till he finds himself equal to those great Men, whose Praises are capable of no further Addition: Nor let him ever be satisfied with himself, if there is that Thing any where that can possibly be of Use to him, and that can be obtained either by Diligence or Thought, which he is not thoroughly Master of, till he is arrived at the Summit of Perfection in the Art which he professes. The Arts which are useful, and indeed absolutely necessary to the Architect, are Painting and Mathematics. I do not require him to be deeply learned in the rest; for I think it ridiculous, like a certain Author, to expect that an Architect should be a profound Lawyer, in order to know the Right of conveying Water or placing Limits between Neighbors, and to avoid falling into Controversies and Lawsuits as in Building is often the Case: Nor need he be a perfect Astronomer, to know that Libraries ought to be situated to the North, and Stoves to the South; nor a very great Musician, to place the Vases of Copper or Brass in a Theater for assisting the Voice: Neither do I require that he should be an Orator, in order to be able to display to any Person that would employ him, the Services which he is capable of doing him; for Knowledge, Experience and perfect Mastery in what he is to speak of, will never fail to help him to Words to explain his

Sense sufficiently, which indeed is the first and main End of Eloquence. Not that I would have him Tongue-tied, or so deficient in his Ears, as to have no Taste for Harmony: It may suffice if he does not build a private Man's House upon the public Ground, or upon another Man's: If he does not annoy the Neighbors, either by his Lights, his Spouts, his Gutters, his Drains, or by obstructing their Passage contrary to Law: If he knows the several Winds that blow from the different Points of the Compass, and their Names; in all which Sciences there is no Harm indeed in his being more expert; but Painting and Mathematics are what he can no more be without, than a Poet can be without the Knowledge of Feet and Syllables; neither do I know whether it be enough for him to be only moderately tinctured with them. This I can say of myself, that I have often started in my Mind Ideas of Buildings, which have given me wonderful Delight: Wherein when I have come to reduce them into Lines, I have found in those very Parts which most pleased me, many gross Errors that required great Correction; and upon a second Review of such a Draught, and measuring every Part by Numbers, I have been sensible and ashamed of my own Inaccuracy. Lastly, when I have made my Draught into a Model, and then proceeded to examine the several Parts over again, I have sometimes found myself mistaken, even in my Numbers. Not that I expected my Architect to be a *Zeuxis* in Painting, nor a *Nicomachus* at Numbers, nor an *Archimedes* in the Knowledge of mixed Lines and Angles: It may serve his Purpose if he is a thorough Master of those Elements of Painting which I have wrote; and if he is skilled in so much practical Mathematics, and in such a Knowledge of mixed Lines, Angles and Numbers, as is necessary for the Measuring of Weights, Superficies and Solids, which Part of Geometry the *Greeks* call *Podismata* and *Emboda*. With these Arts, joined to Study and Application, the Architect may be sure to obtain Favor and Riches, and to deliver his Name with Reputation down to Posterity.

There is one Thing that I must not omit here, which relates personally to the Architect. It is, that you should not immediately run and offer your Service to every Man that gives out he is going to build; a Fault which the inconsiderate and vain-glorious are too apt to be guilty of. I know not whether you ought not to wait till you are more than once importuned to be concerned. Certainly they ought to repose a free and voluntary Confidence in you, that want to make use of your Labors and Advice. Why should I offer those Inventions which have cost me so much Study and Pains, to gain perhaps no other Recompence, but the Confidence of a few Persons of no Taste or Skill? If by my Advice in the Execution of your intended Work, I either save you from an unnecessary Expense, or procure you some great Convenience or Pleasure; surely such a Service deserves a suitable Recompence. For this Reason a prudent Man should take care to maintain his Reputation; and certainly it is enough if you give honest Advice, and correct Draughts to such as apply themselves to you. If after-

wards you undertake to supervise and compleat the Work, you will find
it very difficult to avoid being made answerable for all the Faults and
Mistakes committed either by the Ignorance or Negligence of other Men:
Upon which Account you must take care to have the Assistance of honest,
diligent, and severe Overseers to look after the Workmen under you. I
would also have you, if possible, concern yourself for none but Persons of
the highest Rank and Quality, and those too such as are truly Lovers of
these Arts: Because your Work loses of its Dignity by being done for mean
Persons. Do you not see what Weight the Authority of great Men is to
advance the Reputation of those who are employed by them? And, indeed,
I insist the more upon this Piece of Advice, not only because the World
has generally a higher Opinion of the Taste and Judgment of great Men,
than for the most Part they deserve, but also because I would have the
Architect always readily and plentifully supplied with every thing that is
necessary for completing his Edifice; which those of lower Degree are
commonly not so able, and therefore not so willing to do: to which add,
what we find very frequent Instances of, that where the Design and Invention has been perfectly equal in two different Works, one has been much
more esteemed than the other, for the Sake of the Superiority of the
Materials. Lastly, I advise you not to be so far carried away by the Desire
of Glory, as rashly to attempt any thing entirely new and unusual: Therefore be sure to examine and consider thoroughly what you are going to
undertake, even in its minutest Parts; and remember how difficult it is
to find Workmen that shall exactly execute any extraordinary Idea which
you may form, and with how much Grudging and Unwillingness People
will spend their Money in making Trial of your Fancies. Lastly, beware of
that very common Fault, by means of which there are so few great Structures but what have some unpardonable Blemishes. We always find People
very ready to criticize, and fond of being thought Counselors and Direc-
tors. Now as, by reason of the Shortness of Man's Life, few great Works
are compleated by the first Undertaker, we that succeed him, either out
of Envy or Officiousness, are vain of making some Alteration in his original Design. By this means what was well begun is spoiled in the finishing.
For this Reason I think we should adhere to the original Design of the
Inventor, who we are to suppose had maturely weighed and considered it.
It is possible he might have some wise Inducement to do what he did,
which upon a more diligent and attentive Examination, you may at length
discover yourself. If however you do make any Alteration, never do it
without the Advice, or rather absolute Direction of the most approved
and experienced Masters: By which means you will both provide for the
Necessities of the Structure, and secure yourself against the Malice of
envious Tongues. We have now treated of public Buildings, and of private;
of sacred, and of profane; of those which relate to Dignity, and those of
Pleasure. What remains is to show how any Defects in an Edifice, which
have arisen either from Ignorance or Negligence, from the Violence of

Men or Times, or from unfortunate and unforeseen Accidents, may be repaired and amended: Still hoping that these Arts will meet with the Favor and Protection of the Learned.

✦ *Leonardo da Vinci*

*L*eonardo da Vinci was born in 1452 near Florence, the natural son of a Florentine notary. He was sent to Florence as an apprentice in the workshop of the painter and sculptor Andrea Verrocchio, where he was to remain until 1477, although he was admitted as a master in the painters' guild in 1472. In 1482–1483 he left for Milan to enter the court of Duke Lodovico Sforza. He was to work in Milan until forced to flee during the French invasions. Returning to Florence, he worked on important civic commissions for the Republic, such as the now lost frescos decorating the Palazzo della Signoria.

Leonardo was the ideal genius of the Italian Renaissance. His almost unsurpassed skill in so many areas is truly remarkable: painting, architecture, sculpture, drawing, and many aspects of scientific observation and experimentation, including anatomy, hydraulics, mathematics, and botany. He recorded his original thoughts and observations in his notebooks, a large collection of his personal notes designed for his own use. They are written in his tiny, almost illegible handwriting, in which the letters were formed backwards and in reverse, requiring a mirror to read them now, although Leonardo himself could write naturally and quickly in this manner and read it with ease. Containing thousands of drawings and preliminary sketches for many known pictures and some wonderful ideas for machines such as aircraft and tanks, these notebooks also record Leonardo's unequaled talent for observing and reproducing plants, animals, rushing water, and human anatomy. The writings in his notebooks are a sample of his wide-ranging mind and boundless curiosity about every aspect of human experience and the natural world.

On his return to Milan in 1506, he was appointed royal painter and engineer by King Francis I of France. In 1517, he left Italy for France, where the king had given him a chateau at Cloux. It was there he died in 1519.

SELECTIONS FROM THE NOTEBOOKS

Two weaknesses leaning together create a strength. Therefore the half of the world leaning against the other half becomes firm.

SOURCE: Excerpts from *The Notebooks of Leonardo da Vinci*, ed. by Edward MacCurdy (London: Jonathan Cape), pp. 57–59, 61–66, 81–85, 852–856, 902–903.

While I thought that I was learning how to live, I have been learning how to die.

Every part of an element separated from its mass desires to return to it by the shortest way.

Nothingness has no center, and its boundaries are nothingness.

My opponent says that nothingness and a vacuum are one and the same thing, having indeed two separate names by which they are called, but not existing separately in nature.

The reply is that whenever there exists a vacuum there will also be the space which surrounds it, but nothingness exists apart from occupation of space; it follows that nothingness and a vacuum are not the same, for the one is divisible to infinity,and nothingness cannot be divided because nothing can be less than it is; and if you were to take part from it this part would be equal to the whole, and the whole to the part.

Aristotle in the Third [Book] of the *Ethics:* man is worthy of praise and blame solely in respect of such actions as it is within his power to do or to abstain from.

He who expects from experience what she does not possess takes leave of reason.

For what reason do such animals as sow their seed sow with pleasure and the one who awaits receives with pleasure and brings forth with pain?

Intellectual passion drives out sensuality.

The knowledge of past time and of the position of the earth is the adornment and the food of human minds.

Among the great things which are found among us the existence of Nothing is the greatest. This dwells in time, and stretches its limbs into the past and the future, and with these takes to itself all works that are past and those that are to come, both of nature and of the animals, and possesses nothing of the indivisible present. It does not however extend to the essence of anything . . . .

Therefore O students study mathematics and do not build without foundations.

Mental things which have not passed through the understanding are vain and give birth to no truth other than what is harmful. And because such discourses spring from poverty of intellect those who make them are always poor, and if they have been born rich they shall die poor in their old age. For nature, as it would seem, takes vengeance on such as would work miracles and they come to have less than other men who are more quiet. And those who wish to grow rich in a day shall live a long time in great poverty, as happens and will to all eternity happen to the alchemists, the would-be creators of gold and silver, and to the engineers who think to make dead water stir itself into life with perpetual motion, and to those supreme fools, the necromancer and the enchanter.

[*The Certainty of Mathematics*]

He who blames the supreme certainty of mathematics feeds on confusion, and will never impose silence upon the contradictions of the sophistical sciences, which occasion a perpetual clamor.

The abbreviators of works do injury to knowledge and to love, for love of anything is the offspring of knowledge, love being more fervent in proportion as knowledge is more certain; and this certainty springs from a thorough knowledge of all those parts which united compose the whole of that thing which ought to be loved.

Of what use, pray, is he who in order to abridge the part of the things of which he professes to give complete information leaves out the greater part of the matters of which the whole is composed?

True it is that impatience, the mother of folly, is she who praises brevity; as though such folk had not a span of life that would suffice to acquire complete knowledge of one particular subject such as the human body. And then they think to comprehend the mind of God which embraces the whole universe, weighing and dissecting it as though they were making an anatomy. O human stupidity! Do you not perceive that you have spent your whole life with yourself and yet are not aware of that which you have most in evidence, and that is your own foolishness? And so with the crowd of sophists you think to deceive yourself and others, despising the mathematical sciences in which is contained true information about the subjects of which they treat! Or you would fain range among the miracles and give your views upon those subjects which the human mind is incapable of comprehending and which cannot be demonstrated by any natural instance. And it seems to you that you have performed miracles when you have spoiled the work of some ingenious mind, and you do not perceive that you are falling into the same error as does he who strips a tree of its adornment of branches laden with leaves intermingled with fragrant flowers or fruits, in order to demonstrate the suitability of the tree for making planks. Even as did Justinus, maker of an epitome of the histories of Trogus Pompeius, who had written an elaborate account of all the great deeds of his ancestors which lent themselves to picturesque description, for by so doing he composed a bald work fit only for such impatient minds as conceive themselves to be wasting time when they spend it usefully in study of the works of nature and of human things.

Let such as these remain in the company of the beasts, and let their courtiers be dogs and other animals eager for prey and let them keep company with them; ever pursuing whatever takes flight from them, they follow after the inoffensive animals who in the season of the snow drifts are impelled by hunger to approach your doors to beg alms from you as from a guardian.

If you are as you have described yourself, the king of the animals—it would be better for you to call yourself king of the beasts since you are the greatest of them all!—why do you not help them so that they may presently be able to give you their young in order to gratify your palate, for the sake of which you have tried to make yourself a tomb for all the animals? Even more I might say if to speak the entire truth were permitted me.

But do not let us quit this subject without referring to one supreme form of wickedness which hardly exists among the animals, among whom are none that devour their own species except for lack of reason (for there are insane among them as among human beings though not in such great numbers). Nor does this happen except among the voracious animals as in the lion species and among leopards, panthers, lynxes, cats, and creatures like these, which sometimes eat their young. But not only do you eat your children, but you eat father, mother, brothers, and friends; and this even not sufficing you, you make raids on foreign islands and capture men of other races and then, after mutilating them in a shameful manner, you fatten them up and cram then down your gullet. Say does not nature bring forth a sufficiency of simple things to produce satiety? Or if you cannot content yourself with simple things can you not by blending these together make an infinite number of compounds as did Platina and other authors who have written for epicures?

And if any be found virtuous and good drive them not away from you but do them honor lest they flee from you and take refuge in hermitages and caves or other solitary places in order to escape from your deceits. If any such be found, pay him reverence, for as these are as gods upon the earth they deserve statues, images, and honors. But I would impress upon you that their images are not to be eaten by you, as happens in a certain district of India; for there, when in the judgment of the priests these images have worked some miracle, they cut them in pieces being of wood and distribute them to all the people of the locality—not without payment.

And each of them then grates his portion very fine and spreads it over the first food he eats; and so they consider that symbolically by faith they have eaten their saint, and they believe that he will then guard them from all dangers. What think you Man! of your species? Are you as wise as you set yourself up to be? Are acts such as these things that men should do, Justinus?

Let no one read me who is not a mathematician in my beginnings.

Every action of nature is made along the shortest possible way.

Thou, O God, dost sell unto us all good things at the price of labor. . . .

Comparison of the Arts

If you know how to describe and write down the appearance of the forms, the painter can make them so that they appear enlivened with lights and shadows which create the very expression of the faces; herein you cannot attain with the pen where he attains with the brush.

How painting surpasses all human works by reason of the subtle possibilities which it contains:

The eye, which is called the window of the soul, is the chief means whereby the understanding may most fully and abundantly appreciate the infinite works of nature; and the ear is the second, inasmuch as it acquires its importance from the fact that it hears the things which the eye has seen. If you historians, or poets, or mathematicians had never seen things with your eyes you would be ill able to describe them in your writings. And if you, O poet, represent a story by depicting it with your pen, the painter with his brush will so render it as to be more easily satisfying and less tedious to understand. If you call painting "dumb poetry," then the painter may say of the poet that his art is "blind painting." Consider then which is the more grievous affliction, to be blind or to be dumb! Although the poet has as wide a choice of subjects as the painter, his creations fail to afford as much satisfaction to mankind as do paintings, for while poetry attempts to represent forms, actions, and scenes with words, the painter employs the exact images of these forms in order to reproduce them. Consider, then, which is more fundamental to man, the name of man or his image? The name changes with change of country; the form is unchanged except by death.

And if the poet serves the understanding by way of the ear, the painter does so by the eye, which is the nobler sense.

I will only cite as an instance of this how if a good painter represents the fury of a battle and a poet also describes one, and the two descriptions are shown together to the public, you will soon see which will draw most of the spectators, and where there will be most discussion, to which most praise will be given, and which will satisfy the more. There is no doubt that the painting, which is by far the more useful and beautiful, will give the greater pleasure. Inscribe in any place the name of God and set opposite to it His image, you will see which will be held in greater reverence!

Since painting embraces within itself all the forms of nature, you have omitted nothing except the names, and these are not universal like the forms. If you have the results of her processes we have the processes of her results.

Take the case of a poet describing the beauties of a lady to her lover and that of a painter who makes a portrait of her; you will see whither nature will the more incline the enamoured judge. Surely the proof of the matter ought to rest upon the verdict of experience!

You have set painting among the mechanical arts! Truly, were painters as ready equipped as you are to praise their own works in writing, I doubt whether it would endure the reproach of so vile a name. If you call it mechanical because it is by manual work that the hands represent what the imagination creates, your writers are setting down with the pen by manual work what originates in the mind. If you call it mechanical because it is done for money, who fall into this error—if indeed it can be called an error—more than you yourselves? If you lecture for the schools do you not go to whoever pays you the most? Do you do any work without some reward?

And yet I do not say this in order to censure such opinions, for every labor looks for its reward. And if the poet should say, "I will create a fiction which shall express great things," so likewise will the painter also, for even so Apelles made the Calumny. If you should say that poetry is the more enduring—to this I would reply that the works of a coppersmith are more enduring still, since time preserves them longer than either your works or ours; nevertheless they show but little imagination; and painting, if it be done upon copper in enamel colors, can be made far more enduring.

In Art we may be said to be grandsons unto God. If poetry treats of moral philosophy, painting has to do with natural philosophy; if the one describes the workings of the mind, the other considers what the mind effects by movements of the body; if the one dismays folk by hellish fictions, the other does the like by showing the same things in action. Suppose the poet sets himself to represent some image of beauty or terror, something vile and foul, or some monstrous thing, in contest with the painter, and suppose in his own way he makes a change of forms at his pleasure, will not the painter still satisfy the more? Have we not seen pictures which bear so close a resemblance to the actual thing that they have deceived both men and beasts?

If you know how to describe and write down the appearance of the forms, the painter can make them so that they appear enlivened with lights and shadows which create the very expression of the faces; herein you cannot attain with the pen where he attains with the brush.

How he who despises painting has no love for the philosophy of nature:
If you despise painting, which is the sole imitator of all the visible works of nature, it is certain that you will be despising a subtle invention which with philosophical and ingenious speculation takes as its theme all the various kinds of forms, airs and scenes, plants, animals, grasses

and flowers, which are surrounded by light and shade. And this truly is a science and the true-born daughter of nature, since painting is the offspring of nature. But in order to speak more correctly we may call it the grand-child of nature; for all visible things derive their existence from nature, and from these same things is born painting. So therefore we may justly speak of it as the grandchild of nature and as related to God himself.

That sculpture is less intellectual than painting, and lacks many of its natural parts:

As practicing myself the art of sculpture no less than that of painting, and doing both the one and the other in the same degree, it seems to me that without suspicion of unfairness I may venture to give an opinion as to which of the two is the more intellectual, and of the greater difficulty and perfection.

In the first place, sculpture is dependent on certain lights, namely those from above, while a picture carries everywhere with it its own light and shade; light and shade therefore are essential to sculpture. In this respect, the sculptor is aided by the nature of the relief, which produces these of its own accord, but the painter artificially creates them by his art in places where nature would normally do the like. The sculptor cannot render the difference in the varying natures of the colors of objects; paint-ing does not fail to do so in any particular. The lines of perspective of sculptors do not seem in any way true; those of painters may appear to extend a hundred miles beyond the work itself. The effects of aerial perspective are outside the scope of sculptors' work; they can neither represent transparent bodies nor luminous bodies nor angles of reflection nor shining bodies such as mirrors and like things of glittering surface, nor mists, nor dull weather, nor an infinite number of things which I forbear to mention lest they should prove wearisome.

The one advantage which sculpture has is that of offering greater resistance to time; yet painting offers a like resistance if it is done upon thick copper covered with white enamel and then painted upon with enamel colors and placed in a fire and fused. In degree of permanence it then surpasses even sculpture.

It may be urged that if a mistake is made it is not easy to set it right, but it is a poor line of argument to attempt to prove that the fact of a mistake being irremediable makes the work more noble. I should say indeed that it is more difficult to correct the mind of the master who makes such mistakes than the work which he has spoiled.

We know very well that a good experienced painter will not make such mistakes; on the contrary, following sound rules he will proceed by removing so little at a time that his work will progress well. The sculptor also if he is working in clay or wax can either take away from it or add to it, and when the model is completed it is easy to cast it in bronze; and this is the last process and it is the most enduring form of sculpture, since that which is only in marble is liable to be destroyed, but not when done in bronze.

But painting done upon copper, which by the methods in use in painting may be either taken from or altered, is like the bronze, for when you have first made the model for this in wax it can still be either reduced or altered. While the sculpture in bronze is imperishable this painting upon copper and enameling is absolutely eternal; and while bronze remains dark and rough, this is full of an infinite variety of varied and lovely colors, of which I have already made mention. But if you would have me speak only of panel painting I am content to give an opinion between it and sculpture by saying that painting is more beautiful, more imaginative, and richer in resource, while sculpture is more enduring, but excels in nothing else.

Sculpture reveals what it is with little effort; painting seems a thing miraculous, making things intangible appear tangible, presenting in relief things which are flat, in distance things near at hand.

In fact, painting is adorned with infinite possibilities of which sculpture can make no use.

One of the chief proofs of skill of the painter is that his picture should seem in relief, and this is not the case with the sculptor, for in this respect he is aided by nature.

[Of Poetry and Painting]

When the poet ceases to represent in words what exists in nature, he then ceases to be the equal of the painter; for if the poet, leaving such representation, were to describe the polished and persuasive words of one whom he wishes to represent as speaking, he would be becoming an orator and be no more a poet or a painter. And if he were to describe the heavens he makes himself an astrologer, and a philosopher or theologian when speaking of the things of nature or of God. But if he returns to the representation of some definite thing he would become the equal of the painter if he could satisfy the eye with words as the painter does with brush and color, [for with these he creates] a harmony to the eye, even as music does in an instant to the ear.

Painting and Sculpture

Why the picture seen with two eyes will not be an example of such relief as the relief seen with two eyes; this is because the picture seen with one eye will place itself in relief like the actual relief, having the same qualities of light and shade. . . .

How from age to age the art of painting continually declines and deteriorates when painters have no other standard than work already done:

The painter will produce pictures of little merit if he takes the works of others as his standard; but if he will apply himself to learn from the objects of nature he will produce good results. This we see was the case with the painters who came after the time of the Romans, for they continually imitated each other, and from age to age their art steadily declined.

After these came Giotto the Florentine, and he—reared in mountain solitudes, inhabited only by goats and such like beasts—turning straight from nature to his art, began to draw on the rocks the movements of the goats which he was tending, and so began to draw the figures of all the animals which were to be found in the country, in such a way that after much study he not only surpassed the masters of his own time but all those of many preceding centuries. After him art again declined, because all were imitating paintings already done; and so for centuries it continued to decline until such time as Tommaso the Florentine, nicknamed Masaccio, showed by the perfection of his work how those who took as their standard anything other than nature, the supreme guide of all the masters, were wearying themselves in vain. Similarly I would say about these mathematical subjects, that those who study only the authorities and not the works of nature are in art the grandsons and not the sons of nature, which is the supreme guide of the good authorities.

Mark the supreme folly of those who censure such as learn from nature, leaving uncensured the authorities who were themselves the disciples of this same nature!

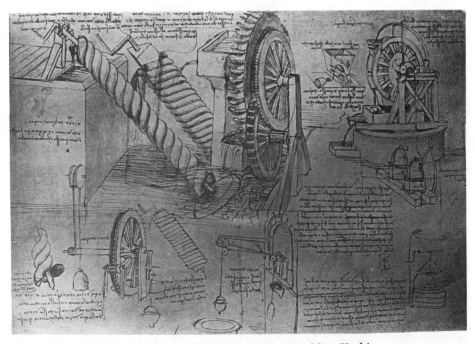

Water Wheel (Uffizi, Florence; Alinari/Art Resource, New York)

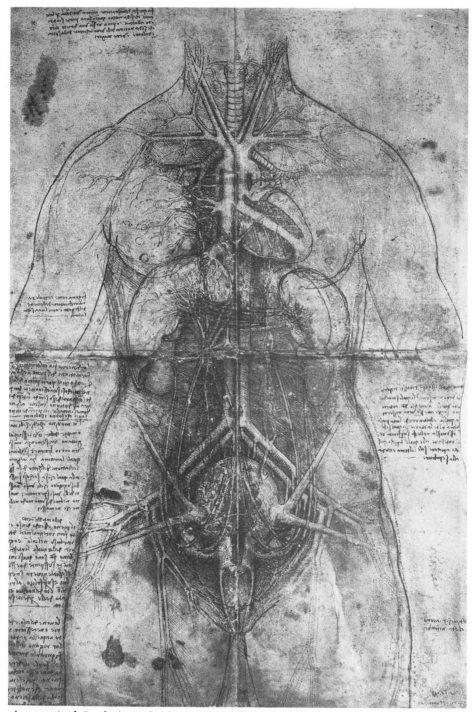

Anatomical Study (Royal Library, Windsor; Alinari/Art Resource, New York)

Caricatures (Accademia, Venice; Alinari/Art Resource, New York)

Flowers (Accademia, Venice, Alinari/Art Resource, New York)

Rural Life in the Renaissance. These illustrations from a Renaissance calendar illustrate the tasks of farmers in Italy. Agriculture was based entirely on animal power and manual labour. (Biblioteca Medicea Laurenziana, Florence)

The burning of Girolamo Savonarola in the Piazza della Signoria, 23 May 1498. (Museo di San Marco, Florence; Alinari/Art Resource, New York)

Domenico Ghirlandaio, detail of fresco portrait of Lodovica Tornabuoni and her attendants. These fresco cycles of Ghirlandaio (1449–1494) in Florence are among the best sources for detailed knowledge of Renaissance costume. (Santa Maria Novella, Florence; Scala/Art Resource, New York)

Palazzo Strozzi (courtyard). Designed by Benedetto da Maiano in 1489 for the very wealthy patrician Strozzi family, the palace was not completed until 1536. The interior courtyard was a standard feature in palace construction to permit natural light to enter as many rooms as possible, and often these courtyards included both open colonnades and enclosed galleries. (Palazzo Strozzi, Florence; Alinari/Art Resource, New York)

Leon Battista Alberti, Palazzo Rucellai, Florence (1446), main facade. Alberti designed this palace for Giovanni Rucellai, although its construction was supervised by Bernardo Rossellino, who completed it in 1451. Alberti used the three classical orders of columns in the three stories of the elevation, as found in the Roman architectural theorist, Vitruvius. The self-conscious classicism of this palace illustrates the application of humanist principles to building. (Rucellai Palace, Florence; Alinari/Art Resource, New York)

Sandro Botticelli, *The Birth of Venus* (c. 1486). Botticelli (c. 1445–1510) produced this painting for Lorenzo the Magnificent's cousin, Lorenzo di Pierfrancesco de'Medici. The inspiration for this picture was probably the *Stanze* of the poet Poliziano, another close associate of the circle of Lorenzo the Magnificent, whose neoplatonic ideals are quite evident in the work. This painting is also one of the earliest idealized depictions of the nude female form in the Renaissance. (Uffizi, Florence; Alinari/Art Resource, New York)

Sandro Botticelli, *Primavera (Springtime)* (1477–1478). As in *The Birth of Venus*, the poet Poliziano probably provided the program for this painting, which was also for Lorenzo di Pierfrancesco de'Medici. Again, neoplatonic and classical sources abound. Assuming the patron's knowledge not only of Poliziano but also of Ovid, Botticelli has introduced the figures of Zephyr pursuing the nymph Chloris, transforming her into Flora, goddess of Spring. At the left of the painting, Mercury is dispelling the mist of winter while the three graces dance and Venus presides with her attendant Cupid. (Galleria Antica e Moderna, Florence; Alinari/Art Resource, New York)

Sandro Botticelli, *Adoration of the Magi* (c. 1475). This painting was commissioned by the banker and political associate of the Medici, Giovanni Lami, for his family's chapel in Santa Maria Novella in Florence. The picture is important not only for an understanding of Botticelli but for the portraits of the members of the Medici faction in the time of Lorenzo the Magnificent. Indeed, the work contains the likenesses of Lorenzo himself (far left at front); Poliziano (next to Lorenzo); the patron, Lami (second row at left, looking out of the picture); Lorenzo's father, Piero; the Gouty, (center, kneeling in the robe); Cosimo il Vecchio (center left, holding the feet of the Christ child); and Botticelli himself (far right, looking out of the painting). (Uffizi, Florence; Alinari/Art Resource, New York)

On the Cover: Melozzo da Forli, *Pope Sixtus IV and his Nephews* (1477). This fresco by Melozzo da Forli (1438–1494) in the Vatican records Sixtus IV appointing the humanist Platina as papal librarian. The pope was ambitious for his nephews, and this papal nepotism brought about the events of the Pazzi Conspiracy in Florence. Melozzo was celebrated in his time for this skill in pespective, especially extreme foreshortening, which is evidenced in the architectural background of this fresco. The papal nephews depicted here are from the left: Giovanni della Rovere, Girolamo Riario, Giuliano della Rovere, Pietro Riario. (Pinacoteca Vaticana, Rome; Scala/Art Resource, New York)

Justus van Ghent, detail of *Federigo and Guidobaldo da Montefeltro, Dukes of Urbino* (c. 1476). This portrait of the great condottiere Federigo, Duke of Urbino, and his son and successor, Guidobaldo, has sometimes been attributed to the Spaniard Berruguete, although the Flemish artist is more likely. Justus (Joos) van Ghent (active c. 1460–c. late 1470s) was a Netherlander who had worked in Antwerp and Ghent before leaving for Italy. He was in Urbino in 1473–1474 and in Rome the following year. He painted a series of portraits of famous men about 1476. This double portrait is interesting because it depicts Duke Federigo in full armor, surmounted by his ducal robes, wearing the English Order of the Garter bestowed upon him by Henry VII, and in the company of his young son. However, the warrior duke is shown reading one of the volumes from the great library he collected. (Ducal Palace, Urbino; Alinari/Art Resource, New York)

Andrea del Verrocchio, *Lorenzo the Magnificent* (c. 1485). Verrocchio (c. 1436–1488) fashioned this painted terra-cotta bust of Lorenzo, which reflects not only the likeness of its subject but also his subtle strength of character. Lorenzo is portrayed wearing the costume of a well-to-do Florentine merchant. (National Gallery of Art, Washington; Samuel H. Cress Collection)

Leonardo da Vinci, *Self-Portrait* (c. 1512). Leonardo (1452–1519) was one of the greatest of the universal geniuses of the Italian Renaissance. His gifts in all the arts, as well as in engineering, science, anatomy, and almost every other aspect of human endeavour are well known. This drawing is a self-portrait of the artist in old age. (Biblioteca Reale, Turin; Scala/Art Resource, New York)

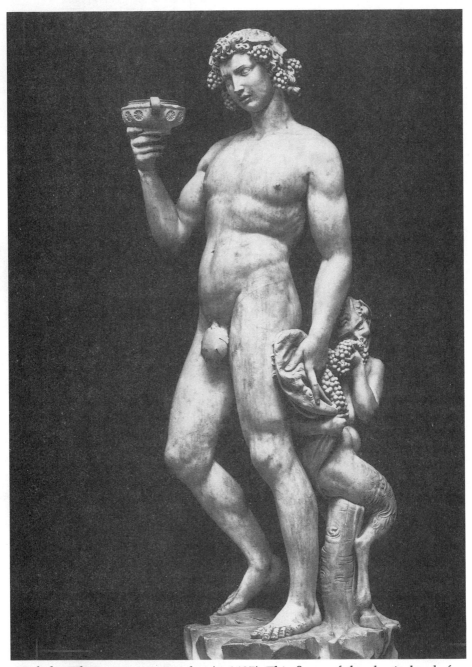

Michelangelo Buonarroti, *Bacchus* (c. 1497). This figure of the classical god of wine was commissioned originally by Cardinal Riario but was purchased by a Roman collector of ancient statues, among which it stood in the garden of his house. Nothing better illustrates Michelangelo's success in recovering both the form and the spirit of ancient sculpture, especially the ideal nude male body. (Museo Nazionale, Florence; Alinari/Art Resource, New York)

Michelangelo Buonarroti, *David* (1501–1504). This huge (16 feet high) sculpture was commissioned originally for the facade of the cathedral in Florence but was judged too fine a work to place so far from easy view. Eventually it was set up in front of the Palazzo della Signoria. Carved from a single block of marble that had been damaged and abandoned by earlier sculptors, the *David* became a symbol of the republic and an example of the Renaissance humanist celebration of the idealized human form, despite the fact that Michelangelo altered normal proportions somewhat in his heroic figure. (Academia, Florence; Alinari/Art Resource, New York)

Michelangelo Buonarroti, *The Temptation of Man and the Expulsion From Eden*, detail of Sistine Chapel ceiling fresco, the Vatican (1508–1512). Pope Julius II commissioned Michelangelo to fresco the ceiling of the Sistine Chapel, despite the artist's objections that he was a sculptor not a painter. Michelangelo altered the order of some of his biblical sources for the huge fresco to achieve the greatest possible dramatic effect and suit best the spaces offered to him on the ceiling. The representation of the fall illustrated here records the human weakness of mankind expressed through the sensuous nature of both the nude figures. (Vatican, Sistine Chapel, Rome; Alinari/Art Resource, New York)

Michelangelo Buonarroti, *The Medici Chapel, San Lorenzo, Florence* (1520–1534). San Lorenzo was the Medici family church, and the chapel was to serve as a burial chamber to extend the function of the Old Sacristy, built by Brunelleschi, whose architectural vocabulary is reminiscent in Michelangelo's design. It was probably Cardinal Giulio de'Medici who began the commission; and, as was so common with the artist, the project grew beyond the original scheme and was never completed. Reproduced here is the lifesized figure and sarcophagus of Lorenzo de'Medici, Duke of Urbino. On the sarcophagus are allegorical figures of evening and dawn. At left is a Madonna and child flanked by the two Medici patron saints, SS Cosmas and Damian, completed by other artists after Michelangelo's designs. (Medici Chapel, Florence; Foto Marburg/Art Resource, New York)

Raphael, *Pope Leo X* (1519). This portrait is of Giovanni de'Medici, son of Lorenzo the Magnificent, who became pope in 1513, together with his cousin, Cardinal Giulio de'Medici (the illegitimate son of Lorenzo's brother, Guiliano, and
eventually Pope Clement VII), and Cardinal Luigi de'Rossi, another Florentine.
Leo was a celebrated patron of the arts and an excellent example of a refined
humanist pope. Raphael (1483–1520), born in Urbino, the son of Federigo da
Montefeltro's court artist, has captured not only the luxury and elegance of the
Renaissance papacy in this brilliant portrait but also the characters of his three
subjects. (Pitti Palace, Florence; Alinari/Art Resource, New York)

Raphael, detail of *The School of Athens* (1509–1511). This fresco from the Stanza della Segnatura in the Vatican represents one of the great moments of Renaissance art and its connections with the ancient world. Illustrated in a grand and splendid architectural frame are the great thinkers of antiquity. The central places of honour are accorded to Plato and Aristotle, the founders of the two fundamental systems of thought, while Diogenes the Cynic, half naked, is sprawled below, and Socrates engages in dialogue with his students. Pythagorus, Euclid, Heraclitus, Zoroaster are all present, often as likenesses of the most celebrated artists and thinkers of Renaissance Italy: Leonardo da Vinci is Plato, Michelangelo is Heraclitus, Bramante, the architect, is Euclid. To the extreme right, Raphael portrayed himself with his friend, the painter Sodoma. (Vatican, Stanze, Rome, Alinari/Art Resource, New York)

Raphael, *The Triumph of Galatea* (1514). Commissioned by the rich Sienese banker Agostino Chigi for his villa on the Tiber in Rome (a summer palace now known as the Farnesina after the Farnese family who owned it later), this ceiling fresco represents the ideal world of classical mythology with an exuberant delight, expressed in a manner far more sensuous than the highly allegorized work of Botticelli, with which it is sometimes compared. Gods, nymphs like Galatea herself, tritons, and sea creatures cavort in this celebration of mythology and rich color. (Villa Farnesina, Rome; Giraudon/Art Resource, New York)

Benvenuto Cellini, *Salt Cellar* (c. 1540). Cellini (1500–1571) was a justly celebrated goldsmith and sculptor, as well as an autobiographer. He was influenced by the style of Michelangelo and produced a number of very important pieces, such as his *Perseus* (1545–1554) and his *Nymph of Fontainebleau*, as well as medals and coins. At the court of France between 1540 and 1545, Cellini crafted the exquisite salt cellar for King Francis I. (Kunsthistorisches, Vienna; Foto Marburg/Art Resource, New York)

Sofonisba Anguissola, *Three of the Artists' Sisters Playing Chess* (1555). One of the great women artists of the Renaissance, Sofonisba (1535/40–1625) was born into a noble family in Cremona, near Milan. Her father gave her a good education and sent her to the household of a local artist to learn painting. She became celebrated in her own lifetime, eventually moving to the court of Philip II of Spain where she resided for over 20 years as a court painter. Her sisters, Lucia, Europa, and Anna Maria were also painters. (Muzeum Narodowe W Poznaniu, Poland)

Titian, *Pietro Aretino*. Tiziano Vecelli (c. 1487/90–1576) was born in the Veneto and became one of the greatest of Venetian artists during a long and very productive life. He was ennobled and named court painter to the emperor Charles V in 1533, and the emperor became his personal friend as well as patron. Titian's portrait of his friend Aretino illustrates well the artist's genius for depicting individuals with distinct characters, full of life and vitality. (Pitti Palace, Florence; Alinari/Art Resource, New York)

VIII

Learning and Education

INTRODUCTION

*L*earning was the medium through which humanism was spread and consolidated. The desire to reconcile Renaissance Latin with the elegance of Cicero's prose, the growing interest in Greek studies, and the search for lost ancient texts all reflect the central role that learning played in Italy during the Renaissance.

How that learning was acquired was through education. Giovanni Villani remarks in his Chronicle that before the middle of the fourteenth century there were about 8000 to 10,000 young Florentine boys being taught by private tutors and in schools. Most of these boys would learn only the most rudimentary skills of reading and writing in the vernacular, and perhaps basic arithmetic. Of these, perhaps ten percent would continue to learn more sophisticated mathematics and business practices such as book keeping to permit them to enter business. About five percent would learn Latin, logic, and rhetoric to equip them to enter a university to study arts, law, or medicine. Thus Renaissance education for the great majority of boys was instrumental, designed to assist them in their work. Humanism was the prerogative of the social as well as the intellectual elite.

The schools designed to teach the new curriculum of humanism, centered on rhetoric, moral philosophy (ethics), good Latin style and Greek, were confined to a relatively few students. Nevertheless, these humanist academies had a wide influence not only because the subjects taught became the basis for European liberal arts education for centuries, but also because the graduates of these humanist schools consisted of the most influential men, and occasionally women, of their times.

Vittorino da Feltre (1378–1446), for example, established a court academy at Mantua in 1423 that united a sound classical education with

269

physical training and instruction in social grace in an attempt to recreate the classical ideal of the well-rounded individual. He insisted that some poor boys be taught with the sons of Mantuan courtiers to ensure social cohesion and permit talented youngsters of poor parents to advance intellectually. Religious training was added so that each pupil emerged from Vittorino's school ready to assume responsible positions in the public service of the court, communal government, or even the curia.

da Feltre's contemporary, Guarino of Verona (1374–1460), was one of the great teachers of the Renaissance and a founder of the practical humanist curriculum. He lived in Constantinople for five years, learning written and spoken Greek and collecting Greek books. After an unhappy period as a teacher in Florence, Guarino traveled to Ferrara in 1429 as tutor to the son of the Marquis. He established a school there to teach Latin and Greek and the subjects necessary to understand the ancient world. Latin for Guarino had to correspond to the style of Cicero, and Greek studies were given equal importance with Latin.

The education of women tended to be another matter. Some girls, because of their father's or mother's interests, did acquire a good education in the classics. However, with the exception of women like Isabella d'Este, who emerged as rulers of states or perhaps learned nuns, there was little opportunity to practice their learning. The vast majority of girls, if they had any education at all, learned the practical skills of managing a household: basic reading and writing in Italian, rudimentary arithmetic, spinning, weaving, and much devotional instruction. Religious studies constituted a great part of their restricted education, which was to make them useful to a still male-dominated society rather than to develop their own talents as individuals.

✦ Petrarch

*F*or information about the life and writings of Petrarch, see above, p. 17.

ON HIS OWN IGNORANCE

Much too vagrantly am I rambling along at the heels of my ignorance, much too much am I indulging my mind and my pen. It is time to return. These and similar reasons brought me before the friendly and nevertheless unfair court of my friends—a strange combination of attributes! As far as

SOURCE: E. Cassirer et al., eds., *The Renaissance Philosophy of Man* (Chicago: University of Chicago Press, 1948), pp. 113–133. Reprinted by permission of the University of Chicago Press.

I understand, none has so much weight as the fact that, though I am a sinner, I certainly am a Christian. It is true, I might well hear the reproach once launched at Jerome, as he himself reports: "Thou liest, thou art a Ciceronian. For where thy treasure is, there is thy heart also." Then I shall answer: My incorruptible treasure and the superior part of my soul is with Christ; but, because of the frailties and burdens of mortal life, which are not only difficult to bear but difficult merely to enumerate, I cannot, I confess, lift up, however ardently I should wish, the inferior parts of my soul, in which the irascible and concupiscible appetites are located,[1] and cannot make them cease to cling to earth. I call upon Christ as witness and invoke Him: He alone knows how often I have tried again and again, sadly and indignantly and with the greatest effort, to drag them up from the ground and how much I suffer because I have not succeeded. Christ will perhaps have compassion on me and lend me a helping hand in the sound attempt of my frail soul, which is weighed down and depressed by the mass of its sins.

In the meantime I do not deny that I am given to vain and injurious cares. But among these I do not count Cicero. I know that he has never done me harm; often has he brought me benefit. Nobody will be astonished to hear this from me, when he hears Augustine assert that he has had a similar experience. I remember discussing this a little while ago and even more explicitly. Therefore, I shall now be content with this simple statement: I do not deny that I am delighted with Cicero's genius and eloquence, seeing that even Jerome—to omit countless others—was so fascinated by him that he could not free his own style from that of Cicero, not even under the pressure of the terrible vision and of the insults of Rufinus. It always retained a Ciceronian flavor. He feels this himself, and in one place he apologizes for it.

Cicero, read with a pious and modest attitude, did no harm to him or to anybody else at any time. He was profitable to everybody, so far as eloquence is concerned, to many others as regards living. This is especially true in Augustine's case, as I have already said. Augustine filled his pockets and his lap with the gold and silver of the Egyptians when he was about to depart from Egypt.[2] Destined to be the great fighter for the Church, the great champion of Faith, he girded his loins with the weapons of the enemy, long before he went into battle. When such weapons are in

---

1. The threefold division of the soul into the rational, irascible, and concupiscent parts is ultimately based on Plato and appears quite frequently in ancient and medieval Latin writers.
2. Augustine never returned from Egypt, where he never was in his life; but he took over into his Christian life what he had learned from his pagan teachers and from pagan authors, to enrich and adorn Christian literature, just as the Jews, when they left Egypt, took with them the silver and golden vessels they had borrowed upon Moses' command; Exod. 3:21–22; 11:2; 12:35–36.

question, especially when eloquence is concerned, I confess, I admire Cicero as much or even more than all whoever wrote a line in any nation. However, much as I admire him, I do not imitate him. I rather try to do the contrary, since I do not want to be too much of an imitator of anybody and am afraid of becoming what I do not approve in others.

If to admire Cicero means to be a Ciceronian, I am a Ciceronian. I admire him so much that I wonder at people who do not admire him. This may appear a new confession of my ignorance, but this is how I feel, such is my amazement. However, when we come to think or speak of religion, that is, of supreme truth and true happiness, and of eternal salvation, then I am certainly not a Ciceronian, or a Platonist, but a Christian. I even feel sure that Cicero himself would have been a Christian if he had been able to see Christ and to comprehend His doctrine. Of Plato, Augustine does not in the least doubt that he would have become a Christian if he had come to life again in Augustine's time or had foreseen the future while he lived. Augustine relates also that in his time most of the Platonists had become Christians and he himself can be supposed to belong to their number. If this fundament stands, in what way is Ciceronian eloquence opposed to the Christian dogma? Or how is it harmful to consult Cicero's writings, if reading the books of heretics does no harm, nay, is profitable, according to the words of the Apostle: "There must be heresies that they which are approved may be made manifest to you." Besides, any pious Catholic, however unlearned he may be, will find much more credit with me in this respect than Plato or Cicero.

These, then, are the more valid arguments for our ignorance. By God, I am so glad they are true that I wish them to become more true every day. Indeed, I agree perfectly with what certain eminent men have said— that these arrogant and ignorant people will charge any philosopher, however famous, and even their god Aristotle, with being rude and ignorant, as soon as they hear that one of them has come to life again and has become a Christian. In their arrogant ignorance they will look down on the same man to whom they before looked up in reverence, as if he had forgotten what he had learned just because he had turned away from the beclouded and loquacious ignorance of this world to the wisdom of God the Father: so rare is truth and so much is it hated. "Victorinus" was reputed to be such a brilliant man that he "deserved and got a statue in the Roman Forum," while he was still teaching rhetoric. I have no doubt that as soon as he professed Christ and the true Faith with clear and saving voice, he was considered dull and downright delirious by those arrogant demon-worshipers whom he feared so much to offend that, as Augustine reports in his *Confessions,* he delayed his conversion for quite a while. Just the same I suspect Augustine did himself. I suspect it all the more, because he was a more brilliant figure and his conversion was more conspicuous. The enemies of Christ and His Church were the more exasperated and grieved the more propitious and gratifying it was for the faithful when he resigned his chair of rhetoric in Milan—as he mentions in his same *Confessions*—grasped the heavenly wisdom under the guidance of Ambrose, that most faithful and holy herald of truth, and, ceasing to be a commentator of Cicero, was about to become a preacher of Christ.

Here let me tell what I once heard said of him, for I want you to understand how grave, how pestiferous, how deeply rooted this disease is. It happened that I once quoted some maxim of Augustine's to a man with a great name, and he took a deep breath and said, "What a pity that a genius like him was so deeply entangled in empty fables!"

I replied: "How miserable are you to say such a thing; most miserable if you really believe it."

But he smiled and retorted: "On the contrary, it is you who are stupid, if you believe what you say, though I hope better for you." What else might he hope for me than that I should silently agree with him in his contempt of piety?

By all faith in God and men, in the judgment of such people nobody can be a man of letters unless he is also a heretic and a madman besides being impertinent and impudent, a two-legged animal disputing about four-legged animals and beasts everywhere in the streets and squares of every city. No wonder my friends declare me not only ignorant but mad, since they doubtless belong to that sort of people who despise piety without regard to the attitude in which it is practiced and take diffidence to be a religious habit. They believe that a man has no great intellect and is hardly learned unless he dares to raise his voice against God and to dispute against the Catholic Faith, silent before Aristotle alone. The more boldly a man ventures to attack Faith—for he will not be able to seize this fortress by the power of intelligence or by violence—the more these men think him highly gifted and learned. The more faithful and pious he proves to be when defending Faith, the more he is supposed to be slow of perception and unlearned, the more he is suspected of using Faith as a veil to cover and mask himself, in consciousness of his ignorance. They act just as if the old fables they tell were not inconsistent and shaky and their silly talk empty and void; as if there could be had certain knowledge of ambiguous and unknown matters and not merely vague, loose, and uncertain opinions; as if knowledge of the true Faith were not the highest, most certain, and ultimately most beatifying of all knowledge. If one deserts it, all other knowledge is not a path but a road with a dead end, not a goal but a disaster, not knowledge but error. However, these friends of ours have a strange mentality and a peculiar way of forming their judgments. I am not sure whether the two philosophers of whom I have just now spoken, or others like them, would—I will not say: "have begun to displease the Jews, whom they had pleased all the while before," as Jerome tells us in his interpretation of Paul's *Epistle to the Galatians*, but appear to these our friends just as raving mad as Paul appeared to the Pharisees and priests, since he had become a lamb instead of a wolf, an Apostle of Christ instead of a persecutor of the Christian name.

Therefore, it can be a comfort to me to be charged with ignorance.

Even were I charged with madness, it would be a comfort—since such great men are my companions. And it *is* a comfort to me: sometimes I am even delighted in my heart and happy to be accused, for honorable reasons, not only of ignorance, but even of madness.

Thus I am happy for myself but feel sorry for my friends. Still other arguments were brought before their court. They are perhaps of lighter weight, though they are not free from crime and impiety. To them they are deadly and infamous; for me they are so glorious that I would suffer with perfect peace of mind to be deprived not only of fame but above all of life, if it came to it. It is exceedingly painful that a grudge is the true reason for their biased judgment, the only true reason, or at any rate the most prominent of all. A grudge has infected many a man's eyes and made him see things distorted, though to sound and clear eyes this could never happen. It is something new to me, amazing and unheard of, that, much against my will, I have had to experience in my own case that an envious grudge may dwell in the hearts of friends. Of friends, I say, but not of those whose friendship is perfect and complete: such friendship means to love a friend as one's self. These friends of mine love me, but not with all their hearts. I should rather say that they love me with all their hearts but not all of me. They certainly love my life, my body and soul, and whatever is mine, except my fame, and this so far as it is literary fame. This fame I would hand over confidently and without reluctance to all of them, every single one of them. And this exception is caused not by hatred or lukewarm friendship but, as I have said, by envy, such as dwells even in the midst of friendship.

This may be hard to hear, and I had better say that it is an exception caused not by any grudge but by grief. They are perhaps grieved, indeed they are surely grieved, that in the estimate of learned men they are neither men of letters nor known at all, while they hear me called by that name which, rightly or wrongly, I have acquired. Therefore, they wish to tear from me what they lack and what they cannot hope to acquire if they are reasonable. It must lead to great conflict and discordance of wishes if you wish a person all that is good, even the best, and begrudge him the most trifling thing. They do so, I believe, out of deep regret, which they feel not so much because I enjoy fame but because they do not. They wish to be equal in friendship, and this, I admit, is not unjust; but they are trying to achieve it in such a way that we are to be equally obscure, all of us, because they believe this to be the easier way, since we cannot all be brilliant and famous. I do not deny that equality among friends is something extremely beautiful. As soon as one party is noticeably preponderant, the souls of the friends seem to be not well teamed under the yoke of friendship, like unequal young bullocks. However, this parity ought to be a parity of love and confidence, not necessarily of fortunes and fame. This is proved by unequal pairs of friends like Hercules and Philoctetes, Theseus and Pirithous, Achilles and Patroclus, Scipio and

Laelius, not to mention those that remain unknown. Therefore, it is up to these friends of mine to see how they are disposed toward my fame. For, if I am not mistaken, they are most kindly disposed toward me.

I do not want you to lack knowledge of anything that concerns me, my friend. You shall know where and in what mood I am writing you this. Know then that I am sitting in a small boat amid the whirling waves of the Po. Thus you shall not wonder when you find both the hand and the speech of the writer fluctuating: I am driving against the current of this huge river with all my ignorance. Once when I was still young, I wrote much on its banks and meditated a good deal, all of which was destined to please the old men of those days, long before these youths trapped my senile ignorance. The fate of men is indeed unstable. The Po himself seems to feel compassion for me somehow, remembering as it were my studies and conscious of my ancient sorrows, since he saw me —if it can be said without arrogance—glorified by fame when I was young and now sees me as an old man inglorious and despoiled of the brilliantly shining attire of fame. With all the might of his current he urges me incessantly back to demand my right from my unfair judges.

However, I am tired of the toilsome burden of my fame, which arouses the envy of those from whom I do not in the least expect it. I flee from quarrels and lawsuits and despise contempt. Therefore, I leave my spoils to these dear robbers. They may have them; willingly I give my spoils up to them, if fame can be handed over to a robber in the way money can when it is snatched from its owner. Let them have learning or, what is the same in the opinion of the stupid mass, the confidence that they have it. I shall get along without both or, at any rate, without the latter, that is to say, without this confidence. Happier and richer I shall be in my humble nakedness than they in the superb spoils, which in my view do not belong to them. I proceed onward, glad enough that I am relieved of a brilliant but heavy burden. With oars, sails, and ropes I master the Po that resists me on my way home to Padua, this old city of studies. There, if I care to, I shall get back the old robe of fame I have lost among the seafaring people, for I can never get rid of it, however intensely I may want to. It shall always be my aim and wish to be called illiterate, as long as I am a good man or, at any rate, not a bad one, and therein I wish to find repose at last. Nothing is more gratifying to a weary man than repose. My literary fame had deprived me of this quiet rest, and, as I now hear, it was lying all the time. This repose will be restored to me by the reputation of being ignorant, whether it is true or untrue. Thus, late but still in time, everything will turn out all right.

But I am afraid my endeavors and wishes will be in vain. There are so many whose opinions are so much opposed to those of my judges. Not only in the city to which I am now traveling, but wherever they make this their verdict public all over our world it will return upon their heads by the judgment of more and greater men, although with me it has become a settled case by now, as you have already heard. One single exception will perhaps be that most noble and good city where they dare sit in court. Because of its large population and its manifold variety, there are many in that city who practice philosophy and pass judgment without any knowledge. Much freedom reigns there in every respect, and what I should call the only evil prevailing—but also the worst—far too much freedom of speech. Confiding in this freedom, the extremely inept often insult famous men, much to the indignation of the good. Of this latter kind there are there so many that I do not know whether as many good and modest people live in any other city. However, the horde of stupid fellows is everywhere so much greater that the indignation of the wise is of no avail. So sweet does the word freedom sound to everyone that Temerity and Audacity please the vulgar crowd, because they look so much like Freedom. Thus the night owls insult the eagle with impunity; so do the ravens the swan and the monkeys the lion; thus the nasty rend the honest to pieces, the ignorant the learned, the cowards the brave, the bad the good. And the good do not oppose the licentiousness of the bad, because the bad are the greater number and more in favor with the public, which believes it to be expedient to let everyone talk as he likes. So deeply fixed in the mind is that word of Tiberius Caesar: "In a free state tongue and mind ought to be free." They ought to be free, of course, but so that freedom remains free from injustice and injuriousness.

◆ *Leonardo Bruni*

*F*or information about the life and work of Leonardo Bruni, see above, p. 97.

A LETTER TO BATTISTA MALATESTA ON THE STUDY OF LITERATURE

I am led to address this Tractate to you, Illustrious Lady, by the high repute which attaches to your name in the field of learning; and I offer it, partly as an expression of my homage to distinction already attained, partly as an encouragement to further effort. Were it necessary I might urge you by brilliant instances from antiquity: Cornelia, the daughter of Scipio, whose Epistles survived for centuries as models of style; Sappho, the poetess, held in so great honor for the exuberance of her poetic art;

SOURCE: J. Woodward, ed., *Vittorino da Feltre and Other Humanist Educators* (New York: Columbia University Press, 1963), pp. 123–133.

Aspasia, whose learning and eloquence made her not unworthy of the intimacy of Socrates. Upon these, the most distinguished of a long range of great names, I would have you fix your mind; for an intelligence such as your own can be satisfied with nothing less than the best. You yourself, indeed, may hope to win a fame higher even than theirs. For they lived in days when learning was no rare attainment, and therefore they enjoyed no unique renown. Whilst, alas, upon such times are we fallen that a learned man seems well-nigh a portent, and erudition in a woman is a thing utterly unknown. For true learning has almost died away amongst us. True learning, I say: not a mere acquaintance with that vulgar, threadbare jargon which satisfies those who devote themselves to Theology, but sound learning in its proper and legitimate sense, *viz.*, the knowledge of realities—Facts and Principles—united to a perfect familiarity with Letters and the art of expression. Now this combination we find in Lactantius, in Augustine, or in Jerome; each of them at once a great theologian and profoundly versed in literature. But turn from them to their successors of to-day: how must we blush for their ignorance of the whole field of Letters!

This leads me to press home this truth—though in your case it is unnecessary—that the foundations of all true learning must be laid in the sound and thorough knowledge of Latin: which implies study marked by a broad spirit, accurate scholarship, and careful attention to details. Unless this solid basis be secured it is useless to attempt to rear an enduring edifice. Without it the great monuments of literature are unintelligible, and the art of composition impossible. To attain this essential knowledge we must never relax our careful attention to the grammar of the language, but perpetually confirm and extend our acquaintance with it until it is thoroughly our own. We may gain much from Servius, Donatus and Priscian, but more by careful observation in our own reading, in which we must note attentively vocabulary and inflexions, figures of speech and metaphors, and all the devices of style, such as rhythm, or antithesis, by which fine taste is exhibited. To this end we must be supremely careful in our choice of authors, lest an inartistic and debased style infect our own writing and degrade our taste; which danger is best avoided by bringing a keen, critical sense to bear upon select works, observing the sense of each passage, the structure of the sentence, the force of every word down to the least important particle. In this way our reading reacts directly upon our style.

You may naturally turn first to Christian writers, foremost amongst whom, with marked distinction, stands Lactantius, by common consent the finest stylist of the post-classical period. Especially do I commend to your study his works, *Adversus falsam Religionem*, *De via Dei*, and *De opificio hominis*. After Lactantius your choice may lie between Augustine, Jerome, Ambrose, and Cyprian; should you desire to read Gregory of Nazianzen, Chrysostom, and Basil, be careful as to the accuracy of the translations you adopt. Of the classical authors Cicero will be your constant pleasure: how unapproachable in wealth of ideas and of language, in force of style, indeed, in all that can attract in a writer! Next to him ranks Vergil, the glory and the delight of our national literature. Livy and Sallust, and then the chief poets, follow in order. The usage of these authors will serve you as your test of correctness in choice of vocabulary and of constructions.

Now we notice in all good prose—though it is not of course obtrusive—a certain element of rhythm, which coincides with and expresses the general structure of the passage, and consequently gives a clue to its sense. I commend, therefore, to you as an aid to understanding an author the practice of reading aloud with clear and exact intonation. By this device you will seize more quickly the drift of the passage, by realizing the main lines on which it is constructed. And the music of the prose thus interpreted by the voice will react with advantage upon your own composition, and at the same time will improve your own Reading by compelling deliberate and intelligent expression.

The art of Writing is not limited to the mere formation of letters, but it concerns also the subject of the diphthongs, and of the syllabic divisions of words; the accepted usages in the writing of each letter, singly and in cursive script, and the whole field of abbreviations. This may seem a trivial matter, but a knowledge of educated practice on these points may fairly be expected from us. The laws of quantity are more important, since in poetry scansion is frequently our only certain clue to construction. One might ask, further, what capacity in poetic composition or what critical ability or taste in poetical literature is possible to a man who is not first of all secure on points of quantity and meter? Nor is prose, as I have already hinted, without its metrical element; upon which indeed Aristotle and Cicero dwelt with some minuteness. A skillful orator or historian will be careful of the effect to be gained by spondaic, iambic, dactylic or other rhythm in arousing differing emotions congruous to his matter in hand. To ignore this is to neglect one of the most delicate points of style. You will notice that such refinements will apply only to one who aspires to proficiency in the finer shades of criticism and expression, but such a one must certainly by observation and practice become familiar with every device which lends distinction and adornment to the literary art.

But the wider question now confronts us, that of the subject matter of our studies, that which I have already called the realities of fact and principle, as distinct from literary form. Here, as before, I am contemplating a student of keen and lofty aspiration to whom nothing that is worthy in any learned discipline is without its interest. But it is necessary to exercise discrimination. In some branches of knowledge I would rather restrain the ardor of the learner, in others, again, encourage it to the uttermost. Thus there are certain subjects in which, whilst a modest proficiency is on all accounts to be desired, a minute knowledge and excessive devotion seem to be a vain display. For instance, subtleties of Arithmetic and Geometry are not worthy to absorb a cultivated mind and the same must be said of Astrology. You will be surprised to find me suggesting (though with much more hesitation) that the great and complex art of Rhetoric should be placed in the same category. My chief reason is the obvious one, that I have in view the cultivation most fitting to a woman. To her neither the intricacies of debate nor the oratorical artifices of action and delivery are of the least practical use, if indeed they are not positively unbecoming. Rhetoric in all its forms—public discussion, forensic argument, logical fence, and the like—lies absolutely outside the province of woman.

What disciplines then are properly open to her? In the first place she has before her, as a subject peculiarly her own, the whole field of religion and morals. The literature of her Church will thus claim her earnest study. Such a writer, for instance, as St Augustine affords her the fullest scope for reverent yet learned inquiry. Her devotional instinct may lead her to value the help and consolation of holy men now living; but in this case let her not for an instant yield to the impulse to look into their writings, which, compared with those of Augustine, are utterly destitute of sound and melodious style, and seem to me to have no attraction whatever.

Moreover, the cultivated Christian lady has no need in the study of this weighty subject to confine herself to ecclesiastical writers. Morals, indeed, have been treated of by the noblest intellects of Greece and Rome. What they have left to us upon Continence, Temperance, Modesty, Justice, Courage, Greatness of Soul, demands your sincere respect. You must enter into such questions as the sufficiency of Virtue to Happiness; or whether, if Happiness consist in Virtue, it can be destroyed by torture, imprisonment or exile; whether, admitting that these may prevent a man from being happy, they can be further said to make him miserable. Again, does Happiness consist (with Epicurus) in the presence of pleasure and the absence of pain: or (with Xenophon) in the consciousness of uprightness: or (with Aristotle) in the practice of Virtue? These inquiries are, of all others, most worthy to be pursued by men and women alike; they are fit material for formal discussion and for literary exercise. Let religion and morals, therefore, hold the first place in the education of a Christian lady.

But we must not forget that true distinction is to be gained by a wide and varied range of such studies as conduce to the profitable enjoyment of life, in which, however, we must observe due proportion in the attention and time we devote to them.

First amongst such studies I place History: a subject which must not on any account be neglected by one who aspires to true cultivation. For it is our duty to understand the origins of our own history and its development; and the achievements of Peoples and of Kings.

For the careful study of the past enlarges our foresight in contemporary affairs and affords to citizens and to monarchs lessons of incitement or warning in the ordering of public policy. From History, also, we draw our store of examples of moral precepts.

In the monuments of ancient literature which have come down to us History holds a position of great distinction. We specially prize such authors as Livy, Sallust and Curtius; and, perhaps even above these, Julius Caesar; the style of whose Commentaries, so elegant and so limpid, entitles them to our warm admiration. Such writers are fully within the comprehension of a studious lady. For, after all, History is an easy subject: there is nothing in its study subtle or complex. It consists in the narration of the simplest matters of fact which, once grasped, are readily retained in the memory.

The great Orators of antiquity must by all means be included. Nowhere do we find the virtues more warmly extolled, the vices so fiercely decried. From them we may learn, also, how to express consolation, encouragement, dissuasion or advice. If the principles which orators set forth are portrayed for us by philosphers, it is from the former that we learn how to employ the emotions—such as indignation, or pity—in driving home their application in individual cases. Further, from oratory we derive our store of those elegant or striking turns of expression which are used with so much effect in literary compositions. Lastly, in oratory we find that wealth of vocabulary, that clear easy-flowing style, that verve and force, which are invaluable to us both in writing and in conversation.

I come now to Poetry and the Poets—a subject with which every educated lady must shew herself thoroughly familiar. For we cannot point to any great mind of the past for whom the Poets had not a powerful attraction. Aristotle, in constantly quoting Homer, Hesiod, Pindar, Euripides and other poets, proves that he knew their works hardly less intimately than those of the philosophers. Plato, also, frequently appeals to them, and in this way covers them with his approval. If we turn to Cicero, we find him not content with quoting Ennius, Accius, and others of the Latins, but rendering poems from the Greek and employing them habitually. Seneca, the austere, not only abounds in poetical allusions, but was himself a poet; whilst the great Fathers of the Church, Jerome, Augustine, Lactantius and Boethius, reveal their acquaintance with the poets in their controversies and, indeed, in all their writings. Hence my view that familiarity with the great poets of antiquity is essential to any claim to true education. For in their writings we find deep speculations upon Nature, and upon the Causes and Origins of things, which must carry weight with us both from their antiquity and from their authorship. Besides these, many important truths upon matters of daily life are suggested or illustrated. All this is expressed with such grace and dignity as demands our admiration. For example, how vividly is the art of war portrayed in Homer: the duties of a leader of men: the chances of the field: the varying temper of the host! Wise counsel, too, is not wanting, as when Hector upbraids

Aeneas for too rashly urging the pursuit. Would, indeed, that in our own day our captains would deign to profit by this ancient wisdom, to the security of the commonwealth and the saving of valuable lives! Consider, again, how fitly Iris, descending upon Agamemnon in his sleep, warns against the sloth of rulers—could Socrates, Plato or Pythagoras more pointedly exhibit the responsibility of a king of men? There are the precepts also, not fewer nor less weighty, which pertain to the arts of peace. But it is time to pass to our own Poets, to Vergil, who surpasses, it seems to me, all philosophers in displaying the inner secrets of Nature and of the Soul:

> Know first, the heaven, the earth, the main,
> The moon's pale orb, the starry train,
>   Are nourished by a soul,
> A bright intelligence, whose flame
> Glows in each member of the frame
>   And stirs the mighty whole.
> Thence souls of men and cattle spring,
> And the gay people of the wing,
> And those strange shapes that ocean hides
> Beneath the smoothness of the tides.
> A fiery strength inspires their lives,
> An essence that from heaven derives,
> Though clogged in part by limbs of clay
> And the dull "vesture of decay."

Nor can we deny a certain inspiration to a poet who, on the very eve of the Redeemer's birth, could speak of "the Virgin's return" and "the Divine offspring sent down from on High." So thought Lactantius, who held that the Sibyl here alludes directly to the Savior. Such power of reading the future is implied in the name "vates," so often given to the true poet, and we must all recognize in such one a certain "possession," as by a Power other and stronger than himself.

✦ *Battista Guarino*

*B*attista Guarino, born in Ferrara in 1434, was the son of the great Guarino of Verona. He was educated by his father and eventually joined him as a master in his palace school. In 1455, however, Battista was appointed to the chair of rhetoric at the University of Bologna, even though he was only 21 years old, but he kept this position for only two years before returning to Ferrara and his father's school.

Battista Guarino began his treatise on education, On the Means of Teaching and Learning, *about 1459, probably to record his father's pedagogical principles, developed during his many years at Ferrara.*

ON THE MEANS OF TEACHING AND LEARNING

Battista Guarino to Maffeo Gambara, of Brescia

In offering this short Treatise for your acceptance, I am fully aware that you need no incentive to regard the pursuit of Letters as the most worthy object of your ambition. But you may find what I have written a not unwelcome reminder of our past intercourse, whilst it may prove of use to other readers into whose hands it may fall. For I have had in view not only students anxious for guidance in their private reading, but masters in search of some definite principles of method in teaching the Classics. Hence I have treated both of Greek and of Latin Letters, and I have confidence that the course I have laid down will prove a thoroughly satisfactory training in literature and scholarship. I should remind you that the conclusions presented in this little work are not the result of my own experience only. It is indeed a summary of the theory and practice of several scholars, and especially does it represent the doctrine of my father Guarino Veronese; so much so, that you may suppose him to be writing to you by my pen, and giving you the fruit of his long and ripe experience in teaching. May I hope that you will yourself prove to be one more example of the high worth of his precepts?

Let me, at the outset, begin with a caution. No master can endow a careless and indifferent nature with the true passion for learning. That a young man must acquire for himself. But once the taste begins to develope, then in Ovid's words "the more we drink, the more we thirst." For when the mind has begun to enjoy the pleasures of learning the passion for fuller and deeper knowledge will grow from day to day. But there can be no proficiency in studies unless there be first the desire to excel. Wherefore let a young man set forward eagerly in quest of those true, honorable, and enduring treasures of the mind which neither disease nor death has power to destroy. Riches, which adventurers seek by land and sea, too often win men to pleasure rather than to learning; for self-indulgence is a snare from whose enticements it is the bounden duty of parents to wean their children, by kind word, or by severity if need arise. Perchance then in later years the echo of a father's wise advice may linger and may avail in the hour of temptation.

In the choice of a Master we ought to remember that his position should carry with it something of the authority of a father: for unless respect be paid to the man and to his office regard will not be had to his words. Our forefathers were certainly right in basing the relation of teacher and pupil upon the foundation of filial reverence on the one part and

SOURCE: J. Woodward, ed., *Vittorino da Feltre and Other Humanist Educators* (New York: Columbia University Publications, 1963), pp. 161–177.

fatherly affection on the other. Thus the instinct of Alexander of Macedon was a sound one which led him to say that, whilst he owed to his father Philip the gift of life, he owed to his tutor Aristotle an equal debt, namely, the knowledge how to use it. Care must be taken therefore from the outset to avoid a wrong choice of master: one, for instance, who is ill-bred, or ill-educated. Such a one may by bad teaching waste precious years of a boy's life; not only is nothing rightly learnt, but much of that which passes as instruction needs to be undone again, as Timotheus said long ago. Faults, moreover, imbibed in early years, as Horace reminds us, are by no means easy to eradicate. Next, the master must not be prone to flogging as an inducement to learning. It is an indignity to a free-born youth, and its infliction renders learning itself repulsive, and the mere dread of it provokes to unworthy evasions on the part of timorous boys. The scholar is thus morally and intellectually injured, the master is deceived, and the discipline altogether fails of its purpose. The habitual instrument of the teacher must be kindness, though punishment should be retained as it were in the background as a final resource. In the case of elder boys, emulation and the sense of shame, which shrinks from the discredit of failure, may be relied upon. I advise also that boys, at this stage, work two altogether with a view to encouraging a healthy spirit of rivalry between them, from which much benefit may be expected. Large classes should be discouraged, especially for beginners, for though a fair average excellence may be apparently secured, thorough grounding, which is so important, is impossible. In the case of more advanced pupils, however, numbers tend rather to stimulate the teacher.

2. As regards the course of study. From the first, stress must be laid upon distinct and sustained enunciation, both in speaking and in reading. But at the same time utterance must be perfectly natural; if affected or exaggerated the effect is unpleasing. The foundation of education must be laid in Grammar. Unless this be thoroughly learnt subsequent progress is uncertain—a house built upon treacherous ground. Hence let the knowledge of nouns and verbs be secured early, as the starting point for the rest. The master will employ the devices of repetition, examination, and the correction of erroneous inflexions purposely introduced.

Grammar falls into two parts. The first treats of the rules which govern the use of the different Parts of Speech, and is called therefore "Methodice," the second includes the study of continuous prose, especially of historical narrative, and is called "Historice."

Now these Rules can be most satisfactorily learnt from the Compendium written by my father which briefly sets out the more important laws of composition. In using this or a similar text-book the pupil must be practiced both in written and in oral exercises. Only by rapid practice in oral composition can fluency and readiness be gained. And this will be further secured if the class is accustomed to speak in Latin. Certain general Rules of a crucial nature must be early learnt, and constantly practiced, by the whole class. Such are those by which we recognize the differences between active, passive and deponent verbs, or between those of transitive or intransitive meaning. It is most important that each boy be required to form examples in illustration of the main rules of accidence and syntax, not only with accuracy but also with a certain propriety of style, as for instance with due attention to the order of words in the sentence. In this way the habit of sound and tasteful composition is imbibed during the earliest stages of education. A master who is properly qualified for his work will be careful to use only such transcripts of texts as can be relied upon for accuracy and completeness. The work just referred to has been much disfigured by additions and alterations due to the ignorance or conceit of the would-be emendator. As examples of what I mean you may turn to the rule as to the formation of the comparative of adjectives of the second declension where an inept correction is added in some copies ("vowel before a vowel" is turned into "vowel before -us"); and in another place the spelling "Tydites" is substituted for my father's (and, of course, the correct) form "Tydides."

But to return. Let the scholar work at these Rules until they are so ingrained, as it were, into the memory that they become a part and parcel of the mind itself. In this way the laws of grammar are accurately recalled with effort and almost unconsciously. Meanwhile rules of quantity and meter have been entered upon. This branch of Letters is so important that no one who is ignorant of it can claim to be thought an educated man. Hence it is significant that so much attention was paid to the subject by the ancients; even Augustine, that great pillar of the Church, did not disdain to publish a tract upon Scansion. In reading the Poets a Knowledge of Prosody is indispensable to the enjoyment, nay even the understanding, of their works. An acquaintance with metrical structure enables us to enter into the beauties of the rhythm, whilst our only clue to the exact meaning of the writer is not seldom given by the quantity of a vowel. Nor is the artifice of rhythm confined to poetical composition. Orators often shew themselves masters of this art; and in order to duly appreciate the flow of their eloquence, much more to reproduce it for ourselves, we must be skilled in the ordinary laws of meter. On this ground it is possible to commend the use of the manual of grammar which passes under the name of Alexander; it is founded upon the great work of Priscian, but it is much more readily committed to memory on account of its metrical form. When the rudiments of prosody have been carefully learnt we shall find that proficiency is best gained by the daily reading of the poets. The works of Vergil must be learnt by heart, and recited as a regular task. In this way the flow of the hexameter, not less than the quantity of individual syllables, is impressed upon the ear, and insensibly molds our taste. Other meters may afterwards be attempted, so that no form of ancient poetry be left neglected.

3. I have said that ability to write Latin verse is one of the essential

marks of an educated person. I wish now to indicate a second, which is of at least equal importance, namely, familiarity with the language and literature of Greece. The time has come when we must speak with no uncertain voice upon this vital requirement of scholarship. I am well aware that those who are ignorant of the Greek tongue decry its necessity, for reasons which are sufficiently evident. But I can allow no doubt to remain as to my own conviction that without a knowledge of Greek Latin scholarship itself is, in any real sense, impossible. I might point to the vast number of words derived or borrowed from the Greek, and the questions which arise in connection with them; such as the quantity of the vowel sounds, the use of the diphthongs, obscure orthographies and etymologies. Vergil's allusion to the Avernian Lake:

> O'er that dread space no flying thing
> Unjeoparded could ply its wing

is wholly missed by one who is ignorant of the relation between the name of the lake and the Greek word ὄρνιδ. Or again the lines of Ovid,

> Quae quia nascuntur dura vivacia caute
> Agrestes aconita vocant

is unintelligible unless we can associate "cautes" with the Greek (ἀκόνη). So too the name *Ciris* (κείρω), and the full force of *Aphrodite* (ἄφρων) are but vaguely understood without a clear perception of their Greek etymologies. The Greek grammar, again, can alone explain the unusual case-endings which are met with in the declension of certain nouns, mostly proper names, which retain their foreign shape; such as "Dido" and "Mantus." Nor are these exceptional forms confined to the poetic use. But I turn to the authority of the great Latins themselves, to Cicero, Quintilian, Cato and Horace: they are unanimous in proclaiming the close dependence of the Roman speech and Roman literature upon the Greek, and in urging by example as well as by precept the constant study of the older language. To quote Horace alone:

> Do you, my friends, from Greece your models draw,
> And day and night to con them be your law.

And again,

> To Greece, that cared for nought but fame, the Muse
> Gave genius, and a tongue the gods might use.

In such company I do not fear to urge the same contention.

Were we, indeed, to follow Quintilian, we should even begin with Greek in preference to Latin. But this is practically impossible, when we consider that Greek must be for us, almost of necessity, a learned and not a colloquial language; and that Latin itself needs much more elaborate and careful teaching than was requisite to a Roman of the imperial epoch.

On the other hand, I have myself known not a few pupils of my father—
he was, as you know, a scholar of equal distinction in either language—
who, after gaining a thorough mastery of Latin, could then in a single year
make such progress with Greek that they translated accurately entire
works of ordinary difficulty from that language into good readable Latin
at sight. Now proficiency of this degree can only be attained by careful
and systematic teaching of the rudiments of the Grammar, as they are
laid down in such a manual as the well-known Ἐρωτήματα of Manuel
Chrysoloras, or in the abridgement which my father drew up of the original
work of his beloved master. In using such a text-book the greatest attention must be paid to the verb, the regular form, with its scheme of moods
and tenses; then the irregular verbs must be equally mastered. When the
forms of noun and verb can be immediately distinguished, and each inflex-
ion of voice, mood and tense recognized—and this can only be tested by
constant *vivâ voce* exercises—then a beginning should be made with
simple narrative prose. At this stage all authors whose subject matter
requires close thought should be avoided, for the entire attention must be
concentrated upon vocabulary and grammatical structure. Only when
some degree of freedom in these latter respects has been secured should
the master introduce books of increasing difficulty.

Our scholar should make his first acquaintance with the Poets through
Homer, the sovereign master of them all. For from Homer our own poets,
notably Vergil, drew their inspiration; and in reading the *Iliad* or the
Odyssey no small part of our pleasure is derived from the constant parallels we meet with. Indeed in them we see as in a mirror the form and
manner of the *Aeneid* figured roughly before us, the incidents, not less
than the simile or epithet which describe them, are, one might say, all
there. In the same way, in his minor works Vergil has borrowed from
Theocritus or Hesiod. After Homer has been attempted the way lies open
to the other Heroic poets and to the Dramatists.

In reading of this wider range a large increase of vocabulary is gained,
and in this the memory will be greatly assisted by the practice of making
notes, which should be methodically arranged afterwards. The rules of
Accentuation should now be learnt and their application observed after
the same method. It is very important that regular exercises in elementary
composition be required from the first, and this partly as an aid to con-
struing. The scholar will now shortly be able to render a Latin author into
Greek, a practice which compels us, as nothing else does, to realise the
appropriateness of the writer's language, and its dignity of style, whilst at
the same time it gives us increased freedom in handling it. For though
delicate shades of meaning or beauties of expression may be overlooked
by a casual reader they cannot escape a faithful translator.

But whilst a beginning is being thus made with Greek, continued
progress must at the same time be secured in Latin. For instance the
broader rules of grammar which sufficed in the earlier stages must give

place to a more complete study of structure, such as we find in Priscian, and irregularities or exceptions, hitherto ignored, must be duly noted. At the same time the *Epistles* of Cicero will be taken in hand for purposes of declamation. Committed to memory they serve as one of the finest possible aids to purity, directness, and facility of style, and supply admirable matter in no less admirable form for adaptation to our own uses. Yet I would not be understood to claim the *Letters* of Cicero as alone offering a sufficient training in style. For distinction of style is the fruit of a far wider field of study. To quote Horace once more:

> Of writing well, be sure, the secret lies
> In wisdom: therefore study to be wise.

4. But we are now passing from the first, or elementary, to the second, or more advanced, stage of grammar which I called "Historice," which is concerned with the study of continuous prose authors, more particularly the Historians. Here we begin with a short but comprehensive view of general history, which will include that of the Roman people, by such writers as Justin or Valerius Maximus. The latter author is also valuable as affording actual illustrations of virtuous precepts couched in attractive style. The scholar will now devote his attention to the Historians in regular order. By their aid he will learn to understand the manners, laws and institutions of different types of nation, and will examine the varying fortunes of individuals and states, the sources of their success and failure, their strength and their weakness. Not only is such Knowledge of interest in daily intercourse but it is of practical value in the ordering of affairs.

Side by side with the study of history a careful reading of the poets will be taken in hand. The true significance of poetic fiction will now be appreciated. It consists, as Cicero says, in the exhibition of the realities of our own life under the form of imaginary persons and situations. Thus Jerome could employ Terence in bringing home his exhortations to Temperance. Let us not forget that Vergil as a subject of deep and regular study must always stand not first, but alone. Here we have the express authority of Augustine, who urges the supreme claim of the great poet to our life-long companionship. Lucan may perhaps with good reason be postponed to a later stage. Quintilian regarded him as "the rhetorical poet": and undoubtedly his poem has much affinity with certain aspects of the forensic art. There is a certain strain of the keen debater in particular portions of his work. So I should advise that Vergil be followed by Statius, whose *Thebais*, fashioned upon the *Aeneid*, will be found easy reading. The *Metamorphoses* of Ovid form a useful introduction to the systematic knowledge of Mythology—a subject of wide literary application—and as such deserves close attention. The rest of the works of this poet, if I except the *Fasti*—unique as a source of antiquarian lore, and, alas! as incomplete as it is interesting—may very wisely be omitted from the school course. The Tragedies of Seneca attract us by the gravity of their situations and the moral distinction of their characters by which they are rendered specially useful for teaching purposes. Terence has the sanction of Cicero as regards grace and appropriateness of diction; he urged that parts of the Comedies should be committed to memory upon those grounds. If with Terence we couple Juvenal, the greatest of Satirists, we shall find that these two writers afford us a copious and elastic vocabulary for all the needs of ordinary intercourse, and not that alone, but that they provide us with a store of sound and dignified judgments. It is objected, indeed, without sufficient reason, that Juvenal is unsuitable for educational purposes in that he describes too freely the vicious morals which come under his lash. But in the first place this applies to but very few passages, whilst the rest of the Satires must command the admiration of all earnest men: in the second, if we must shew our indignation in the matter we should direct it rather against the vices themselves than against their critic. Plautus is marked by a flow of eloquence and wit which secures him a high place in Latin literature. That the Muses, if they spoke in Latin, would choose "the Plautine diction" was a common saying; and Macrobius placed the comic poet, in company with Cicero, at the head of the great masters of the Roman tongue. Horace throws unusual light upon the Art of poetry: he has a specially delicate sense of expression; and in his choice of epithets is only surpassed by Vergil. His *Satires* again form the best introduction to that type of poetry: for Persius is much less clear. There are other poets of literary importance, but their study may be postponed to a later period. It will be of advantage that the reading of the poetical authors should be accompanied by occasional perusal of writers who have treated of Astrology and of Geography: such as Pomponius Mela, Solinus, and Strabo, which latter author has been lately translated from the Greek by my father. A clear conception, too, ought to be attained of the Ptolemaic Geography, to enable us to follow descriptions of countries unfamiliar to us.

The course of study which I have thus far sketched out will prove an admirable preparation for that further branch of scholarship which constitutes Rhetoric, including the thorough examination of the great monuments of eloquence, and skill in the oratorial art itself. The first work to claim our attention in this subject is the *Rhetoric* of Cicero, in which we find all the points of Oratory concisely but comprehensively set forth. The other rhetorical writings of Cicero will follow, and the principles therein laid down must be examined in the light of his own speeches. Indeed the student of eloquence must have his Cicero constantly in his hand; the simplicity, the lofty moral standard, the practical temper of his writings render them a peculiarly noble training for a public speaker. Nor should the admirable Quintilian be neglected in this same connection.

It will be desirable also to include the elements of Logic in our course of studies, and with that the *Ethics* of Aristotle, and the Dialogues of Plato; for these are necessary aids to the proper understanding of Cicero.

The Ciceronian Dialogue, in form and in matter, seems often to be modeled directly upon Plato. None of his works however are so attractive to myself personally as the *De Officiis* and the *Tusculans.* The former reviews all the main duties of life; the latter exhibits a wealth of knowledge most valuable—both as to material and expression—to every modern writer. I would add that some knowledge of the principles of Roman Law will be helpful to the full understanding of Latin authors.

A master who should carry his scholars through the curriculum which I have now laid down may have confidence that he has given them a training which will enable them, not only to carry forward their own reading without assistance, but also to act efficiently as teachers in their turn.

✦ *Coluccio Salutati*

LETTER TO CATERINA DI MESSER VIERI DI DONATINO D'AREZZO[1]

I know, Caterina, beloved daughter in Christ, that it arouses suspicion when a man writes to a woman, especially to a young one, and, committed to the worldly life as she is, one with whom he might hope to have contact.[2] The same slanders have been made about the most holy women when they have written to very devout men. However, not only my age —for I am now in my sixty-eighth year—exempts me from such charges,

---

1. The Latin original of this letter is found in *Epistolario di Coluccio Salutati,* 3:337–41. I am deeply indebted to Novati's detailed notes in making my own.
2. On the death of her father, under strong pressure from her mother, Caterina di messer Vieri became a nun of Santa Chiara in Montepulciano at the age of eleven. Her mother's motives are unclear, but Caterina herself seems to have had no religious vocation. Consequently, when an occasion presented itself she fled the convent and presumably left Tuscany. Because she already enjoyed some reputation for intellectual gifts rarely recognized in women of the time, her flight probably received wide attention. After wandering for a time, however, she resolved to return home, to marry, and to have children. She wrote Salutati, obviously hoping for some kind of approval of her intention from the leading Italian intellectual. Instead the old man roundly rebuked her. Undaunted, Caterina married within a short time and began to raise her family. After a few years, wishing to have her offspring recognized as legitimate, she appealed to the pope to have her childhood vow annulled. A favorable decision was rendered by a papal representative in Arezzo in 1403.

SOURCE: B. Kohl and R. Witt, eds., *The Earthly Republic* (Philadelphia: University of Pennsylvania Press, 1978), pp. 115–118. Reprinted with permission of University of Pennsylvania Press.

but more than this a right conscience and a sincere intention. This being so, I do not fear the tongues or depraved thoughts of those imagining evil in everything. Therefore, I write to advise you, so that you might look at yourself; so that I might attempt to recall you to the road of salvation, to reason, and to your God whom you have left at such a distance. If God grants this—and he will if you have not entirely abandoned yourself to perverted ideas—I will be responsible for giving you a holier life, one full of glory and honor.

You may be a bit superior to other women in having some notion of letters; you may have seen Seneca and other, lowly authors and cite them. But do not flatter yourself that you are adorned with eloquence or that you possess secular learning, which in God's eyes is foolishness. Believe me, you are indeed far from both. You can boast of this among simple women and those who are not properly educated in these studies. If you encounter something of moral or poetic significance, do not think that it is automatically a sure basis for truth. For you say:

> O fortune envious of strong men!

This is not the assertion of the Tragic Poet but rather of the crowd, the chorus! Why do you, woman, complain about fortune? Why do you blame it for your crime or your guilt as you do? You are badly instructed in the art of organizing a speech according to the nature and condition of the listener. You dare accuse fortune to me? You are not speaking to simple women who follow what you say with sighs, tears, and fawning acquiescence. Divine Providence, which is fortune, ruling and governing all things, and your precious mother, of whom you are unworthy, dedicated you to God, delivered you to him, and consecrated you in the most holy fashion as the bride of Christ. Had you sincerely followed this rule of life as your vow demands, and, laying aside the trifles probably learned with your natural genius in the convent, had you devoted yourself to love of God with all your heart, all your soul, and all your powers as is fitting and as we are commanded—had you done these things you would not have left the cloister. You would not have wandered over the earth, moved by unfulfilled desires, notorious, ridiculed, and despised like the daughter of Inachus who was turned into a cow, according to the poets. Now, however, warned by heaven, as you say, you have returned home, or rather to the cradle of your exile; for if you do not know it, this world is an exile, a way, not a homeland. Rather, our sublime home is Jerusalem, the vision of peace, the eternal and immeasurable fullness of peace that passes all understanding. I want you to long for this true home, to direct yourself toward it, to prepare yourself for it, so that you do not disgrace your bridegroom. You labor in the vain confusion of the world, burdened with passions, fouled by infinite evil deeds.

Hear, I pray, the voice of your bridegroom! For he calls you and others:

"Come to me all you who labor and are burdened and I will refresh you. Bear my yoke upon you and learn from me because I am mild and humble in heart and you will find rest for your souls. For my yoke is pleasant and my burden light." By returning reconcile yourself with him whom you offended by leaving. See how sweetly he calls you. See how humanely he encourages you. See what he promises: refreshment and rest for your soul! O if you would decide to return to him! O if you could see the difficulties that await you on your present path! If you do not know, worse than incest, more serious than debauchery is the marriage that you so ardently desire. Although you call it marriage, you cover a crime with this name. You are not able to be the legitimate wife of another. When you embrace this man, whoever he shall be, you will know that you embrace not your husband but a fornicator, an adulterer. I beg you not to listen to those who advise you badly, with a view to bodily delights. This approval, this flattery will not lead you to peace of mind or serve your honor but, rather, will bring you to infamy, confuse your mind, and vex your body.

Return to your husband, your beloved, your king! Leaving your depraved path of passion, let the winter and rainstorms of your labors pass, so that you will merit hearing His sweetest voice: "Arise, hasten, my love, my dove, my fair one, and come." You will merit being called "love" when, abandoning the world, you shall resolve to follow Christ. You will deserve the name "dove" when it can be truly said that you have vomited the gall of passion. You will indeed be fair when, devoted to the spirit, you do whatever you do for God's sake. Then you will hear what Christ added many words later: "Arise, my love, my beautiful one, and come, my dove, in the clefts of the rock, in the cave under the cliff; show me your face, let your voice sound in my ears; for your voice is sweet and your face comely." Your husband calls for you to show him your face, that is, your works, in the clefts of the rock and the cave under the cliff, that is, in the cloister and in the monastery built of stones. Your voice sounds in his ears with frequent prayers and devotions. Do not enter into the depravity and incest that you call marriage, but allow yourself to be brought back to the cloister, not to the service of a man but of Christ, not to carnal delights but to the joy and happiness of the spirit. Believe me, Caterina, the more things of carnal nature are possessed and known, the more they burden, the more they afflict. Things of the spirit give more pleasure, the more they are possessed; the more they are known, the more they are loved.

I will make an end here although my mind is alive with many thoughts and the subject demands that a good deal more be said. But I must consider my other obligations and you, unless you are otherwise disposed, should not be afflicted further. Farewell and be happy. And you will fare well if you open your ears to my sincere and salubrious warnings and meditate on them. Florence, May 14 [1399].

♦ *Laura Cereta*

LETTER TO BIBULUS SEMPRONIUS: A DEFENSE OF THE LIBERAL INSTRUCTION OF WOMEN

My ears are wearied by your carping. You brashly and publicly not merely wonder but indeed lament that I am said to possess as fine a mind as nature ever bestowed upon the most learned man. You seem to think that so learned a woman has scarcely before been seen in the world. You are wrong on both counts, Sempronius, and have clearly strayed from the path of truth and disseminate falsehood. I agree that you should be grieved; indeed, you should be ashamed, for you have ceased to be a living man, but have become an animated stone; having rejected the studies which make men wise, you rot in torpid leisure. Not nature but your own soul has betrayed you, deserting virtue for the easy path of sin.

You pretend to admire me as a female prodigy, but there lurks sugared deceit in your adulation. You wait perpetually in ambush to entrap my lovely sex, and overcome by your hatred seek to trample me underfoot and dash me to the earth. It is a crafty ploy, but only a low and vulgar mind would think to halt Medusa with honey. You would better have crept up on a mole than on a wolf. For a mole with its dark vision can see nothing around it, while a wolf's eyes glow in the dark. For the wise person sees by [force of] mind, and anticipating what lies ahead, proceeds by the light of reason. For by foreknowledge the thinker scatters with knowing feet the evils which litter her path.

I would have been silent, believe me, if that savage old enmity of yours had attacked me alone. For the light of Phoebus cannot be befouled even in the mud. But I cannot tolerate your having attacked my entire sex. For this reason my thirsty soul seeks revenge, my sleeping pen is aroused to literary struggle, raging anger stirs mental passions long chained by silence. With just cause I am moved to demonstrate how great a reputation for learning and virtue women have won by their inborn excellence, manifested in every age as knowledge, the [purveyor] of honor. Certain, indeed, and legitimate is our possession of this inheritance, come to us from a long eternity of ages past.

[To begin], we read how Sabba of Ethiopia, her heart imbued with divine power, solved the prophetic mysteries of the Egyptian Salomon. And the earliest writers said that Amalthea, gifted in foretelling the future, sang her prophecies around the banks of Lake Avernus, not far from Baiae. A sibyl worthy of the pagan gods, she sold books of oracles to Priscus

SOURCE: M. King and A. Rabil, *Her Immaculate Hand* (Binghamton, N.Y.: MARTS, 1983), pp. 81–86. Reprinted by permission of the publisher.

Tarquinius. The Babylonian prophetess Eriphila, her divine mind penetrating the distant future, described the fall and burning of Troy, the
fortunes of the Roman Empire, and the coming birth of Christ. Nicostrata
also, the mother of Evander, learned both in prophecy and letters, possessed such great genius that with sixteen symbols she first taught the
Latins the art of writing. The fame of Inachian Isis will also remain eternal
who, an Argive goddess, taught her alphabet to the Egyptians. Zenobia of
Egypt was so nobly learned, not only in Egyptian, but also in Greek and
Latin, that she wrote histories of strange and exotic places. Manto of
Thebes, daughter of Tiresias, although not learned, was skilled in the arts
of divination from the remains of sacrificed animals or the behavior of
fire and other such Chaldaean techniques. [Examining] the fire's flames,
the bird's flight, the entrails and innards of animals, she spoke with spirits
and foretold future events. What was the source of the great wisdom of
the Tritonian Athena by which she taught so many arts to the Athenians,
if not the secret writings, admired by all, of the philosopher Apollo? The
Greek women Philiasia and Lasthenia, splendors of learning, excite me,
who often tripped up, with tricky sophistries, Plato's clever disciples.
Sappho of Lesbos sang to her stone-hearted lover doleful verses, echoes, I
believe, of Orpheus' lyre or Apollo's lute. Later, Leontia's Greek and poetic
tongue dared sharply to attack, with a lively and admired style, the eloquence of Theophrastus. I should not omit Proba, remarkable for her
excellent command of both Greek and Latin and who, imitating Homer
and Virgil, retold the stories from the Old Testament. The majesty of
Rome exalted the Greek Semiamira, [invited] to lecture in the Senate on
laws and kings. Pregnant with virtue, Rome also gave birth to Sempronia,
who imposingly delivered before an assembly a fluent poem and swayed
the minds of her hearers with her convincing oratory. Celebrated with
equal and endless praise for her eloquence was Hortensia, daughter of
Hortensius, an oratrix of such power that, weeping womanly and virtuous
tears, she persuaded the Triumvirs not to retaliate against women. Let me
add Cornificia, sister of the poet Cornificius, to whose love of letters so
many skills were added that she was said to have been nourished by waters
from the Castalian spring; she wrote epigrams always sweet with Heli-
conian flowers. I shall quickly pass by Tulliola, daughter of Cicero, Ter-
entia, and Cornelia, all Roman women who attained the heights of
knowledge. I shall also omit Nicolosa [Sanuto] of Bologna, Isotta Nogarola
and Cassandra Fedele of our own day. All of history is full of these examples. Thus your nasty words are refuted by these arguments, which compel
you to concede that nature imparts equally to all the same freedom to
learn.

Only the question of the rarity of outstanding women remains to be
addressed. The explanation is clear: women have been able by nature to
be exceptional, but have chosen lesser goals. For some women are concerned with parting their hair correctly, adorning themselves with lovely

dresses, or decorating their fingers with pearls and other gems. Others delight in mouthing carefully composed phrases, indulging in dancing, or managing spoiled puppies. Still others wish to gaze at lavish banquet tables, to rest in sleep, or, standing at mirrors, to smear their lovely faces. But those in whom a deeper integrity yearns for virtue, restrain from the start their youthful souls, reflect on higher things, harden the body with sobriety and trials, and curb their tongues, open their ears, compose their thoughts in wakeful hours, their minds in contemplation, to letters bonded to righteousness. For knowledge is not given as a gift, but [is gained] with diligence. The free mind, not shirking effort, always soars zealously toward the good, and the desire to know grows ever more wide and deep. It is because of no special holiness, therefore, that we [women] are rewarded by God the Giver with the gift of exceptional talent. Nature has generously lavished its gifts upon all people, opening to all the doors of choice through which reason sends envoys to the will, from which they learn and convey its desires. The will must choose to exercise the gift of reason.

[But] where we [women] should be forceful we are [too often] devious; where we should be confident we are insecure. [Even worse], we are content with our condition. But you, a foolish and angry dog, have gone to earth as though frightened by wolves. Victory does not come to those who take flight. Nor does he remain safe who makes peace with the enemy; rather, when pressed, he should arm himself all the more with weapons and courage. How nauseating to see strong men pursue a weakling at bay. Hold on! Does my name alone terrify you? As I am not a barbarian in intellect and do not fight like one, what fear drives you? You flee in vain, for traps craftily-laid rout you out of every hiding place. Do you think that by hiding, a deserter [from the field of battle], you can remain undiscovered? A penitent, do you seek the only path of salvation in flight? [If you do] you should be ashamed.

I have been praised too much; showing your contempt for women, you pretend that I alone am admirable because of the good fortune of my intellect. But I, compared to other women who have won splendid renown, am but a little mousling. You disguise your envy in dissimulation, but cloak yourself in apologetic words in vain. The lie buried, the truth, dear to God, always emerges. You stumble half-blind with envy on a wrongful path that leads you from your manhood, from your duty, from God. Who, do you think, will be surprised, Bibulus, if the stricken heart of an angry girl, whom your mindless scorn has painfully wounded, will after this more violently assault your bitter words? Do you suppose, O most contemptible man on earth, that I think myself sprung [like Athena] from the head of Jove? I am a school girl, possessed of the sleeping embers of an ordinary mind. Indeed I am too hurt, and my mind, offended, too swayed by passions, sighs, tormenting itself, conscious of the obligation to defend my sex. For absolutely everything—that which is within us and that which is without—is made weak by association with my sex.

I, therefore, who have always prized virtue, having put my private concerns aside, will polish and weary my pen against chatterboxes swelled with false glory. Trained in the arts, I shall block the paths of ambush. And I shall endeavor, by avenging arms, to sweep away the abusive infamies of noisemakers with which some disreputable and impudent men furiously, violently, and nastily rave against a woman and a republic worthy of reverence. January 13 [1488]

LETTER TO LUCILIA VERNACULA: AGAINST WOMEN WHO DISPARAGE LEARNED WOMEN

I thought their tongues should have been fine-sliced and their hearts hacked to pieces—those men whose perverted minds and inconceivable hostility [fueled by] vulgar envy so flamed that they deny, stupidly ranting, that women are able to attain eloquence in Latin. [But] I might have forgiven those pathetic men, doomed to rascality, whose patent insanity I lash with unleashed tongue. But I cannot bear the babbling and chattering women, glowing with drunkenness and wine, whose impudent words harm not only our sex but even more themselves. Empty-headed, they put their heads together and draw lots from a stockpot to elect each other [number one]; but any women who excel they seek out and destroy with the venom of their envy. A wanton and bold plea indeed for ill-fortune and unkindness! Breathing viciousness, while she strives to besmirch her better, she befouls herself; for she who does not yearn to be sinless desires[in effect] license to sin. Thus these women, lazy with sloth and insouciance, abandon themselves to an unnatural vigilance; like scarecrows hung in gardens to ward off birds, they tackle all those who come into range with a poisonous tongue. Why should it behoove me to find this barking, snorting pack of provocateurs worthy of my forebearance, when important and distinguished gentlewomen always esteem and honor me? I shall not allow the base sallies of arrogance to pass, absolved by silence, lest my silence be taken for approval or lest women leading this shameful life attract to their licentiousness crowds of fellow-sinners. Nor should anyone fault me for impatience, since even dogs are permitted to claw at pesty flies, and an infected cow must always be isolated from the healthy flock, for the best is often injured by the worst. Who would believe that a [sturdy] tree could be destroyed by tiny ants? Let them fall silent, then, these insolent little women, to whom every norm of decency is foreign, inflamed with hatred, they would noisily chew up others, [except that] mute, they are themselves chewed up within. Their inactivity of mind maddens these raving women, or rather Megaeras, who cannot bear even to hear the name of a learned woman. These are the mushy faces who, in their vehemence, now spit tedious nothings from their tight little mouths, now to the horror of those looking on spew from their lips thunderous trifles. One becomes disgusted with human failings and grows weary of these women who [trapped in their own mental predicament], despair of attaining possession of human arts, when they could easily do so with the application of skill and virtue. For letters are not bestowed upon us, or assigned to us by chance. Virtue only is acquired by ourselves alone; nor can those women ascend to serious knowledge who, soiled by the filth of pleasures, languidly rot in sloth. For those women the path to true knowledge is plain who see that there is certain honor in exertion, labor, and wakefulness. Farewell. November 1 [1487]

IX

The Church and the Papacy

❦

INTRODUCTION

*T*he Roman Catholic Church remained throughout the Renaissance
the religion of Italy. The Church united all members of the community through ritual, devotion, and a common faith, and those very rituals
provided the basic markers of an individual's and the community's life.
Baptism, marriage, and burial were functions of the Church; saints' days,
religious festivals, and the bells tolling the ecclesiastical hours punc-
tuated the year; and sincere piety served well to comfort men and women
in a time of great change and upheaval.

The vast majority of Italians, then, remained sincere Christians
throughout the Renaissance. The importance of popular preachers, religious leaders like Savonarola, and the examples of simple holy men
attested to the continuation of religious devotion. Certainly, members of
the intellectual elite were attracted by the world of pagan antiquity as a
consequence of their humanist studies. These, however, remained a tiny
minority who usually continued to exhibit all the characteristics of Christians in public, even if they held private doubts.

In Italy, the Church remained powerful and effective and as ubiqui-
tous as ever during the Renaissance. There were challenges to the authority of the pope and doubts raised about specific elements of tradition.
However, like many Renaissance churches, these constituted only a clas-
sically inspired facade superimposed over a medieval foundation.

THE PAPACY

*I*t must be stressed that to Renaissance Italians the papacy was both a
spiritual office directing the Church or defining doctrine for the faithful
and just another—if more unstable—state of the peninsula, striving for

balance or superiority with the other major states of Italy, such as Venice, Florence, Milan, and Naples. Because of this dualism, the papacy often used spiritual weapons to fight political or diplomatic wars. Interdicts or excommunications were applied for political purposes, and money collected from the faithful for the religious functions of the Church was spent instead on armies or luxurious living, suitable to an Italian principality. Also, qualities more suited to administration or warfare were sought in popes, cardinals, and high Church officials rather than the elements of personal sanctity or religious fervor appropriate to their ecclesiastical callings. The papal court, or Curia, then, often became the realm of ambitious men seeking favor or power and willing to use the revenues and authority of the Church for purely secular goals.

This divergence of purpose was often exacerbated by attempts on the part of individual popes to use their authority to establish hereditary dynasties for their families, either in the states of the Church or at the expense of weaker neighbors. These attempts led to more warfare and to a further weakening of the moral force of the heirs of St Peter.

Moreover, between 1309 and 1377, the papacy was not even resident in Rome but in Avignon, a territory in the southern part of France. Unable to operate because of the continuous warfare among the Roman noble families, the pope fled to the territory of Avignon, where a succession of French popes was elected, and it appeared that the papacy was an appendage of the kings of France. Subsequently, between 1378 and 1417, this unhealthy situation was rendered far worse by the Great Schism, which saw the election of two and, after 1409, three popes, each claiming to be the rightful pontiff.

The deposition of all three popes and the election of Martin V as the sole pontiff restored some order and authority to the office. Returning to Rome, the pope found the city half abandoned and in ruins. He and his successors set about rebuilding of the city, and in so doing, the culture of humanism and the Italian Renaissance entered Rome and the Curia. Popes such as Nicholas V (1446–1555), who collected a great library and attracted leading artists to the holy city, Pius II (1458–1464), the humanist Aeneas Silvius Piccolomini, Sixtus IV (1471–1484), a founder of the Capitoline Museum and a great builder and patron of humanists, Julius II (1503–1513), a warrior pope and brilliant administrator who commissioned Michelangelo to paint the Sistine Chapel and Raphael to decorate the Stanze della Segnatura, and Leo X (1513–1521), son of the Magnificent Lorenzo de' Medici, who surrounded himself with men of letters and great artists—but who was also pope during the outbreak of the Lutheran revolt—all served to beautify Rome and turn the city into the great repository of Renaissance art and culture it became by the early sixteenth century.

The sack of Rome in 1527 by soldiers of the Emperor Charles V destroyed much of the city and a great many works of art. The pope, Leo

X's cousin, Clement VII, became virtually a prisoner of the Habsburgs and the great moment of the Renaissance papacy declined together with the rest of Italy as the peninsula became the battlefield between France and the Habsburgs for the hegemony of Europe.

✦ *Aeneas Silvius Piccolomini (Pius II)*

*A*eneas Silvius Piccolomini (1405–1464) was born into a noble Sienese family and received an excellent humanist education. His skill at Latin style resulted in numerous appointments as secretary to high Church officials and to the Emperor Frederick III. He became a cleric in 1446 and entered the Curia, eventually entering the sacred college as a cardinal.

After the death of Calixtus II in 1458, Aeneas Silvius was elected pope, taking the name Pius II. As pope he attempted to impose order and papal authority on the states of the Church and especially to mount a crusade against the Turks, who had captured the Byzantine capital of Constantinople in 1453. Unable to secure much military support for his crusade, Pius died at Ancona in 1464 while waiting for a Christian fleet to assemble.

In addition to his ecclesiastical achievements, Pius was an important patron of the arts and a significant literary figure in his own right. He had built an ideal Renaissance city (Pienza) on the site of the village of his birth, Corsignano. As a young man he had written erotic Latin literature—which he later repudiated—and as a diplomat and Church official he composed works of history and geography, education, biography, and an important autobiography, his Commentaries, *which trace the pattern of his life and career and supply an insightful commentary on his times.*

THE ELECTION OF POPE PIUS II

The conclave was held in the apostolic palace at St. Peter's, where two halls and two chapels were set apart for it. In the larger chapel were constructed cells in which the cardinals might eat and sleep; the smaller, called the chapel of San Niccolò, was reserved for discussion and the election of the pope. The halls were places where all might walk about freely.

On the day of their entrance nothing was done about the election. On

SOURCE: Aeneas Silvius Piccolomini (Pope Pius II), *Commentaries*, in F. Gragg and L. Gabel, *Memoirs of a Renaissance Pope* (New York: Putnam, 1959). Reprinted by permission.

the next day certain capitulations were announced, which they agreed should be observed by the new pope, and each swore that he would abide by them, should the lot fall on him. On the third day after mass, when they came to the scrutiny, it was found that Filippo, Cardinal of Bologna, and Aeneas [Sylvius], Cardinal of Siena, had an equal number of votes, five apiece. No one else had more than three. On that ballot, whether from strategy or dislike, no one voted for Guillaume, Cardinal of Rouen.

The cardinals were accustomed, after the result of the scrutiny was announced, to sit and talk together in case any wished to change his mind and transfer the vote he had given one to another (a method called "by accession"), for in this way they more easily reach an agreement. This procedure was omitted after the first scrutiny owing to the opposition of those who had received no votes and therefore could not now be candidates for accession. They adjourned for luncheon and then there were many private conferences. The richer and more influential members of the college summoned the rest and sought to gain the papacy for themselves or their friends. They begged, promised, threatened, and some, shamelessly casting aside all decency, pleaded their own causes and claimed the papacy as their right. Among these were Guillaume, Cardinal of Rouen, Pietro, Cardinal of San Marco, and Giovanni, Cardinal of Pavia; nor did the Cardinal of Lerida neglect his own interests. Each had a great deal to say for himself. Their rivalry was extraordinary, their energy unbounded. They took no rest by day or sleep by night.

Rouen, however, did not fear these men so much as he did Aeneas and the Cardinal of Bologna, toward whom he saw the majority of the votes inclining. But he was especially afraid of Aeneas, whose silence he had no doubt would prove far more effective than the barkings of the rest. Therefore he would summon now some, now others, and upbraid them as follows:

> What is Aeneas to you? Why do you think him worthy of the papacy? Will you give us a lame, poverty-stricken pope? How shall a destitute pope restore a destitute church, or an ailing pope an ailing church? He has but recently come from Germany. We do not know him. Perhaps he will even transfer the Curia thither. And look at his writings! Shall we set a poet in Peter's place? Shall we govern the church by the laws of the heathen? Or do you think Filippo of Bologna is to be preferred?—a stiff-necked fellow, who has not the wit to rule himself, and will not listen to those who show him the right course. I am the senior cardinal. You know I am not without wisdom. I am learned in pontifical law and can boast of royal blood. I am rich in friends and resources with which I can succor the impoverished church. I hold also not a few ecclesiastical benefices, which I shall distribute among you and the others, when I resign them.

He would then add many entreaties and if they had no effect, he would resort to threats. If anyone brought up his past simony as an indication that in his hands the papacy would be for sale, he did not deny that his past life had been tainted with that stain but swore that in the future his hands should be clean. He was supported by Alain, Cardinal of Avignon, who lent him every assistance in his power, not so much because he was a Frenchman siding with a Frenchman as because, at the elevation of Guillaume, he expected to obtain his house in Rome, the church of Rouen, and the vice-chancellorship. Not a few were won over by Rouen's splendid promises and were caught like flies by their gluttony. And the tunic of Christ without Christ was being sold.

Many cardinals met in the privies as being a secluded and retired place. Here they agreed as to how they might elect Guillaume pope and they bound themselves by written pledges and by oath. Guillaume trusted them and was presently promising benefices and preferment and dividing provinces among them. A fit place for such a pope to be elected! For where could one more appropriately enter into a foul covenant than in privies? Guillaume could certainly count on the two Greeks, the Cardinals of Genoa, San Sisto, Avignon, Colonna, and Pavia. The Vice-Chancellor, the Cardinals of Bologna, Orsini, and Sant' Anastasia were doubtful and seemed likely to accede to him if pushed a little. Indeed they had almost given him definite grounds for hope. Since it now appeared that eleven were agreed, they did not doubt that they would at once get the twelfth. For when it has come to this point, some one is always at hand to say, "I too make you pope," to win the favor that utterance always brings. They thought therefore that the thing was as good as done and were only waiting for daylight to go to the scrutiny.

Some time after midnight the Cardinal of Bologna went hurriedly to Aeneas's cell and waking him said, "Look here, Aeneas! Don't you know that we already have a pope? Some of the cardinals have met in the privies and decided to elect Guillaume. They are only waiting for daylight. I advise you to get up and go and offer him your vote before he is elected, for fear that if he is elected with you against him, he will make trouble for you. I intend to take care not to fall into the old trap. I know what it means to have the pope your enemy. I have had experience with Calixtus, who never gave me a friendly look, because I had not voted for him. It seems to me expedient to curry favor beforehand with the man who is going to be pope. I offer you the advice I am taking myself."

Aeneas answered, "Filippo, away with you and your advice! No one shall persuade me to vote for a man I think utterly unworthy to be the successor of St. Peter. Far from me be such a sin! I will be clean of that crime and my conscience shall not prick me. You say it is hard not to have the pope well-disposed to you. I have no fears on that score. I know he will not murder me because I have not voted for him. 'But,' you say, 'he will not love you, will not make you presents, will not help you. You will feel the pinch of poverty.' Poverty is not hard for one accustomed to it. I have led a life of indigence heretofore; what matter if I die indigent? He will not take from me the Muses, who are all the sweeter in humble fortunes.

"But I am not the man to believe that God will allow the Church, His

Bride, to perish in the hands of the Cardinal of Rouen. For what is more alien to the profession of Christ than that His Vicar should be a slave to simony and lewdness? The Divine Mercy will not endure that this palace, which has been the dwelling of so many Holy Fathers, shall become a den of thieves or a brothel of whores. The apostleship is bestowed by God, not by men. Those who have conspired to commit the papacy to Rouen are men; and men's schemes are vain—who does not know it? Well has their conspiracy been made in the privies! Their plots too will have to retire and, like the Arian heresy, their most foul contrivings will end in a most foul place. Tomorrow will show that the Bishop of Rome is chosen by God not by men. As for you, if you are a Christian, you will not choose as Christ's Vicar him whom you know to be a limb of the devil." With these words he frightened Filippo from going over to Rouen.

Next Aeneas went at daybreak to Rodrigo, the Vice-Chancellor, and asked whether he had sold himself to Rouen. "What would you have me do?" he answered, "The thing is settled. Many of the cardinals have met in the privies and decided to elect him. It is not for my advantage to remain with a small minority out of favor with a new pope. I am joining the majority and I have looked out for my own interests. I shall not lose the chancellorship; I have a note from Rouen assuring me of that. If I do not vote for him, the others will elect him anyway and I shall be stripped of my office." Aeneas said to him, "You young fool! Will you then put an enemy of your nation in the Apostle's chair? And will you put faith in the note of a man who is faithless? You will have the note; Avignon will have the chancellorship. For what has been promised you has been promised him also and solemnly affirmed. Will faith be kept with him or with you? Will a Frenchman be more friendly to a Frenchman or to a Catalan? Will he be more concerned for a foreigner or for his own countryman? Take care, you inexperienced boy! Take care, you fool! And if you have no thought for the Church of Rome, if you have no regard for the Christian religion and despise God, for Whom you are preparing such a vicar, at least take thought for yourself, for you will find yourself among the hindmost, if a Frenchman is pope."

The Vice-Chancellor listened patiently to these words of his friend and completely abandoned his purpose.

After this Aeneas, meeting the Cardinal of Pavia, said to him, "I hear the you too are with those who have decided to elect Rouen. is this true?" He replied, "You have heard correctly. I have agreed to give him my vote so that I may not be left alone. For his victory is already certain; so many have declared for him." Aeneas said, "I thought you a different man from what I find you. Only see how much you have degenerated from your ancestors! Your father's brother (or was he your mother's?), Branda, Cardinal of Piacenza, when the papacy was beyond the mountains in Germany (for John XXIII, when he appointed the Council of Constance, had carried the Roman Curia across the Alps) never rested till he brought the Holy

See back to Italy. It was owing to his diplomacy, devotion, and genius that on the withdrawal of the contestants for the papacy, Martin V, a Roman of the house of Colonna, was elected pope. Branda brought the Apostolic Curia back from Germany to Italy; you, his nephew, are going to transfer it from Italy to France. But Rouen will prefer his own nation to Italy and a Frenchman will be off to France with the supreme office.

"You say, 'He is under oath. He will not go outside this province without the decree of the senate and if he wishes to go, we will not consent.' What cardinal will dare oppose him when he is once seated on the apostolic throne? You will be the first, when you have secured some rich benefice, to say, 'Go where you will, Holy Father.' And what is our Italy without the Bishop of Rome? We still have the Apostleship though we have lost the Imperium, and in this one light we see light. Shall we be deprived of this with your sympathy, persuasion, help? A French pope will either go to France—and then our dear country is bereft of its splendor; or he will stay among us—and Italy, the queen of nations, will serve a foreign master, while we shall be the slaves of the French. The kingdom of Sicily will come into the hands of the French. The French will possess all the cities and strongholds of the Church. You might have taken warning from Calixtus, during whose papacy there was nothing the Catalans did not get. After trying the Catalans are you so eager to try the French? You will soon be sorry if you do! You will see the college filled with Frenchmen and the papacy will never again be wrested from them. Are you so dull that you do not realize that this will lay a yoke upon your nation forever?

"And what shall I say of this man's life? Are you not ashamed to entrust Christ's office to a slippery fellow who would sell his own soul? A fine bridegroom you are planning for the bride of Christ! You are trusting a lamb to a wolf. Where is your conscience? your zeal for justice? your common sense? Have you so far fallen below your true self? I suppose we have not often heard you say that it would be the Church's ruin if it fell into Rouen's hands? and that you would rather die than vote for this very man? What is the reason for this change? Has he suddenly been transformed from a demon to an angel of light? Or have you been changed from an angel of light to the devil, that you love his lust and filth and greed? What has become of your love for your country and your continual protestations that you preferred Italy above all other nations? I used to think that if everyone else fell away from devotion to her, you never would. You have failed me; nay, more, you have failed yourself and Italy, your country, unless you come to your sense."

The Cardinal of Pavia was stunned by these words and, overcome alike with grief and shame, he burst into tears. Then stifling his sobs he said, "I am ashamed, Aeneas. But what am I to do? I have given my promise. If I do not vote for Rouen, I shall be charged with treachery." Aeneas answered, "So far as I can see, it has come to the point where you will be guilty of treachery whichever way you turn. You now have to choose whether you prefer to betray Italy, your country, and the Church or the Bishop of Rouen." Convinced by these arguments Pavia decided it was less shameful to fail Rouen.

When Pietro, Cardinal of San Marco, learned of the conspiracy of the French and had lost hope of getting the papacy himself, actuated alike by patriotism and hatred of Rouen, he began to go to the Italian cardinals urging and warning them not to abandon their country; and he did not rest until he had gathered all the Italians except Colonna in the cell of the Cardinal of Genoa, revealed the conspiracy that had been made in the privies, and showed them that the Church would be ruined and Italy a slave forever, if Rouen should obtain the papacy. He implored them individually to show themselves men, to consult for the good of Mother Church and unhappy Italy, to put aside their enmities for one another and choose an Italian rather than a foreigner for pope. If they listened to him, they would prefer Aeneas to all others. There were present seven cardinals: Genoa, Orsini, Bologna, San Marco, Pavia, Siena, and Sant' Anastasia. All approved Pavia's words except Aeneas, who thought himself unworthy of so exalted an office.

The next day they went as usual to mass and then began the scrutiny. A golden chalice was placed on the altar and three cardinals, the Bishop of Ruthen, the Presbyter of Rouen, and the Deacon of Colonna, were set to watch it and see that there should be no cheating. The other cardinals took their seats and then, rising in order of rank and age, each approached the altar and deposited in the chalice a ballot on which was written the name of his choice for pope. When Aeneas came up to put in his ballot, Rouen, pale and trembling, said, "Look, Aeneas! I commend myself to you"—certainly a rash thing to say when it was not allowable to change what he had written. But ambition overcame prudence. Aeneas said, "Do you commend yourself to a worm like me?" and without another word he dropped his ballot in the cup and went back to his place.

When all had voted, a table was placed in the middle of the room and the three cardinals mentioned above turned out upon it the cupful of votes. Then they read aloud the ballots one after another and noted down the names written on them. And there was not a single cardinal who did not likewise make notes of those named, that there might be no possibility of trickery. This proved to be to Aeneas's advantage, for when the votes were counted and the teller, Rouen, announced that Aeneas had eight, though the rest said nothing about another man's loss, Aeneas did not allow himself to be defrauded. "Look more carefully at the ballots," he said to the teller, "for I have nine votes." The others agreed with him. Rouen said nothing, as if he had merely made a mistake.

This was the form of the ballot: The voter wrote with his own hand, "I, Peter (or John or whatever his name was) choose for pope Aeneas, Cardinal of Siena, and Jaime, Cardinal of Lisbon"; for it is permitted to vote for one or two or more, on the understanding that the one first named is the one preferred, but if he does not have enough votes to be elected, the next is to be counted in his place, that an agreement may more easily be reached. But a thing advantageous in itself some men pervert to base ends, as Latino Orsini did on that day. He named seven in the hope that those he named might be influenced by that good turn either to accede to him in that scrutiny or to vote for him in another; although he who has the reputation of a cheat does not gain much by tricks.

When the result of the scrutiny was made known, it was found, as we have said before, that nine cardinals (Genoa, Orsini, Lerida, Bologna, San Marco, Santi Quattro Coronati, Zamora, Pavia, and Portugal) had voted for Aeneas; the Cardinal of Rouen had only six votes, and the rest were far behind. Rouen was petrified when he saw himself so far outstripped by Aeneas and all the rest were amazed, for never within the memory of man had anyone polled as many as nine votes by scrutiny. Since no one had received enough votes for election, they decided to resume their seats and try the method that is called "by accession," to see if perhaps it might be possible to elect a pope that day. And here again Rouen indulged in empty hopes. All sat pale and silent in their places as if entranced. For some time no one spoke, no one opened his lips, no one moved any part of his body except the eyes, which kept glancing all about. It was a strange silence and a strange sight, men sitting there like their own statues; no sound to be heard, no movement to be seen. They remained thus for some moments, those inferior in rank waiting for their superiors to begin the accession.

Then Rodrigo, the Vice-Chancellor, rose and said, "I accede to the Cardinal of Siena," an utterance which was like a dagger in Rouen's heart, so pale did he turn. A silence followed and each man looking at his neighbor, began to indicate his sentiments by gestures. By this time it looked as if Aeneas would be pope and some, fearing this result, left the conclave, pretending physical needs, but really with the purpose of escaping the fate of that day. Those who thus withdrew were the Cardinals of Ruthen and San Sisto. However, as no one followed them, they soon returned. Then Jacopo, Cardinal of Sant' Anastasia, said, "I accede to the Cardinal of Siena." At this all appeared even more stunned, like people in a house shaken by unprecedented earthquakes, and lost the power of speech.

Aeneas now lacked but one vote, for twelve would elect a pope. Realizing this, Cardinal Prospero Colonna thought that he must get for himself the glory of announcing the pope. He rose and was about to pronounce his vote with the customary dignity, when he was seized by the Cardinals of Nicaea and Rouen and sharply rebuked for wishing to accede to Aeneas. When he persisted in his intention, they tried to get him out of the room by force, resorting even to such means to snatch the papacy from Aeneas. But Prospero, who, though he had voted for the Cardinal of Rouen on his ballot, was nevertheless bound to Aeneas by ties of old friendship, paid no attention to their abuse and empty threats. Turning to the other cardinals, he said, "I too accede to the Cardinal of Siena and I make him pope." When they heard this, the courage of the opposition failed and all their machinations were shattered.

All the cardinals immediately fell at Aeneas's feet and saluted him as Pope. Then they resumed their seats and ratified his election without a dissenting vote. At this point Bessarion, Cardinal of Nicaea, speaking for himself and for the others who had voted for the Cardinal of Rouen, said, "Your Holiness, we approve your election, which we do not doubt is of God. We thought before and still think that you are worthy of this office. The reason we did not vote for you was your infirmity. We thought your gout the one thing against you; for the Church needs an active man who has the physical strength to take long journeys and meet the dangers which we fear threaten us from the Turks. You on the contrary need rest. It was this consideration that won us to the side of the Cardinal of Rouen. If you were physically strong, there is no one we should have preferred. But, since God is satisfied, we must needs be satisfied too. God Himself, who has chosen you, will make good the defect in your feet and will not punish our ignorance. We revere you as Pope, we elect you again, so far as is in our power, and we will serve you faithfully."

Aeneas answered, "Your Eminence of Nicaea, your opinion of us, as we understand it, is much higher than our own, when you attribute to us no defect except that in our feet. We are not ignorant that our imperfection is more general and we realize that our failings, which might justly have caused us to be rejected as pope, are almost innumerable. As to any virtues which might raise us to this post, we know of none; and we should declare ourselves utterly unworthy and should refuse the honor offered us, if we did not fear the judgment of Him Who has called us. For what is done by two thirds of the sacred college, that is surely of the Holy Ghost, which may not be resisted. Therefore we obey the divine summons and we praise you, Your Eminence of Nicaea, and those who voted with you. If, following the dictates of your conscience, you thought we ought not to be elected as being inadequate, you will still be welcomed by us, who attribute our calling not to this man or that but to the whole college and to God Himself, from Whom cometh every good and perfect gift."

With these words he took off the garments he was wearing and put on the white tunic of Christ. When asked by what name he wished to be called, he answered, "Pius," and he was at once addressed as Pius II. Then after swearing to observe the capitulations that had been announced in the college two days before, he took his place by the altar and was again reverenced by the cardinals, who kissed his feet, hands, and cheek. After that the election of a pope was proclaimed to the people from a high window and it was announced that he who had been Cardinal of Siena was now Pope Pius II [August 19, 1458].

The attendants of the cardinals in the conclave plundered Aeneas's cell and meanly carried off all the plate (though it was very modest), his clothes, and his books; and the infamous rabble not only pillaged his house in the city but actually demolished it, taking away even the blocks of marble. Other cardinals, too, suffered losses, for while the people were waiting in suspense, various rumors got about and as now this cardinal, now that was reported elected, Vicar.

✦ *Lorenzo Valla*

*L*orenzo Valla (1407–1457) was born in Rome and received a humanist education. As a young man he moved to Pavia to teach rhetoric, but in 1435 he traveled to Naples, where he entered the court of Alfonso I. It was there, in the midst of a strongly antipapal environment, that Valla wrote his On the False Donation of Constantine (1440), which proved, using the techniques of textual criticism, that the first Christian emperor could not have been the author of the document that supposedly trans-ferred the Western Empire to the papacy.

Also, Valla's deep understanding of Latin style produced books that were to influence the study of Latin and ancient literature for centuries. His On the Elegance of the Latin Language *became a standard textbook throughout Europe, and his biblical studies,* Annotations on the New Testament, *began the great period of Renaissance biblical textual schol-arship, which led ultimately to Erasmus' 1516* New Testament, *a work heavily influenced by Valla.*

These works led to charges of heresy against him, but nevertheless he was called to Rome by the humanist pope Nicholas V in 1448 to assist in the establishment of the papal library and the collection of Greek editions. Valla died in Rome in 1457.

THE PRINCIPAL ARGUMENTS FROM THE FALSELY-BELIEVED AND FORGED DONATION OF CONSTANTINE

I, 1—There are those who are offended because in the numerous books I have made public, in almost every field of learning, I disagree with some great authors who have been acclaimed for a long time. They accuse me of being sacrilegiously bold. Well, I wonder, what will they do, how

SOURCE: Lorenzo Valla, *The Profession of the Religious and The Principal Argu-ments from the Falsely-Believed and Forged Donation of Constantine,* trans. and ed. by O. Z. Pugliese (Toronto: CRRS, 1985), pp. 63–72. Reprinted by permission of Dovehouse Editions, Inc., Ottawa.

enraged will they be against me, and how eagerly and hastily would they drag me off to torture, if they only could, now that I am writing not just against the dead but against the living too, not just against this or that individual but against a multitude of men, not merely private citizens but even public officials? And which officials? Why, even the Supreme Pontiff who is armed not only with a temporal sword, like kings and rulers, but with a spiritual one too, so that you can not defend yourself from being visited with excommunication, anathema, or curse, not even by seeking refuge beneath the shield of princes, so to speak. . . .

2— . . . Many have run the risk of dying in order to defend their country on earth; shall I be afraid to risk death in order to reach the celestial fatherland? Indeed it is those who please God, not men, who reach Heaven. So, away with trepidation, anxiety begone, fears disappear! One must defend the cause of truth, the cause of justice, the cause of God, with steadfast courage, great confidence, and undying hope. For he who has the ability to speak well should not be considered a true orator unless he also has the courage to speak. Let us, then, venture to accuse whomever it is that carries out actions deserving of accusation. And let him who sins against everyone be reproached by the voice of one individual on behalf of all. . . .

4—My purpose is not to speak ill of any person and write Philippics against him; far be this misdeed from me. Rather, I seek to eradicate error from men's minds, to remove them from vice and evil, either through warnings or reproach. I hardly dare say it, but my aim is to instruct those who, with an iron blade, will prune the Papal See, that is, Christ's vineyard, which is rife with over-abundant undergrowth, and force it to bear plentiful grapes rather than meager wild vines. As I do this, is there perhaps someone who will want to shut my mouth or his own ears and threaten me with the death penalty, so that I shall be silent? What should I call one who would do this, even if he is the Pope? A "good shepherd" (John 10:11), perhaps? Or a "deaf adder that stoppeth her ear: Which will not hearken to the voice of charmers" (Psalm 58:4–5 [57:5–6]) and wants to strike the enchanter's limbs with her poisonous sting?

II, 5—I understand that the ears of men have been waiting for a long time to hear with what crime I am about to charge the Roman Pontiffs. Surely it is a most serious crime, of either lackadaisical ignorance or enormous greed, which is a form of idolatry, or the vain will to power, which is always accompanied by cruelty. In fact, for several centuries now either the Popes have not understood that the donation of Constantine is a forgery and a fabrication, or they have invented it themselves, or else, as followers treading in the footsteps of their predecessors' deceit, they have defended it as being true, even while knowing it was false. Thus they have disgraced the dignity of the Pontificate and the memory of the early Popes, dishonored the Christian religion and caused general confusion with their massacres, destruction, and shameful actions. They say that theirs are the city of Rome, the Kingdom of Sicily and Naples, the whole of Italy, Gaul, Spain, the lands of the Germans and Britons, and, finally, all of the West. And all these things, purportedly, are contained in the document describing the donation. Are these lands then all yours, oh Supreme Pontiff? Do you intend to recover all of them? Do you plan to strip all the kings and princes in the West of their cities or compel them to pay annual taxes to you? On the contrary, I deem it to be more just if the rulers are allowed to deprive you of all the dominion you hold, since, as I shall demonstrate, that donation, from which the Popes claim their rights derive, was unknown either to Pope Sylvester or to the Emperor Constantine.

6—However, before I come to the confutation of the text of the donation, the only defense they have, and one that is foolish as well as false, I must go back to an earlier period for the sake of order. And, first of all, I maintain that neither Constantine nor Sylvester was able to carry out the transaction: the former had no motive to make the donation, had no right to make it, and no power to hand over his possessions to someone else; while the latter had no motive to accept the gift and had no right to do so. Secondly, even if this were not absolutely true and evident, as it is, the Pope did not receive nor did the Emperor transmit possession of what is supposed to have been donated. It always remained in the power and dominion of the Caesars. Thirdly, Constantine gave nothing to Sylvester, but rather to the previous Pope, even before he received Baptism, and those gifts were modest ones on which the Pope could barely subsist. Fourthly, it is incorrect to say that the deed of the donation is to be found in the *Decretum* or that it was taken from the Life of Sylvester since it is not included either in this or in any other historical work. Moreover, it contains certain elements that are contradictory, impossible, foolish, strange, and ridiculous. . . . I shall add, in supernumerary argument, that even if at one time Sylvester had held title, yet, because either he himself or some successive pope was dispossessed, it cannot, after such a long interval of time, be reclaimed either according to divine law or to human law. Finally, the Pope's possessions could not have been won through prescription, no matter how long he held them.

III, 7— . . . Thus, I am going to pretend I am delivering a speech to an assembly of kings and leaders (as in reality I am doing, since this oration of mine will probably come into their hands), and I shall address them as though they were present before me: "I ask you, kings and rulers . . . , is there anyone among you who, had he been in Constantine's position, would have deemed it proper to donate to someone else, as a mark of generosity, the city of Rome, his place of birth, the capital of the world, the queen of all cities, the most powerful, most noble, and richest of all peoples, the conqueror of nations, sacred in her very appearance, and then retire to a humble town and later to Byzantium? Would he, furthermore, have given away, together with Rome, all of Italy, which is not one

province but the conqueror of other provinces? Would he have relinquished the three Gauls, the two Spains, the Germanic peoples, the Britons, all of the West? Would he have deprived himself of one of the two
eyes of the Empire? I can not be led to believe that anyone in his right
mind would do such a thing.

8—What can befall you that is more desired, delightful, and pleasant
than to augment your empires and kingdoms, than to extend your rule as
far and wide as possible? It seems to me that you devote every care,
thought, and effort, day and night, to this purpose. It is from this that you
derive your chief hope for glory, it is for this that you sacrifice pleasure,
face a thousand risks, and bear uncomplainingly the loss of your dear ones
or of part of your own body. Indeed, I have never heard or read that any
of you has been deterred from striving to increase his dominion, even if
one of his eyes or hands or legs or any other part were to be cut away.
And this passion, this desire for immense rule agitates and torments most
intensely those who are most powerful . . . ."

IV, 11— . . . As for you, Constantine, if you wish to show you are a
Christian, that you are devout and care not only for the Church of Rome,
but also for the Church of God, precisely for this reason you must act like
a ruler now and fight on behalf of those who cannot and should not engage
in combat, and protect with your authority those who are exposed to
snares and insults. . . . Have you become a Christian, Constantine? Yet it
is absolutely shameful for you to have less power now as a Christian
Emperor than when you were an infidel. Sovereignty is indeed a special
gift from God; because of it even pagan rulers are considered to be chosen
by God.

12—"But he had been cured of leprosy and therefore it is likely that
he wanted to show his gratitude and repay in greater measure what he
had received," an objector might say. Really? If Naaman the Syrian, when
he was cured by Elisha, simply offered a few gifts, not half of his possessions, can it be that Constantine offered half of his Empire? I regret having
to respond to an impudent fable as though it were indisputable history.
In fact this legend must have been designed on the basis of the Biblical
story of Naaman and Elisha. . . . And you would have it that Constantine
donated his kingdom to God . . . when, by so doing, he would have offended
his children, humiliated his friends, neglected his relatives, harmed his
country, brought sorrow upon everyone, and forgotten himself?

V, 13—And even if he had been capable of doing this and if he had
almost been transformed into a different man, surely there would have
been some to warn him, above all his children, relatives, and friends.
Would not everyone agree that these people would have gone to the
Emperor immediately? You can imagine how, after hearing of Constantine's plan, they would have rushed in alarm to kneel before the ruler and,
sighing and crying, would have pronounced this speech: "So this is how
you, father, who were once so affectionate to your children, now strip,

disinherit, and disown us? We do not so much deplore the fact that you should wish to strip yourself of the best and largest part of your Empire as we are surprised by it. But we complain because by conferring it on others you cause us harm and dishonor. Why is it that you defraud your children of the succession they expected to the Empire which you yourself have ruled as did your father? . . ."

V, 14— . . . And if Constantine had not wanted to listen to them, would there not have been those who would have objected with words and deeds? And would the Roman Senate and People not have judged it appropriate to take action in such an important matter? . . .

VII, 27— . . . Do not those who state that the donation took place insult Constantine, judging, as they do, that he wished to despoil his own family and break apart the Roman Empire? Are they not injurious to the Senate and People of Rome, to Italy, and the whole West who would have allowed a change in the Empire that went against human and divine law? Would they not be slandering both Sylvester, by alleging he accepted a donation that is unworthy of a holy man, and also the Holy Pontificate which, they think, was allowed to take possession of earthly kingdoms and to govern the Roman Empire? Yet all this tends to make it evident that, in the midst of so many obstacles, Constantine would never have donated the greater part of the Roman Empire to Sylvester, as those persons claim. . . .

VIII, 30— . . . Oh, what an astonishing event! The Roman Empire that was created through so much hardship and bloodshed, was both acquired and lost by Christian priests so calmly and quietly, without any bloodshed, war, or conflict! And what is even more amazing, it is altogether unknown by whom, when, or how this was carried out, or how long it lasted. You would think that Sylvester had reigned in sylvan places amid trees, rather than in Rome among men, and that he was driven out by the rains and cold of winter, rather than by men. Whoever has read more than a little, knows how many kings, consuls, dictators, tribunes of the people, censors, and aediles were created in Rome. . . . Yet, even in the city of Rome itself, no one has the slightest knowledge how, when, or by whose efforts the Roman, or Sylvestrian, Empire began or ended. I ask you, what witnesses, what sources can you produce for these events? "None," you reply. Are you not ashamed to say, like beasts rather than men, that it is plausible that Sylvester did possess the Empire?

IX, 31—Since you can not prove your theory, I shall demonstrate, on the contrary, that Constantine ruled over the Empire until the last day of his life, as did all the other Caesars who followed him. Thus I shall silence you, who tell me it is a very difficult and laborious task to demonstrate this. Let all the Latin and Greek histories be consulted, let all the other authors who mention that period be cited; you will find discrepancies in none regarding this matter. Of the thousand testimonies available, one will suffice: Eutropius saw Constantine and wrote that, when he died, his three sons were made rulers over the whole world. . . . This historian would not have kept silent about the donation of the Western Empire had it taken place. . . .

32—At this point I wish to summon all of you recent Roman Pontiffs although you are dead and you, Eugenius, who are living. . . . Why do you boast loudly of the donation of Constantine and often present yourselves threateningly before certain kings and rulers as claimants of the Empire which has been usurped? Why do you force the Emperor and other rulers—the King of Naples and Sicily, for instance—to acknowledge submission at the time of their coronation? None of the early Popes of Rome did this. . . . They always recognized that Rome and Italy along with the provinces belonged to the Emperors. Furthermore, golden coins exist, not to mention other monuments and temples in Rome, that bear not Greek but Latin inscriptions of Constantine, when he was already a Christian, and of almost all the successive emperors. I own many of these myself. . . . If ever you had ruled over Rome, an infinite number of coins would be found commemorating the Supreme Pontiffs, whereas none are to be found either of gold or silver, and no one remembers having seen any. Yet, at that time, whoever ruled over the Roman Empire would have had to mint his own currency, probably with the image of the Savior or of Saint Peter. . . .

X, 34—But, so as not to be tedious, it is now time to deal the fatal blow to my adversaries' cause, which has already been beaten and torn to bits, and to slit its throat with a single slash. Almost every history which deserves the name narrates that, right from childhood, Constantine was a Christian (as was his father), and thus a long time before Sylvester became Pope. So writes Eusebius, author of the *Ecclesiastical History*, which Rufinus, not an unlearned man himself, translated into Latin and to which he added two books on his own times. Both of these writers were virtually contemporaries of Constantine. There is, besides, the testimony of the Roman Pontiff too, who not only participated in these events but actually directed them. He was not merely a witness but also a protagonist who recounts not someone else's but his own actions. I mean Pope Miltiades, Sylvester's immediate predecessor. This is what he writes:

> The Church reached such a stage that not only the peoples of Rome but the rulers too, who held sway over the whole world, flocked to the religion of Christ and to the sacraments of the faith. Among these Constantine, a most religious man, who was the first to embrace the true faith publicly, not only allowed those who, anywhere in the world, lived within his Empire to become Christians, but he arranged for the building of churches to which he granted lands. And finally the aforementioned ruler contributed immense temples and began the building of the church which was the first seat of the blessed Peter.

He even left his imperial palace and donated it for the benefit of Saint Peter and his successors.

Behold! Miltiades states that Constantine gave only the Lateran palace and some land. . . . Where are those who would prevent us from questioning the validity of the donation of Constantine, when that donation occurred before Sylvester's time and involved the transfer of private possessions only? Although the matter is clear and evident it is still necessary to discuss the document itself which those fools commonly cite.

XI, 35—First of all, one must not only accuse of dishonesty the person who tried to pass himself off as Gratian, and added interpolations in Gratian's work, but one must also accuse of ignorance all those who maintain that the document of the privilege is contained in Gratian—something that learned men have never believed. It is not to be found in the oldest copies of the *Decretum*. And if Gratian had mentioned this event anywhere he would not have mentioned it at the point where they put it, interrupting the flow of the discourse. . . . Some say that the name of the person who added this chapter on the donation was Palea ("Straw"), either because this was actually his name, or else because the things he added, compared to Gratian's, can be likened to straw, or chaff, as opposed to grain. In any case, it is most shameful to believe that the compiler of the *Decretum* was either unaware of such insertions or that he attached great significance to them and considered them true.

Well, that is enough; we have won. First of all because Gratian does not say what those liars claim; rather, as a great number of passages indicate, he denies and refutes it. Next, because they cite a single author, one who is unknown and without authority or consequence, and who is, moreover, so stupid as to attribute to Gratian things that could not be reconciled with his other affirmations. Is this, then, the source you are adducing? Are you relying exclusively on this testimony? Do you quote the paltry screed of such an individual in order to verify a matter of such great importance, even though six hundred categories of proof to the contrary can be enumerated? I was expecting you to show golden seals, marble inscriptions, and a thousand written authorities. . . .

44—As for the text of the document, it is still more absurd and unnatural that Constantinople should be referred to as one of the patriarchal sees, when it was not yet either patriarchal or a see or a Christian city; it was not yet called Constantinople; it had not yet been founded or even planned. In fact, the privilege was supposedly granted three days after Constantine was converted to Christianity, when Byzantium still existed and not Constantinople. . . . Who fails to see, therefore, that he who drew up the privilege lived a long time after the age of Constantine? . . .

49—Oh holy Jesus, will you not answer with storm and with thunder this man who twists phrases in his uncouth speeches? Will you not hurl avenging thunderbolts against such blasphemy? Will you endure such disgrace in your servants? Can you listen to and watch all this and yet close your eyes to it for so long? But "thou . . . art . . . longsuffering, and plenteous in mercy" (Psalm 86 [85]: 15). . . .

50— . . . Now, let us speak to this deceiver about his crude language. Through his babbling, he reveals his most impudent forgery himself. . . . Where he deals with the gifts, he says "a diadem . . . made of pure gold and precious jewels." The ignoramus did not know that the diadem was made of cloth, probably silk. . . . He thinks it had to be made of gold, since nowadays kings usually wear a circle of gold set with jewels. But Constantine was not a king and he would never have dared to call himself a king or to adorn himself in regal fashion. He was Emperor of the Romans, not a king. . . .

XVIII, 58— . . . Is the barbarousness of his style not sufficient proof that such a piece of nonsense was forged not in Constantine's day but much later? . . .

XX, 65— . . . Therefore this text is not by Constantine but by some foolish petty cleric who does not know what to say or how to say it. Fat and full, he belches out ideas and words enveloped in fumes of intoxicating wine. But these sentences do not touch others; rather, they turn against the originator himself. . . .

XXII, 69—The text ends with the words "Dated at Rome, the third day before the Kalends of April, in the fourth consulate of Constantine Augustus . . . ." The word "dated" [Latin *datum* "given"] is used only in letters and nowhere else, except by the ignorant. For letters are given to the addressees or to the courier who brings them to the addressees. But since the so-called privilege of Constantine was not to be delivered to anyone, one should not have said it was "dated." Thus it is plain to see that the person who wrote this was lying and was unable to feign what, according to verisimilitude, Constantine would have said and done. . . .

98—Besides, can we believe that God would have allowed Sylvester to accept opportunities for sin? I will not allow this insult to be brought against a most holy man, or this offense to be made against an excellent Pontiff, by saying that he accepted empires, kingdoms, and provinces, things which are renounced even by those who want to become mere priests. Sylvester possessed little, as did the other holy Popes. . . . But the Supreme Pontiffs of our time, who abound in wealth and pleasure, strive, it appears, to be wicked and foolish just as much as the early Popes strove to be wise and holy; they try to outdo with every kind of infamy the brilliant glory of their predecessors. Can anyone who deserves to be called a Christian tolerate this calmly?

99—Even so, in this first discourse of mine, I do not wish to exhort rulers and peoples to stop the Pope as he hastens on his unbridled course and force him to remain within his own territory. I simply want them to warn him. Once he has been apprised of the truth, perhaps he will leave others' lands and make his way home of his own will; abandoning the furious waves and violent storms, he will return into port. If he refuses to do so, then I shall set about writing another discourse and a much harsher one. Oh, how I hope (and there is nothing that I desire more, especially if it comes about through my advice) that one day the Pope will be the vicar of Christ only and not that of Caesar. No longer will one hear those terrible words: "supporters of the Church" or "opponents of the Church." . . . It is the Pope, not the Church, who is warring against Christians. The Church, instead, fights only "against spiritual wickedness in high places" (Paul, Ephesians 6: 12). Then the Pope will be deemed (and will truly be) a holy father, the father of all, the father of the Church. He will not stir up wars among Christians; on the contrary, if they are initiated by others, he will terminate them with his apostolic censure and his papal majesty.

✦ *Roderigo Borgia (Alexander VI)*

R oderigo Borgia (c. 1431–1503) was the nephew of Pope Calixtus III, and as a result, he rose rapidly in the Church, becoming a cardinal in 1456 and vice-chancellor of the Church in 1457. His style of life was known for its luxury, nepotism, and sensuality. His mistress, Vanozza Catanei, was virtually queen and gave him four children, all of whom he advanced in the Church or through dynastic marriages. His eldest son, Juan, was trained to be the military commander of the Church but was murdered before he had the opportunity. This role was then given to Cesare Borgia, who resigned his cardinal's hat in 1498 to become his father's general. Alexander's daughter, Lucrezia Borgia, was used as a dynastic pawn. The pope married her first to a Sforza prince but later annulled the marriage so that she might marry the Duke of Bisceglie, who was subsequently murdered in 1500. Ultimately, Lucrezia became the Duchess of Ferrara (1501).*

The rapacity and cruelty of Cesare (the Duke Valentino of Machiavelli's Prince*), together with the lascivious character of the papal court, made Alexander the model of the wicked pope. Balanced against this, however, was his skill at administration, which helped strengthen the authority of Rome, his support of Catholic orthodoxy, and his decision in 1493 that divided the New World (the Line of Demarcation) between Spain and Portugal. He was not a patron of art, although Pinturicchio worked for him at the Vatican. He failed to recognize the danger posed by Charles VIII's invasion of Italy in 1494, a campaign he initially encouraged, and after his death, the powerful papal state his son Cesare had built collapsed.*

Much is known of the daily life in Rome under Alexander from his master of ceremonies, Johannes Burchardus, whose diary recorded the character of the court in the Vatican palace under the Borgias.

SELECTIONS FROM *POPE ALEXANDER VI AND HIS COURT*

The Accession of Alexander VI

In the year of the Lord 1492, on Saturday, the 11th of August, at noon, Roderigo Borgia, vice-chancellor and the nephew of Calixtus III, was created Pope and named Alexander VI.

On the 27th of August Alexander was crowned in St. Peter's. Then he went in the customary manner to the Church of St. John Lateran while the greatest honor was done to him throughout the city by the Roman people with triumphal arches and with more than there was ever done to other Popes.

And in the first consistory he held, he created the Archbishop of Mount Royal, his nephew from a sister, a cardinal.

After his coronation it was brought to his knowledge that from the day of the last illness of Innocent until his coronation more than two hundred and twenty men had been assassinated in various places and at various times. It was also brought to his knowledge who the murderers were and the reasons and success they had had. Of all this that had gone on in Rome he received full knowledge. . . .

The Year of the Jubilee

February, 1500. In former days the major-domo of the papal palace, Petrus de Aranda, Bishop of Calahorra, had been arrested as suspected of heresy, and brought to the castle San Angelo, where he was imprisoned. The governor of Rome, Cardinal Isuagli, and the Bishop of Cesena, Pietro Menzi, as deputy-auditors of the papal camera, had been charged with the investigation and procedure. To justify himself Aranda brought up, as I was later informed, a hundred witnesses who, however, all without exception gave evidence against him. It was ascertained that he asserted and maintained among other things that the Mosaic law had only one principle, while the Christian had three, Father, Son and Holy Ghost, that Christ had not suffered as a real God, and that he had in praying said "Gloria Patri" leaving away "Filio" and "Spiritu sancto," that he had eaten before celebrating the mass and had eaten meat on Good Friday and other forbidden days, that he had stated that indulgences were void and inefficacious and had been invented by the fathers for their own advantage,

SOURCE: Johannes Burchardus, *Pope Alexander VI and His Court*, ed. by F. L. Glase (New York: Brown, 1921), pp. 53–66, 119–141, 179–187.

and that there was no hell or purgatory but only paradise, and many other things.

On the 25th of February, 1500, a papal letter was posted at the doors of St. Peter's and the Lateran Church which stated that the roads and inns for the pilgrims to Rome ought to be safeguarded during the year of the jubilee and that the vassals of the Church would be held responsible for damage sustained and that reprisals would be made against them.

On Monday, the 26th of February, 1500, by order of the Pope it was urged upon all the cardinals that they should send their suites on this day at four o'clock in the afternoon out to the Porta Santa Maria del Popolo to meet Cesare Borgia as he approached the city and furthermore upon all ambassadors, conservators and officials of Rome as well as upon the abbreviators, clerics, etc., of the Roman Curia that they should go out personally to meet him. On the previous Friday, the 21st, Cardinal Orsini had gone to meet the Duke Cesare as far as Castello; and there followed him on Saturday, the 22nd, the Cardinal Farnese. On this morning the Cardinal Lopez, with my colleague in his suite, went out to meet him about three to four miles beyond the Ponte Molle. All the ambassadors also rode out beyond the bridge as far as the meadows to await the duke there. When it had sounded the hour of four Cardinal Pallavicini went on horseback from the palace to the residence of Cardinal Orsini who awaited him there outside on his mule. They rode together to the church of Santa Maria del Popolo to receive the duke there. He entered through the gate between seven and eight o'clock and was greeted by all the ambassadors, retainers and officials of the said cardinal. When they heard that the duke was outside the gate, they mounted their mules and awaited him at the said place before the gate, where they saluted him with bared heads while he thanked them also in the same manner. Then he rode between them to the Vatican.

In the train of the duke there came first in good order a hundred sumpters provided with new black covers and then about fifty others without any order. I could not arrange the escort in proper order as there were about a thousand ducal soldiers on foot, Swiss and Gascons, who marched in their own order in five sections and under five banners with the ducal arms, and took no heed of our order. There were also papal soldiers marching on foot to meet the duke and lansquenets with the flag of St. Andrew. The Swiss wanted the lansquenets to roll up their banner but they would not consent and a great quarrel started among them. But the conflict was settled by the duke with little effort. The Swiss and Gascons marched first with their banners, behind them came the lansquenets with theirs, and then about fifty noblemen of the duke. He himself had a hundred men around him of whom every one bore a new halberd and wore a coat of black velvet and shoes of black cloth.

He had also many trumpeters wearing his arms as well as two heralds of his own and one of the King of France, who wanted to march under all conditions behind the soldiers. The duke, however, when appealed to, decided that he ought to precede them, which he did only with great reluctance. By order of the duke the trumpeters and the other musicians did not play.

Behind them rode the Duke of Bisceglia at the right and the Prince of Squillace, the son of the Pope, at the left. Then came the duke between the aforementioned cardinals, behind them the Archbishop of Ragusa, de Sachis, at the right and the Bishop of Tréguier, Robert Guibé, Ambassador of the King of France, at the left, the Bishop of Zamora at the right and the ambassador of the King of Spain at the left, and so on, the others according to their rank. Two ambassadors of the King of Navarre got into a quarrel with the ambassadors of the Kings of Naples and of England, who retorted in a very hot-headed manner. The two ambassadors of Navarre had to give in and departed. There were also present the ambassadors of Florence, Venice, Savoy, and others. Behind them followed a large crowd in such confusion that the prelates were not able to take their places and the majority of them therefore departed.

The Pope stood in the loggia of the chamber above the portal of the palace, and with him were the Cardinals Juan Borgia, San Giorgio, Lopez, Cesarini and Farnese. When the duke came to the chamber of paraments, the Pope entered the Camera Papagalli, bringing with him five cushions of gold brocade, one of which he had laid on the elevated seat where he himself sat, another one under his feet and the three others upon the floor before his footstool. The door to the Camera Papagalli was opened and there entered the noblemen of the duke and after them, between the cardinals, the duke himself, who knelt down before the Pope and made a short speech in Spanish wherein he thanked the Pope that he had deigned to do him during his absence such a—I do not know what. The Pope replied to him in the same idiom, which I did not understand. Then the duke kissed both feet of the Pope as well as his right hand and was allowed also to kiss his mouth. After the duke the noblemen also approached at their pleasure to kiss the foot.

The castle of San Angelo was splendidly decorated and I never saw such pomp and triumph as from this castle.

On Thursday, the 27th of February, 1500, there was a festive procession in the Agone with the customary gorgeous display, twelve triumphal chariots and the victory of Julius Cæsar, who sat on the last chariot. All these chariots were taken to the palace and back again with the exception of the last one with Julius Cæsar, which remained there. The duke rode from the palace to the Agone where the festivities of the Romans were held in the customary way.

On Thursday, the 5th of March, Cesare Borgia began with his calls on the cardinals. He had no bishop or prelate with him but was only accompanied by one of his retainers. When calling on Cardinal Piccolomini he went with him from the chamber down to the foot of the stairs walking on his left side, as he did not want to take the right one in any case, although the cardinal offered it to him with eager insistency. As I hear, he did the same with the other cardinals but I do not know how far the cardinals went to meet him when he arrived and therefore I could not put it down.

On the fourth Sunday of Lent the Pope, with the intention of making Cesare Borgia Captain-General and Gonfaloniere of the Roman Church, decided to bestow upon him the Golden Rose. On Sunday Laetare, therefore, the fourth of Lent and the 29th of March, 1500, the Pope had come into the small audience room in the morning at the usual hour with the cardinals, who had assembled in the Camera Papagalli, and decided with their consent to bestow the aforesaid Rose on Cesare Borgia of France, Duke of Valentinois, his dearest son, and to nominate him Captain-General and Gonfaloniere of the Holy Roman Church. From there the Pope went with the cardinals into the chamber, blessed the Rose in the customary way, and went in procession on his portable chair with the Rose in his left hand to the church of St. Peter. Immediately before him walked a papal shield-bearer in a garment of frilled brocade which came down to his knees. He walked before the chamberlains and carried over his arm a new garment, that is a coat and barret, the insignia of the dignity of a Gonfaloniere. The barret was of crimson, two spans high, and lined with ermine. In the middle there was a small piece of gold brocade with four large buttons, that is to say pearls of the size of ordinary nuts. At the four corners and inside there was a stripe of ermine fur about five fingers broad and above there was attached a dove composed of pearls, four fingers wide and adorned with many pearls. While the Pope was still sitting in his portable chair, Cardinal Cibó appeared, who was officiating in the church, and dressed himself as usual in the sandals and the holy garments. After arriving at the main altar the Pope took down the miter and prayed in his folding-chair; then he made the confession of faith together with the celebrant.

In the meantime the duke stepped up to the papal throne and placed himself at the right side. After the obeisance of the cardinals the duke in his short tunic stepped before the Pope and kneeled down before him at the last step above. He was joined by the Cardinal delle Rovere as an assistant of the Pope, who now with the miter in his hand rose and said: "Our assistance in the name of the Lord who made heaven and earth. The Lord be with you and with your spirit.—Let us Pray: 'God, who Thou has promised to be an aid to Thy servants assembled in Thy name, grant to this Thy servant Cesare, our Gonfaloniere, the mercy that has been granted to Abraham at the burnt offering, to Moses with his legions, to Elia in the desert, to Samuel in the temple. Give, O Lord, the unity, that Thou gavest to the patriarchs, that Thou hast preached to the peoples, that Thou hast handed down to the Apostles, that Thou hast ordered to the victors. Bless, O Lord, we ask Thee, this our Gonfaloniere, who has been given to us certainly for the welfare of our people. Let him grow rich in years, let him be blooming and healthy in vigor of body until a ripe old age and let him arrive finally at a blessed end. May the trust remain with us that he will receive the same compassion in favor of his people that Aaron received in the sanctuary, Elisha by the stream, Ezekiel on his bed and the old Zachary in the temple. May the force and power of dominion be granted to him as Joshua possessed it in the camp and Gideon in battle, and as Peter received it with the keys and Paul used it in doctrine. Thus the care of the shepherds may be a blessing to the sheep as Isaac prospered in his fruits and Jacob in his herds. This grant us mercifully the One who lives and reigns with the Father and the Holy Ghost in eternity.'"

After these words the Pope put the miter on his head and sat down again. I took the coat from the hands of that shield-bearer, and handed it over to the assisting Cardinal delle Rovere who took off the coat of the duke. I received it and had it sent quickly through my servant to my house before anything further was said about it. For it was worth about four hundred ducats. The Pope took the coat from the hands of Cardinal delle Rovere and hung it around the duke, so that the clasp was lying on the right shoulder of the duke, with the following words: "May the Lord clothe you with this garment of blessing and wrap you in the garb of joy, in the name of the Father, the Son and the Holy Ghost. Amen."

Then the same cardinal took from my hands the aforementioned crimson barret and handed it over to the Pope, who put it on the head of the duke with these words: "Receive the sign of the dignity of the Gonfaloniere that is being put on your head by us in the name of the Father, the Son and the Holy Ghost, and remember that from now on you are pledged to defend the faith and the Holy Church. That success may be true to you, may be granted to you mercifully by Him that is blessed in all eternity."

A cleric of the Camera brought the Rose from the altar, and the Pope took it from the hands of the Cardinal delle Rovere and handed it over to the duke who knelt before him with the following words: "Receive from our hands as we are, although undeservedly God's representative on earth, as a symbol of the joy of Jerusalem triumphant as well as of the church militant. To all who believe in Christ it means the most precious flower as it is the joy and crown of all saints. Receive it, my most-beloved son, you who are of secular nobility, powerful and rich in virtue, in order that you may win furthermore the nobility of every virtue in Christ, the Lord, similar to the Rose that has been planted on the bank of many waters. This favor may grant you in its overflowing kindness the One who is the triune in eternity. Amen."

The duke took the Rose in his right hand and kissed first the hand then the foot of the Pope. Both rose, the duke covered himself with the barret, and with the Rose in his right hand, walked, for the entire time, before the Pope. The holy handkerchief was shown as usual and the cardinals besides the duke accompanied the Pope as far as the courtyard, where the cardinals usually ride away. From there the Pope went up to his palace after he had dismissed the duke and the cardinals, who then all mounted their horses. The older cardinals rode first and last between Piccolomini and Cesarini, the duke still wearing the barret of the Gonfaloniere on his head. The Rose, however, he did not bear in his hand all the way, but he had it carried most of the way by one of his servants, of whom he had only six or eight around himself while the others followed.

In riding back the usual order was observed, the banners were carried by those two armed men on horseback, both Spaniards of the lower class. They rode behind all the ambassadors, preceded by eight trumpeters and before these four drummers. After the trumpeters there came three heralds, after these the armed men, then all the cardinals and among the last of these the cardinal with all his servants. There followed the prelates and the men of the duke in a crowd as this could not be helped. In this order we rode to the residence of Cardinal Sclafenata, where the duke intended to have dinner. Before the entrance the duke thanked with bared head every one of the cardinals, who had stopped here and there. Finally he turned around once again before the door to the cardinals who then departed.

On Tuesday, the 12th of May, 1500, a certain Baron René d'Agrimont, ambassador of the King of France, while on his way to Rome with his sumpters and about thirteen horses and servants was robbed completely by twenty-two highwaymen and brigands in the mountains of Viterbo. One of his noblemen together with a servant was wounded severely.

The ambassador entered Rome on the 13th May without pomp and escorted only by his men. The Pope, indignant at the incident, sent out the Bargello to capture the malefactors, and wrote numerous *breves* to Fabrizio Colonna, from whose territory the brigands had come, and to others in order that they should send the highwaymen to the city. Fifteen of them were apprehended and brought to Rome.

On Wednesday, 27th May, 1500, the day before Assumption, eighteen men were hanged at noon while the cardinals passed over the bridge of San Angelo, nine on each side of the bridge. The hanged men fell down with the gallows on the bridge but were immediately set up again so that the cardinals when they returned from the palace could see all of them hanged.

The first of the eighteen was a doctor of medicine, physician and surgeon to the hospital of St. John Lateran, who had left the hospital every day early in the morning in a short tunic and with a crossbow and had shot every one who happened to cross his path and pocketed his money. It was also said that the confessor of the hospital communicated with the physician when a patient confided to him during confession that he possessed any money, whereupon he gave an efficacious remedy to the patient and they divided the money between them. Thirteen belonged to the twenty-two who had robbed Baron d'Agrimont. The four others had committed various misdeeds.

After vespers, on the 28th of May, 1500, the eighteen hanged men were taken down, laid on carts, and brought to the chapel by the society of Misericordia, where they were buried in the usual way.

On Wednesday, the 24th of June, 1500, the feast of St. John, the place of St. Peter was railed in by beams on all sides from the corner of the house of the palace-guard to the fountain of Innocence and from there to the corner of the house St. Martinelli, as well as both approaches of the Via Sancta towards the church of St. Peter. After dinner a bullfight was held in this enclosure with five or six bulls. Cesare on horseback and several others administered numerous thrusts to them until they were dead.

On Wednesday, 15th July, 1500, the Duke Alphonse of Aragon, the husband of Lucretia Borgia, was suddenly attacked on the steps of St. Peter before the outer entrance about ten o'clock at night and severely wounded in the head, the right arm, and the leg. The assailants fled down the stairs of St. Peter, where about forty men on horseback were waiting for them and they rode out with these through the Porta Pertusa.

On Tuesday, 18th August, 1500, Alphonso of Aragon, who had been brought after his recent injuries to the new tower above the papal cellar in the main garden of the Vatican, and had been carefully guarded, was strangled in his bed at four o'clock in the afternoon, as he did not die of his wounds. In the evening at ten o'clock the body was carried to the church of St. Peter and buried in the chapel of Maria delle Febbri. The archbishop of Cosenza, Francesco Borgia, the treasurer of the Pope, accompanied the body with their suites.

The physicians of the deceased and a hunchback who had nursed him almost all the time were arrested and brought to the castle of San Angelo where an investigation was started against them. They were set free later on as they were found not guilty, a fact that was very well known to those who had made out the warrants.

The same day and almost at the same hour Lucas de Dulcibus, the chamberlain of Cardinal delle Rovere and master of the Register of Papal Decrees, was wounded to death on the back of his mule before the house of the Roman citizen Domenico de Massimi, and his membrum virile was cut off by a man of Reiti whose wife he had kept as a concubine. He was brought into the house of the said Domenico where he died after three or four hours. In the evening he was carried to the church of Maria Transpontina and the next morning, Wednesday, the 19th, the body was transferred to the church of Santa Maria del Popolo with the suite of the Cardinal delle Rovere and many others in the funeral procession. May he rest in peace!

On Sunday, 23d August, 1500, there arrived in Rome, Lord Lucas de Villeneuve, Baron de Trans, chamberlain of the King of France and his ambassador. To the inn of Domenico Attavanti, where the ambassador stayed, near the hospital of St. Lazarus, a masked rider came in great haste, accompanied by a man on foot. He dismounted, embraced the ambassador with the mask over his face and had a conversation with him. After a short while the masked person returned to the city. It has been said that it was Cesare Borgia.

The ambassador mounted his horse and rode to the city. The suite of the Pope and of all the cardinals present in Rome went to meet him as well as the ambassadors of the Kings of Spain and Naples, who said to him: Be welcome! I asked them if they wanted to say anything more. They answered: No. The ambassador who heard this, added: Who does not want to say anything else does not expect an answer. He rode then between the Archbishop of Cosenza, the governor of the city, and the Archbishop of Ragusa through the Via Papae to the inn of the Holy Apostles were he took up his quarters.

On Monday, 31st of August, 1500, Lucretia, once of Aragon, the daughter of the Pope, betook herself from the city to Nepi accompanied by six hundred on horseback in order to find some consolation and rest after the grief and consternation in which she had been thrown by the recent death of her husband, Alphonse of Aragon.

On 20th December, 1500, a bull was posted on the doors of St. Peter, concerning the prolongation of the jubilee year until the coming feast of Epiphany in favor of those abroad. The Pope granted to Italy the unlimited indulgence until the next feast of Pentecost and nominated for this purpose as commissaries the Minorities of the strict observance through an Apostolic letter.

After the beginning of the last year of the jubilee the penitentiaries of St. Peter saw from cases that came before them in confession that the rights of indulgence granted to them were not broad enough. In the course of a conversation I had with one of them I asked him to let me hear some of the cases that were submitted daily to his colleagues. He told me that there were varied and curious cases reported to them but that he could not retain all of them in his memory. He told me, however, a few he remembered.

Some one had concluded matrimony with a virgin and after he had slept with her and had had intercourse with her for a certain time, he had deserted her in order to contract a marriage with a second and a third one. The same he did with a fourth one and had thus four wives living at the same time. The same case he told me of a woman who married four men one after the other without any one of them having died.

A monk of the order of the Benedictines who had been ordained as a priest contracted a marriage with a woman and consummated it through cohabitation. They lived together for about thirty years and had six children. After the death of the woman he contracted another marriage and lived and slept with his second wife for about seven years. Then he came to the jubilee and acknowledged his error himself. Another one, who had married and had consummated the cohabitation, let himself be ordained as a priest and contracted another marriage although he had been ordained.

One had had intercourse with a woman and then married her daughter. He came to the jubilee and acknowledged his error.

A priest slept with his niece who became pregnant through him and bore him a son. The priest father christened him after his birth, then killed him immediately and buried him in the stable. Nevertheless he had celebrated mass for eighteen years after this without dispensation or rehabilitation for his deed.

Another one had taken monastic vows and entered the order of the Franciscans of the strict observance. Still within the first four months of the year of probation he left the convent, threw off the cowl and contracted a marriage with a married woman whom he later deserted after intercourse. Now he entered another order which he left within the probationary year in order to contract a marriage with another married woman. When he heard after cohabitation with her that she was the wife of some one else he left her and married another free woman with whom he also cohabited. He ran away from this one too and married a fourth one with whom he also cohabited. Finally he deserted the fourth one also and entered the order of Santa Maria of the Teutons, of which he confessed to be a member. When the fourth one heard of this she went to the convent in the belief that he was her husband and demanded his surrender. He fled before the imminent danger and came to Rome with the request to render him appropriate aid. It was said that the case was known in Strasburg.

The two principals of a merchant firm in Provins, Pierre and Jean, had both beautiful wives. Pierre, acting on information from his servants, told his wife, that he would go on a certain day to Bruges so that she could make an appointment with Jean. On that day Pierre pretended to set forth on a journey but went instead to the house of a friend and arranged with his servants that they should let him know as soon as Jean had shut up himself with his wife. This they faithfully did. Pierre then went to his house and knocked violently at the door. The frightened wife locked the naked Jean into a chest in her room. Pierre was admitted, went to his wife's chamber and sent immediately for Jean's wife, who appeared soon afterwards. He asked her about her husband and she answered she did not know where he was. He often left the house early in the morning and returned in the late evening. Often he would stay away for one or two days. Pierre said: "Your husband is locked up in this chest here and he has often slept with my wife, although you are much more beautiful than she is. I give you the choice, either you surrender yourself to me on the top of this chest or you will see your husband cruelly murdered." The woman asked her husband in the chest what she should do. He answered from the chest that one could more easily compromise with decency than with death. So Pierre took Jean's wife on the top of the chest, then he let him out and they were the best friends. The incident had been kept secret for years.

A similar case happened in Lübeck. Philip had a very beautiful sister, and Anton whom she loved very much slept with her. She climbed through the window of her chamber over the roof and went to the room of her lover. When Philip found out that his sister had gone to Anton he sent for the sister of Anton who came to his room without any hesitation. Philip said to her: "Your brother Anton has often slept with my sister and now they are lying together again. I decided to lie with you or your brother will die an evil death." She consented in order to free her brother. After he had lain with her, he sent her back to her house through the window over the roof the same way by which his sister usually returned. When Anton heard of it, he came to an understanding with Philip that the matter should be kept secret. Nevertheless it came finally to our knowledge.

When Angelo went through a church at noon, he cast a glance into the chapel of St. Florence situated in a corner. There he saw how Grada was lying under Paolo and how they amused themselves together. For this Angelo later on reproached Paolo in public. Paolo denied the incident stubbornly, and as Angelo did not cease his pointed remarks, he sued him for libel before the magistrate. Proceedings were started against Angelo and his insults were proven while he could not justify his accusation. Judgment was rendered therefore against Angelo that he had to recant his abuse and libellous speeches publicly in the church from the pulpit and to restore the good reputation of Paolo. When therefore, on a Sunday, the principal of the church came down from the pulpit after the sermon, Angelo stepped up and told before all the people of his trial before the magistrate and of the decision rendered and recanted the abuse and libellous speeches by admitting his error in appropriate words. Then, however, he added at the end: "But as a matter of fact, my dear co-citizens, when I saw that woman lying on the floor and Paolo above her and her nakedness exposed and what they were doing together just as one is acting usually in performing the fleshly act, then I was firmly convinced that they had performed this act." So this last error proved to be still worse for Paolo then the one before. . . .

The Death and Funeral of Alexander

On Saturday, the 12th of August, 1503, the Pope fell ill in the morning. After the hour of vespers, between six and seven o'clock a fever appeared and remained permanently.

On the 15th of August thirteen ounces of blood were drawn from him and the tertian ague supervened.

On Thursday, the 17th of August, at nine o'clock in the forenoon he took medicine.

On Friday, the 18th, between nine and ten o'clock he confessed to the Bishop Gamboa of Carignola, who then read mass to him. After his communion he gave the Eucharist to the Pope who was sitting in bed. Then he ended the mass at which were present five cardinals, Serra, Juan and Francesco Borgia, Casanova and Loris. The Pope told them that he felt very bad. At the hour of vespers after Gamboa had given him extreme unction, he died.

There were present, in addition, only the datary and the papal grooms. Cesare, who was lying sick in bed, sent Michelotto with many men, who locked all doors at the entrance to the residence of the Pope. One of them drew a dagger and threatened Cardinal Casanova, if he did not give him the keys and the money of the Pope, he would stab him and throw him out of the window, whereupon the frightened cardinal surrendered the keys to him. One after the other they entered the room behind the chamber of the Pope and took all the silver they could find as well as two chests with 100,000 ducats each. At eight o'clock they opened the doors again and the death of the Pope became known. In the meantime his servants had appropriated whatever was left in the wardrobes and they left nothing but the papal armchairs, a few cushions, and the rugs on the walls. Cesare did not appear during the whole illness of the Pope and not even at his death. Nor did the Pope mention him or Lucretia with one word.

After seven o'clock my colleague arrived at the Vatican, and was recognized and admitted. He found the Pope dead and had him washed by the servant of the sacristy, Balthasar, and a papal servant. Then they put on him all his everyday garments and a white coat without a train which he had never worn while alive. Over this they put a surplice. And thus they laid him on a bier in the ante-chamber of the hall, where he had died, with a crimson silk and a beautiful carpet over him.

After eight o'clock my colleague sent for me and I came. The cardinals in the city had not yet received any announcement, but during the time that I went to the Vatican, it was communicated to them. But none of them made any move nor did they meet anywhere else. I suggested to Carafa that he ought to prepare for imminent dangers and after nine o'clock he notified all the cardinals, through his secretary, that they should deign to appear the next morning in Santa Maria Minerva. There, in the middle of the sacristy, four benches were placed for the cardinals in a quadrangle. When I came to the Pope I dressed him in red robes all of brocade, with a short fanon, a beautiful chasuble, and with stockings. And as there was no cross on the shoes, I put on instead his daily slippers of crimson velvet with the golden cross which I bound with two strings to the back of the heels. His ring was missing and I could not recover it. Thereupon we carried him through the two rooms, the hall of the Pontiffs, and the audience room, to the Camera Papagalli, where we prepared a beautiful table of one rod in length with a crimson cover and a beautiful rug over it. We obtained four cushions of brocade and one of crimson velvet. The one of old crimson velvet we did not use, but of the others we laid one under the shoulders of the Pope, two besides and one beneath the head and over this an old carpet. And so he lay throughout the night with two torches, quite alone, although the protonotaries had been invited to read the burial service.

I returned to the city during the night, after twelve o'clock, accompanied by eight palace-guards. In the name of the Vice-chancellor I ordered the runner Carlo, together with his companions, under penalty of the loss of his office, to inform the whole clergy of Rome, both regular and secular, that they should be at the Vatican on the morrow at nine o'clock in the morning to escort the body from the main chapel to St. Peter's. Two hundred torches were prepared for the escort of the Pope.

On the following Monday, the 19th of August, 1503, I had the coffin brought to the Camera Papagalli and laid the body in it. The subdeacon, in his cloak, stood ready to carry the cross, but we could not find the papal cross. The shield-bearers and a few servants of the chamber were called together to bear forty-three torches as well as four penitentiaries, namely the Bishop of Milopotamo, Claudius, Cataleni, Andreas Frisner, and Arnold de Bedietto of the order of the Minorites. During the night they sung the requiem, sitting on the window-bench and laying their hands on the bier of the Pope, which was then carried by the poor who stood around in order to see the Pope. I then put a double mattress into the coffin and over it a beautiful new bishop's cloak of brocade of pale mauve with two new veils on which were embroidered the arms of Pope Alexander. I then laid the Pope on this and covered him with an old rug and placing an old pillow beneath his shoulders and two cushions of brocade beneath his head. Two new crimson hats with golden strings I took home with me. The body thus wrapped up was borne by our servants, but they became apprehensive that they would not be able to carry it out of the palace which they were quite well, and they left it to the chaplain of the palace, the Bishop of Sessa, to guard him.

We brought the Pope to the main chapel, where the regular clergy of Rome, the clergy of St. Peter's, and the canons with the cross assembled. Then he was carried from the main chapel to the center of St. Peter's. First came the cross, then the monks of St. Onofrio, the Paulist Fathers, the Franciscans, Augustinians and Carmelites, three brethren only of the Order of the Predicants together with the clergy of St. Peter's and the chamberlain of the Roman clergy in stole and pluviale with a few priests. About a hundred-and-forty torches were borne for the most part by the clerics and beneficiaries of St. Peter's and by servants and retainers of the Pope. Then came the body. The beneficiaries and clerics surrounded the coffin without any order, and it was carried by the poor who had stood around it in the chapel, while four or six canons went beside them with their hands on the bier. Only four prelates followed the coffin, two by two, namely, the major-domo, Bishop Deza of Zamora, his vicar Gamboa, and the bishops of Narni and Sessa.

When the coffin was deposited in the center of the church, the *Non intres in judicium*, etc., should have been recited, but there was no book there. While we were waiting for it in vain, the clergy intonated the responsorium: *Libera me, Domine*. During the singing some soldiers of the palace-guard attempted to appropriate several torches. The clergy defended itself against them and the soldiers turned their weapons against the clergy, who left their singing and fled to the sacristy. And the Pope was left lying there almost alone. I took up the bier together with three others and we carried him up to the main altar and the papal throne and placed him with the head towards the altar, closing the choir behind the coffin. The bishop of Sessa feared that if the people came near to the dead, there might be a scandal, that is, some one whom the dead had injured might take revenge upon him. Therefore he had the coffin taken away again and had it deposited at the entrance of the chapel between the stairs, the feet so near to the rails and the door that one could touch them easily with the hand through the railing. There it remained the whole day through behind the well-closed railing.

In the meantime sixteen cardinals had assembled in Sta. Maria Minerva after nine o'clock. They appointed Archbishop Sachis of Ragusa as governor of Rome and assigned two hundred soldiers to him. The office of the chamberlain they handed over to Cardinal Vera. And to these two they entrusted the supervision of the gates of Rome and of the populace and the clergy. The leaden seal of Alexander VI was broken before them in their presence by the plumbators, and they ordered that the papal ring should be handed over to the datary, which was done by Cardinal Casanova, while Pallavicini and Borgia charged themselves with the task of taking an inventory of the possessions of the Pope in his chamber. The congregation ended about three o'clock.

After dinner the cardinals before named, together with the clerics of the Camera, took an inventory of the silver and costly furnishings. They found the papal crown and two precious tiaras, all the rings which the Pope used at the mass, and the whole service of vessels used by the Pope when officiating, as much as could be packed into eight large chests. There were furthermore silver vessels in the first chamber behind the papal apartment, which Michelotto Neri had overlooked, and a box of cyprus wood which was covered with a green cloth and had also not been discovered. In this box were precious stones and rings to the value of about twenty-five thousand ducats, many papers, among them the oath of the cardinals, the bull of investiture of the kingdom of Naples and various other documents.

The cleric of the chamber, Fernando Ponzetto, made arrangements during my absence with the carpenters, Michaele and Buccio, for a catafalque in the middle of the church of St. Peter fifteen spans in length, twelve spans in width and six spans in height; furthermore, for a railing in the aisle, besides the catafalque to hold fifty torches and a hundred-and-fifty torchholders, also for benches for the mourners and a hundred prelates—everything for the price of a hundred-and-fifteen ducats, the ducat at ten carlines. He also arranged for a credence for the celebrant and that they should execute the catafalque and everything else during the whole of the following day.

Meanwhile the Pope, as has been told before, stood between the rails of the main altar and beside him there burned four torches. The decomposition and blackness of his face increased constantly so that he looked at eight o'clock, when I saw him, like the blackest cloth or the darkest negro, completely spotted, the nose swollen, the mouth quite large, the tongue swollen up, doubled so that it started out of his lips, the mouth open, in short so horrible that no one ever saw anything similar or declared to know of it.

In the evening after nine o'clock he was brought from there to the chapel of Santa Maria delle Febbri and deposited in the corner on the wall at the left of the altar by six porters who made jokes and allusions to the Pope all the while. The two carpenters had made the coffin too narrow and too short. They laid the miter by his side, covered him with an old carpet and helped with their fists to fit him into the coffin. All this without torches or any other illumination, without a priest or any person who took care of his body! Thus told me Lord Chrispolit of St. Peter.

> Hardness and falseness, madness and hate, rage, lustful desire,
> Thirsty for blood and for gold, a sponge that can never be filled,
> Alexander the sixth, here I lie; Roma rejoice thee
> Free now at last; for my death was to mean new life for you.
> Alexander the sixth has smothered the world in carnage,
> Pius revives it again, worthy in name and in deed,
> Alexander has sold the altars and crosses and Christum:
> What he had gotten before, now he distributes again.

✦ *Girolamo Savonarola*

G irolamo Savonarola (1452–1498) was born in Ferrara, the son of the court physician. In 1475 he entered a Dominican monastery, where he found fame as a preacher and theologian. In 1491 Savonarola became prior of the monastery of San Marco in Florence, having been invited there by Lorenzo the Magnificent, whose family had some rights of appointment to the foundation. The Dominican preacher used his position to speak out strongly against abuses in both the Church and the Florentine Republic, attacking the Medici in particular for subverting the freedom of the Florentine people.

As a result, Savonarola found himself the spokesman for the anti-Medicean faction following the expulsion of Lorenzo's son, Piero, in 1494 as a consequence of the French invasion of Italy. As the power behind the government, Savonarola used his influence to attempt to purify the city by extirpating what he considered unchristian activities as well as the traditions of classical humanism, which he identified as pagan. Many ancient texts were destroyed, including Latin poets such as Catullus and Ovid; Boccaccio's Decameron was deemed unfit for moral Florentines, as were the paintings of certain artists. Huge pyres of works of art—including paintings of Botticelli, who became a follower of the preacher—books, manuscripts, musical instruments, mirrors, cosmetics, clothing, cards, dice, and similar "ungodly" objects were burned in the Piazza della Signoria.

Moreover, Savonarola began an assault on the failings of the Renaissance papacy, calling for the deposition of pope Alexander VI (Roderigo Borgia). Although excommunicated, Savonarola continued to preach, but political defeats and Florence's isolation during the dangerous period of the French invasions weakened his power. Eventually, in 1498, Savonarola was arrested by the opposing faction, which had secured power. With the blessing of the pope, Savonarola was burned in Florence in the Piazza della Signoria.

O SOUL, BY SIN MADE BLIND

O soul, by sin made blind—and sorely robbed of rest,
God hates in you mankind—for this your life unblest;
your bridegroom, Jesus Christ—you've lost indeed,
nor do you plead—for pity, help, or peace.
                    Alas, alas, alas,
                fear of the Lord is dead in us.

In Prato and in Bibbona—a thousand signs are shown,
yet not the smallest corner—new faith can light and own;
on vice your mind alone—is still intent:
what punishment—will soon against you pass!
                    Alas, alas, alas . . .

Italy is at war—and famine finds new room;
the plague wins every shore—and spreads God's wrathful doom:
such is the food of gloom—left for your blind,
lost life, mankind—of faith as frail as glass.
                    Alas, alas, alas . . .

SOURCE: Girolamo Savonarola, "O Soul, By Sin Made Blind," in J. Tusiani, trans. and ed., Italian Poets of the Renaissance (Long Island, N.Y.: Baroque Press, 1971), p. 81.

Prophets, astrologers—learned and saintly men,
preachers with sermons terse—your woes had in their ken;
yet madly over again—you sing and play
your sinful way:—virtue's no more with us.
                Alas, alas, alas . . .

Tell me each gift and grace—God did you assign;
how many thoughts, not base—did in your heart once shine,
and how much help divine!—But, thankless still
you are of will—and sloth too deep to pass.
                Alas, alas, alas . . .

Go back to Jesus Christ—and to His Mother dear;
no more by vice enticed—desert your path of fear.
Our Virgin Mary's near—and full of grace:
tears on her face—she begs her Son for us.
                Alas, alas, alas
            fear of the Lord is dead in us.

SELECTIONS FROM A DRAFT
CONSTITUTION FOR FLORENCE

Every Florentine citizen who wants to be a good member of his city and to help her, as everyone should wish to do, must first of all believe that this council and this civil government were ordained by God. This is true, indeed, not only because all good government comes from God, but also and especially because of the providential care which God has recently manifested in preserving the city. No one who has lived here for the past three years and is not blind and devoid of judgment would deny that, but for the hand of God, this government would never have been created against so much and such powerful opposition, nor would it have maintained itself to this day among so many traitors and so few friends. God, however, demands of us that we ourselves use the intellect and the free will he has given us. He has made all that pertains to government imperfect at first, so that with his help we can improve it. This government is still imperfect and has many flaws. We have hardly more than the foundation. Every citizen, therefore, should strive to perfect it. It can be made perfect only if all or at least the majority are blessed with the following four virtues.

First, fear of God. It is known that every government comes from God, for everything does. He is the first cause of all things and he governs all things. The government of things in nature is visibly perfect and stable,

SOURCE: R. Watkins, ed., *Humanism and Liberty* (Columbia, S.C.: University of South Carolina, 1978), pp. 253–260. Reprinted by permission of Renee E. Watkins.

because natural things are subject to him and do not disobey. As they submit to all his commandments, he will always guide them to the perfection of their order and show them whatever they must do.

Second, love of the common good. When they hold offices and other dignities, the citizens must put aside all private interests and all the special needs of their relatives and friends. They must think solely of the common good. This concern will illuminate the eye of the intellect. With their own affections put aside, they will not see falsely. With a firm grasp of the true ends of government they will not tend to go wrong in their decisions. They will deserve God's help, indeed, in fostering the growth of the common good. This, it is said, is one of the reasons for the expansion of the Roman empire, that they loved the common good of the city very much, and therefore God, to reward this virtue (for he does not want any good to go unrewarded, and yet their virtue, lacking the sanctification of grace, did not merit eternal life) rewarded them with temporal goods corresponding to their virtue. He caused the common good of their city to grow and extended their empire over the whole earth.

Third, love of one another. The citizens must drop feuds and forget all past offenses. Hatred, bad feelings, and envy blind the eye of the intellect and do not let it see the truth. Sitting in councils and in public offices, anyone who is not well purged in this regard will make many mistakes. For this God will let them suffer, for their own sins and those of others. But when they are well purged of such feelings, He will enlighten them. Beyond this, if they are peaceful and love one another, God will reward their benevolence with perfect government and growing power. This again is one of the reasons God gave such an empire to the Romans, for they loved one another and in the beginning lived in concord. Theirs was not divine charity, but it was good and natural charity, and God therefore rewarded it with temporal goods. If the citizens of Florence love each other with charity natural and divine, God will multiply their temporal and their spiritual goods.

Fourth, justice. Justice purges the city of bad men, or makes them live in fear. The good and just endure in high authority because they are gladly elected to office by those who love justice. They are enlightened by God in legislation and in guiding the city to a happy state. Justice will make the city fill up with goodness because it always rewards goodness; and the good men, wanting to live where there is justice, will congregate there in great numbers. God, for justice also, will increase the city's empire, as he did that of the Romans. Because the Romans exercised strict and severe justice, He gave them imperial power over the whole world. He wanted justice to make his peoples righteous.

The Florentine citizens, if they deliberate and use rational judgment, will see that they require no other government than the one we have described. If they have faith, moreover, that it was given to them by God, and exercise the four virtues we have named, their government will doubtless be soon perfected. They will arrive at good counsels together, in which

God will illuminate their minds concerning whatever they seek to do. God will give them special light, moreover, because they are his servants, and they will know many things that they could not have found out for themselves. They will create on earth a government like that of heaven. They will be blessed with many spiritual and temporal blessings. If they will not have faith, however, that this government is given to them by God, and that they must truly fear God and love the common good, and if they follow only their own wills, without love for one another but with factionalism as always before, and if they fail to do justice, the government ordained by God will still remain. Only they and their children will be wholly consumed rather than receive the grace of it.

God has shown signs of his anger already, but they do not want to open their ears. God will punish them in this world and in the next. In this one they will always be restless and full of passions and sadness; in the other they will burn in the eternal fire. For they refused to follow the natural light, and even the divine signs which have been vouchsafed them, and to realize that this truly is their government. Some who failed to act righteously under this regime and were always restless with it are already suffering the pains of hell. Florentines! You have seen that God wants this government and signs have been given you, you know that it has not faltered despite attacks from within and without, and you realize that those who attack it are threatened by God with many punishments. I beg you by the bowels of mercy of our lord Jesus Christ, that you be content now to accept it. If you are not, God will send a greater scourge to assail you than he has done before. You will lose then both this world and the other. But if you support it, you will gain the happiness that I shall attempt to describe in the next chapter.

◆ ◆ ◆

This government is made more by God than by men, and those citizens who, for the glory of God and for the common good, obey our instructions and strive to make it perfect, will enjoy earthly happiness, spiritual happiness, and eternal happiness.

First, they will be free from servitude to a tyrant. How great that servitude is we have declared above. They will live in true liberty, which is more precious than gold and silver. They will be safe in their city, caring with joy and peace of mind for their own households and for making an honest profit in business. When God increases their property or their status, they will not be afraid of someone taking these away. They will be free to go to the country or wherever they want without asking permission from the tyrant. They will marry their sons and daughters to whomever they choose. They will be free to have weddings and celebrations and friends and to pursue science or art, whichever they please, and in other ways too, to build for themselves a certain earthly happiness.

Second, spiritual happiness will follow. Everyone will be able to dedicate himself to the good Christian life, and no one will prevent him. No one when in office will be forced by threats not to give justice, because everyone will be free. Nor will a man be forced by poverty to make evil pacts. The government of the city being good, riches will abound and everyone will work. The poor will earn money. The boys and girls will receive a holy upbringing. Good laws will protect the honor of women and girls. Religion especially will flourish, for God, seeing the people's good will, will send them good clergy. As the Scripture says: "God gives priests to suit the peoples." And these priests will be able to govern their flocks without hindrance, and good church officials and good monks too will become numerous. The bad, indeed, will not be able to live here, since contrary expels contrary.

Thus in a short time the city will be filled with true religion. It will be like a paradise on earth. The people will live amidst rejoicing and singing of psalms. The boys and girls will be like angels growing up in both the Christian and the civic life combined. They, in time, will create a government in this city that is more heavenly than earthly. The happiness of the good will be so profound that they will enjoy in this world a certain spiritual beatitude.

Third, not only will this earn the people eternal happiness, but it will raise the level of that happiness by a great deal. Their merits and therefore their reward in heaven will be increased. For God gives to those that govern well the greatest reward, since beatitude is the prize of virtue, and the greater a man's virtue, the greater his actions, the greater the prize. It is certainly greater virtue to rule oneself and others, and especially a community and a kingdom, than merely to rule oneself. It follows that he who rules a community merits in eternal life the greatest prize. Greater reward as we see in all the arts is given to the master who governs the undertaking than to the servants who obey his directions. In the military art, more is given the captain of the army than the soldiers; in building, greater reward is given the master builder and the architect than the manual workers. And so on in all the arts. The better the actions of a man, moreover, the more he honors God and makes himself useful to his neighbors, the more deserving he is. Certainly to govern a community well, especially one like the Florentine, is an excellent action. It will, as we have shown, bring great glory to God and benefit the souls and bodies and temporal prosperity of men. There can be no doubt, then, that it merits a high reward and great glory.

We know that one who gives to charity or feeds a few poor is greatly rewarded by God, for our Savior says that in the day of judgment he will turn to the just and say: "Come, blessed of the Father, receive the kingdom prepared for you from the beginning of the world, for when I was hungry and when I was thirsty and when I was naked and wandering, you fed me and dressed me and took me in. And you came to visit me when I was ill, for what you have done to my little ones, you have done to me also." If

God, then, gives great rewards for each man's particular charity, what reward will he give to the man who governs a large city well? Good government feeds many poor, provides for many who are wretched, defends widows and orphans, and takes out of the hands of the powerful and wicked the persons who otherwise could not defend themselves from their power, liberates the country from thieves and assassins, protects the good, and maintains good living and religious practice. Beyond all this it does infinitely more good. Similar loves similar, moreover, and he will love most whoever most resembles him. All creatures are similar to God, and all are loved by him, but because some are more similar to him than others, he loves them more. He who governs is more similar to God than he who is governed, and therefore surely, if he governs justly, is more loved and rewarded by God for this than for private actions when he is not governing. Whoever governs also takes more risk and suffers more weariness of mind and body than he who does not govern, for which again he deserves greater reward.

But the would-be tyrant is unhappy. First, he has no earthly happiness, for though he has riches, he cannot enjoy them because of the affliction of his spirit, his fears and continual worries, and especially because of the vast sums he must spend to remain in power. And though he wants to make everyone else a mere subject, he is the merest subject of all, forced to wait upon everyone in order to win people over. He is deprived of friendship, which is the greatest and best thing a man can enjoy in this world, because he does not want anyone to be his equal, because he is afraid of everyone, and especially because a tyrant is almost always generally hated for the evils he perpetrates. If bad men love him, it is not because they really wish him well, but because they want to profit from him. No true friendship, therefore, can exist among them. Because of the evils he does, he does not have fame and honor. Others always hate and envy him. He can never really be consoled and free of melancholy, because he must always be vigilant and suspicious that his enemies may try something. He is necessarily always afraid. He does not trust even his guards. He is spiritually unhappy also, moreover, for he lacks the grace of God, and all knowledge of him. Surrounded by sinners and by the perverse characters who make up his assiduous following, he is bound to fall into evil ways. He will, therefore, be eternally unhappy, for tyrants are almost always incorrigible. The multitude of his sins means that sin has become a habit with him, extremely hard to abandon. To give back all the property he has stolen, also, and to offer reparations for so many evil deeds would mean being left in his underwear, a thing one can imagine would be difficult to one accustomed to a life of such pride and indulgence. He is also prevented by his flatterers, who make light of his sins and convince him that wicked things are good, even by the tepid monks who confess and absolve him, showing him white when they should show him black. Thus he is wretched in this world and goes to hell in the other, where he is more severely punished than other men. There stands against him the multitude of his sins and of the sins he has caused others to commit. He is also condemned for the office he has usurped, for, as the good ruler earns God's greatest rewards, the bad one is most severely punished.

The tyrant's followers all participate in his wretchedness in temporal, in spiritual, and in eternal things. They lose their liberty, which is the greatest of treasures, as well as their property and honors and sons and wives. For all these come into the tyrant's power. They are always imitating his sins, in order to please him and to be as like him as they can. In hell, too, therefore, they will participate in his terrible punishment.

The citizens who dislike civil government because it stops them from being tyrants all participate in the same wretchedness even though they are not actually tyrants. They lack riches, honors, reputation, and friendship. All the lean ones congregate around them hoping to repair their fortunes, and all the bad men surround them. They must be always spending money, and the good people avoid them. They have not a single real friend, for their followers try to rob them. Their bad companions lead them into a thousand sins which they would not otherwise commit. They are restless in heart and at all times filled with hatred, envy, and complaints. Thus they have hell both in this world and the next.

Since (as we have shown), therefore, those who rule well are happy and are like God, and those who rule badly are unhappy and like the devil, every citizen should abandon his sins and his private affections to strive to rule well. Everyone should work to preserve and increase and perfect this civil government, for the honor of God and for the salvation of souls. God gave this government especially to Florence because of his love for this city. Through this government, it can be happy in this world and the other, by the grace of our Savior Jesus Christ, king of kings, lord of lords, who with the Father and the Holy Spirit lives and rules *in saecula saeculorum.*

♦ *Gregorio Dati*

INDIVIDUAL PIETY: SELECTIONS FROM THE *RICORDANZE*

1 January 1404.

I know that in this wretched life our sins expose us to many tribulations of soul and passions of the body, that without God's grace and mercy

SOURCE: G. Brucker, ed., *Two Memoirs of Renaissance Florence* (New York: Harper and Row, 1967), pp. 124–126, 128–133. Reprinted by permission of HarperCollins Publishers.

which strengthens our weakness, enlightens our mind and supports our will, we would perish daily. I also see that since my birth forty years ago, I have given little heed to God's commandments. Distrusting my own power to reform, but hoping to advance by degrees along the path of virtue, I resolve from this day forward to refrain from going to the shop or conducting business on solemn Church holidays, or from permitting others to work for me or seek temporal gain on such days. Whenever I make exceptions in cases of extreme necessity, I promise, on the following day, to distribute alms of one gold florin to God's poor. I have written this down so that I may remember my promise and be ashamed if I should chance to break it.

Also, in memory of the passion of Our Lord Jesus Christ who freed and saved us by His merits, that He may, by His grace and mercy preserve us from guilty passions, I resolve from this very day and in perpetuity to keep Friday as a day of total chastity—with Friday I include the following night—when I must abstain from the enjoyment of all carnal pleasures. God give me grace to keep my promise, yet if I should break it through forgetfulness, I engage to give 20 *soldi* to the poor for each time, and to say twenty Paternosters and Avemarias.

I resolve this day to do a third thing while I am in health and able to, remembering that each day we need Almighty God to provide for us. Each day I wish to honor God by some giving of alms or by the recitation of prayers or some other pious act. If, by inadvertence, I fail to do so, that day or the next day I must give alms to God's poor of at least 5 *soldi*. These however are not vows but intentions by which I shall do my best to abide.

3 May 1412. On 28 April, my name was drawn as Standard-bearer of the Militia Company. Up until then I had not been sure whether my name was in the purses for that office, although I was eager that it should be both for my own honor and that of my heirs. I recalled that my father Stagio had held a number of appointments in the course of his life, being frequently a consul of the Guild of Por Santa Maria, a member of the Merchants' Court and one of the officials in charge of gabelles and the treasurers. Yet he was never drawn for any of the Colleges during his lifetime, though shortly after his death he was drawn as a prior. I recalled that I had aroused a great deal of animosity eight years ago because of my business in Catalonia, and that last year I only just escaped being arrested for debt by the Commune. On the very day my name was drawn for this office, only fifteen minutes before it was drawn, I had taken advantage of the reprieve granted by the new laws and finished paying off my debt to the Commune. That was a veritable inspiration from God, may His name be praised and blessed! Now that I can obtain other offices, it seems to me that, having had a great benefit, I should be content to know that I have sat once in the Colleges and should aspire no further. So, lest I should ungratefully give way to the insatiable appetites of those in whom success breeds renewed ambition, I have resolved and sworn to myself that I shall

not henceforth invoke the aid of any or attempt to get myself elected to public offices or to have my name included in new purses. Rather, I shall let things take their course without interfering. I shall abide by God's will, accepting those offices of the guilds or Commune for which my name shall be drawn, and not refusing the labor but serving and doing what good I may. In this way I shall restrain my own presumption and tendency towards ambition and shall live in freedom without demeaning myself by begging favors from any. And if I should depart from this resolve, I condemn myself each time to distribute two gold florins in alms within a month. I have taken this resolution in my fiftieth year.

Knowing my weakness in the face of sin, I make another resolve on the same day. In order to ensure the peace and good of my own conscience, I vowed that I would never accept any office, if my name should be drawn, wherein I would have power to wield the death penalty. If I should depart from this resolution, I condemn myself to give 25 gold florins in alms to the poor within three months for each such office that I have agreed to accept. And I shall in no way attempt to influence those who make up the purses for such offices, either asking them to put or not put in my name, but shall let them do as they think fit. If I should do otherwise, I condemn myself to distribute a gold florin.

◆ ◆ ◆

After that it was God's will to recall to Himself the blessed soul of my wife Ginevra. She died in childbirth after lengthy suffering, which she bore with remarkable strength and patience. She was perfectly lucid at the time of her death when she received all the sacraments: confession, communion, extreme unction, and a papal indulgence granting absolution for all her sins, which she received from Master Lionardo, who had been granted it by the Pope. It comforted her greatly, and she returned her soul to her Creator on 7 September, the Eve of the Feast of Our Lady, at nones: the hour when Our Blessed Lord Jesus Christ expired on the cross and yielded up his spirit to our Heavenly Father. On Friday the 8th she was honorably buried and on the 9th, masses were said for her soul. Her body lies in our plot at S. Spirito and her soul has gone to eternal life. God bless her and grant us fortitude. Her loss has sorely tried me. May He help me to bring up the unruly family which is left to me in the best way for their souls and bodies.

God who shows his wisdom in all things permitted the plague to strike our house. The first to succumb was our manservant Paccino at the end of June 1420. Three days later it was the turn of our slave-girl Marta, after her on 1 July my daughter Sandra and on 5 July my daughter Antonia. We left that house after that and went to live opposite, but a few days later Veronica died. Again we moved, this time to Via Chiara where Bandecca and Pippa fell ill and departed this life on 1 August. All of them bore the marks of the plague. It passed off after that and we returned to our own house. May God bless them all. Bandecca's will and her accounts appear on page . . . of my ledger A.

X

Life in Renaissance Italy

❖

INTRODUCTION

B *eneath the large-scale facades of church and state and below the level of self-conscious humanist prose and the monuments of high culture, most Italian men and women of the Renaissance lived their daily lives. Obviously, the larger contexts of their social, economic, and political positions influenced them greatly, but what mattered most usually was their families, friends, occupations, holidays, and special personal moments. To reveal this level of daily life is difficult because even personal letters are often carefully fashioned public documents. However, it is possible to provide an insight into some aspects of the experience of men and women from different social classes, with different levels of education, in different occupations, and from different parts of Italy. In so doing, an impression of the individual living his or her daily life might emerge that may serve to balance the traditional emphasis placed on the great figures of the Renaissance in their public rather than their private personas.*

THE ELITE

✦ *Pietro Aretino*

P ietro Aretino (1492–1556) was born in Arezzo, hence his name. He was from a modest family, and he received very little formal education. However, friends of his mother helped his rise in society so that by

341

1517 he was in the service of the very rich banker, Agostino Chigi, in Rome. Still, Aretino was hardly a humanist, preferring scurrilous verse and satire. Consequently, he was employed by powerful clerics to embarrass their rivals. This use of his biting pen and razor wit—and his publication of pornographic materials—made Aretino many enemies in Rome, which he had to flee on several occasions. Finally, he moved to Venice in 1527, where he would stay until his death.

In Venice, Aretino made his living by writing satire and by publishing his letters, as well as by collecting information about important people and events. These activities made him rich, since some men paid him to write scandalously about their rivals and those rivals paid him not to do so. His letters were immensely popular, as were his comedies and dialogues. In addition, this "scourge of princes" wrote religious literature of a high quality, which, together with his close association with the leading artists, writers, and politicians of the day and the importance of his letters as an insight into his times, has kept his reputation alive, despite the often scandalous content of his writings.

LETTER TO MESSER GIANNANTONIO DA FOLIGNO

The Defence of Genius Against Powerful Men

My happiness would be too great, my distinguished friend, if anyone who doubted whether the talent given me by God were true gold or not were to assay it for himself; for then I feel certain that everyone would give me my due as you have done in the letter you kindly sent me. So I bless the fact that you previously disdained reading my writings, because as a result of this I have acquired a true friend. Certainly my compositions are so feeble that they do not deserve to be read; but this is not because there is any malice in them. I laugh at the vulgar mob that has found fault with them, because it is its usual custom to blame what is praiseworthy and praise what is disgraceful; and it is the nature of the mob to try to stir things up if it possibly can. You see, if I have a go at someone important, as I lay into him this or that fawning courtier starts to fume and contrives to grow purple with anger, and he calls me by all the names he deserves himself, hoping for favors for himself. Another does the same in order to appear important, and not because there's any sense or decency in him. And in this way the countless tribe of ignoramuses wickedly besmirch the honor of others.

SOURCE: Excerpts from Pietro Aretino, *Selected Letters*, trans. by G. Bull (Harmondsworth, England: Penguin, 1976). Reproduced by permission of Penguin Books Ltd.

All that I have written has been in honor of genius, whose glory was usurped and blackened by the avarice of powerful lords. And before I began to scourge these lords, talented men had to beg even for the ordinary necessities of life and if anyone did secure himself against want, it was by acting the clown and not because of his merits. And so my pen, armed with all its terrors, has succeeded in forcing them to reform themselves and to receive men of intelligence and distinction with extreme courtesy, which is more hateful to them than any hardship. So true men should always cherish me, because I always fought for genius with my life's blood, and it is only because of me that genius goes about the world today wearing brocade, drinks from gold cups, adorns herself with gems, owns necklaces and money, rides proudly as a Queen, is served like an Empress and revered as a Goddess. If anyone says that I have not restored her to her ancient status he is a liar and blasphemer. But as I am in fact the savior of genius, who cares whether the envious mob criticizes and complains?

My dear brother, I am boasting of this, not out of pride, but in order to answer those who assert that the gospel I preach is evil. On the contrary, the learned now make their way along the paths built for them by my strength of arm, whenever they want to attack and ridicule the intrigues and treacheries of the powerful. So they too should sing the praises of God just as I have done, because I know that I succeeded through His grace and not through any wit of my own. This is now my resolve for the future, and so I trust that when I die even those who would once have mocked will grieve over my death.

Now let us make a pact of everlasting friendship, and let the penalty you anxiously ask me to inflict on you for your past incredulity be the brotherhood that I now proclaim between us. [From Venice, the 3rd of April 1537]

LETTER TO MESSER DOMENICO BOLLANI

The Spectacle from Aretino's Marvellous House on the Grand Canal

It would seem to me, most honored sir, a great sin of ingratitude were I not to repay at least a part of my great indebtedness by praising the divine beauty of the site where your house stands, and where, to the daily delight of my life, I have my lodging. For the house is in a spot that is completely without blemish either above or below, this side or that. So I am as shy of speaking of its merits as one would be of discussing those of the Emperor. For sure, he who built it did so on the noblest side of the Grand Canal. And as the Grand Canal is the patriarch of all waterways and Venice is the feminine Pope of all cities, I can truly say that I enjoy the finest highway and the loveliest view in all the world.

Never do I lean out of the windows but that I see at market time a thousand persons and as many gondolas. In my field of vision to the right stand the Fish Market and the Meat Market; in the space to the left, the Bridge and the Fondaco dei Tedeschi; where both views meet I see the Rialto, packed with merchants. I have grapes in the barges, game and game birds in the shops, vegetables on the pavement. I do not hanker after meadows irrigated by streams when at dawn I admire the water covered with every kind of produce in season. And it's a real joy to watch those who have brought vast loads of fruits and green vegetables distribute them to others for carrying to their various destinations.

It is all fascinating, including the spectacle of the twenty or twenty-five sailboats, choked with melons, which are lashed together to make a kind of island where people run and assess the quality of the melons by snuffing them and weighing them. In order not to detract from their famous pomp and splendor, I won't say a word about those beautiful ladies of the town, shimmering in silk and gold and jewels, and seated so proudly in their boats. But let me tell you I split my sides laughing when the hoots, whistles and shouts of the boatmen explode behind those who are rowed along by servants who aren't wearing scarlet breeches. And who wouldn't have pissed himself on seeing capsize in the bittermost cold a boat packed with Germans just escaped from the tavern, as did I and the famous Giulio Camillo? It was he who used to say affably that the land entrance of the house I have described, being dark, lop-sided, with nasty stairs, was like the terrible name I have acquired through airing the truth; and then he added that whoever gets to know me intimately finds in my pure, sincere and honest friendship the tranquil contentment experienced on coming out onto the portico and looking out over those balconies.

And so that nothing may be lacking to delight the eyes, on one side I am charmed by the orange trees which gild the foot of the Palazzo del Camerlinghi, and on the other by the waters and bridge of San Giovan Crisostomo. Nor does the winter sun ever dare to rise without first sending word to my bedside, to my study, to my kitchen, my living-rooms and my hall.

And what I most appreciate is the nobility of my neighbors. Opposite me, I have his eloquent and honorable Magnificence, Maffio Lioni, on whose supreme virtues are grounded the learning, knowledge and good manners that characterize the knowledge and behavior of Girolamo, Piero and Luigi, his remarkable sons. I also have Sirena, the life and soul of my own studies. I have the magnanimous Francesco Mocenigo, whose liberality is at the continuous service of knights and gentlemen. Next door I see the good Messer Giambattista Spinelli, in whose paternal home live my friends, the Cavorlini, and may God forgive Fortune for the wrongs that chance has made them suffer. Nor do I hold as the least of my blessings the beloved and dignified proximity of Signora Jacopa.

In short, if my sense of touch and my other senses were to be nourished as well as my sight, the apartments I am praising would be a veritable paradise, seeing my eyes are supplied with all the objects that can give them pleasure. Nor do I lack delight in the great noblemen from Venice and elsewhere who flock to my doors, and I swell with tremendous pride when I see the *Bucentaur*[1] going to and fro; and the regattas and the festivals which are always so resplendent on the Canal which I oversee like a lord.

But what of the lights which after nightfall seem like scattered stars, shining on the place where we buy what is needed for our supper-parties and dinners? And then the music, whose strains thrill my ears during the night with the harmony of their melodies? One would sooner explain the profound judgment you possess in letters and state affairs, before I could come to the end of the delights that I experience from what is displayed before me. And so, if I am inspired by any spirit of genius in the trifles I write down on paper, it comes from the benefit I derive not from the light, or the shade, or the violet, or the verdant, but from the graces received by me through the airy enchantment of your dwelling-place, in which may God grant that I shall spend in health and vigor all the years that a good man deserves to live. [From Venice, the 27th of October 1537]

LETTER TO MESSER SIMONE BIANCO

The Joys of a Recluse and the Burden of Servants

A thousand times I, who wouldn't change places with a half duke, have had the fantasy that I would like to be you; not so much because I know that you're a fine fellow, a good sculptor and the best of friends, as because you know how to live in the world and stay aloof from it, and living there and remaining aloof, you can laugh at the expense both of those who are better off and those who are worse off than you.

You take things as they come, avoiding company when you're at home and seeking it when you go out: so you're both a private recluse and a public figure. But what happiness, what beatitude, what glory equal that of the man who knows how to, is able to and wishes to imitate you? Pity me, wasting my life, squandering my money and blighting my spirit because of the asinine demands of my servants!

What luxury they enjoy who return to the simplicity of Nature, observing her modest laws with a sober disposition, and who, refusing to allow the blessings of their humble state to be corrupted by the vain pursuits of

---

1. The *Bucentaur* was the State barge of Venice, used for the annual ceremony of the city's marriage with the sea.

ambition, are content to keep themselves to themselves, and won't allow
the animals to keep this privilege to themselves.

Just consider: you return in the evening to your retreat, which is
exactly suited to the style of life you have chosen, to escape the wifely
nagging which afflicts a man just as much when he comes home early as
when he comes home late. If your coals banked with ashes have not burned
out, you can kindle your light with a bit of sulfur taper; if they are cold,
you call out to your neighbor and she passes through the window a
burning-brand or else lets you have some live coals on a shovel: and then
when you have scattered a bundle of wood on the hearth, you're like an
abbot warming his front in the heat of a roaring fire, and intoning a little
song you wait to grow hungry. And as soon as you are, turning your back
to the blaze, you attack the salad you've prepared and the sausage you've
fried, with a fisherman's appetite, drinking from the jug with no worry
about the faces being made behind your back by some sluttish maid or
treacherous servant.

Then you go back to the fire and gaze at your own shadow which sits
down when you sit and rises when you rise, paying court to your Lordship
while you chat with the cat or fill your stomach reading about the adventures of others. When you're assailed by sleep, saying "happy dreams" or
"good night" to yourself, you climb into bed, which you've made up
yourself scarcely twice a month; and finishing a "Hail Mary" and an "Our
Father" and making the sign of the Cross (there's no need for any more
prayers since a single man doesn't sin) you snuggle your head into your
feather-pillow in such a way that even the thunder would have to work
miracles to wake you up.

Come the morning and you get up and taking the greatest delight in
your delectable skill you wait till a couple of chops or an omelette or a
cutlet call you to table; and after you've lifted up your mug and shaken
the napkin and put it back on a table which is always laid and always
presided over by the jug of wine, standing in front of it with constant
lovingness, you eat to live rather than live to eat.

You go out for a walk whenever it suits you, providing yourself out
of your own money with some liver or tasty sheeps' heads for a stew. You
buy a little fish or some eggs all fresh from the country, honoring Easter
with a fat capon and solemn feast-days with a chicken or two, not forgetting the goose for All Saints and never returning to your lodgings without
a radish in your hand and a salad in your handkerchief, singing as you go.

Come the summer and it brings you your plums, with a handful of
figs, two flasks of Moscatello and a bunch of grapes, and having ventured
to buy a nicely ripened melon, small but very heavy, you take it along
home. Enjoying fresh water on the dinner-table, you fill your jug full from
the tub, and plunging your nose and your knife together into that melon,
finding it sweet and succulent, you are as pleased as Punch, and after
you've eaten two slices, you guzzle the lot and the flavor penetrates your
very bones; and, despising what's eaten in all the courts in the world, you

finish your meal with a scrap of meat or some cheese, and you're convinced that to live any other way would be folly; for it's a vile thing to make one's gullet a Paradise of food or one's body a packing-case for provisions.

I tell you, I feel quite drowsy when I think of you reposing in your kitchen-chair or letting your head sink to your chest and dozing off for a pleasant cat-nap. Then you get to your feet and bundle up all your dirty clothes to hand them over to the woman who lights your lamp and kindles your fire, without cursing and complaining about the firewood and soap that have to be expended on the laundry work. With money, it's easy come easy go and so why not give it to the laundry-woman?

As I praise your solitary kind of life, someone might object: "Where can he turn when he's ill or has an accident?" Well, he can turn to the goodness of God and he can depend on the will of Christ. For Christ's mercy deserts no one and through His grace you remain in good health while you exhaust yourself working on a fine block of marble which you transform into heads similar to those the Chinese sent to the King of France.

If you are troubled by lust, bang away with your hammer and chisel; and if it still chases after you and you can't escape it, remember not only your friend "the five-fingered widow" but also that "whores are cheap at the price." But it would be just as well, to placate its insistent demands, to walk a couple of times from the Rialto to San Marco, to collect news of the truce made at Nice or the Council dissolved at Vicenza.

But now let's turn from your comforts to just one of my afflictions, which are so many that they are greater in number than all the tickets of the lottery. I am not referring to the murder of my reputation, or the way I'm swindled over my accounts, or have my coffers rifled, since all this is nothing. I mean instead the cruel way I've been assassinated by Ambrogio. Let's hope this is the end of it.

But if only you were here. I am utterly convinced that to do what he did he could have been moved only by conceit, which is natural to those who grow arrogant over some modest talent or other and start to think they are better suited to command than to obey. It's true that I think I've taken my revenge on him through the torment of a wife that I've made him take, though I regret I can't inflict another one on him, so that he should have to scurry every day from Purgatory into Hell and from Hell back into Purgatory.

But talking of servants, a bishop who was one of the best of priests certainly knew what was what. When he was at the point of death he remarked to the friar who was reminding him of spiritual matters: "I don't care a damn about Hell, if there are no servants there."

Giannozzo Pandolfini vowed that, if he recovered from an illness, he would kill himself so as never to employ servants again, because he had one who apart from other tortures split his fevered head day and night playing on a fiddle. So you are a lucky man, since when you need assistance you are your own servant as well as your own master. [From Venice, the 25th of June 1538]

LETTER TO MESSER AGOSTINO RICCHI

Venice, 10 July, 1537

If knowledge and learning, my son, were as important as living well, I would implore you to go on with your appointed studies. But since living well comes first, I beg you instead to hie you hither. For here you need not torment your mind about the devilish subtleties of Aristotle. Here your one occupation will be to keep yourself sane while the frenzy of this heat wave endures which is so trying to our patience and our poor frames.

As far as I am concerned, I would much rather see the snow falling from the sky than to be scorched by the so-called balmy breezes. God's truth, indeed, winter seems to me an abbot who floats downstream in comfortable ease, taking just a little too much pleasure in eating and sleeping and doing that other thing. But summer is a rich and noble harlot, who, drenched with cheap perfume, throws herself down disgusted and does nothing but drink and drink again. Nor are the iced wines and flower-decked rooms, with whatever man-made breezes and dishes of galantined meat that June or July can imagine, worth the crust of buttered bread which you eat before the fire in December or January, tossing off several glasses of wine, the while, turning the spit, you steal a piece of roast pork therefrom, and do not trouble yourself about your mouth and your fingers, both of which are burned during the theft.

At night—this is in winter—you climb into a bed which a warming pan has already made ready for you, and there you embrace your companion, or better still, all huddled up and under the covers, you take comfort in the pervasive heat. The rain and the thunder and fury of the north wind only keep you firm in your resolve not to get up until day.

In contrast, who can put up with the cruel torturing of fleas, bed-bugs, mosquitoes, and flies? Especially when they are added to the other unpleasantnesses of summer? You lie stark naked upon your pallet, and your rogue off as soon as he thinks you have closed your eyes. You wake up in the midst of the first good sleep you have had. You begin to sweat again. You drink and pant and toss this way and that. You wish that it were possible to flee from yourself and to get out of your own body. So great is the unpleasantness of the suffocating heat that it almost makes you die even as it drenches you.

Indeed, if it were not for your craving for melons, those pimps of the appetite, which almost overpowers you, and makes you long for the days when they are in season, you would cry a pox on the hot weather just as ragged beggars cry a pox on the cold. But there are many who like the

SOURCE: R. Clements and L. Levant, eds., *Renaissance Letters* (New York: New York University Press, 1976), pp. 437–438.

summer just because of its plentiful fruit. They praise the artichokes, the cherries, the figs, the peaches, and the grapes as if the truffles, the olives, and the chard of winter were not worth them all.

Over and above that, there is better conversation around a roaring fire than there is under the shadow of a handsome beech tree, for under the beech tree you need a thousand harlot tricks to whet your appetite. You must have the song of birds, the murmur of the water, the sighing of the breezes, the freshness of the grass and other such trifles. But you only need four well-seasoned logs to provide all that is necessary for a conversation of four or five hours, with chestnuts on a platter and a jug of wine between your knees.

Yes, we should love winter, for it is the spring of genius. But, to return to our own affairs, I tell you again that you should hie yourself hither. For our Messer Niccolo Franco,[1] that best and most learned of youths, has found himself his own room where he can lie off and take his ease and he has summoned to it a thousand gay young blades.

I have nothing more to say to you, except that you must deign to commend me to Signor Sperone[2] and to Ferraguto.[3]

✦ *Michelangelo Buonarroti*

*M*ichelangelo Buonarroti (1475–1564) was among the greatest artists Europe has ever produced. He was a pupil of Ghirlandaio, and he absorbed much humanism and neo-Platonism during the years (1490–1492) he lived in the Medici palace under the patronage of Lorenzo the Magnificent. His early sculptures from this period exhibit the strong influence of classical marbles, but he was equally able to create great Christian art, such as his Pietà *of 1499. These two influences merged to some degree in his* David *of 1504, which represents the youthful slayer of Goliath (and a popular Florentine image of the Republic itself) in a manner equal to the best surviving sculptures of antiquity.*

In 1505, Pope Julius II summoned him to Rome to carve a huge tomb for him that was originally to comprise 40 figures. Although the project was never finished, the Moses, *created for the project, is among the greatest of Michelangelo's work. Subsequently, Pope Julius set Michelangelo to painting the ceiling of the Sistine Chapel, a huge undertaking that proved that the Florentine was as gifted a painter as a sculptor.*

---

1. Secretary of Aretino later hanged for writing satires against Pope Paul IV.
2. Sperone Speroni, a learned playwright and philologist who died the year this letter was written.
3. Ferraguto di Lazzara, a close friend who "supposedly twice saved Aretino's life from assassins in Rome" (Chubb).

Michelangelo also was an architect of brilliance. He designed and carved the figures for the new sacristy of San Lorenzo in Florence, where the Medici are buried. Moreover, he designed the Laurentian Library in the same church to house the great collection of manuscripts collected first by Niccolo Niccoli and later added to by the Medici. Finally, back in Rome, he was given the commission to complete the new St Peter's, whose huge dome was Michelangelo's creation.

Besides his artistic genius, Michelangelo was a poet of great sensitivity, especially in his religious and his neo-Platonic poetry, some of which was written for his very close friend Tommaso Cavalieri, as was the letter reproduced here.

LETTER TO TOMMASO CAVALIERI

Without due consideration, Messer Tomao, my very dear Lord, I was moved to write to your Lordship, not by way of answer to any letter received from you, but being myself the first to make advances, as though I felt bound to cross a little stream with dry feet, or a ford made manifest by paucity of water. But now that I have left the shore, instead of the trifling water I expected, the ocean with its towering waves appears before me, so that, if it were possible, in order to avoid drowning, I should gladly retrace my steps to the dry land whence I started. Still, as I am here, I will e'en make of my heart a rock, and proceed further; and if I shall not display the art of sailing on the sea of your powerful genius, that genius itself will excuse me, nor will be disdainful of my inferiority in parts, nor desire from me that which I do not possess, inasmuch as he who is unique in all things can have peers in none. Therefore your Lordship, the light of our century without paragon upon this world, is unable to be satisfied with the productions of other men, having no match or equal to yourself. And if, peradventure, something of mine, such as I hope and promise to perform, give pleasure to your mind, I shall esteem it more fortunate than excellent; and should I ever be sure of pleasing your Lordship, as is said, in any particular, I will devote the present time and all my future to your service; indeed, it will grieve me much that I cannot regain the past, in order to devote a longer space to you than the future only will allow, seeing I am now too old. I have no more to say. Read the heart and not the letter, because "the pen toils after man's good will in vain."

I have to make excuses for expressing in my first letter a marvelous astonishment at your rare genius; and thus I do so, having recognized the error I was in; for it is much the same to wonder at God's working miracles as to wonder at Rome's producing divine men. Of this the universe confirms us in our faith.

It would be permissible to give the name of the things a man presents,

SOURCE: R. Clements and L. Levant, eds., *Renaissance Letters* (New York: New York University Press, 1976), pp. 392–393.

to him who receives them; but proper sense of what is fitting prevents its being done in this letter.

✦ *Niccolo Machiavelli*

*N*iccolo Machiavelli (1469–1527) is perhaps the best known writer of the Italian Renaissance. He was born in Florence to a patrician family and received a good humanist education. After the Medici were expelled from Florence, Machiavelli entered the service of the republic and rose rapidly, enjoying many important diplomatic missions. However, this success meant that he was seen as hostile to the Medici, who took away his appointments after their restoration in 1512.

Forced by poverty and the suspicions of the Medici that he was plotting against them, Machiavelli retired to a farm he owned at San Casciano, just outside of Florence. There he wrote the books for which he is still famous: The Prince and The Discourses on Livy (1513). In those works he explored the nature of men and of politics, trying to learn how to succeed, despite the fickleness of fortune and the generally low character exhibited by most men in high office. He wrote of the need to reinvigorate the Florentine people by establishing a citizen militia rather than relying on mercenaries, and he called upon his city to emulate the virtue of the ancient Roman Republic.

Although he attempted to regain some position in the Medici's service, Machiavelli was never to reenter the lofty spheres of government he had enjoyed in his youth. The Medici did give him some small appointments, and Cardinal Giuliano did commission him to write his great History of Florence. It was in part his desire to keep in contact with the political, intellectual, and social life of Florence that drove Machiavelli to write many letters to his friends. These letters, thoughtful, amusing, and astute as they are, provide significant commentaries on the Italy and Florence of the period after the French invasions and give a wonderful perspective on the private life of a humanist politician.

LETTER TO FRANCESCO VETTORI

Cascine, 10 December 1513

Magnificent Ambassador:

"Never late were favors divine." I say this because I seemed to have lost—no, rather mislaid—your good will; you had not written to me for a long time, and I was wondering what the reason could be. And of all those that came into my mind I took little account, except of one only,

SOURCE: R. Clements and L. Levant, eds., *Renaissance Letters* (New York: New York University Press, 1976), pp. 64–67.

when I feared that you had stopped writing because somebody had written to you that I was not a good guardian of your letters, and I knew that, except Filippo and Pagolo, nobody by my doing had seen them. I have found it again through your last letter of the twenty-third of the past month, from which I learn with pleasure how regularly and quietly you carry on this public office, and I encourage you to continue so, because he who gives up his own convenience for the convenience of others, only loses his own and from them gets no gratitude. And since Fortune wants to do everything, she wishes us to let her do it, to be quiet, and not to give her trouble, and to wait for a time when she will allow something to be done by men; and then will be the time for you to work harder, to stir things up more, and for me to leave my farm and say: "Here I am." I cannot, however, wishing to return equal favors, tell you in this letter anything else than what my life is; and if you judge that you would like to swap with me, I shall be glad to.

I am living on my farm, and since I had my last bad luck, I have not spent twenty days, putting them all together, in Florence. I have until now been snaring thrushes with my own hands. I got up before day, prepared birdlime, went out with a bundle of cages on my back, so that I looked like Geta when he was returning from the harbor with Amphitryon's books. I caught at least two thrushes and at most six. And so I did all September. Then this pastime, pitiful and strange as it is, gave out, to my displeasure. And of what sort my life is, I shall tell you.

I get up in the morning with the sun and go into a grove I am having cut down, where I remain two hours to look over the work of the past day and kill some time with the cutters, who have always some bad-luck story ready, about either themselves or their neighbors. And as to this grove I could tell you a thousand fine things that have happened to me, in dealing with Frosino da Panzano and others who wanted some of this firewood. And Frosino especially sent for a number of cords without saying a thing to me, and on payment he wanted to keep back from me ten lire, which he says he should have had from me four years ago, when he beat me at *cricca* at Antonio Guicciardini's. I raised the devil, and was going to prosecute as a thief the waggoner who came for the wood, but Giovanni Machiavelli came between us and got us to agree. Batista Guicciardini, Filippo Ginori, Tommaso del Bene and some other citizens, when that north wind was blowing, each ordered a cord from me. I made promises to all and sent one to Tommaso, which at Florence changed to half a cord, because it was piled up again by himself, his wife, his servant, his children, so that he looked like Gabburra when on Thursday with all his servants he cudgels an ox. Hence, having seen for whom there was profit, I told the others I had no more wood, and all of them were angry about it, and especially Batista, who counts this along with his misfortunes at Prato.

Leaving the grove, I go to a spring, and thence to my aviary. I have a book in my pocket, either Dante or Petrarch, or one of the lesser poets, such as Tibullus, Ovid, and the like. I read of their tender passions and their loves, remember mine, enjoy myself a while in that sort of dreaming. Then I move along the road to the inn; I speak with those who pass, ask news of their villages, learn various things, and note the various tastes and different fancies of men. In the course of these things comes the hour for dinner, where with my family I eat such food as this poor farm of mine and my tiny property allow. Having eaten, I go back to the inn; there is the host, usually a butcher, a miller, two furnace tenders. With these I sink into vulgarity for the whole day, playing at *cricca* and at trich-trach, and then these games bring on a thousand disputes and countless insults with offensive words, and usually we are fighting over a penny, and nevertheless we are heard shouting as far as San Casciano. So, involved in these trifles, I keep my brain from growing moldy, and satisfy the malice of this fate of mine, being glad to have her drive me along this road, to see if she will be ashamed of it.

On the coming of evening, I return to my house and enter my study; and at the door I take off the day's clothing, covered with mud and dust, and put on garments regal and courtly; and reclothed appropriately, I enter the ancient courts of ancient men, where, received by them with affection, I feed on that food which only is mine and which I was born for, where I am not ashamed to speak with them and to ask them the reason for their actions; and they in their kindness answer me; and for four hours of time I do not feel boredom, I forget every trouble, I do not dread poverty, I am not frightened by death; entirely I give myself over to them.

And because Dante says it does not produce knowledge when we hear but do not remember, I have noted everything in their conversation which has profited me, and have composed a little work *On Princedoms*, where I go as deeply as I can into considerations on this subject, debating what a princedom is, of what kinds they are, how they are gained, how they are kept, why they are lost. And if ever you can find any of my fantasies pleasing, this one should not displease you; and by a prince, and especially by a new prince, it ought to be welcomed. Hence I am dedicating it to His Magnificence Giuliano. Filippo Casavecchia has seen it; he can give you some account in part of the thing in itself and of the discussions I have had with him, though I am still enlarging and revising it.

You wish, Magnificent Ambassador, that I leave this life and come to enjoy yours with you. I shall do it in any case, but what tempts me now are certain affairs that within six weeks I shall finish. What makes me doubtful is that the Soderini we know so well are in the city, whom I should be obliged, on coming there, to visit and talk with. I should fear that on my return I could not hope to dismount at my house but should dismount at the prison, because though this government has mighty foundations and great security, yet it is new and therefore suspicious, and there is no lack of wiseacres who, to make a figure, like Pagolo Bertini, would place others at the dinner table and leave the reckoning to me. I beg you to rid me of this fear, and then I shall come within the time mentioned to visit you in any case.

I have talked with Filippo about this little work of mine that I have spoken of, whether it is good to give it or not to give it; and if it is good to give it, whether it would be good to take it myself, or whether I should send it there. Not giving it would make me fear that at the least Giuliano will not read it and that this rascal Ardinghelli will get himself honor from this latest work of mine. The giving of it is forced on me by the necessity that drives me, because I am using up my money, and I cannot remain as I am a long time without becoming despised through poverty. In addition, there is my wish that our present Medici lords will make use of me, even if they begin by making me roll a stone; because then if I could not gain their favor, I should complain of myself; and through this thing, if it were read, they would see that for the fifteen years while I have been studying the art of the state, I have not slept or been playing; and well may anybody be glad to get the services of one who at the expense of others has become full of experience. And of my honesty there should be no doubt, because having always preserved my honesty, I shall hardly now learn to break it; and he who has been honest and good for forty-three years, as I have, cannot change his nature; and as a witness to my honesty and goodness I have my poverty.

I should like, then, to have you also write me what you think best on this matter, and I give you my regards. Be happy.

Niccolò Machiavelli, in Florence

LETTER TO FRANCESCO VETTORI

Florence, 3 August, 1514

You, my friend, have with many accounts of your love at Rome kept me all rejoicing, and you have removed from my mind countless worries, through my reading and thinking of your pleasures and your angers, because one is not good without the other. And truly Fortune has brought me to a place where I can render you just recompense for it, because being at my farm I have encountered a creature so gracious, so delicate, so noble, both by nature and environment, that I cannot praise her so much or love her so much that she would not deserve more. I ought to tell you, as you did me, the beginning of this love, with what nets he took me, where he spread them, of what sort they were; and you would see that they were nets of gold, spread among flowers, woven by Venus, so pleasant and easy that though a villainous heart might have broken them, nonetheless I did not wish to, and for a bit I enjoyed myself in them, until the tender threads became hard and secured with knots beyond untying.

SOURCE: R. Clements and L. Levant, eds., *Renaissance Letters* (New York: New York University Press, 1976), p. 387.

And you should not believe that Love, in order to take me, has used ordinary methods, because knowing that they would not have been enough for him, he used extraordinary ones, of which I knew nothing, and from which I could not protect myself. May it be enough for you that, already near fifty years, neither do these suns harm me, nor do rough roads tire me, nor the dark hours of the night frighten me. Everything to me seems level, and to all her desires, even though unlike mine and opposed to what mine ought to be, I adapt myself. And though I seem to have entered into great labor, nevertheless I feel in it such sweetness, both through what the face so wonderful and soft brings me, and also through having laid aside the memory of all my troubles, that for anything in the world, being able to free myself, I would not wish it. I have abandoned, then, the thoughts of affairs that are great and serious; I do not any more take delight in reading ancient things or in discussing modern ones; they all are turned into soft conversations, for which I thank Venus and all Cyprus. So if it occurs to you to write anything about the lady, write it, and of the other things talk with those who estimate them higher and understand them better, because I never have found in them anything but harm, and in these of love always good and pleasure. Farewell.

Your Niccolò Machiavelli

✦ *Lorenzo de' Medici*

*L*orenzo the Magnificent (1449–1492) was the grandson of Cosimo de' Medici, who led the faction that took control of Florence in 1434. Lorenzo's father, Piero, managed the city for only five unstable years (1464–1469) before dying and passing the unofficial rule of the republic to his just 20-year-old son.

Lorenzo was a brilliant patron of the arts and a great friend to learned humanists. Pico della Mirandola, Marsilio Ficino, Sandro Botticelli, Michelangelo, and Angelo Poliziano were all part of the cultural entourage of the great Lorenzo. As a collector, Lorenzo was most interested in antique pieces and small objects of great value. He was also a fine vernacular poet himself, writing excellent verses with both a ribald content and great religious sensitivity.

In addition, Lorenzo was a consummate politician who succeeded in holding the republic and his faction together, despite difficult times. For example, he survived an attempt on his life during the Pazzi Conspiracy, in which the pope, Sixtus IV, plotted with the disaffected Florentine Pazzi family to murder Lorenzo and his brother Giuliano in church. The conspiracy failed, although Guiliano was killed, but war with the papacy and Naples resulted, a war that Lorenzo ended by sailing to Naples to convince King Alfonso to break his alliance with the pope. Such states-

manship and personal qualities of courage and humanity characterized Lorenzo the Magnificent.

At the time of his death, the Medici family's control of the city passed peacefully to his eldest son, Piero. However, Savonarola's power was growing rapidly in Florence, and the French invasion of 1494 and Piero's personal weakness led to the expulsion of the Medici in that year and the humiliation of Italy by the French.

SONG FOR DANCE

> O fair lasses, long around
> have I looked for my heart lost.
> But, O Love, I thank you most,
> for my heart I now have found.

> In this dance perhaps is she
> who did steal it from my breast:
> hers it is and will it be,
> while in me my life shall last:
> she's so kind and heaven-blest
> that she'll ever hold it bound.
> But, O Love, I thank you most,
> for my heart I now have found.

> O fair lasses, shall I say
> how my heart I now have found?
> When I knew it ran astray,
> I began to look around;
> soon two lovely eyes I met,
> where my heart was safe and sound.
> But, O Love, I thank you most,
> for my heart I now have found.

> Now that pain must this thief face,
> who did steal my heart like this?
> Oh, how fair and full of grace!
> How she brings love in her eyes!
> Her I never will release:
> let her heart burn, with mine abound.
> But, O Love, I thank you most,
> for my heart I now have found.

SOURCE: J. Tusiani, trans. and ed., *Italian Poets of the Renaissance* (Long Island, N.Y.: Baroque Press, 1971), pp. 68–69.

Bind, O Love, this thief indeed,
burn her with the thing she stole:
if she begs you, do not heed,
do not look at her at all;
let your darts and arrows fall
till my heart revenge has found.
But, O Love, I thank you most,
for my heart I now have found.

SONG OF GIRLS AND OF CICADAS

The Girls

We are women, as you see,
youthful lasses fair and gay,
and are seeking our delight
for this is Carnival day.
Envious people and Cicadas
much resent an alien glee;
so they vent their evil rancor,
the Cicadas that you see.
Most unfortunate are we!
The Cicadas' prey we are:
the whole summer chattering,
they still chatter the whole year:
and from those who do far worse
comes the worst of gossiping.

The Cicadas

O fair lasses, we but do
what within our nature is;
often, though, the fault is yours,
for it's you who tell all this.
One must act, but also know
how to hide one's happiness.
One who's quick can run away
from the peril of the word:
does it pay to make one die
in a long, long agony?
Without chattering too much,
act at once, while you still may.

SOURCE: J. Tusiani, trans. and ed., *Italian Poets of the Renaissance* (Long Island, N.Y.: Baroque Press, 1971), pp. 72–73.

The Girls

> What's the purpose of our beauty?
> It's worth nothing if it goes.
> Long live love and gentleness!
> Death to envy and Cicadas!
> Want to gossip? Very well:
> we shall act, and you will tell.

♦ *Johannes Burchardus*

LIFE IN PAPAL ROME DURING THE
REIGN OF ALEXANDER VI

Alexander and His Family

On Friday, the 20th of May, 1496, at six o'clock in the afternoon an entry was made into Rome through the Lateran gate by one Gofredo Borgia of Aragon, a son of the Pope, about fourteen years old and his wife, Sancia of Aragon, with about six ladies of her household. There went out to meet them the captain of the squadron with his men-at-arms, about two hundred of them, the suites of all the cardinals and the papal prelates. For every single cardinal had been requested that morning by papal runners at the instigation of Cesare to send their chaplains and men-at-arms to meet his brother Gofredo, upon his entry into the city. This they all did and dispatched their men as far as beyond the aforementioned gate, and here Lucretia Sforza, also a daughter of the Pope, and wife of Giovanni Sforza, Lord of Pesaro and sister of Gofredo met them with twelve other women. Two pages preceded her bearing two cloaks and riding on two horses one of which was covered with precious gold brocade, the other with crimson velvet. She greeted her brother and his wife with affection.

When we had come to the palace, the Pope went to the hall of the Pontiffs and sat down on an elevated seat that had been prepared for him there in the center of the left wall with a green carpet before it on which was depicted the Savior laying His fingers on the side of St. Thomas. Another similar carpet was laid over the seat. Eleven cardinals were standing around in their coats. We entered the hall through the three ordinary halls, the chamber of paraments, the Camera Papagalli and the others. Before the footstool of the Pope there stood a small stool on which lay a cushion of brocade, and before it four larger cushions of crimson velvet

SOURCE: J. Burchardus, *Pope Alexander VI and His Court*, ed. by F. L. Glase (New York: Brown, 1921), pp. 85–93, 154–155.

crosswise on the floor. Gofredo made obeisance to the Pope in the customary way and kissed his foot and hand. The Pope took the head of Gofredo between both his hands bowing his head over him but without kissing him. There followed Sancia, who in the same way kissed the foot and hand of the Pope and whose head he took in the same way between his hands. Also Lucretia was thus received by the Pope. After this Gofredo approached every cardinal beginning with Pallavicini and kissed their hands, whereupon each of them gave him a kiss upon the mouth. Sancia too kissed the hands of the cardinals and these took her head between their hands as if they wanted to kiss it. During this the daughter of the Pope stood before her father. Then Gofredo placed himself between the cardinals Sanseverino and Cesare Borgia, his brother. Lucretia sat down on a cushion on the floor at the right of the Pope, Sancia on another one at the left of the Pope, and the other ladies approached to kiss the papal foot. The Pope, Sancia and Lucretia exchanged together a few hilarious remarks.

After this Gofredo, Sancia, and Lucretia and all the others went away while the Pope remained in the hall, and in the same order as we had come we rode to the house of the former Cardinal della Porta, where Gofredo and Sancia found quarters and reception. At the entrance they thanked those who had escorted them in the proper way; then Gofredo, Sancia, and Lucretia entered, where they were greeted by many Roman ladies who were awaiting them there.

On Whitsunday, the 22nd of May, 1495, the Pope went to St. Peter's under the miter without the canopy and there Cardinal Cibo celebrated solemn mass in his presence. The sermon was preached by a Spaniard, a chaplain of the Bishop of Segorbe, who was rather wordy and wearisome, to the disgust of the Pope and all the others. He announced a full indulgence which the Pope granted from the beginning of the mass until he should be carried out again from the church. Lucretia and Sancia were standing on the marble staircase, on which the canonics usually sing the epistle and the Evangile, as well as many other ladies, and they occupied the whole stairway and the floor around it which aroused great disgust and scandal among us and the populace.

On Wednesday, the 14th of June, 1497, Cesare Borgia and Juan Borgia, Duke of Aragon, the Captain General of the guards, the favorite sons of the Pope, dined at the house of Donna Vanozza, their mother, who lived in the neighborhood of the Church of Saint Peter in Chains. Their mother and various other people were present at the dinner. After the meal, when night had fallen, Cesare urged his brother to return to the Apostolic palace. And so they both mounted the horses or mules with a few attendants, as they had not many servants with them, and rode together until they approached the neighborhood of the palace of the Vice-chancellor Ascanio Sforza, which the Pope had erected and usually occupied during his tenure of the office of Vice-chancellor.

At this point the duke declared that he would like to find entertainment somewhere and took leave of his brother, the Cardinal. He dismissed all his servants except one and retained further a masked man who had already presented himself before the dinner and had visited him in the Apostolic palace almost every day for a month. The duke took him up behind him on his mule and rode to the Square of the Jews, where he dismissed the one groom and sent him back to the palace. He instructed him, however, that he should wait for him about eight o'clock in the square, and if he had not appeared at the end of an hour he should return to the palace. Thereupon the duke departed from the groom with the masked man behind him on the back of the mule and rode no one knows whither and was murdered.

The corpse was thrown into the river at the point besides the fountain where the refuse of the streets is usually dumped into the water, near or beside the Hospital of Saint Hieronymus of the Slavonians on the road which runs from the Angel's Bridge straight to the Church of Santa Maria del Popolo. The groom who had been dismissed on the Square of the Jews was hurt seriously and wounded unto death. He was mercifully taken into the house of some one unknown to me and cared for. Unconscious as he was he could tell nothing about his instructions and the expedition of his master.

When the duke did not return to the palace on the next morning, which was Thursday, the 15th of June, his trusted servants became uneasy and one of them carried to the Pope the news of the late expedition of the duke and Cesare and the vain watch for the return of the former. The Pope was much disturbed at the news, but tried to persuade himself that the duke was enjoying himself somewhere with a girl and was embarrassed for that reason at leaving her house in broad daylight, and he clung to the hope that he might return at any rate in the evening. When this hope was not fulfilled, the Pope was stricken with deadly terror and set on foot all possible inquiries through a few of his trusted men.

Among those who were questioned was a Slavonian dealer in wood by the name of Giorgio, who had unloaded his wood on the bank of the Tiber near the above-mentioned fountain and who had spent the night on his boat guarding his wood to prevent it being stolen. The question was put to him whether he had seen anything thrown into the river during the middle of the night just past, to which he made answer that at about two o'clock in the morning two men came out of a lane by the hospital on to the public road along the river. They looked about cautiously to see whether any one was passing and when they did not see anybody they disappeared again in the lane. After a little while two others came out of the lane, looked about in the same way and made a sign to their companions when they discovered nobody. Thereupon a rider appeared on a white horse who had a corpse behind him with the head and arms hanging down on one side and the legs on the other and supported on both sides by the two men who had first appeared. The procession advanced to the place where the refuse is thrown into the river. At the bank they came to a halt and turned the horse with its tail to the river. Then they lifted the corpse, one holding it by its hands and arms, the other by the legs and feet, dragged it down from the horse and cast it with all their strength into the river.

To the question of the rider if it was safely in, they answered, "Yes, Sir!" Then the rider cast another look at the river and, seeing the cloak of the corpse floating on the water, asked his companions what that black thing was floating there. They answered, "the cloak," whereupon he threw stones at the garment to make it sink to the bottom. Then all five, including the other two who had kept watch and now rejoined the rider and his two companions, departed and took their way together through another lane that leads to the Hospital of Saint James.

The servants of the Pope asked Giorgio why he had lodged no information of such a crime with the governor of the city, to which he answered: "In my day I have seen as many as a hundred corpses thrown into the river at that place on different nights without anybody troubling himself about it, and so I attached no further importance to the circumstance."

After this fishermen and boatmen were summoned from all Rome and ordered to drag the corpse out of the river with the assurance of a large reward for their pains.

Three hundred fishermen and boatmen, as I have heard, came together and dragged the bed of the river, and finally brought up the corpse of a man. It was just before vespers when they found the duke still fully clad, with his stockings, shoes, coat, waistcoat and cloak, and in his belt there was his purse with thirty ducats. He had nine wounds, one in the neck through the throat, the other eight in the head, body and legs. The duke was laid in a boat and was carried into the castle of San Angelo, where his clothing was removed. The corpse was then washed and clothed in princely raiment. Everything was done at the order of my colleague, Bernardino Gutieri, cleric in charge of ceremonies.

On the evening of this day, at nine o'clock the corpse of the duke was brought by his noble retainers, if I remember rightly, from the castle of San Angelo to the church of Santa Maria del Popolo, preceded by 120 torchbearers and all the prelates of the palace, together with the papal servitors and pages. With loud lamentations and weeping they proceeded without any orderly formation. The corpse was borne upon a bier with pomp and ceremony in public view and looked more as if sleeping than dead. In the aforementioned church it was consigned to the vault, where it reposes up to the present day.

When the Pope was informed that the duke had been murdered and thrown into the river like refuse and there discovered, violent grief overcame him, and in his deep sorrow he locked himself in his chambers and wept bitterly. Only after long pleading, persuasion and solicitation before his door did the Cardinal Bartolommeo Marti finally succeed after several hours in being admitted with a few attendants. The Pope took no food or drink from the evening of Wednesday, the 14th of June, until the following Saturday, and he let no sleep come to his eyes from the morning of Thursday until the next Sunday. Upon varied and ceaseless appeals of his trusted friends he admitted himself to be won over and finally began to conquer his grief as well as he could. This he did also out of considerations for the risk and danger to his own person.

✦ ✦ ✦

On the following Monday two jugglers, to one of whom on horseback Donna Lucretia had given her new robe of brocade worn only once on the previous day and worth three hundred ducats, went through all the main streets and alleys of Rome with the loud cry: "Long live the noble Duchess of Ferrara, long live Pope Alexander! Long may they live." And then the other one on foot to whom Donna Lucretia had also given a robe went along with the same cry.

On Thursday, the 9th of September, 1501, there was hung at the wall of the Torre di Nona a woman who had stabbed her husband to death with a knife during the previous night.

On Saturday, the 25th of September, the Pope went early in the morning to Nepi, Civita Castellana, and to the other places in the neighborhood, and with him Cesare Borgia and the Cardinals Serra, Francesco and Ludovico Borgia with a small suite. Donna Lucretia remained in the chamber of the Pope in order to guard it and with the same orders as upon the previous absence of the Pope. He returned to Rome on Saturday, the 23rd of October, 1501.

On the evening of the last day of October, 1501, Cesare Borgia arranged a banquet in his chambers in the Vatican with fifty honest prostitutes, called courtesans, who danced after the dinner with the attendants and the others who were present, at first in their garments, then naked. After the dinner the candelabra with the burning candles were taken from the tables and placed on the floor, and chestnuts were strewn around, which the naked courtesans picked up, creeping on hands and knees between the chandeliers, while the Pope, Cesare, and his sister Lucretia looked on. Finally prizes were announced for those who could perform the act most often with the courtesans, such as tunics of silk, shoes, barrets, and other things.

On Monday, the 11th of November, 1501, there entered the city through the Porta Viridarii a peasant leading two mares laden with wood. When these arrived in the place of St. Peter the men of the Pope ran towards them and cut the saddle-bands and ropes, and throwing down the wood they led the mares to the small place that is inside the palace just behind the portal. There four stallions freed from reins and bridles were sent from the palace and they ran after the mares and with a great struggle and noise fighting with tooth and hoof jumped upon the mares and covered them, tearing and hurting them severely. The Pope stood together with Donna Lucretia under the window of the chamber above the portal of the palace and both looked down at what was going on there with loud laughter and much pleasure.

✦ *Giovanni Boccaccio*

TALE OF ANDREUCCIO

Andreuccio from Perugia, having gone to Naples to buy horses, is caught up in three unfortunate adventures in one night; escaping from them all, he returns home with a ruby.

There once was in Perugia, according to what I have been told, a young man whose name was Andreuccio di Pietro, a dealer in horses, who, when he heard that in Naples horses were being sold at a low price, put five hundred gold florins in his purse, and, though he had never been outside of his town before, set out for Naples with some other merchants and arrived there on Sunday evening around vespers, and at the advice of his landlord, the following morning he went to the market place, where he saw many horses, a good number of which he liked, but he was not able to strike a bargain no matter how hard he tried; in fact, to show that he was really ready to do business, being the crass and incautious fool that he was, more than once, in the presence of whoever came and went by, he would pull out his purse full of florins. While he was in the midst of these dealings, with his purse on full display, a young and very beautiful Sicilian lady—one who, for a small price, would be happy to please any man—passed close to him, and without being seen by him, she caught a glimpse of his purse and immediately said to herself:

"Who would be better off than I if that money were mine?"—and she walked on.

There was with this young lady an old woman, also Sicilian, who, when she saw Andreuccio, let her young companion walk ahead while she ran up to him and embraced him affectionately; when the young girl saw this, she said nothing, and waited nearby for her companion. Andreuc-

SOURCE: Giovanni Boccaccio, *The Decameron*, trans. and ed. by M. Musa and P. Bondanella (New York: Norton, 1977), pp. 37–47. Reprinted with the permission of W. W. Norton & Company.

cio turned around, recognized the old woman and greeted her with a great deal of pleasure, and after she had promised to visit him at his inn, they parted company without further conversation, and Andreuccio returned to his bargaining; but he bought nothing that morning.

The young woman, who had first seen Andreuccio's purse and then his familiarity with her older companion, cautiously began to ask who that man was and where he came from and what he was doing there and how her friend knew him, in order to try and see if she could find a way of getting that money of his—if not all of it, at least some of it. The old woman told her everything about Andreuccio almost as well as he himself might have done, for she had lived a long time in Sicily and then in Perugia with Andreuccio's father; she also told her where he was staying and why he had come. Once the young woman was completely informed about his relatives and their names, she devised a cunning trick, based on what she had learned, to satisfy her desires. As soon as she returned home, she sent the old woman on errands for the entire day so that she would not be able to return to Andreuccio; then, around vespers, she sent one of her young servant girls, whom she had well trained for such missions, to the inn where Andreuccio was staying. Arriving there, the servant girl found Andreuccio by chance alone at the door, and she asked him about Andreuccio's whereabouts; when he told her he was standing before her, drawing him aside, she said:

"Sir, a gentle lady who lives in this city would like to speak to you at your leisure."

When Andreuccio heard this, he immediately assumed, for he considered himself a handsome young man, that such a woman as that must be in love with him (as if no man as handsome as he could be found in all of Naples), and he replied immediately that he was ready and asked her where and when this lady wished to speak to him. To this, the young servant girl answered:

"Sir, whenever you wish to come, she awaits you at her home."

Quickly, and without mentioning anything to anyone at the inn, Andreuccio replied:

"Let's go, then, you lead the way; I'll follow you."

Whereupon the servant girl led him to her house which was in a district called the Malpertugio, which was as respectable a district as its own name implies.[1] But Andreuccio knew or suspected nothing, believing he was going to a most respectable place and to the house of a respectable woman, and so he calmly followed the servant girl into the house. Climbing up the stairs, the servant girl called to her mistress: "Here's Andreuccio!" and he saw her appear at the head of the stairs to greet him.

---

1. This ill-famed district of Naples actually existed in Boccaccio's day, and its name might best be rendered into English as "Evilhole."

She was still very young, tall, with a very beautiful face, and elegantly dressed and adorned. Andreuccio started toward her, and she descended three steps to greet him with open arms, and throwing her arms around his neck, she remained in that position for a while without saying a word—as if some overpowering emotion had stolen her words—then she started crying and kissing his forehead, and with a broken voice she said:

"Oh my Andreuccio, what a pleasure to welcome you!"

Andreuccio, amazed at such tender greetings, and completely astonished, replied:

"My lady, the pleasure is mine!"

Then, she took his hand and led him through her sitting room, and from there, without saying a word, into her bedchamber, which was all scented with roses, orange blossoms, and other fragrances; and he saw there a most beautiful curtained bed, and many dresses hanging on pegs (as was the custom there), and other very beautiful and expensive things. And, since all those lovely things were new to him, Andreuccio was convinced that she had to be nothing less than a great lady. They sat together on a chest at the foot of her bed, and she began speaking to him:

"Andreuccio, I am quite sure that you are amazed at my tears and caresses, for perhaps you do not know me or do not remember hearing of me; but you are about to hear something that will amaze you even more: I am your sister! And, now that God has granted me the favor of seeing one of my brothers before I die (Oh, how I wish I could see them all!), I assure you I shall pass away content. Since you know nothing about this, I shall tell you. Pietro, your father and mine, as I think you probably know, resided for a long time in Palermo, and because of his kindness and friendliness, he was dearly loved and still is loved by those who knew him; but among those who loved him very much, my mother, who was a lady of noble birth and then a widow, was the one who loved him the most, so much so that she put aside the fear of her father and brothers and her own honor and lived with him in so intimate a way that I was born, and here I am as you see me. Then when Pietro had to leave Palermo and return to Perugia, he left me, a tiny child, with my mother, and as far as I know, he never thought of me or my mother again: if he were not my father, I would criticize him severely for his ingratitude towards my mother (to say nothing of the love he owed me, his daughter, not born from any servant girl or from some woman of low birth), who had put herself, as well as her possessions, into his hands, moved by a true love for a man she did not really know.

"But what does it matter? Things done badly in the past are more easily criticized than amended—that's how it all ended. He abandoned me as a little girl in Palermo where, grown up almost as much as I am now, my mother, who was a rich lady, gave me as a wife to a rich man of noble birth from Agrigento who, out of his love for me and my mother, came to live in Palermo: and there, as he was an avid supporter of the

Guelfs, he began to carry on some kind of intrigue with our King Charles.[2] But King Frederick[3] discovered the plot before it could be put into effect, and this was the cause of our fleeing from Sicily—and just when I was about to become the greatest lady ever to be on that island. Taking with us those few things we could (I say "few" as compared to the many things we owned), we abandoned our lands and palaces and took refuge in this land, where we found King Charles so grateful to us that he restored in part the losses which we had suffered on his account, and he gave us property and houses, and he continues to provide my husband, who is your brother-in-law, with a good salary, as you can see for yourself; and so, my sweet brother, here I am, and with no thanks to you but rather through the mercy of God I have come to meet you."

And when she had said all this, she embraced him once more, and continuing to weep tenderly, she kissed his forehead. Hearing this fable so carefully and skillfully told by the young lady who never hesitated over a word or fumbled in any way, Andreuccio recalled that it was indeed true that his father had been in Palermo, and since he himself knew the ways of young men who easily fall in love when they are young and since he had just witnessed the piteous tears, the embraces, and the pure kisses of this young lady, he took everything she said to be the absolute truth; and, when she had finished speaking, he said:

"My lady, it should not be surprising to you if I am amazed; for to tell the truth, either my father never spoke of you and your mother, or, if he did, I never heard a word about it, for I had no more knowledge of you than if you never existed; but I am all the more delighted to have found a sister, for I am completely alone here, and I never hoped for such a thing, and, truly, I don't know of any man of whatever rank or station to whom you would not be very dear, not to mention an insignificant merchant like me. But I beg you to clarify one thing for me: how did you know I was here?"

To this she answered:

"I was told about it this morning by a poor woman whom I often see, and according to her story, she was with our father for a long time both in Palermo and in Perugia; and if it were not for the fact that it seemed to me more proper for you to come to my house than for me to visit you in a stranger's house, I would have come to see you much sooner."

Then, she began to ask about all his relatives individually by name, and Andreuccio replied to all her questions about them; and her questions

---

2. A reference to Charles of Anjou, King of Naples from 1285 until 1309. The ruling family to which he belonged lost Sicily during the popular uprising known as the Sicilian Vespers, in 1282.

3. King Frederick II of Aragon, king of Sicily from 1296 until 1337.

made him believe even more of what he should not have believed at all. They talked for a long time and it was a hot day, so she had Greek wine and sweets served to Andreuccio; then it was supper time, and Andreuccio got up to leave, but the lady would not hear of this, and pretending to get angry, she said as she embraced him:

"Alas, poor me! How clearly I see that you care very little for me! How is it possible? Here you are with a sister of yours that you have never seen before, and she is in her own house, where you ought to be lodging, and you want to leave her, to eat at some inn? You shall certainly dine with me, and though my husband is not here (a fact which displeases me a great deal) I shall honor you as best a woman can."

Not knowing what to say to this, Andreuccio replied:

"I hold you as dear as one can hold a sister, but if I don't leave, they'll wait all evening for me to come to supper and I'll make a bad impression."

And she said:

"God be praised! As if I did not have anyone to send to tell them not to wait for you! But you would do me an even greater courtesy by inviting all of your companions to have supper here and then, if you still wished to leave, you could all leave together."

Andreuccio replied that he did not want to be with his companions that evening, and that he would stay as she wished. Then, she pretended to send someone to notify the inn that he should not be expected for supper; and, after much conversation, they finally sat down to supper and were served a number of splendid courses, and she cleverly prolonged the supper until night came; and when they got up from the table and Andreuccio decided to leave, she said that she would not permit it under any circumstances, for Naples was not the kind of town to wander around in at night, especially if you are a stranger, and furthermore, she said that when she sent the message telling them not to expect him for supper, she also told them not to expect him back that night. Since he believed everything she said and enjoyed being with her, because of his false belief, he decided to stay with her. After supper, and not without her reasons, she kept him engaged in a lengthy conversation; and when a good part of the night had passed, she left Andreuccio in her bedchamber in the company of a young boy who would assist him if he wanted anything, and she withdrew into another bedroom with her women servants.

The heat of the night was intense, and because of this and since he was alone, Andreuccio quickly stripped to his waist and took off his pants and placed them at the head of the bed; and then the natural need of having to deposit the superfluous load in his stomach beckoned him, so he asked the boy-servant where he should do it, and the boy pointed to a place in one corner of the bedroom and said: "Go in there."

Andreuccio entered without suspecting anything, and, by chance, he happened to place his foot upon a plank which was not nailed to the beam it rested on; this overturned the plank, and he, together with the plank, plunged down. But God loved him so much that He saved him from hurting himself in the fall, in spite of the height from which he fell; he was, however, completely covered by the filth that filled the place. In order for you to understand better what just took place and what is going to take place, I shall now describe to you the kind of place it was. Andreuccio was in a narrow alley like the kind we often see between two houses; some planks had been nailed on two beams placed between one house and the other, and there was a place to sit; and one of the planks which plunged with him to the bottom was precisely one of these two supporting planks.

Andreuccio, finding himself down there in the alley, to his great discomfort, began calling the boy, but as soon as the boy heard Andreuccio fall, he ran to tell the lady, and she rushed to Andreuccio's bedchamber and quickly checked to see if his clothes were still there. She found his clothes and with them his money, which he stupidly always carried with him, for he did not trust anyone; and when this woman of Palermo, pretending to be the sister of a Perugian, had gotten what she had set her trap for, she quickly locked the exit he had gone through when he fell, and she no longer was concerned about him.

When the boy did not answer, Andreuccio began to call him more loudly but that didn't help either; then he became suspicious, and began to realize (only too late) that he had been tricked. He climbed over a small wall which closed that alley from the street and ran to the door of the house which he recognized all too well, and there he shouted and shook and pounded on the door for a long time, but all in vain. Then, as one who sees clearly his misfortune, he began to sob, saying:

"Alas, poor me! I have lost five hundred florins and a sister and in so short a time!"

And after many such laments, he began all over again to beat on the door and to scream; and he kept this up for so long that many of the neighbors were awakened and forced out of bed by the disturbance; one of the lady's servants, appearing to be sleepy, came to the window and said in a complaining tone of voice: "Who's knocking down there?"

"Oh," said Andreuccio, "don't you recognize me? I am Andreuccio, brother of Madame Fiordaliso."[4]

To this the servant replied:

"My good man, if you've drunk too much, go sleep it off and come back in the morning; I don't know what Andreuccio you are talking about or any other nonsense: off with you, and let us sleep, if you please!"

"What," said Andreuccio, "you don't know what I'm talking about?

---

4. The irony of this shrewd prostitute's name, "Lily of the Valley," should not be overlooked, as it is a traditional symbol for nobility and chastity, both of which Andreuccio's "sister" lacked. The story, of course, abounds in such irony.

You've got to know; but if this is what it is like to be related in Sicily—that you forget your ties so quickly—then at least give me back the clothes I left up there, and in God's name I'll gladly be off!"

To this, in a laughing voice the woman replied:

"You must be dreaming, my good man!"

No sooner had she said this than she shut the window. Andreuccio, now most certain of his loss, was so vexed that his anger was turning to rage, and he decided to get back by force what he could not get back with words: he picked up a large stone and began all over again, but with harder blows than before, to beat furiously at the door, and many of the neighbors who had been aroused from their beds not long before thought that he was some sort of pest who had invented all this to bother that good lady, and so, they took offense at the racket he was making; they appeared at their windows, and began to shout in a way not unlike all the dogs in a neighborhood who bark at a stray:

"It's an outrage to come at this hour to a decent lady's house and shout such foul things. In God's name leave, good man; let us sleep, if you don't mind; if you have any business with her, come back tomorrow and don't bother us any more tonight."

The good woman's pimp, who was inside the house and whom Andreuccio had neither seen nor heard, taking courage from his neighbor's words, exclaimed in a horrible, ferocious, roaring voice:

"Who's down there?"

Andreuccio raised his head at the sound of that voice and saw someone who seemed, as far as he could tell, to be some big shot; he had a thick black beard and was yawning and rubbing his eyes as if he had just been awakened from a sound sleep. Andreuccio, not without fear, replied:

"I am the brother of the lady who lives here . . ."

But the man did not wait for Andreuccio to finish what he had to say; with a voice more menacing than the first time, he exclaimed:

"I don't know what's keeping me from coming down there and beating the shit out of you, you dumb ass, you drunk—you're not going to let anybody get any sleep tonight, are ya?"

He turned inside and banged the window shut. Some of the neighbors, who knew this man for what he was, said to Andreuccio in a kindly way:

"For God's sake, man, get out of here quick unless you want to stick around for your own murder tonight! For your own good, leave!"

Frightened by the voice and face of the man at the window and persuaded by the advice of the neighbors, who seemed kindly disposed toward him, Andreuccio, as sorrowful as anyone ever could be and despairing over the loss of his money, and not knowing which way to go, started moving in the direction that the servant girl had led him that day, as he tried to find his way back to the inn. Even *he* found the stench he was giving off disgusting; so, turning to the left, he took a street called Catalan Street and headed for the sea in order to wash himself off; but he was heading towards the upper part of town, and in so doing, he happened to see two men with lanterns in their hands coming in his direction, and fearing that they might be the police or other men who could do him harm, he cautiously took shelter in a hut he saw nearby. But the two men were headed for the very same spot and they, too, entered the hut; once inside, one of them put down the iron tools he was carrying and began examining them and discussing them with the other. All of a sudden, one of them remarked:

"What's going on here? That's the worst stink I've ever smelled!"

As he said this, he tilted his lantern up a bit and saw Andreuccio, the poor devil. Amazed, he asked:

"Who's there?"

Andreuccio did not utter a word; the two men drew closer with the light, and one of them asked him how he had become so filthy; Andreuccio told them every detail of what had happened to him. Having guessed where all this must have taken place, they said to each other:

"This guy really knows the head of the Mafia—he's been to Butta-fuoco's place!"[5]

Turning to Andreuccio, one of them said:

"My good man, you might have lost your money, but you still have God to thank for not going back into the house after you fell; if you had not fallen, you can be sure that before you fell asleep, you would have been murdered and, along with your money, you would have lost your life.[6] You have as fat a chance of getting a penny of your money back as you do of getting a snowball out of hell! You could even get killed if that guy finds out you ever said a word about it!"

After telling him this, he consulted with his companion for a while, then said:

"Look, we've taken pity on you, so, if you want to come with us and do what we plan to do, we're sure that your share of what we all get will be more than what you've lost."

---

5. Buttafuoco's name underlines his evil nature, since it means "fire belcher"; further-more, he is called a "scarabone" by the two men in the original Italian, meaning an important figure in the local criminal underworld, what is known today as the Camorra, a Neapolitan equivalent of the Sicilian Mafia.

6. Here, Boccaccio seems to be using Andreuccio's mishap to poke fun at a central tenet of Christian doctrine, the theory of the *felix culpa* or the "fortunate fall." In its proper context, the idea refers to the happy consequences of Adam's fall from grace and his expulsion from Paradise, for this original sin made possible Christ's salvation of the human race from sin. In Andreuccio's case, however, a man is supposed to thank God for having literally fallen into a cesspool, thereby avoiding an even greater evil—his murder. The agent of his salvation is no heaven-sent savior, but rather his natural need to relieve himself!

Andreuccio was so desperate that he said he was willing to go along. That day an archbishop of Naples named Messer Filippo Minutolo[7] had been buried and with him, the richest of vestments and a ruby on his finger which was worth more than five hundred gold florins; this is what they were out to get, and they let Andreuccio in on their plan. More avaricious than wise, he set off with them, and as they made their way towards the cathedral, Andreuccio stank so badly that one of them said:

"Can't we find some way for this guy to wash up a little, so that he doesn't stink so bad?"

The other answered:

"O.K. We're near a well that should have a pulley and a large bucket; let's go give him a quick washing."

When they reached the well, they discovered that the rope was there but the bucket had been removed; so they decided between themselves that they would tie Andreuccio to the rope and lower him into the well, and he could wash himself down there; then, when he was washed, he could tug on the rope and they would pull him up. And this is what they did. It happened that no sooner had they lowered him into the well than some police watchmen, who had been chasing someone else and were thirsty because of the heat, came to the well for a drink; when the two men saw the police heading for the well, they immediately fled without being seen.

Andreuccio, who had just cleaned himself up at the bottom of the well, gave a pull on the rope. The thirsty night watchmen had just laid down their shields, arms, and other gear and were beginning to pull up the rope, thinking that a bucket full of water was at the other end. When Andreuccio saw himself nearing the rim of the well, he dropped the rope and grabbed the edge with his two hands; when the night watchmen saw him, they were terrified and dropped the rope without saying a word and began to run as fast as they could. Andreuccio was very surprised at all this, and if he had not held on tightly, he would have fallen back to the bottom of the well and perhaps have hurt himself seriously or even killed himself; when he climbed out and discovered these weapons which he knew his companions had not brought with them, he became even more puzzled. Afraid, not understanding a thing, lamenting his misfortune, he decided to leave that spot without touching a thing; and off he went, not knowing where he was going.

But on his way, he ran into his two companions who were on their way back to pull him out of the well, and when they saw him, they were

---

7. As various scholars have demonstrated, much of this story refers both to real locations in Naples and to actual historical figures. The archbishop in question died on October 24, 1301, thus setting the tale in a period immediately preceding Boccaccio's birth.

amazed and asked him who had pulled him out of the well. Andreuccio replied that he did not know, and then he told them exactly what had happened and what he had discovered near the well. They then realized what had actually taken place and laughing, they told him why they had run away and who the people were who had pulled him up. And without any further conversation (for it was already midnight), they went to the cathedral and managed to get in without any trouble at all; they went up to the tomb which was very large and made of marble; with their iron bars, they raised up the heavy cover as far as was necessary for a man to get inside, and then they propped it up. And when this was done, one of them said:

"Who'll go inside?"

To this, the other replied:

"Not me!"

"Not me either," answered the other. "You go, Andreuccio."

"Not me," said Andreuccio.

Both of them turned toward Andreuccio and said:

"What do you mean, you won't go in? By God, if you don't, we'll beat your head in with one of these iron bars till you drop dead!"

This frightened Andreuccio, so he climbed in, and as he entered the tomb, he thought to himself:

"These guys are making me go into the tomb to cheat me: as soon as I give them everything that's inside and I am trying to get out of the tomb, they will take off with the goods and leave me with nothing!"

And so, he thought about protecting his own share from the start: he remembered the two men had talked about an expensive ring, so, as soon as he had climbed into the tomb, he took the ring from the archbishop's finger and placed it on his own; then, he handed out the bishop's staff, his miter, his gloves, and stripping him down to his shirt, he handed over everything to them, announcing, finally, that there was nothing left, but they insisted that the ring must be there and told him to look all over for it; but Andreuccio answered that he could not find it, and he kept them waiting there for some time while he pretended to search for it. The other two, on the other hand, were just as tricky as Andreuccio was trying to be, and at the right moment they pulled away the prop that held the cover up and fled, leaving Andreuccio trapped inside the tomb.

When Andreuccio heard this, you can imagine how he felt. He tried time and again, both with his head and his shoulders to raise the cover, but he labored in vain; overcome with despair, he fainted and fell upon the dead body of the archbishop (and anyone seeing the two of them there together would have had a hard time telling which one of them was really dead: he or the archbishop). Regaining consciousness, he began to sob bitterly, realizing that he being where he was, without any doubt one of two kinds of death awaited him: either he would die in the tomb from hunger and from the stench of the maggots on the dead body (that is, if no one came to open the tomb) or, if someone were to come and find him in the tomb, he would be hanged as a thief.

With this terrible thought in his head, and filled with grief, he heard people walking and talking in the church; they were people, it seemed to him, who had come to do what he and his companions had already done —this terrified him all the more! As soon as these people raised the cover of the tomb and propped it up, they began arguing about who should go in, and no one wanted to do so; then, after a long discussion, a priest said:

"Why are you afraid? Do you think he is going to eat you? The dead don't eat the living! I'll go inside myself."

After saying this, he leaned his chest against the rim of the tomb, then swung around and put his legs inside, and he was about to climb down when Andreuccio saw him and rose to his feet, grabbing the priest by one of his legs and pretending to pull him down. When the priest felt this, he let out a terrible scream and instantly jumped out of the tomb. This terrified all the others who, leaving the tomb open, began to flee as if a hundred thousand devils were chasing them.

Andreuccio, happy beyond all his hopes, jumped out of the tomb and left the church by the street from which he had come in. It was almost dawn, and he started wandering about with that ring on his finger until finally he reached the water front and stumbled upon his inn where he found that the innkeeper and his companions had been up all night worried about him.

He told them the story of what had happened to him, and the innkeeper advised him to leave Naples immediately; he did so at once and returned to Perugia, having invested his money in a ring when he had set out to buy horses.

THE POOR

PENSIONS FOR RETIRED EMPLOYEES

Moved by compassion for the poor, the lord priors . . . have been informed that Cristoforo di Ture, Tommaso di Giovanni of Savoy, and Giovanni di Ser Francesco of Ortignano were formerly employed as servants in the palace of the priors and worked there, Cristoforo for some ten years, Tommaso for eighteen years or thereabouts, and Giovanni for more than twenty-two years. And since they are now old and can no longer work, they were removed from their posts, and they have very little with which to sustain themselves. So, desiring to provide them with some charitable

SOURCE: G. Brucker, ed., *The Society of Renaissance Florence* (New York: Harper, 1991), pp. 229–239. Reprinted by permission of HarperCollins Publishers.

subsidy, [the priors] . . . have provided . . . that the treasurer of the
Commune . . . shall pay the sum of 5 lire per month to Cristoforo,
Tommaso, and Giovanni for the remainder of their lives. . . .

PLAGUE, FAMINE, AND CIVIL DISORDER

[June 8, 1383] Uberto di Schiatta Ridolfi, [speaking] for the [Sixteen] *gonfalonieri*, said that the officials in charge of the grain supply should be
instructed to lend to the poor up to four *staiora* [three bushels] of . . .
grain, according to the size of their families. Those who receive [the grain]
should be recorded as debtors of the Commune.

Master Giovanni di Master Ambrogio, [speaking] for the Twelve *buo-
nuomini*, said that the indigent should receive either bread or flour according to their needs, for the love of God. . . .

[July 1, 1383] Uberto di Schiatta Ridolfi, for the *gonfalonieri*, said that
the shortage of grain should be kept secret, and that a plentiful supply of
victuals should be made available by every means possible. And if this
cannot be arranged quickly, then forced loans should be levied on the
citizenry so that money is available. . . . And [the grain officials] should
be instructed to obtain grain for the market by breaking into the houses
of those [citizens] who are absent. And arrange for the baking of bread
marked with a sign, and give that only to the poor.

[June 15, 1417] Messer Lorenzo Ridolfi, speaking for both colleges, said
that . . . it is to be feared that the pestilence will become worse. The poor
are in a very bad condition, since they earn nothing, and in future they
will earn less. . . .

Antonio Alessandri said that on account of the plague which is imminent, it is necessary to provide for the preservation of our regime, keeping
in mind the measures which were taken at similar times in the past. First,
we should acknowledge our obligation to God, taking into account the
poverty of many [citizens], that is, by distributing alms to the needy and
indigent persons, appointing [for this task] men who are devoted to God
and who lead good lives, and not those who are active in the affairs of
state. But since not all are quiet, and in order to instill fear into some,
foot soldiers should be hired who are neither citizens nor residents of the
contado, and who will serve the needs of the Commune and not those of
private [citizens]. . . .

Marsilio di Vanni Vecchietti said that nothing will be more pleasing
to God than to help the needy and the poor who are dying of hunger. By
this means we will placate God so that he will remove this pestilence
from us. . . .

Messer Rinaldo Gianfigliazzi said that the poor should be subsidized
with public funds since they are dying of hunger. God will be pleased and

their evil thoughts will disappear. God should be placated with processions and prayers. . . .

Bartolomeo di Niccolò Valori said that the poor are not earning anything and they are dying like dogs. Many are in prison. . . . The poor who are sick should be helped, and God in his mercy will remove this plague from us.

Paolo di Francesco Biliotti said that up to 20,000 florins should be spent to succor the poor, and this will be most acceptable to God. . . . The rich should be willing to support the burdens of others and especially the poor, since it is not possible for the poor to help themselves. . . .

Buonaccorso di Neri Pitti said that the poor should be assisted so they can feed themselves. Those of our indigent citizens who are capable of doing evil should be hired [as soldiers] and sent to those places where troops are stationed, and their salaries should be increased.

APPEAL FOR TAX RELIEF

Lord priors of Florence! You should do something about the taxes which the poor people of Florence must pay, the forced loans and the extra levies. . . . If you don't do something, you will discover that no one in Florence will be able to save you. There will be an uprising if these forced loans and special levies are not reduced, for there is great privation here. People are living in misery since they earn little and prices have been so high for thirteen months and more. Just think about those who have three or four or five children, and who are assessed two or three florins, and who have to live from the labor of their hands and those of their wives. . . . How can they stay here and live? . . .

JUSTICE FOR THE POOR

Lord executor. Among the priors and the colleges, the rumor circulates that you are here at the behest of the magnates of Florence, and that you will not investigate any case involving them. It would have redounded more to your honor if you had not accepted the office, than to refuse to do what your honor requires. Many secret accusations have been delivered to you and you have done nothing about them. When those who have been offended have no other recourse, they have gone to the palace of the Signoria. . . .

There have been many executors here . . . and they have punished both magnates and *popolani*. There have been executors from Lombardy of the highest rank and they have punished the magnates who committed crimes, and they always favored the *popolani*. But it is widely believed that . . . you call witnesses who don't appear, and that you favor the magnates and the greater citizens. . . . Do your duty, lord executor, so that you will gain honor in a Commune such as ours, and so that in the future you will be acclaimed for the high reputation which you possess. . . . Do not besmirch your honor by listening to the petitions of private citizens. . . .

THE CONDEMNATION OF A LABOR ORGANIZER, 1345

. . . This is the inquisition which the lord captain [of the *popolo*] and his judge . . . have conducted . . . against Ciuto Brandini, of the parish of S. Piero Maggiore, a man of low condition and evil reputation. . . . Together with many others who were seduced by him, he planned to organize an association . . . of carders, combers, and other laborers in the woolen cloth industry, in the largest number possible. In order that they might have the means to congregate and to elect consuls and leaders of their association . . . he organized meetings on several occasions and on various days of many persons of lowly condition. And among other things done in these meetings, Ciuto ordered that there should be a collection of money from those who attended these assemblies. . . . [This was done] so that they would be stronger and more durable in this wicked organization, and so that they could accomplish the above-mentioned outrages and in order that—with arguments, force, and other means—they could oppose those citizens of good condition who wished to prevent Ciuto and the others in these assemblies from accomplishing those objectives, and their iniquitous thoughts, decisions, and activities.

Moving from bad to worse, he sought . . . to accomplish similar and even worse things, seeking always [to incite] noxious disorders, to the harm, opprobrium, danger, and destruction of the citizens of Florence, their persons and property, and of the stable regime of that city. And the above-mentioned illegal plots planned by him would have taken place, from which there would have arisen tumult, sedition, and disorder among the *popolani* and guildsmen of Florence, except that [Ciuto] was seized and detained by an official of the captain and his court. And the above-mentioned [acts] were committed and perpetrated in the present year and in the month of May in the city of Florence, in the church of S. Croce . . . and in the church of S. Maria de' Servi. [Ciuto confessed and was condemned to death on the gallows; the sentence was executed.]

THE DEMANDS OF THE CIOMPI, 1378

[July 21, 1378] When the *popolo* and the guildsmen had seized the palace [of the podestà], they sent a message to the Signoria . . . that they wished to make certain demands by means of petitions, which were just and reasonable. . . . They said that, for the peace and repose of the city, they wanted certain things which they had decided among themselves . . . and they begged the priors to have them read, and then to deliberate on them, and to present them to their colleges. . . .

The first chapter [of the petition] stated that the Lana guild would no longer have a [police] official of the guild. Another was that the combers, carders, trimmers, washers, and other cloth workers would have their own [guild] consuls, and would no longer be subject to the Lana guild. Another chapter [stated that] the Commune's funded debt would no longer pay interest, but the capital would be restored [to the shareholders] within twelve years. . . . Another chapter was that all outlaws and those who had been condemned by the Commune . . . except rebels and traitors would be pardoned. Moreover, all penalties involving a loss of a limb would be cancelled, and those who were condemned would pay a money fine. . . . Furthermore, for two years none of the poor people could be prosecuted for debts of 50 florins or less. For a period of six months, no forced loans were to be levied. . . . And within that six months' period, a schedule for levying direct taxes [*estimo*] was to be compiled. . . .

The *popolo* entered the palace and [the podestà] departed, without any harm being done to him. They ascended the bell tower and placed there the emblem of the blacksmiths' guild, that is, the tongs. Then the banners of the other guilds, both great and small, were unfurled from the windows of the [palace of] the podestà, and also the standard of justice, but there was no flag of the Lana guild. Those inside the palace threw out and burned . . . every document which they found. And they remained there, all that day and night, in honor of God. Both rich and poor were there, each one to protect the standard of his guild.

The next morning the *popolo* brought the standard of justice from the palace and they marched, all armed, to the Piazza della Signoria, shouting: "Long live the *popolo minuto!*" . . . Then they began to cry "that the Signoria should leave, and if they didn't wish to depart, they would be taken to their homes." Into the piazza came a certain Michele di Lando, a wool-comber, who was the son of Monna Simona, who sold provisions to the prisoners in the Stinche . . . and he was seized and the standard of justice placed in his hands. . . . Then the *popolo* ordered the priors to abandon the palace. It was well furnished with supplies necessary [for defense] but they were frightened men and they left [the palace], which was the best course. Then the *popolo* entered, taking with them the standard of justice . . . and they entered all the rooms and they found many ropes which [the authorities] had bought to hang the poor people. . . . Several young men climbed the bell tower and rang the bells to signal the victory which they had won in seizing the palace, in God's honor. Then they decided to do everything necessary to fortify themselves and to liberate the *popolo minuto*. Then they acclaimed the wool-comber, Michele di Lando, as *signore* and standard-bearer of justice, and he was *signore* for two days. . . . Then [the *popolo*] decided to call other priors who would be good comrades and who would fill up the office of those priors who had been expelled. And so by acclamation, they named eight priors and the Twelve and the [Sixteen] standard-bearers. . . .

When they wished to convene a council, these priors called together the colleges and the consuls of the guilds. . . . This council enacted a decree that everyone who had been proscribed as a Ghibelline since 1357 was to be restored to Guelf status. . . . And this was done to give a part to more people, and so that each would be content, and each would have a share of the offices, and so that all of the citizens would be united. Thus poor men would have their due, for they have always borne the expenses [of government], and only the rich have profited.

. . . And they deliberated to expand the lower guilds, and where there had been fourteen, there would now be seventeen, and thus they would be stronger, and this was done. The first new guild comprised those who worked in the woolen industry: factors, brokers in wool and in thread, workers who were employed in the dye shops and the stretching sheds, menders, sorters, shearers, beaters, combers, and weavers. These were all banded together, some nine thousand men. . . . The second new guild was made up of dyers, washers, carders, and makers of combs. . . . In the third guild were menders, trimmers, stretchers, washers, shirtmakers, tailors, stocking-makers, and makers of flags. . . . So all together, the lower guilds increased by some thirteen thousand men.

The lord priors and the colleges decided to burn the old Communal scrutiny lists, and this was done. Then a new scrutiny was held. The Offices were divided as follows: the [seven] greater guilds had three priors; the fourteen [lower] guilds had another three, and the three new guilds had three priors. And so a new scrutiny was completed, which satisfied many who had never before had any share of the offices, and had always borne the expenses.

XI

The Late Italian Renaissance

※━━━◆━━━※

INTRODUCTION

*I*taly became, after 1494, the battlefield of Europe in which the rival
claims of France, Spain, and the Holy Roman Empire competed for
supremacy. Charles VIII's invasion began a series of wars that disrupted
the carefully arranged balance of power among the Italian states determined in the middle of the century (the Peace of Lodi 1454). Before the
greater resources of large northern dynastic kingdoms, the city-states of
Italy collapsed and fell under foreign domination or retreated from
dynamic policies. Spain captured all of southern Italy and Sicily by 1504;
France and Spain fought for Milan, which moved from one foreign power
to the other until it finally fell to the Spanish Habsburg Emperor Charles
V in 1535; Venice was soundly defeated by a northern alliance led
by Emperor Maximilian in 1509 and lost almost all its mainland territory for a time; Florence was returned to the Medici in 1512 by a
Spanish army working for Pope Leo X (Lorenzo the Magnificent's son,
Giovanni); France occupied Piedmont and Savoy after 1535; and in
1527, the terrible sack of Rome by imperial troops took place, which
made Pope Clement VII a creature of the Habsburgs and destroyed
much of the legacy of Renaissance rebuilding begun a century
before. In 1559, most of these victories of the Habsburgs were
codified in the Treaty of Cateau-Cambresis, by which France acknowledged imperial hegemony in the peninsula, leaving Venice the
only major independent Italian state, although Florence, now ruled
by hereditary Medici Grand Dukes of Tuscany, would soon throw
off the imperial protectorate and sustain a measure of independence
as well.

379

It was in this environment that Italian humanists, artists, and writers worked at the beginning of the sixteenth century. Much of the confidence and optimism reflected in the belief that man was the measure of all things and that man could do anything if he but willed was shattered by the total failure of the apparently more civilized Italians to thwart the ambitions of the northern "barbarians," as Machiavelli termed them. Brute force seemed to be victorious over reason and compromise; villany defeated virtue; and human nature had proved itself not almost divine and prejudiced toward the good, but rather vicious, petty, self-seeking, and cowardly. In other words, many of the elemental precepts of classical humanism had to be reevaluated in the context of the reality of the Italian situation after 1494.

Cynicism and unsentimental realism were the characteristics of political observers like Guicciardini, who was an active participant in many of the cataclysmic events of the day. A new search for rules and order, heavily influenced by the still-rigid class structure of the northern monarchies now dominating the peninsula, resulted in a closing of the Italian social structure, making texts like Della Casa's Galateo *necessary; artists became increasingly courtiers attached to the service of princes and aware of the political and social circumstances of their times.*

Italian Renaissance society therefore became more aristocratic, mannered, ordered, and pessimistic. Great art was still created (Michelangelo lived to 1564), and classical scholarship continued, as did the writing of literature. However, the mood was very different. Italy not only had lost much of its political independence, but also was in the process of losing much of its economic vitality, with formerly republican patrician families in cities like Florence taking money out of trade and investing in landed estates to sustain an aristocratic style of life now expected of the titled courtiers surrounding the Medici dukes. Similarly, Venetian patricians lost much of their economic nerve after the victories of the Turks in the second half of the fifteenth and through much of the sixteenth centuries (the Turkish onslaught in the Mediterranean was not really stopped until Lepanto in 1571). The Venetians, too, withdrew to country estates in the terrafirma and began to spend heavily in conspicuous consumption to sustain privileged pleasure at the expense of risky trade. And, of course, in 1517 the Lutheran revolt began the Protestant Reformation, shattering forever the unity of the faith and heaping northern opprobrium on Rome and the papacy in addition to reducing its income. The Italian Renaissance, then, did not simply end with the sack of Rome, but it did change in character as a consequence of the same forces that were the cause of that horrible event.

✦ *Francesco Guicciardini*

*F*rancesco Guicciardini (1483–1540) was born into a patrician family in Florence. He was educated in the best humanist traditions and began early to serve the republic. He was advanced in office by the Medici after their restoration in 1512, but soon he went into the papal service under Leo X (Giovanni de' Medici, Lorenzo's son), assuming the office of papal governor of the territories of Modena (1516), Reggio (1517), Parma (1519), and the Romagna (1524). Moreover, as a papal counselor in 1527, Guicciardini must bear some of the responsibility for giving Pope Clement VII the advice that led to the sack of Rome by imperial troops.

In 1530 he was returned to Florence to advise the young, unstable Duke of Florence, Alessandro de' Medici, which he did, despite the young man's unsuitability to govern, and after the Duke's assassination in 1537, Guicciardini expected to continue in the same role with his successor, the 17-year-old Cosimo de' Medici.

The young Cosimo did not want Guicciardini to restrict his authority, however, and the adviser was left without an appointment. This enforced leisure resulted, like Machiavelli's, in the production of some of the most significant works of the century. Guicciardini's celebrated History of Italy discussed the course of Italian affairs beginning with the invasion of the peninsula by Charles VIII in 1494. As a work of history, this text ranks among the greatest of any period. Insightful, carefully researched, and balanced, the History is a classic example of historical scholarship. Also, Guicciardini collected the Ricordi, or maxims, that he had written down during his long and distinguished career close to the important events of the age. These maxims concern a wide variety of subjects, but the study of human nature, politics, and power dominates them, as is appropriate for a humanist politican involved in Italian events in the first decades of the sixteenth century.

SELECTIONS FROM *MAXIMS AND REFLECTIONS*

4. If princes take little account of their servants and scorn them or push them aside for the slightest reason whenever they please, why should a lord be offended or complain when his ministers—provided they do not fall short of their debts of loyalty and honor—leave him or take up with those parties that better serve their interests?

SOURCE: Francesco Guicciardini, *Maxims and Reflections*, trans. by M. Domandi (Philadelphia: University of Pennsylvania Press, 1972), pp. 42–68, 88–89. Reprinted with permission of University of Pennsylvania Press.

5. If men were respectful or grateful enough, it would be the duty of a master to benefit his servants on every occasion, as much as he could. But experience shows—and I have seen this to be the case with my own servants—that as soon as they get their fill, or as soon as the master is unable to treat them as generously as he has in the past, they leave him flat. Thus, to best serve his own interests, a master must be tight-fisted, more readily inclined to be stingy rather than liberal. He must retain their allegiance with hopes rather than deeds. Now, for that to be successful, he must occasionally be very generous to just one of them; and that is enough. For the nature of men is such that hope, as a rule, is stronger than fear. They are more excited and pleased by the sight of one man well rewarded than they are frightened by seeing many men treated poorly.

6. It is a great error to speak of the things of this world absolutely and indiscriminately and to deal with them, as it were, by the book. In nearly all things one must make distinctions and exceptions because of differences in their circumstances. These circumstances are not covered by one and the same rule. Nor can these distinctions and exceptions be found written in books. They must be taught by discretion.

7. Unless you are forced by necessity, be careful in your conversations never to say anything which, if repeated, might displease others. For often, at times and in ways you could never foresee, those words may do you great harm. In this matter, I warn you, be very careful. Even prudent men go wrong here, and it is difficult not to. But if the difficulty is great, so much greater is the reward for him who knows how to do it.

8. If either necessity or contempt induces you to speak ill of another, at least be careful to say things that will offend only him. For instance, if you want to insult a particular person, do not speak ill of his country, his family, or his relatives. It is great folly to offend many if you only want to insult one man.

9. Read these *Ricordi* often, and ponder them well. For it is easier to know and understand them than to put them into practice. But this too becomes easier if you grow so accustomed to them that they are always fresh in your memory.

10. Let no one trust so much in native intelligence that he believes it to be sufficient without the help of experience. No matter what his natural endowments, any man who has been in a position of responsibility will admit that experience attains many things which natural gifts alone could never attain.

11. Do not let the ingratitude of many men deter you from doing good to others. To do good without ulterior motive is a generous and almost divine thing in itself. Moreover, while doing good, you may come across someone so grateful that he makes up for all the ingratitude of others.

12. In every nation, we find nearly all the same or similar proverbs, expressed in different words. The reason is that these proverbs are born of experience, or observation of things; and that is the same, or at least similar, everywhere.

13. If you want to know what the thoughts of tyrants are, read in Cornelius Tacitus the last conversations of the dying Augustus with Tiberius.

14. Nothing is more precious than friends; therefore, lose no opportunity to make them. Men will always get together to talk; and friends can help, and enemies can harm you, in times and places you would never have expected.

15. Like all men, I have pursued honor and profit. And often, I got more than I had wished or hoped. But I never found in them the satisfaction I had anticipated. A powerful reason, if it be well considered, for men to lessen their vain cupidity.

16. Power and position are generally sought, because everything that is beautiful and good about them appears externally, emblazoned on their superficies. But the bother, the toil, the troubles, and the dangers lie hidden and unseen. If these were as obvious as the good things, there would be no reason to seek power and position, except one: the more men are honored, revered, and adored, the more they seem to approach and become similar to God. And what man would not want to resemble Him?

17. Do not believe those who say they have voluntarily relinquished power and position for love of peace and quiet. Nearly always, their reason was either levity or necessity. Experience shows that, as soon as they are offered a chance to return to the former life, they leave behind their much vaunted peace and quiet, and seize it with the same fury that fire seizes dry or oily things.

18. Cornelius Tacitus teaches those who live under tyrants how to live and act prudently; just as he teaches tyrants ways to secure their tyranny.

19. Conspiracies cannot be hatched without the complicity of others, and for that reason they are extremely dangerous. For most men are either stupid or evil, and to take up with such people involves too great a risk.

♦ ♦ ♦

22. How often is it said: if only this had been done, that would have happened; or, if only that had not been done, this would not have happened. And yet, if it were possible to test such statements, we should see how false they are.

23. The future is so deceptive and subject to so many accidents, that very often even the wisest of men is fooled when he tries to predict it. If you look very closely at his prognostications, especially when they concern details—for often the general outcome is easier to guess—you will see little difference between them and the guesses of those who are considered less wise. Therefore, to give up a present good for fear of a future evil is, most of the time, madness—unless the evil is very certain, very near, or very great compared to the good. Otherwise, quite often a groundless fear will cause you to lose a good thing you could have kept.

24. Nothing is more fleeting than the memory of benefits received. Therefore, rely more on those whose circumstances do not permit them to fail you than on those whom you have favored. For often they will not remember the favors, or they will suppose them to have been smaller than they were, or they will even claim that you did them almost because you were obliged.

25. Be careful not to do anyone the sort of favor that cannot be done without at the same time displeasing others. For injured men do not forget offenses; in fact, they exaggerate them. Whereas the favored party will either forget or will deem the favor smaller than it was. Therefore, other things being equal, you lose a great deal more than you gain.

26. Men ought to pay a great deal more attention to substance and realities than to ceremonies. And yet it is incredible how easily people fall for kind, soft words. The reason is that everyone thinks he merits being highly esteemed, and therefore will be indignant if he thinks you are mindless of what he is sure he deserves.

27. If you have doubts about someone, your true and best security consists in having things so arranged that he cannot hurt you even if he wants to. For any security founded on the will and discretion of others is worthless, seeing how little goodness and faith is to be found in men.

28. I know of no one who loathes the ambition, the avarice, and the sensuality of the clergy more than I—both because each of these vices is hateful in itself and because each and all are hardly suited to those who profess to live a life dependent upon God. Furthermore, they are such contradictory vices that they cannot coexist in a subject unless he be very unusual indeed.

In spite of all this, the positions I have held under several popes have forced me, for my own good, to further their interests. Were it not for that, I should have loved Martin Luther as much as myself—not so that I might be free of the laws based on Christian religion as it is generally interpreted and understood; but to see this bunch of rascals get their just deserts, that is, to be either without vices or without authority.

29. I have said many times, and it is very true, that it was harder for the Florentines to achieve their small dominion than for the Venetians to achieve their large territorial gains. For the Florentines are in a region that knew many liberties, and these are very hard to extinguish. These provinces are very hard to conquer and, once conquered, are no less hard to keep. Besides, the Florentines have the Church nearby, which is strong and immortal. Though it sometimes seems to stagger, in the end it reaffirms its rights more strongly than ever. The Venetians have conquered lands accustomed to servitude, stubborn neither in defense nor in rebellion. And as neighbors they have had secular princes, whose lives and memories are not everlasting.

30. If you consider the matter carefully, you cannot deny that Fortune has great power over human affairs. We see these affairs constantly being affected by fortuitous circumstances that men could neither foresee nor avoid. Although cleverness and care may accomplish many things, they are nevertheless not enough. Man also needs good Fortune.

31. Even if you attribute everything to prudence and virtue and discount as much as possible the power of Fortune, you must at least admit that it is very important to be born or to live in a time that prizes highly the virtues and qualities in which you excel. Take the example of Fabius Maximus, whose great reputation resulted from his being by nature hesitant. He found himself in a war in which impetuosity was ruinous, whereas procrastination was useful. At another time, the opposite could have been true. His times needed his qualities, and that was his fortune. To be sure, if a man could change his nature to suit the conditions of the times, he would be much less dominated by Fortune. But that is most difficult, and perhaps even impossible.

32. Ambition is not a reprehensible quality, nor are ambitious men to be censured, if they seek glory through honorable and honest means. In fact,

it is they who produce great and excellent works. Those who lack this passion are cold spirits, inclined more toward laziness than activity. But ambition is pernicious and detestable when it has as its sole end power, as is generally the case with princes. And when they make it their goal, they will level conscience, honor, humanity, and everything else to attain it.

♦ ♦ ♦

34. All things whose end comes about not through violence but through gradual wearing away have a much longer life than you would at first suppose. We can see this in the example of a consumptive who is judged to be at his end but who lives on, not just for days, but for weeks and months. So, too, in a city that must be taken by siege, provisions last much longer than anyone would have thought.

35. How different theory is from practice! So many people understand things well but either do not remember or do not know how to put them into practice! The knowledge of such men is useless. It is like having a treasure stored in a chest without ever being able to take it out.

36. If you are seeking the favor of men, be careful never to give a flat refusal to anyone who makes a request of you. Rather you should give evasive answers, for it may happen that someone who asked for something will not need it later. Or else circumstances may arise that make your excuses seem convincing. Furthermore, many men are foolish and easily swayed by words. Even without doing what you could not or would not do, you can often leave a person well satisfied by answering him cleverly, whereas if you had refused him outright, he would dislike you no matter how things turned out subsequently.

37. Always deny what you don't want to be known, and always affirm what you want to be believed. For, though there be much—even conclusive—evidence to the contrary, a fervent affirmation or denial will often create at least some doubt in the mind of your listener.

38. Although the house of the Medici is powerful and has produced two popes, it is much harder for it to keep control of the Florentine state than it was for Cosimo,[1] a private citizen. Aside from his extraordinary ability,

---

1. Cosimo de' Medici (1389–1464) After a brief exile, Cosimo returned to Florence in 1434, defeated the powerful rival family of the Albizzi, and became the power behind the Florentine government. Though few changes were made in the organization of the state, Cosimo dominated election and voting lists, kept the favor of the public, and

Cosimo was aided by the conditions of his times. With the help of only a few men, he was able to take and keep control of the government, without displeasing the many, who did not yet know freedom. Indeed, in his day, the middle and lowest classes were able to better their conditions every time the strong quarreled, and every time a revolution took place.

Now that the people have had a taste of the Grand Council, however, it is no longer a matter of seizing or usurping power from the hands of four, six, ten, or twenty citizens, but from the entire people. And they are so attached to their liberty that there is no chance of having them forget it—not with all the kindness, with all the good government, or with all the recognition and exaltation of the people that the Medici or any other powers may attempt.

39. Our father had children of such excellent qualities that, in his day, he was considered the most fortunate parent in Florence. Even so, I have often thought that, all things considered, we were more trouble to him than we were solace. Think what must be the plight of those whose children are crazy, evil, or unfortunate.

40. It is a great thing to have authority. If you use it well, men will fear you even more than your powers warrant. Not knowing exactly the extent of your authority, they will quickly decide to yield rather than contest whether you can do what you threaten.

41. If men were wise and good, those in authority should certainly be gentle rather than severe with them. But since the majority of men are either not very good or not very wise, one must rely more on severity than on kindness. Whoever thinks otherwise is mistaken. Surely, anyone who can skillfully mix and blend the one with the other would produce the sweetest possible accord and harmony. But heaven endows few with such talents; perhaps no one.

42. Do not strive harder to gain favor than to keep your good reputation. When you lose your good reputation, you also lose good will, which is replaced by contempt. But the man who maintains his reputation will never lack friends, favor, and good will.

43. In my various administrative posts I have observed that when I wanted to bring about peace, civil accord, and the like, it was better, before stepping in, to let matters be debated thoroughly and for a long time. In

---

made other powerful families come to depend upon him. He enjoyed uncontested dominion until his death in 1464, when the city conferred upon him the title *Pater Patriae.*

the end, out of weariness, both sides would beg me to reconcile them. Thus, at their invitation, with good reputation, and without a single note of cupidity, I could accomplish what seemed impossible at first.

44. Do all you can to seem good, for that can be infinitely useful. But since false opinions do not last, it will be difficult to seem good for very long, if you are really not. My father once told me this.

45. He also used to say, in praise of thrift, that a ducat in your purse does you more credit than ten you have spent.

46. In my administrations I never liked cruelty or excessive punishments. Nor are they necessary. Except for certain cases that must serve as example, you can sufficiently maintain fear if you punish crimes with three quarters of the penalty, provided you make it a rule to punish all crimes.

47. Learning imposed on weak minds does not improve them, and it may ruin them. But when it is added to natural talent, it makes men perfect and almost divine.

48. Political power cannot be wielded according to the dictates of good conscience. If you consider its origin, you will always find it in violence —except in the case of republics within their territories, but not beyond. Not even the emperor is exempt from this rule; nor are the priests, whose violence is double, since they assault us with both temporal and spiritual arms.

49. Tell no one anything you want kept secret, for there are many things that move men to gossip. Some do it through foolishness, some for profit, others through vanity, to seem in the know. And if you unnecessarily told your secret to another, you need not be surprised if he does the same, since it matters less to him than to you that it be known.

50. Waste no time with revolutions that do not remove the causes of your complaints but that simply change the faces of those in charge. For you will still remain dissatisfied. To take an example: what good does it do to rid the Medici of Ser Giovanni da Poppi, if he is replaced by ser Bernardino da San Miniato,[2] a man of the same quality and caliber?

---

2. Ser Giovanni da Poppi was secretary to Lorenzo, duke of Urbino; Bernardino da San Miniato was Lorenzo's military chargé d'affaires in Genoa. Both men were, apparently, universally disliked.

51. In Florence, anyone who tries to overthrow the regime is very unwise, unless he do it out of necessity, or because he hopes to be head of the new government. For if the attempt should fail, he has endangered himself and all his possessions. And if it succeeds, he will gain only a fraction of what he had envisaged. What folly it is to play a game in which you can lose incomparably more than you can win. And what matters perhaps even more, once you have brought about your revolution, you will face a constant torment: the fear of a new revolution.

✦ ✦ ✦

60. A superior intellect is bestowed upon men only to make them unhappy and tormented. For it does nothing but produce in them greater turmoil and anxiety than there is in more limited men.

61. Men have different temperaments. Some are so full of hope that they count as certain what they do not yet have; others are so fearful that they do not count on anything not yet in their hands. I am closer to the second than the first. And men of my temperament will be less often deceived but will live with greater torment.

62. People generally—and inexperienced men always—are more easily moved by the hope of gain than by the danger of loss. And yet the contrary should be true, for the desire to keep is more natural than the desire to gain. The reason for the mistake is that, ordinarily, hope is stronger than fear. Men easily allay their fears, even when they are warranted; and hope, even when there is no hope.

63. We see that the old are more avaricious than the young. And yet the contrary should be true, for, having less time to live, they need less. The reason is said to be that the old are more timorous. But I don't believe it, for I see many of them who are more cruel, more lecherous—in thought if not in deed—and more afraid of death than the young. The reason, I believe, is that the longer a man lives, the more does he become accustomed to and fond of the things of this world. Thus, the old are more strongly attached to those things, and more easily moved by them.

106. Nothing in our civic life is more difficult than marrying off our daughters well. The reason is that all men think more of themselves than others do, and thus they begin to reach for heights which in fact they cannot attain. I have seen many fathers refuse matches which, after they had looked around, they would have accepted gratefully. Men should, therefore, measure accurately their own conditon as well as that of others, and not be led astray by a higher opinion of themselves than is warranted. I know all this well, though I do not know whether I shall use the

knowledge well. Nor do I know whether I shall fall into the common error of presuming more than I should. But neither ought this *ricordo* serve to disgust anyone so much that, like Francesco Vettori,[3] he give his daughters to the first man who asks for them.

107. Best of all is not to be born a subject.[4] But if it must be, then it is better to be the subject of a prince than of a republic. For a republic represses all its subjects and gives only its own citizens a share of power. A prince acts more equably towards all; the one is as much his subject as the other. Thus, everyone may hope to receive benefits and employment from him.

◆ ◆ ◆

109. The fruit of liberties and the end for which they were instituted is not government by everyone—for only the able and deserving should govern—but the observance of just laws and order, both of which are more secure in a republic than under the rule of one or few. And therein lies the difficulty that so troubles our city. Men are not satisfied to be free and secure: they also want to govern.

110. How wrong it is to cite the Romans at every turn. For any comparison to be valid, it would be necessary to have a city with conditions like theirs, and then to govern it according to their example. In the case of a city with different qualities, the comparison is as much out of order as it would be to expect a jackass to race like a horse.[5]

111. Common men find the variety of opinions that exists among lawyers quite reprehensible, without realizing that it proceeds not from any defect in the men but from the nature of the subject. General rules cannot possibly comprehend all particular cases. Often, specific cases cannot be decided on the basis of law, but must rather be dealt with by the opinions of men, which are not always in harmony. We see the same thing happen with doctors, philosophers, commercial arbitrators, and in the discourses of those who govern the state, among whom there is no less variety of judgment than among lawyers.

---

3. Francesco Vettori (1474–1539). Florentine diplomat and statesman, and intimate friend of G. and Machiavelli. His principal work was the *Storia d'Italia dal 1511 al 1527,* but he is far better known for his correspondence with Machiavelli.
4. By "subject" G. means here someone born in a state dominated by or dependent upon another state.
5. This *ricordo* seems to be aimed directly at Machiavelli.

112. Messer Antonio da Venafra used to say very rightly, "Put six or eight wise men together, and they become so many madmen." The reason is that whenever they disagree on any matter, they would rather argue than resolve it.

◆ ◆ ◆

137. If the harmful results of bad government were visible in detail, those who do not know how to govern would either try to learn or would willingly relinquish the government to able men. But the trouble is that men, and especially the common people, are too ignorant to understand the cause of disorders, and thus do not attribute them to the mistake that brought them about. Not recognizing how much harm is caused by unskilled leaders, they persevere in the error of doing themselves what they do not understand, or of letting themselves be governed by incompetents. From that is often born the ultimate ruin of a city.

◆ ◆ ◆

139. It is true that cities, like men, are mortal. But there is a difference. Men, being made of corruptible matter, will perish, even though they do nothing irregular. Cities do not perish from a defect in their substance, for that renews itself constantly. Rather they perish either because of bad fortune or because of bad government—that is to say, because of the imprudent measures taken by their rulers. Ruin through bad fortune alone is very rare. Being a vigorous body of such great resistance, it would take extraordinary and intense violence to destroy a city. The ruin of cities, then, is almost always caused by the mistakes of rulers. If a city were always well governed, it is possible that it would last forever, or at least have an incomparably longer life than has been the case hitherto.

140. To speak of the people is really to speak of a mad animal gorged with a thousand and one errors and confusions, devoid of taste, of pleasure, of stability.

141. You need not be surprised at our ignorance of things that happened in past ages, or of things that happen in the provinces and in far off places. If you think about it carefully, you will find we do not have any true information about the present or about the things that happen every day in our own city. Often there is such a dense cloud or a thick wall between the palace and the market place that the human eye is unable to penetrate it. When that is the case, the people will know as much about what the rulers are doing or the reason for doing it as they know about what is happening in India. And thus the world is easily filled with erroneous and idle opinions.

142. One of the greatest pieces of good fortune a man can have is the chance to make something he has done in his own interest appear to have been done for the common good. That was what made the enterprises of His Catholic Majesty so glorious. They were always undertaken for his own security or power, but often they would appear to be done either to strengthen the Christian faith or to defend the Church.

143. It seems to me that all historians without exception have erred in leaving out of their writings many facts well known to their contemporaries, simply because they presupposed everyone knew them. That is why we now lack information on so many points in Roman, Greek, and all other history. For instance, we lack information concerning the authority and diversity among magistrates, the constitution of government, the art of warfare, the size of cities, and many such things well known in the time of the writers and therefore omitted by them. They should have remembered that in time cities perish and the memory of things is lost, and that the sole purpose for writing history is to preserve the memories forever. Then they would have taken more care to write so that someone born in a far distant age would have all those things as much before his eyes as did those who were then present. That is indeed the aim of history.

✦ ✦ ✦

185. Men always praise the lavish spending, the generosity, and magnificence of others. But in their own lives the majority of men practice just the opposite. Therefore, measure your expenditures by your means and by the profit they may honestly and reasonably bring. And do not be swayed by the opinions and words of the mob or by the belief that you will gain praise and reputation among them. When all is said and done, they will not praise in others what they do not practice themselves.

✦ Giovanni Della Casa

Giovanni Della Casa (1503–1556) was born near Florence into a politically active and wealthy patrician family. He studied law at Bologna and continued his studies of classical literature at Padua, where he entered the literary community of Pietro Bembo. Having decided upon a literary career himself, he left for Rome in 1528, where he enjoyed the company of fashionable men of letters and led a life of sensual pleasure.

While in Rome he became an associate of Cardinal Farnese, nephew of Pope Paul III, who encouraged him to seek a career in the Church. In 1537 he took Holy Orders and soon after was appointed clerk of the

Apostolic Camera, the papal treasury. By 1541 he was living in Florence again as papal collector, taking advantage as well of the literary opportunities available in the city. Della Casa was then appointed Archbishop of Benevento in 1544 and Papal Nuncio to Venice, an extremely delicate position, given that he had to see to the implementation of the decrees coming from the Council of Trent. He also was instrumental in the foundation of the Venetian heresy tribunal in 1547 and was active in prosecuting heretics.

Della Casa returned to Rome in 1548, where he was largely responsible for the creation of the Index of Prohibited Books. The following year, however, saw his hopes for further advancement dashed with the death of Pope Paul and the election of Julius III, who was hostile to the officials of his predecessor. As a result, Della Casa lost his appointment as Nuncio and retired to a villa near Treviso, where from 1552 to 1555 he wrote much excellent poetry and Galateo.

The election of Paul IV in 1555 brought Della Casa to Rome once again as Secretary of State, although he was not named a cardinal, as he had hoped. He died in Rome in 1556.

SELECTIONS FROM *GALATEO*

[1]

In as much as you are now just starting that journey that is this earthly life which I, as you can see, have for the most part completed, and because I love you as much as I do, I have taken it upon myself to show you (as someone who has had experience) those places in which I fear you may easily either fail or fall, as you proceed through them, so that, if you follow my advice, you may stay on the right path towards the salvation of your soul as well as for the praise and honor of your distinguished and noble family. And since your tender age would not be capable of grasping more important or subtle teachings, I will save them for a more suitable time and start with what many others might perhaps consider frivolous, that is, how I believe one ought to behave when speaking or dealing with other people so as to be polite, pleasant, and well-mannered. If this is not a virtue, it is at least something very similar. And although liberality, courage, or generosity are without doubt far greater and more praiseworthy things than charm and manners, none the less, pleasant habits and decorous manners and words are perhaps no less useful to those who have them than a noble spirit and self-assurance are to others. This is so because everyone must deal with other men and speak to them every day; thus, good manners

SOURCE: Giovanni Della Casa, *Galateo*, trans. by K. Eisenbichler and K. Bartlett (Ottawa, Canada: Dovehouse, 1990), pp. 3–16. Reprinted by permission of Dovehouse Editions, Inc., Ottawa.

must also be practiced many times daily, whereas justice, fortitude, and the other greater and nobler virtues are called into service much more seldom. Generous and magnanimous persons are not called upon to put such virtues into practice on a daily basis; rather, no one could behave in this way very often. Similarly even men who are strong and courageous are rarely required to demonstrate their valor and virtue by their works. Thus, while the latter virtues easily surpass the former in greatness and weightiness, yet the qualities I speak of surpass the others in number and frequency. I could very easily, if it were appropriate, mention to you many men who, though not worthy of high praise in other things, nevertheless are or have been highly esteemed only by reason of their pleasant manner. Thus helped and sustained, they have attained high rank, leaving far behind those who were gifted with those nobler and more outstanding virtues which I mentioned earlier. And, just as pleasant and polite manners have the power to stimulate the benevolence of those with whom we live, rough and uncouth manners lead others to hate and disdain us.

For this reason, even though the laws have not decreed any penalty for unpleasant and rough manners (for this fault has been considered light—and in fact it is not grave), we see none the less that nature herself punishes us severely for it by depriving us of the company and benevolence of others. And just as great sins harm us greatly, these lighter faults are a nuisance and bother us often. Men fear wild beasts but have no fear of smaller animals such as mosquitoes or flies; still, because these insects are constant pests, men complain more often about them than about wild beasts. Similarly, most people hate unpleasant and bothersome people as much as, if not more than, evil ones.

Because of this no one will deny that knowing how to be gracious and pleasant in one's habits and manners is a very useful thing to whomever decides to live in cities and among men, rather than in desert wastes or hermit's cells. Moreover, the other virtues require greater resource, without which they amount to little or nothing, while these, quite on their own, are rich and powerful precisely because they involve nothing but words and gestures.

[2]

So that you may learn this lesson more easily, you must know that it will be to your advantage to temper and adapt your manners not according to your own choices but according to the pleasure of those with whom you are dealing and act accordingly. This you must do with moderation, for when someone delights too much in favoring someone else's wishes in conversation or in behavior he appears to be more of a buffoon or a jester, or perhaps, a flatterer, rather than a well-mannered gentleman. And, on the contrary, someone who does not give a thought to another's pleasure or displeasure is boorish, unmannered, and unattractive.

Therefore, our manners are considered pleasant when we take into consideration other people's pleasures and not our own. And if we try to distinguish between the things which generally please the majority of men and those which displease them we can easily discover what manners are to be shunned and what manners are to be selected for living in society.

Let us say, then, that every act which is disgusting to the senses, unappealing to human desire, and also every act that brings to mind unpleasant matters or whatever the intellect finds disgusting, is unpleasant and ought to be avoided.

[3]

Dirty, foul, repulsive or disgusting things are not to be done in the presence of others, nor should they even be mentioned. And not only is it unpleasant to do them or recall them, but it is also very bothersome to others even to bring them to mind with any kind of behavior.

Therefore, it is an indecent habit practiced by some people who, in full view of others, place their hands on whatever part of their body it pleases them. Similarly, it is not proper for a well-mannered gentleman to prepare to relieve his physical needs in the presence of others. Or, having taken care of his needs, to rearrange his clothing in their presence. And, in my opinion, when returning from nature's summons, he should not even wash his hands in front of decent company, because the reason for his washing implies something disgusting to their imaginations.

For the same reason it is not a proper habit when, as sometimes happens, one sees something disgusting on the road to turn to one's companions and point it out to them. Even less so should one offer something unpleasant to smell, as some insist on doing, placing it even under a companion's nose saying: "Now Sir, please smell how this stinks," when instead he should be saying: "Don't smell this because it stinks."

And just as these and similar actions disturb those senses which they affect, so grinding one's teeth, or whistling, or shrieking, or rubbing together rough stones, or scraping metal is unpleasant to the ear, and a man ought to abstain as much as possible from doing such things. Not only this, but he must avoid singing, especially solo, if his voice is out of tune and unharmonious. But few refrain from doing this; in fact it seems that whoever has the least natural talent for singing is the one who sings most often.

There are also some who cough or sneeze so loudly that they deafen everybody. And some who are so indiscreet in such actions that they spray those near them in the face.

You will also find the type who, when he yawns, howls and brays like an ass; or someone who opens his mouth wide as he begins to speak or carries on with his argument, producing thus a voice, or rather a noise, that a mute makes when he attempts to speak. And these vulgar manners are to be avoided because they are bothersome to the ear and to the eye.

Indeed, a well-mannered man ought to abstain from yawning too much because, besides the above-mentioned reasons, it seems that yawning is caused by boredom and regret, because whoever yawns would much rather be somewhere else and dislikes the company he is with, their conversation, and their activities. Certainly, even though a man is inclined to yawn at any time, it will not occur to him to do it if he is involved in some pleasure or thought; but when he is inactive and indolent he easily remembers to yawn. And so when someone else yawns in the presence of idle and carefree persons, everybody else will immediately start to yawn, as you may have seen many times, as if that person had reminded them of something which they would already have done themselves, had they thought of it first. And many times have I heard learned men say that in Latin the word for yawning is the same as that for lazy and careless. It is therefore advisable to avoid this habit which, as I have said, is unpleasant to the ear, the eyes, and the appetite, because by indulging in it we show that we are not pleased with our companions, and we also give a bad impression of ourselves, that is to say, that we have a drowsy and sleepy spirit which makes us little liked by those with whom we are dealing.

And when you have blown your nose you should not open your handkerchief and look inside, as if pearls or rubies might have descended from your brain. This is a disgusting habit which is not apt to make anyone love you, but rather, if someone loved you already, he is likely to stop there and then. The spirit in the Labyrinth, whoever he may have been, proves this: in order to cool the ardour of Messer Giovanni Boccaccio for a lady he did not know very well, he tells Boccaccio how she squats over ashes and coughs and spits up huge globs.

It is also an unsuitable habit to put one's nose over someone else's glass of wine or food to smell it. By the same token I would not want someone to smell even his own drink or food for fear that some things that men find disgusting may drop from his nose, even if it should not happen. And I would advise you not to offer your glass of wine to someone else after you have had your lips to it and tasted it, unless he were someone very close to you. And even less should you offer a pear or some other fruit into which you have bitten. Do not consider the above things to be of little importance, for even light blows can kill, if they are many.

♦ ♦ ♦

[5]

Now what do we think the bishop and his noble friends would have said to those we sometimes see who, totally oblivious like pigs with their snouts in the swill, never raise their faces nor their eyes, let alone their hands, from the food in front of them? or to those who eat or rather gulp down their food with both their cheeks puffed out as if they were blowing a trumpet or blowing on a fire? or to those who soil their hands nearly up to the elbows, and dirty their napkins worse than their toilet towels? Often they are not ashamed to use these same napkins to wipe away the sweat which, because of their hurry and their over-eating, drips and drops from their foreheads, their faces and from around their necks. They even use them to blow their noses whenever they feel like it. Truly, men like these are not worthy of being received, not just in the very elegant house of that noble bishop, but should even be banished from any place where there are well-mannered men. A well-mannered man must therefore take heed not to smear his fingers so much that his napkin is left soiled, for it is a disgusting thing to see. And even wiping one's fingers in the bread one is about to eat does not seem to be a polite habit.

The servants who wait on gentlemen's tables must not, under any circumstances, scratch their heads—or anything else—in front of their master when he is eating, nor place their hands on any part of the body which is kept covered, nor even appear to do so, as do some careless servants who hold them inside their shirt or keep them behind their backs hidden under their clothes. They must rather keep their hands in sight and out of suspicion, and keep them carefully washed and clean, with no sign of dirt anywhere upon them.

Those who serve the dishes of food and the drinks must diligently abstain during that entire time from spitting, coughing and, even more, from sneezing. Since in such actions suspicion of misconduct is just as disturbing to the diners as the certainty of it, so the servants must take care not to give their masters reason to suspect their actions, for in this case what may have taken place disturbs as much as what has taken place.

If you have placed a pear to cook by the fireplace, or roasted bread on the coals, you must not blow on it if it is covered with a few ashes, for the saying is that "there never was wind without rain." You must rather tap the dish gently, or by some other means brush off the ashes. You will not offer your handkerchief to anyone, even though it is fresh out of the laundry, because the man to whom you offer it may not know this and could then be disgusted by it.

When one speaks with someone, he should not get so close to the man that he breathes on his face, for you will find that many men do not like to smell someone else's breath, even though it may not have any bad odor to it. These and other such manners are unpleasant and should be avoided for, as I said above, they could bother some of the senses of those with whom we are dealing.

Let us now mention those manners which are not obnoxious to any of the senses in particular, but still offend the majority of persons when they are committed.

[6]

You must know that men naturally desire different and varied things: some want to satisfy their wrath, some their gluttony, others their sexual desires, others their avarice, and still others some other appetite. When dealing with other men, however, it does not seem that one asks, or could ask or desire, any of the above-mentioned things, in as much as these appetites are not evident in their manners of behavior or in their speech, but elsewhere. They therefore desire whatever can facilitate this act of social intercourse; and this appears to be kindness, honor, and pleasure, or some similar thing. For this reason one must not say or do anything which may give an indication that one holds the other person in little affection or harbors a low opinion of him. Thus, the habit of many people of falling asleep quite eagerly wherever a respectable group of persons is sitting in conversation appears to be impolite. By doing this, they show that they have a low opinion of the company and appreciate very little indeed both them and their discussion. Not to mention that whoever falls asleep, especially if he is in an uncomfortable position—which is inevitable—most of the time succumbs to the tendency to do something which is unpleasant to see or to hear. Very often he wakes up sweaty and slobbery.

For this same reason it appears to be a bothersome habit to get up where other persons are sitting in conversation and pace about the room. There are some who so fidget, writhe, stretch, and yawn, turning first to one side, then to the other, that it looks as if they have just caught the fever. These are obvious signs that they are unhappy with the company.

Those who occasionally pull a letter out of their pockets and read it act just as badly. Someone who pulls out his nail clippers and devotes himself to his manicure acts even worse, appearing to hold the company in no esteem at all and so tries to find some other amusement for himself in order to pass the time.

One must not indulge in the habits of some other men, such as humming to oneself, or tapping one's fingers, or moving one's leg to and fro, for they indicate that the person does not care for others.

In addition, one must not turn one's back to someone, nor hold one's leg so high that those parts covered up by clothing become visible, for these acts should not be done among persons one respects. However, it is true that if a gentleman did them among very close friends or in the presence of a friend of lower social rank he would show not arrogance but rather love and intimacy.

A man must stand erect and not lean against or over someone else. When he speaks he must not elbow others, as many are in the habit of doing with every sentence, saying: "Isn't that right? What do you say about that? What about Mr So-and-so?" all the while rubbing you with their elbows.

[7]

Everyone must dress well according to his status and age, because if he does otherwise it seems that he disdains other people. For this reason the people of Padua used to take offense when a Venetian gentleman would go about their city in a plain overcoat as if he thought he was in the country. Not only should clothing be of fine material, but a man must also try to adapt himself as much as he can to the sartorial style of other citizens and let custom guide him, even though it may seem to him to be less comfortable and attractive than previous fashions. If everyone in your town wears his hair short, you should not wear it long; and where other citizens wear a beard, you should not be clean shaven, for this is a way of contradicting others, and such contradictions, in your dealings with others, should be avoided unless they are necessary, as I will tell you later. This, more than any other bad habit, renders us despicable to most other persons. You should not, therefore, oppose common custom in these practices, but rather moderately adapt yourself to them, so that you will not be the only one in your neighborhood to wear a long gown down to your feet while everyone else wears a short one, just past the belt. It is like having a very pug face, that is to say, something against the general fashion of nature, so that everybody turns around to look at it. So it is also with those who do not dress according to the prevailing style but according to their own taste, with beautiful long hair, or with a very short-cropped beard or a clean-shaven face, or who wear caps, or great big hats in the German fashion. Everyone turns around to look at them and crowds around to see them, as one does, for example, with those people who seem ready to come to blows with everyone in their neighborhood.

Clothes must also fit well and suit the wearer, for men who wear rich and noble clothes that are so ill-made that they do not seem made for them indicate one of two things: either they have no conception that they could please or displease others, or they have no conception of what grace and measure are. With their manners these men then make their companions suspect that they have a low opinion of them, and so are ill-received by most groups and are not well liked.

[8]

There are others who are more than suspect, for they act and behave in such a manner that it is impossible to put up with them. They always cause delay, annoyance, and discomfort for everybody; they are never ready, never orderly, never satisfied. When everybody is ready to sit down at the table, for example, and the food is ready to be served, and everyone has washed his hands, they ask for pen and paper, or for a urinal, or complain that they missed their daily exercise and say: "It's still early. Surely you can wait a while. What's the hurry this morning?" and by being concerned so much with themselves and their own needs, totally oblivious of others, they hold up the entire company. Moreover, they want to have an advantage over others in all things; they want to sleep in the best beds, in the most beautiful rooms, and sit in the most comfortable chairs and take the place of honor, and expect to be served or seated before anyone else, and never like anything unless they themselves thought it up, turning up their noses at everything else, and think that others ought to wait for them before taking a meal, going out riding, playing a game, or being entertained.

Some other people are so touchy, contrary-minded, or strange that nothing can be done to please them. They always answer with a sour face, no matter what is said to them. They never cease yelling at or scolding their servants, and keep the entire company in constant misery. "Some fine hour you called me this morning! Look here how well you shined this shoe! And you didn't come to church with me! You ass, I don't know what's keeping me from punching you right in the snout!" All of these are unsuitable and rude manners which must be avoided like the plague. Even if a man were full of humility and had displayed such manners not out of malice but out of carelessness and bad habits, he would still be hated because his outward behavior would suggest he was haughty. For arrogance is nothing else but lack of respect for others, and, as I said at the beginning, everybody wishes to be respected even if he does not deserve it.

Not long ago there was in Rome a worthy man gifted with a sharp mind and profound learning and his name was Messer Ubaldino Bandinelli. This man used to say that whenever he came or went from the Vatican palace, although the streets were full of noble courtiers, prelates, and lords, and also of poor, or middle-class, or even low-class people, none the less he never thought he met anyone who was more or less worthy than he was. Undoubtedly there were few he could see that matched him, if we keep in mind his own virtue which truly was very great. However, in these matters men must not be judged in this way; rather, they must be weighed with the miller's scales, not those of the goldsmith. It is proper to accept them readily not for what they are truly worth but rather, as with money, for their stated value. Therefore, nothing must be done in front of those people we wish to please which denotes lordship rather than companionship. Every action of ours, instead, must imply reverence and respect towards the people in whose company we find ourselves.

For this reason, whatever is not worthy of blame at the proper time may be reprehensible in another context, or with other persons, such as speaking roughly to servants, or reprimanding them—as we mentioned above—or, worse still, beating them. Doing such things is a way of lording it over someone and exercising one's jurisdiction, which no one does in front of those one respects without shocking the company and ruining the conversation, especially if it is done at the dinner table, which should be a place for merriment and not indignation. Thus, Messer Currado Gianfigliazzi acted correctly when he did not prolong the discussion with his cook Chichibio so as not to trouble his guests, even though the servant deserved great punishment for having chosen to please his girl Brunetta rather than his lord. If Currado had made even less of a fuss, he would have been even more praiseworthy, for it was not right to threaten his servant and call upon the name of the Lord blasphemously, as he did.

Returning to our matter, however, I will say that it is not pleasant that someone should lose his temper at the table, no matter what happens. If he should become upset he should not show it nor give any indication of his anger, for the reason I have already mentioned, especially if you have strangers dining with you; you have called them to enjoy themselves and now you are causing them anxiety. When we see other people eat bitter, tart fruits our own mouths will pucker; similarly when we see someone else become upset, this will upset us as well.

[9]

Those people who want what is opposite to the wishes of most people are called contrary-minded, as the word itself shows; for contrary is a synomym for opposite. You can therefore easily judge on your own how useful being contrary is to those who want to have the affection and the love of other people, for it consists in being opposed to the pleasure of others and this tends to make enemies rather than friends. Those who wish to have the affection of others should always try to avoid this vice, for it produces neither pleasure not goodwill, but rather hatred and displeasure. On the contrary, if there is no danger of harm or shame, one should make other people's desires one's own, and do and say rather what others like to hear than what you yourself like.

One should not be either uncouth or awkward, but pleasant and friendly, for there is no difference between the myrtle and the butcher's-broom except that one is a cultivated plant and the other a wild one.

I want you to know that a man is considered pleasant if his manners conform to the common practices between friends, whereas someone who is eccentric will, in all situations, appear to be a stranger, that is, alien. On the contrary, men who are affable and polite will appear to have friends and acquaintances wherever they may be.

For this reason it is advisable to accustom oneself to greet, speak, and answer gracefully, and to treat everyone like a neighbor or a friend. Those who are never kind to anybody behave wrongly when they eagerly say no to everything, or appreciate no honor or kindness which is rendered to them. They are like foreigners and barbarians. They do not appreciate visitors, not do they like company; they do not enjoy witty remarks or pleasantries, and refuse all offers. If someone should say: "A short time back Messer So-and-so asked me to extend his greetings." They answer: "And what am I to do with his greetings?" Or if someone says: "Messer So-and-so asked how you were." They respond: "Let him come and take my pulse." These persons really deserve not to be well liked by others.

It is not fitting to be melancholy or distracted in the company of others. This may be accepted of people who have long pursued studies in the arts which, as I have heard, are called "liberal arts," but it should not, under any condition, be allowed of other people. Even those who are allowed such introspection would do well to withdraw from the company of others when they want to devote themselves to thinking.

✦ Giorgio Vasari

G iorgio Vasari (1511–1574) was born in Arezzo to humble parents, but he attracted the attention of the cardinal responsible for the education of the young Medici princes. Vasari was taught with them and studied painting with Michelangelo and Andrea del Sarto. His earlier close association with the Medici led to an invitation from Cardinal Ippolito de' Medici to travel to Rome. There he was able to study classical monuments and begin his long career as a painter and architect himself.

When the Medici were restored to Florence in 1527, Vasari accompanied them and consequently entered the Medici court, where he was to work between 1555 and 1572 as the virtually official artist of Duke Cosimo I. Very gifted and facile as a painter, architect, and cultural bureaucrat, Vasari impressed his style on the rule of Duke Cosimo I. He decorated the Palazzo Vecchio (the former Palazzo della Signoria, which the Medici Duke used as a private residence) for his master and designed the Uffizi to house the offices of the growing, centralized state. In addition, he painted altarpieces, portraits, and other significant works both in Florence and in Rome.

It is, however, as the author of the Lives of the Most Excellent Painters, Sculptors, and Architects (first published in 1550 and dedicated to Cosimo) that Vasari is most remembered today. He in many ways created the concept of art criticism and in so doing helped define the Renaissance itself. His humanism taught him that his biographies could serve as spurs to the development of excellence in the arts, and his belief in the improvement over time of artistic style gave rise to art history as a discipline.

SELECTIONS FROM THE LIVES OF THE ARTISTS

The Life of Raphael of Urbino, Painter and Architect, 1483–1520

With wonderful indulgence and generosity heaven sometimes showers upon a single person from its rich and inexhaustible treasures all the favors and precious gifts that are usually shared, over the years, among a

SOURCE: Giorgio Vasari, The Lives of the Artists, trans. by G. Bull (Harmondsworth, England: Penguin, 1965), pp. 284–287, 318–322. Reproduced by permission of Penguin Books Ltd.

great many people. This was clearly the case with Raphael Sanzio of Urbino, an artist as talented as he was gracious, who was endowed by nature with the goodness and modesty to be found in all those exceptional men whose gentle humanity is enhanced by an affable and pleasing manner, expressing itself in courteous behavior at all times and towards all persons.

Nature sent Raphael into the world after it had been vanquished by the art of Michelangelo and was ready, through Raphael, to be vanquished by character as well. Indeed, until Raphael most artists had in their temperament a touch of uncouthness and even madness that made them outlandish and eccentric; the dark shadows of vice were often more evident in their lives than the shining light of the virtues that can make men immortal. So nature had every reason to display in Raphael, in contrast, the finest qualities of mind accompanied by such grace, industry, looks, modesty, and excellence of character as would offset every defect, no matter how serious, and any vice, no matter how ugly. One can claim without fear of contradiction that artists as outstandingly gifted as Raphael are not simply men but, if it be allowed to say so, mortal gods, and that those who leave on earth an honored name in the annals of fame may also hope to enjoy in heaven a just reward for their work and talent.

Raphael was born in Urbino, a notable Italian city, on Good Friday in the year 1483, at three o'clock in the night. His father was Giovanni Santi, a mediocre painter but an intelligent man who knew how to set his children on the right path which, through bad fortune, he himself had not been shown when young. Giovanni also understood how important it was that children should be reared on the milk of their own mothers rather than of wet-nurses; and so he insisted that Raphael (the name he chose, very felicitously, for the baptism) should, being his first child (and as it happened his last), be suckled by his own mother and should be trained in childhood in the family ways at home rather than in the houses of peasants or common people with their less gentle, indeed, their rough manners and behavior. And as Raphael grew up Giovanni began to instruct him in painting, because he saw that the boy was attracted by the art and was very intelligent. So before many years passed Raphael came to be of great help to his father in the numerous works that Giovanni executed in the state of Urbino.

Eventually Raphael's kind and devoted father, knowing that his son could make little progress under him, resigned himself to placing him with Pietro Perugino who, as he had heard, was the most outstanding painter of the time.[1] He went, therefore, to Perugia, but he failed to find Perugino, and so to occupy his time usefully he started work on some paintings for San Francesco.

After Pietro had returned from Rome, Giovanni, who was a man of

---

1. Pietro Perugino (*c.* 1445/50–1523).

good breeding and manners, struck up a friendship with him, and when the time seemed ripe he told him what he wanted as tactfully as he could. Pietro who was also very courteous and a great admirer of talent agreed to take Raphael; and so Giovanni returned in high spirits to Urbino and then took the boy back with him to Perugia, not without many tears from his mother who loved him dearly. When Pietro saw how well Raphael could draw and what fine manners and character he had he formed a high opinion of him, which in time proved to be completely justified.

Is is very remarkable that, in studying Pietro's style, Raphael imitated his work so exactly in every detail that it was impossible to tell the difference between the copies he made and his master's originals. And it was also impossible to distinguish clearly between Raphael's own original works and Pietro's, as is evident from some figures that he painted in oils on a panel in San Francesco in Perugia for Maddalena degli Oddi; these represent the Assumption of Our Lady into heaven and her Coronation by Jesus Christ, and among them are the twelve apostles standing about the tomb of Our Lady and contemplating the celestial vision. At the foot of the panel, in a predella divided into three scenes, are some little figures enacting the Annunciation, with Our Lady and the angel, the Adoration of Christ by the Magi, and the Presentation in the Temple, where Simeon takes the Child in his arms. This work was executed with marvelous diligence, and anyone who is not an expert would swear that it was by Pietro and not, as it undoubtedly is, by Raphael.

After Pietro had gone to Florence on business, Raphael left Perugia in company with some friends for Città di Castello, where he painted a panel for Sant'Agostino in the same style as the picture he had just finished. For San Domenico he did a similar work, showing the crucifixion, and if his name were not written on it everyone would think it was by Pietro. For the church of San Francesco in the same city he painted a small panel picture of the Marriage of Our Lady which shows very forcefully the way his own style was improving as he surpassed the work of Pietro. This painting contains a temple in perspective drawn with great care and devotion and showing what amazingly difficult problems Raphael was ready to tackle.

The pictures he did in the style of Perugino brought Raphael considerable fame, and in the meanwhile it happened that Pope Pius II commissioned Pintoricchio to decorate the library of the cathedral at Siena; so being a friend of Raphael's and knowing his excellence as a draughtsman Pintoricchio took him to Siena, where he did some of the drawings and cartoons for the library.[2] The reason he left what he was doing unfinished was that while in Siena he heard some painters enthusiastically praising

---

2. Bernardino Pintoricchio (c. 1454–1513) left as his chief works fresco cycles in the Borgia Apartments at the Vatican and in the Piccolomini library at Siena.

the fine cartoon for the great hall that Leonardo had drawn in the Hall of the Pope at Florence and the nudes that Michelangelo Buonarroti had executed in rivalry with Leonardo, and with even better results. And so, because of his love of painting, Raphael became so anxious to see these works that he put aside what he was doing and, ignoring his own immediate interest, went off to Florence.

On his arrival the city pleased him as much as did the works of Leonardo and Michelangelo (which indeed came as a revelation to him) and he made up his mind to stay in Florence for some time. He became friendly with a group of painters including Ridolfo Ghirlandaio, Aristotile Sangallo, and others, and he was held in great respect in Florence, especially by Taddeo Taddei, who liked to see him always in his house or at his table, being a great admirer of talented men. In order not to be outdone in kindness Raphael, who was courtesy itself, painted for Taddei two pictures executed in his original style derived from Pietro but also in the manner he was then starting to adopt and which, as I shall explain, was far superior. (These pictures are still in the house belonging to Taddeo Taddei's heirs.) Raphael also became a close friend of Lorenzo Nasi, and as Lorenzo had just got married he painted for him a picture which showed Our Lady and between her legs the Christ-Child to whom a laughing St John is offering a bird, to the great joy and delight of them both. The children are shown in an attitude of youthful simplicity, which is lovely to see, and, moreover, the figures are so well colored and finished so meticulously that they seem to be made of living flesh rather than paint. Our Lady as well seems truly full of grace and divinity; and lastly, the foreground, the landscape, and all the rest of this painting are extremely beautiful. It was held in great veneration by Lorenzo Nasi as long as he lived, as much in memory of Raphael, whose dear friend he had been, as for its majesty and excellence. But subsequently, on 17 November 1548, it came to grief when a landslide on the hill of San Giorgio destroyed Lorenzo's house along with other nearby dwellings, including the ornate and beautiful houses belonging to the heirs of Marco del Nero. However, the pieces were found among the debris of the ruined house and they were put together again as best he could by Lorenzo's son, Battista, who was very devoted to the art.

◆ ◆ ◆

When he had decided what to do, Raphael turned his attention to the work of Bartolommeo di San Marco. Fra Bartolommeo was a competent painter and a sound draughtsman with a pleasant style of coloring, although sometimes for the sake of greater relief he made too much use of shadows. From this painter Raphael took what suited his needs and inclination, namely, a middle course as regards drawing and coloring; and to this he added various methods chosen from the finest works of other painters to form from many different styles a single manner which he made entirely his own and which always was and always will be the object of tremendous admiration. He brought this style to perfection when he painted the sibyls and prophets for the work executed, as I mentioned, for Santa Maria della Pace. And when he did this it was of great benefit to him to have seen Michelangelo's paintings in the Sistine Chapel.

If Raphael had rested content with his own style and not tried to show by striving to give his work more variety and grandeur that he understood how to depict the nude as well as Michelangelo he would not have lost some of his fine reputation; for despite their many qualities the nudes that he painted in the room in the Borgia Tower (where the Fire in the Borgo was represented) fall short of perfection. Nor are those that Raphael made on the ceiling of the palace of Agostino Chigi in the Trastevere completely satisfying, since they lack his characteristic grace and sweetness. To a large extent this was because he had them colored by others after his designs. However, regretting his mistake, like the judicious man he was he then made up his mind to paint without the assistance of anyone else the altarpiece for San Pietro in Montorio, showing the Transfiguration of Christ, where are displayed all the qualities which, as I described, a good picture needs and must have. And if he had not on some whim or other used printer's black (which, as has often been pointed out, becomes gradually darker with time and damages the other colors with which it is mixed) this work would be as fresh as when it was first executed, whereas today it seems to be a mass of shadowy tints.

I wanted to discuss these matters toward the end of Raphael's *Life* to show the painstaking study and diligence with which that renowned artist applied himself and, above all, to assist other painters to learn how to avoid the mistakes from which Raphael was rescued by his wisdom and genius. Let me say this as well: that everyone should be content to do what he feels is natural to him and should never, merely to emulate others, want to try his hand at something for which he has no natural gift; otherwise he will labor in vain, and often to his own shame and loss. Moreover, when he has done his best a painter should not try to do even better in order to surpass those whom God and nature have made so gifted that their work seems almost miraculous. For if he lacks the ability, whatever his efforts he will never be able to achieve what another painter, with the help of nature, can take in his stride.

Among the early painters we have as an instance of this Paolo Uccello, who worked in opposition to his natural talents in order to improve his painting and who succeeded merely in slipping back. In our own time (only a short while ago) the same misfortune befell Jacopo Pontormo; and, as I have said already and shall say again, there are many other artists to whom the same thing has clearly happened. And perhaps this is so everyone may be satisfied with the talent he is born with.

But now that I have discussed these questions, perhaps at too great a length, I must return to the life and death of Raphael. It happened that he was very friendly with Cardinal Bernardo Dovizi of Bibbiena, who for many years kept pestering him to get married. Without giving the cardinal a direct yes or no, Raphael had delayed the issue for a good while by saying that he wanted to wait for three or four years. So the years passed, and then when he was not expecting it the cardinal reminded him of his promise. Thinking himself under an obligation, like the courteous man he was Raphael refused to go back on his word and he agreed to marry a niece of the cardinal's. But he resented this entanglement and kept putting things off; and after several months still the wedding had not taken place. All the same, his motives were not dishonorable; for the truth of the matter was that as he had served the court for many years and Pope Leo owed him a great deal of money he had been dropped the hint that, when the hall he was painting was finished, to reward him for his labor and talent the Pope would give him a red hat. (For the Pope had already decided to create a number of new cardinals, among whom there were several less deserving than Raphael.)

Meanwhile, Raphael kept up his secret love affairs and pursued his pleasures with no sense of moderation. And then on one occasion he went to excess, and he returned home afterwards with a violent fever which the doctors diagnosed as having been caused by heat-stroke. Raphael kept quiet about his incontinence and, very imprudently, instead of giving him the restoratives he needed they bled him until he grew faint and felt himself sinking. So he made his will: and first, as a good Christian, he sent his mistress away, leaving her the means to live a decent life. Then he divided his belongings among his disciples, Giulio Romano, whom he had always loved dearly, the Florentine Giovanni Francesco, called Il Fattore, and a priest I know nothing about who was a relation of his and came from Urbino. Next he stipulated that some of his wealth should be used for restoring with new masonry one of the ancient tabernacles in Santa Maria Rotonda and for making an altar with a marble statue of Our Lady; and he chose this church, the Pantheon, as his place of rest and burial after death. He left all the rest of his possessions to Giulio and Giovanni Francesco, and he appointed as his executor Baldassare da Pescia, then the Pope's datary. Having made his confession and repented, Raphael ended his life on Good Friday, the same day he was born. He was thirty-seven when he died; and we can be sure that just as he embellished the world with his talent so his soul now adorns heaven itself.

As he lay dead in the hall where he had been working they placed at his head the picture of the Transfiguration which he had done for Cardinal de' Medici; and the sight of this living work of art along with his dead body made the hearts of everyone who saw it burst with sorrow. In memory of Raphael, the cardinal later placed this picture on the high altar of San Pietro in Montorio, where because of the nobility of everything that

Raphael ever did it was afterwards held in great reverence. Raphael was given the honorable burial that his noble spirit deserved, and there was no artist who did not weep with sorrow as he followed him to the grave.

His death also plunged into grief the entire papal court, first since when he was alive he had held the office of Groom of the Chamber, and then because of the affection in which he had been held by the Pope, who wept bitterly when he died. How blessed and happy is the soul of Raphael! Everyone is glad to talk of him and to celebrate his actions and admire all the drawings that he left. When this noble craftsman died, the art of painting might well have died with him; for when Raphael closed his eyes, painting was left as if blind.

For those of us who survive him, it remains to imitate the good, or rather the supremely excellent method that he left for our example and, as is our duty and as his merits demand, always to remember what he did with gratitude and to pay him the highest honor in what we say. For to be sure, because of Raphael, art, coloring, and invention have all three been brought to a pitch of perfection that could scarcely have been hoped for; nor need anyone ever hope to surpass him. Apart from the benefits that he conferred on painting, as a true friend of the art, while he was alive he never ceased to show us how to conduct ourselves when dealing with great men, with those of middle rank or station, and with the lowest. And among his exceptional gifts I must acknowledge one of great value that fills me with amazement; namely, that heaven gave him the power to bring about in our profession a phenomenon completely alien to our character as painters. What happened was that craftsmen who worked with Raphael began to live in a state of natural harmony and agreement. (This was true not only of artists of ordinary talent but also of those who made some pretense to be great men, and painting produces any number of those.) At the sight of Raphael, all their bad humor died away, and every base and unworthy thought left their minds. This harmony was never greater than while Raphael was alive; and this state of affairs came about because the artists were won over by his accomplishments and his courteous behavior, and above all by the loving-kindness of his nature. Raphael was so gentle and so charitable that even animals loved him, not to speak of men.

It is said that if any painter who knew Raphael (and even any who did not) asked him for a drawing, he would leave what he was doing himself in order to help. And he always kept employed a vast number of artists whom he helped and instructed with a love that belonged rather to children of his own than to his fellow craftsmen. He was never seen leaving his house to go to court but that he was accompanied by fifty painters, all able and excellent artists, going with him to do him honor.

In short, Raphael lived more like a prince than a painter. The art of painting was supremely fortunate in securing the allegiance of a craftsman who, through his virtues and his genius, exalted it to the very skies. It is fortunate also in having disciples today who follow in the footsteps of

Raphael. For he showed them how to live and how to combine virtue and art; and in him these qualities prevailed on the magnificent Julius II and the munificent Leo X, despite their exalted dignity and rank, to make him their intimate friend and show him every mark of favor. Because of their favors and rewards Raphael was able to win great honor both for himself and his art. Happy, too, may be called all those who were employed in Raphael's service and worked under him; for whoever followed him discovered that he had arrived at a safe haven. Just so, those who follow Raphael in the future will win fame on earth, and if they follow also the example of his life they will be rewarded in heaven.

The Life of Michelangelo Buonarroti, Florentine Painter, Sculptor, and Architect, 1475–1564

Enlightened by what had been achieved by the renowned Giotto and his school, all artists of energy and distinction were striving to give the world proof of the talents with which fortune and their own happy temperaments had endowed them. They were all anxious (though their efforts were in vain) to reflect in their work the glories of nature and to attain, as far as possible, perfect artistic discernment or understanding. Meanwhile, the benign ruler of heaven graciously looked down to earth, saw the worthlessness of what was being done, the intense but utterly fruitless studies, and the presumption of men who were farther from true art than night is from day, and resolved to save us from our errors. So he decided to send into the world an artist who would be skilled in each and every craft, whose work alone would teach us how to attain perfection in design (by correct drawing and by the use of contour and light and shadows, so as to obtain relief in painting) and how to use right judgment in sculpture and, in architecture, create buildings which would be comfortable and secure, healthy, pleasant to look at, well-proportioned and richly ornamented. Moreover, he determined to give this artist the knowledge of true moral philosophy and the gift of poetic expression, so that everyone might admire and follow him as their perfect exemplar in life, work, and behavior and in every endeavor, and he would be acclaimed as divine. He also saw that in the practice of these exalted disciplines and arts, namely, painting, sculpture, and architecture, the Tuscan genius has always been pre-eminent, for the Tuscans have devoted to all the various branches of art more labor and study than all the other Italian peoples. And therefore he chose to have Michelangelo born a Florentine, so that one of her own citizens might bring to absolute perfection the achievements for which Florence was already justly renowned.

So in the year 1474 in the Casenino, under a fateful and lucky star,

SOURCE: Giorgio Vasari, *The Lives of the Artists,* trans. by G. Bull (Harmondsworth, England: Penguin, 1965), pp. 325–339, 351–355, 418–419. Reproduced by permission of Penguin Books Ltd.

the virtuous and noble wife of Lodovico di Leonardo Buonarroti gave birth
to a baby son. That year Lodovico (who was said to be related to the most
noble and ancient family of the counts of Canossa) was visiting magistrate
at the township of Chiusi and Caprese near the Sasso della Vernia (where
St Francis received the stigmata) in the diocese of Arezzo. The boy was
born on Sunday, 6 March, about the eighth hour of the night; and without
further thought his father decided to call him Michelangelo, being inspired
by heaven and convinced that he saw in him something supernatural and
beyond human experience. This was evident in the child's horoscope
which showed Mercury and Venus in the house of Jupiter, peaceably
disposed; in other words, his mind and hands were destined to fashion
sublime and magnificent works of art. Now when he had served his term
of office Lodovico returned to Florence and settled in the village of Settig-
nano, three miles from the city, where he had a family farm. That part of
the country is very rich in stone, especially in quarries of greystone which
are continuously worked by stone-cutters and sculptors, mostly local people; and Michelangelo was put out to nurse with the wife of one of the
stone-cutters. That is why once, when he was talking to Vasari, he said
jokingly:

"Giorgio, if my brains are any good at all it's because I was born in
the pure air of your Arezzo countryside, just as with my mother's milk I
sucked in the hammer and chisels I use for my statues."

As time passed and Lodovico's family grew bigger he found himself,
as he enjoyed only a modest income, in very difficult circumstances and
he had to place his sons in turn with the Wool and Silk Guilds. When
Michelangelo was old enough he was sent to the grammar school to be
taught by Francesco of Urbino; but he was so obsessed by drawing that
he used to spend on it all the time he possibly could. As a result he used
to be scolded and sometimes beaten by his father and the older members
of the family, who most likely considered it unworthy of their ancient
house for Michelangelo to give his time to an art that meant nothing to
them. It was about this time that Michelangelo became friendly with the
young Francesco Granacci, who had been sent as a boy to learn the art of
painting from Domenico Ghirlandaio.[1] Francesco saw that Michelangelo
had a great aptitude for drawing, and as he was very fond of him he used
to supply him every day with drawings by Ghirlandaio, who was then
regarded, throughout all Italy let alone in Florence, as one of the finest
living masters. As a result Michelangelo grew more ambitious with every
day that passed, and when Lodovico realized that there was no hope of
forcing him to give up drawing he resolved to put his son's aspirations to

---

1. Domenico Ghirlandaio (1449–1494), a competent painter, chiefly in fresco, who ran a
large family studio in Florence.

some use and make it possible for him to learn the art properly. So on the advice of friends he apprenticed him to Domenico Ghirlandaio.

When this happened Michelangelo was fourteen years old. And incidentally, the author of a biography of Michelangelo which was written after 1550 (when I wrote these *Lives* the first time) says that some people, because they did not know Michelangelo personally, have said things about him that were never true and have left out others that deserved to be mentioned.[2] For instance, he himself taxes Domenico with envy and alleges that he never gave any help to Michelangelo. But this accusation is plainly false, as can be judged from something written by Michelangelo's father, Lodovico, in one of Domenico's record books, which is now in the possession of his heirs. The entry reads as follows:

> 1488. This first day of April I record that I, Lodovico di Leonardo Buonarroti, do apprentice my son Michelangelo to Domenico and David di Tommaso di Currado for the next three years, under the following conditions: that the said Michelangelo must stay for the stipulated time with the above-named to learn and practice the art of painting, and that he should obey their orders, and that the same Domenico and David should pay him in those three years twenty-four florins of full weight: six in the first year, eight in the second year, and ten in the third year, to a total of ninety-six lire.

And below this, also in Lodovico's handwriting, is the following entry or record:

> The above-named Michelangelo received this sixteenth day of April two gold florins, and I, Lodovico di Leonardo, his father, received twelve lire and twelve soldi on his account.

I have copied these entries straight from the book in order to show that everything I wrote earlier and am writing now is the truth; nor am I aware that anyone was more familiar with Michelangelo than I or can claim to have been a closer friend or more faithful servant, as can be proved to anyone's satisfaction. Moreover, I do not believe there is anyone who can produce more affectionate or a greater number of letters than those written by Michelangelo and addressed to me. I made this digression for the sake of truth, and it must suffice for the rest of his *Life*. And now let us go back to Michelangelo himself.

The way Michelangelo's talents and character developed astonished Domenico, who saw him doing things quite out of the ordinary for boys of his age and not only surpassing his many other pupils but also very often rivalling the achievements of the master himself. On one occasion it happened that one of the young men studying with Domenico copied in ink some draped figures of women from Domenico's own work. Michel-

---

2. Ascanio Condivi, Michelangelo's pupil, whose *Life of Michelangelo*, closely supervised by Michelangelo himself, was published in 1553.

angelo took what he had drawn and, using a thicker pen, he went over the contours of one of the figures and brought it to perfection; and it is marvellous to see the difference between the two styles and the superior skill and judgment of a young man so spirited and confident that he had the courage to correct what his teacher had done. This drawing is now kept by me among my treasured possessions. I received it from Granaccio, along with other drawings by Michelangelo, for my book of drawings; and in 1550, when he was in Rome, Giorgio Vasari showed it to Michelangelo who recognized it and was delighted to see it again. He said modestly that as a boy he had known how to draw better than he did now as an old man.

Another time, when Domenico was working on the principal chapel of Santa Maria Novella, Michelangelo came along and started to draw the scaffolding and trestles and various implements and materials, as well as some of the young men who were busy there. When Domenico came back and saw what Michelangelo had done he said: "This boy knows more about it than I do." And he stood there astonished at the originality and skill in imitation that his inborn sense of judgment enabled so young an artist to display. Certainly, the work showed all the qualities to be expected of an artist with years of experience. This was because the instinctive grace of Michelangelo's work was enhanced by study and practice; and every day he produced work that was still more inspired. For example, it was at that time that he made the copy of an engraving by Martin the German that brought him considerable fame.[3] Michelangelo did a perfect pen-and-ink copy of this copper engraving, which showed St Anthony being tormented by devils, soon after it had been brought to Florence. He also did the scene in colors; and for this purpose in order to copy some of the strange-looking demons in the picture he went along to the market and bought some fishes with fantastic scales like theirs. The skill with which he did this work won him a considerable reputation. Michelangelo also copied the works of other masters, with complete fidelity; he used to tinge his copies and make them appear black with age by various means, including the use of smoke, so that they could not be told apart from the originals. He did this so that he could exchange his copies for the originals, which he admired for their excellence and which he tried to surpass in his own works; and these experiments also won him fame.

At that time the custodian or keeper of all the fine antiques that Lorenzo the Magnificent had collected at great expense and kept in his garden on the Piazza di San Marco was the sculptor Bertoldo.[4] He had been a pupil of Donatello's, and the chief reason why Lorenzo kept him in his service was because he had set his heart on establishing a school of

---

3. Martin Schongauer (1453–1491), a painter and engraver of Colmar.
4. Giovanni di Bertoldo (c. 1420–1491).

first-rate painters and sculptors and wanted Bertoldo to teach and look after them. Bertoldo was now too old to work; nevertheless, he was very experienced and very famous, not only for having polished the bronze pulpits cast by Donatello but also for the many bronze casts of battle-scenes and the other small things he had executed himself with a competence that no one else in Florence could rival. So Lorenzo, who was an enthusiastic lover of painting and sculpture, regretting that he could find no great and noble sculptors to compare with the many contemporary painters of ability and repute, determined, as I said, to found a school himself. For this reason he told Domenico Ghirlandaio that if he had in his workshop any young men who were drawn to sculpture he should send them along to his garden, where they would be trained and formed in a manner that would do honor to himself, to Domenico, and to the whole city. So Domenico gave him some of the best among his young men, including Michelangelo and Francesco Granacci. And when they arrived at the garden they found Torrigiano (a young man of the Torrigiani family) working there on some clay figures in the round that Bertoldo had given him to do.[5] After he had seen these figures, Michelangelo was prompted to make some himself; and when he saw the boy's ambitious nature Lorenzo started to have very high hopes of what he would do. Michelangelo was so encouraged that some days later he set himself to copy in marble an antique faun's head which he found in the garden; it was very old and wrinkled, with the nose damaged and a laughing mouth. Although this was the first time he had ever touched a chisel or worked in marble, Michelangelo succeeded in copying it so well that Lorenzo was flabbergasted. Then, when he saw that Michelangelo had departed a little from the model and followed his own fancy in hollowing out a mouth for the faun and giving it a tongue and all its teeth, Lorenzo laughed in his usual charming way and said:

"But you should have known that old folk never have all their teeth and there are always some missing."

In his simplicity Michelangelo, who loved and feared that lord, reflected that this was true, and as soon as Lorenzo had gone he broke one of the faun's teeth and dug into the gum so that it looked as if the tooth had fallen out; then he waited anxiously for Lorenzo to come back. And after he had seen the result of Michelangelo's simplicity and skill, Lorenzo laughed at the incident more than once and used to tell it for a marvel to his friends. He resolved that he would help and favor the young Michelangelo; and first he sent for his father, Lodovico, and asked whether he could have the boy, adding that he wanted to keep him as one of his own sons. Lodovico willingly agreed, and then Lorenzo arranged to have

---

5. Pietro Torrigiano (1472–1528), a Florentine sculptor who worked in England, notably on the tomb of Henry VII.

Michelangelo given a room of his own and looked after as one of the Medici household. Michelangelo always ate at Lorenzo's table with the sons of the family and other distinguished and noble persons who lived with that lord, and Lorenzo always treated him with great respect. All this happened the year after Michelangelo had been placed with Domenico, when he was fifteen or sixteen years old; and he lived in the Medici house for four years, until the death of Lorenzo the Magnificent in 1492. During that period, as salary and so that he could help his father, Michelangelo was paid five ducats a month; and to make him happy Lorenzo gave him a violet cloak and appointed his father to a post in the Customs. As a matter of fact all the young men in the garden were paid salaries varying in amount through the generosity of that noble and magnificent citizen who supported them as long as he lived. It was at this time that, with advice from Politian, a distinguished man of letters, Michelangelo carved from a piece of marble given him by Lorenzo the Battle of Hercules with the Centaurs. This was so beautiful that today, to those who study it, it sometimes seems to be the work not of a young man but of a great master with a wealth of study and experience behind him. It is now kept in memory of Michelangelo by his nephew Lionardo, who cherishes it as a rare work of art. Not many years ago Lionardo also kept in his house in memory of his uncle a marble Madonna in bas-relief, little more than two feet in height. This was executed by Michelangelo when he was still a young man after the style of Donatello, and he acquitted himself so well that it seems to be by Donatello himself, save that it possesses more grace and design. Lionardo subsequently gave this work to Duke Cosimo de' Medici, who regards it as unique, since it is the only sculpture in bas-relief left by Michelangelo.

To return to the garden of Lorenzo the Magnificent: this place was full of antiques and richly furnished with excellent pictures collected for their beauty, and for study and pleasure. Michelangelo always held the keys to the garden as he was far more earnest than the others and always alert, bold, and resolute in everything he did. For example, he spent many months in the church of the Carmine making drawings from the pictures by Masaccio; he copied these with such judgment that the craftsmen and all the others who saw his work were astonished, and he then started to experience envy as well as fame.

It is said that Torrigiano, who had struck up a friendship with Michelangelo, then became jealous on seeing him more honored than himself and more able in his work. At length Torrigiano started to mock him, and then he hit him on the nose so hard that he broke and crushed it and marked Michelangelo for life. Because of this, Torrigiano, as I describe elsewhere, was banished from Florence.

When Lorenzo the Magnificent died, Michelangelo went back to live with his father, filled with sorrow at the death of a great man who had befriended every kind of talent. While he was with his father he obtained a large block of marble from which he carved a Hercules eight feet high, which stood for many years in the Palazzo Strozzi. This work, which was very highly regarded, was later (when Florence was under siege) sent to King Francis in France by Giovanbattista della Palla. It is said that Piero de' Medici, who had been left heir to his father, Lorenzo, often used to send for Michelangelo, with whom he had been intimate for many years, when he wanted to buy antiques such as cameos and other engraved stones. And one winter, when a great deal of snow fell in Florence, he had him make in his courtyard a statue of snow, which was very beautiful. Piero did Michelangelo many favors on account of his talents, and Michelangelo's father, seeing his son so highly regarded among the great, began to provide him with far finer clothes than he used to.

For the church of Santo Spirito in Florence Michelangelo made a crucifix of wood which was placed above the lunette of the high altar, where it still is.[6] He made this to please the prior, who placed some rooms at his disposal where Michelangelo very often used to flay dead bodies in order to discover the secrets of anatomy; and in this way he started to perfect the great powers of design that he subsequently enjoyed.

It happened that a few weeks before the Medici were driven out of Florence Michelangelo had left for Bologna and then gone on to Venice, since he feared, when he saw the insolence and bad government of Piero de' Medici, that because of his connexion with the Medici family he would run into trouble himself. Being unable to find any means of living in Venice, he went back to Bologna. But thoughtlessly he failed to find out when he entered through the gate the password for going out again. (As a precaution, Giovanni Bentivogli had ordered that foreigners who could not give the password should pay a penalty of fifty Bolognese lire.) Now when he found himself in this predicament, without the money to pay the fine, by chance Michelangelo was seen by Giovanfrancesco Aldovrandi, one of the Sixteen of the Government, who felt sorry for him, and after he had heard his story secured his release and then gave him hospitality in his own home for more than a year. One day Aldovrandi took Michelangelo to see the tomb of St Dominic which had been executed (as I describe elsewhere) by the early sculptors, Giovanni Pisano and, later, Niccolò dell'Arca. There were two figures missing: an angel holding a candelabrum and a St Petronius, both about two feet high. Aldovrandi asked Michelangelo if he had the courage to do them, and he answered yes. So he had the marble given to Michelangelo, who executed the two figures, which proved to be the finest on the tomb. Aldovrandi paid him thirty ducats for this work.

Michelangelo stayed in Bologna just over a year, and he would have stayed longer in order to repay Aldovrandi for his kindness. (Aldovrandi

---

6. This is the crucifix (disputedly) discovered in Florence in 1963, carved in white poplar.

loved him for his skill as an artist and also because of his Tuscan accent, which he enjoyed when Michelangelo read him work by Dante, Petrarch, Boccaccio, and other poets.) However, as he realized that he was wasting time, Michelangelo was only too happy to return to Florence. And there, for Lorenzo di Pierfrancesco de'Medici, he made a little St John in marble, and then immediately started work on another marble figure, a sleeping Cupid, life-size. When this was finished, Baldassare del Milanese showed it as a beautiful piece of work to Lorenzo di Pierfrancesco, who agreed with his judgment and said to Michelangelo:

"If you were to bury it and treat it to make it seem old and then send it to Rome, I'm sure that it would pass as an antique and you would get far more for it than you would here."

Michelangelo is supposed to have then treated the statue so that it looked like an antique; and this is not to be marvelled at seeing that he was ingenious enough to do anything. Others insist that Milanese took it to Rome and buried it in a vineyard he owned and then sold it as an antique for two hundred ducats to Cardinal San Giorgio. Others again say that Milanese sold the cardinal the statue that Michelangelo had made for him, and then wrote to Pierfrancesco saying that he should pay Michelangelo thirty crowns since that was all he had got for the Cupid; and in this way he deceived the cardinal, Lorenzo di Pierfrancesco, and Michelangelo himself. But then afterwards, the cardinal learned from an eyewitness that the Cupid had been made in Florence, discovered the truth of the matter through a messenger, and compelled Milanese's agent to restore his money and take back the Cupid. The statue later came into the possession of Duke Valentino who presented it to the marchioness of Mantua; and she took it back to her own part of the world where it is still to be seen today. Cardinal San Giorgio cannot escape censure for what happened, since he failed to recognize the obviously perfect quality of Michelangelo's work. The fact is that, other things being equal, modern works of art are just as fine as antiques; and there is no greater vanity than to value things for what they are called rather than for what they are. However, every age produces the kind of man who pays more attention to appearances than to facts.

All the same this work did so much for Michelangelo's reputation that he was immediately summoned to Rome to enter the service of Cardinal San Giorgio, with whom he stayed nearly a year, although the cardinal, not understanding the fine arts very much, gave him nothing to do.[7] At that time the cardinal's barber, who had been a painter and worked very studiously in tempera, though he had no draughtsmanship, struck

---

7. Michelangelo went to Rome first in 1496. The Popes he served were Julius II (1503–1513), Leo X (1513–1521), Clement VII (1523–1534), Paul III (1534–1549), Julius III (1550–1555), Paul IV (1555–1559), and Pius IV (1559–1565).

up a friendship with Michelangelo, who drew for him a cartoon showing St. Francis receiving the stigmata; and this was very carefully painted by the barber on a panel which is to be found in the first chapel on the left, as one enters the church of San Pietro in Montorio. Michelangelo's abilities were then clearly recognized by a Roman gentleman called Jacopo Galli, and this discerning person commissioned from him a marble life-size statue of Cupid and then a Bacchus, ten spans high, holding a cup in his right hand and the skin of a tiger in his left, with a bunch of grapes which a little satyr is trying to nibble. In this figure it is clear that Michelangelo wanted to obtain a marvellous harmony of various elements, notably in giving it the slenderness of a youth combined with the fullness and roundness of the female form. This splendid achievement showed that Michelangelo could surpass every other sculptor of the modern age. Through the studies he undertook while in Rome he acquired such great skill that he was able to solve incredibly difficult problems and to express in a style of effortless facility the most elevated concepts, to the sheer amazement not only of those who lacked the experience to judge but also of men accustomed to excellent work. All the other works then being created were regarded as trivial compared with what Michelangelo was producing. As a result the French cardinal of Saint-Denis, called Cardinal Rouen,[8] became anxious to employ his rare talents to leave some suitable memorial of himself in the great city of Rome; and so he commissioned Michelangelo to make a Pietà of marble in the round, and this was placed, after it was finished, in the chapel of the Madonna della Febbre in St Peter's, where the temple of Mars once stood. It would be impossible for any craftsman or sculptor no matter how brilliant ever to surpass the grace or design of this work or try to cut and polish the marble with the skill that Michelangelo displayed. For the Pietà was a revelation of all the potentialities and force of the art of sculpture. Among the many beautiful features (including the inspired draperies) this is notably demonstrated by the body of Christ itself. It would be impossible to find a body showing greater mastery of art and possessing more beautiful members, or a nude with more detail in the muscles, veins, and nerves stretched over their framework of bones, or a more deathly corpse. The lovely expression of the head, the harmony in the joints and attachments of the arms, legs, and trunk, and the fine tracery of pulses and veins are all so wonderful that it staggers belief that the hand of an artist could have executed this inspired and admirable work so perfectly and in so short a time. It is certainly a miracle that a formless block of stone could ever have been reduced to a perfection that nature is scarcely able to create in the flesh. Michelangelo put into this work so much love and effort that (something he never did again) he left his name written across the sash over Our

---

8. This was Jean Villier de la Grolaie, abbot of Saint-Denis and cardinal of Santa Sabina.

Lady's breast. The reason for this was that one day he went along to where the statue was and found a crowd of strangers from Lombardy singing its praises; then one of them asked another who had made it, only to be told: "Our Gobbo from Milan."[9]

Michelangelo stood there not saying a word, but thinking it very odd to have all his efforts attributed to someone else. Then one night, taking his chisels, he shut himself in with a light and carved his name on the statue. And a fine poet has aptly described the Pietà, which is full of truth and life, as follows:

> Bellezza ed onestate,
>   E doglia, e pieta in vivo marmo morte,
>   Deh, come voi pur fate,
>   Non piangete sí forte,
>   Che anzi tempo risveglisi da morte.
>   E pur, mal grado suo,
>   Nostro Signore, e tuo
>   Sposo, figliuolo e padre,
>   Unica sposa sua figliuola e madre.[10]

This work did wonders for Michelangelo's reputation. To be sure, there are some critics, more or less fools, who say that he made Our Lady look too young. They fail to see that those who keep their virginity unspotted stay for a long time fresh and youthful, just as those afflicted as Christ was do the opposite. Anyhow, this work added more glory and luster to Michelangelo's genius than anything he had done before.

Then some of his friends wrote to him from Florence urging him to return there as it seemed very probable that he would be able to obtain the block of marble that was standing in the Office of Works. Piero Soderini, who about that time was elected Gonfalonier for life,[11] had often talked of handing it over to Leonardo da Vinci, but he was then arranging to give it to Andrea Contucci of Monte Sansovino, an accomplished sculptor who was very keen to have it. Now, although it seemed impossible to carve from the block a complete figure (and only Michelangelo was bold enough to try this without adding fresh pieces) Buonarroti had felt the desire to work on it many years before; and he tried to obtain it when he came back to Florence. The marble was eighteen feet high, but unfortunately an artist called Simone da Fiesole had started to carve a giant figure,

---

9. Cristoforo Solari.

10. The verse was by Giovan Battista Strozzi il Vecchio, poet and madrigalist, and is very obscure. Roughly and literally: "Beauty and goodness, And grief and pity, alive in the dead marble, Do not, as you do, weep so loudly, Lest before time should awake from death, In spite of himself, Our Lord, and thy Spouse, son and father, Oh virgin, only spouse, daughter and mother."

11. Soderini was elected Gonfaloniere di Justizia for life (in effect, head of the Florentine Republic) in 1502.

and had bungled the work so badly that he had hacked a hole between the legs and left the block completely botched and misshapen. So the wardens of Santa Maria del Fiore (who were in charge of the undertaking) threw the block aside and it stayed abandoned for many years and seemed likely to remain so indefinitely. However, Michelangelo measured it again and calculated whether he could carve a satisfactory figure from the block by accommodating its attitude to the shape of the stone. Then he made up his mind to ask for it. Soderini and the wardens decided that they would let him have it, as being something of little value, and telling themselves that since the stone was of no use to their building, either botched as it was or broken up, whatever Michelangelo made would be worthwhile. So Michelangelo made a wax model of the young David with a sling in his hand; this was intended as a symbol of liberty for the Palace, signifying that just as David had protected his people and governed them justly, so whoever ruled Florence should vigorously defend the city and govern it with justice. He began work on the statue in the Office of Works of Santa Maria del Fiore, erecting a partition of planks and trestles around the marble; and working on it continuously he brought it to perfect completion, without letting anyone see it.

As I said, the marble had been flawed and distorted by Simone, and in some places Michelangelo could not work it as he wanted; so he allowed some of the original chisel marks made by Simone to remain on the edges of the marble, and these can still be seen today. And all things considered, Michelangelo worked a miracle in restoring to life something that had been left for dead.

After the statue had been finished, its great size provoked endless disputes over the best way to transport it to the Piazza della Signoria. However, Giuliano da Sangallo, with his brother Antonio, constructed a very strong wooden framework and suspended the statue from it with ropes so that when moved it would sway gently without being broken; then they drew it along by means of winches over planks laid on the ground, and put it in place. In the rope which held the figure suspended he tied a slip-knot which tightened as the weight increased: a beautiful and ingenious arrangement. (I have a drawing by his own hand in my book showing this admirable, strong, and secure device for suspending weights.)

When he saw the David in place Piero Soderini was delighted; but while Michelangelo was retouching it he remarked that he thought the nose was too thick. Michelangelo, noticing that the Gonfalonier was standing beneath the Giant and that from where he was he could not see the figure properly, to satisfy him climbed on the scaffolding by the shoulders, seized hold of a chisel in his left hand, together with some of the marble dust lying on the planks, and as he tapped lightly with the chisel let the dust fall little by little, without altering anything. Then he looked down at the Gonfalonier, who had stopped to watch, and said:

"Now look at it."

"Ah, that's much better," replied Soderini. "Now you've really brought it to life."

And then Michelangelo climbed down, feeling sorry for those critics who talk nonsense in the hope of appearing well informed. When the work was finally finished he uncovered it for everyone to see. And without any doubt this figure has put in the shade every other statue, ancient or modern, Greek or Roman. Neither the Marforio in Rome, nor the Tiber and the Nile of the Belvedere, nor the colossal statues of Monte Cavello can be compared with Michelangelo's David, such were the satisfying proportions and beauty of the finished work. The legs are skilfully outlined, the slender flanks are beautifully shaped and the limbs are joined faultlessly to the trunk. The grace of this figure and the serenity of its pose have never been surpassed, nor have the feet, the hands, and the head, whose harmonious proportions and loveliness are in keeping with the rest. To be sure, anyone who has seen Michelangelo's David has no need to see anything else by any other sculptor, living or dead.

♦ ♦ ♦

Pope Julius himself was always keen to see whatever Michelangelo was doing, and so naturally he was more anxious than ever to see what was being hidden from him. So one day he resolved to go and see the work, but he was not allowed in, as Michelangelo would never have consented. (This was the cause of the quarrel described earlier, when Michelangelo had to leave Rome as he would not let the Pope see what he was painting.) Now when a third of the work was completed (as I found out from Michelangelo himself, to clear up any uncertainty) during the winter when the north wind was blowing several spots of mold started to appear on the surface. The reason for this was that the Roman lime, which is white in color and made of travertine, does not dry very quickly, and when mixed with pozzolana,[12] which is a brownish color, forms a dark mixture which is very watery before it sets; then after the wall has been thoroughly soaked, it often effloresces when it is drying. Thus this salt efflorescence appeared in many places, although in time the air dried it up. When Michelangelo saw what was happening he despaired of the whole undertaking and was reluctant to go on. However, his holiness sent Giuliano da Sangallo to see him and explain the reason for the blemishes. Sangallo explained how to remove the molds and encouraged him to continue. Then, when the work was half finished, the Pope who had subsequently gone to inspect it several times (being helped up the ladders by Michelangelo) wanted it to be thrown open to the public. Being hasty

---

12. A volcanic dust found near Pozzuoli.

and impatient by nature, he simply could not bear to wait until it was perfect and had, so to say, received the final touch.

As soon as it was thrown open, the whole of Rome flocked to see it; and the Pope was the first, not having the patience to wait till the dust had settled after the dismantling of the scaffolds. Raphael da Urbino (who had great powers of imitation) changed his style as soon as he had seen Michelangelo's work and straight away, to show his skill, painted the prophets and sibyls of Santa Maria della Pace; and Bramante subsequently tried to persuade the Pope to let Raphael paint the other half of the chapel. When Michelangelo heard about this he complained of Bramante and revealed to the Pope, without reserve, many faults in his life and in his architectural works. (He himself, as it happened, was later to correct the mistakes made by Bramante in the fabric of St Peter's.) However, the Pope recognized Michelangelo's genius more clearly every day and wanted him to carry on the work himself; and after he had seen it displayed he was of the opinion that Michelangelo would do the other half even better. And so in twenty months Michelangelo brought the project to perfect completion without the assistance even of someone to grind his colors. Michelangelo at times complained that because of the haste the Pope imposed on him he was unable to finish it in the way he would have liked; for his holiness was always asking him importunately when it would be ready. On one of these occasions Michelangelo retorted that the ceiling would be finished "when it satisfies me as an artist."

And to this the Pope replied: "And we want you to satisfy us and finish it soon."

Finally, the Pope threatened that if Michelangelo did not finish the ceiling quickly he would have him thrown down from the scaffolding. Then Michelangelo, who had good reason to fear the Pope's anger, lost no time in doing all that was wanted; and after taking down the rest of the scaffolding he threw the ceiling open to the public on the morning of All Saints' Day, when the Pope went into the chapel to sing Mass, to the satisfaction of the entire city.

Michelangelo wanted to retouch some parts of the painting *a secco*, as the old masters had done on the scenes below, painting backgrounds, draperies, and skies in ultramarine, and in certain places adding ornamentation in gold, in order to enrich and heighten the visual impact.[13] The Pope, learning that this ornamentation was lacking, and hearing the work praised so enthusiastically by all who saw it, wanted him to go ahead. However, he lacked the patience to rebuild the scaffolding, and so the ceiling stayed as it was. His holiness used to see Michelangelo often and

---

13. *Fresco secco*—as opposed to *buon fresco*—is painted on dry plaster and was rarely used, even for retouching, by Michelangelo's time.

he would ask him to have the chapel enriched with colors and gold, since it looked impoverished. And Michelangelo would answer familiarly:

"Holy Father, in those days men did not bedeck themselves in gold and those you see painted there were never very rich. They were holy men who despised riches."

For this work Michelangelo was paid by the Pope three thousand crowns in several instalments, of which he had to spend twenty-five on colors. He executed the frescoes in great discomfort, having to work with his face looking upwards, which impaired his sight so badly that he could not read or look at drawings save with his head turned backwards; and this lasted for several months afterwards. I can talk from personal experience about this, since when I painted five rooms in the great apartments of Duke Cosimo's palace if I had not made a chair where I could rest my head and relax from time to time I would never have finished; even so this work so ruined my sight and injured my head that I still feel the effects, and I am astonished that Michelangelo bore all that discomfort so well. In fact, every day the work moved him to greater enthusiasm, and he was so spurred on by his own progress and improvements that he felt no fatigue and ignored all the discomfort.

The painting on the ceiling of the chapel is arranged with six pendentives on either side and one in the center of the walls at the foot and the head; and on these Michelangelo painted prophets and sibyls, twelve feet high.[14] In the middle of the vault he depicted from the Creation up to the Flood and the Drunkenness of Noah; and in the lunettes he showed all the Ancestors of Jesus Christ. For the foreshortenings in these compartments he used no consistent rule of perspective, nor is there any fixed point of view. He accommodated the various compartments to the figures, rather than his figures to the compartments, for he was resolved to execute both the draped figures and the nudes so that they should demonstrate the perfect quality of his draughtsmanship. There is no other work to compare with this for excellence, nor could there be; and it is scarcely possible even to imitate what Michelangelo accomplished. The ceiling has proved a veritable beacon to our art, of inestimable benefit to all painters, restoring light to a world that for centuries had been plunged into darkness. Indeed, painters no longer need to seek new inventions, novel attitudes, clothed figures, fresh ways of expression, different arrangements, or sublime subjects, for this work contains every perfection possible under those headings. In the nudes, Michelangelo displayed complete

---

14. In fact, five pendentives on either side. Vasari's description, however, is substantially accurate, though in describing the histories he follows the logical sequence of the frescoes rather than the order in which they were painted. Michelangelo started work on the ceiling in 1508, the frescoes were unveiled in the summer of 1511, and the project was completed in 1512, setting the seal on his reputation as the greatest living artist.

mastery: they are truly astonishing in their perfect foreshortenings, their wonderfully rotund contours, their grace, slenderness, and proportion. And to show the vast scope of his art he made them of all ages, some slim and some full-bodied, with varied expressions and attitudes, sitting, turning, holding festoons of oakleaves and acorns (to represent the emblem of Pope Julius and the fact that his reign marked the golden age of Italy, before the travail and misery of the present time). The nudes down the middle of the ceiling hold medallions painted like gold or bronze with subjects taken from the Book of Kings. Moreover, to show the perfection of art and the greatness of God, in the histories Michelangelo depicted God dividing Light from Darkness, showing him in all his majesty as he rests self-sustained with arms outstretched, in a revelation of love and creative power.

◆ ◆ ◆

Michelangelo had a strong vocation for the arts on which he labored, and he succeeded in everything he did, no matter how difficult. For nature gave him a mind that devoted itself eagerly to the great arts of design. And in order to achieve perfection he made endless anatomical studies, dissecting corpses in order to discover the principles of their construction and the concatenation of the bones, muscles, nerves, and veins, and all the various movements and postures of the human body. He studied not only men but animals as well, and especially horses, which he loved to own. Of all these he was anxious to learn the anatomical principles and laws in so far as they concerned his art; and in his works he demonstrated this knowledge so well that those who study nothing else except anatomy achieve no more. As a result everything he made, whether with the brush or the chisel, defies imitation, and (as has been said) is imbued with such art, grace, and distinctive vitality that, if this can be said without offense, he has surpassed and vanquished the ancients, for the facility with which he achieved difficult effects was so great that they seem to have been created without effort, although anyone who tries to copy his work finds a great deal of effort is needed.

Michelangelo's genius was recognized during his lifetime, not, as happens to so many, only after his death.[15] As we have seen, Julius II, Leo X, Clement VII, Paul III, Julius III, Paul IV, and Pius IV, all these supreme pontiffs, wanted to have him near them at all times; as also, as we know, did Suleiman, emperor of the Turks, Francis of Valois, king of France, the Emperor Charles V, the Signoria of Venice, and lastly, as I related, Duke Cosimo de' Medici, all of whom made him very honorable offers, simply to avail themselves of his great talents. This happens only to men of

---

15. Michelangelo died on 18 February 1564.

tremendous worth, like Michelangelo, who, as was clearly recognized, achieved in the three arts a perfect mastery that God has granted no other person, in the ancient or modern world, in all the years that the sun has been spinning round the world. His imagination was so powerful and perfect that he often discarded work in which his hands found it impossible to express his tremendous and awesome ideas; indeed, he has often destroyed his work, and I know for a fact that shortly before he died he burned a large number of his own drawings, sketches, and cartoons so that no one should see the labors he endured and the ways he tested his genius, and lest he should appear less than perfect. I have some examples of his work, found in Florence and placed in my book of drawings; and these not only reveal the greatness of his mind but also show that when he wished to bring forth Minerva from the head of Jove, he had to use Vulcan's hammer: for he used to make his figures the sum of nine, ten, and even twelve "heads"; in putting them together he strove only to achieve a certain overall harmony of grace, which nature does not present; and he said that one should have compasses in one's eyes, not in one's hands, because the hands execute but it is the eye which judges. He also used this method in architecture.

✦ Benvenuto Cellini

*B*envenuto Cellini (1500–1571) was born in Florence, the son of a mason who expected him to become a flute player. However, his talent as an artist was apparent, and his father permitted him to be apprenticed to a goldsmith. In 1519 he traveled to Rome, where he studied classical art and entered the service of Pope Clement VII, first as a flutist but later as an engraver in the papal mint. During the sack of Rome in 1527, Cellini claims to have been an expert gunner; indeed, he says he fired the shot that killed the constable of Bourbon, the leader of the imperial troops, and again earned the favor of the pope. Clement's successor, Paul III, initially continued Cellini's employment, but the jealousy of the pope's nephew drove Cellini to France first in 1537 and again from 1540 until 1545. It was during these years that Cellini created his wonderful saltcellar and other works for King Francis I.

Returning to Florence in 1545, he began work for Duke Cosimo de' Medici, for whom he cast his bronze Perseus, still to be seen in the Loggia dei Lanzi in Florence. Cellini remained in Florence until his death in 1571.

Cellini is remembered almost as much for his **Autobiography** as for his works of art. Written between 1558 and 1562, the book is the remarkable story of a full, brawling, bragging, almost lawless life. Cellini describes his escapades with almost salacious candor, and he tries to

ruin the reputations of his enemies while enhancing his own. The Autobiography *is a unique insight into the life of a Renaissance artist who
apparently used his skill at literary hyperbole as effectively as his gifts
as a goldsmith and sculptor.*

SELECTIONS FROM *THE AUTOBIOGRAPHY*
OF *BENVENUTO CELLINI*

XXXIV

The whole world was now in warfare.[1] Pope Clement had sent to get some
troops from Giovanni de' Medici, and when they came, they made such
disturbances in Rome, that it was ill living in open shops.[2] On this account
I retired to a good snug house behind the Banchi, where I worked for all
the friends I had acquired. Since I produced few things of much importance
at that period, I need not waste time in talking about them. I took much
pleasure in music and amusements of the kind. On the death of Giovanni
de' Medici in Lombardy, the Pope, at the advice of Messer Jacopo Salviati,
dismissed the five hands he had engaged; and when the Constable of
Bourbon knew there were no troops in Rome, he pushed his army with
the utmost energy up to the city. The whole of Rome upon this flew to
arms. I happened to be intimate with Alessandro, the son of Piero del
Bene, who, at the time when the Colonnesi entered Rome, had requested
me to guard his palace.[3] On this more serious occasion, therefore, he
prayed me to enlist fifty comrades for the protection of the said house,
appointing me their captain, as I had been when the Colonnesi came. So
I collected fifty young men of the highest courage, and we took up our
quarters in his palace, with good pay and excellent appointments.

Bourbon's army had now arrived before the walls of Rome, and Alessandro begged me to go with him to reconnoitre. So we went with one of
the stoutest fellows in our Company; and on the way a youth called

SOURCE: Benvenuto Cellini, *Autobiography*, trans. by J. A. Symonds (Garden
City, N.Y.: Garden City Publishing, 1927), pp. 62–75, 252–269.

---

1. War had broken out in 1521 between Charles V and Francis I, which disturbed all
   Europe and involved the states of Italy in serious complications. At the moment when
   this chapter opens, the imperialist army under the constable of Bourbon was marching
   upon Rome in 1527.
2. These troops entered Rome in October 1526. They were disbanded in March 1527.
3. Cellini here refers to the attack made upon Rome by the great Ghibelline house of
   Colonna, led by their chief captain, Pompeo, in September 1526. They took possession
   of the city and drove Clement into the Castle of S. Angelo, where they forced him to
   agree to terms favoring the imperial cause. It was customary for Roman gentlemen to
   hire bravi for the defence of their palaces when any extraordinary disturbance was
   expected, as, for example, upon the vacation of the papal chair.

Cecchino della Casa joined himself to us. On reaching the walls by the Campo Santo, we could see that famous army, which was making every effort to enter the town. Upon the ramparts where we took our station several young men were lying killed by the besiegers; the battle raged there desperately, and there was the densest fog imaginable. I turned to Alessandro and said: "Let us go home as soon as we can, for there is nothing to be done here; you see the enemies are mounting, and our men are in flight." Alessandro, in a panic, cried: "Would God that we had never come here!" and turned in maddest haste to fly. I took him up somewhat sharply with these words: "Since you have brought me here, I must perform some action worthy of a man;" and directing my arquebuse where I saw the thickest and most serried troop of fighting men, I aimed exactly at one whom I remarked to be higher than the rest; the fog prevented me from being certain whether he was on horseback or on foot. Then I turned to Alessandro and Cecchino, and bade them discharge their arquebuses, showing them how to avoid being hit by the besiegers. When we had fired two rounds apiece, I crept cautiously up to the wall, and observing among the enemy a most extraordinary confusion, I discovered afterwards that one of our shots had killed the Constable of Bourbon; and from what I subsequently learned, he was the man whom I had first noticed above the heads of the rest.[4]

Quitting our position on the ramparts, we crossed the Campo Santo, and entered the city by St. Peter's; then coming out exactly at the church of Santo Agnolo, we got with the greatest difficulty to the great castle; for the generals Renzo di Ceri and Orazio Baglioni were wounding and slaughtering everybody who abandoned the defense of the walls.[5] By the time we had reached the great gate, part of the foemen had already entered Rome, and we had them in our rear. The castellan had ordered the portcullis to be lowered, in order to do which they cleared a little space, and this enabled us four to get inside. On the instant that I entered, the captain Pallone de' Medici claimed me as being of the Papal household, and forced me to abandon Alessandro, which I had to do, much against my will. I ascended to the keep, and at the same instant Pope Clement came in through the corridors into the castle; he had refused to leave the palace

---

4. All historians of the sack of Rome agree in saying that Bourbon was shot dead while placing ladders against the outworks near the shop Cellini mentions. But the honor of firing the arquebuse which brought him down cannot be assigned to any one in particular. Very different stories were current on the subject. See Gregorovius, *Stadt Rom.*, Vol. viii. p. 522.

5. Orazio Baglioni, of the semiprincely Perugian family, was a distinguished Condottiere. He subsequently obtained the captaincy of the Bande Nere, and died fighting near Naples in 1528. Orazio murdered several of his cousins in order to acquire the lordship of Perugia. His brother Malatesta undertook to defend Florence in the siege of 1530, and sold the city by treason to Clement.

of St. Peter earlier, being unable to believe that his enemies would effect their entrance into Rome.[6] Having got into the castle in this way, I attached myself to certain pieces of artillery, which were under the command of a bombardier called Giuliano Fiorentino. Leaning there against the battlements, the unhappy man could see his poor house being sacked, and his wife and children outraged; fearing to strike his own folk, he dared not discharge the cannon, and flinging the burning fuse upon the ground, he wept as though his heart would break, and tore his cheeks with both his hands.[7] Some of the other bombardiers were behaving in like manner; seeing which, I took one of the matches, and got the assistance of a few men who were not overcome by their emotions. I aimed some swivels and falconets at points where I saw it would be useful, and killed with them a good number of the enemy. Had it not been for this, the troops who poured into Rome that morning, and were marching straight upon the castle, might possibly have entered it with ease, because the artillery was doing them no damage. I went on firing under the eyes of several cardinals and lords, who kept blessing me and giving me the heartiest encouragement. In my enthusiasm I strove to achieve the impossible; let it suffice that it was I who saved the castle that morning, and brought the other bombardiers back to their duty.[8] I worked hard the whole of that day; and when the evening came, while the army was marching into Rome through the Trastevere, Pope Clement appointed a great Roman nobleman named Antonio Santacroce to be captain of all the gunners. The first thing this man did was to come to me, and having greeted me with the utmost kindness, he stationed me with five fine pieces of artillery on the highest point of the castle, to which the name of the Angel specially belongs. This circular eminence goes round the castle, and surveys both Prati and the town of Rome. The captain put under my orders enough men to help in managing my guns, and having seen me paid in advance, he gave me rations of bread and a little wine, and begged me to go forward as I had begun. I was perhaps more inclined by nature to the profession of arms than to the one I had adopted, and I took such pleasure in its duties that I discharged them better than those of my own art. Night came, the enemy had entered Rome, and we who were in the castle (especially myself, who

---

6. Giovio, in his *Life of the Cardinal Prospero Colonna*, relates how he accompanied Clement in his flight from the Vatican to the castle. While passing some open portions of the gallery, he threw his violet mantle and cap of a monsignore over the white stole of the pontiff, for fear he might be shot at by the soldiers in the streets below.

7. The short autobiography of Raffaello da Montelupo, a man in many respects resembling Cellini, confirms this part of our author's narrative. It is one of the most interesting pieces of evidence regarding what went on inside the castle during the sack of Rome. Montelupo was also a gunner, and commanded two pieces.

8. This is an instance of Cellini's exaggeration. He did more than yeoman's service, no doubt. But we cannot believe that, without him, the castle would have been taken.

have always taken pleasure in extraordinary sights) stayed gazing on the indescribable scene of tumult and conflagration in the streets below. People who were anywhere else but where we were, could not have formed the least imagination of what it was. I will not, however, set myself to describe that tragedy, but will content myself with continuing the history of my own life and the circumstances which properly belong to it.

XXXV

During the course of my artillery practice, which I never intermitted through the whole month passed by us beleaguered in the castle, I met with a great many very striking accidents, all of them worthy to be related. But since I do not care to be too prolix, or to exhibit myself outside the sphere of my profession, I will omit the larger part of them, only touching upon those I cannot well neglect, which shall be the fewest in number and the most remarkable. The first which comes to hand is this: Messer Antonio Santacroce had made me come down from the Angel, in order to fire on some houses in the neighborhood, where certain of our besiegers had been seen to enter. While I was firing, a cannon shot reached me, which hit the angle of a battlement, and carried off enough of it to be the cause why I sustained no injury. The whole mass struck me in the chest and took my breath away. I lay stretched upon the ground like a dead man, and could hear what the bystanders were saying. Among them all, Messer Antonio Santacroce lamented greatly, exclaiming: "Alas, alas! we have lost the best defender that we had." Attracted by the uproar, one of my comrades ran up; he was called Gianfrancesco, and was a bandsman, but was far more naturally given to medicine than to music. On the spot he flew off, crying for a stoop of the very best Greek wine. Then he made a tile red-hot, and cast upon it a good handful of wormwood; after which he sprinkled the Greek wine; and when the wormwood was well soaked, he laid it on my breast, just where the bruise was visible to all. Such was the virtue of the wormwood that I immediately regained my scattered faculties. I wanted to begin to speak; but could not; for some stupid soldiers had filled my mouth with earth, imagining that by so doing they were giving me the sacrament; and indeed they were more like to have excommunicated me, since I could with difficulty come to myself again, the earth doing me more mischief than the blow. However, I escaped that danger, and returned to the rage and fury of the guns, pursuing my work there with all the ability and eagerness that I could summon.

Pope Clement, by this, had sent to demand assistance from the Duke of Urbino, who was with the troops of Venice; he commissioned the envoy to tell his Excellency that the Castle of S. Angelo would send up every evening three beacons from its summit accompanied by three discharges of the cannon thrice repeated, and that so long as this signal was continued, he might take for granted that the castle had not yielded. I was charged with lighting the beacons and firing the guns for this purpose; and all this while I pointed my artillery by day upon the places where mischief could be done. The Pope, in consequence, began to regard me with still greater favor, because he saw that I discharged my functions as intelligently as the task demanded. Aid from the Duke of Urbino never came; on which, as it is not my business, I will make no further comment.[9]

XXXVI

While I was at work upon that diabolical task of mine, there came from time to time to watch me some of the cardinals who were invested in the castle; and most frequently the Cardinal of Ravenna and the Cardinal de' Gaddi.[10] I often told them not to show themselves, since their nasty red caps gave a fair mark to our enemies. From neighboring buildings, such as the Torre de' Bini, we ran great peril when they were there; and at last I had them locked off, and gained thereby their deep ill-will. I frequently received visits also from the general, Orazio Baglioni, who was very well affected toward me. One day while he was talking with me, he noticed something going forward in a drinking-place outside the Porta di Castello, which bore the name of Baccanello. This tavern had for sign a sun painted between two windows, of a bright red color. The windows being closed, Signor Orazio concluded that a band of soldiers were carousing at table just between them and behind the sun. So he said to me. "Benvenuto, if you think that you could hit that wall an ell's breadth from the sun with the demi-cannon here, I believe you would be doing a good stroke of business, for there is a great commotion there, and men of much importance must probably be inside the house." I answered that I felt quite capable of hitting the sun in its center, but that a barrel full of stones, which was standing close to the muzzle of the gun, might be knocked down by the shock of the discharge and the blast of the artillery. He rejoined, "Don't waste time, Benvenuto. In the first place, it is not possible, where it is standing, that the cannon's blast should bring it down; and even if it were to fall, and the Pope himself was underneath, the mischief would not be so great as you imagine. Fire, then, only fire!"

---

9. Francesco Maria della Rovere, Duke of Urbino, commanded a considerable army as general of the Church, and was now acting for Venice. Why he effected no diversion while the imperial troops were marching upon Rome, and why he delayed to relieve the city, was never properly explained. Folk attributed his impotent conduct partly to a natural sluggishness in warfare, and partly to his hatred for the house of Medici. Leo X had deprived him of his dukedom, and given it to a Medicean prince. It is to this that Cellini probably refers in the cautious phrase which ends the chapter.

10. Benedetto Accolti of Arezzo, Archbishop of Ravenna in 1524, obtained the hat in 1527, three days before the sack of Rome. He was a distinguished man of letters. Niccolò Gaddi was created cardinal on the same day as Accolti. We shall hear more of him in Cellini's pages.

Taking no more thought about it, I struck the sun in the center, exactly as I said I should. The cask was dislodged, as I predicted, and fell precisely between Cardinal Farnese and Messer Jacopo Salviati.[11] It might very well have dashed out the brains of both of them, except that just at that very moment Farnese was reproaching Salviati with having caused the sack of Rome, and while they stood apart from one another to exchange opprobrious remarks, my gabion fell without destroying them. When he heard the uproar in the court below, good Signor Orazio dashed off in a hurry; and I, thrusting my neck forward where the cask had fallen, heard some people saying: "It would not be a bad job to kill that gunner!" Upon this I turned two falconets toward the staircase, with mind resolved to let blaze on the first man who attempted to come up. The household of Cardinal Farnese must have received orders to go and do me some injury; accordingly I prepared to receive them, with a lighted match in hand. Recognizing some who were approaching, I called out; "You lazy lubbers, if you don't pack off from there, and if but a man's child among you dares to touch the staircase, I have got two cannon loaded, which will blow you into powder. Go and tell the Cardinal that I was acting at the order of superior officers, and that what we have done and are doing is in defense of them priests,[12] and not to hurt them." They made away; and then came Signor Orazio Baglioni, running. I bade him stand back, else I'd murder him; for I knew very well who he was. He drew back a little, not without a certain show of fear, and called out: "Benvenuto, I am your friend!" To this I answered: "Sir, come up, but come alone, and then come as you like." The general, who was a man of mighty pride, stood still a moment, and then said angrily: "I have a good mind not to come up again, and to do quite the opposite of that which I intended toward you." I replied that just as I was put there to defend my neighbors, I was equally well able to defend myself too. He said that he was coming alone; and when he arrived at the top of the stairs, his features were more discomposed than I thought reasonable. So I kept my hand upon my sword, and stood eyeing him askance. Upon this he began to laugh, and the color coming back into his face, he said to me with the most pleasant manner: "Friend Benvenuto, I bear you as great love as I have it in my heart to give; and in God's good time I will render proof of this. Would to God you had killed those two rascals; for one of them is the cause of all this trouble, and the day perchance will come when the other will be found the cause of something even worse." He then begged me, if I should be asked, not to say that he was with me when I fired the gun; and for the rest bade me be of good cheer. The commotion which the affair made was enormous, and lasted a long while. However, I will not enlarge upon it further, only adding that

---

11. Alessandro Farnese, Dean of the Sacred College, and afterwards Pope Paul II.
12. *Loro preti.* Perhaps *their priests.*

I was within an inch of revenging my father on Messer Jacopo Salviati, who had grievously injured him, according to my father's complaints. As it was, unwittingly I gave the fellow a great fright. Of Farnese I shall say nothing here, because it will appear in its proper place how well it would have been if I had killed him.

XXXVII

I pursued my business of artilleryman, and every day performed some extraordinary feat, whereby the credit and the favor I acquired with the Pope was something indescribable. There never passed a day but what I killed one or another of our enemies in the besieging army. On one occasion the Pope was walking round the circular keep,[13] when he observed a Spanish Colonel in the Prati; he recognized the man by certain indications, seeing that this officer had formerly been in his service; and while he fixed his eyes on him, he kept talking about him. I, above by the Angel, knew nothing of all this, but spied a fellow down there, busying himself about the trenches with a javelin in his hand; he was dressed entirely in rose-color; and so, studying the worst that I could do against him, I selected a gerfalcon which I had at hand; it is a piece of ordnance larger and longer than a swivel, and about the size of a demi-culverin. This I emptied, and loaded it again with a good charge of fine powder mixed with the coarser sort; then I aimed it exactly at the man in red, elevating prodigiously, because a piece of that caliber could hardly be expected to carry true at such a distance. I fired, and hit my man exactly in the middle. He had trussed his sword in front, for swagger, after a way those Spaniards have; and my ball, when it struck him, broke upon the blade, and one could see the fellow cut in two fair halves. The Pope, who was expecting nothing of this kind, derived great pleasure and amazement from the sight, both because it seemed to him impossible that one should aim and hit the mark at such a distance, and also because the man was cut in two, and he could not comprehend how this should happen. He sent for me, and asked about it. I explained all the devices I had used in firing; but told him that why the man was cut in halves, neither he nor I could know. Upon my bended knees I then besought him to give me the pardon of his blessing for that homicide; and for all the others I had committed in the castle in the service of the Church. Thereat the Pope, raising his hand, and making a large open sign of the cross upon my face, told me that he blessed me, and that he gave me pardon for all murders I had ever perpetrated, or should ever perpetrate, in the service of the Apostolic Church. When I left him, I went aloft, and never stayed from

---

13. The Mastio or main body of Hadrian's Mausoleum, which was converted into a fortress during the Middle Ages.

firing to the utmost of my power; and few were the shots of mine that missed their mark. My drawing, and my fine studies in my craft, and my charming art of music, all were swallowed up in the din of that artillery; and if I were to relate in detail all the splendid things I did in that infernal work of cruelty, I should make the world stand by and wonder. But, not to be too prolix, I will pass them over. Only I must tell a few of the most remarkable, which are, as it were, forced in upon me.

To begin then: pondering day and night what I could render for my own part in defence of Holy Church, and having noticed that the enemy changed guard and marched past through the great gate of Santo Spirito, which was within a reasonable range, I thereupon directed my attention to that spot; but, having to shoot sideways, I could not do the damage that I wished, although I killed a fair percentage every day. This induced our adversaries, when they saw their passage covered by my guns, to load the roof of a certain house one night with thirty gabions, which obstructed the view I formerly enjoyed. Taking better thought than I had done of the whole situation, I now turned all my five pieces of artillery directly on the gabions, and waited till the evening hour, when they changed guard. Our enemies, thinking they were safe, came on at greater ease and in a closer body than usual; whereupon I set fire to my blow-pipes.[14] Not merely did I dash to pieces the gabions which stood in my way; but, what was better, by that one blast I slaughtered more than thirty men. In consequence of this maneuver, which I repeated twice, the soldiers were thrown into such disorder, that being, moreover, encumbered with the spoils of that great sack, and some of them desirous of enjoying the fruits of their labor, they oftentimes showed a mind to mutiny and take themselves away from Rome. However, after coming to terms with their valiant captain, Gian di Urbino,[15] they were ultimately compelled, at their excessive inconvenience, to take another road when they changed guard. It cost them three miles of march, whereas before they had but half a mile. Having achieved this feat, I was entreated with prodigious favors by all the men of quality who were invested in the castle. This incident was so important that I thought it well to relate it, before finishing the history of things outside my art, the which is the real object of my writing: forsooth, if I wanted to ornament my biography with such matters, I should have far too much to tell. There is only one more circumstance which, now that the occasion offers, I propose to record.

---

14. *Soffioni,* the cannon being like tubes to blow a fire up.
15. This captain was a Spaniard, who played a very considerable figure in the war, distinguishing himself at the capture of Genoa and the battle of Lodi in 1522, and afterwards acting as lieutenant-general to the prince of Orange. He held Naples against Orazio Baglioni in 1528, and died before Spello in 1529.

XXXVIII

I shall skip over some intervening circumstances, and tell how Pope Clement, wishing to save the tiaras and the whole collection of the great jewels of the Apostolic Camera, had me called, and shut himself up together with me and the Cavalierino in a room alone.[16] This Cavalierino had been a groom in the stable of Filippo Strozzi; he was French, and a person of the lowest birth; but being a most faithful servant, the Pope had made him very rich, and confided in him like himself. So the Pope, the Cavaliere, and I, being shut up together, they laid before me the tiaras and jewels of the regalia; and his Holiness ordered me to take all the gems out of their gold settings. This I accordingly did; afterwards I wrapt them separately up in bits of paper and we sewed them into the linings of the Pope's and the Cavaliere's clothes. Then they gave me all the gold, which weighed about two hundred pounds, and bade me melt it down as secretly as I was able. I went up to the Angel, where I had my lodging, and could lock the door so as to be free from interruption. There I built a little draught-furnace of bricks, with a largish pot, shaped like an open dish, at the bottom of it; and throwing the gold upon the coals, it gradually sank through and dropped into the pan. While the furnace was working I never left off watching how to annoy our enemies; and as their trenches were less than a stone's-throw right below us, I was able to inflict considerable damage on them with some useless missiles, of which there were several piles, forming the old munition of the castle. I chose a swivel and a falconet, which were both a little damaged in the muzzle, and filled them with the projectiles I have mentioned. When I fired my guns, they hurtled down like mad, occasioning all sorts of unexpected mischief in the trenches. Accordingly I kept these pieces always going at the same time that the gold was being melted down; and a little before vespers I noticed some one coming along the margin of the trench on muleback. The mule was trotting very quickly, and the man was talking to the soldiers in the trenches. I took the precaution of discharging my artillery just before he came immediately opposite; and so, making a good calculation, I hit my mark. One of the fragments struck him in the face; the rest were scattered on the mule, which fell dead. A tremendous uproar rose up from the trench; I opened fire with my other piece, doing them great hurt. The man turned out to be the Prince of Orange, who was carried through the trenches to a certain tavern in the neighborhood, whither in a short while all the chief folk of the army came together.

---

16. This personage cannot be identified. The Filippo Strozzi mentioned as having been his master was the great opponent of the Medicean despotism, who killed himself in prison after the defeat of Montemurlo in 1539. He married in early life a daughter of Piero de' Medici.

When Pope Clement heard what I had done, he sent at once to call for me, and inquired into the circumstance. I related the whole, and added that the man must have been of the greatest consequence, because the inn to which they carried him had been immediately filled by all the chiefs of the army, so far at least as I could judge. The Pope, with a shrewd instinct, sent for Messer Antonio Santacroce, the nobleman who, as I have said, was chief and commander of the gunners. He bade him order all us bombardiers to point our pieces, which were very numerous, in one mass upon the house, and to discharge them all together upon the signal of an arquebuse being fired. He judged that if we killed the generals, the army, which was already almost on the point of breaking up, would take flight. God perhaps had heard the prayers they kept continually making, and meant to rid them in this manner of those impious scoundrels.

We put our cannon in order at the command of Santacroce, and waited for the signal. But when Cardinal Orsini[17] became aware of what was going forward, he began to expostulate with the Pope, protesting that the thing by no means ought to happen, seeing they were on the point of concluding an accommodation, and that if the generals were killed, the rabble of the troops without a leader would storm the castle and complete their utter ruin. Consequently they could by no means allow the Pope's plan to be carried out. The poor Pope, in despair, seeing himself assassinated both inside the castle and without, said that he left them to arrange it. On this, our orders were countermanded; but I, who chafed against the leash, when I knew that they were coming round to bid me stop from firing, let blaze one of my demi-cannons, and struck a pillar in the courtyard of the house, around which I saw a crowd of people clustering. This shot did such damage to the enemy that it was like to have made them evacuate the house. Cardinal Orsini was absolutely for having me hanged or put to death; but the Pope took up my cause with spirit. The high words that passed between them, though I well know what they were, I will not here relate, because I make no profession of writing history. It is enough for me to occupy myself with my own affairs.

XXXIX

After I had melted down the gold, I took it to the Pope, who thanked me cordially for what I had done, and ordered the Cavalierino to give me twenty-five crowns, apologizing to me for his inability to give me more. A few days afterwards the articles of peace were signed. I went with three hundred comrades in the train of Signor Orazio Baglioni toward Perugia;

---

17. Franciotto Orsini was educated in the household of his kinsman Lorenzo de' Medici. He followed the profession of arms, and married; but after losing his wife took orders, and received the hat in 1517.

and there he wished to make me captain of the company, but I was unwilling at the moment, saying that I wanted first to go and see my father, and to redeem the ban which was still in force against me at Florence. Signor Orazio told me that he had been appointed general of the Florentines; and Sir Pier Maria del Lotto, the envoy from Florence, was with him, to whom he specially recommended me as his man.[18]

In course of time I came to Florence in the company of several comrades. The plague was raging with indescribable fury. When I reached home, I found my good father, who thought either that I must have been killed in the sack of Rome, or else that I should come back to him a beggar. However, I entirely defeated both these expectations; for I was alive, with plenty of money, a fellow to wait on me, and a good horse. My joy on greeting the old man was so intense, that, while he embraced and kissed me, I thought that I must die upon the spot. After I had narrated all the devilries of that dreadful sack, and had given him a good quantity of crowns which I had gained by my soldiering, and when we had exchanged our tokens of affection, he went off to the Eight to redeem my ban. It so happened that one of those magistrates who sentenced me, was now again a member of the board. It was the very man who had so inconsiderately told my father he meant to march me out into the country with the lances. My father took this opportunity of addressing him with some meaning words, in order to mark his revenge, relying on the favor which Orazio Baglioni showed me.

Matters standing thus, I told my father how Signor Orazio had appointed me captain, and that I ought to begin to think of enlisting my company. At these words the poor old man was greatly disturbed, and begged me for God's sake not to turn my thoughts to such an enterprise, although he knew I should be fit for this or yet a greater business, adding that his other son, my brother, was already a most valiant soldier, and that I ought to pursue the noble art in which I had labored so many years and with such diligence of study. Although I promised to obey him, he reflected, like a man of sense, that if Signor Orazio came to Florence, I could not withdraw myself from military service, partly because I had passed my word, as well as for other reasons. He therefore thought of a good expedient for sending me away, and spoke to me as follows: "Oh, my dear son, the plague in this town is raging with immitigable violence, and I am always fancying you will come home infected with it. I remember, when I was a young man, that I went to Mantua, where I was very kindly received, and stayed there several years. I pray and command you,

---

18. Pier Maria di Lotto of S. Miniato was notary to the Florentine Signoria. He collected the remnants of the Bande Nere, and gave them over to Orazio Baglioni, who contrived to escape from S. Angelo in safety to Perugia.

for the love of me, to pack off and go thither; and I would have you do this to-day rather than to-morrow."

✦ ✦ ✦

XV

When I returned to Paris, the great favor shown me by the King made me a mark for all men's admiration. I received the silver and began my statue of Jupiter. Many journeymen were now in my employ; and the work went onward briskly day and night; so that, by the time I had finished the clay models of Jupiter, Vulcan, and Mars, and had begun to get the silver statue forward, my workshop made already a grand show.

The King now came to Paris, and I went to pay him my respects. No sooner had his Majesty set eyes upon me than he called me cheerfully, and asked if I had something fine to exhibit at my lodging, for he would come to inspect it. I related all I had been doing; upon which he was seized with a strong desire to come. Accordingly, after his dinner, he set off with Madame de Tampes, the Cardinal of Lorraine, and some other of his greatest nobles, among whom were the King of Navarre, his cousin, and the Queen, his sister; the Dauphin and Dauphiness also attended him; so that upon that day the very flower of the French court came to visit me.[19] I had been some time at home, and was hard at work. When the King arrived at the door of the castle, and heard our hammers going, he bade his company keep silence. Everybody in my house was busily employed, so that the unexpected entrance of his Majesty took me by surprise. The first thing he saw on coming into the great hall was myself with a huge plate of silver in my hand, which I was beating for the body of my Jupiter; one of my men was finishing the head, another the legs; and it is easy to imagine what a din we made between us. It happened that a little French lad was working at my side, who had just been guilty of some trifling blunder. I gave the lad a kick, and, as my good luck would have it, caught him with my foot exactly in the fork between his legs, and sent him spinning several yards, so that he came stumbling up against the King precisely at the moment when his Majesty arrived. The King was vastly amused, but I felt covered with confusion. He began to ask me what I was engaged upon, and told me to go on working; then he said that he would much rather have me not employ my strength on manual labor, but take as many men as I wanted, and make them do the rough work;

---

19. These personages were Madame d'Etampes, the king's mistress; John of Lorraine, son of Duke Renée II, who was made cardinal in 1518; Henri d'Albret II and Marguerite de Valois, his wife; the Dauphin, afterwards Henri II, and his wife, the celebrated Caterina de' Medici, daughter of Lorenzo, duke of Urbino.

he should like me to keep myself in health, in order that he might enjoy my services through many years to come. I replied to his Majesty that the moment I left off working I should fall ill; also that my art itself would suffer, and not attain the mark I aimed at for his Majesty. Thinking that I spoke thus only to brag, and not because it was the truth, he made the Cardinal of Lorraine repeat what he had said; but I explained my reasons so fully and clearly, that the Cardinal perceived my drift; he then advised the King to let me labor as much or little as I liked.

XVI

Being very well satisfied with what he had seen, the King returned to his palace, after bestowing on me too many marks of favor to be here recorded. On the following day he sent for me at his dinner-hour. The Cardinal of Ferrara was there at meat with him. When I arrived, the King had reached his second course; he began at once to speak to me, saying, with a pleasant cheer, that having now so fine a basin and jug of my workmanship, he wanted an equally handsome salt-cellar to match them; and begged me to make a design, and to lose no time about it. I replied: "Your Majesty shall see a model of the sort even sooner than you have commanded; for while I was making the basin, I thought there ought to be a salt-cellar to match it; therefore I have already designed one, and if it is your pleasure, I will at once exhibit my conception." The King turned with a lively movement of surprise and pleasure to the lords in his company—they were the King of Navarre, the Cardinal of Lorraine, and the Cardinal of Ferrara—exclaiming as he did so: "Upon my word, this is a man to be loved and cherished by every one who knows him." Then he told me that he would very gladly see my model.

I set off, and returned in a few minutes; for I had only to cross the river, that is, the Seine. I carried with me the wax model which I had made in Rome at the Cardinal of Ferrara's request. When I appeared again before the King and uncovered my piece, he cried out in astonishment: "This is a hundred times more divine a thing than I had ever dreamed of. What a miracle of a man! He ought never to stop working." Then he turned to me with a beaming countenance, and told me that he greatly liked the piece, and wished me to execute it in gold. The Cardinal of Ferrara looked me in the face, and let me understand that he recognized the model as the same which I had made for him in Rome. I replied that I had already told him I should carry it out for one who was worthy of it. The Cardinal, remembering my words, and nettled by the revenge he thought that I was taking on him, remarked to the King: "Sire, this is an enormous undertaking; I am only afraid that we shall never see it finished. These able artists who have great conceptions in their brain are ready enough to put the same in execution without duly considering when they are to be accomplished. I therefore, if I gave commission for things of such magnitude, should like to know when I was likely to get them." The King replied that if a man was so scrupulous about the termination of a work, he would never begin anything at all; these words he uttered with a certain look, which implied that such enterprises were not for folk of little spirit. I then began to say my say: "Princes who put heart and courage in their servants, as your Majesty does by deed and word, render undertakings of the greatest magnitude quite easy. Now that God has sent me so magnificent a patron, I hope to perform for him a multitude of great and splendid master-pieces." "I believe it," said the King, and rose from table. Then he called me into his chamber, and asked me how much gold was wanted for the salt-cellar. "A thousand crowns," I answered. He called his treasurer at once, who was the Viscount of Orbec, and ordered him that very day to disburse to me a thousand crowns of good weight and old gold.

When I left his Majesty, I went for the two notaries who had helped me in procuring silver for the Jupiter and many other things. Crossing the Seine, I then took a small hand-basket, which one of my cousins, a nun, had given me on my journey through Florence. It made for my good fortune that I took this basket and not a bag. So then, thinking I could do the business by daylight, for it was still early, and not caring to interrupt my workmen, and being indisposed to take a servant with me, I set off alone. When I reached the house of the treasurer, I found that he had the money laid out before him, and was selecting the best pieces as the King had ordered. It seemed to me, however, that that thief of a treasurer was doing all he could to postpone the payment of the money; nor were the pieces counted out until three hours after nightfall.

I meanwhile was not wanting in despatch, for I sent word to several of my journeymen that they should come and attend me, since the matter was one of serious importance. When I found that they did not arrive, I asked the messenger if he had done my errand. The rascal of a groom whom I had sent replied that he had done so, but that they had answered that they could not come; he, however, would gladly carry the money for me. I answered that I meant to carry the money myself. By this time the contract was drawn up and signed. On the money being counted, I put it all into my little basket, and then thrust my arm through the two handles. Since I did this with some difficulty, the gold was well shut in, and I carried it more conveniently than if the vehicle had been a bag. I was well armed with shirt and sleeves of mail, and having my sword and dagger at my side, made off along the street as quick as my two legs would carry me.

XVII

Just as I left the house, I observed some servants whispering among themselves, who also went off at a round pace in another direction from the one I took. Walking with all haste, I passed the bridge of the Exchange,[20] and went up along a wall beside the river which led to my lodging in the castle. I had just come to the Augustines—now this was a very perilous passage, and though it was only five hundred paces distant from my dwelling, yet the lodging in the castle being quite as far removed inside, no one could have heard my voice if I had shouted—when I saw four men with four swords in their hands advancing to attack me. My resolution was taken in an instant. I covered the basket with my cape, drew my sword, and seeing that they were pushing hotly forward, cried aloud: "With soldiers there is only the cape and sword to gain; and these, before I give them up, I hope you'll get not much to your advantage." Then crossing my sword boldly with them, I more than once spread out my arms, in order that, if the ruffians were put on by the servants who had seen me take my money, they might be led to judge I was not carrying it. The encounter was soon over; for they retired step by step, saying among themselves in their own language: "This is a brave Italian, and certainly not the man we are after; or if he be the man, he cannot be carrying anything." I spoke Italian, and kept harrying them with thrust and slash so hotly that I narrowly missed killing one or the other. My skill in using the sword made them think I was a soldier rather than a fellow of some other calling. They drew together and began to fall back, muttering all the while beneath their breath in their own tongue. I meanwhile continued always calling out, but not too loudly, that those who wanted my cape and blade would have to get them with some trouble. Then I quickened pace, while they still followed slowly at my heels; this augmented my fear, for I thought I might be falling into an ambuscade, which would have cut me off in front as well as rear. Accordingly, when I was at the distance of a hundred paces from my home, I ran with all my might, and shouted at the top of my voice: "To arms, to arms! out with you, out with you! I am being murdered." In a moment four of my young men came running, with four pikes in their hands. They wanted to pursue the ruffians, who could still be seen; but I stopped them, calling back so as to let the villains hear: "Those cowards yonder, four against one man alone, had not pluck enough to capture a thousand golden crowns in metal, which have almost broken this arm of mine. Let us haste inside and put the money away; then I will take my big two-handed sword, and go with you whithersoever you like." We went inside to secure the gold; and my lads, while expressing deep concern for the peril I had run, gently chided me, and said: "You risk yourself too much alone; the time will come when you will make us all bemoan your loss." A thousand words and exclamations were exchanged between us; my adversaries took to flight; and we all sat down and supped

---

20. The Pont du Change, replaced by the Pont Neuf.

together with mirth and gladness, laughing over those great blows which fortune strikes, for good as well as evil, and which, what time they do not hit the mark, are just the same as though they had not happened.[21] It is very true that one says to oneself: "You will have had a lesson for next time." But that is not the case; for fortune always comes upon us in new ways, quite unforeseen by our imagination.

XVIII

On the morning which followed these events, I made the first step in my work upon the great salt-cellar, pressing this and my other pieces forward with incessant industry. My workpeople at this time, who were pretty numerous, included both sculptors and goldsmiths. They belonged to several nations, Italian, French, and German; for I took the best I could find, and changed them often, retaining only those who knew their business well. These select craftsmen I worked to the bone with perpetual labor. They wanted to rival me; but I had a better constitution. Consequently, in their inability to bear up against such a continuous strain, they took to eating and drinking copiously, some of the Germans in particular, who were more skilled than their comrades, and wanted to march apace with me, sank under these excesses, and perished.

While I was at work upon the Jupiter, I noticed that I had plenty of silver to spare. So I took in hand, without consulting the King, to make a great two-handled vase, about one cubit and a half in height. I also conceived the notion of casting the large model of my Jupiter in bronze. Having up to this date done nothing of the sort, I conferred with certain old men experienced in that art at Paris. and described to them the methods in use with us in Italy. They told me they had never gone that way about the business; but that if I gave them leave to act upon their own principles, they would bring the bronze out as clean and perfect as the clay. I chose to strike an agreement, throwing on them the responsibility, and promising several crowns above the price they bargained for. Thereupon they put the work in progress; but I soon saw that they were going the wrong way about it, and began on my own account a head of Julius Cæsar, bust and armor, much larger than the life, which I modeled from a reduced copy of a splendid antique portrait I had brought with me from Rome. I also undertook another head of the same size, studied from a very handsome girl, whom I kept for my own pleasures. I called this Fontainebleau, after the place selected by the King for his particular delight.

We constructed an admirable little furnace for the casting of the bronze, got all things ready, and baked our molds; those French masters undertaking the Jupiter, while I looked after my two heads. Then I said:

---

21. Cellini's philosophy is summed up in the proverb: "A miss is as good as a mile."

"I do not think you will succeed with your Jupiter, because you have not provided sufficient vents beneath for the air to circulate; therefore you are but losing your time and trouble." They replied that, if their work proved a failure, they would pay back the money I had given on account, and recoup me for the current expenses; but they bade me give good heed to my own proceedings, for the fine heads I meant to cast in my Italian fashion would never succeed.

At this dispute between us there were present the treasurers and other gentlefolk commissioned by the King to superintend my proceedings. Everything which passed by word or act was duly reported to his Majesty. The two old men who had undertaken to cast my Jupiter postponed the experiment, saying they would like to arrange the molds of my two heads. They argued that, according to my method, no success could be expected, and it was a pity to waste such fine models. When the King was informed of this, he sent word that they should give their minds to learning, and not try to teach their master.